MILLER'S

glass
fact file a–z

GLASS IN VARIOUS LANGUAGES

Afghan (dari): *peahala*, *glass* (pashtu): *khikha*; Bahasa Malaysia/Indonesia: *kaca*; Bulgarian: *staklo*; Catalan: *vidre*; Mandarin *boli*; Cantonese: *poli*; Croatian: *staklo*; Czech *sklo*; Danish: *glas*; Dutch: *glas*; Egyptian Arabic: *zuggag*; Estonian: *Klaas*; Finnish: *lasi*; French: *verre*; Georgian: *mina*; German: *glas*; Gujarati: *kaanch*; Greek: *gyali*; Hebrew: *zchuchit*; Hindi: *kach*; Hungarian: *üveg*; Icelandic: *gler*; Iranian: *shishe*; Italian: *vetro*; Japanese: *galasu*; Korean: *yuri*; Latvian: *stikls*; Letzeburgisch: *glas*; Lithuanian: *stiklas*; Malay: *gelas*; Norwegian: *glass*; Omani arabic: *zigag*; Pashtu: *khikha*; Polish: *szklo*; Portuguese: *vidro*; Romanian: *geam*; Russian: *steklo*; Scottish, Gaelic: *gloinne*; Slovak: *sklo*; Slovenian: *steklo*; Spanish: *vidrio*; Sri Lankan: *veeduru*; Swedish: *glas*; Taiwanese: *bolei*; Thai: *gaew*; Uto-Atzecan: *güishte*; Urdu: *sheesha*; Welsh: *gwydr*

MILLER'S

glass
fact file a–z

IVO HAANSTRA

Miller's Glass Fact File A-Z
Ivo Haanstra

First published in Great Britain in 2001 by Miller's
a division of Mitchell Beazley,
imprints of Octopus Publishing Group Ltd.,
2-4 Heron Quays, London E14 4JP

Commissioning Editor Anna Sanderson
Executive Art Editor Rhonda Fisher
Editor Claire Musters, Samantha Stanley
Designer Peter Gerrish
Jacket Design Colin Goody
Editorial Assistant Rhoda Sweeting, Frazer Bell
Production Nancy Roberts

A CIP catalogue record for this book is available from the British Library

ISBN 1840004290

The publishers will be grateful for any information that will assist them in
keeping future editions up to date. Although all reasonable care has been
taken in the preparation of this book, neither the publishers nor the
author can accept liability for any consequence arising from the use
thereof, or the information contained therein.

Set in Helvetica Neue Light
Produced and printed by Toppan

Cover images left to right: English amethyst cased-glass decanter,
c.1900 (OPG/Tanner/Mark West); Late 19thC Continental
"Chrysanthemum" vase (OPG/Tanner/Mark West); Coquille vase by Paul
Kedelv for Flygsfors, 1952 (Smålands Museum, Växjö, Sweden)

CONTENTS

USING THIS BOOK

All entries are organized alphabetically and particular abbreviations and conventions have been adopted to illustrate the information as clearly as possible (see below). Entries include particular glassworks or manufacturers, designers, engravers and makers, plus techniques, terms, and types of ware. Some of the larger glassworks have been split up into different entries for ease of use so you will find a general information entry followed by another on designers, another on marks and signatures etc. If a glassworks or studio is usually known by an abbreviated term the complete entry will be found there and there will be a cross reference at the full entry. At the back of the book are a bibliography for further reading and a list of museums with specialist glass collections, plus collectors' clubs and Internet resources.

KEY FOR DATES

Factory dates are enclosed in square brackets with the following variations:

• Beginning and end dates have a straightfoward notation of [1865–1912].
• The earliest and/or last recorded dates are shown: [c.1865–c.1912].
• If there is no record of a start or an end date this is shown: [1900–?] or [?–1950]
• If no concrete dates known but there is evidence of production this is shown: "[–], active c. 1945".
• If a company is currently dormant this is shown: [1945–*].
• If a company was in existence in the year 2000 this is shown: [–present].

A typical glassworks entry will show production dates within square brackets at the start of the entry (see above for other variations) followed by location, details of designers and production

---

Abis, Mario Glass designer from Italy [1924], worked for Vistosi 1968.
Aborigeni Barovier & Toso art glass type by Ercole Barovier, 1954..
Abrasion Shallow, unpolished wheel decorations.
Abrasive wheel Disc rotated at variable speed and pressure for cutting and grinding, often made of stone or synthetic stone powders.
Absolon, William Glass decorator from Great Yarmouth, Great Britain [–], did gilding and enamelling on souvenir pieces c.1790–c.1820. **Sig:** sometimes inscribed with WA.
Ace Glass, Inc Glassworks in USA [–], producing c.1940.
Ace Line Glass refinery located in Napajedla, Czechoslovakia [?–present]. (Schwarzlot painting, high rise enamels, engraving, cutting).

Acmelite Trade name of Gill Brothers.
Acorn Trade name used by Fostoria.
Adam Kristall, Peter Adam Glass-cutting works located in Döbern, Germany [?–present], (cut glass).
Adamantine lustre Diamond-like reflection, see lustre.
Adams & Co/US Glass A Glassworks in Pittsburgh, PA, USA [1851–91]. Named Adams, Macklin & Co 1851–61, then Adams & Co until 1891 when it merged into US Glass, (tableware, pressed glass). See also US Glass.
Adle, Josef Thomas Glass decorator from Bohemia who worked in the 1880s.
Adlerhütten, Glashüttenwerke Glassworks in Penzig, Thuringen, Germany [1872–c.1937]. Designers include Richard Süssmuth, (tableware).
Adnet, Jacques Glass designer from France [–]. Worked for Baccarat c.1930s and Walther Nancy.
Adolfhütte, Adolfov Glassworks in Adolfov nad Vimperk, Czechoslovakia [1816–1972]; (art glass, enamel, pressed glass reported 1836, decorative glass and high quality blanks for refining, Bohemia glass). See also Lobmeyr, Meyr's Neffe, Moser.
Aetna Glass & Manufacturing Co Glassworks in Bellaire, OH, USA [1880–91], (pressed glass).

Sig: gives details of marks or signatures which are sometimes followed by examples of the mark or label. "Sig: always" means the signature is the full name of the company or person unless stated otherwise

Details of the different types of ware produced are shown within the square brackets (see box below for details)

The individual's birth and death dates (if applicable) are shown within square brackets

Acmelite Trade name of Gill Brothers.

Acorn Trade name used by Fostoria.

Adam Kristall, Peter Adam Glass-cutting works located in Döbern, Germany [?–present], (cut glass).

Adamantine lustre Diamond-like reflection, see lustre.

Adams & Co/US Glass A Glassworks in Pittsburgh, PA, USA [1851–91]. Named Adams, Macklin & Co 1851–61, then Adams & Co until 1891 when it merged into US Glass, (tableware, pressed glass). **See also US Glass.**

Adle, Josef Thomas Glass decorator from Bohemia who worked in the 1880s.

Adlerhütten, Glashüttenwerke Glassworks in Penzig, Thuringen, Germany [1872–c.1937]. Designers include Richard Süssmuth, (tableware).

Adnet, Jacques Glass designer from France [–]. Worked for Baccarat c.1930s and Walther Nancy.

A & Co, AG Co Bottlemarks for Agnew & Son.

A (encircled) Trademark of American Glassworks.

A & DHC Trade name of A & DH Chambers, Pittsburgh, PA, [1842–86], **(bottles)**.

Aalto, Aino Marsio Architect/glass designer from Finland [1894–1949]. Worked for Iittala 1932; her tableware is still in production.

Aalto, (Hugo Henrik) Alvar Architect/glass designer from Finland **[1898–1976]**. Worked for Riihimaki Glass c.1932 and Karhula-Iittala c.1936. Designed Savoy vase, 1937.

Aarikka, Kaija Glass designer from Finland [1929–]. Worked for Aarikka 1954–present as well as Humppila 1972–87.

Aaronson, Adam Glass artist from Great Britain [1957–]. Works at Aaronson-Noon Glass studio in Earls Court, London 1986–present.

AB (linked) Trade name of Adolphus Busch Glass Mfg, Belleville, IL and St Louis, MO, USA [1904–7], (aka ABGM Co, 1886–1928) (bottles).

Cross refernces to other entries will be made where appropriate

---

DEFINITIONS OF TYPES OF WARE

Art Glass includes all types of decorative wares, coloured, refined, embellished, painted, engraved, shaped etc. without a direct everyday household function.

Borosilicate refers to labware, cookware and similar heat-resistant applications.

Carnival refers to lustred pressed glass.

Cut glass refers to items that have been refined by cutting; in many cases this would be on crystal, not glass, but the term is used to refer to the technique not the material.

Full lead crystal refers to material containing 24% PbO or more.

Paperweights include not only millefiori and lampworked weights but also pressed crystal items.

Pharmaceutical or apothecary glass includes small bottles, vials and often some labware.

Pressed Glass refers to moulded, pressed and similar machine made wares.

Refinery refers to secondary glass making, i.e. using blanks supplied by another firm for cutting, enamelling, painting etc.

Sodalime refers to standard glass.

Semi-crystal refers to quality glass.

Tableware refers to glass for table and general household use: stems, goblets, decanters up to and including flower vases and ornamental items, usually in clear glass or crystal.

A & Co

A & Co, AG Co Bottlemarks for Agnew & Son.

A (encircled) Trademark of American Glassworks.

A & DHC Trade name of A & DH Chambers, Pittsburgh, PA, [1842–86], (bottles).

Aalto, Aino Marsio Architect/glass designer from Finland [1894–1949]. Worked for Iittala 1932; her tableware is still in production.

Aalto, (Hugo Henrik) Alvar Architect/glass designer from Finland [1898–1976]. Worked for Riihimaki Glass c.1932 and Karhula-Iittala c.1936. Designed Savoy vase, 1937.

Aarikka, Kaija Glass designer from Finland [1929–]. Worked for Aarikka 1954–present as well as Humppila 1972–87.

Aaronson, Adam Glass artist from Great Britain [1957–]. Works at Aaronson-Noon Glass studio in Earls Court, London 1986–present.

AB (linked) Trade name of Adolphus Busch Glass Mfg, Belleville, IL and St Louis, MO, [1904–7], (aka ABGM Co, 1886–1928) (bottles).

Abbe, Ernst Professor of optics from Jena, Germany [1840–1905] developed the scientific basis for optics c.1866. Also co-founder of Schott glass 1884 and owner of Carl Zeiss after 1888.

AB Co Trade name of American Bottle.

ABC-plates Clear or milk glass plates with alphabet in rim made in Great Britain c.1780–1860.

Abelmann Glass-making studio located in Van Nuys, CA, USA [1980s–present]. Artists include Mayauel Ward, (paperweights, art glass).

Abels, Gustav Glass engraver from Sweden [–], worked for Orrefors c.1910.

Abis, Mario Glass designer from Italy [1924], worked for Vistosi 1968.

Aborigeni Barovier & Toso art glass type by Ercole Barovier, 1954.

Abrasion Shallow, unpolished wheel decorations.

Abrasive wheel Disc rotated at variable speed and pressure for cutting and grinding, often made of stone or synthetic stone powders.

Absolon, William Glass decorator from Great Yarmouth, Great Britain [–], did gilding and enamelling on souvenir pieces c1790–c.1820. Sig: sometimes inscribed with WA.

Ace Glass, Inc Glassworks in USA [–], producing c.1940.

Ace Line Glass refinery located in Napajedla, Czechoslovakia [?–present]. (Schwarzlot painting, high rise enamels, engraving, cutting).

ACI Crown Glassware Glassworks in Sydney, Australia and in Hobart, Tasmania [?–present]. (Tumblers, barware).

Acid cutback Design produced by acid etching the outside of two or more layers of cased glass.

Acid engraving Surface treatment using hydrofluoric acid and potassium fluoride. First the object is covered in wax or glue, the design is cut into the coating and etched onto the glass surface. Developed in Germany; first used on a commercial scale in 1857 by Richardson's of Stourbridge, Great Britain. (In US known as needle etching.)

Acid etching Matt-surface treatment, obtained by exposing the glass to fumes of hydrofluoric acid or baths of hydrofluoric acid. Designs are made by first coating the glass with wax, then scratching the pattern through the wax layer. When applied, the acid will eat away the glass but not the wax.

Acid finish Aka Satin finish; matt surface obtained by acid etching.

Acid polishing (Cut glass) High-gloss polished surface obtained by dipping the object into hydrofluoric and sulphuric acid. Possible from 1883, common since 1889. Items are immersed either once in a strong solution or repeatedly in a weaker one to burn away dull edges.

Acid stamping Signature applied to glass using etching acid on a rubber stamp.

ACME Trade name of Acme glass, Olean, NY [1920–30], (bottles).

Acme Cut Glass Co Glassworks in USA [–], (cut glass, Brilliant period).

Acmelite Trade name of Gill Brothers.

Acorn Trade name used by Fostoria.

Adam Kristall, Peter Adam Glass-cutting works located in Döbern, Germany [?–present], (cut glass).

Adamantine lustre Diamond-like reflection, see lustre.

Adams & Co/US Glass A Glassworks in Pittsburgh, PA, USA [1851–91]. Named Adams, Macklin & Co 1851–61, then Adams & Co until 1891 when it merged into US Glass, (tableware, pressed glass). See also US Glass.

Adle, Josef Thomas Glass decorator from Bohemia who worked in the 1880s.

Adlerhütten, Glashüttenwerke Glassworks in Penzig, Thuringen, Germany [1872–c.1937]. Designers include Richard Süssmuth, (tableware).

Adnet, Jacques Glass designer from France [–]. Worked for Baccarat c.1930s and Walther Nancy.

Adolfhütte, Adolfov Glassworks in Adolfov nad Vimperk, Czechoslovakia [1816–1972]; (art glass, enamel, pressed glass reported 1836, decorative glass and high quality blanks for refining, Bohemia glass). See also Lobmeyr, Meyr's Neffe, Moser.

Aetna Glass & Manufacturing Co Glassworks in Bellaire, OH, USA [1880–91], (pressed glass).

Åfors Glasbruk AB Glassworks in Eriksmåla, Småland, Sweden [1876–present]. Merged with Kosta and Boda in 1946. Currently operated by Orrefors. Designers include Bertil Vallien, Ulrika Hydman-Vallien and Gunnel Sahlin. Sig: Engraved Åfors + model + designer 1946–76, then Kosta Boda 1976–present. The following marks indicate the various artists: GSA = Sahlin, BVA = Vallien, UHV = Hydman-Vallien). (Tableware and art glass.)

Agata A type of glass patented in 1887 by Joseph Locke of New England Glass, but produced for less than a year. Has shading from white at the base to deep pink at the top, with a shiny, mottled purple or brown metallic stain.

Agate Glass See calcedonio.

Agee Trade name used by Hazel Atlas [1921–5].

Agnew & Son Glassworks in Pittsburgh, PA, USA [c.1854–c.1892], marks include "A" 1854–66, "A & Co" 1854–92 and "A G Co" 1854–92), (bottles).

Agnew Co Glassworks in USA [c.1891], (tableware).

Agostinho, Vitor Glass designer from Portugal [–], worked for Mglass in Marinha Grande c.1999.

Agterberg, Chris Glass designer from the Netherlands [1883–1948], designed enamel decorated tableware for Leerdam c.1925. His vases and dishes were produced in Bohemia.

Agussol see VFA.

AGW, AGW Co Trade name of American Glassworks Ltd.

Ahne Family of glass decorators from Czechoslovakia includes Josef [1830–1909], Gustav [1861–1925] and Theodor [1863–1907].

Ahne Glassworks in Kamenický Šenov Czechoslovakia [1860–?].

Ahola, Hilkka Liisa Glass designer from Finland [–], worked for Wärtsilä, Notsjö c.1956/7.

Aigremont, SA des Verreries Nouvelles d' See Nouvelles d'Aigremont, SA des Verreries.

Air trap, air lock Air bubble in glass. Air traps in stems are frequently tear-shaped or spirally twisted. See Diamond air trap and Twist.

Air twist Stem type with twisted elongated air bubbles inside.

Ajka Üveggyár Glassworks in Ajka, Hungary [1878–present]. Designers include Magda Nemeth after 1960 and Zsuzsa Csala after 1997. Sig: no sigs before 2000; sanded Ajka mark after 2000). (Tableware, cut glass, cut-to-clear, cut glass museum copies, 24% lead crystal and sodalime.)

Åkerdahl, Anna Glass designer from Sweden [1879–1957], worked for SAIAR Ferro Toso in 1921.

Akro Agate Co Glassworks in Clarksburg, WV, USA [1911–51], moved to Akron, OH in 1914 and took over Westite moulds 1931. Was sold to Clarksburg Glass 1951. Sig: many pieces marked "Made in USA" + mould number; Westite pieces have a W in a diamond. (Thickwalled glass; marbles, pressed glass; floral ware after 1935.)

Aksyonov, Roman N Glass designer from Russia [1939–], worked at Gus-Krushtalny, Vladimir region as a glass blower 1954–64 and a designer 1969–present.

Alabaster glass Translucent white, opal-like glass, first developed in Bohemia in the 19thC. Steuben introduced alabaster glass in 1920, with an iridescent finish.

Aladdin Lamps Trade name used both by Aladdin Manufacturing and by the Mantle Lamp Company 1919–35.

Aladdin Manufacturing Co. Glassworks in Muncie, IN, USA [1919–59]. Renamed General Lamps Co after trade name dispute with Mantle in 1935, (lamps and lighting).

Aladin, Tamara Glass designer from Finland, [1932–], worked for Riihimäen Lasi Oy 1959–75), designed Koralli ware.

A La Paix Glass shop located in Paris, [c.1880–c.1900], (tableware, art glass). See Jules Mabut and Geo Rouard

Alaska Glass designed by Sven Palmqvist for Orrefors, 1939 (light blue, cut glass, marked PA2133/1–12).

Albany Glass Co Glassworks in Albany, NY, USA [c.1780-1820], (flat glass, bottles, some tableware).

Albatros SRL Glassworks in Fosso, Venezia [?–present], (fused, slumped art glass, picture frames, lamps and lighting).

Alberius, Olle Glass designer from Sweden [1926–], worked for Orrefors 1971–present.

Albert Brothers Glassworks in USA [–], active c.1913, (cut glass).

Albert Glassworks Glassworks in Vauxhall Walk Lambeth, London, Great Britain [1879–1920]. Operated by Charles Henry Kempton whose son Richard founded Nazeing in 1928.

Albertine glass Art glass produced by Mt Washington; aka Crown Milano.

Albian Glassworks See Stykes & Macvay Co.

Albiglass See Vidrio Ecologico.

Albion Bottle Co Glassworks in Birmingham, Great Britain [–]. Sig: ABC; AG BCo, (bottles).

Albrechtice u Jiretin Glassworks in Albrechtsdorf, Georgenthal/Albrechtice, Jiretin, Czechoslovakia [1919–50], (earlier glassworks reported here c.1860), (lighting, pressed glass, tableware).

Albret Signature found on paperweights from Cristallerie de Vianne, France.

Alcobaça SA, Cristais de Glassworks in Alcobaça, Portugal [1945–present]. Cut glass trade name Atlantis for 30% lead crystal; Sig: sandblasted "Atlantis" in semi-circle. Barware has trade name Crisa. Also makes sodalime glass.

Aldridge, Peter Studio artist from USA [1947–], worked for Steuben.

Alexandrite 1. A form of the mineral chrysoberyl that changes from green to red under artificial light. 2. Thomas Webb transparent glass shading yellow to rose to blue named after Princess Alexandra, first made in Great Britain in the 1880s. 3. Stevens and Williams cased glass in yellow, rose and blue. 4. A. Douglas Nash amethyst-coloured glass 5. Any glass containing Neodymium with colour shift from purple to blue under electric light. First made by Moser as "Rare Earth" glass (after 1925/8), aka Rosalith, Royalith, as Luxodine by ZBS, as Wisteria by Steuben. Also made by Heisey, Tiffin, Fostoria, Morgantown, Mosser, Lotton, Zanetti, RCM and Arques.

Alford, CG & Co Inc Glassworks in New York, NY, USA [1872–1918], (jewellery, cut glass).

Alga Type of glass made by Venini, designed by Tomaso Buzzi, 1932/3.

Alga-Laguna Venini term for lattimo cased with

Älghults Glasbruk

a layer of coloured glass with an even application of gold leaf; Alga is green, Laguna red. First presented by Venini 1933 (designed by Tomasso Buzzi).

Älghults Glasbruk Glassworks in the Kingdom of Crystal, Sweden [1995–present]. Currently operated by Orrefors. Designers include Rolf Sinnemark, Berit Johansson, Vivianne Karlsson; Sigurd Persson) (tableware, restaurant ware, art glass).

Alhambra glass Type of art glass made by Rindskopf at Barbarahütte.

Alicja huta skla i krysztalow Glassworks in Tarnów, Poland [1981–present]; (tableware, art glass, giftware, coloured, laminated, cased, powdered, clouded, sand-blasted, metal-cased glass).

Alkali Soluble salt of potassium or sodium carbonate; one of the essential ingredients of glass, generally accounting for about 15–20% alkali (aka "flux") lowers the melting point of the batch.

Alkaline earths The alkaline earth metal oxides of barium, beryllium, calcium, magnesium and strontium are all used in glassmaking: calcium and magnesium in sodalime glass, and barium as a lead substitute in crystal.

Allan & Co, AM Glassworks located at Forth Glass Works, Glasgow, Scotland [c.1870s–c.1899], (pressed glass, tableware).

Allen Cut Glass Co Glassworks in USA [–], (cut glass, Brilliant period).

Allglass Trade name used by ITALIA2 srl

Alloa Glass Ltd Glassworks in Alloa, Scotland [–]. Sig: AGW, (bottles).

Almahütte Glassworks in Grossräschen and/or Senftenberg/Elster, near Calau NL, Germany [1868–c.1937], operated by Julius Fahdt, (bottles, lamps and lighting).

Alméric Walter Glassworks in Nancy, France [c.1900–present], (pressed glass). See Walter, Nancy.

Almorrata, almorrataxa (Sp) A rose water sprinkler with many spouts, made in northern Spain between the 16thC and 18thC.

Almy & Thomas Glass refinery located in USA [1903–18], previously known as Knickerbocker Cut Glass Co, (cut glass on Corning blanks).

Alscher, Anja Studio artist from Germany [1966–], works at Devidrio Glaswerk, Germany.

Alsterbro Glassworks Glassworks in Sweden [–], active in 1959.

Alsterfors Glasbruk Glassworks in Sweden [–], active in 1940.

Alston, Margaret Studio artist from Great Britain [1956–].

Alt AG/VEB Glaswerk Ilmenau Glassworks in Ilmenau, Germany [1923–89], founded by Alt, Eberhardt and Jäger, (technical glass, coloured glass, tubes and hollow ware).

ALT Luci Alternativi Glassworks in Murano, Italy [c.1980–present], Designers include Lorenzo Bertocco. (lamps and lighting, art glass, paperweights).

AltaGlass Glassworks in Canada [1950–c.1987].

Altare Traditional glassmaking centre near Genoa, Italy.

Altenburger, Brigitte Glass designer from Austria [1942–]. Worked for Tiroler Glashütte (Kufstein) c.1960 and Leerdam 1963–70. Sig: on Leerdam "Unica", AT.

Altenburger Glashütte Glassworks in Altenburg OL, Germany [–], operated by Hermann Hirsch, (bottles, lamps and lighting, pressed glass).

Altmann Manufacturer of costume jewellery from Jablonec, Czechoslovakia [c.1920s–c.1936].

Alton Manufacturing Co Glassworks located Sandwich, MA, USA [1907–8]. (Trevaise art glass, resembles Favrile, Aurene).

Aluminosilicate glass Technical glass used in Halogen lights.

Amadi, Bruno Glass worker/artist located in Murano, Italy [–], was working c.1980.

Amalienhütte Glassworks in Bunzlau OL, Germany [1872–present], operated by Adolf Hirsch, (tableware)

Amberette Pressed glass that is frosted or amber-stained to resemble art glass.

Amberg, Kristall-Glasfabrik Glassworks in Amberg, Germany [?–present], taken over by Rosenthal 1997.

Amberina A heat sensitive glass that varies in colour from light amber to dark ruby red in the same object (used in art glass). Patented in 1882 by Joseph Locke from New England Glass Co. The shading is owed to the presence of gold in the batch. The glass has an amber colour when it emerges from the lehr, but partial reheating causes the colour to change to red. If the colours are reversed, it is called reverse amberina. This was produced at Mount Washington as "Rose Amber". Iridescent Bohemian amberina from Rindskopf was called "Grenada". Contemporary production occurs at Boyd and other places. Variations are Bluerina and plated (opaque) amberina, patented 1886 by Locke in the US, which is identical to Webb's 1885 peach glass.

Ambiente Kristall GmbH Glassworks in Zwiesel, Bavaria, Germany [?–present].

Amblecote Glass Co.Ltd Glassworks in Stourbridge, Great Britain [–], was producing c.1950.

Amblève, Verrerie Glassworks in Amblève near Liège, Belgium [c.1750–].

Ambrati Barovier & Toso art glass type by Ercole Barovier, 1956.

Ambrolite see emeralite.

Amelung glass Glassworks in USA [c.1780s–c.1800].

American Bottle Bottle manufacturer from Chicago, IL, USA [–], (bottles).

American Cut Crystal Corp Glassworks in USA [–], active c.1945.

American Cut Glass Co Glassworks in Chicago, IL, USA [1897–1920], moved to Lansing, MI c.1902, (cut glass, Brilliant period).

American cutting Cut glass that has been decorated all over.

American Flint Glass Works Glassworks in Wheeling, WV, USA [–], active 1840s, (pressed glass, tableware, flint, lead, colour).

American Glass First glass houses in Mexico (1535), Argentina (1592) Jamestown, VA (1608), Salem (1641), Philadelphia (1682) and New Amsterdam (1650s) but these were all short-lived. First successful plant for bottles, flatglass and tableware Wistarburgh, NJ (1739) "South Jersey", New Bremen Glass near Baltimore (1785) and Stiegel (3 Glassworks near Philadelphia, 1763). Dozens of glass houses sprung up between 1780 and 1820. Invented hinged moulds (early 1800s) and the invention of the glass pressing machines was by US companies Bakewell, Page & Co. (Pittsburgh, PA 1825) and by Boston & Sandwich (Sandwich, MA, 1828). Pittsburgh remained the most important glass centre in the US throughout the 1850s, also during the ensuing fashion for cut glass in the Brilliant period. A fashion for colourful art glass followed in the 1880s, followed by Art Nouveau, Carnival (1908–20) and Depression glass. US consumers have embraced pressed glass from its earliest days, while in Europe blown glass has remained the norm.

American Glass Co Glassworks in Anderson, IN, USA [1889–90], (from 1890 known as Hoosier Glass Co when taken over).

American Glass Co Glassworks in Indiana, PA, USA [1899–1913]. Bought Dugan/Northwood then sold to Diamond Glass Co in 1913. (Pressed glass.)

American Glassworks Glassworks based in Richmond, VA and Paden City, WV, USA [1909–36], (bottles).

American Glassworks Ltd Glassworks in Great Britain [1860–1905], marks include AGW and AGW Co, (bottles).

American Opalescent Werke Glassworks in Muskau near Rothenburg, OL, Germany [1901–c.1937].

American overlay see Silver deposit glass.

American Silver Plate Co Glassworks in USA [–], active c.1898, (tableware).

Amiable, Alexandre Glassmaker from Liège [–]. Worked for Nizet/Liège 1841, VSL 1849/50, Laken, Namur 1851 and 1857 and Jambes et Chênée, (filigrane, tableware).

Amiable, Baiwir & Cie Glassworks in Chênée, Belgium [1883–present], previously known as Cristallerie et Verreries de l'Ourthe, (filigrane, paperweights, art glass).

Amiable, Louvet, Berneau et Belleflamme Glassworks in Chênée Belgium [1872–88]. Started by Alexandre Amiable in Jambes/Namur, 1870, moved to Chênée 1872), (tableware).

Amorino (It) Decorative cherub.

Amoroso, Giampaolo Glass artist working at Gala, Liège, Belgium c.1989.

Amour, Paul Verreries Glassworks in Paris, France [–], active c.1890.

Ampoule Glass capsule for liquid, sealed ready for use.

Anchor Cap and Closure Co Glassworks located Long Island, NY, USA [1904-1937]. Producer of containers merged with Hocking 1937 to form Anchor Hocking, see below.

Anchor Hocking Glass Co Glassworks in Lancaster, OH USA [1906–present]. Began as Hocking Glass Co in 1906, merged with Ohio Flint Glass Co, was renamed Anchor Hocking Glass Company in 1937 after merger with Anchor Cap and Closure Co. The word "glass"' is dropped from the name in 1969. Acquisition of Phoenix Glass in 1970, Anchor Hocking taken over by Newell 1987 and since acquiring Rubbermaid in 1999 has been renamed Newell Rubbermaid. The subsidiary company is known as Fire King. Sig: HGCO monogram in shield or HGC in a circle 1906–37, Anchor in H 1937–77, Anchor in a square + Anchor Hocking 1977–present. Fire King or Lightning logo on ovenware. (Tableware, depression glass, pressed glass.)

Anchor Hocking Specialty Glass Co (Pressed glass, tableware, bottles, lamps and lighting, novelties, souvenirs.)

Anco Flint Trade name of Gill Brothers.

Andelys, Verreries des Glassworks in Andelys, France [–], active c.1932, (tableware, lamps and lighting). See also Verlys.

Ander, Gunnar Architect and Glass designer from Sweden [1908–], designed for Alsterbro and for Lindshammar Glasbruk c.1957/66.

Andersen, Doug Studio artist from USA. [–].

Andersen, William C Glass designer from the USA [–], worked for Libbey c.1890s, (cut glass).

Anderson & Lewis Glassworks in USA [–], active c.1904, (cut glass).

Andolfato Francesco Glass refinery located in Venice, Italy [c.1948–c.1967]. Designers include Mirko Casaril, F Quaia 1954 and Giulio Padoan 1954. (Cut glass; engraved glass.)

Andreashütte Glassworks in Wehrau-Klitschdorf near Bunzlau OL, Germany [1840–c.1937], operated by Gräfl zu Solm'sche Glasfabrik, (tableware).

Andrews Glass Ltd Glassworks in Vineland, NJ, USA [1992–present], (bottles, tubing).

Anfora, Vetrerie L' Glassworks in Murano, Italy [c.1980–present], artists include Vittorio Ferro, (art glass).

Anglo Dutch Bottle Works Glassworks in Capelle a/d IJssel, Netherlands [1861–1924]. Founded 1861 as vd Kloot & Mijnlieff, renamed Anglo Dutch 1908, taken over by AG/Gerresheimer Glashüttenwerke vorm. Ferd Heye in 1919, joint venture with NV Verenigde Glasfabrieken 1924, which took over Van Deventer Schiedam & Delft in 1926, Bottle Works in Zwijndrecht in 1938, Leerdam in 1938 and Nieuw Buinen in 1938).

Anglo-Irish glass Cut glass style from England/Ireland c.1780–c.1825.

Aniche, Verrerie: Glassworks in Aniche near Douai, France [1814–?], aka Verrerie d'en Bas, (flat glass, bottles).

Ankerglas Bernsdorf Glassworks in Bernsdorf near Hoyerswerda, OL, Germany [1872–1987]. Began as Glasfabrik Gebrüder Hoffmann in 1872, then Ankerglas Bernsdorf AG für Glasfabrikation vorm. Gebr. Hoffmann 1889–1941, Ankerglas Bernsdorf/OL 1941–6, VEB Ankerglas 1946–1975, VEB Behälterglas Bernsdorf/OL 1975–87. Sig: anchor impressed 1933–65; anchor in a bell 1965–present, triangular sail shape in a circle for Behälterglas Bernsdorf 1974–present. (Lamps and lighting 1872–1914, pressed glass 1914–69, bottles 1969–present.)

Annagrün Bright yellow or green glass, obtained by adding uranium oxide to the batch. Discovered in 1830 by Franz-Anton Riedel of Polaun (1816–94), who named it after his daughters, Anna Maria and Eleonora ("Eleonorengrün"). See Uranium glass.

Annahütte, Annahütte Glassworks in Annahütte near Calau, Germany [1865–?], operated by Heye.

Annahütte, Annathal Glassworks in Annín u Sušice, Czechoslovakia [1836–c.1873]. Owned by E J Schmidt (enamelled and hot decorated glass, iridized glass c.1873).

Annahütte, Döbern Glassworks in Döbern near Sorau, NL, Germany [1872–present]. Merged into Heye, H, known as AnnaHütte VEB [1945–72], as Annahütte, Grossräschen/Döbern [recent], operated by Concorde Kristal1glas since 1994. (Pressed crystal.)

Annahütte, Penzing Glassworks in Penzig near Görlitz, OL, Germany [–].

Annahütte, Polevsko Glassworks in Polevsko, Czechoslovakia [1907–43], operated by Rudolf Handschke; produced blanks for local refineries.

Annealing The process of gradual cooling a completed object in a "lehr" or annealing oven, to eliminate stresses. The outside of molten glass will cool more rapidly than the centre, resulting in internal stresses that may cause the object to crack, shatter or explode at some later time. The glass is brought to the "annealing point" and the temperature is stabilized for a specific duration, depending on glass type, thickness and expansion coefficient, to allow stress to relax. Then follows a period of cooling with a pre-defined temperature gradient.

Antica Murrina Veneziana Glassworks in Venice, Italy [1968–present], (murrina).

Antimony Refining/decolourizing agent – as antimonate of lead with arsenic it produces yellows. Antimony is found as the mineral stibnite, antimony oxide, Sb2O3.

Antique glass Flat glass with an uneven texture and bubbles, made to look like pre-industrial glass.

Anton, Ernst Glass decorator from Bohemia [–], worked 1880s.

Antonienhütte Glassworks in Grossräschen near Calau, NL, Germany [1904–c.1937].

Antoniwald, Zenknerhütte Glassworks in Antonínov (u Jabloneč nad Jizerou), Zenknerova Hut, Czechoslovakia [1697–1909].

Antonova, Galina A Glass designer from Moscow, Russia [1926–], worked at the Workshops of Applied Arts, Moscow after 1947, at the Leningrad Factory of Decorative Glassware, at Dzherzhinski Glassworks and at Lvov factory of sculpture and ceramics.

Anverre Glasatelier Glass studio located in Antwerp, Belgium [1972–present], founded by Edward Leibovitz, Cristian and Laura Klepsch, Sem Schanzer and Peter Soetens.

Anversoises, Verreries Glassworks in Merxem, Antwerp, Belgium [–].

Anzin, Verrerie Glassworks in Anzin near Valenciennes, France [1814–?], (flat glass, bottles).

Apelt & Sohn, Glashütte Glassworks in Haidemühl near Spremberg, NL, Germany [1909–c.1937].

Apollonov, Ivan G Glass designer from Kiev, Ukraine [1933–], designer at Kiev Factory 1960–6 and after 1970 and chief designer at UkrGlass Trust 1966–9.

Appert Frères Glassworks in Batignolles/Clichy, France [1835–c.1878], founded by Louis, run by sons Léon and Adrien, Rousseau had works made by them c.1880s. (Flat glass, art glass; coloured glass, opalines, slag, iridescence.)

Applied Any handle(s) or part of a vessel applied separately.

Applied decoration Separate glass elements (trails, prunts) applied during manufacture to a glass object. Applied decorations can be on the surface or rolled in.

Applied lip Bottle top with ring of glass trailed around the neck, before 1880.

Applied top Aka blob top, c.1850–80s.

Appliqué Any type of decorative glass with hand-applied three-dimensional trim.

Aqua-graal Glass type by Orrefors (with inclusions of colour and bubbles).

Aqua marine Trade name for art glass produced by Frederick Carder at Steuben. Resembles verre-de-soie with a greenish colour.

Aquatoll Glassworks in Sumperk, Czechoslovakia [?–present], (paperweights).

Arabia Glass See Nuutajärvi-Notsjö 1971–6.

Arcade International Glass company located in Bolzano, Italy with manufacturing in Murano, Italy [1990–present]. Designers include director Laura de Santillana, Ivan Baj, Anna Galli, Ernst Gamperl, James Irvine, Ross Lovegrove, Paola Navone, Marcello Panza, Franco Poli, Kazuhiko Tomita and Master Simone Cenedese. Sig: all pieces signed in full "Arcade" in needle script + edition number + designer + year). (Art glass esp. with cut, frosted and battuto decoration, tableware).

Architectural glass 1. Glass elements used in buildings, such as glass bricks, decorative panels, church windows etc. 2. Glass designed by architects (eg Aalto, Berlage, de Bazel).

Arcopal Trade name from J G Durand for tempered glass, introduced 1958.

Arcoroc Trade name from J G Durand for tempered and heat resistant glass, introduced 1958.

Arcotherm Trade name from J G Durand for heat resistant glass, introduced 1988.

Arcuisine Trade name from J G Durand for clear and smoke coloured cookware, introduced 1986.

Arculus & Co, Alfred Glassworks in Birmingham, Great Britain [c.1920s–1930s], (fake paperweights 1848 canes).

Argand lamps Oil or gas lamp having an Argand burner (patented 1784 by Aimée Argand). Features two hollow tubes, a tubular wick and a chimney. Produced in USA after 1824; improved as Astral lamps.

Argental d' Glassworks in Müntzthal, France [c.1900], see Nicolas, Paul.

Argentan Type of art glass made by Loetz.

Argenthal, D' Signature on art glass from St Louis.

ə͗ argental

Argentine Art glass by Edward Webb, c.1880s, includes foil.

Argentor Glassworks or refinery located in Vienna, Austria [–], operating c.1905.

Argo Barovier & Toso art glass type by Ercole Barovier, 1959.

Argy-Rousseau, Gabriel Glass artist from France [1885–1953]. Developed pâte-de-verre technique c.1906–c.1914, founded Les Pâtes-de-Verre d'Argy-Rousseau, Paris [1921–1932]. His works were sold exclusively by Galerie Moser-Millot until 1932; continued working until 1952. Designers include Marcel Bouraine 1928–31. Sig: G A R or full name impressed; "Bouraine" on items designed by Bouraine).

G.ARGY-ROUSSEAU

Aricò, Gianni Glass maker located in Murano, Italy [1941–c.1980].

Ariel Technique developed by Orrefors 1936/7, which was named after the spirit from Shakespeares *The Tempest*. It is submerged air pattern décor on art glass. Ariel designers include Lindstrand 1937–40, Öhrström 1940–c.1960 and Lundin c.1960–present. Ariel numbering Sequential 1937–1949 starting 1=1937 66=1938 81=1939 221=1940 241=1946 570=1949 up to 865=1949). Encoded from 1950: 51B=1950 53E=950 833E=1951 1451E=1952

1756=1953 2023=1954 50F=1955 243F=1956 409F=1957 100G=1958 100H=1959 268H=1960 100K=1961 101L=1962 100M=1963 101N=1964 100O=1965 100P=1965 104A=1966 100B=1967 100C=1968 100D=1969 100E=1970 101F=1971 100G=1972 100E3=1973 101E4=1974 100E5=1975 100E6=1976 100E7=1977 100E8=1978 100E9=1979 500F1=1980 500F2=1981.

Arlecchini See clowns.

Arlt, Heinz Glass designer from Germany [1921–], worked at Arnstadt Bleikristall 1955–86.

Armstrong, Wendy Glass designer from Belgium [–], worked for VSL in the 1980s.

Arnimische, Gräflich Glassworks in Jämlitz bei Muskau, Germany [–], active c.1924, see also Jamlitz Glashutte.

Arnstadt-Kristall GmbH Glassworks in Arnstadt, Germany [1947–present], (cut glass, tableware, cut-to-clear, giftware, engraved, sanded, gilt).

Arques, Cristallerie d' Glassworks in Arques, France [1825–present], see Durand, J G, (mass-produced tableware).

Arrowhead cane A millefiori cane with a three-pronged arrow design (paperweights).

ARS Trade name for Samuels Glass Co, AR.

Arsall Glass studio located in Weisswasser near Rothenburg, Germany [1918–38], was operated by VLG. Produced floral cameo 1918–29. Designers include Nicolas Rigot 1918–24 and Wilhelm Krause 1924–38. Sig: "Arsall" or "Lusa" in cameo script, often with a pattern number on pieces in 1918–29.

Arsall

Art Deco Style characterized by linear, geometric design [1920s–c.1939].

Art Design AB Design company located in Vadstena, Sweden [1985–present], designers include Berit and Jan Johansson.

Art et Verre, Sté Coopérative See Gobbe-Hocquemiller.

Arte '80 Glassworks in Murano, Italy [–], active c.1980, (glass art).

Artel, Kunstgewerbliches Atelier Glass group located in Praha, Czechoslovakia [1908–35], various artist members include Kotěra, Rosipal, Kysela, Brunner. (Designer glass, cubist after 1916, decorative until 1926, expressionist after 1926, souvenir glass after 1920.)

Arte Nuova Murano Glassworks in Murano, Italy [–], active c.1967, members of Quality Circle, (art glass).

Arte Vetraria Muranese (AVEM) Muranese Glassworks in Murano, Italy [1932–*]. Founded by Antonio Ferro, Egidio Ferro and Emilio Nason. Designers include Vittorio Zecchin c.1932, Giulio Radi 1935–52, Aldo Nason 1934–67, Giorgio Ferro 1951–5, Ansolo Fuga 1955–62. Styles include pulegoso 1932, zanfirico 1932, opaque

Arte Vetro

metallic lustre glasses 1948 and 1950, anso volante 1952–5; vaso astrale 1960. Sig: AVEM pieces are never signed, instead have labels: circular foil label in red, green or blue 1940–1964 while typewritten paper labels on factory bought glass c.1980s only. (Art glass.)
Arte Vetro, Alberto Seguso Glassworks in Murano [1947–54], designers include Martinuzzi 1950/2 and Vinicio Vianello 1952/4.
Art Glas SA Glassworks in Bistrita, Romania [?–present].
Art glass Glass made for decorative purposes.
Art glass baskets Victorian novelties, "whimsies" in the shape of a basket.
Artifice, Verrerie Glassworks in Vallauris, France [?–present].
Artigianato Artistico Veneziano di Nicolò Barbini Glassworks in Murano, Italy [–], active c.1980.
Artiglass Glassworks in Albignasego, near Padua, Italy [?–present], (bottles).
Artistica La Piana, Cristalleries Glassworks in Colle Val d'Elsa, Italy [1967–present], merger of Cristalleria Artistica Lavorazioni Brevettate and Cristalleria La Piana resulted in the start of this company in 1967, Trade names include RCR, Primavera di Cristallo and DaVinci Crystal, (crystal tableware); automated production after c.1973).
Artistique Collection Series of miniature art glass designed by Bertil Vallien for Boda c.1980s. Sig: Boda artistique # B Vallien.
Art Moderne 1. See Art Deco. 2. Trade name for Artistic glass from Verreries de Momignies, Belgium, discontinued 1962, designers include Charles Conrad c.1958.
Art Nouveau Style from late 19thC and early 20thC characterized by naturalistic shapes and long curved lines. Art Nouveau started around 1880, reached the peak of its popularity around 1900, and fell in decline around 1915. See also entries for Gallé, Tiffany, Daum, Val St. Lambert, Loetz; Followed by Art Deco in the 1920s.
Arts and Crafts Arts and Crafts Exhibition Society started in 1887 to promote good design and quality for all, greatly influenced the Art Nouveau style. British movement linked to William Morris, Liberty retailers and Christopher Dresser.
Arts du Verre, Ateliers des Glass studio located in Seraing near Liège, Belgium [1983/5–?], aka Les Compagnies du Val, designers include Alfred Collard, Philippe Coyette, Eugène Moureau, (art glass).
Art Vannes Mark used by Vannes-le-Chatel.
Art Verrier SL Mark used by Saint-Louis.
Artver Signature found on art glass produced by Boom, [c.1927–81]. Sand-blasted geometric designs on blown black glass, sometimes with silver, gold; usually signed, were produced until 1937 and the designer was Paul Heller.
Arvid Böhlmarks Lampfabrik Manufacturer from Sweden [–], designers include Eva Englund c.1966/7, (lamps and lighting as well as vases etc.)
Asch van Wijck, Cornélie van Glass designer from the Netherlands [1900–32], designed

matt bust for Leerdam 1929.
Åseda Glasbruk Glassworks in Sweden [c.1960s–c.1970s], designers include Bo Borgström c.1969, (art glass, tableware).
Åsélius-Lidbeck, Catherina Glass designer from Sweden [1941–], designed for Gullaskrufs after 1967.
Asfour Crystal Intl Glassworks in Cairo, Egypt [1961–present], (chandeliers, cut glass, tableware, pressed glass, decorative items, figures, beads, bracelets, crystal, sodalime, opal).
Ashi, Kabey Studio glass artist from Japan [–].
Asnières, Verrerie de Glassworks in Asnières, France [–], active c.1865, (tableware).
Association des Gobeletiers Belges et Holandais Export group of tableware producers [c.1900–c.1920], comprising: Verreries de Braine-le-Comte, Verreries Réunies à Familleureux; Verreries de Fauquez à Virginal, Cristalleries de Manage, Verreries St. Laurent à Manage, Verreries de Scailmont à Manage, Le Progrès à Manage, Verreries St. Louis à Neufville, Verreries de Manage, all in Belgium.
Astera Glassworks in Nový Bor, Czech Republic [?–present], (tableware).
Asti, Sergio Glass designer from Italy [1926–], worked for Salviati c.1961–c.1983, Venini 1968–74, Seguso Vetri d'Arte 1986–8, Barovier e Toso 1988 and Peruzzi & Bozzi c.1970/1.
Asträa glass Type of art glass made by Loetz in the early 1900s.
Astral lamps Burning fluid lamp that has an Argand burner and a circular reservoir; patented 1843 by Cornelius & Co, aka Sinumbral.
Astvatsaturyan, Aknuny Glass designer from Rostov, Russia [1925–], worked at Vosstanie Glassworks 1961–2 and the Leningrad Factory 1965–present.
Ateliers Artistique V.de Winner Glassworks in Liège, Belgium [1930–53], (lamps and lighting, satinated, blown, pressed glass).
Athena Cattédrale Barovier & Toso art glass type by Ercole Barovier, 1964.
Atkins, Lloyd Glass designer from USA [1922–], worked for Steuben 1948–84.
Atlantis/Cristais de Alcobaça Glassworks in Alcobaça, Marinha Grande, Portugal [1945–present]. Trade names includes Atlantis, Royal Crystal, Crisal – see also Marinha Grande and Mglass. Atlantis is the largest of the Portugese glass makers, (cut glass, tableware.)
Atlas Trade name of Atlas Glass Co, Washington, PA, USA [1896–1965], later known as Hazel Atlas.
Atmosphere The mix of oxygen and fuel in a kiln. Fuel rich atmosphere causes reduction; oxygen rich atmosphere causes oxidation, aka redox. These both affect colouring metallic oxides.
Ätta Glashyttan Glass studio located in Sweden [?–present].
Atterberg, Ingrid Glass designer from Sweden [1920–].
Atterbury & Co Glassworks in Pittsburgh, PA, USA [1859–c.1902], (pressed glass, milk glass).

14

Aubervilliers, Verreries & Cristalleries d' Glassworks in Aubervilliers, France [c.1865–c.1890], also known as Verrerie Parisienne, Mellerio Frères and as Gerspach, (lamps and lighting).

Augarten Porcelain manufacturer from Vienna, Austria [1718–present], has a range of luxury glass tableware including designs by Josef Hoffmann.

Augustahütte Glassworks in Wiesau near Sprottau NL, Germany [1677–c.1937].

Aulenti, Gae Glass designer from Italy [1927–], worked for Vistosi c.1968–c.1973.

Aureliano Toso see Toso.

Aurene Glass Metallic iridescent glassware developed in 1904 by Frederick Carder of the Steuben Glass Works, NY. Usually a lustrous gold or blue, but green and red also occur. Sig: acid-etched fleur-de-lis. For similar glass types see Tiffany, Myra, Quezal, Kew Blas

Aurora 1. Trade name of Macbeth-Evans Glass Co. 2. Aurora Glass Company: original name for Vasa Murrhina glass company, London c.1880s. See also D'Humy.

Austenglashütte Glassworks in Bodenmais, Bavaria, Germany [?–present].

Australian Glass Manufacturing Co Glassworks in Kilkenny, S. Australia [–]. Sig: gm inside dip A, (bottles).

Austria Glas Glassworks in Bad Ischl, Austria [–], active c.1947.

Automatic bottle machine (ABM) Aka as Owens machine, invented in 1903. In ABM-produced bottles the seam extends to the top of the mouth. By 1913 ABMs had replaced all previous methods. See Side seams.

Autunnale Barovier & Toso art glass type by Ercole Barovier, 1954

AVEM See Arte Vetraria Muranese.

Aventurine Glass type developed in 15th-century Venice. It contains copper shavings to produce a brilliant sparkle; most often brownish in colour, sometimes black. Does not look like the mineral of the same name. Often used as colour accent, seldom solid; it does not allow high temperatures. Green aventurine includes chromium and was developed in France 1865 – also used by Orrefors.

Aventurine Glistening reflections of leaf-like inclusions on an almost opaque background.

Averbeck, MJ Glass distributor located in New York, NY, USA [1892–1923], (cut glass; jewellery, mail order).

Averkov, Pavel P Glass designer from Kiev, Ukraine [1924–], chief designer at Kiev Factory 1954–69.

Avesn, Verreries Paul d' Glassworks in France [–].

Avesn, Paul d' Glass designer from France [–], worked for Belle-Etoile c.1927–c.1930 and for Verreries Paul d'Avesn.

Avesn, Pierre d' Glass designer from France [–], worked for Choisy-le-Roi c.1928–c.1930).

AVH Trade name of A van Hoboken & Co, Rotterdam, Netherlands [1800–98], (bottles).

AV Mazzega Vetri d'Arte See Mazzega.

Avolio A dot of glass added as an attachment point for additonal parts.

Avon Cosmetic marketing organization

[1886–present]. Sig: CPC = California Perfume Co. 1886–1939; Avon brand used since 1929, (perfume bottles, giftware, pressed glass).

Avondale Glass producer or refinery located in Wales [–], active c.1980.

Avroy, SA des Verreries d' Glassworks in Quai d'Avroy, Liège, Belgium [1837–52], previously named Nizet 1709–1816 and Mélotte-Nizet 1816–37, (crystal, semi-crystal, tableware).

Awashima Masakichi Glass designer from Japan [1914–], worked for Hoya Crystal Corporation 1946–50 and Awashima Glass Company 1956–75, and developed waterdrop textured "Shizuku" glass.

Axenbrandt, Mikael Glass designer from Sweden [–], worked for Strombergshyttan.

Ayotte, Rick (Roland) Lampwork and paperweights artist from Nashua, NH, USA [1944–], has had a studio with Paul Stankard 1970–present.

B

B in a square diamond Boyd Art Glass mark (line on top and bottom).

Baasler Bohemian engraver [–], worked at Stevens & Williams after 1876.

Baccarat, Cristalleries de Glassworks in Baccarat (near Lunéville, Nancy) [1765–present], early production included flat glass, tableware, mining lamps, were bought by Aimé Gabriel d'Artigues who also owned Vonêche in Namur, Belgium, in 1816. Renamed Verrerie de Vonêche à Baccarat, 1817–24, renamed Vonêche-Baccarat 1824–42. Invention of opaline, 1823, joint sales with St-Louis 1832–57, introduction of colour 1838, paperweights millefiori and sulfures 1846–60 and 1957–present. Exposition Internationale, 1855 and 1878, cut glass and crystal, enamel, pressed glass, cased glass, limited production of Art Nouveau glass. Designers include Berlage (c.1900, tableware), Georges Chevalier (c.1916–1960, animal figures, tableware, lamps and lighting) and Jean Sala (tableware, vases). Sig: circular paper label 1860–1936 features stem + decanter + tumbler, Baccarat on pressed glass after 1870s, acid-etched marks after c.1920s on perfumes and after 1936 on tableware, sand-blasted marks after 1971, laser cut signatures added after 1990. (Tableware, cut glass, pressed glass, art glass, paperweights, lamps and lighting all of high quality.)

Bacchante Nude stems crystal tableware made by Bayel, France c.1970s–present.

Bacchus & Sons, George Glassworks in

Birmingham, Great Britain [–], active 19thC, (tableware, paperweights, pressed glass).
Bachmetov Glass Factory Glassworks located at Nikol'sko/St Petersburg, Russia [1763–?], (coloured glass).
Back painted Decorated from the rear, esp. snuff bottles, icons, aka Hinterglasmalerei.
Backström, Monica Glass designer from Sweden [1939–], worked for Kosta Boda after 1965, married to Höglund.
Bacquart, Francoise Glass designer from Belgium [–], worked for Vereno 1974–86, Boussu 1987–present.
Bacri, Clotilde Glass designer from France [–], worked for Daum & Cie after 1986.
Badalona, Cristall Glassworks in Badalona, Spain [1866–1983] and [1984–present], founded as Badia Grau I Companyia, 1866, became Cristall Badalona 1874, A Farrés i Cia. 1908; Unión Vidriera de España, 1908, now known as Cristall Badalona SAL.
Bad Ischl, Glasmanufaktur Glassworks in Bad Ischl, Austria [–], active c.1947.
Bad Karlshafen Glashütte GmbH Glassworks in Bad Karlshafen, Germany [1985–present], (part of Glashütten Rolf Wiemers).
Bad Reichenhall, Glashütte Glassworks in Bad Reichenhall, Germany [1994–?], uses the trade name Riedl glass, (giftware, art glass, Graal).
Badalona SAL, Cristall Glassworks in Badalona, Spain [1866–present], founded as Badia Grau I Cia, (tableware).
Badger & Co Thos Glassworks located in Dudley, Great Britain [c.1772–1859], aka Phoenix Glassworks, operated by T Badger 1820–59, (cut glass, pressed glass).
Badging Glass etching technique using acid paste applied with a rubber stamp.
Bagley & Co Ltd Glassworks in Knottingley, N. Yorkshire, Great Britain [1871–1975], aka Crystal Glass Co. Taken over and closed by Rockwell group 1975. (Bottles only 1871–1912). Designers include Alexander Hardie Williamson after 1933. Sig: paper labels only 1929, B & Co L on bottles. (pressed glass and lead crystal from 1912, crystaltynt 1932 Art Deco style, Jetique black glass c.1930–c.1950, "Polkadot").

Bagneux, Verrerie de Glassworks in Bagneux, France [–], active c.1924.
Baguière Small dish with a single vertical pin for depositing rings.
BAG Vsetin Glassworks in Vsetin, Czechoslovakia [1993–present], owned and operated by Barovier & Toso Czech Republic, designers include Jiri Suhajek, Rony Plesl, Otto Macek, Mojmir Cermak, Jan Votava and Petr Vlcek. Sig: BAG vases are marked "Designed + artist name" in needle-etched script, (art glass, giftware).

Bahr, Walter Flamework artist from Wertheim, Germany [1949–], set up own studio 1978. Sig: WB. (Combined blown and flameworked glass after 1982, fused glass 1986, esp. combined techniques, paperweights, mosaics.)
Bailey & Co, WA Glass maker located in London, Great Britain [–], active c.1908, trade names include Rockware Glass.
Bailey, Banks & Biddle Co Glassworks in USA [–], active c.1930, (cut glass, Brilliant period).
Baird, James Engraver worked at Couper & Sons in Glasgow, Scotland c.1870s/80s.
Bakalowits & Söhne Glass dealer located in Vienna, Austria [1845–?], commissioned works from artists that were manufactured by Loetz, Meyr's Neffe. Designers include Josef Olbrich, Kolo Moser c.1900, Robert Holubetz, Antoinette Krasnik, Jutta Sika, Otto Prutscher, Emil Hoppe, Hans Vollmer. No sig.
Baker Brothers & Co Glassworks in Baltimore, USA [–], active c.1880, aka Baltimore Glass Works, (bottles).
Baker, de Glass outlet in Brussels, Belgium, sig. found on Schneider pieces.
Bakewell & Ensell Glassworks in Pittsburgh, PA, USA [1807–44], became Bakewell, Pears & Co, was the first US company to produce flint glass, (pressed glass).
Bakewell, Payn & Page Co Glassworks in Pittsburgh, PA 1808–70s, later known as Bakewell, Pears & Co.
Bakewell, Pears & Co Glassworks in Pittsburgh, PA [1807–88], started as Bakewell & Ensell 1807–44, later Bakewell, Payn & Page Co, (pressed glass, tableware, barware).
Bakhmetyevsky Glassworks Glassworks in Vladimir Province, Russia [18thC], see Krasny Ghigant.
Bakkene, Arvid Glass designer from Norway [1947–], worked for Hadeland 1964–1976.
Bakker, AJ Glassworks in Nieuw-Buinen, Netherlands [1921–67], merged with NV Nederlandse Glasfabrieken Leerdam in 1938, closed 1967, (bottles).
Baku Glassworks Glassworks in Baku, Azerbaijan [1950s–?]. Designers have included Ibraghimov since 1967.
Balabin, Albert G Glass designer from Kiev, Ukraine [1934–], worked at The Neman Glassworks 1962–4, at Kerch packaging 1964–8 and at Kiev Factory after 1968.
Balboa Glassworks Glassworks in Murano, Italy [c.1960s–?].
Ball Trade name for Ball Brothers Glass Manufacturing Company, Muncie, IN, USA [1887–1973], later known as Ball Corp. Sig: Ball in caps or script, (bottles).
Ball gatherer A machine for collecting a portion of molten glass from the furnace to feed a forming machine.
Ball stopper 1. Ball-shaped stopper rests on the everted neck of a decanter 2. Internal ball

stopper used in soda bottles, introduced in 1873.

Ballarin, Francesco e Mario Glass makers located in Murano, Italy [c.1980–present], (lampwork).

Balmain Glass Works, The Glassworks in Rozelle, Australia [1919–26], merged with Crystal Glassworks, (bottles, lamps and lighting, pressed glass, carnival).

Balsamo Stella, Guido Glass designer from Italy [1882–1941], worked for Artisti Barovier 1918, started own workshop 1925, worked for SALIR 1926–c.1932.

Baltimore Glass Works Glassworks in Baltimore, USA [–], run by Baker Brothers & Co, (bottle plant).

Baluster Short round pillar narrower towards the top, part of a balustrade, it is called an inverted baluster if it is narrower at the bottom.

Banford, Ray and Bob Paperweight artists from NJ, USA [1918– and 1951–], (paperweights from 1971).

Bang, Jacob E Glass designer from Denmark [1899–1965], worked for Holmegaard 1925–42 and Kastrup 1955–63.

Bang, Michael Glass designer from Denmark [1944–], worked for Björn Wiinblad 1960–2 and 1964–6, Ekenäs Glasbruk 1966–8, Kastrup & Holmegaard at Odense 1968–74, Fensmark after 1974 and at Royal Copenhagen after 1975, (tableware, lamps and lighting).

Bank Quay Glass Works See Perrin Geddes & Co.

Barateiro, Sandra Glass designer from Portugal [–], worked for Mglass at Marinha Grande c.1999.

Barbarahütte, Mstišov, Emina Hut/Barborina Hut Glassworks in Mstišov, Teplic v Cechách, Czechoslovakia [?–1927], acquired by Rindskopf, 1900 (art glass, iridized glass Grenada, Alhambra, Pepita, pressed glass after the 1920s, later coloured tableware only).

Barbárico Barovier & Toso art glass type by Ercole Barovier, 1951.

Barbe, Jules Glass decorator from France [–], worked for Thomas Webb 1879–1901, freelance after 1901), (enamelling, gilding).

Barber bottle US term for decorative bottle for lotions used in barber shops c.1850s–c.1920.

Barber, Ralph Glass maker from Millville, NJ, USA [–], (paperweights 1900s–1910s).

Barbican Glassworks Glassworks in Plymouth, Great Britain [?–present], operated by Dartington Crystal.

Barbini, Alfredo Glass designer from Murano, Italy [1912–], worked for SAIAR Ferro Toso after 1920, Cristalleria Murano after 1930, Zecchin Martinuzzi 1932–7, Seguso Vetri d'Arte/VAMSA 1936–44, Gino Cenedese 1947–50, own company founded 1950, (art glass; hot-formed glass animals, monumental works, chandeliers).

Barbini, Flavio Glass designer from Italy [1948], worked for Barbini c.1968–c.1980).

Barbini Guglielmo Glass engraver from Murano, Italy [c.1967–], worked for SALIR 1923–35, own workshop after 1936, also worked for Aureliano Toso, (cut glass and engraved glass).

Barbini Vetri d'Arte di Murano Glassworks in Martellago/Venice, Italy [1964–present], operated by Francesco Barbini, (decorated glassware; speciality raised enamel on gold – "terzo fuoco").

Barbini Vetri Artistici, Alfredo Glassworks in Murano, Italy [1950–present], (member of Quality Circle), designers include Vinicio Vianello 1950, Napoleone Martinuzzi c.1960s, Flavio Barbini c.1968–c.1980, Toffoloni & Palange c.1980. Creations include sommerso 1960, tulipani 1962, pesce c.1962, murrine 1969, vetri scavi c.1969. Sig: circular foil label early 1950s, needle-etched name on bottom c.1950–present, square paper label 1971–present, needle-etched name on side c.1971–9, plastic labels c.1979–present, signatures on all commercial items since the 1970s), (art glass).

A.Barbini **BARBINI**

Bärenhütte, Glasfabrik Weisswasser GmbH Glassworks in Weisswasser near Rothenburg, Germany [1897–?]. Operated by Hirsch & Janke, Malky, Müller & Co, by Philips after 1920, known as Weisswasser GmbH section Bärenhütte after 1945 and VEB Kombinat Lausitzer Glas Section Bärenhütte 1969, 1979. (Goblets, cut glass, tableware, bottles, lead glass; automatic stemware production since 1962.)

Barnes, Hobbs & Co/US Glass See Hobbs.

Barney, ACJ Studio artist from USA, [–].

Barocchi Barovier & Toso art glass type by Ercole Barovier, 1948.

Barolac Trade name for pressed glass vases made by Libochovice Sklarny in Czechoslovakia [c.1930–45], designer Prof Drahonovsky. Sig: Barolac, although not always present. Re-issued in the 1970s, (heavy moulded vases in various colours, including opalescent).

Barovier & Toso Glassworks in Murano, Italy [1883–present], (members of Quality Circle), founded 1883; name changed from Fratelli Barovier e Co to Artisti Barovier 1886. Copies of old glass produced c.1900, murrine flowers after 1910, murrine glass by Vittorio Zecchin and Teodoro Wolf-Ferrari c.1913. Name changed to Vetreria Artistica Barovier e Co in 1919. Designers include Nicolo and Ercole Barovier, Piero Toso, Umberto Bellotto c.1919–c.1923, Angelo Barovier after 1947. Merged with SAIAR Ferro Toso 1935, new names Ferro Toso Barovier e Co, Barovier & Toso & Cie 1936–42 then Barovier e Toso in 1942. Art glass types include vetro primavera 1927, rostrati technique 1938, vetro gemmato c.1936–8, rugiada glass 1940, Oriente technique 1940, murrini 1947, damasco 1948, corinto 1948, barbarico 1951, aborigeni

1954, cobaltei 1956, dorici 1960, efeso c.1963. Current designers include Toni Zuccheri, Renato Toso, Noti Massari and Matteo Thun. (Art glass, lamps and lighting, chandeliers.)

Barovier & Toso signatures Square tear-off paper label "Artisti Barovier Murano" 1878–1914, murrine "AB" in murrine pieces, paper label "Verreries Artistiques Barovier & C" 1919–34, circular foil label "Ars Murano FTB" 1935–42; rectangular tear-off paper label "Barovier & Toso Murano Made in Italy" 1936–55, rectangular peel-off paper label in red/white 1956–70, circular relief foil label "Barovier & Toso Made in Italy" 1936–55; circular foil label "Barovier & Toso Murano" 1956–70; rectangular peel-off labels with company logo 1971–84, square label with text at 45° angle under logo, and rectangular label with text only since 1985.
Barovier e Toso Czech Republic sro Glassworks in Vsetin, Czech Republic [1991–present], aka B A G.
Barovier Seguso e Ferro Glassworks in Murano, Italy [1933–present], designers include Vittorio Zecchin 1933–35.
Barovier, Ercole Glass designer from Italy [1889–1974], worked for Barovier & Toso, 1924–74, credited with more than 25,000 art glass designs.
Barovier, various people Angelo 1927–, Benedetto 1857–1930, Benvenuto 1855–1932, Ercole 1889–1974, Giuseppe 1853–1942, Giovanni 1839–1908, Jacopo 1950–, Napoleone 1881–1957, Nicolò 1895–1947.
Bars Large diameter glass rods made by fusing a number of thinner glass canes; bars cut into sections are used in paperweights or mosaics. See murrina.
Bar-Tal, Ariël Glass designer from Hungary [1920–present], has worked in Israel since c.1950.
Barthélemy, Louis Glass engraver from Belgium [–], worked at VSL 1950s–60s.
Bartlett-Collins Glass Co Glassworks in Sapulpa, OK, USA [1907–present], (located in Coffeyville, KY 1903–11), (tableware, pressed glass, lamps and lighting).
Bartsch, Quilitz & Co Glashütte Glassworks in Finsterwalde near Luckau NL, Germany [1908–45]. Sig: G/FK in hexagons in a circle 1923–45.
Baruth Glashütte Glassworks in Baruth, Brandenburg, Germany [1234–1980], (lamps and lighting, milk glass globes and chimneys after 1830).
Bas, Verrerie d'en Glassworks in Aniche, France [1865–].
Basal ring The circular rim around a base that a piece rests on.

Basalto Barovier & Toso art glass type by Ercole Barovier, 1950.
Baskemölla, Glashyttan på Glass studio located in Baskemölla, Sweden [?–present], owned and run by Anders Wingård.
Batanova, Ekatarina I Glass designer from Moscow, Russia [1925–], worked at Leningrad Factory 1952–4, art director at central offices 1956–60 and 1960–present. Works realized at Leningrad Factory, Krasny May, The Neman, Vorovsky Glassworks.
Báthory, Júlia Glass designer from Budapest, Hungary [1901–], worked in Munich and Dessau (Bauhaus) 1929–32, in Paris 1932–9 and in Budapest 1939–1990s, (stylized figurative engraving, glass panels).
Battledore Glass maker's tool/wooden spatula for smoothing bottoms etc.
Battuto 1. Developed in the 1930s, in Vetro battuto the entire surface of the glass is ground to form small, irregular, adjacent markings running in the same direction. 2. Venini art glass designed by Carlo Scarpa in 1940, by Tobia Scarpa after 1957 and by Tobia Scarpa and Ludovico Diaz de Santillana in 1960.
Bauduin Glass maker from France [1943–].
Bauer Co, The Glasshouse located in Philadelphia, PA, USA [–], active c.1890s, (gas shades).
Bauer, Leopold Glass designer from Austria [1872–1938]. Designed 60 different models for Loetz 1900–6.

B

Bauer, Lisa Glass decorator from Sweden [–], worked for Kosta. Sig: P/Bauer on Kosta pieces designed by Sigurd Persson.
Bauzot-Ledoux & Cie Glassworks in Jumet, Belgium [1855–79], previously Ledoux Frères, engraved tableware 1855–60, closed 1860–7, flat glass only 1867–79, taken over by Verreries Nationales 1879.
Bavarian Forest Glass-making region in Germany near the Czech border that has many glass makers and cut glass refineries. Towns include Arnbruck, Bodenmais, Frauenau, Freyung, Riedlhütte, Spiegelau, Zwiesel. Makers include Ambiente, Austenglas, Eisch, Hirtreiter, Joska, Köck, Krauspe, Nachtmann, Theresienthal, Poschinger, Rimpler, Schmid, Schott, Seemann, TRS, Wandtner, Weinfurtner.
Baxley, Gene Glass maker from Corydon, IN, USA [–], made paperweights 1960s–80s for Zimmerman Art Glass Co.
Baxter, Geoffrey P Glass designer from Great Britain [1922–], worked for James Powell & Sons/Whitefriars as resident designer 1954–61 and for Dartington Crystal, (Scandinavian style, paperweights).
Bayel (Aube) et Fains (Meuse), Verreries de Glassworks in Bayel (Aube), France [1666–present], names have included Alexis

Marquot 1854, Gustave Marquot 1872, Veuve Gustave Marquot et ses Fils 1895, Veuve Gustave Marquot et Fils after 1914, Bayel Cristalleries de Champagne, Cristalleries Royales de Champagne. Currently known as Royales de Champagne. Sig: circular acid stamp "Bayel Cristal", (pressed glass, tableware, novelties).

Bayer, Karl Painter/decorator from Bohemia [–], worked in Weisswasser after 1945.

Bazel, KPC de Architect and glass designer from the Netherlands [1869–1923], worked for Leerdam 1916–23. Sig: etched monogram in a double circle 1916–21, simplified/single circle 1922–45, sand-blasted monogram 1946/7.

BBR See Bouteilleries Belges R Réunies, des SA.

Beads Glass beads (or rocailles) are made from pieces of coloured glass tubing that are spun in a heated drum (in ancient times by trailing a glass thread around a metal wire). Centres of production are Murano, Bohemia and Japan. Venetian millifiori beads that were imported by traders of the 17thC were used as currency in African countries until quite recently.

Beam bottles, Jim The whisky maker has released more than 500 different collectable bottles since 1953, inspiring colleagues Ezra Brooks, JW Dant, Lionstone, McCormick, Old blue ribbon, Old Commonwealth and Old Fitzgerald to do the same.

Beardslee Chandelier Manufacturing Glassworks, location unknown [c.1910–c.1920], (lamps and lighting).

Beatson, Clark & Co Ltd Glassworks in Rotherham, Yorkshire, Great Britain [–], active c.1950, (bottles).

Beatty, Alexander J & Sons/US Glass R Glassworks in Steubenville, OH, USA [1845–92], moved to Tiffin, OH in 1888, joined US Glass as Factory R in 1892, previously known as Beatty & Stillman, later Tiffin Glass, (tableware & pressed glass).

Beatty-Brady Glass Co. Glassworks in Steubenville, OH, USA [1850–1907], also located in Dunkirk, IN, 1898, National Glass 1899, was taken over by Indiana Glass 1907–present], (pressed glass).

Beaumont Glass Co Glassworks in Morgantown, WV, USA [1895–1905], situated in Martins Ferry, OH 1895–1902, Grafton, WV 1903–5 and Morgantown, WV after 1906, where part of it continued as Hocking & Co, the other part remained in Grafton as Tygart Valley Glass Co, (tableware, pressed glass).

Beaver Falls Cooperative Glass Co Glassworks in Beaver Falls, PA, USA [1879–1937], renamed Beaver Falls Glass Co 1887, (pressed glass).

Beaver Flint Glass Co Glassworks in Toronto, Ontario, Canada [1897–1920]. Sig: beaver, (bottles).

Beaver Valley Glass Co Glassworks in USA [–], owned and operated by Fry Glass Co, HC.

Becht, Alfred Glassworks in Offenburg in Baden, Bermany [–], used trade name Derfla, (heat resistant opal glass; dentist ware).

Beckert, Adolf Glass designer from Česká Lípa, Bohemia [1884–1929], trained at Nový Bor school, worked for the company Pietsch c.1915, art director at Loetz 1909–11; at Kamenický Šenov school 1911–26. Sig: AB.

Bečvář, Karel Glass designer from the Strakonice, Czech Republic [1955–].

Bedřichov Glassworks in Bedřichov, Friedrichswald, Czechoslovakia [1558–1806].

Beecham, Gary Studio glass artist from USA [–].

Beer, Erwin Glass worker located in Pfaffenhofen, Austria [1970–present], (lampwork, tableware).

Begou, Alain Glass designer from France [1945–].

Begou, Marysa Glass designer from France [1948–].

Behrens, Peter Glass designer from Germany [1868–1940], worked for Rheinische Glashütten c.1901, three of his glass service designs reissued by Poschinger 1999.

Behrmann, Prof Glass designer from Germany [–], worked for WMF c.1930.

Beilby glassware Enamelled glassware in the style of William and Mary Beilby, see above.

Beilby, William and Mary Glass decorators from Great Britain [1740–1819] and [1749–97]; (son and daughter of William Beilby 1706–65).

Bel Art Römische Glashütte Glassworks in Bad Münstereifel [?–present], (Roman-style glass).

Belga Lamp Works, SA Glassworks in Belgium [–], active c.1928, (lamps and lighting).

Belgian Glass Production centres are Liège (Jemeppe, Seraing, Chênée), Charleroi (Jumet, Roux, Gilly, Courcelles), Namur (Jambes, Floreffe), Mons (Boussu, Ghlin, Havré) as well as Antwerp, Brussels, Braine-le-Comte, Gent.

Bellaire Goblet Co/US Glass M. Glassworks in Bellaire, OH, USA [1876–91], Findlay, OH [1888–91] and from 1891 part of US Glass – known as Factory M.

Belle-Etoile, Verreries de Glassworks in Croismare, Meurthe-et-Moselle, France [c.1927–c.1930], founded by Daum, art director Paul d'Avesn. Sig: Lorrain, (art glass & opalescent glass).

Bellefroid, Edmond Glass designer from the Netherlands [1893–1971], (worked for Maastricht 1939].

Belleville Glass Co Glassworks in Belleville, IL, USA [–], active c.1882, (bottles).

Bellevue Verreries de Glassworks in France [–], active c.1844, (flat glass).

Bell Fruit Bottle Co Glassworks in Fairmount, IN, USA [–], producing c.1910, (bottles).

Bellis Glassworks in Jablonec nad Nisou, Czech Republic [?–present], (beads).

Bellotto, Umberto Glass designer from Italy [1882–1940], worked for Artisti Barovier,

19

Salviati and Pauly e Co.

Belmont Glass Co Glassworks in Bellaire, OH, USA [1866–90], started by J H Leighton from Wheeling, WV, named Belmont Glass works from 1888, (pressed glass).

Belmont Tumbler Co Glassworks located Bellaire, OH, USA [1890–1952], (pressed glass, depression glass, tumblers).

Belopal Ltd Glassworks locaed in Beloslav, Bulgaria [?–present], (bottle, jars, vials, glasses, vases, tumblers).

Benda, Eduard Glass cutter from Jablonec, Czechoslovakia [c.1800–49].

Bendel, Hugo Glass decorator from Bohemia [1881–1953].

Benedict Kimber Glassworks in Bridgeport and Brownsville, PA, USA [1822–40], (bottles).

Benedict, MS Manufacturing Co Glassworks, location unknown [–], active c.1890, (tableware).

Beniganim see Vidrios.

Bennert-Bivort et Courcelles Réunies, SA Glassworks in Jumet-Coupe [1923–31], (bottles, flat glass).

Bennett Brothers Inc Glassworks in USA [–], active c.1941, (tableware).

Benson, John Glass cutter from Dudley, Great Britain [–], (cut glass).

Bent glass, Bending 1. Process for curving flat glass in a hollow shape for bowls, plates, ashtrays, etc, the tailored glass plate is placed on a talc-coated steel mould in the oven and "slumps" into shape (aka slumping). 2. Curved flat glass made by US Art Bent Glass Co and subsidiaries in many countries c.1920–c.1960, including flamingo glass, often with printed lace.

Beránek, Emanuel Glass designer from Czechoslovakia [–]; works at Škrdlovice, Czech Republic [1943–present]. Sig: paper labels only, many variations include "Škrdlovice", "Bohemia", "Beranek", contemporary pieces usually engraved with artist's name, (art glass, esp. thickwalled).

BERÁNEK

Berckemeyer Drinking glass of the 16th/17thC, from Germany and Holland, see replicas.

Bercy, Cristallerie de Glassworks in Bercy, near Paris, France [–], 19thC, (opalines).

Bereg Crystal Glassworks in Vasarosnameny, Hungary [?–present].

Berezhanski Sklozavod (Berezhany Glass Factory) Glassworks in Berezhany, Ukraine [1961–present], linked to Raduga factory. Marks may include Eurosklo, (coloured, decorated tableware, enamelled giftware, art glass, lamps and lighting).

Bergamini, Aldo Glass designer from Italy [1903–],worked for AVEM 1954, Dalla Venezia Martinuzzi 1956, IVR Mazzega c.1950s and Fucina 1953.

Bergdala Glassworks in the Crystal Kingdom,

Sweden [1889–present], designers include Thommy Bremberg, Bengt Lindberg, Lena Linderholm and Mats Theselius.

Bergé, Henri Glass decorator from France [1870–1930], chief decorator for Daum 1900–14, worked for Almaric Walter c.1918–30.

Bergen, JD, Co Glassworks in Meriden, CT, USA [1885–1922], aka Bergen Cut Glass Co, (cut glass, esp. Brilliant period).

Berger lamps Style of perfume burner introduced 1898/1910 by Berger company in France and still produced today. Luxury models by Baccarat, Saint-Louis, d'Argenthal, Czech crystal, Boussu crystal; Valérysthal, and other makers. There have also been special issues for the collector's market. Berger lamps and precursor Müller lamps are avidly collected in France and Belgium.

Bergh, Elis Glass designer from Sweden [1881–1954], worked for Pukeberg 1906–16, Kosta 1929–54). Sig: in the early 1930s only B and model number; later also includes year and "Kosta"; sequential numbering starts 1=1929, 101=1930, 199=1931, 320=1932, 389=1933, 549=1934, 750=1935, 1134=1937, 1332=1938, 1509=1939, 1673=1940 1928=1942, 2032=1943, 2248=1945, 2310=1946, 2379=1947, 2427=1948, 2494=1949, 2577=1950; re-issues in the 1950s and 1960s are marked BH plus model number.

Bergkvist, Gustav Master glass blower from Sweden [–], developed Ariel with Öhrström and Lindstrand at Orrefors c.1936.

Bergkvist, Knut Master glass designer from Sweden [–], developed Graal with Simon Gate in 1916.

Berglund, Ture Glass designer from Sweden [–], worked for: Stockholms Glasbruk.

Bergslien, Gro Glass designer from Norway [1940–], worked for Hadeland 1964.

Bergström, Lena Glass designer from Sweden [1961–], works for Orrefors 1994–present.

Berlage, Hendrik P Architect and glass designer from the Netherlands [1856–1934], worked for Pantin 1902, Val St Lambert 1903, Leerdam 1923–9. Sig: HB monogram.

Berluze Long-necked vase for one single flower. Produced by Daum, Delatte, Legras, Müller in the 1920s and Jemeppe, Monart, WMF in the 1930s.

Berman, Eugene Glass designer from Russia [1899–], US citizen since 1944, has been based in Rome since 1958, worked for Venini 1951.

Bernard, Paul Glass designer from Belgium [1910–72], worked for Familleureux c.1931 and for Gobeleterie Nationale in Manage. Sig: P Bernard Gobena, P B or P Bernard for works done in own studio.

Berndt, Victor Glass designer from Sweden [1919–], designed for Flygsfors 1950–61.

Bernschein, Glasbläserei Christian Glass-making workshop located in Stade, Germany [?–present].

Bernsdorf Glassworks in Kamenz and Bernsdorf, OL Germany [1845–?], operated by Gebr. Hoffmann, see Ankerglas. Sig: Anchor, (lamps and lighting, bottles, tableware).

Berry bowl US term for a round bowl.

Berskinskaya, Svetlana M Glass designer from Moscow, Russia [1930–], designer at Kalinin Cut Glass factory, Moscow 1955–7, Krasny May after 1957, works were also realized in the Lvov factory.

Bertolini See Soffiera Bertolini.

Bestiario Type of art glass made by Venini, which was designed by Toni Zuccheri in1964.

Bettarini, Enrico Glass designer from Italy [–], worked for La Fenice, Italy c.1960/1.

Bettencourt, Sylvia Glass designer from Portugal [–], worked for Mglass in Marinha Grande c.1999.

Betti Torino, Vetrerie Glassworks in Settimo Torinese, TO, Italy [?–present], (bottles, decorative bottles).

Bevelled edge Cut to a bevel, cut at an angle or slant. The cut edge can be ground and polished to obtain a prismatic effect.

Beyer & Co Kristallglas GmbH Glassworks in Neustadt, Germany [?–present], (cut glass, crystal giftware, coloured glass)

Beyermann & Co Glassworks in Nový Bor, Czechoslovakia [c.1915–28].

Beyers, Scott Glass designer from USA [–], worked for Orient & Flume, (paperweights).

Bezon, Verrerie de Glassworks in Bezon, France [–], active c.1928.

Biaglass Ltd Glassworks in Bialystock, Poland [c.1977–present], glass blowers include Mariusz Rynkiewicz 1978–85, (tableware, lamps and lighting).

Bianconi, Fulvio Glass designer from Italy [1915–], worked for Venini 1946–55, Cenedese 1954, Danese gallery, Vistosi 1963, Galliano Ferro 1966 and Toso Vetri d'Arte c.1980.

Bicolori Barovier & Toso art glass type by Ercole Barovier, 1967.

Biedermeier Decorative style mainly used in 1815–50 in Germany, Austria and Bohemia. Techniques include enamel decoration, schwarzlot painting, engraving, gilding, colour overlays and cut-to-clear. Vessel type used were mainly goblets and recurring themes were portraits, flowers, horses, town views, rural life and well-dressed scenes of domestic bliss. Known artists include Kothgasser, Mohn, Mildner and Egerman.

Biemann, Dominick Master of Biedermeier glass engraving [1800–57], specialized in portraits, worked in Prague and in Franzensbad according to the season.

Biemann, Vincenz Glass engraver from Bohemia [1811–48].

Bigaglia, Pietro Glass maker from Murano, Italy [c.1850s], the first to show millefiori paperweights on the 1845 Vienna exhibition, (beads, paperweights, mosaics).

Bigelow and Kennard Lighting manufacturer located in USA [–], (lamps and lighting, leaded glass shades c.1920).

Bilek, Ilja Glass artist from Liberec, Czech Republic [1948–], designer at ŽBS 1981–present.

Billeci, André Glass artist from Alfred, NY, USA [–], (studio glass).

Billinghurst, A Noel Glass designer from Great Britain [–], worked for Gray-Stan Glass 1926–36, (figurative designs, engraving).

Billnäsin Lasihytti Glassworks in Billnäs, Finland [?–present], (bottles, flasks).

Bimann, Dominick Alternative spelling for Biemann.

Bimini Werkstätte Glassworks in Vienna, Austria [1923–38], some glasses were realized by Venini c.1925–c.1930, (light lampworked glassware and table glass).

Bin, Guido See Deluigi, Mario.

Bing, S European agent for Tiffany c.1900.

Biniranger & Co Grocery business located in New York City, USA [c.1826–c.1880], (figural whisky bottles, packaging).

Biocolore Type of art glass made by Venini, designed by Carlo Scarpa, 1940.

Biondi, Caterina Glass dealer or refinery from Venice, Italy [–], active c.1960.

Biot, Verrerie de Glassworks in Biot (near Nice), France [1956–present], founded by Eloi Monod. Sig: all items stamped "biot", (characteristic air bubble glass in clear, green, blue).

Bipezzati Barovier & Toso art glass type by Ercole Barovier, 1956.

Bird swing A string of glass on the inside of a defective glass container, aka birdcage.

Birkhill, Fred Flamework artist from Pinkney, Michigan, USA [–], has worked since c.1977/1980.

Bisazza Vetro srl Glassworks in Murano, Italy [?–present], (tableware).

Biščan-Bertoša, Srebrenka Glass designer from Croatia [1952–], worked for Kristal in Samobor c.1980, (colour, figures).

Bischoff & Co, Glashütte Glassworks in Kunzendorf near Sorau NL, Germany [c.1937–?].

Bischoff Glass Inc, AF Glassworks in Huntingdon, WV, USA [1922–?], (has been known as Bischoff Glass Co and Bischoff Sons & Co), (tableware, crackle 1942–63).

Bischofswerda Glassworks in Bischofswerda near Bautzen OL, Germany [–], operated by F Greiner & Sohn, (lamps and lighting, milk glass, opal, alabaster shades).

Bishop's Trade name of Bishop & Co, Los Angeles, CA and San Diego, CA, USA [1890–1920], (bottles).

Bismarkhütte Glassworks in Welzow near Spremberg, NL, Germany [1894–c.1937].

Bistro glass Thickwalled drinking glass used in French cafés [19thC] looks as if it contains more than it does, in Great Britain aka deception glass, in US as cheater.

Bits Snippets of molten glass applied hot to a glass shape.

Bitters bottles Small bottle for tonic made in US from 1862 until prohibition 1920, Taiwan replicas abound.

Bittner, Paul Glass maker/designer from Weisswasser, Germany [1910], worked at Weisswasser 1930–72, Schönborn 1972–5 and Rietschen 1975–82.

BK Trade name of Benedict Kimber.

Black bottles Dark green, almost black bottles made in the UK c.1650–1850s.

Black glass Contains oxide or manganese and iron oxide; very dark purple is aka black amethyst and was made from 17th century; see also Obsidian glass and Hyalith.

Blacking bottle Square-shaped bottles with a short neck 10–15cm (4–6in) made [1803–c.1850].

Blackmer Cut Glass Co Glassworks in New Bedford, MA, USA [1894–1916], known as AL Blackmer Inc after 1902, (cut glass).

Blackwell Wielandy Co Glassworks, location unknown [–], active c.1940, (tableware).

Blades, John Glass cutter located in London, Great Britain [c.1820–c.1830], (cut glass, tableware, Regency style).

Blakewell Glass Company Glassworks in Pittsburgh, PA, USA [–], active19thC, (lamps and lighting).

Blanc-Nisseron, Verrerie de Glassworks in Belgium [?–1888], merged into Gobeleterie Nationale in 1888.

Blank A glass object ready for further decoration or finishing.

Blanthorn, Brian Studio artist from Great Britain [–].

Blaschka, Leopold Glass maker from Bohemia, worked in Dresden, Germany [1822–95], specialized in lampwork models of flowers and sea creatures for museums of natural history 1860–95. The Harvard Botanical Museum commissioned him and his son to make botanical models of plants; in over 50 years, some 850 model sets of plants were produced, including magnified parts and anatomical sections. Some 3,000 models are in the Harvard Botanical Museum today.

Blaschka, Rudolf Glassmaker from Dresden, Germany [1857–1936], worked with his father Leopold after 1870.

Blažek, J Glass refinery located in Poděbrady and in Nový Bor, Czech Republic [1933–present], (the refinery in Poděbrady closed down in 1948), currently producing as Blažek J Sklo Poděbrady, (cut glass, raised enamel, miniatures; decorated black glass).

Bleeding Glass See cupping jar, ventouse.

Blenko Glass Co Glassworks in Milton, WV, USA [1922–present], Joel Myers was design director 1964–72. Sig: sand-blasted Blenko mark 1959–60 only, DS + year engraved for Don Sheperd/studio range, labels Blenko Handcraft in hand 1930s–1960s, stylized B 1970s–present, four digit numbers start with production year, 3-digit numbers on tableware, S=small, L=large, HT=Highball tumbler etc, some client marks may occur), (stained glass, tableware [from 1929], pressed glass, 1950s glass).

Blijk, Jacobus van den Glass decorator from Holland [1736–1814], (stippled glass 1770–1814).

Blob seal Applied blob of glass on a bottle neck with a logo etc.

Blob top Bottles that have a heavy knob-like glass top to allow closure, especially mineral/soda water bottles c.1850–80s, aka applied top.

Bloch, Luciënne Glass designer from the Netherlands [1905–], designed frosted figures for Leerdam 1929/30, which were produced until c.1980. Sig: B inside a square.

Block Forming tool made from cherry wood or graphite that is used for shaping glass.

Blocker The person who blows the first bubble of air into the glass, before passing it on to colleagues.

Blohme & Rode Glassworks in Germany [–], see Brockwitz Glasfabrik AG (its factory).

Blom, Håkan Glass designer from Sweden, see Ulven AB, Glashyttan.

Blomberg, Kjell Glass designer from Sweden [1931], worked for Gullaskruf 1954–75.

Bloom Condensation of vaporized glass, usually removed in the working and annealing process. Glasses high in metallic oxides bloom more readily than other glasses.

Bloomingdale Flint Glass Works Glass works located in Manhattan, NY, USA [1820–?], established by John L Gilliland, (cut glass).

Blow-and-blow Process Production process for bottles.

Blower Person who inserts the glass into a mould and then blows it out.

Blowpipe A steel tube, usually c.1.5m (5ft) long, with a mouthpiece at one end and a metal ring on the other, used for blowing molten glass into a bubble.

Blue Ribbon Trade name for Standard Glass Co.

Bluerina US term for a type of glass which shades from light blue to ruby, also known as blue amberina.

Boam, HJ Glass engraver from Great Britain [–], worked for Webb c.1937.

Bobêche Disc used with candlesticks to stop candles dripping.

Boda Bruks AB Glassworks in Boda, Sweden [1864–1946], merged with Kosta to form Kosta Boda 1946. Currently operated by Orrefors. Designers include Fritz Kallenberg, Erik Höglund 1953–73, Monica Backström, Kjell Engmann, Bertil Vallien since 1963. Sig: no sigs pre-1953, H + 3-digit number on Höglund pieces, MB=Backström 1960s, MB/MBA + pattern number=Backström 1971–present, engraved artist name or monogram + either Boda or Kosta Boda 1970s–present, KEN=Engmann), (tableware, decorative glass).

BodaNova Trade name from BodaNova-Höganäs Keramik AB, Höganäs, Sweden [c.1970–present]. The collection includes designer glassware by Liselotte Henriksen, Erik

Espmark, Lovisa Wattman, Ann-Carin Wiktorsson, Barbro Wesslander, Anki Spets and Signe Persson.

Bodum Trade name for borosilicate tableware from Pi design AG, Switzerland (present).

Bohemia Crystalex Trading AS Glass exporter located in Liberec, Czech Republic [1996–present]. Groups include Crystalex in Nový Bor, Sklo Bohemia as in Svetla nad Sazavou, Sklarny Kavalier as in Sazava and Sklarny Bohemia Poděbrady), (tableware).

Bohemia Glassworks: Glassworks in Poděbrady, Nižbor, Jihlava, Zámecka and Svetla nad Savazou, all Czech Republic [1965–present], resulted from merger of all crystal manufacturers in Czechoslovakia in 1965. Designers include Ladislav Oliva and Vladimir Zahour. Sig: various stickers, (cut glass, tableware, giftware, lead crystal).

Bohemia Heritage Trade name for contemporary Biedermeier glass from Bohemia Crystalex Trading (cut-to-clear, engraved, gilded, enamelled etc, traditional style).

Bohemian glass Glass made in Bohemia, the traditional glass-making area in the Czech Republic and neighbouring Austria, Bavaria (Germany) and Silesia (Poland). Also refers to a style of glass making: heavy, brilliant and colourful. The first recorded glass in Bohemia dates from the 6thC; around 1300 there were approx. 20 glass houses in operation making blown vessels. In the 16thC, Bohemian products rivalled Venetian glass in quality and ingenuity. In the 18thC cut glass became important, and new colour techniques were introduced: ruby glass, gilded glass, gold decoration between layers (Zwischengoldglas), enamelling, cut-to-clear. Bohemia in the 19thC had many small glass houses, but no large ones. Specific areas Nový Bor (Haida, 3,200 inhabit.) and Kamenický Šenov (Steinschönau, 5,200 inhabit.) had more than 90 glassworks, and hundreds of cottage refineries. Technical schools had their own glass-working facilities. Many works produced Baroque, Neoclassical and Biedermeier glass. Innovation was driven by Lobmeyr and Loetz. Other important glassworks included Goldberg, Harrach, Kralik, Oertel and Schappel. After World War II, most

of the German glassworkers and factory owners were expelled; the remaining industry was nationalized and reorganized during the communist years (1948–89). In recent years, many new glass houses have sprung up on the (privatized) remains of state corporations, or as new enterprises.

Böhm, August Glass engraver from Bohemia [1812–90], (worked various locations in the UK and in the USA).

Bohnert, Gertrude Glass decorator/engraver from Switzerland [–], worked c.1945–c.1960.

Böhnisch, Josef Glass maker working in Nový Bor, Czechoslovakia c.1912.

Bohus, Zoltan Studio artist from Budapest, Hungary [1941–], independent artist since c.1970.

Bois, Verreries du Glassworks in Manage, Belgium [1906–?].

Boissier, Phyllis Glass engraver from Great Britain [–], worked c.1945–c.1970.

Boldini, Andrea Glass maker from Murano [–], worked for Salviati in the 1890s and for LC Tiffany in New York.

Bolek, Hans Glass designer from Austria [1890–1970], worked for Loetz c.1915.

Bolle Type of art glass made by Venini designed by Tapio Wirkkala, 1966.

Bolton & Sons, Edward Glassworks in Warrington, Great Britain [–], active 19thC, pressed glass from the 1860s.

Bolotino Glassworks in Russia [19thC].

Boman, Axel Enoch Glass designer/cutter/engraver from Sweden [1875–1949], worked for Kosta after 1895, Norrala Glassworks 1906–9, Hadeland 1911, own workshop 1913–20 and 1923–39, Orrefors 1915/6 and Holmegaard 1922.

Bomax Trade name used by Kimble for borosilicate glass (labware).

Bon, Aldo Glass blower/designer from Italy [1906–88], worked for Aureliano Toso 1939–55 and set up Vetreria Artigiana Aldo in 1960.

Bon, Antonio Glass designer from Belgium [–], worked for Val St Lambert c.1950.

Bon Bon A candy dish, open or covered.

Bon, Guido Glass worker from Venice [–], worked for VSL 1950–5 and Vannes after 1955.

Bon, Vetreria Artigiana Aldo Glassworks in Murano [1960–present], designers include Aldo Bon after 1960 and Bruno Bon.

Bonaventura, Skelné Hute Glassworks in Skelné Hute, Czechoslovakia [–].

Bonetti, Mattia Glass designer from France [1953–], worked for Daum c.1989.

Bongard, Herman Glass designer from Norway [1921–], worked for Hadeland 1947–55 and Plus 1960–4.

Bonhomme, Verrerie Glassworks in Liège, Belgium [17thC–1804], (Venetian style).

Bontemps Glass maker from France [1799–1884], re-invented filigrane and millefiori and wrote Le guide du Verrier in 1868. Was director at Choisy-le-Roi 1823–49.

Book family Glass engravers from Sweden; see BSA.

Boom, Glasfabriek de Rupel Glassworks in

Antwerp, Belgium [1920–45], (art glass, tableware, esp. black, gold).

Booth Art Glass Co Glassworks in USA [–], active c.1909, (stained glass).

Booz Bottle Figural whisky bottle named after Philadelphia merchant Edmund Booz c.1860.

Boral Gmbh Glassworks in Rosbach, Germany [1968–present], (bottles).

Bordeaux, Verreries de Glassworks in Bordeaux, France [18thC–c.1865], (tableware).

Borgfeldt, George & Co Glassworks in USA [–], (cut glass, Brilliant period).

Borgonovo/o Vetrai del Borgo Glassworks in Borgonovo, Italy [?–present], full name Vetreria di Borgonovo SpA, (tableware, giftware, barware, household glass, all mechanical).

Borgström, Bo Glass designer from Sweden [1929–], worked for Åseda Glasbruk c.1969.

Borgström, Carl-Einar Glass Designer from Sweden [1914–], worked for Bjorkhults Glas.

Borgstrom, Matz Studio artist from Sweden [1954–], worked for Orrefors c.1984.

Boric oxide (B2O3) This is used as a glass constituent and flux, reducing thermal expansion while improving corrosion resistance and refractive index in tableware, optical glass and glass fibre.

Bormioli Rocco Glassworks in Parma, Italy [1825–present], founded c.1800, became Vetrerie Bormioli SpA, took over Reale Fabbrica delle Maioliche e dei Vetri di Parma to become Vetreria Fratelli Bormioli in 1880, glassworks destroyed in WWII and then reconstructed 1946. The Bormioli Rocco group operates 13 plants including Vetreria Parmense BR, Vetreria BR, BR Casa, Neubor, Verreries de Masnières/F, Verrerie de Gier/F, VMC, Vetropack. Trade names includes Duralex, Bormioli Rocco Basic and Bormioli Rocco Professional, (bottles, tableware, barware, kitchenware, tableware, vases, pressed glass, crystal, sodalime, opal glass, perfume bottles).

Bormioli SpA, Luigi Glassworks in Parma, Italy [?–present], trade name is Light & Music, (tableware and giftware).

Bornholm Glass Workshop Glassworks in Bornholm, Denmark [1978–present].

Borocrystal Conglomerate of nationalized glassworks/refineries in Czechoslovakia, founded 1948, merged with Umělecké Sklo to form Crystalex in 1974.

Boromica Trade name for borosilicate glass by VSL, c.1930.

Borosil Glass Works Ltd Glassworks in Bombay and Marai Malai Nagar, India [1965–present], (lamps and lighting, tubes & rods, tableware, flat glass, cookware, borosilicate glass).

Borosilicate glass Composed mainly of silica (70–80%) and boric oxide (7–13%) with smaller amounts of alkalis (sodium and potassium oxides) and aluminium oxide, featuring a relatively low alkali content. Has good chemical durability and thermal shock resistance due to a much lower thermal coefficient of expansion. Used for lab equipment, cookware, lampwork, lighting,

glass fibre and technical applications. Brand names include Pyrex, Jena-er Glass, Duralex, Hysil and Duran.

Borowski, Stanislaw Glass artist from Poland [1944–], worked for Krosno in the 1960s, started own studio in Lichtenberg, Germany in 1982 and set up his own studio in Boleslawiec, Poland in 1991 with his sons Pawel and Wiktor, (art glass, paperweights).

Borsella Italian term for tongs used for shaping glass.

Borské Sklo Glassworks in Chripska, Nový Bor, Harrachóv, Czechoslovakia [1870–present], its glass-making school was founded in Nový Bor in 1870. Designers include René Roubicek, Ladislav Oliva 1957–64, Pavel Hlava 1956–64, Stanislav Honzik c.1961/2, Josef Hospodka c.1961/2, Ludvika Smrčkova c.1962/3, Vratislav Sotola 1958–69 and Maria Stráhliková c.1960/1. Sig: labels only, (art glass)

Borussia glass Type of triple cut-to-clear (black over white over clear) developed by Karl Schappel c.1913, (art glass).

Boston & Sandwich Glass Co Glassworks in Sandwich, MA, USA [1825–88], (pressed glass, cut glass, paperweights in the 1850s–80s).

Boston Crown Glass Manufactory Glassworks in Boston, MA, USA [1793–1827], (flat glass, tableware).

Boston Silver Glass Co Glassworks in East Cambridge, MA, USA [1857–73], (pressed glass and silver plating).

Bott, Thomas Glass decorator from Great Britain, worked for Richardson c.1851.

Bottle moulds, various Open mould: leaves vertical seams going up to the shoulder whereas closed mould leaves vertical seams extending to neck and lip. A three-piece mould (1809-80) leaves seams along the shoulder while the wooden three-part turn mould (c.1880–1900) leaves no seams. The paste mould (c.1880–1900) is a steel turn mould filled with paste to smoothen ripples.

Bottles and flasks, dating An unfinished pontil mark indicates a date before c.1845. A metallic residue from an iron pontil points to c.1845–c.1860. A seam reaching from base to lip indicates mechanical production after c.1903. An applied or handmade lip indicates an early mould-blown bottle. The crown cap was patented in 1892. If the bottle mould seam extends to the shoulder it indicates it is pre-1860, if it extends ¾ down toward the neck it means 1860–80, if it extends down to the neck it indicates 1880–1900 and if it extends over neck and lip it is post-1900.

Bottles Avon, ball stopper, bottle moulds, desert glass, embossing, fruit jars, Garnier bottle, gob feeder, Heinz, Hutchinson stopper; Jim Beam bottles, laid-on-ring lip, lighting stopper; Mason fruit jar, miniature bottles, Owens machine, press-and-blow, screwtop, sheared lip, slug plate, snap cases, TBMBR.

Bottleworks NV Glassworks in Zwijndrecht, Holland [1838–1932], known as Glasfabriek Swerijn 1838–55, Zwijndrechtse Glasfabriek/Van Hoboken de Bie 1855–1905, Bottleworks NV 1905 then closed in 1932), (bottles in black and green).

Boudin process A flat glass production method enabling horizontal drawing; also suitable for producing wire mesh.

Boudnik, Maximilian Glass artist from Germany [–], worked in Ullersdorf Liegnitz, Germany c.1900–c.1914, sold mostly France, (art glass; combination of enamel, metallic lustre, threading and bronze mounting).

Boulton & Mills Glassworks in Audnam, Stourbridge, Great Britain [–], produced autumnal tinted cameo 1880s, Old gold c.1886, crackled primrose c.1886, "Nacre de Perle" 1888, "Algerine", "Tunisian" and "Verre d'Iris" in 1887, (art glass, table ornaments, rigarees).

Bouquet de Mariage A millefiori mushroom paperweight entirely composed of white stardust canes.

Bouraine, Marcel Sculptor from France [–], designed pâte-de-verre statuettes and plaques for Argy-Rousseau 1928–31.

Bourgeois, Emile Sales outlet in Paris [1862–?] aka Le Grand Depot, selling tableware and ceramics as well as art glass produced by various manufacturers including Baccarat under a private label.

Bournique Glass Co Glassworks, location unknown [–], active c.1913, (lamps and lighting, glass).

Boussu, Cristalleries de Glassworks in Boussu, Belgium [1960–88], known as Manufacture Boussu until merger with Doyen in 1968 when it became Manuverbel/Manubervel, bought up by Gelb 1974 and became part of Vereno/Verreries du Hainaut 1982–86. Closure in 1988 meant the last of hand-made glass in Belgium. Designers include Z Busine c.1960–c.1965, Laurent c.1965, Ferreau c.1966, Faidherbe c.1967, Marcquebreucq c.1970, Vincent 1974–86, Smith, M c.1981 and Bacquart c.1987, (tableware, cut glass, opalines, colour glass and fantasy glass).

Boussu Crystal Crystal manufacture located in Boussu, Belgium [1986–8].

Boussu, Nouvelle SA des Verreries de Glassworks in Boussu, Belgium [1884–?], (in decline 1905–18), (bottles, tableware, clear and coloured crystal, lamps and lighting, cut glass, engraving, sanding and guilloche).

Boussu, Verreries du Glassworks in Boussu [1836–49], renamed Meuse after 1949, (bottles, tableware, semi-crystal, colour, cut glass c.1850, pressed glass).

Bouteilleries Belges Réunies, des SA (BBR) [1963–present], includes Bennert-Bivort, Hamendes, Land van Luiken Kempen, continuation of Comptoir des Bouteilles Belges, (bottles).

Bowen, WO Glass engraver from Great Britain [–], worked for Sèvres & Williams.

Bowl 1 Cuppa (stemware). 2 Unfooted open vessel wider than it is high.

Boyadjiev, Latchezar Studio artist from Bulgaria [1959–].

Boyds (script) Trade name used by Illinois Glass Co.

Boyd's Crystal Art Glass Co Glassworks in Cambridge, OH, USA [1947–present], aka Crystal Art Glass Co, bought moulds from Degenhart 1978. Sig: B inside diamond 1978–83; another line added every 5 years, (pressed glass and animal figures).

Bracquemond, Félix Master etcher from France [1833–1914], designed innovative tableware for Sèvres c.1900.

Bradley & Hubbard Lighting manufacturer located in Meriden, CT, USA [1854–c.1920s], (table lamps, sconces, hanging lamps, burners are marked B & H).

Braine-le-Comte Glassworks in Braine-le-Comte, Belgium [1905–74], became part of Association de Gobeletiers Belges c.1916, operated by Artisanat Braine-le-Comte 1954, subcontracted for VSL before 1964, taken over by Vs du Hainaut 1974, (hot modelled glass, cut-to-clear, blanks for cutting).

Brandt, Åsa Glass designer from Sweden [1940–], set up Brandt Contemporary Glass in Torshälla, Sweden 1968–present, (studio glass).

Brandt, Marianne Glass designer from Germany [1893–1983], worked for Loetz.

Brantenberg, Ulla-Mari Glass designer from Norway [1947–], worked for Randsfjord, Hadeland, Bornholm 1976–?.

Branzell, Sten Glass designer from Sweden [1893–1959], worked for Eda, Reijmyre and Kosta 1922–3, 1929–30 and 1950. Sig: often unsigned or engraved with SB monogram + year + Kosta.

Bratt, Monica Glass designer from Sweden [1913–61], worked for Reijmyre 1937–58.

Brázda, Josef Glass engraver from Bohemia [–], worked 1920s.

Brditschka Manufacturer of costume jewellery from Jablonec, Czechoslovakia [c.1920s–c.1936].

Bread & butter plate Pressed plate or tray made in the USA, dating from the last quarter of the 19thC, often featuring historical events.

Breit, Ludwig, Glas und Glasperlenfabrik Glassworks in Jabloneč nad Nisou, Czechoslovakia [c.1916–1934], closed during World War II but from 1948 part of Jablonec

Glass Works; since 1990 Jizera Glass/Jizerské Sklo, (coloured bars and rods for jewellery making).

Briard, Georges Glass decorator from USA [1917–]; (alias of Jascha Brojdo; worked for Bent Glass Co. c.1950–?; founded Glass Guild, NY Jamaica; operation ceased 1989); (gold decorated bent glass, barware).

Briati, Vetri d'Arte srl Glassworks in Murano, Italy [–], active c.1967, (art glass).

Bride's baskets Decorated baskets in art glass, pressed glass or cut glass, fashionable between 1893 and 1905.

Bridge Crystal Glass Co Glassworks in Great Britain [–], designers include Robert Welch.

Brierly Crystal, Royal (previously Stevens & Williams) Glassworks in Stourbridge, Great Britain [1847–2000]. Designers include David Redman and engravers include Stewart Davies, Lenny Jones and Michael Pargeter. Sig: Brierly/Royal/Crystal with a fleur-de-lis etched mark 1924–7, Circular stamp S & W after 1927, Keith Murray signature over S & W Brierly 1934–9, sand-blasted marks after 1945; Royal/Brierly/England 1945–50, Royal/Brierly/Crystal 1950s, Brierly, RBC or Royal Brierly after 1960. (Cut and engraved crystal, cut-to-clear, luxury tableware, giftware.)

Brierly Hill Glass Co Ltd Glassworks in Brierly Hill, Great Britain [1930–c.1950].

Brilliant Glass Works Glassworks in Brilliant, OH, USA [1880–93], LaGrange 1880–2, burned down and rebuilt in Brilliant, OH 1882–3, operated by Dalzell Bros & Gilmore 1883–4, sold to Central Glass Co in Wheeling, WV 1884–6, moved to Greensburg, PA 1888/9, closed in 1893 and finally burned down again 1895, (pressed glass).

Brilliant period The period between approximately 1880–1915 when more than 1,000 small cut glass shops operated in the eastern USA, all producing similar, mostly unsigned cut glass patterns.

Brillantati Barovier & Toso type of art glass designed by Ercole Barovier, 1939.

Brisbane, Amanda Studio artist from Great Britain [–].

Bristol Glass-making centre in Great Britain from c.1700. In 1725 there were 15 glass houses. The most successful period was 1780–1820.

Bristol Blue Greenish blue to dark blue lead glass, so named because its main colouring agent (zaffre, containing cobalt oxide) was produced in or imported via Bristol c.1760–90 and c.1820–40.

Bristol Glass A type of opaline named after the town in Great Britain where it was first produced . It was imported from there in the late 1700s. Also made in France, Germany, Italy, USA and Czechoslovakia. Very difficult to attribute correctly to a manufacturer. Bristol glass is often decoated with cold enamel painting.

British American Glass Co Glass importer/distributor located in London, Great Britain [–], active c.1930s, distributor for Cambridge Glass, (pressed glass).

British Heat-resisting Glass Co Ltd Glassworks in Bilston, Staffordshire, Great Britain [–], c.1950. Sig: impressed logo Phoenix/Made in England.

Broad glass Cylinder glass.

Brocard, Joseph Glass maker from France [?–1896], set up Brocard & Fils 1884, later Verrerie Brocard 1896–1900. Sig: enamelled or gilt, (historic, islamic type enamelled and gilt glass 1867–1900).

Brockway Glass Glassworks in Wheeling, WV, USA [-1964], bought Continental Can Co in 1964.

Brockwitz Glasfabrick, AG Glassworks in Sornewitz, Meissen, Germany [1903–32]. Brockwitz, together with Fenne/Saar and August Walther, were the largest suppliers of pressed glass in Germany. Sig: normally unmarked, logo c.1928 is B over two crossed swords, GAB, (tableware, pressed glass, carnival glass).

Brodegaard, RF & Co Inc Glassworks in USA [–], c.1950, (tableware).

Brody Co EO Glassworks in Cleveland, OH USA [?–present], owned by Lancaster Colony since 1990s, (pressed glass; florist supplies).

Bronzit Black and/or gold decoration introduced 1910 by Lobmeyr until c.1920; artists include Josef Hoffmann.

Bronze glass Iridescent glass type by Thomas Webb & Sons, after 1878. There has been green bronze, scarabeous and bronze crackle glass.

Brooklyn Flint Glass Works Glassworks in Brooklyn, NY, USA [–], c.1851, owned by John Gilliland, (cut glass, tableware, high quality clear flint).

Brörby, Severin Glass designer and engraver from Norway [1932–], worked for Hadelands 1956–c.1967.

Brosse, Verreries Glassworks in Rouen, France [?–present], (bottles, decanters & pressed glass).

Brougba Glassworks in Bulgaria [–]. Sig: hat, (bottles).

Brown & Co Ltd, Dale Glassworks in

Mesborough, York, Great Britain [–]. Sig: DB in a book frame, (bottles).

Brownsville Glass Works Located in Brownsville, PA, USA [1824–8], (bottles).

Brox & Mader Glassworks in Döbern near Sorau NL, Germany [–], see Döbern.

Brummer, Arttu Glass designer from Finland [1891–1951], worked for Riihimäki Glass c.1913–51.

Brunner, Vratislav Glass decorator from Bohemia [–], worked early 1900s.

Bryce Brothers/US Glass B Glassworks in Pittsburgh, PA [1850–2], aka Bryce, McKee & Co 1850–4, Bryce, Walker & Co/Bryce, Richards & Co 1854–82, located in Hammondsville, PA after 1889, became part of USG as Factory B in 1891, moved to Mt Pleasant, PA 1896–1952, (tableware, barware, etched, engraved, decorated ware, coloured glass since 1920, iridescent shades c.1920s, aurene colours, black 1930s).

Bryce, Higbee & Co Glassworks in Homestead, PA, USA [1879–1911], also ran JB Higbee Glass Co 1907–16 at Bridgeville, Pennsylvania, aka Homestead Glass, (pressed glass).

Brychta, Jaroslav Glass designer from Pohodli Czechoslovakia [1896–1971], worked at schools in Nový Bor and Kamenický Šenov c.1920 and Železný Brod 1921–1960); (small sculptures, figures).

Brychtová-Zahradníková, Jaroslava Glass designer from Železný Brod, Czechoslovakia [1924–], worked with Stanislav Libenský after 1954, worked for Železný Brod 1952–84), (tableware, art glass, sculpture, architectural projects).

BSA Glasbruks Produkter Glass refinery located in Sweden [1929–present], designer Karl-Erik Book, (engraving on blanks from Kosta, small series).

BS & Co Mark used by Burgun, Schwerer & Co, see Meisenthal.

BSN Vidro España SA Glassworks in Madrid, Spain [1952–present], additional plant located in Castellar, Barcelona, part of BSN group, aka Giralt Laporta SA, (bottles).

Bubacco, Lucio Flamework artist from Venice, Italy [1957–].

Bubbles Gas in the melt is normally removed by firing. Large bubbles are called blisters, small ones seeds, while stretched bubbles are called airlines. Bubbles may be intentional. See also pulegoso, foam glass, nail mould.

Buckeye Glass Co Glassworks in Wheeling, WV, USA [1849–c.1903], situated in Martins Ferry, OH in 1879 but burned down 1894, and its other factory situated in Bowling Green, OH 1888–c.1903, (pressed glass).

Budenheim GmbH, Glashütte Glassworks in Budenheim, Germany [?–present].

Buffalo Cut Glass Co Glassworks in USA [–], (cut glass, Brilliant period).

Bugnati Barovier & Toso art glass type by Ercole Barovier, 1938.

Bulinato Barovier & Toso art glass type by Ercole Barovier, 1950.

Bulle de Savon French term meaning soap bubble glass, grainy opaline that has been produced since c.1822.

Bullions Bullions or bulls eyes are decorative window panes made by spinning out a bowl-shaped piece, (flat glass).

Bull's eye cane A paperweight cane with red and white concentric design.

Bumper See Toastmaster's glass, aka Firing glass.

Bunamo, Philip Glass maker from USA [–], his paperweights were made at Union Glass Co, Somerville, MA, USA 1900s–1910s.

Bundtzen, Brigitte Glass designer from Germany [1937–], worked at Weisswasser 1951–4, Döbern 1954–73 and at Kristallglaswerk Essen since 1981.

Bundtzen, Friedrich Glass designer from Brühl, Germany [1910–], worked at VLG 1932–9 and 1949–76.

Bunte & Remmler Glassworks in Germany [–], active c.1936, (lamps and lighting).

Bunzlau, Glashütte Glassworks in Bunzlau OL, Germany [1866–?], operated by Raffinerie Vogt, later by Christinenhütte AG vorm. W Nitschke, (art glass, bottles, tableware, lamps and lighting).

Buquoy, Count Jiří František August Glass maker from Bohemia [1781–1851], (specialized in hyalith, lithyalin, gold decorated).

Buquoy Glassworks Glassworks in Nove Hrady, south Bohemia, Czechoslovakia [1608–1835]. Count Georg Franz August Longueval von Buquoy (1781–1851) owned numerous glass houses in South Bohemia and is credited with the invention of opaque red c.1803 and hyalith black glass c.1807.

Burger, Edwin Glass artist from Austria [–],worked in Milan, Italy c.1945, (cut glass, engraving).

Burgun, Schwerer & Cie Glassworks in Lemberg, France [c.1867–c.1969], (tableware, art glass). See Meisenthal.

Burian, Ivan Glass designer from Czechoslovakia [1939–], did designs for Železný Brod c.1965.

Burley & Tyrrell Co Glassworks, location unknown [–], active c.1908, (tableware).

Burlington Glass Works Glassworks in Hamilton Ontario, Canada [1874–97].

Burmeister, Gabriel Glass designer from Sweden [–], worked for Boda in 1923.

Burmese glass Nearly opaque art glass shading from pale lemon yellow to salmon pink, achieved by using Uranium oxide and gold. The first patent (given to Mount Washington Glass Co) was granted in 1885. It comes in either a glossy or satin finish, and is sometimes decorated or gilded. Also produced under license by Thomas Webb ("Queen's Burmese", 1886), further production in the US in the 1930s, Italy in the 1960s, and by Gunderson-Pairpoint, Bryden and Fenton in recent times.

Burner Flamework tool, runs on gas and oxygen or air.

Burn-off The separation of a blown glass by rotating it in a ring of gas burners.

Burtles, Tate and Company Glassworks in Manchester, Great Britain [19thC–1924], moulds sold to Butterworth in Manchester, 1924, (pressed glass 1858–1924, novelties, "topas opalescent" glass (opal to opaque in various colours) after 1891).

Burton, John Glass designer from Great Britain [–], went to CA USA 1927, (lampwork, developed new colours in borosilicate glass).

Bush Glass Co Glassworks in USA [–], (cut glass, Brilliant period).

Busine, Zéphyr Painter from Gerpinnes, Belgium [1916–76], designed for Boussu c.1960–c.1965.

Butler Brothers Glassworks, location unknown [c.1905–c.1925], (tableware).

Butt seal An end-to-end seal between two pieces of tube or rod in lampwork.

Butter plate Miniature dish.

Butterworth Bros Ltd Glassworks in Newton Heath, Manchester, Great Britain [c.1860–c.1950], uses the trade names Bulldog and Invincible, (pressed glass after the 1860s).

Button A tiny amount of glass used to seal two pieces together.

Buzzi, Tommaso Architect/designer from Italy [1900–81], worked for Venini 1932–4 and Fontana Arte 1933.

Buzzini, Chris Paperweight artist from USA [–], has worked at Correia since 1982.

Byakov, Yury M Glass designer from St Petersburg, Russia [1938–], worked at Leningrad Factory after 1965.

Byakova, Alexandra P Glass designer from St Petersburg, Russia [1938–], worked at Leningrad Factory after 1965.

Bychkov, Boris T Glass designer from Irkutsk, Russia [1928–], was designer and chief designer at Gus-Krushtalny, 1958–62.

C

C (encircled) Mark used by Chattanooga Bottle and Glass Co.

C (in a square) Mark used by Crystal Glass Co.

C (in a star) Mark used by Star City Glass Co, Star City, WV [1949–present], (bottles).

C (in a triangle) Mark used by Cambridge.

C & H Trade name used by Coffin & Hay.

C Co/C & Co Trade name of Cunninghams & Co

C Conrad & Co Located in USA [1878–83], trade mark used is CCCo, (bottles).

C Milw Trade name used by Chase Valley Glass Co.

Cabral, Ricardo Glass designer from Portugal [–], worked for MGlass, c.1999.

Caccia Barovier & Toso type of art glass by Ercole Barovier, 1960.

Cadalso Glassworks in Madrid, Spain [?–1908], merged into Union Vidriera de España, 1908.

Cadmium sulphide (CdS) Colouring agent used with selenium produces strong reds and yellows; it occurs as the mineral greenockite.

Cadorin, Guido Painter and glass artist from Italy [1892–]; worked for Fratelli Toso c.1923.

Caerleon glass Type of art glass by Stevens and Williams c.1919 produced at the Lighting Glass Factory, Tipton. The surface imitates Roman glass.

Caithness Glass Ltd Glassworks in Wick and in Perth, Scotland [1961–present]. Part of the Royal Doulton group. Sig: most items unmarked; paperweights may have edition number engraved, some items acid-etched "Caithness", the logo "CG" was in use in the 1960s, label "Caithness" since c.1970s. Paul Ysart weights made at Caithness had a PY cane, date canes were also used in some pieces, (art glass produced in Wick, paperweights in Perth).

Cake plate Glass plate for serving cakes, usually footed or with three legs.

Calcedonio Marbled glass (brown, blue, green, yellow) imitating chalcedony or agate. First recorded in Venice in the 15thC, aka Jasper glass in the 17thC; popular as "Slag" at the end of the 19thC. The effect is obtained by adding blast furnace slag to the melt.

Calcite glass Cream-coloured type of art glass produced by Steuben in the 1910s; named after the mineral which is, however, not one of its constituents.

Calcium carbonate (CaCO3) It is used to introduce calcium oxide into the batch. Found in nature as calcite/limestone; in the melt it releases carbon dioxide that helps the fining process.

Calcium fluoride (CaF2) Aka fluorspar, fluorite or "Blue John". This is a purple mineral used as a source of fluorine for producing opal glass and enamels is rarely used any more due to noxious fluorine vapours.

Calcium oxide (CaO) see lime.

Caldier Trade name from Vetri delle Venezie 1999–present, (pressed glass, tableware in modern style)

Caliper Glassmaker's tongs.

Calme Channel profiles used for stained glass, normally made from lead but also found in brass, copper and zinc, aka cames.

CALP SpA See Artistica La Piana, Cristalleries.

Cambridge Glass Co Glassworks in Cambridge, OH USA [1901–57], constructed for National Glass Co, privatized in 1910 and became AJ Bennett, with a subsidiary in Byesville, OH 1910–17). Sig: C in a triangle 1920–54, paper label 1935–54, (blown and pressed tableware, coloured wares, cut glass, pressed glass).

Camden City Cut Glass Co Glassworks, location unknown [–], active c.1914.

Cameo, floral Producers include: Arsall/VLG, Baccarat, Bourgeois, Choisy, Cristalleries de Nancy, Daum, Damon, Degué, Delatte, Gallé, Gus Crystal, Hadelands, Harrach, Heckert, Imperial China and Glass, Kosta, Kralik, Lagny, Le Verre Français, Legras, Lorrain/Meisenthal, Moser, Müller, Mt Washington, Pantin, Pilgrim, Raspiller, Richard, Saint-Louis/D'Argental, Schappel, Schneider/Charder, Sèvres, Sovánka, Stevens & Williams, Tip, Ujantalvölgy, Val, Valérysthal, Val St Lambert, de Vez, Villeroy & Boch, Thomas Webb, Wennerberg and Zayngróc.

Cameo-fleur Cameo type of art glass by Richardson c.1928/30s, aka pseudo-cameo.

Cameo Glass: Roman technique of cutting through layers of different coloured glass to obtain a raised design. The most famous example of cameo glass is the Portland Vase in the British Museum, which dates between 300BC and 50AD. The Chinese used a similar technique for making intricately carved snuff bottles in the 18thC and 19thC. European glassmakers revived the process in the 19thC – Thomas Webb in Great Britain (mostly white outside, coloured ground with classical or botanical motifs), Gallé and Daum (naturalistic work in multiple colours) perfected this difficult and expensive technique. Aka cameo engraving and relief cutting.

Camerino, Maurizio Glass maker from Italy [1859–1931], worked for Salviati 1896–1920, children Olga, Mario and Renzo worked for Salviati after 1931.

Campanella Glass srl Glassworks in Murano, Italy [1993–present], (art glass, decorative glass, figures).

Campbell, Jones & Co Glassworks in PA Pittsburgh, USA [1865–84], became Jones, Cavitt & Co 1884, burned down 1891, some moulds then sold to US Glass. (pressed glass).

Campbell Street Glass Works Glass cutting shop in Dudley, Great Britain [c.1870–c.1900], operated by Richard Wilkes, (cut glass, engraved glass, gilt and silver mounts; subcontracting for Stevens & Williams).

Camphene Lighting fluid consisting of turpentine and alcohol.

Camphor Glass Cloudy white glassware, blown or pressed, made by many factories in the middle of the 19thC.

Canadian glass First glass maker began at Rice Lake, Ontario in 1819 but closed after a year. First production at Mallorytown, Ontario in 1839 (flat glass, bottles) and at Saint Jean Que and Como Que in the 1850s. After 1880, glass production was based at Montreal Quebec, Wallaceburg Ontario and New Glasgow Nova Scotia (bottles, lighting and tableware). Pressed glass production at Burlington Glass, Nova Scotia Glass, Jefferson Glass and Dominion Glass, who took over the other three in 1913.

Canary glass 1. Bright yellow glass made with sulphur, iron oxide and carbon. 2. Misnomer for Annagrün 3. Misnomer for Vaseline Glass. 4. Heisey green colour .

Candelabrum Candlestick with several branches.

Candlewick Pressed glass pattern aka beaded edge or kugelrand (Ger). It was introduced in 1936 and produced at Imperial until 1984 and by various manufacturers after that; produced in Germany since the 1950s and currently in production in the Czech Republic.

Candy containers, figural US containers for sweets; earliest examples from 1876 while the most popular were made after 1900, such as milk glass 1906–12. Toys and animals were made after 1930. Markings postdate the Food & Drink Act of 1912, which aids dating, and a list of contents has been compulsory since the 1940s. Manufacturers include West Bros, Cambridge, LE Smith, Victory, Jeannette, TH Stough and Summit.

Candy stripe US term for a glass with colour stripes. See Zanfirico and Lutz.

Cane A thin glass rod, of a single colour or in multiple colours drawn out in a design only visible in cross section.

Canna Coloured glass thread.

Canne, A Venini art glass designed by Gio Ponti, 1946.

Canne Diafano Barovier & Toso art glass type by Ercole Barovier, 1959

Canne Policrome Barovier & Toso art glass type by Ercole Barovier, 1956

Cannette 1. Slender, coloured glass threads. 2. Type of art glass made by Venini designed by Ludovico Diaz de Santillana and Mario Ticco, 1965.

Canning jars Wide-mouthed vessel used for storing preserved foodstuffs after 1810. Flange top wax seal used before 1850, inner flange wax seal introduced after c.1850, the screw top/Mason jar after 1858 and the clamp seal after 1875.

Cannington, Shaw & Co Bottle plant located in St Helens, Great Britain [1872–1916]. Sig: CS & Co, (bottles).

Cántir, cántaro Spanish vessel that has two spouts.

Canton Glass Co Glassworks in Canton, OH, USA [1883–c.1903], situated in Marion, IN 1883–present (founded in, and named after Canton, OH), then became part of National Glass 1899–present. Their fruit jar, which is embossed with Canton Domestic Fruit Jar, was produced 1890–1904), (pressed glass, novelties).

Canvidrio/Fabricaçao de Vidro Glassworks in the Marinha Grande region of Portugal [?–present], see Marinha Grande and MGlass, (tableware, decorative items, lamps and lighting, bottles).

Cape Cod Glass Works Glassworks in Sandwich, MA, USA [1858–69], took over c.1869 by Dr Flower who operated the company until 1882, (pressed glass, tableware, art glass, peachblow, gold ruby and Sandwich alabaster).

Capellemans Glass shop in Brussels, Belgium [1827–43], was both a cut glass refinery and sales outlet – used blanks from VSL and Zoude.

Capello del Doge Venini art glass type

designed by Thomas Stearns, 1962.

Capodimonte Porcelain maker from Naples, Italy [?–present], produced a range of giftware fashioned from flat glass.

Cappellin Glassworks in Paris, France [1936–?], (perfume bottles).

Cappellin, MVM Glassworks in Murano, Italy [1921–31], from 1921–25 with Venini, designers include Zecchin 1921–5 and Carlo Scarpa 1927–8. See MVM Cappellin.

Capredoni, Alfred Glass engraver from Italy [–], works at Dartington Crystal Ltd at present, producing "iceberg" engraving that is marketed as the Capredoni collection.

Capstan Glass Co Glassworks in Connellsville, PA [1910–18], had offices in Pittsburgh PA before 1915.

Capuzzo, Enrico Glass designer from Italy [1924–], worked for Vistosi in 1966.

Carafe (Fr) Decanter, stoppered bottle.

Caramel slag Glass the colour of coffee with milk; often found in French pressed glass where it is normally called opaline. Similar in colour to chocolate glass.

Caranza, Amédée de Glass artist from Istanbul, Turkey [–], worked as ceramic designer in France1870–90, had own art glass workshop in Noyon, 1890–WWI, sigs: include H Copillet and Duc A de Caranza, (enamels, etching and engraving).

Carboys Large wide-necked glass bottles containing up to 60 litres. Used for storing chemicals, often fitted in a wicker or steel frame, see demijohn.

Card tray US term for a dish used to hold two standard packs of playing cards.

Carder, Frederick Glassmaker from Great Britain [1863–1963], worked for Stevens & Williams 1880–1903, emigrated to USA 1903, co-founder of Steuben 1903–18, art director of the Steuben Division of Corning Glassworks 1918–32, then of Corning Glassworks 1932–59, (Carder developed over 100 colours, 7,000 forms and dozens of techniques, including Aurene, Intarsia, Tyrian and Lost Wax).

F. Carder

Cardin Venini art glass designed by Ludovico Diaz de Santillana, 1969.

Cardinal International Inc Glassworks in USA [–], active c.1920, (tableware).

Cardoso, Paulo Glass designer from Portugal [–], worked for Mglass c.1999.

Carib Glassworks Ltd Glassworks in Port of Spain, Trinidad [1955–present], (bottles and mugs).

Carlshütte Glassworks in Teplice, Czechoslovakia [–], active c.1908, C Slanina & Co was based there, (blanks for local refineries and hot-finished glass).

Carlson, William Studio artist from USA [1950–].

Carlsson, Birgita Glass designer from Sweden [–], worked for Venini c.1974/5.

Carlsson, Sven-Åke Glass designer from Sweden [–], works at Transjö Hytta AB.

Carlswerke Glassworks in Bunzlau OL, Germany [–].

Carmaux, Verrerie de Glassworks in Carmaux, Tarn, France [–], active c.1865, (tableware and bottles).

Carnival glass Pressed glass coated with a lustre finish, first made in the US in 1905, then mass produced 1908–18 and for export until the 1930s. Iridescence is a distinguishing characteristic of this type of glass. Reproductions have been done since the 1950s, especially since the 1970s. Colours include marigold, green, blue and purple, but many other colours exist. Main producers were Fenton, Northwood & Co, Imperial, Millersburg, Dugan Glass Co, US Glass, Cambridge, Westmoreland and McKee. Carnival has been produced in Great Britain by Sowerby, in Finland by Riihimäki Glass, in Holland by Leerdam, in Germany by Brockwitz, in Sweden by Eda Glasbruk, in Czechoslovakia by Inwald, in Argentina by Piccardo, in Australia by Crystal Glass, in Canada by Dominion and in India by Jain.

Carnival glass, contemporary US manufacturers include Crescent, Degenhart, Fenton, Gibson, Imperial, Indiana, New Northwood Art Glass, Robert Hansen, LE Smith, St Clair, Terry Crider, Weatoncraft, Wetzel and LG Wright.

Carpenter, AF Paperweight artist from Pasadena, CA, USA [–], active in the 1960s and 1970s.

Carpenter, James Glass designer from USA [1950–], worked for Venini in 1972, Fostoria 1976-80, Toso c.1972, Chihuly/Pilchuck 1969–76 and Steuben 1973–81. Now has own company, James Carpenter Design Associates, located in New York (since 1979).

Carr-Lowrey Glass Co Glassworks based in Baltimore, MD, USA [1889–1920], (bottles).

Carson Pirie Scott & Co Glassworks in USA [–], active c.1920, see Northwood & Co, (tableware).

Carter Glass Works/National Glass Glassworks in Marion, IN, USA [?–1898], merged into National Glass in 1899.

Carving: Removing glass from the surface of an object using hand tools.

Cascade Glass Works Glassworks, location unknown [–], see King, Son & Co, which it became.

Cash, Sydney Studio artist from USA [1941–].

Casing Refers to the application of one layer of glass over a differently coloured one. Technique first done in Bohemia c.1804. Sometimes the outer layer is cut, carved or etched to produce cut-to-clear or cameo glass, while the combination with lattimo produces opalina.

Castille, Willy Painter decorator from Belgium [–], worked on opaline from Valérysthal c.1960–78.

Casting: 1 The technique of producing glass pieces by pouring hot glass in a mould, or by heating glass until it assumes the mould shape. 2 A flat glass production method.

3 The application of a second layer of glass over a vessel.

Castle Foot Glassworks See Joseph Guest & Co.

Castleford Glassworks in Yorkshire, Great Britain [–], active 1850s–90s, (paperweights).

Castor Covered container for sugar, spice, salt etc that has been used since the 17thC.

Castor sets: Table set for sugar, mustard, oil and vinegar popular until the 18thC until the 1920s. Aka cruet sets.

Castro, DH de Chemist from Amsterdam, Holland [?–1863], revived diamond-point engraving c.1850, see Andries Melort.

Catteau, Charles Potter/ceramicist from Belgium [1880–1966], works produced at Verreries de Scailmont after 1927.

Cattelan, Vetreria Glassworks in Murano, Italy [–], active c.1967, (lamps and lighting).

Cavalier Glass Co Glassworks, location unknown [–], active c.1930, (tableware).

Cavalieri Alice see Nazionali, Cristallerie.

Cazaux, Edouard Glass artist from France [–],(sig Guéron, Guéron cazaux), (art glass vases, sculptures in cast glass c.1927/c.1937, executed by Maison Guéron).

CCC Mark used by Continental Can Company (HazelWare) (ccc wrapped together as concentric circles).

CCCo Trade name used by C Conrad & Co, USA [1878–83], (bottles).

Cecchelin, Antonio Glass maker located in Murano, Italy, works produced c.1980.

Cecchinato Illuminazione Glassworks in Marcon, Italy (lighting, chandeliers, shades)

Celery 1. A table vase for holding celery sprigs; 2. A long flat dish for serving celery sprigs.

Celestialite Trade name used by Gleason-Tiebout for lamps and lighting.

Cenedese Gino & Figlio Glassworks in Murano, Italy [1946–?], designers include Alfredo Barbini 1947–50, Riccardo Licata 1952, Fucina degli Angeli 1954, Fulvio Bianconi 1954, Napoleone Martinuzzi 1953/8 and Antonio Da Ros after 1959, produced sommerso, (art glass, lamps and lighting, lustres).

Cenedese labels Hexagonal foil label "Cenedese Vetri" 1946–59 and re-issued in the 1990s, rectangular paper tear-off label c.1959–c.1972 with typewritten number/design year, similar label in peel-off paper c.1978–present, shield-shaped label "Murano Cenedese Vetri" used now.

Cenedese, Gino Glass designer from Italy [1907–73], worked for Cappelin c.1926, had own company from 1946, see above.

Central Glass Co/US Glass/National Glass: Glassworks in Wheeling, WV [1863–98] and then Summitville, IN [1898–1939]. Started as

Oesterling & Henderson 1863–93, taken over by US Glass as Factory O in 1891 and closed 1893, re-opened 1896, moved to Summitville 1898 and then was operated by National Glass 1899–1924 as "National 03", (bottles, lamps, tableware, pressed glass, coin glass, depression glass, crystal after1900, decorated tableware after 1900 and Chippendale after 1919).

Centro Studio Pittori nell'arte del Vetro Glass studio in Murano, Italy [1953–?], executed glass sculptures by Picasso, Kokoschka, Chagall, Le Corbusier etc; better known as Fucina degli Angeli.

Centro Vidreiro do Norte de Portugal Glassworks in the Marinha Grande region of Portugal [c.1930–present], see Marinha Grande and Mglass, (hand moulding and bottles).

Centrovetro Glass consortium from Empoli, Italy [?–present].

Ceonix Blown marbled glass type produced by Richardson after c.1904.

CERFAV Centre Européen de Recherche et Formation aux Arts Verriers. See Vannes.

Cerium oxide The oxide of the rare earth cerium used as a polishing agent.

Cerné Údoli/Cernodol Glassworks in Nové Hrady v jižních Cechách, Czechoslovakia [1836–94], (pressed glass)

Cerve Spa Glass decorator located in Parma, Italy [1953–present], operates 1 plant in France, 8 in Italy. Decorates 500 million items each year, mostly bottles, (enamel printing, sanding, drilling, gilding etc).

Cervera Marti, Joan Glass designer from Spain [1912–], worked for UVE c.1926–34 and Marti c.1941–c.1966.

César Artist from France [–], worked for Daum c.1975.

Cesare Glassworks in France [–], active c.1930s, (opalescent glass).

CFC See Cie Française de Cristal.

Chaikov, Iosif M Sculptor from Moscow, Russia [1888–], studied in Paris, produced painted panels 1912, designed a crystal fountain for the world fair in New York 1937/8.

Chair 1. Glass maker's bench. 2. Team of glass workers who assist the gaffer.

Chalet Artistic Glass Glassworks in Montreal, Canada [1958–81], started as Les Industries de Verre & Miroirs Ltée 1958–60, became Murano Glass Inc 1960–2, known as Chalet Artistic since 1963, moved to Cornwall Ontario and has operated as Rossi Artistic Glass since 1981. Sig: acid stamp.

Chalice Ornamented drinking vessel with a wide bowl, normally footed.

Challenge Incandescent Mfg Co Lighting works located in USA [–], operated by Block light Co.

Challinor, Charles Glass maker from USA [–], worked at Gillinder & Sons, (paperweights after 1867).

Challinor, Taylor & Co/US Glass C Glassworks in Tarentum, USA [1866–93], began in Pittsburgh, PA as Challinor, Hogan Glass Co 1866–84, then moved to Tarentum, PA in 1884 and known as Challinor, Taylor & Co.

Merged with US Glass as Factory C in 1891 then burned down in 1893, (pressed glass, lamps and lighting, novelties, milk glass and slag).

Chamäleon glass 1. Type of mixed colour art glass introduced by Egermann in 1835. 2. Type of art glass produced by Fritz Heckert c.1900.

Chambord Trade name used by Fratelli Toso.

Champagne glass 1. Stemmed glass with a wide flat bowl. 2. A tall and slender flute. 3. A glass with a hollow stem.

Chance Brothers Glassworks in Smethwick, Birmingham, Great Britain [1824–1981], aka W E Chance & Co Ltd, designers include WM Harris c.1960/1. Sig: moulded Orlak or Orlak/British Made, labels include Chance Glass, Chance and Fiesta. Script logo of the 1930s was revamped in the 1970s, (flat glass, bottles & lighting).

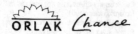

Chandelier Lighting device with hanging prismatic drops made in many places: France, Italy, Austria, Czechoslovakia, Ireland, England and the US, aka lustre. (A gas light chandelier is also known as Gasolier; an electric one as Electrolier.)

Changeant glass Type of art glass produced by Fritz Heckert c.1900.

Charder Art glass signature, see Schneider.

Charleroi, Glaces de Glassworks in Roux near Charleroi, Belgium [–], part of Glaver group, (flat glass, ornamental flat glass).

Charleroi, SA des Verreries et Verres Spéciaux de: Glassworks in Gilly near Charleroi, Belgium [–], active after 1920, (flat glass).

Charleroi, Verreries de Glassworks in Charleroi, Belgium [1790–1887], last bottles/tableware produced in Charleroi in 1889, (bottles, flat glass, tableware).

Charlottenburg Glashütten FW Otte Glassworks in Charlottenburg, Germany [–], active c.1890, (bottles).

Charlottenhütte 1. Glassworks in Germany [–], active c.1970. 2. Glassworks in Karolinka, Czechoslovakia [1813–c.1920], operated by Reich & Co.

Chase Scientific Glass Glassworks in Rockwood, TN, USA [1935–present], (bottles).

Chase Valley Glass Co Glassworks based in Milwaukee, WI, USA [–], active c.1880, (bottles).

Chattanooga Bottle and Glass Co Located in the USA [1927–present], (bottles).

CHB Trade name of Cristallerie de Haute Bretagne.

Cheater Thick-bottomed whisky tumbler, see deception glass and bistro glass.

Checkered diamond Describes cut glass that

has several diamonds in a larger diamond pattern.

Cheese dish A covered dish, usually a bell on a flat plate.

Cheese-and-cracker dish US term for a serving dish with two levels.

Chênée, Verrerie de Glassworks in Chênée, Liège, Belgium [–], active c.1880–c.1910, aka Delhaise-Dethier.

Chestnut bottle US term for a bottle with a flattened shape like a chestnut, sometimes aka Ludlow bottle.

Chetkov, Boris A Glass designer from St Petersburg, Russia [1926–], chief designer of First Communist VDG after 1966.

Chevalier, Georges Glass designer from France [1894–1987], worked for Baccarat c.1916–60.

Chiesa, Pietro Glass designer from Italy [1892–1948], worked for SALIR and Fontana Arte.

Chihuly, Dale Glass artist from USA [1941–], (studio glass).

Chilla, Leo Glass designer from Czechoslovakia [–], worked for School at Kamenický Šenov c.1890.

Chiné glass Type of art glass made by Loetz (irregular spun threads).

Chinese cameo glass Intricately carved glass, esp. snuff bottles, made in China since the 18thC.

Chintz glass Type of art glass patented by A Douglas Nash [–].

Chippendale Popular pressed glass pattern designed in1907 and first made at Ohio Flint. Production soon transferred to Jefferson Glass Co, its trade name, Krys-Tol, was registered in 1911. Production transferred to Central Glass in 1919, moulds were bought by London agent Charles Pratt c.1933, who continued production at Davidson in Great Britain until 1939.

Chirivi, Romano Architect and glass designer from Italy [1931–], worked for Salviati 1960–c.1981.

Chlum, Ceský Krištál Glassworks in Chlum u Trebone, Czechoslovakia [1891–present], part of Ceský Krištál, (pressed glass reported 1895, tableglass).

Chocolate glass US term for opaque brown glass, sometimes mistaken for caramel slag, first made around 1900 at the Indiana Tumbler and Goblet Co, and produced for three years only. Fenton produced chocolate glass c.1907–c.1915.

Choisy-le-Roi Glassworks in Choisy-le-Roi, near Paris. [1821–?], merged with Houdaille et Triquet in 1928 and used new name, Cristalleries et Verreries Réunies de Choisy-le-Roi. Art director Pierre d'Avesn c.1928–c.1930s, designers include d'Avesn, Chaudron, Landier, Houdaille, (tableware, millefiori rediscovered 1838, opalines, art glass Japanese décor cameo c.1890–1900).

Choisy-le-Roi, Cristalleries de & de Lyon Glassworks in Choisy-le-Roi, France [–], active c.1930.

Choisy-le-Roi, Houdaille et Triquet, Cristalleries de Glassworks in Choisy-le-Roi, France

[1820–1928], see Houdaille et Triquet and Choisy-le-Roi above.

Chop plate See salver.

Chribská Glass refinery/cutting works located in Varnsdorf, Czechoslovakia [14thC–c.1972], aka Umitkove Sklo, (cut glass and pressed glass).

Christian, Désiré Painter and glass decorator from Lemberg, Meisenthal [1846–1907], worked for Burgun, Schwerer & Co [1864–85] and was an independent collaborator until 1907, then became the main artist for Gallé, (art glass enamel and cameo).

Christiansthal Glassworks in Kristiánov, Czechoslovakia [1776-?].

Christinenhütte Glassworks in Germany [?–present], owned by Schott-Zwiesel.

Christofle Cutlery manufacturer from Saint-Denis, France; also deals in crystal under its own brandname.

Chrysoprase Opaque green glass, first made by Baccarat, 1843. Is an opaque version of uranium glass.

Chudovo Glassworks in Russia [–], active from c.1918.

Chukanov, Rudolf V Glass designer from Vladimir Region, Russia [1939–], craftsman/designer at Gus-Krushtalny after c.1967.

Chunked US term meaning "badly damaged".

Cie Française de Cristal Glassworks in Levallois-Perret, France [1970–present], mother company of Sèvres, Daum and Vannes, production based at Vannes and Nancy.

Cifuentes y Pola Glassworks in Gijon, Spain [–], active from c.1890, (tableware).

Cigler, Václav Glass artist from Vsetin, Czech Republic [1929–], taught at the Bratislava Academy 1965–79 and independent artist from 1979.

Cimaver SA Glassworks in Houdeng-Coegnies, Belgium [?–present], (paperweights, lighting, novelties, globes, bells, and tubes).

Cinesi Type of art glass made by Venini, designed by Carlo Scarpa, 1940.

Cintra Type of art glass produced by Steuben c.1917 (bubbles, interior decorated).

Cioni, Mario Glass producer located in Capraia e Limite, Firenze, Italy [1958–present]. Sig: all tableware items sand marked while cut glass items have a needle sig, (luxury crystal cut glass, cut-to-clear, tableware).

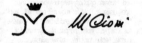

Cire Signature found on enamelled glassware made by Moser for the Portuguese market (c.1920s).

Cire Perdu Method of casting one-off glass vessels or sculptures, aka Lost Wax.

Cirera Casanovas, Genis Glass designer from Spain [1890–1970], worked 1901–1960s.

Ctrulis, Raimonds Contemporary designer from Latvia, designs for Livanu Stiklas.

Citroen, Paul Painter from Holland [1896–1983], designed 54 unica for Leerdam in 1960. Sig: engraved Unica PCD #/Pcitroen.

CIVE See Cooperativa Industria Vetro Empoli.

Clairay, Verrerie de Glassworks in Clairay, Vosges, France [–], c.1951–c.1960/5 designs by Heiligenstein. Sig: Clairistal.

Clambroth glass Grey-white semi-transparent glass type popular in the Victorian era.

Claret A glass for drinking claret wine.

Clark, TB & Co Glassworks in Honesdale, PA, USA [1884–1930], (cut glass on blanks by Dorflinger, Brilliant period).

Classic Light srl Glass firm located in Maerne, Venezia, Italy [?–present], uses the trade name Cristal de Settat, (chandeliers, crystal drops, cut glass)

Clausthal Glashütte Glassworks in Clausthal-Zellerfeld, Germany [?–present], see Wiemers Glashütten Rolf.

Claw beakers Drinking glass from the Middle Ages, mainly found in Germany and Holland. See replicas.

Claye, L Glassworks in Paris, France [–].

Clayman, Daniel Studio artist from USA [1957–].

Clayton Mayers & Co Glass seller/broker located in London, Great Britain [–], active c.1920s, introduced the famous Jacobean pattern in 1923, (tableware, pressed glass).

Cleemann Glashütte Glassworks in Rauscha near Görlitz, OL, Germany [1792–c.1937].

Clegg, Tessa Studio glass artist from Scotland [–].

Clements, Richard Flamework artist from Tasmania, Australia [1950–], worked at Argyle Glass, Sydney 1972–4 and in Tasmania after 1972.

Clessidre Type of art glass made by Venini designed by Paolo Venini, 1957.

Clevenger Bros Glassworks in Clayton, NJ, USA [1929–c.1950], (tableware).

CLG Co Trade name used by Carr-Lowrey Glass Co., MD Baltimore [1889–1920]; (bottles)

Clichy, Cristallerie de Glassworks in Pont-de-Sèvres [1838–44] and then in Clichy [1844–85], bought by Landier, the owner of Sèvres in 1885 and renamed Cristallerie de Sèvres et de Clichy Réunis. Sig: none on tableware/art glass but C or Clichy on paperweights, (paperweights 1849–60s, art glass engraved, gilded and etched, coloured tableware).

Clichy-la-Garenne, Verreries & Cristallerie de See Schmitt a Clichy.

Closset et Cambresier Glassworks in Chênée, Belgium [18thC–1888], taken over by Verreries de Vaux-sous-Chèvremont 1888 and in 1895 renamed Verreries de Chênée, (bottles, flat glass, coloured glass, lamps and lighting, spa bottles after 1840).

Cloud glass Type of pressed glass with dark swirls, produced since 1922 at Davidson's, popular throughout the 1920s and 1930s. Produced in a wide range of bold Art Deco-style shapes. Colours include amber, brown, purple, blue, green, orange, red and grey, although the latter two rare and expensive.

33

Re-introduced after World War II with a new colour, topaz, a mix of green base with purple cloud

Cloudiness Glass is attacked by acidity in water, which dissolves metallic components such as sodium, lead and potassium and replaces their atoms with hydrogen. If glass is subsequently subjected to alkaline conditions, the crystalline bonds in the glass can be hydrolyzed. This is called etched cloudiness and is irreversible. Polishing can solve the problem, but not on the inside of decanters etc. Cloudiness caused by calcium deposits due to hard water can be removed by using anti-calcium products. Cloudiness caused by biological deposits in flower vases can be removed using a solution of chlorine bleach, or denture cleaning tablets. A cosmetic cure for cloudiness is to rub or spray the surface with silicon oil.

Clowns Murano clown are made by many companies and can normally not be attributed to a particular glass house. The fashion started around 1950 when Fulvio Bianconi designed a series of "Arlecchini" for Venini.

Clutha Type of art glass with cloudy streaks, silver foil and a pitted surface. Developed by J Couper & Sons c.1885.

Cluthra Cloudy type of art glass with bubble inclusions made by Steuben (c.1903) and by Kimball (after c.1925).

Clyde NY Bottle mark used by Clyde Glass Works, Clyde, NY, USA [1870–82]. It is also found as "The Clyde" in script lettering around 1885, (bottles).

Coalburn Hill Glass Works Glassworks in Great Britain [–], see Webb, Joseph.

Coalbournebrook Glassworks See Haden.

Coasters Shallow plates normally made from cut glass or pressed glass in boxes of 12. Popular in the 20thC until the 1950s.

Cobaltei Barovier & Toso type of art glass by Ercole Barovier, 1956.

Cochrane, John Glass designer from Great Britain [–], worked for George Davidson & Co c.1962/3.

Cocktail glass Stemmed glass with funnel shaped cuppa.

Coquille Signature found on art glass made at Flygsfors, designed by Paul Kedelv, in production 1956–65.

COE Stands for Coefficient of Expansion, aka Thermal Coefficient of Expansion.

Coffin & Hay Glassworks based in Winslow, NJ, USA [1838–42], (bottles).

Cofrac Export Trade name used by Vannes /CFC c.1980s.

Cog cane Describes a cane with a cogged edge, (paperweights).

Cohansey Trade name used by Cohansey Glass Manufacturing Co, Philadelphia, PA [1870–1900], (bottles).

Coin glass Type of pressed glass – coins were incorporated in glasses from the 18thC.

Colcothar Polishing agent aka Jeweller's Rouge.

Cold end Refers to all processes undertaken after the glass has cooled.

Cold seal A temporary seal used in lampwork that can be easily cracked off later.

Colinet, Englebert Glassworks in Beauwelz, Belgium [–].

Collar A ring for holding canes in place in paperweights.

Collard, Alfred Glass designer from Belgium [–], worked at VSL after 1984.

Colle, Cristalleria srl Glassworks in Colle Val d'Elsa,Si, Italy [1960s–present], part of the Bormioli Rocco group, designers include Roberto Licenziato Monti and Setsu Ito. Sig: Sand-blasted shield mark, (tableware, stemware, giftware, paperweights, vases in full lead crystal).

Colle Val d'Elsa Medieval town near Siena, Italy, centre of glass production, factories include CALP, Colle and Stiver.

Colle, Michel Artist and glass designer from France [1872–1949], worked for Baccarat and Cristalleries de Nancy.

Colleoni Vetreria Artistica Glassworks in Murano, Italy [?–present], (art glass, vases, objects, figures, limited editions, clear crystal, gold leaf).

Collet Venini art glass type designed by Ludovico Diaz de Santillana, 1962.

Colon, A Venini art glass type designed by Fulvio Bianconi and Paolo Venini, 1950.

Colonial Trade name of Dorflinger & Sons, C.

Colony Glassworks in USA [1962–present], bought by Lancaster to become Lancaster Colony in 1962, acquired by Indiana Glass and the Lancaster Glass Company in Lancaster, OH, USA, (became Lancaster Colony Commercial Products, 1978).

Colopal Opaque glass type in pale lemon colour; rarer in pastel green, grey and lavender, Leerdam 1930s.

Colora Coloured variety of Orrefors Fuga glass, (centrifugally cast), designed by Palmqvist.

Colorlites Glass refinery located in Chatham, Kent, Great Britain [–], (glass colouring).

Colotte, Aristide Crystal sculptor from Nancy [1885–1959], worked 1920–39 only, (geometric and Art Deco shapes chiselled into thick-walled Baccarat blanks).

Colour chemistry Adding antimony to the glass melt produces brown or yellow glass; add Antimony sulphide for red; Cadmium sulphide for yellow; Carbon and sulphur for amber and brown; Cerium for yellow, Chromium for green, yellow and pink, Cobalt for light and dark blue, green, pink; Copper for turquoise, blue, green, red; Fluoride or phosphate compounds for opal, opaque; Gold for ruby red and pink; Iron for green, blue, yellow and brown; Manganese for amethyst, violet, purpur; Neodymium for purple; Nickel for grey; yellow, purple; Praseodymium for green; Selenium for pink, red; Silver for yellow; Tin, bone ash, phosphate, cryolite and arsenic for opaque white; Titanium for purple, brown; Uranium for luminous green, yellow, brown and Vanadium for green, blue and grey.

Coloured glass Many glass colours were developed after 1840. Before then, most glassworks were limited to using green, brown, clear and blue glass. Many works now have their own specific names for colours.

Columbia Glass Co/US Glass Factory J Glassworks in Findlay, OH, USA [1886–91], in 1891 merged into US Glass as Factory J, (pressed glass).

Combing Pulling apart an applied decoration. See also feathering and festooning.

Comet Glass Ltd Glassworks in New Delhi, India [1993–present], (pressed glass tableware, barware, giftware, paperweights and tumblers).

Commedia dell'Arte, La Venini art glass designed by Fulvio Bianconi, 1948.

Comolla Contemporary gold engraved crystalware from Italy

Compagnies du Val See Arts du Verre.

Compiègne, Cristalleries Glassworks in Compiègne, north of Paris [–], active c.1927 and 1930. Sig: Degue, (art glass cameo, colour, etched, lamps and lighting).

Composto Venini art glass type designed by Carlo Scarpa, 1940

Comptoir des Bouteilles Belges Manufacturing group from Belgium [1931–63], includes Bennert-Bivort in Jumet; Hamendes in Merksem and Jumet, Glasfabriek Mol, they regrouped 1963 as BBR, (bottles).

Con Macchie Venini art glass designed by Carlo Scarpa, 1940 and by Fulvio Bianconi and Paolo Venini, 1950

Concorde Kristallglas GmbH Glassworks in Windischeschenbach, Germany [1994–present], a continuation of Annahütte, Dobern, 1994. Trade names include Annahütte, Glassics and Evita Crystal), (cut glass, pressed crystal, tableware, giftware, lustre, colour).

Condiment set See castor set.

Conne The name of several glass engravers from Great Britain: Augustin worked c.1851, Nicholas worked at Richardson 1823–54 and Emily worked at Richardson c.1860s.

Conrad, Charles Glass artist from Belgium [1912–], worked for Val St Lambert in 1961.

Conradsminds Glasvaerk Glassworks in Aalborg, Denmark [–].

Console bowl See Milieu de Table.

Console set A US term for a fruit bowl with two matching candlesticks, popular in the 1920s and 1930s.

Consolidated Lamp & Glass Co Glassworks in Corapolis, PA, USA [1893–1964], created from merger of Wallace & McAfee with Fostoria Shade and Lamp in 1893, located in Fostoria, OH 1893–1896, sold in 1962 and burned down 1963, (lighting, shades and chimneys, giftware after 1925, Martele and Catalonian art glass after 1925, "Florentine", "Chintz" after 1927 and "Ruba Rombic" after 1928).

Consorzio Murano da Mula Glassworks located in Murano, Italy [–], active c.1980, (art glass).

Constantini, Cleto Glassworks in Murano, Italy [–], active c.1967, (conterie etc).

Constantini Glassbeads Glassworks in Murano, Italy [–], active c.1967, (conterie etc).

Constantini, Vittorio Flamework artist from Murano, Italy [1944–], has had own shop in Venice since 1973.

Contardi Glassworks in Colle Brianza, CO, Italy [1948–present], (tubes & lighting).

Contat & Cie Glassworks in Monthey, Switzerland [–], active c.1910, (tableware).

Contemporary glass Refers to studio glass, which means the artists execute their own work instead of designing for a factory.

Conterie Beads, from contare to count. Beads were considered currency in the 16thC.

Conterie et Cristallerie, Società Veneziana Glassworks in Murano, Italy [c.1948–c.1967], designers include Maria Damerini; Flavio Poli, Antonio Pagan, (beads, art glass and lustres).

Continental Can Company Glassworks in USA [–]. Sig: three Cs interlocked, (pressed glass and HazelWare).

Convolvulus vase Art glass vase made by Richardson c.1885,which has convoluted pincered applications.

Cook, John Heald Glass designer from Great Britain [1942–], active c.1970.

Cooperativa Industria Vetro Empoli Glassworks in Empoli, FI, Italy [1950–present], merged with Fornace da Vinci into Vetreria in Toscane, 2000, most designs by Studio Cive, additional designs by Sandro Bessi 1997, Antonio Rossi 1995, Christina Cappelli and Laura Gennai 1992, Antonella Martinelli 1996 and Claudio Marturano 1997, (tableware, vases, coloured glass, moulded ware, tortoise shell, spatter).

Co-operative Flint Glass Co Glassworks in Beaver Falls, PA, USA [1879–1937], previously known as Beaver Falls Co-Operative Glass Co, (pressed glass, reverse amberina "sunset" 1925–7).

Coopzen, Glasblzazerij Willem Glassworks in Isselt, near Amersfoort, Netherlands [1731–1828], (green bottles).

Copier, Andries Glass designer from the Netherlands [1901–91], worked for Leerdam 1923–72, and with various glassmakers in Italy, Czechoslovakia, US and the Netherlands 1977–91. Famed for tableware, art glass and pressed glass he is classed as one of the top glass designers of all time. Unica (one-off) pieces are signed, serica (limited editions) and some tableware are marked. Sig: LC (c reversed) in acid stamp or moulded on pressed pieces and needle etched on unica.

Copier unica Letter, year and quantity produced: none=1923/4 (unknown); none=1925 (min of 420), none=1926 (min of 953), A=1926/7 (min of 413), B=1927 (min of 273), C=1927/8 (min of 831), D=1928 (min of 475), E=1928/9 (min of 468), F=1929/30 (min of 457), G=1930/1 (416), H=1930/1 (712), K=1931/2 (530), L=1931/2 (475), M=1931/2 (446), N=1932 (277), O=1933/4 (max of 200), O=1935/6 (200–300), O=1937 (300–400), O=1938 (400–662), P=1939 (111), R=1940 (189), S=1941 (789), T=1942 (313), V=1943 (1273), W=1944 (1841), none=1945 (unknown), X=1946 (1750), Z=1947 (647), none=1948 (unknown), AA=1949 (366), AB=1950 (273), AC=1951 (approx. 75), AD=1952 (approx. 350), AE=1953 (approx. 370), AF=1954 (approx. 270), AH=1955 (approx. 420), AM=1956 (approx. 675), none=1957 (unknown), CB=1958 (186),

CC=1959 (16), CD=1960 (17), none=1961 (unknown), CF=1962 (6), CH=1963 (70), CK=1964 (259), CL=1965 (13), CO=1966 (11) and CP=1967 (3).

Copillet See Caranza.

Copper foil A mounting technique for flat glass using foil and soldering, esp. used for lamp shades. Aka Tiffany.

Copper wheel engraving Surface-decorating technique using abrasive coated copper disks on a spindle. Allows detailed pattern cutting.

Coralene Surface decorating technique using small glass beads which are fused onto the glass. First patented in Germany in 1883 and later also produced in Italy, Great Britain, Czechoslovakia and the US from around 1880 onwards. There are many reproductions around.

Corba SpA, Cristalleria Glassworks in San Giovanni Valdarno, Italy [?–present], (pressed glass, frosted).

Cord Flaw in glass tubes; visible streaks ("striata" or "striae") due to the irregular viscosity of the glass or rods caused by uneven mixing of ingredients

Cordial A small goblet or stem for drinking bitters etc.

Cordonato d'Oro Barovier & Toso art glass type by Ercole Barovier, 1950.

Core The clay form around which molten glass was applied to make small flasks in Egyptian and Roman times. The technique is known as core forming.

Coreano Type of art glass made by Venini and designed by Tapio Wirkkala, 1969.

Corinto Barovier & Toso art glass type by Ercole Barovier, 1948.

Cork Glass Company Glassworks in Cork, Irish Republic [–], (old Irish cut glass).

Cornelius & Co Glassworks in Pittsburgh, PA USA [19thC], (lighting, esp. lard oil lamps).

Corning Cut Glass Co Glassworks in Corning, NY, USA [–], active c.1901, (cut glass).

Corning Flint Glass Works Glassworks in Corning, NY, USA [1868–75], continued as Corning Glass Works, see below.

Corning Glass Works Glassworks in Corning, NY, USA [1875–present], took over Steuben in 1933 as well as Macbeth-Evans in 1936. Trade names include Pyrex, invented photochromatic glass, (tableware, art glass and cut glass).

Corniola Barovier & Toso art glass type by Ercole Barovier, 1959.

Cornucopia Glass vessels in the shape of a shell, esp. by Loetz.

Corona Special quality piece produced by Orrefors.

Corona Trade name used by Will and Baumer Co.

Coronet Trade name of Gill Brothers.

Correia Art Glass Glassworks in Santa Monica, CA, USA [1974–?], designers include Chris Buzzini and Steven Correia, (art glass).

Correia, Steven V Glass maker from Santa Monica, CA, USA [1949–], (paperweights).

Corroso 1. Having an acid-etched surface. 2. Type of art glass made by Venini, designed by Carlo Scarpa and Tyra Lundgren, 1936. 3. Art glass designed by Flavio Poli c.1951. "Vetro Corroso" introduced around 1951.

Cosmos Pressed glass pattern in milk glass from Consolidated produced 1894–1915.

Costebelle, Verreries de Glassworks in Costebelle, France [–], c.1926, (lamps and lighting).

Costoloni Barovier & Toso art glass type by Ercole Barovier, 1945.

Coudersport Tile and Ornamental Glass Co Glassworks in Coudersport, PA USA [1900–4].

Coughlan, John Glass engraver from Great Britain [–], working c.1975.

Couper & Sons, J Glassworks in Glasgow, Scotland [–], (clutha glass 1880s), designers include Christopher Dresser and George Walton.

Courcelles-Nord, Manufacture des Verres Spéciaux de Glassworks in Courcelles, Belgium [1919–37], (flat glass, including ornamental flat glass).

Courtney, Giselle Flamework artist from Australia [–], worked at Glass Artist's Gallery in Sydney 1982–92.

Couterier, Robert Designer from France [–], worked for Daum c.1975.

Coventry Glass Factory Co Glassworks in Coventry, CT, USA [1813–50], (bottles, inkwells, demijohns and tumblers).

Coverpla SA Glassworks in Nice, France [1946–present], (bottles, perfume).

CP signature used by Pantin.

CPC See Avon.

Crachoir See Cuspidor.

Cracker jar A biscuit or cookie jar.

Cracking off Detaching a glass object from a blowpipe or pontil.

Crackle glass Aka ice glass or craquelé. Produced using an old Venetian technique (16thC) in which the parison is rolled in moist sawdust/sand to condition the surface, then plunged in water to make the surface crack. A new layer of glass is added and the cracks fused. The result looks like cracked ice. Sometimes mistaken for overshot glass.

Craftsman Trade name of Nazeing Glass Works, Great Britain.

Cranberry Glass Dark red transparent colour first made in England, later also in the US and Czechoslovakia c.1870s.

Cream soup US term for a soup bowl with handles.

Creamer A small jug used for serving cream.

Cremax Opaque beige glass from Macbeth-Evans.

Crepuscoli Type of art glass made by Venini and designed by Toni Zuccheri, 1964.

Crepuscolo Aurato Barovier & Toso art glass type by Ercole Barovier, 1968.

Crescent Glass Co Glassworks in Wellsburgh,

WV [1879–1907], became part of National Glass in 1899 then closed in 1907, (automobile lenses and blown tumblers).

Crespin, Verrerie de Glassworks in Crespin, France [?–1897], merged into Gobeleterie Nationale, Belgium 1879.

Crest and Company Lighting manufacturer located in Chicago, IL, USA [–], (leaded glass shades c.1910–c.1920).

Creusot-Montcenis, Le Glassworks in Le Creusot (Bourgogne), France [1253–1910], manufacture des Cristaux de la Reine, (cut glass, opalines 1783–1832 and sulphures 1810–30s).

Cribbs, Keke Studio artist from USA [1951–].

Crieff Town in Scotland, where Perthshire paperweights and Stuart Crystal are based.

Crimp 1. A decoration technique for rims and edges popular after 1875. 2. A metal tool for pushing coloured glass into a paperweight. 3. A crimped cane in a paperweight is one with an ondulating edge.

Crisa Glass Trade name used by Vitrocrisa, Mexico.

Crisal Glass Trade name used by Cristais de Alcobaça.

Cristal d'Arques Trade name from JG Durand for machine-made 24% lead crystal pressed glass, which was first introduced in 1968.

Cristal De Paris Glassworks in Montbronn, Vosges [1980–present], tableware, ornamental glass, tumblers, vases in full lead crystal.

Cristal de Settat Trade name of Classic Light.

Cristal de Sèvres See Sèvres and CFC.

Cristalcolor Glassworks in Napoli, Italy [?–present], artists include Antonio Procentese, (crystal silver combination giftware).

Cristalerias De Mataro SCOCL See Mataro SCOCL, Cristalerias de.

Cristalerias Papini See Papini, Cristalerias.

Cristalerias Piccardo See Piccardo, Cristalerias.

Cristalex Sklarna Janstejn Glassworks in Horní Dubenky, Czech Republic [1809–present], (lamps and lighting).

Cristall Badalona See Badalona, Cristall.

Cristalleria e Vetreria Veneziana gia Franchetti See Veneziana gia Franchetti, Cristalleria e Veteria.

Cristalleria Europa Srl See Europa srl, Cristalleria.

Cristalleria Corba SpA See Corba SpA, Cristalleria.

Cristalleria Matarese Sas See Matarese Sas, Cristalleria.

Cristalleria Murano See Murano, Cristalleria.

Cristalleria Santi See Santi, Cristalleria.

Cristallerie de Haute Bretagne See Haute Bretagne, Cristallerie de.

Cristallerie de Montbronn See Montbronn, Cristallerie de.

Cristallerie de Nancy See Nancy, Cristallerie de.

Cristallerie de Puteaux See Puteaux, Cristallerie de.

Cristallerie de Saint-Paul See Saint-Paul, Cristallerie de.

Cristallerie des Papes See Papes, Cristallerie des.

Cristallerie des Vosges du Nord See Vosges du Nord, Cristallerie de.

Cristallerie du Creusot see Creusot-Montcenis, Le.

Cristallerie en Emaillerie St Joseph du Bourget See Saint Joseph du Bourget, Cristallerie en Emaillerie.

Cristallerie La Rochère See Rochère La, Cristallerie.

Cristallerie Livellara srl See Livellara Srl, Cristallerie.

Cristallerie Lorraine See Lorraine, Cristallerie.

Cristallerie Rube See Rube, Cristallerie.

Cristalleries & Verreries Namuroises Cie Anon Des See Namuroises, Cristalleries & Verreries Cie Anon Des.

Cristalleries de Compiègne See Compiègne, Cristalleries.

Cristalleries de Lyon See Lyon, Cristalleries de.

Cristalleries de Manage See Association & Manage, Cristalleries de.

Cristalleries de Portieux see Portieux, Cristalleries de.

Cristalleries de Saint-Louis See Saint-Louis, Cristalleries de.

Cristallo (It) Light clear glass used in Venice since the Middle Ages.

Cristallo Filigana Viola Type of art glass made by Venini and designed by Tommaso Buzzi, 1932.

Cristalux SA Glassworks in Buenos Aires, Argentina [1896–present], (bottles, barware, tableware and giftware).

Cristul/Fábrica de Vidros Glassworks in the Marinha Grande region of Portugal [1990–present], see Marinha Grande and Mglass, (decorative glass, lamps and lighting).

Crivisa Cristalerias SA Glassworks in Azuqueca de Henares, Spain [?–present]. It is a Bormioli Rocco production plant for Bormioli Rocco.

Crizzling, Criseeling Chemical instability caused by improper glass recipe (surplus alkali or insufficient lime), causing small cracks in the surface. Also seen on glass from antiquity.

Crocheting See Stitching.

Crodes, Charles Glass decorator from France [1894–1973], worked at VLG c.1937.

Croismare, Grandes Verreries de Glassworks in France [–], see Müller Frères, Hinzelin and Véssière.

Cros, Henri Glass designer from Narbonne, France [1840–1907], (relief panels after 1885/1893–1903, sculptures in pâte-de-verre produced at Sèvres after 1891 and had his own kiln in Sèvres after 1897).

Cros, Jean Glass designer from France [1884–1932], son of Henri Cros, worked at Sèvres before 1912, then continued producing pâte-de-verre plaques 1918–32.

Crosshatching Parallel or crossed fine lines on cut glass.

Crown Hollow-blown paperweights.

Crown cap Introduced in 1891, became the standard closing system for beer bottles.

Crown Crystal Glass Co Ltd Glassworks in Waterloo, NSW, Australia [1927–?], incorporates Balmain, Crown, Crystal Glass and Zetland, sigs: include Crown with three dots.

Crown glass 1. Window glass produced by spinning out a bowl-shaped piece of glass (bullion) to a flat disk. Aka Bull's eye. 2. An alkali-lime silicate optical glass used in the production of lenses. 3. Types of window glass: London Crown (standard) and Bristol Crown (good quality) 4. Standard glass (as opposed to Flint glass).

Crown Glassworks, The Glassworks in Alexandria, Australia [1920–7], started in 1920 as Alexandria Bottle Works, merged into Crown Crystal Glass Co in 1927.

Crown Milano Trade name of art glass patented in 1893 by Mt Washington Glass Co. It is decorated with enamel and gold, aka Albertine. Sig: crowned CM monogram.

Crown top Type of bottle top in use after c.1900.

Crown Tuscan Trade name used by Cambridge Glass Company.

Crozara Ezio Glassworks in Murano, Italy [–], active c.1967, (cut glass and engraved glass).

Crucible A refractory vessel used for melting a batch of glass.

Cruet sets Table set for sugar, mustard, oil and vinegar popular from the 18thC until the 1920s. Aka Castor sets.

Crystal 1. Glass containing at least 24% lead oxide. 2. Any glass having particular refraction qualities.

Crystal Art Glass Co/Degenhart Glassworks in Cambridge, OH USA [1947–78]. See Degenhart and Boyd's Art Glass Co .

Crystal balls Used for magic and divination in the spirited 19thC. Originally made from mountain crystal, later crystal and glass. Examples known from Baccarat and Val St Lambert.

Crystal composition Cristallin has 10% lead oxide, Cristal 24% and Crystal Supérieur 30%.

Crystal fabrication The ingredients are mixed and placed in refractory pots. Inside the pot a ring of refractory earth floats on the surface of the viscous paste to isolate the fusing materials (at 1,500°C), then impurities accumulate at the side of the pot. the gatherer dips in the centre of the ring when the crystal is mixed and melted (takes 20–40 hours).

Crystal Glass Co Glassworks in Knottingley, Yorkshire, Great Britain, active 1930s, see Bagley.

Crystal Glass Co/National Glass 04 Glassworks in Pittsburgh, PA, USA [1879–1908], La Belle Glass Co, sold to Crystal Glass Co 1888 then merged into National Glass 1899, (pressed glass).

Crystal Glass Works, The Glassworks in Waterloo, Sydney, Australia [1919–27], merged with Balmain in 1926 then merged with Zetland to form Crown Crystal in 1927, (pressed glass and carnival glass)

Crystal Kingdom Region in southern Sweden (in the Kronoberg and Kalmar counties) with around 20 glassworks including: Kosta, Boda, Orrefors, Skrufs, Bergdala, Johansfors, Sandviks, Målerås, Nybro, Rosdala, Sea, Älghult, Strömbergshyttan, Lindshammar, Pukeberg.

Crystal RPC/Glass Research Institute Glassworks in Gus-Krushtalny, Russia [–], (enamel, souvenirs, coloured glassware; art

glass, tableware, barware, cookware and jewellery).

Crystales de Mexico: Glassworks in Nuevo Leon, Mexico [–]. Sig: M inside C, (pressed glass, carnival glass and bottles).

Crystalex Glassworks conglomerate [1974–present] with works located in Chribska, Harrachóv, Kamenický Šenov, Nový Bor, all in the Czech Republic, (Český Krištal, Rosice, Karolinka, Kvetna, Vrbno, Zahn). Began as a state enterprise and was completely reorganized in 1994, (art glass, tableware, barware, cookware, paperweights, pressed glass; full lead crystal, sodalime, opal glass).

Crystalia Glass studio located in Istanbul, Turkey [1985–present], (crystal figures and promotional items).

Crystaltynt Glassware made by Bagley's after 1934. There are Art Deco designs in blue, pink, amber, green, clear or matt.

CS & Co Trade name of Cannington, Shaw & Co.

Csala, Zsuzsa Glass designer from Hungary [1972–], has worked for Ajka Üveggyár since 1997.

CSS Glassworks in Czechoslovakia [?–present], (pressed glass and black glass).

CT Abbreviation for crown top.

Cuijpers, Ed Architect/Glass designer from the Netherlands [1859–1927], worked for Maastricht in 1927.

Cukmanti, Pozorka Glassworks in Teplic v Cechách, Czechoslovakia [19thC–1950], (pressed glass).

Culemborgse Glasfabriek, NV Glassworks in Culemborg, Netherlands [1861–1928], owned by distillers Hoytema, production stopped in 1917, (gin & storage bottles).

Cullet The mixture of raw materials for glass making is known as the batch. Cullet, or scrap glass, is added to the batch to help the melting process (which can take up to 36 hours). Cullet must always be of the same composition, and the batch can contain as much as 50–75% of cullet.

Cumberland Glass Co/National Glass 05 Glassworks in Cumberland, MD USA [?–1899], in 1899 it merged into National Glass and became known as Factory 05, (pressed glass).

Cumberland Glass Manufacturing Co Bridgeton, NJ, USA [1890–1900], (bottles).

Cunha, Isabel Glass designer from Portugal [–], worked for MGlass c.1999.

Cunningham Glass Co, DO Located in Pittsburgh, PA USA [1883–1937], (bottles).

Cunninghams & Co Located in Pittsburgh, PA [1880–1907], trade names include C Co and C & Co, (bottles).

Cuny, Jutta Glass designer from France [1940–1983]

Cup Drinking or decorative vessel, with or without stem or handles, having a rounded cavity.

Cupola Dome.

Cupping glass Open-mouthed glass jar applied to the skin to create suction in 18th ,19th and early 20thC. medicine. Esp. used in Great Britain and France.

Curio Crafts Glassworks/refinery located in New Delhi, India [1991–present], (bottles, perfumes, tableware, barware, paperweights, stemware, lamps and lighting, chandeliers, Christmas ornaments and glass-metal combinations).

Curling, Robertson & Co (Curling, Price & Co) Glassworks in Pittsburgh, PA, USA [1827–1901], became Dithridge & Sons in 1860, (pressed glass).

Curran, Patrick J Studio artist from USA [–].

Cuspidor A wide-necked vase for spitting. Aka spittoon (US) or Crachoir (Fr).

Custard cup A small dessert glass, with or without handle.

Custard glass Ivory-coloured glass type first made in Great Britain in the 1880s. Soon made in the US by Northwood, Heisey, Tarentum, Fenton and McKee. Is highly collectable and expensive. Contains uranium salts, hence it glows under UV light.

Cut Glass Products Co Glassworks in USA [–], (cut glass, Brilliant period).

Cut glass This type of glass came into fashion around 1750 in Great Britain, Ireland (by Waterford) and France (by Baccarat) as well as in the US in 1810 (by Bakewell & Page). By the middle of the 19thC, thicker glass and deeper cuts were used (this was known as the "Rich Cut" Period). Patterns became more elaborate, often covering the entire surface around 1880 during the "Brilliant period", which lasted until 1915.

Cut overlay Glass with two or more layered colours, cut to show the underlying one(s); see cut-to-clear.

Cut velvet Art glass of the c.1880s, made in relief-moulded patterns to allow white casing to show through the pastel outer layer.

Cutting: Grinding a pattern into glass using a rotating wheel coated with abrasives. See also copper wheel engraving, carving and wheel engraving.

Cut-to-clear Glass with two or more layered colours, cut through to show the underlying one. Developed in Silesia and Bohemia (by Egermann) c.1804, new colours appeared in the 1820s–1830s, 2-colour casing after 1836. The main producers have been: Choisy-le-Roi since 1825, Baccarat since 1837, Saint-Louis since 1837, Clichy since the 1840s, Bacchus since c.1844, Pellatt since c.1844, Rice Harris since c.1844, Richardson since c.1844 and Val St Lambert since the 1840s.

Cuypers, Eduard Architect from Holland [1859–1927], designed tableware for Maastricht together with Kannegieter. Sig: CK monogram.

CVM See Venezia e Murano, Compagnia di.

Cvrček Glass refinery located in Železný Brod, Czechoslovakia [?–present], (engraving and sand-blasting).

Cylinder glass This is a flat glass production method that uses a long cylinder cut lengthwise and subsequently slumped on a flat table.

Cypriot glass Type of art glass made by Tiffany – has surface corrosion.

Cyrén, Gunnar Glass designer/goldsmith from Sweden [1931–], worked for Orrefors 1959–70 and 1976-present. Sig: monogram: B.

Czechoslovakian glass Glass has been made in the forest regions of Bohemia since the Middle Ages. Czechoslovakia came into being as a country in 1918. Slovakia became independent in 1993 and Bohemia and Moravia, continued as the Czech Republic. The main glass-making centres are North Bohemia (Nový Bor, Jablonec nad Nisou and Teplice) and South Bohemia (Sušice and Vimperk).

D

Da Ros, Antonio Glass designer from Italy [1936–], worked for Cenedese after 1958.

Dabrowa See Huta Skla.

Daden, Frederick Glassworker and designer from Great Britain [–], worked for Whitefriar's 1942–61.

Dahl, Oskar Glass designer from Sweden [–]; worked for Kosta 1939-40

Dahle Glashütte, P. Glassworks in Teplitz near Sorau, NL, Germany [1885–c.1937].

Dahlskog, Evald Glass designer from Sweden [1894–1950], worked for Kosta 1926–9. Sig: E Dahlskog Kosta on cut and engraved art glass but none on brown coloured tableware.

Daisy and Greek Key Famous pressed glass design from Davidson in 1886. Was also made by Holmegaard in Denmark, Leerdam in Holland, Karhula-Iittala in Finland, Kosta in Sweden, AG für Glasfabrikation vorm Gebr Hoffmann in Germany, Villeroy & Boch in Germany, Rheinische Glashütten in Germany and by unknown manufacturer(s) in Czechoslovakia.

Dal Mas Renato & Ongaro Renzo Glassworks in Murano, Italy [–], active c.1967, (cut glass and engraved glass).

Dal Maschio, Serena Glass designer from Venice, Italy [1920–74], worked for SALIR after 1951.

Dal Moro See Soffiera Dal Moro.

Dali, Salvador Artist designer from Spain [–], designed works in pâte-de-verre for Daum c.1968–c.1989.

Dalla Venezia Martinuzzi Glassworks in Murano, Italy [–], active c.1954, designers include Ezio Rizzetto, 1960.

Dalle de verre Aka faceted or slab glass, which comes in sheets 30 x 20 x 2.5cm (12in x 8in x1in). It is worked with diamond saws, hammers and chisels. It is made by casting in an epoxy matrix.

Dalzell Brothers & Gilmore/National Glass Glassworks in Wellsburgh, WV [1883–1902], located in Brilliant, OH, USA 1883–88, was known as Dalzell, Gilmore & Leighton Co in Findlay, OH 1888-1902 then became part of National Glass in 1899, (pressed glass).

Dalzell-Viking Glass Glassworks in New Martinsville, WV [1987–present], (pressed glass, tableware, barware, paperweights and giftware).

Damara Glassworks Glassworks in Tarnów, Poland [1989–present], (tableware, lighting).

Damasco Barovier & Toso art glass type by Ercole Barovier, 1948.

Dâmaso/Vidros de Portugal Glassworks in the Marinha Grande region of Portugal [?–present], (tableware, decorative items, tiles and bricks), see Marinha Grande and Mglass.

Dammouse, Albert Louis Glass designer from France [1848–1926], designed glass after 1898 and specialized in pâte-de-verre.

Damon, Louis Glass artist from France [?–1947], owner of Au Vase Etrusque art glass shop in Paris after 1887. Sig: L.Damon, Paris, (art glass cameo on blanks supplied by Daum).

Damprémy, Verreries de Glassworks in France [–], aka A Fourcault-Frison & Cie.

Danese Glassworks in Murano, Italy [–], active c.1950s, designs by Fulvio Bianconi after 1955, (art glass).

Daniolo Glassworks in France [–], active c.1930s, (opalescent glass).

Danone Second-largest bottle producer in Europe churning out 2.4 million tons of glass a year in 20 works in France, Holland and Spain. Their main site is Verreries Souchon Neuvesel with 4.2 billion items but they also have works in Gironcourt, Wingles, Vayres, Reims, Labegude and Veauche. Further companies include Verdôme, producer of perrier bottles at Puy Guillaume and Verrières de Masnières. The activities of tableware producer VMC, including 3 works at Givors, Rive-de-Gier, Reims were sold in 1996 to the Italian group Bormioli Rocco.

D'Argenthal Signature on art glass from Saint-Louis.

Darmstadt Glassworks in Darmstadt [1901–11], its full name is Grossherzogliche Hessische Edelglasmanufaktur. The designer was Schneckendorf; sig: monogram, (art glass iridescent, bronze mounted).

Dartington Crystal Glassworks in Torrington, Devon, Great Britain [1967–present], designers include Frank Thrower 1967–c.1973 and Geoffrey Baxter. Sig: D inside a square on barware only, (tableware, giftware, bowls, vases, wine suits, 24% lead crystal and the Capredoni collection).

Dartington Studio Glass studio part of Dartington Crystal [1998–present], designers include Hilary Green and John Ford. Sig: all items are stamped with their logo: 2 blowpipes in a circle. Their gold crackle technique is called alchemy and the marbled crackle is called farrago, (art glass, crackle, graal, gold foil).

Daum & Cie, Verrerie de Belle-Etoile Glassworks in Nancy, France [–], (produce of "Lorrain" industrial art glass).

Daum, Antonin Glass designer from France [1864–1930], worked for Daum c.1909.

Daum, Michel Glass designer from France [1900–1986], worked for Daum c.1935–66.

Daum, Nancy Glassworks in Nancy, France [1875–present], family members involved were: Antonin (1864–1930), Auguste (1853–1901), Jacques (1909–87), Jean (1825–85), Michel (1900–86) and Paula (1888–1944). Designers who worked for Daum include Jacques Gruber, Almaric Walter, Henri Bergé, Charles Schneider, Emile Wirtz, Roger Tallon, Dan Dailey, Philippe Druillet, Hilton McConnico, Elisabeth Garouste, Mattia Bonetti and Philippe Starck. It is currently known as CFC-Daum and it produces at Nancy and in Vannes. Sig: gold-painted Daum with a Lorraine cross and Nancy 1890–96, then the same in various techniques 1896–1914, wheel-engraved Daum, the Lorraine cross and Nancy France 1924–39 and needle script "Daum France" 1945–75, (art glass using all techniques and colours).

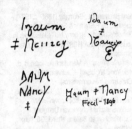

DAVC Glassworks in Murano, Italy [–], active c.1967, (cut glass and engraved glass).

Davenport, John Glass refinery located in Longport, Staffordshire [1765–1887], known as William Davenport & Co 1848–87, patented a decoration technique in 1806.

Davidson, George & Co Ltd Glassworks in Gateshead, Great Britain [1867–1987], George Davidson founded it in 1867 making lamps and lighting, which was soon followed by a full range of pressed glass tableware imitating cut glass designs. They also produced vitroporcelain in c.1880s in white, blue and slag colours, "Pearline" was produced in 1889–c.1918 and "Cloud Glass" produced in 1922–39 and re-introduced in the 1950s. Designers include John Cochrane and Milner Gray c.1962/3. Sig: marks on 19thC pressed glass is a lion on a turret in a circle, 20thC glass usually unmarked, there are labels saying GD and sometimes a trade name.

Davies Glass & Manuf Co Glassworks in Martins Ferry, OH, USA [1922–5].

DaVinci Crystal Trade name used by CALP.

Davis & Co, Thomas Glassworks located in Dudley, Great Britain [c.1750–1833], aka Dixons Green, (cut glass).

Davis, Greathead & Green Glassworks in Stoubridge, Great Britain [1837–?], production was based at Dial Glasshouse, Amblecote, (tableware, etruscan-decorated opaque ware, cut glass, gilding, figurative, coloured wares).

Daxhelet, Paul Painter from Belgium [–], worked at VSL 1966–71.

Day-Impex Ltd Glassworks in Earls Colne, Colchester, Great Britain [1946–present], (giftware, borosilicate).

De Majo Guido Glassworks in Murano, Italy [1947–present], designers included Guido De Majo, Yoichi Ohira, Fulvio Bianconi, Toni Zuccheri and, recently, Danilo de Rossi, O Favaretto, C Nason and Cristiano Bianchin, (lighting, art glass).

De Steiger Glass Co Based in LaSalle, IL, USA [1867–96], (bottles).

De Vez Signature used by Camille Tutré de Varreux on vases produced at Pantin c.1908–c.1920 (esp. landscape and floral cameo).

De Vilbiss Co Atomizer works located in Toledo, OH, USA [c.1900s–c.1938], (perfume bottles).

Deacons, John Glassmaker located in Crieff, Scotland [–], worked on paperweights in the 1970s.

Dean, Henry Glass company located in Massenhoven, Belgium [?–present], Sig: all products are needle signed, (art glass designed in Belgium, produced elsewhere).

Decal A transfer decoration.

Decanter Stoppered bottle for wine, port or spirits.

Deception glass Glass that looks as if it contains more than it does, mainly produced in the UK in the 18thC and 19thC. See also Cheater and Bistro glass.

Decho, Ilse Glass designer from Leipzig, Germany [1915–78], created designs for OLG Weisswasser in the 1950s.

Décorchemont, Francois-Emile Glass maker from Conches, Eure, France [1880–1971], first enamel pastes, pâte-d'émail art glass after 1903 with metallic oxides and colour effects, worked for St-Denis c.1909, produced Pâte-de-verre 1907–14 and 1919–1970, did glass window design c.1933. His works compare to Despret, Cros and Dammouse.

Decover Srl Glass-decorating company located in Borgonovo Val Tidone, Italy [1993–present], it is a subsidiary of Vetreria di Borgonovo, (tableware and barware).

Defries & Sons, J Manufacturer from London, Great Britain [–], active c.1862, (lighting, cut glass chandeliers).

Deganello, Paolo Glass designer from Italy [1940–], worked for Venini c.1985.

Degenhart, Charles Glassmaker from Cambridge, OH USA [1884–1964], (paperweights 1930s–60s).

Degenhart Crystal Art Glass Co Glassworks in Cambridge, OH, USA [1947–78]. Its moulds were sold to Boyd in 1978. Sig: items from 1947–72 were unmarked or, rarely, had an impressed D, D inside heart was used c.1972–8, (pressed glass; novelties; covered animal dishes)

Degué Signature found on vases made by Cristalleries de Compiègne, designed by director David Guérin [c.1925–after WWII], (art glass vases in the style of Gallé, Schneider and Daum).

Dejonghe, Bernard Glass designer from France [1942–].

Delatte, André Glass artist from Nancy, France [–], founded Les Verreries de l'Est in 1921. Sig: Delatte or Jarville, (art glass, enamelled, engraved, cameo, berluzes).

Deleersnijder, Albert Painter from Liège, Belgium [1945–], worked at VSL 1966–9.

Delf, Dorothea Glass cutter/engraver from Germany [1929–], worked at VEB Bleikristall Arnstadt 1959–64, Weisswasser 1964–73 and Olbernhau after 1973.

Delft, Flesschenfabriek Glassworks in Delft, Netherlands [1798–1963], known as Macalester Loup 1798 and then Jan Boers & Co after 1806. Used the first Owens bottles machine in Holland in 1912, merged into NV Verenigde Glasfabrieken, Schiedam in 1926 and then closed in 1963, (bottles).

Delft glass: Mount Washington glass that has blue decoration on white ground, with a gloss or satin finish, produced c.1900–1920s.

Delius & Co, Glasfabrik "Anna" Glassworks in Diemen, Netherlands [1907–11]. Sig: D&C, (medicine bottles).

Delhaise-Dethier Glassworks in Chênée and Liège, Belgium [c.1880–c.1910], (see Chênée).

Delobel, Verrerie Glassworks in Ghlin near Mons, Belgium [1750–?], (flat glass bottles).

Deluigi, Mario Glass designer from Italy [1908–89], alias Guido Bin, worked for Salviati in 1936.

Delvaux Sales outlet in the Rue Royale, Paris [?–present] with its own decoration department [c.1923–c.1934], artists include Mme Zillhardt and M Neilz. Sig: sometimes enamelled or gilt, mostly paper labels, (enamelled, cut art glass).

Delvenne, René Glass designer from Belgium [1902–72], worked for Val St Lambert 1919–67, was their designer from 1922 and art director 1958–1967, designed their "Luxval" range c.1930.

Dema Glass Ltd Glassworks in Doncaster, S Yorkshire and in Chesterfield, Derbyshire, Great Britain [1922–present], companies include Dema tableware, lighting and pharmaceutical. Sig: unmarked, (tableware, barware, stemware, vases, bulbs, Christmas ornaments).

Demardi, Jean-Pierre Glass designer from France [–], worked for Daum c.1975.

Demitasse A small cup & saucer.

Demitz/Thumitz Glassworks in Demitz/Thumitz near Bautzen, OL, Germany [1866–c.1937], operated by F Greiner & Sohn, (lighting).

Demptos Glass Company LLC Glassworks in Louisville, KY, USA [1982–present], (bottles, giftware).

Demuth, William A Manufacturer located in New York, NY, USA [–], active c.1891, (Christmas tree ornaments).

Demyon en Ballonfabriek, NV Glassworks in Tiel, Holland [1916–65] known as NV Nederlandsche Fabriek van Demyons, Korfflesschen en Ballons after 1930, (large bottles).

Denizli Cam Sanayi ve Ticaret AS Glassworks in Denizli, Turkey [?–present], subsidiary of Sisecam, (handmade tableware, lead crystal, barware, paperweights).

Dennis Glassworks Glassworks located near Stourbridge, Great Britain [1855–present], see Thomas Webb.

Denoël, Modeste Glass designer from Belgium [1869–1940], worked for Val St Lambert 1923–5.

Depression glass American term for cheap glass made during the depression years (1929–c.1940). Europe had a similar period of low-quality glass, sometimes referred to as "crisis-glass".

Derbyshire & Brother, James Glassworks in Manchester, Great Britain [1858–93], named James, John and Thomas Derbyshire after 1870 then James Dc and Sons after 1876, moulds sold at the closure in 1893, (pressed glass).

Derbyshire, John Glassworks in Salford, Manchester, Great Britain [1873–?], aka Regent Road Flint glass works. Sig: not always; embossed J-anchor-D, (pessed glass, figures).

Derfla Trade name for dentists' glassware from Alfred Becht, Offenburg in Baden, Germany c.1930s.

Desaedeler, Joseph Glass designer from Belgium [–], worked at VSL c.1960–6.

Desert glass Common name for glass turned amethyst under influence of sunlight or irradiation, most often found in glass produced c.1880–1915. Glass 1915–30 is more likely to turn pale straw amber. Aka sun coloured glass.

Design Registration, British Lozenge-shaped mark that identifies that a piece is registered. Placed on top a circle to identify the group: III=glass. Symbols surround the central registration mark.

From 1842–67, the year letter is on top, the month letter to the left, the date to the right and the part number at the bottom. Years: X=1842, H=1843, C=1844, A=1845, I=1846, F=1847, U=1848, S=1849, V=1850, P=1851, D=1852, Y=1853,

J=1854, E=1855, L=1856, K=1857, B=1858, M=1859, Z=1860, R=1861, O=1862, G=1863, N=1864, W=1865, Q=1866, T=1867.
Month letters: Jan=C Feb=G Mar=W Apr=H May=E Jun=M Jul=I Aug=R Sep=D Oct=B Nov=K Dec=A.
From 1868–83 the day is on top, part number on the left, year letter to the right, month at bottom.
Year letters: X=1868, H=1869, C=1870, A=1871, I=1872, F=1873, U=1874, S=1875, V=1876, P=1877, D=1878, Y=1879, J=1880, E=1881, L=1882, K=1883. Month letters as before. Sequential numbering after 1884, beginning 1=1884, 19754=1885, 40480=1886, 64520=1887, 90483=1888, 116648=1889, 141273=1890, 163767=1891, 185713=1892, 205240=1893, 224720=1894, 246975=1895, 268392=1896, 291241=1897, 311658=1898, 331707=1899, 351202=1900 and 368154=1901.
Numbering errors have been reported for 1857 (R for September), 1860 (K for December) and 1878 (G for March and W for year letter).

Design Registration numbers, USA 1=1843, 15=1844, 27=1845, 44=1846, 103=1847, 163=1848, 209=1849, 258=1850, 341=1851, 431=1852, 540=1853, 626=1854, 683=1855, 753=1856, 860=1857, 973=1858, 1,075=1859, 1,183=1860, 1,336=1861, 1,508=1862, 1,703=1863, 1,879=1864, 2,018=1865, 2,239=1866, 2,533=1867, 2,858=1868, 3,304=1869, 3,810=1870, 4,547=1871, 5,452=1872, 6,336=1873, 7,083=1874, 7,969=1875, 8,884=1876, 9,686=1877, 10,385=1878, 10,975=1879, 11,567=1880, 12,082=1881, 12,647=1882, 13,508=1883, 14,528=1884, 15,678=1885, 16,451=1886, 17,046=1887, 17,995=1888, 18,830=1889, 19,553=1890, 20,439=1891, 21,275=1892, 22,092=1893, 22,994=1894, 23,922=1895, 25,037=1896, 26,482=1897, 28,113=1898, 29,916=1899, 32,055=1900, 33,813=1901, 35,547=1902, 36,187=1903, 36,723=1904, 37,280=1905, 37,766=1906, 38,391=1907, 38,980=1908, 39,737=1909, 40,424=1910, 41,063=1911, 42,073=1912, 43,415=1913, 46,098=1914, 46,813=1915, 48,358=1916, 50,117=1917, 51,629=1918, 52,836=1919, 54,359=1920, 56,844=1921, 60,121=1922, 61,748=1923, 63,675=1924, 66,346=1925, 69,170=1926, 71,772=1927, 74,159=1928, 77,347=1929, 80,254=1930, 82,966=1931, 85,903=1932, 88,847=1933, 91,258=1934, 94,179=1935, 98,045=1936, 102,601=1937, 107,738=1938, 112,765=1939, 118,358=1940. See also patent dates and trademark registration.
Desjonqueres, Henri, SA Glass firm located in Paris, France [–], (bottles).
Desná 1. Town in the Czech Republic (Desná v Jizerských Horách) near Jablonec, formerly known as Polubný or Polaun. Glassworks located there include Pustiny c.1680 and Potočna 1688–1835 and after 1851, (beads, cut glass) 2. Trade name used by Atelier Ornela, Czech Republic.
Despret, Georges Glass maker from Belgium [1862–1952], mirror factory in Jeumont, 1884, Requingnies 1893 and Boussois. Renamed Cie Réunie des Glaces et Verres spéciaux du Nord de la France in 1903. Did first experiments with pâte-de-verre c.1890. Took part in the Exposition Universelle 1900, workshop destroyed WWI, production resumed 1920–37. Sculptors/designers include Yvonne Serruys, Pierre Le Faguays, Charles Touché, M de Glori, Jean Goujon, Georges Nicollet and Alexandre Charpentier. Sig: Despret glass is always marked.
Desprez Glass maker located in France [–], (paperweights 1780s–1820s).
Desvignes, Jean-Baptiste Glass decorator from Tournay, France [1786–1826].
Deventer, AMF van Glassworks in Schiedam, Holland [1853–1907], founded as Jacobus Sirks in 1853, took over Delft in 1907, (gin bottles in black after 1853, in green after 1886 and in clear glass after 1898).
Devidrio Glaswerk Glass studio located in Houverath near Bad Münstereifel [1994–present], designers include Anja Alscher and Mauricio Vargas.
Devillers, Freddy Glass designer from Malmédy, Belgium [1946–], worked at VSL 1972–4.
Devon PM Glassworks in Jablonec nad Nisou, Czech Republic [?–present], (beads and jewellery).
Dexel, Walter Glass designer from Germany [1890–1973]; worked for WMF 1937/8.
Dexter Trade name for Franklin Flint Glass Works.
D'Humy, Paul Raoul de Facheux Glass maker from London, Great Britain [c.1876–c.1888], operated Aurora Glass Company and Vasa Murrhina Glass Company, (gold-decorated tableware, decorative glass, Venetian-style glass).
Diaconescu, Dino Master glass blower from Valculesti, Romania [1955–], worked in Romania 1974–91 and 1996–8 and then in France and Murano 1991–5, has had his own workshop since 1999. Sig: all pieces signed "Dino D" in needle + numbers + "La Vida".
Diafani Barovier & Toso art glass type by Ercole Barovier, 1954.
Dial Glassworks See Plowden & Thompson.
Diamantati 1. Type of art glass made by

Venini, designed by Paolo Venini, 1934. 2. Barovier & Toso art glass type by Ercole Barovier, 1968.

Diamond air trap Bubbles of air trapped in the glass in a diamond-shaped pattern. Glass is blown in a pre-shaped mould, retrieved and covered again, leaving the air bubbles trapped in the pattern, often with a satin finish. It was patented in 1857 by WH, B & J Richardson of Great Britain and was popular after 1880. Some examples of this include "Nacre de Perle" by Boulton & Mills, "Verre de Soie" by Stevens & Williams after 1886, "Tartan" by Richardson after 1886, "Broche" by Walsh Walsh after 1886, "Octopus" by Loetz after 1888. It is aka "Plush" "Mother-of-Pearl" or "Pearl Satin" in the US.

Diamond cut V-grooves that are cut parallel and at right angles (sometimes called a Strawberry cut or Hobnail cut).

Diamond Glass Co, Ltd Glassworks in Montreal, Quebec, Canada [1890–1902], sig on bottles: crown with crown figure, previously from Excelsior Glass, (pressed glass, lighting, tableware).

Diamond Glass-ware Co Glassworks in Indiana, PA [1913–31], previously named Dugan Glass Co. 1892–1913, (pressed glass, tableware and carnival).

Diamond-point engraving: Decoration technique using diamond engraving, introduced by the Venetians in the 16thC and carried to great artistic heights in the Netherlands in the 17thC along with the stippling technique.

Diamond quilted A decorative pattern of diamonds used in pressed glass.

Dias, Pierre Glass designer from Belgium [–], worked at VSL in the 1980s.

Diaspora glass Type of etched, floral art glass made by Loetz.

Diatreta Roman technique of cutting through the surface, with just a few links remaining to the underlying vessel.

Diaz de Santillana, Alessandro Glass designer from Italy [1959–], worked for Venini c.1985.

Diaz de Santillana, Laura Glass designer from Italy [1955–], worked for Venini 1976-85.

Diaz de Santillana, Ludovico Glass designer from Italy [1931–89]; manager of Venini after 1960.

Dichroic coating A thin layer of metallic oxide such as titanium, silicon or magnesium is used as a coating on glass to allow passage of some wavelengths of light while reflecting others. The resulting interference is similar in appearance to iridescence.

Dichroic glass Glass showing different colours under different light conditions. Baccarat in the 1840s made "Verre Dichroide", which was their name for uranium glass. See also alexandrite.

Dichromatic glass See Dichroic glass.

Dickenson, Anna Maria Studio artist from Great Britain [1961–].

Didymium glass Violet-coloured glass acting as sodium flare filter; used in protective eyewear for hot-glass workers.

Dieupart, Henri-Germain-Etienne Sculptor

from Paris [1888–?], designed lighting and Deco vases for Simonet Frères after 1924.

Diluvium glass Iridized opaque marble art glass, produced by Rindskopf c.1900 at Barbarahütte.

Dip mould A cylindrical one-piece mould, open at the top. Usually made from waterlogged wood. The hot glass generates a thin layer of steam between mould and glass.

Dirmar, R Glassworks in Wien, Austria [–].

Disaster glass Souvenir glass commemorating disasters, popular in NE England in the 19thC and 20thC.

Distortion The deviation of light passing through a glass surface, either due to changes in the refractive index or thickness and/or shape of the glass.

Dithridge & Co Glassworks in Pittsburgh, PA, USA [1860–1903], in Martins Ferry, OH until 1887 and in New Brighton, PA after 1887. It then became Dithridge & Sons and was named Dithridge Flint Glass Co 1881–91, aka Fort Pitt Glassworks, (pressed glass, cut glass & blanks).

Dithridge Flint Glass Works Glassworks in Ellwood, PA [1854–?], located in Pittsburgh, PA before 1880, Bellaire, OH before 1880, bought Union Flint Glass Works in 1882 and started a new plant at Martins Ferry OH in 1895. Was taken over by Northwood Co in 1896.

Dixons Green See Thomas Davis & Co.

Döbbrick, Bleikristallschleiferei Karin Glass-cutting works located in Bad Muskau, Germany [?–present], (cut glass).

Döbern 1. Town near Cottbus, Germany, the location of several glass makers. Glashütte Döbern is still open while Hedwigshütte and Niederlausitzer hohl- und kristallglaswerke are no longer in existence. 2. Glassworks in Döbern near Sorau, NL, Germany [1867–present], operated by Hirsch Bros; Glashüttenwerke Fettke & Ziegler, TBH Hohlglashütte Döbern 1946–52, Glaswerke Döbern 1953–6, VEB Glaswerk Döbern 1956–after 1987. Trade names include: Dresden Crystal and Döbern Crystal. Sig: GD linked in a circle, GD in a circle 1955–75, (tableware, bottles, after 1969 only lead crystal and barware were made, currently lead crystal, both machine and handmade as well as pressed glass, cut-to-clear and gift items).

Dobson & Pearce Glass engraving company from London, Great Britain [–], active c.1862.

Dohln, Ernst von Glass maker who worked at Dorflinger Glass Works, White Mills, PA, USA c.1900s, (paperweights).

Dolní Maxov, Riedlovská Sklárna Glassworks in Tanvald u Jablonce, Czech Republic [1875–1990], since 1990 part of Jizerské Sklo (pressed crystal, esp. flasks).

Dolní Polubný u. Desná Czech name for the town of Polaun, Dessendorf; location of several Glassworks from the Riedel conglomerate, nationalized as Jablonecké Sklárny after 1945; privatized as Ornela from 1990, see Desná.

Dolní Prysk Glassworks in Ceské Kamenice, Czechoslovakia [1900–c.1972], (pressed crystal).

Dominion Glass Co Glassworks in Montreal, Quebec, Canada [1886–?] with factories in Toronto, Hamilton, Wallaceburg, Winnipeg, Redcliff and Burnaby. Dominion took over Burlington glass, Nova Scotia Glass and Jefferson glass in 1913. Sig: D inside diamond, (pressed glass, lighting, depression glass, bottles).

Domus Important interior decorating magazine from Italy founded in 1928 by Gio Ponti.

Domus Vetri d'Arte Glassworks in Murano, Italy [c.1954–c.1967], designers include Anzolo Fuga, (art glass).

Dona Ugo & F Glassworks in Murano, Italy [–], c.1967, (Smalti, enamel for mosaics).

Door Stop Large glass ball for keeping doors open, usually in greenish glass with air bubbles, made in the second half of the 19thC.

Doppio Incalmo, A Venini art glass designed by Paolo Venini, 1956.

Dores Glasstudio Herbert Böhm Glass studio located in Lindau, Germany [1974–present]. Sig: needle-engraved Böhm-Dores + year, (lampwork).

Dorflinger C, & Sons Glassworks in White Mills, PA, USA [1846–1921], French glass maker Christian Dorflinger worked at Saint-Louis before 1846, moved to the USA after 1846 and then founded Dorflinger Glass Works in Green Point, Long Island in 1863. Moved to White Mills, Long Island 1863–1921 and operations ceased in 1921. Designers include Ernst von Dohln c.1900, (cut glass, blanks, paperweights 1850s–1910s).

Dorlodot, Verreries Glassworks in Lodelinsart, Charleroi, Belgium [–], active before 1771, (tableware, bottles, flat glass, decanters, goblets).

Dorotheenhütte Glassworks in Wolfach, Schwarzwald, Germany [–], active c.1960, see also Ichendorf.

Dorothy Taylor Glass distributor located in Kansas City, MO [?–present]. Sig: Encore Taylor KC MO, (pressed glass, souvenirs).

Dostálova, Hana Glass designer from Bohemia, working 1920s.

Double cruet Two bottles that are joined; used for oil and vinegar. Popular in 17thC–20thC.

Double overlay Glass that is cased twice, usually in order to cut a design through the outer layer.

Doverbel Trade name for cookware from Verreries et Gobeleteries Doyen in Havré, Belgium.

Dowler, David P Studio artist from USA [1944–], worked for Steuben.

Downing, John Glassworks in Birmingham, Great Britain [–], active c.1894, (bottles).

Doyen, Verrerie et Gobeleterie Glassworks in Havré-Ville, near Mons Belgium [1918–?], previously known as Havré-Ville, 1910–18, merged with Boussu in 1968 and became Manuverbel/Manubelver. Designers include Faidherbe 1968–75, (blown tableware, organic crystal, lighting after 1964, cookware "Doverbel").

Doyle & Co Glassworks in Pittsburgh, PA, USA [1866–91], became part of US Glass in 1891, (pressed glass).

DRGM (Deutsches Reich Geschützte Marke) Trade mark indication from Germany, used until WWII.

Dr Hütte, Glashütte Glassworks in Weisswasser near Rothenburg, OL, Germany [1894–c.1937].

Drahoňovský Josef Sculptor/decorator/gem cutter from Praha, Czechoslovakia [1877–1938], taught in Prague 1904–38, worked on glass after 1920, worked for Libochovicke Sklárny/Barolac, (large plaques, engraving, stone cutting c.1920–c.1930).

Dram glass Small glass for a single shot of liquor; popular 1750–1850.

Drebkau Glassworks in Drebkau near Calau, NL, Germany [–],sig: wide-necked bottle in a D-frame, (bottles).

Dreisbach, Fritz Studio artist from USA [–].

Dreiser, Peter Glass engraver from Cologne, Germany [1936–], worked in Great Britain after 1955, went freelance after 1970.

Dresden Glassworks in Dresden, Germany [?–1945]. Sig: G over D in an oval.

Dresden Crystal Trade name used by Glashütte Döbern GmbH.

Dresser set Matching bathroom set usually incorporating powder boxes, comb dishes, atomizer, baguières, hat pin vases, videpoches etc. Popular in the Art Deco period in Czechoslovakia, France and Great Britain.

Dresser, Christopher Artist/Glass designer from Great Britain [1834–1904], created "Clutha" glass for J Couper 1885–95.

Dressler, Eduard, Glaswaren-Fabrik Glassworks in Berlin, Germany [–], active c.1901, (tableware).

Dreutler-Zirnsack, Hanne Glass designer from Germany [1942–], worked for Målerås 1968–71, Flygsfors 1968–71.Kosta 1971–5 and Studio Glashyttan i Åhus after 1977.

Drobnik, Antonin Glass artist from Czechoslovakia [1925–], (sculpture, etched flat glass).

Drood Society Ltd Glassworks in London, Great Britain [–], (cut glass).

DSG Co Trade name of De Steiger Glass Co.

Dubí, Rudolfova Hut Glassworks in Teplic v Cechách, Czechoslovakia [1905–c.1972], part of Sklo Union, (pressed glass).

Dublin Crystal Glassworks in Ireland [?–present], (cut glass, crystal, tableware).

Dubois Brewing Co Based in Pittsburgh, PA, USA [–], active c.1918, (bottles).

Dubreuil, André Glass designer from France [–], worked for Daum c.1990

Dudley Flint Glass Works See Thomas Hawkes.

Duffield Trade name Duffield, Parke & Co., MI Detroit [1866–1875]; (bottles)

Duffner and Kimberly Co Lamp and lighting manufacturer located in NY, USA [–]; (lighting; leaded glass shades 1906–1911)

Dug Term used to describe a bottle with a film of water stain on the glass.

Dugan Glass Co Glassworks in Indiana, PA, USA [1892–1913], became Diamond Glass-Ware Co 1913–31, previously known as The Northwood Co, NG 1890–1904, aka Indiana Glass Co, Dugan. Sig: rarely signed, if it is then usually a D inside a diamond, (pressed glass; carnival).

Dugan Glass Co of Indiana Glassworks owned by Harry Northwood 1893–5. Sig: no marks.

Dumich, Pyotr K Glass blower/designer from Lvov, Ukraine [1935–], worked at Lvov factory after 1963.

Dumond & Leloup Glass designers from France [–], worked together for Markhbein SA, France c.1965/66, (tableware).

Dump A glass ball, often internally decorated with colour streaks or air bubbles, popular since the mid-1900s.

Dunaime, Georges Glass artist from Paris, France [–], sig.G Dunaime, (1920s and 1930s lighting and glass objects in thick cast glass).

Dunbar Flint Glass Co Glassworks in Dunbar, WV, USA [1913–1953], renamed Dunbar Glass Co in 1938, (tableware, chimneys, coloured tableware, thinwalled).

Duncan & Miller Glass Co Glassworks in Tiffin, OH USA [1903–1955], the moulds were then taken over by US Glass/Duncan & Miller Division 1955–present, (tableware, pressed glass, novelties and depression glass).

Duncan, George & Sons Glassworks in Pittsburgh, PA, USA [1865–92]. Factory became part of US Glass in 1891, burned down in 1892. George A Duncan & Sons became George Duncan's Sons and moved to Washington, PA 1893–1900 and then became Duncan & Miller Glass Co 1903–55, see below, (tableware and pressed glass).

Duncan, John & Sons Based in New York [1880–90], (bottles).

Dunne-Cooke, HJ Glass designer from Sweden [–], worked for Whitefriars 1938.

Duparquet, Huot & Moneuse Co Glassworks, location unknown [–], active c.1928, (tableware).

Duplex burner Kerosene burner with two parallel wicks, which was introduced in 1865. It was improved with circular wick as Rochester burner 1888.

Duraglas Trade name for hardened glass by Owens-Illinois Co.

Duralex Hardened glass type used for table- and kitchenware, invented in 1939 by Saint Gobain. Is cooked at 1,500ºC, then refined and moulded at 700ºC, refrigerated by cool air to 20ºC. The brand name and factories

were sold to Bormioli Rocco (Italy) in 1997.

Duran Trade name used by Schott & Gen Mainz for borosilicate glass, labware.

Durand Art Glass Co Glassworks in Vineland, NJ, USA [1920–31], established by Victor Durand (see below), (art glass).

Durand, JG Glassworks in Arques, France [1825–present], founded as Verrerie Cristallerie d'Arques JG Durand & Cie. This is the largest producer of glassware in the world and it employs 13,000 people to produce 5 million articles per day. It has also operated works in Vicrila, near Bilbao, Spain since 1980 and in Millville, NJ, USA since 1982. It has exported many of its glass-making techniques across the world. Sig: France# or Made in France impressed, (manual production of tableware after 1934, automatic production of pressed glass since 1934, automated glass blowing since 1950, hardened glass Arcoroc and Arcopal since 1958, machine made 24% Pb crystal Crystal d'Arques since 1968, kitchenware Arcoflam since 1984, kitchenware Arcuisine since 1986, high volume utilitarian glass. Brand names include Arcopal, Arcoflam, Arcuisine, Arcoroc, Luminarc, Cristal d'Arques, Vitroflam, JG Durand, collection "JG Durand" crystal tableware has been produced since 1983).

Durand, Victor Glass maker from France [1870–1931], worked in the USA after 1987, at Vineland Flint after 1897 and established Durand Art Glass Co in 1920, (tableware, art glass, lightning from 1920, iridescent glass, "spiderweb" glass).

Durobor Glassworks in Soignies, Belgium [1928–present], its automatic tableware production was founded by Owens-Illinois in 1956. Has a subsidiary company called Ravenhead Glass in Great Britain. Its trade names includes Durobor, Ravenhead, Dur-o-choc, Dur-o-fine and Verreries de Soignies, (mechanical tableware).

Duroglass Ltd Glassworks in London, Great Britain [–], active c.1950, trade names include Durosil and Duroven.

Dyat'kovo Glassworks in Oryol, Bryansk, Russia [–], active c.1850, owned by Maltsov family.

Dyatkovsky Cut Glass Factory Glassworks in Dyatkovo, Bryansk region, Russia [–], active 19th C, designers include Filimonova, Ganf, Grabar, Kolodin after 1969, Kotov after 1968, Lipskaya, Makarenko 1957/8, Matushevskaya, Maximova, Nevskaya, Rostovtseva, Ryazanova, Savelieva, Shevchenko after 1966, Shushkanov, Shuvalov after 1950, Stepanova, Tarkovskaya, Zhigalkina, (cut glass, art glass, tableware, colour, zinc sulphide glass).

Dyottsville Trade name Dyottsville Glass Works, Philadelphia, PA [1833–1923], (bottles).

Dzerzhinsky Glassworks Glassworks, location

unknown Russia [–], designers include Kobylinskaya, Makarenko, Prokofief after 1964 and Rostovtseva was chief designer 1959/60. Dzivinskaya, Valentina G Glass designer from Beryozovka, Grodno, Belarus [1937–], worked at Krasny May 1959–61 and at The Neman after 1967.

E

Eagle Glass and Manufactoring Co Glassworks in Wellsburgh, WV, USA [1894–1913], (pressed glass).

Eagle Glass Works Glassworks in Keota, Iowa, USA [1879–81], set up by J H Leighton from Wheeling, WV.

EAPG Abbreviation for Early American Pattern Glass; more than 3,000 patterns have been given a name in the US.

East Liverpool Glass Co Glassworks in East Liverpool, OH, USA [1882/3–9], Specialty Glass Co started here, (pressed glass 1889).

Ebeling & Reuss Co Glassworks in Sweden [c.1960–c.1975], (tableware, cut glass, blanks from Kosta).

Ecclesiastical glass Liturgical glass such as chalices and candlesticks, stained glass, leaded glass etc.

Eckhardt, Edris Glass artist from Cleveland, USA [1929–], (sculptures, glass from 1959).

Eckhoff, Tias Glass designer from Norway [1926–], worked for Hadeland c.1951.

Ecologico, Vidrio SL Glasworks located in l'Olleria (Valencia), Spain [?–present], groups it runs include Ecoglass, Albiglass and Fabrilglass (tableware from recycled glass).

Economy Glass Co Glassworks in Morgantown, WV, USA [1924–39], was previously known as Economy Tumbler 1903–24 became Morgantown in 1939.

Economy Tumbler Co Glassworks in Morgantown, WV, USA [1903–1924], became Economy Glass Co in 1924, (tableware).

Ecuyer, L' Glass gallery located in Bruxelles, Belgium [–], active after c.1970s, (art glass sales outlet).

Eda Glasbruk Glassworks in Eda, Värmland, Sweden [1835-1953], produced flat glass before 1863 then moved to Surte and produced tableware and cut glass after 1848 and bottles and tableware 1842–1933. Also then made pharmaceutical glass, cut, engraved, painted tableware and art glass. Next it founded Geijersfors Glassverk in Magnor, Norway 1896–1917 (see Magnor Glassverk AS) and produced lustered tableware c.1905 as well as "luster period" carnival 1925–30. Went through "Strömberg period" 1927–33 and the "Worker's period" 1935–40 in which they created tableware including vases, dishes etc esp. in amber with black feet. The "Eklund period" was 1943–53 and included pressed household glass, engraved & painted vases and dishes and silvered glass. The company merged with Kosta and Reijmyre into Svenska Kristallglasbruken in 1903 and also had a partial closure 1933–53. Designers include Edvard and Gerda Strömberg 1927–33. Sig: Eda, year of manufacture 1927–33.

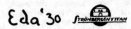

Edelmann, Udo Glass designer from Bergheim, Germany [1938–], had a studio in Rheinbach.

Edelweiss cane A white, star-shaped cane with yellow centres used in Clichy paperweights.

Edenfalk, Bengt Glass designer from Sweden [1924–], worked for Skrufs 1953–78 and Kosta Boda after 1978.

Edinburgh & Leith Flint Glass Works Glassworks in Edinburgh, Scotland [1864–c.1926], became part of Webb's Crystal Glass Co in 1919, (tableware).

Edinburgh Crystal Glass Co Glassworks in Edinburgh, Scotland [1867–present], (cut glass tableware, bottles, giftware and paperweights).

Edison & Swan Utility and Light Co Manufacturer located in London, Great Britain [1880–?], (shades, opalescent, ruffled, pastel).

Edvin glass Type of art glass made by Orrefors. It is like Ariel but has a relief surface. It was designed by Edvin Öhrström. Glasses are marked with the following numbers:
1–60=1944, 61–90=1945 and
91–113=1946/7.

Edwards, B Glass maker or refinery located in Belfast, N Ireland [–], (old Irish cut glass).

Eertwegh, Martien van den Glass designer from Holland [–], worked for Leerdam after c.1968, sig. on Unica: ER=1968, ES=1969.

Efeso Barovier & Toso art glass type by Ercole Barovier, c.1963.

Effe 2 Glassworks in Murano, Italy [–], active c.1980, (art glass).

Effetre International Glassworks in Murano, Italy [1980–present], designers include Guido Ferro and Lino Tagliapietra, (art glass, millefiori, filigrana 5–13mm, lighting).

Egeo Barovier & Toso art glass designed by Ercole Barovier, 1960

Egermann sro Glassworks in Nový Bor, Czech Republic [1861–present], designers include Josef Holeček and Zdeněk Henych, was called Egerman Exbor until c.1990. Trade names include Bohemia Crystal and Bohemia Glass, (ornamented glassware, raised enamel and gold, ruby-flashed engraved, cut-to-clear, transparent enamel, panel-cut glass, glass fruit).

Egermann, Antonin Ambroz Glass decorator from Bohemia [1814–88].

Egermann, Friedrich Glass maker from Nový Bor, Czechoslovakia [1777–1864], his glassworks were located in Harrachóv, Czechoslovakia in 1809 and in Nový Bor, Czechoslovakia c.1820. Egermann Studio was located in Bor c.1830, (art glass, cut glass, enamelled, cased/flashed, cut-to-clear, hyalith, inventor of lythialin).

Eggington, OF Co Glass-cutting studio located in Corning, NY [1899–1920], (cut glass on Corning blanks).

Egipto Cristal Glassworks in Barcelona, Spain [c.1970–present], (giftware, crystal flowers).

Egizia Srl Glass refinery located in Poggibonsi, Siena, Italy [1949–present], their artist collection HWC=Handle With Care and includes designs by Marco Zanini, Flavia Alves de Sousa, Liana Cavallaro, Nathalie du Pasquier, Giovanella Formica, Barbara Forni, Gabriele Giandelli, Johanna Grawunder, James Irvine, Nathalie Jean, Defne Koz, Mario Milizia, Mike Ryan, Ettore Sottsass, Marco Susani, Nanae Umeda and Elisabeth Vidal, (tableware, vases, clocks with sand-blasted, screen-printed decoration).

Egorov, Georghy G Glass designer from Moscow, Russia [1895–?] designer and chief designer at Gus-Krushtalny 1931–41 and 1945–8 respectively, as well as chief designer at the decorative glass section, Institute of Glass Fibre 1946–55.

Ehrenfeld See Rheinische Glashütten.

Ehrner, Anna Glass designer from Sweden [1948–]. worked for Kosta Lampan 1974–6 and Kosta Boda after 1977. Sig: AEH on Kosta pieces.

Eibenstein, Glashütte Gebr Glassworks in Hohenbocka near Hoyerswerda, OL, Germany [1876–c.1937], since 1896 has been known as Glashütte Eibenstein.

Eiff, Wilhelm von Glass engraver/designer from Germany [1890–1943], worked for WMF from c.1904, taught glass engraving until 1943, activities reported for Lalique and Lobmeyr also; sig: sometimes WvE.

Eintrachthütte Glassworks in Mstišov, Czechoslovakia [–].

Eisch, Erwin Glass designer from Germany [1927–], (works at Eisch).

Eisch KG, Glashütte Valentin Glassworks in Bavaria, Germany [?–present], sig: sand-blasted E on tableware, Eisch on giftware while some pieces are engraved with Eisch + designer's initials. E Eisch = Erwin as Erich Eisch signs in full.

Eiselt, J Anton Glassworks in Kamenický Šenov, Czechoslovakia [–], active c.1900], (art glass,cut glass).

Eiselt, Josef Designer from Kamenický Šenov [1896–1975], (protagonist of Czech Art Deco, worked in Kamenický Šenov 1914–17, had own painting studio 1917–45, worked at Nový Bor school 1925–45 then in Hadamar, Germany 1950–6.

Eisenlöffel, Jan Designer from the Netherlands [1876–1957], designed tableware for Maastricht in 1927 that was produced until 1970. Sig: E inside 5-pointed star.

Eisert Family of glass decorators from Bohemia includes Ignacius [1832–1901], Josef [1894–1975] and Peter [working 1870s].

Eismont, Nikolay G Civil engineer/glass designer from St Petersburg, Russia [1906–65], was chief designer at Leningrad Factory 1950–2.

Ekenäs Glasbruk AB Glassworks in Ekenäs, Sweden [–], designers include John-Orwar Lake c.1956/7. Sig: usually marked Ekenäs Sweden L + number, sometimes engraved with JOLake.

El Cristall De Badalona Glassworks in Badalona, Spain [1866–present]. Sig: CB oval monogram, (tableware, paperweights, crystal, borosilicate, opal, lighting).

El-Nasr Glass & Crystal Co Glassworks in Cairo, Egypt [1932–present], has a plant at Kalubia for vials & tubes and plant at Cairo, (bottles, tableware, barware, pressed glass & crystal).

Electric light First incandescent light bulbs produced 1845 and 1859 but first practical ones introduced by Edison in 1879. First power station Holborn Viaduct, 1880. Electricity became widely available from 1882. Frosted bulbs were produced after 1925.

Electric Trade Mark Used by Gayner Glass Works.

Electroplate Silvering or gilding process using electrolysis.

Eleonorenhütte, Lenora Glassworks in Vimperk, Czechoslovakia [1834–1945], founded by Jan Meyr, run by Meyr's Neffe then Wilhelm Kralik after 1881, (decorative glass, furnace finished for export and blanks for other refiners).

Eliades, Elly Engraver from Great Britain [–], working c.1975.

Eliáš, Bohumil Glass artist from Czech Republic [1937–], became an independent artist from 1963.

Elisabeth-Hütte, Wilh Habel Glassworks in Koštany u Teplice, Czechoslovakia [1889–?], (coloured glassware with applied threading/impressed flowers and crystal blanks for the Pallme-König chandelier factory).

Elisabethhütte Glassworks in Jamlitz near Lübben, NL, Germany [1854–c.1937].

Elkington & Co Ltd Glassworks in Birmingham, Great Britain [c.1910–c.1938], (tableware).

Ellenville Glass Works Glassworks in Ellenville,

NY [1836–80], (jars, bottles, carboys and demijohns).

Elliott, George Glass artist from Great Britain [1934–], worked in Norway, Denmark and for Stevens & Williams before setting up own glass studios.

Elliott Ltd, HJ Glassworks in Glamorgan, Wales, Great Britain [c.1950s–1970s],("E-mil" scientific glass).

Elme Glasbruk Glassworks in Almhult, Sweden [1917–70], designers include Edvin Ollers 1926–30. Sig: moulded glass marked Elme/Ollers, art glass engraved Ollers + pattern number+ Elme, shield label *Elme* used in the 1930s, (tableware, engraved glass and also pressed glass after 1921).

Elmhurst, Sheila Glass engraver from Great Britain [1920–], (diamond point since 1951)

Elmira Cut Glass Co Glassworks in USA [–], active c.1900, (cut glass, Brilliant period).

Elric Trade name for export glass from Josef Riedel before WWII.

Elsa Vidrio Cristal SL Glassworks in Barcelona, Spain [?–present].

Elsahütte Glassworks in Poděbrady, Czechoslovakia [1877–?], one of the Inwald works, (cut glass, coloured tableware, blanks for local refineries).

Elson Glass Co, The/National Glass Glassworks in Martins Ferry, OH [1882–94], was previously located in Pittsburgh, PA in the 1870s, became West Virginia Glass Mfg Co 1894–1900 then merged with National Glass 1899, (pressed glass).

Elwell Trade name for Nazeing Glass Works.

Elwell & Co, H Glassworks in Harlow, Essex, Great Britain [–], active c.1950.

Embossed A bottle with raised text on it after c.1870.

Emeralite lamps Green-cased glass shades patented by HG McFaddin Co in 1919 and produced until c.1940 (similar products were made under the brand names of Greenalite, Verdalite and Ambrolite).

Emilienhütte Glassworks in Döbern near Sorau and/or in Senftenberg/Elster near Calau, Germany [1863–72], merged into Annahütte 1872, see H Heye Annahütte, (bottles).

Empire Trade name for Macbeth-Evans Glass Company.

Empire Cut Glass Co Glassworks in New York, NY USA [1896–1904], sold to HC Fry in 1904 and then moved to Flemington, NJ as Flemington Cut Glass Co, (cut glass, Brilliant period).

Empire Lamp & Brass Mfg Co Glassworks, location unknown [–], active c.1915.

Empoli Glass-making town near Florence, Italy known for bottle green art glass/tableware c.1940–c.1960. Factories based here currently include CIVE, Nuova CEV, Cristalleria,

Stelvia, Vetraria SAVE Spa and SVE Societa Vetraria Empoli.

Empoli SpA, Vetrerie di Glass firm in Milano, Italy [1940–present], trade names include "Griffe Montenapoleone", (tableware, decorative glass, gilded & engraved glass).

Enamel 1. (Hot enamel) Ground-coloured glass suspended in eggwhite or a similar medium is then applied with a brush and fired on at 500–700°C. 2. (Cold enamel) This is not fired on and wears off easily. Enamelled glass was popular in the 1870s–1880s; most major art glass producers made enamelled glass at some time. Enamel fused onto semi-crystal was possible from 1836 and could be fired onto lead crystal from 1837.

Enamel incrustation Enamelled sulphures representing coats of arms etc that are incorporated in thick-walled vessels. This was developed by a French jeweller in Paris in the early 19thC and producers included Baccarat, Saint-Louis and Cristallerie de Bercy c.1815–30.

Encased painting Refers to a painted (enamelled) piece with an extra cased layer of glass to cover it.

English Glass Co Ltd Glassworks in Leicester, Great Britain [1934–present], (lenses, reflectors, technical glass, TV, beads).

Englund, Eva Glass designer from Sweden [1937–], worked for Pukeberg 1964–73, Arvid Böhlmarks Lampfabrik c.1966/7 (vases), Målerås and Orrefors in 1974. Sig: monogram: V.

Engman, Kjell Glass designer from Sweden [1946–], has worked for Kosta Boda since 1978.

Engraved or engraving Decoration technique using a wheel, needle, diamond etc. See also carving, cutting and stippling. To test the age of engraving on glass, place a piece of white paper on the inside. New engravings are bright and powder-like, old ones stand out darker.

Engraving in Bohemia Revival began c.1810 esp. in Kamenický Šenov, Nový Svet and Silesia. Designers who worked in the style include Biemann, Simm, Mattoni, Pfeiffer, E.Hofmann, Franz-Anton Pelikan, Moriz Oppitz c.1840s, Franz Hanzel 1803–83, August Böhm 1812–90 and Karl Pfohl 1826–94. Those who have worked in the Pohl style include Karl Günther, Eduard Pelikan, Karel Pietsch, Josef & Anton Sacher and Zach.

Engshyttan Glassworks in Sweden, which closed in the 1970s.

Enot, Edmond Art glass retailer from Paris [–], active c.1884, (Brocard outlet).

Entelis, Fyodor S Designer/engineer from St Petersburg, Russia [1907–], glass making since 1929: designed the crystal fountain at the NY World Fair in 1937/8 with Chaikov, produced jubilee vases with T Smirnov in 1948/9 and a lecturer after 1954.

Enterprise Cut Glass Co Glassworks in Elmira Heights, NY, USA [?–1917], (cut glass, Brilliant period).

Epergnes Fancy centrepiece for the dinner table incorporating candle holders, vases, dishes or a combination of all three. They were popular in late Victorian times. Also known as Milieu de Table.

Epsom Glass Industries Ltd (EGI) Glassworks in Epsom, Surrey, Great Britain [1928–present], (perfume bottles and pharmaceutical glass)

Equarissage, L' Glassworks in Namur, Belgium [1871–?], moved to Chênée in 1873.

Erfurt, Baldermann & Co, Glashütte Glassworks in Dubrauke, Döbern near Sorau, NL, Germany [1906–c.1937].

Erickson, Carl-Ebert Glass designer from Sweden [1899–1966], worked at Pairpoint 1912–32, Libbey 1932–6, Blenko 1936–43 then founded Erickson Glassworks in Bremen in 1943.

Erickson Glass Works Glassworks in Bremen, OH, USA [1943–60], (tableware).

Erickson, Thure Glassmaker from Brockton, MA, USA [–], (paperweights in the 1940s).

Ericsson, Henri Glass designer from Finland; [1898–1933], worked for Riihimäki Glass after c.1928.

Erikson, Gro Glass designer from Norway [1956–], worked at Hadelands, Randsfjord after 1991 and at Magnor after 1998.

Erixson, Sven Painter/glass designer from Sweden [1899–1970], worked for Kosta 1929–32. Sig: usually signed in full.

Erlacher, Max Glass engraver from Innsbruck, Austria [1933–], worked for Lobmeyer after 1954, Steuben 1955–77 then set up own studio after 1977, (engraving, cameo).

Ernstbrunn Glassworks in Arnostov u Budovice, Czechoslovakia [?–1945].

Ernsthütte Glassworks in Vimperk, Czechoslovakia [c.1840s–1945], built by Jan Meyr, operated by Meyr's Neffe then Wilhelm Kralik after the 1880s, (blanks, hot-decorated glass).

Ernstthal, Glaswerk GmbH Glassworks in Ernstthal, Germany [?–present].

Eryomin, Boris A Glass blower/designer from St Petersburg, Russia [1909–], worked at Krasny Ghigant 1924–48 and at Leningrad Factory after 1948.

Escalier de Cristal, A l' Bronze-mounted glass furniture, see Pannier frères.

Escaut, Verreries & Cristalleries de l' Glassworks in Hemiksem, near Antwerp [1896–?].

Espérance, Verreries de l' Glassworks in Manage, Belgium [1910–?].

l'Est, Les Verreries de Glassworks in Nancy, France [1921–], founded and run by Delatte.

Etching Decoration method. Acid etching is when a design is cut into a protective layer (wax, glue) and subsequently treated with acid. Needle etching involeves drawing fine lines on the glass with a special needle. After the development of mechanized blowing, which assured precise dimensions for cuppas, designs could be multiplied by a pantograph. A popular design around the turn of the century was the Meander edge.

Etling, Edmond Sales outlet in Paris, Rue du Paradis [c.1920s–1942], commissioned work from fashionable artists such as Hiesz, Granger and Beal then the actual glass was made by Sèvres or Choisy, trade names include Richard cameo made at Loetz. Sig: always uses "Etling", (pressed glass/art glass frosted, opalescent glass, lighting, figures). There have been recent opalescent re-issues by Sèvres.

Etrusca, Vetreria Glassworks in Montelupo F No (Empoli), Fl, Italy [1951–present], Sig mark: VE linked, (bottles, packaging glass, tableware, giftware, bottle green art glass in the 1950s and 1960s).

Etruscan glass Greek/Roman-style ornamentation on opaque white glass c.1850s made by Webb, Molineaux, Bacchus, Richardson, Davis Greatheat & Green and others.

Eugeneo Barovier & Toso art glass type by Ercole Barovier, 1951.

Euroglas Srl Glassworks in Targu Jiu, Romania [?–present], (giftware, colour-stained, etched, decorated ware).

Europa Srl, Cristalleria Glassworks in Levane, AR, Italy [1964–present], (art glass, tableware, giftware, paperweights, stems, vases).

European glass After the decline of the Roman Empire with its many glass houses, until the emergence of Venice (at the end of the 13thC), glass was produced on a small scale only (eg Merovingien glass). The Venetians revived the art of glass making, most likely re-importing techniques from Syria. Their cristallo, a light, clear glass type, was world famous and exported in huge quantities. By the 16thC Venice had a dominant position in Europe's glass industry. In Germany and Bohemia at the time, relatively simple drinking glasses with a greenish colour were produced, called Waldglas (forest glass, verre de fougère). By the 17thC Bohemia became the second most productive glass-making region in Europe. Late in the 17thC the Englishman George Ravenscroft improved the glass-making recipe by adding lead oxide to the batch, resulting in a brilliant, sparkling type of glass (lead glass) that could be cut.

Evanescenti Barovier & Toso art glass type by Ercole Barovier, 1954.

Evansville Glass Co Glassworks in Evansville, IN, USA [1903–c.1908].

Eve Hill Glassworks See Josiah Lane & Sons.

Evening Star Trade name used by Edward Rorke & Co.

Everted Means turned outward (eg the rim of a tumbler).

Eveson, Stan Glass designer from Great Britain [1913–], worked for Webb 1929–70 and for Dema Glass 1971–8.

Evita Crystal Trade name of Concorde Kristalliglas.

Ewer A footed jug with handle and spout.

Exbor Studio Glassworks in Nový Bor, Czechoslovakia [–], active c.1972.

Excelsior Glass Glassworks in St Johns, Newfoundland, Canada [1879–1913]. Sig: Excelsior in caps 1879–83, Crown with crown figure, sig. passed on to Diamond Glass Co, (bottles).

Excelsior Glass Works/Buckeye Glass Co Glassworks in Wheeling, WV, USA [1849–94], moved to Martins Ferry, OH in 1879 then burned down in 1894. It was later known as Buckeye Glass Works and was run by JH Leighton, (pressed glass).

Excise Act Tax on glass in England introduced 1745, repeatedly increased and repealed in 1845. The Excise Act taxed transparent glass by weight, hence the appearance of hollow stems, milk glass and cut glass.

Exhibitions London 1851, 1862, 1871, 1872, 1873, 1874, 1886; Paris 1855, 1867, 1878, 1889, 1900; New York 1854; Dublin 1853, 1865; Vienna 1873; Santiago 1875; Philadelphia 1876; Cape Town 1877; Sydney 1880; Melbourne 1881, 1888/9; Amsterdam 1883; Boston 1883; Calcutta 1883/4; New Orleans 1884/5; Antwerp 1885; 1894; Adelaide 1887; Barcelona 1888; Brussels 1888, 1897; Glasgow 1888; Kingston 1891; Launceston (Aus) 1891/2; Kimberley South Africa 1893; Chicago 1893; San Francisco 1894; Hobart 1894/5; Guatemala 1897; Brisbane 1897; Buffalo 1901; Glasgow 1901; Turin 1902; Hanoi 1903/4; St Louis 1904.

Exnar, Jan Glass artist from Havlíčkuv Brod, Czech Republic [1951]; (indep. 1975-)

Expo Orrefors exhibition quality glass series 1944–75; designers Hald, Landberg, Lundin, Öhrström, Palmqvist and Selbing. Sequential numbering starts 2=1944, 300=1946, 574=1948, 1391=1950, 2482=1952, 3450=1954, 3604=1956, 3688=1958, 3763=1960, 3774=1962, 3783=1964, 3801=1966, 3814=1968, 3826=1970, 3846=1972, 3856=1975, see also expo number listings for individual artists.

Eygabroadt-Ryon Co Glassworks in USA [–], (cut glass, Brilliant period).

F

F (in jar) Trade name used by CL Flaccus Glass Co.

F (italic in an oval) Fenton Art Glass mark for remakes from other companies' moulds.

F (in a shield) Federal glass mark.

F&A Trade name used by Fahnstock & Albree.

Fabergé Signature found on contemporary tableware for a glass dealer in Frankfurt, Germany.

Fabriglass See Vidrio Ecologico.

Fäcke & Co Glassworks in Kohlfurt, Silesia [?–1945], (pressed glass).

Fagerlund, Carl Glass designer/lighting architect from Sweden [1923–], worked for Orrefors after 1946, (lighting).

Fahnstock & Albree Located in Pittsburgh, PA, USA [1860–2], (bottles).

Faidherbe, Jean-Claude Glass designer from Belgium [–], worked for Boussu c.1967 and Doyen 1968–75.

Fains (Meuse), Verrerie de Glassworks in France [–], active c.1879, see Schmid & Du Houx and Bayel (the combined works).

Fairmont Glass Co/National Glass Glassworks

in Fairmount, WV, USA [?–1899]), in 1899 became part of National Glass, (pressed glass).

Falcon Glasshouse Glassworks in Southwark, Great Britain [1790–1878], founded and operated by Apsley Pellatt I and later by his son Apsley Pellatt II. It had a subsidiary company at New Cross before 1895.

Falkenstein, Claire Glass designer from OR, USA [1909–], worked for Salviati c.1971–80.

Falleur, Pierre Glassworks in Lodelinsart Bon-Air near Charleroi, Belgium [1810–60], (bottles, flat glass, tableware).

Familleureux, Gobeleterie Nationale Glassworks in Familleureux, Belgium [c.1925–1935].

Familleureux, Verreries de Glassworks in Familleureux, Belgium [1865–1908]

Fannyhütte Glassworks in Duchcov, Czechoslovakia [1849–1927], operated by Josef Rindskopf after 1895, (pressed glass after 1920, coloured export glass).

Farbglashütte Reichenbach See Reichenbach.

Färe Glasbruk Glassworks in Sweden [1903–17], merged with Elme in 1917, (tableware).

Farfalla Paperweights distributor for quality paperweights located in Starnberg b. München, Germany [1976–present]. Sig: acid-etched mark "Farfalle + butterfly + München", (paperweights).

Farquharson, William "Clyne" Glass designer from Great Britain [1906–72], worked for John Walsh Walsh 1924–51, (cut glass).

Farrés I Cia Glassworks in Badalona, Spain [1874–1908], merged into Union Vidriera de España, 1908, see Cristall Badalona.

Fasce (Bands) Coloured threads that are trickled hot onto a glass vessel and are worked in, then covered in a thin layer of cristallo.

Fasce, A Venini art glass designed by Fulvio Bianconi and Paolo Venini in 1951/5 and then by Massimo Vignelli in 1956.

Fascia Murrine Type of art glass made by Venini designed by Riccardo Licata and Paolo Venini, 1954.

Fasett Orrefors series glass designed by Palmqvist in 1940, (crystal faceted and polished, marks: PA2424/1–11).

Faustig KG, Kurt Glassworks in Stockdorf, Bavaria, Germany [1960–present], has a plant in Varna, Bolzano, Italy, (lighting, chandeliers).

Fauquez, Verrerie de Glassworks in Fauquez les Virginal, Manage, Belgium [c.1922–present], member of the Association des Gobeletiers Belges, (bottles, flat glass, packaging).

Favrile Trade name for glass produced by Tiffany.

Fazzoletto 1 Type of art glass made by Venini and designed by Fulvio Bianconi and Paolo Venini, 1946/9. 2 A vase in the shape of a handkerchief with the corners pulled up. First designed by Fulvio Bianconi for Venini in 1950, often copied.

Federal Glass Co Glassworks in Columbus, OH, USA [1900–80]. Sig: F in a shield, (cut glass; pressed glass and depression glass).

Federal law See TBMBR.

Fedorkov, Anatoly F Glass blower from Beryozovka, Grodno, Belarus [1934–], worked at Krasny May 1965–68 and at The Neman Glassworks after 1968.

Feet Types of feet that include folded conical, domed, plain, terraced (all 18thC) and flat (19thC), (tableware).

Feix, Gebrüder Export house for beads/costume jewellery located in Jablonec, Czechoslovakia [c.1920s–c.1950].

Felt wheels These are coated with fine abrasive powders (cerium oxide, rouge) and are then used for polishing glass.

Fenice, La Glassworks in Murano, Italy [–], active c.1981, designers include Enrico Bettarini c.1960/1, (art glass and tableware).

Fenicio Type of art glass made by Venini designed by Tyra Lundgren, 1948 or designed by Fulvio Bianconi, 1950.

Fenner Glashütte See Raspiller Cie Fenner Glasshutte.

Fenton Art Glass Co Glassworks in Williamstown, WV, USA [1905–present], originally located in Martins Ferry, OH, USA. Sig: early pieces had label only, the label "Authentic/Fenton/Handmade" was used in the 1950s and 1960s, "Fenton" moulded mark on carnival glass after 1975, an "8" denotes the 1980s and a "9" the 1990s. Sand-blasted "Fenton" mark was also used after the 1980s, an "F" in scripted writing after 1983 and an italic "F" in an oval on pieces made from bought moulds. (Art glass, pressed glass, carnival, novelties, covered animal dishes, opalescent ware, paperweights in the 1960s.)

Fereday, John Thomas Glass engraver from Great Britain [–]; worked for Webb c.1880.

Ferjac Glassworks in France [–], active c.1930s, (opalescent glass).

Fern glass Glasses decorated with a fern leaf motive (etched, cut), popular especially in the UK c.1855–65.

Fero, Shane Flamework artist from Penland, NC [1953–], has been producing flamework since 1968.

Ferreau, Charles Glass designer from Belgium [–], designed for Boussu c.1966.

Ferro & Lazzarini Glassworks in Murano, Italy [1929–present], designers include Ezio Rizzetto 1954; Virgilio Giudi after 1956 and Fulvio Bianconi 1966, (art glass).

Ferro Toso Barovier Glassworks from Murano, Italy [1935–42], was the result of a merger of

SAIAR Ferro Toso and Barovier & Cie and was then renamed Barovier & Toso in 1942.

Ferro Toso Ssee SAIAR Ferro Toso.

Ferro, Egidio Glass blower from Italy [1889–1968], worked for CVM, Andrea Rioda and AVEM after 1932.

Ferro, Fratelli Glassworks in Murano, Italy [–], active c.1967, (tableware).

Ferro, Galliano Glass blower from Italy [1896–1984], worked for Andrea Rioda and then AVEM 1932–55.

Ferro, Giorgio Glass designer from Italy [1931–], worked for AVEM 1951–5 and Ferro Galliano after 1955.

Ferro, Luciano Master glass blower from Murano, Italy [–], worked for AVEM after c.1956 then produced his own designs after 1966. Sig: is sometimes found on AVEM pieces.

Ferro, Vetreria Galliano Glassworks in Murano, Italy [c.1955–c.1981], designers include Aldo Bergamini 1954, Galliano Ferro, Giorgio Ferro (his son, who worked for AVEM before 1955), Ezio Rizzetto, Fulvio Bianconi, Vinicio Vianello, (art glass, lighting).

Ferro, Vittorio Glass maker from Murano, Italy [–], worked at Vetrerie Anfora.

Festonati Barovier & Toso art glass type by Ercole Barovier, 1959.

Festooning A unilateral combed design similar to feathering.

Fettke See Hedwigshütte.

Fettke & Ziegler, Glashütte Glassworks in Döbern near Sorau, NL, Germany [1882–c.1937], see Döbern.

Feure, Georges de Artist from Holland [1869–1928], alias of George van Sluijters, worked in Paris and had own design workshop after 1895, also worked at Rheinische Glashütten. (Designed three items of luxury packaging glass for the Fauchon delicatessen shop in Paris c.1910.)

Fibrilose Green, threaded décor on art glass and silveria glass from Stevens & Williams after the 1880s.

Fidenza, I Vetri di Glassworks in Fidenza, Italy [?–present], (tableware).

Fiedorowich, Ludwik Glass designer from Poland [–], worked for Zabkowice c.1973 and for Staszic Glassworks c.1980.

Figuerras Oliveiras Vidreria Industriale Glassworks in Brazil [–]. Sig: vFo, (bottles).

Figured glass Aka patterned or ornamental glass, it is producing by feeding flat glass between patterned rollers, in order to texture both sides.

Filatov, Vladimir A Glass designer from Almati, Georgia [–], worked at Gus-Krushtalny after 1959, was their chief designer after 1963 and became the art director at the central institute in Moscow after 1968.

Fili, A Venini art glass designed by Carlo Scarpa, 1942.

Filigrana See Zanfirico.

Filimonova, Valentina A Glass designer from Moscow, Russia [1928–], worked at Workshops of Applied Art, Moscow after 1954 and her main works were produced at Dyatkovsky Cut Glass and Kerch packaging.

Filip, Miloš Glass designer from Czechoslovakia [1926–], worked for Moser c.1963/4, (pressed glass, cut glass, engraving, painting).

Findlay Flint Glass Co Glassworks in Findlay, OH, USA [1889–91], (pressed glass).

Findlay onyx Type of art glass in varying shades of brown. Findlay onyx glass Opaque-cased, pattern-moulded glass made by Dalzell, Gilmore & Leighton 1889–c.1891.

Finger tool A special tool with steel fingers used to hold the foot or bowl of a goblet. See also gadget and clamp.

Finial A crowning ornament.

Fining The act of removing gas bubbles from the melt by adding fining agents – these form larger bubbles that make smaller bubbles rise to the surface.

Finisher The worker who puts the finishing touches to a glass – the edges, ruffles, crimps etc.

Fink, Lotte Glass designer from Austria [–], worked for Lobmeyr c.1925.

Finland Over 60 Glassworks are recorded in Finnish history, the three dominant ones are Iittala, Nuutajärvi Notsjö and Riihimäki Glass.

Finn Crystal Glassworks in Nuutajärvi, Finland [1950s–1990s], were operated by Arabia – see Nuutajärvi.

Finne, Gunnar Glass designer from Finland [1886–1952].

Finnigans Glass outlet in London, Great Britain. Sig: found on Schneider pieces.

Fire polishing The method of reheating a finished piece to melt irregularities, seams and dull spots from the surface, developed in Great Britain in 1834 for pressed glass.

Fireclay Refractory material used to make crucibles for melting glass batches.

Fired-on Enamel colour fixed to the glass by reheating.

Firestone Richardson blown, festooned and opalescent range produced c.1905.

Firing glass See Toastmaster's glass.

First Communist Volunteer Detachment Glassworks Glass factory located in St Petersburg, Russia [c.1949–?], designers include Boris Chetkov, who was chief designer after 1966, Prostakov after 1969, Tarkovskaya after 1949 and Yukhvets after 1968, (cut glass, tableware and art glass figures).

First of May, Glassworks Glassworks, located in Russia, designers include Kobylinskaya and Ryazanova.

Fišar, Jan Glass artist from Hořovice, Czech Republic [1933–], designed at ŽBS 1966–71, was independent after 1971.

Fischer-Hütte Glassworks in Ilmenau, Germany [1910–76], (special glass products).

Fišer Liberec̆ Glassworks in Liberec̆, Czech Republic [?–present], (hand-blown glass, historical replicas, stained glass and novelties).

Fisher, Alfred R Glass designer from Great Britain [–], worked for James Powell c.1967/8.

Fishing floats Aka toggle balls these are hollow glass balls for keeping fish nets afloat in various sizes ie 10–40cm (4–15in) in diameter. Blues and greens are most common while yellows, purples are rarer. Japanese fishing floats may have the maker's mark.

Floats first appeared c.1900 and they are still currently in production in many places.

Fistek Glass Glassworks in Tarnow, Poland [?–present].

Fit Refers to the compatibility of different glasses, see also thermal expansion.

Fjaestad, Bo Glass designer from Sweden [–], worked for Eda c.1950.

Flaccus, CL Glass Co Glassworks in USA [1888–1970], (pressed glass).

Flaconneries et Cristalleries de Jumet SA Glassworks in Jumet near Charleroi, Belgium [1930–present], (handmade glass with air bubbles and crackle in the 1950s and flasks and perfume bottles 1963–present).

Flagey, Gerard & Cie Glassworks in Montferrand, Doubs, France [–], active c.1879.

Flame annealing A finished piece is reheated in a relatively cool flame to relax the stresses built up during the construction. This technqiue is only on used small pieces as the work will need to be properly annealed later on, (flamework).

Flameworking Fashioning articles from prefab glass rods and tubes in a burner or torch, aka lampworking or lamp-blowing

Flamingo Glassworks in Halfweg, Netherlands [?–1967], (bent glass)

Flander, Brita Glass designer from Finland [1957–], worked freelance for Rosenthal after 1988 and for Iittala in 1998.

Flared lip Lip of a bottle that has been worked to a flare or flange, produced before 1900.

Flaring Widening the open end of a bubble to create special goblet feet.

Flashed on Colouring technique for glass surfaces. Flashed on colours may wear off whereas fired-on colours will not.

Flashing A thin layer of coloured glass covering either the inside or outside of a piece. Coloured stain (usually ruby red or amber) was etched on, particularly on late 19thC Bohemian goblets. Chemical flashing is achieved through the ion exchange process: glass is heated in cupric oxide vapor until sodium ions are replaced by copper ions. See also overlay.

Flecfrac Trade name for Holophane Lighting Corp.

Flemington Cut Glass Co Glassworks in Flemington, NJ, USA [1904–?], previously known as Empire Cut Glass, operated by HC Fry, (cut glass).

Flint glass 1. Clear glass type with a high lead content, used c.1840–c.1870. 2. US term for pressed glassware made from Flint glass.

Flint Glass Manuf Co Glassworks in Iowa City, Iowa, USA [1880–2], set up by JH Leighton from Wheeling, WV.

Float glass An invention by Pilkington in 1959 for continuous casting of glass on a bed of molten tin. This became a worldwide standard in flat glass production. It represents approximately 20% of production in the EC now. The largest producers include Saint-Gobain, Pilkington, Glaverbel, Guardian and Pittsburgh Plate Glass.

Flôr, Ana Glass designer from Portugal [–], worked for Mglass in Marinha Grande c.1999.

Florahütte Glassworks in Polevsko, Czechoslovakia [1913–48], operated by František Ladisch.

Floret A Murrine with a floral design, (paperweights).

Florida Orrefors series glass designed by Palmqvist 1939, sand-blasted leaf décor, marks: PA2138/1–27.

Flower City Cut Glass Co Glassworks in USA [–], (cut glass, Brilliant period).

Fluogravure Acid-etching procedure used at VSL after 1900. Artists who worked this way include Müller Frères, Denoël Modeste, Lucien Petignot.

Fluorescent lamp A soda-alkaline earth silicate glass tube with an inside fluorescent coating filled with mercury vapour. As the vapour is stimulated it emits UV radiation, which in turn lights up the fluorescent coating.

Fluoval Brand name used at VSL/Jemeppe c.1909–26 for the combined technique of acid etching and cutting.

Fluted Having vertical decoration of grooves or channels.

Flux A substance like potash, boron or soda introduced to lower the melting temperature of the batch; fluxes are also used in enamels.

Fly catcher see Guépière.

Flygsfors Glassworks in Flygsfors, Sweden [1888–1970], taken over by Orrefors 1970 then closed in 1980, designers include Victor Berndt 1950–61. Sig: engraved "Flygsfors+year" after 1945 "Flygsfors Kedelv" 1949–56 and "Flygsfors Coquille" after 1956, (organic fifties glass by Paul Kedelv 1955–65).

flygsfors

FM Ronneby, FM Konstglas See Marcolin.

Foam glass Glass with added gas or gas-forming substances; foam glass has a low density but a high compressive strength and dimensional stability and so it is used in construction materials. See Schaumglas and Pulegoso.

Fogelberg, Anna Glass designer from Sweden [–], worked for Thomas Webb in the 1930s.

Fogelberg, Sven Glass maker from Sweden [–], worked at Kosta before 1932 and was general manager at Thomas Webb & Sons 1932–c.1959.

Folger, JA & Co Located in San Francisco, CA, [1850–present], (bottles).

Foller, Léon Painter from France [–], worked for VSL after c.1878 and was head of the painting studio after 1897.

Foltas, Prof Glass maker located in Nový Bor, Czechoslovakia [–], active c.1930.

Fomina, Lidiya A Glass designer from Moscow, Russia [1942–], worked at Krasny May with, T. Sazhin 1967–71.

Fontana & Co, Luigi Glassworks in Milano, Italy [c.1933–c.1963], designers include Pietro Chiesa, (art glass, lighting, flat glass and tableware).

Fontana Arte Trade name for art glass/lighting made in Milano, Italy after 1934, designers include Gio Ponti, Pietro Chiesa and Max Ingrand c.1957–c.1964.

Footed weight A paperweight with a base flange, unlike the Piedouche, which has a mushroom stem.

Forati Gatto Type of art glass made by Venini and designed by Fulvio Bianconi, 1951.

Forbes Silver Co. Glassworks in USA [–], active c.1911, (tableware).

Ford, John Glass maker at Holyrood Flint Glass Works, Edinburgh, Scotland [1835–1904], (pressed glass and paperweights).

Foreign made Stick-on label for imported glassware in Britain, which was introduced in 1929.

Forest glass See Waldglas.

Formglas of Sweden AB Glassworks in Nybro, Sweden [?–present].

Formia Vetri d'Arte Glassworks in Murano, Italy [?–present], (murano giftware, figures, sculpture, limited editions).

Fornace da Vinci Glassworks in Empoli, Italy [?–present], merged with CIVE. into Vetreria in Toscane in 2000.

Fornasetti, Pietro Glass designer from Italy [1913–88], worked for SALIR c.1940.

Fornasier, Luigi Glassworks in Murano, Italy [–], active c.1981, (lamps and lighting).

Forsell, Ulla-Mari Glass designer from Sweden [1944–], worked independently after 1974.

Fort Dearborn Watch & Clock Co Glassworks in USA [–], active c.1925, (tableware).

Fort Pitt Glassworks Glassworks in Martins Ferry, OH USA [1860–81], was based in Pittsburgh, PA 1881–7 and in New Brighton, PA 1887–c.1903. See Dithridge & Sons.

Forth Glass Works Glassworks in Glasgow, Scotland [–], active c.1899, aka AM Allan & Co, (pressed glass, tableware).

Fortress cane Paperweight cane with a cross-section of a castle made by Baccarat.

Fostoria Glass Co Glassworks in Fostoria, OH, USA [1887–91] moved to Moundsville, WV [1891–1986] and had a factory at Miles, OH after 1910. Fostoria was once the largest producer of handmade glass in America, and it made the first all-glass dinner service in the US. Fostoria also operated Morgantown Glass Co 1965–71 but was then sold to Lancaster Colony Corp in 1983 and closed 1986. Sig: brown paper labels only 1924–57 and red/yellow/blue/black labels 1957–86, (cut glass, tableware, etched, blown, pressed glass, depression glass; paperweights 1880s–1900s and coloured tableware after 1924).

Fostoria Glass Specialty Co Glassworks in Fostoria, OH, USA [–], active c.1908, (lighting).

Fostoria Shade and Lamp Glassworks in

Fostoria, OH USA [?–1893], (lighting); merged into Consolidated Lamp and Glass Co.

Fouarge, Hubert Glass cutter from Belgium [–], worked for Val St Lambert as head cutter after 1893. Sig: HF.

Founding Heating batch material to a temperature c.1400°C. After a maturing period the temperature is lowered to its working temperature of c.1100° C.

Foval Trade name for opalescent glass made by Fry in the 1920s.

Fowler, Suellen Flamework artist from Berkeley, CA, USA [1955–], working since 1974.

Frabel, Hans Godo Flamework artist from Jena, Mainz, Germany [1941–], moved to Atlanta, GA, USA in 1965, had own lampwork studio after 1968.

Frances Ware Pattern name used by Hobbs, Brockunier c.1885 for tableware.

Franchetti Glassworks in Venezia, Italy [–], active c.1907, aka Cristalleria e Vetreria Veneziana gia Franchetti.

Franchini, Giambatista and Jacopo Glass makers from Venice, Italy [–], (paperweights 1840s–1870s).

Franck, Kaj Ceramicist and glass designer from Finland [1911–], worked for Riihimäki after c.1933, Iittala 1946–60, Nuutajärvi 1950–1973.

Franckhauser, Etienne Mould maker from France who supplied pressed glass moulds to Lalique, Sabino, Hunnebelle and Jobling c.1930s.

Frankenwaldglas GmbH Glassworks in Helmbrechts, Germany [?–present], trade name is FW-Glas.

Franklin Trade name used by Gillinder & Sons.

Franklin Flint Glass Co Glassworks in Philadelphia, PA USA [1861–80], operated by Gillinder & Sons, (pressed glass).

Frankonia Kristallglaswerk GmbH Glassworks in Warmensteinach, Germany [1899–present], originally named Glaswerke Warmensteinach but renamed Frankonia in 1997, (pressed glass, tableware, crystal, giftware, flat glass, handmade tableware, also produced beads until 1936).

Franzen & Son, William Glassworks in Milwaukee, WI, USA [1900–29], (bottles).

Franzhütte, Franzensthal Glassworks in Frantiskov u Vimperk, Czechoslovakia [1854–1945], founded by Jan Meyr, part of Meyr's Neffe after 1852, run by Wilhelm Kralik after the 1880s.

Frastagliati Art glass made by Barovier & Toso and designed by Ercole Barovier, 1945.

Fratelli Barovier Glassworks in Murano, Italy [–], active c.1967, (cut glass and engraved glass).

Frauenau Kristallglasfabrik J Gistl Glassworks in Frauenau, Germany [c.1926–c.1970s].

Frederick Lorenz & Co Located in Pittsburgh, PA, USA, [1819–41], trade names include FL and FL & Co, (bottles).

Freij, Edler Glass designer from Norway [1944–], worked for Hadeland after 1976.

Freitas, Paula Glass designer from Portugal [–], worked for Mglass in Marinha Grande c.1999.

Friedlaender, Oscar O Glasshouse located in New York, NY [–], active c.1890. Sig: Lion.

Friedrichglas Glassworks in Germany [–], active c.1975.

Friedrichshain Glassworks in Spremberg, NL, Germany [1767–?], owned by Greiner before 1823, bought by Poncet in 1837 then became von Poncet'sche Glashüttenwerke in 1905). Sig: "Friedrichshain" in a globe, (tableware, bottles in brown and green).

Friedrichsthal Glassworks in Friedrichsthal, NL, Germany [1709–1974], had the first glassworks in Niederlausitz, had its own polishing plant in 1725, became Glashütte Friedrichsthal GmbH, Bartsch, Quilitz & Co in 1923 and was then state operated 1945–68. Became VEB Glaswerk Stralau, Section Finsterwalde Werk Kostebrau 1969–74, (mirrors, tableware after 1787 and bottles after 1923).

Frigger Decorative novelty hats, shoes, rolling pins, snuff bottles etc, see also Nailsea.

Frijns, Bert Glass artist from Holland [1953–], has had own studio since 1980.

Frit Partially fused glass ingredients.

Fritsche, Wilhelm Glass engraver from Bohemia [1853–1924], worked for Thomas Webb and others. Sig: many works are signed with "Fritsche".

Frog A glass block with holes in it for holding flower stems.

Frosting Giving a matt finish to a glass surface, by hydrofluoric acid, sand-blasting or using a grinding wheel. See satin glass and acid etching.

Fruit jars Inside glass lid was used in 1855, outside glass lid (Hero) produced 1856, mason jar/metal screw cap after 1858, mason glass lid after 1868, ball mason jars after 1880, fully automated production after 1903.

Fry Glass Co, HC Glassworks located at Rochester, PA USA [1901–33]. Trade names include Foval. Sig: ovenware is marked "Fry"+no, other pieces are rarely marked apart from silver overlay pieces marked "Rockwell" on Foval, (tableware, art glass "Foval" 1926–7, cut glass 1920s, "Pearl Oven Glass" opalescent ware after 1922).

Frysja Studio, Karen Klim Glassworks in Frysja, Norway [1978–?].

Fucina degli Angeli Glassworks in Murano, Italy [1953–?], see Centro Studio.

Fuga, Aldo Glassworks in Murano, Italy [–], active c.1948.

Fuga, Anzolo Glass designer from Italy [1914–], founded Anzolo Fuga Vetri Decorati e Vetrate Istoriate in 1954. Produced enamelling 1950–60 and did freelance design for AVEM 1955–62. His works were also realized IVR Mazzega. He taught glass making from 1950–70.

Fuga Anzolo e Fratelli Glassworks in Murano, Italy [1947–c.1967], founded by Ansolo and Giuseppe Fuga, (stained glass windows).

Fuga glass Centrifugally cast glass, developed by Sven Palmqvist at Orrefors, 1953–9, the coloured variety is known as Colora.

Full lead crystal Crystal glass containing a

minimum of 30% Lead oxide.

Fuller, Fred H, Co Glassworks in USA [–], active c.1916, (cut glass).

Fuming Surface decoration technique in which a metal-coated (silver or gold) glass rod is held in the flame with the object behind it; the metal fumes condense on the cooler object. Silver fuming gives a yellowish surface; gold turns the surface pink, (lampwork).

Funakoshi, Saburo Glass artist from Japan [1931–], worked for Hoya after 1957, (art glass after 1979).

Funke & Co Glashütte Gebr Glassworks in Penzig near Görlitz, Germany [1914–c.1937].

Furnace Cast Mould cast at the furnace

Fürstenberg an der Oder Glassworks in Fürstenberg, Oder near Guben, Silesia [–], there are two operating: one making lamps and the other pressed glass. The first was operated by Niederlausitzer Glashütten-AG, vorm G Beichler and the second by Max Kray & Co Glas-Industrie AG, Fürstenberg/O and was taken over by VLG in 1930, (lighting, pressed glass and bottles).

Fusamae, Yoyi Glass designer from Japan [–], worked for Joetsu Crystal Glass Co Ltd c.1968/9.

Fused silica/Quartz (SiO2) Glass from pure silica has high thermal expansion, stability and UV-transmission properties so it has to be melted at 2,000°C and is expensive and difficult to produce. It is mainly used in high-temperature research equipment.

Fusing 1. Founding, melting. 2. Heating glass pieces in a kiln until they bond; sodalime glass fuses together between 760°C and 820°C. 3. Binding enamel to a glass surface.

FW-Glas See Frankenwald.

Fyens Glasvaerk Aktieselskabet Glassworks in Odense, Denmark [1874–c.1890], founded as Odense Glasvaerk 1874–88.

G

G (in an outline) Sig used by Gentile Glass.

G & H Trade name used by Gray & Hemingray.

Gadget Gripping device that replaces a pontil rod and leaves no marks, aka finger tool and cramp.

Gadrooning See Knurling.

Gaffer Master glass blower in charge of a "chair" – a team of glass workers.

Gala, Ateliers Glass studio located in Mons, Belgium [c.1989–?], designers include Serge Gallez, Claude Laurent, Giampaolo Amoroso and Lucio Pagnin, (art glass).

Galaica Fine Crystal, La Glassworks in Mos, Pontevedra, Spain [1954–present], founded in Vigo, (tableware, cut glass, silvered glass).

Gall Aka scum, impurities floating to the top of the melting batch.

Gall, Eugène Master glassblower from France [–], worked for Daum 1900–40.

Gallé Emile [1846–1904] Glass artist from Nancy, France, was producing glass after

1874 and earned world fame by 1889. His workshop continued until 1913, (art glass, enamel and cameo).

Gallé works Glassworks in La Garenne, Nancy [1894–1913], was run by Gallé until his death in 1904 and then by Henriette Gallé until 1914. Old designs were reproduced after 1914 and then new designs added after c.1928. Sig: more than 60 different signatures have been recorded 1878–1904, signatures marked * were produced 1909–14.

Gallez, Serge Glass artist from Belgium [–], worked at Gala after c.1989.

Gallo, Ricardo/Vidro De Embalagem SA Glassworks in Lisbon, Marinha Grande, Portugal [1895–present], (bottles).

Galway Irish Crystal Ltd Glassworks in Galway, Ireland [?–present], (tableware, crystal giftware).

Ganf, Natalya Y Glass designer from Moscow, Russia [1926–], worked at Workshops of Applied Art, Moscow after 1950 but main works produced at Ivanischevsky, Dyatkovsky Cut Glass, The Neman and Krasny May.

Garbin, Maria Glass refiner from Venice, Italy [c.1934–].

Gardella, Ignazio Glass designer from Italy [1905–], worked for Venini c.1958.

Gare, Verreries de la SA Glassworks in Lyon, France [1842–c.1890], (tableware).

Garnet & Cie Luxury bottle maker located in France [1858–], (Garnier bottles).

Garnier bottle Figural bottles made by Garnet & Cie, France since 1899.

Garouste, Elisabeth Glass designer from France [1949–], worked for Daum c.1989.

Gas light In 1792 the first home had gas lights in England while the first factory to be lit by gas in England was in 1798 and in Philadelphia 1816 (most major cities before 1860; Coal gas replaced by water gas 1872. In rural areas Acetylene gas was used. Gas light shades point upward (until 1897), electric ones down. Most gas fixtures were converted for electricity c.1920s.).

Gas shades sizes 1½'; 1⅞'; 2½'; 2⅝'; 4' (the most common); and 5'. (Producers include Phoenix, Holophane; Bauer; Gillinder; Hocking; Jeannette shades and Novelty Co.); (electric shades are 2¼).

Gasoline lamps Bright lighting fixture using pressurized gasoline. It was invented in c.1900 and in use until c.1940.

Gaspari, Luciano Glass designer from Italy [1913–], designed for Salviati 1950–68.

Gate numbering on engraved glass number and year G40, 41, 62-117 all=1917/8, G118-127=1919, G128-174=1920, G175-184=1921, G185-213=1922, G214-273=1923, G274-327=1924, 328-358=1925, G359-410=1926, G411-434=1927, G435-509=1928, G510-534=1929, G535-553=1930, G554-570=1931.

Gate, Simon Glass designer from Sweden [1883–1945], worked for Orrefors 1916–5 and developed Graal glass, (cut glass and engraved glasses).

Gates, John Monteith Architect/Glass designer from USA [–], worked for Steuben 1933–70.

Gateshead Stamped Glass Glassworks in Gateshead, Great Britain [–], aka Ellison Glassworks, which was a precursor to Sowerby's, (pressed glass after c.1850s).

Gather Molten glass on the end of a blowpipe, pontil or gathering iron.

Gayner Glass Works Based in Salem, NJ, USA [1900–10], (bottles).

Gebhardsdorf, Glashütte Glassworks in Gebhardsdorf near Lauban, OL, Germany [1918–c.1937].

Gebrüder Felix Glassworks in Schwäbisch Gmünd, Germany [c.1950]; (tableware).

Gebrüder Lorenz Glassworks in Kamenický Šenov, Czechoslovakia [–], active c.1925, (cut glass).

Gebrüder Pallme König GmbH Glassworks in Koštany u Teplice, Czechoslovakia [1913–?].

Geddes & Co, Perrin Glass maker located in Warrington, near Liverpool, Great Britain [c.1806–c.1820], aka Bank Quay Glass Works, (cut glass, tableware, Regency style).

Gehlin, Hugo Glass designer from Sweden [1899–1953], worked for Gullaskruf 1930–53.

Geissler, A Glassworks in Radeberg, Germany [–], active c.1880, (tableware).

Gelsdorf Glashütte W Glassworks in Weisswasser near Rothenburg OL, Germany [1872–?], operated by Görlitzer Glasmacher, W Gelsdorf 1873, taken over by VEB Oberlausitzer Glaswerke Weisswasser in 1952.

GEM Trade name used by Hero Glass Works.

Gemmata Barovier & Toso art glass type by Ercole Barovier, 1940.

General Lamps Co See Aladdin Manufacturing Co.

General Traders Glass Works Glassworks in Firozabad, India [?–present], (tableware, giftware, barware; sodalime, handmade or semi-automatic).

Genesee Cut Glass Co Glassworks in USA [–], (cut glass, Brilliant period).

Genet & Michon Glassworks in France [–]. Sig: Genet et Michon, (Art Deco lighting and Art Deco vases in cast glass since 1921).

Gent, Glasfabrieken Glassworks in Gent, Belgium [1820–?].

Gentile Glass Glassworks in Star City, WV, USA [–], active c.1960s, artists include John and Gertrude Gentile and Frank Hamilton. Sig: G inside outline, (pressed glass and paperweights).

Gentile, Peter Glass maker from USA [–], worked at G-F Glass Co, Morgantown, WV in the 1940s, (paperweights).

Gentili, Giorgio Glass designer from Italy [1928–], designed lighting for Vistosi.

Georgenthal, Jiríkovo Údolí Glassworks in Jiríkovo Údolí, Czechoslovakia [c.1835–?].

Georgian See Style periods.

Gerdlichka Brothers Glassworks in Russia [–], active 19thC.

Gering, Jean Glass designer from Vaals, Belgium [1909–83], worked at VSL 1950–60, (tableware).

German Cut Glass Co Glassworks in Jermyn, PA, USA [1903–5], founded as the German Cut Glass Co in 1903 but was soon renamed Laurel and then renamed Kohinur Cut Glass Co in 1906/7. Finally merged with Quaker City Cut Glass Co in 1918, see Laurel Cut Glass Co, (cut glass).

Germania Glashütte, Glaswerk Glassworks in Weisswasser near Rothenburg OL, Germany [1893–c.1937], Aka Germaniahütte, was operated by VLG Weisswasser 1920, (tableware, bottles, pressed glass, refinery).

Germania, Glashütten Glassworks in Finsterwalde-Friedrichstal NL, Germany [–]. Sig: GG/F in a circle.

Germaniahütte Glassworks in Welzow near Spremberg, Germany [1891–c.1937].

Gerresheimer Glas Glass conglomerate located in Düsseldorf, Germany [?–present], operates 17 plants around the world, (bottles, vials and tubes).

Gerspach, Dubois, Bourgeois & Nicolle Glassworks in France [–], they also made Aubervilliers, Verreries et Cristalleries de.

Gervais et Lambalais Glassworks in France [c.1890–c.1900], (lighting).

Gessner, Hubert Glass designer from Austria [–], worked for Loetz c.1902.

Gevaert, Romain Glass designer from Belgium [1875–1931], worked for Val St Lambert at Jemeppe-sur-Meuse, (used opal and enamel and is known for using black, green, copper red and black filigrane).

GF (Glass Flowers & Figures) Glassworks in Železný Brod, Czech Republic [?–present], (lampwork figures).

G-F Glass Co Glass company located in Morgantown, WV [–], active c.1940s, (paperweights), see Peter Gentile.

Ghenshke, Vladimir N Glass designer from Kiev, Ukraine [1925–], worked in the Kiev Factory after 1948.

Ghisetti Glass maker located in Murano, Italy [–], active c.1980.

Ghlin See Moulineau, Verrerie du.

Gl (intertwined) Glass mark used by Imperial 1951–72.

Gibbs, WH & Co Glassworks, location unknown [–], active c.1914, (cut glass).

Giberson, Dudley Studio artist from USA [1942–].

Gibson Gas Fixture Works, Inc Glassworks in

USA [–], active c.1905, (lighting).

Gibson Glass Glassworks in Milton, WV, USA [1983–?]. Sig: GIBSON in a circle, (paperweights, figures, animals, novelties).

Gidding, Jaap Glass decorator from the Netherlands [1887–1955], worked for Leerdam 1926–30. Sig: curly J inside G inside circle monogram, (abstract, enamelled glass).

Giergl, Henrik Glass refinery located in Budapest, Hungary [–], active c.1890s, (enamelled glass).

Gilberds Trade name used by Gilberds Butter Tub Co, Jamestown, NY [1883–90], (bottles).

Gilbert, Walter Sculptor from Great Britain [1871–1946], designed "Vesta" range of lamps and lighting for John Walsh Walsh in the late 1920s.

Gilchrist, Jane Studio glass artist from Great Britain [–], working c.1975.

Gilding Decorating technique using gold leaf, paint or dust, usually fired onto the glass. Oil gilding is the earliest technique; from 1755 honey gilding was used; from 1790 mercury gilding and from 1850 bright gilding. The technique is aka Liquid Gold. See also Napoli glass.

Gill & Co/Gill Brothers Co Manufacturer located in USA [–], active c.1915. Sig: unicorn, trade names include Acmelite, Coronet, Gloria, Granite, Lucky Cross, OK, Rock, Parian, Sampson and Victor Top, (lighting and pressed shades).

Gillinder & Sons/US Glass G Glassworks in Philadelphia, PA, USA [1861–1930], known as Franklin Flint Glass 1861, Gillinder & Bennett 1863, Gillinder & Sons 1867 moved to Greensburg, PA, Pennsylvania in 1888, in 1891 became part of US Glass and in 1900 was registered as an Inc company, (pressed glass, cut glass, lighting, paperweights 1860s/70s and art glass).

Gillinder Brothers, Inc Glassworks in Port Jervis, NY, USA [1912–present], previously known as Gillinder & Sons before they moved to Port Jervis to start another factory, (pressed glass).

Ginniken, van Glass designer from Holland [–], worked for Leerdam c.1979.

Ginzburg, Vitaly A Flamework artist from Lvov, Ukraine [1938–], produced lampwork after 1960 at Raduga, Lvov.

Giovanni, Giuseppe de Glass engraver from Napoli, Italy [–], worked in London in the 1870s.

Giralt Laporta SA See BSN Vidro España SA.

Girandole Multi-branch candlestick.

Girard, Otto and Rehlender, Georg Glass artists from Austria [–] they worked for Lobmeyr 1872–80 and designed "blue aquamarine" glass.

Girasole Barovier & Toso art glass type by Ercole Barovier, 1939.

Gistl, J See Frauneau Kristallglasfabrik J Gistl.

Gjövik Glasverk Glassworks in Norway [?–1843].

Glacerie Sainte-Marie d'Oignies Mirror works located in Hainaut, Belgium [1837–?], (flat glass, mirrors).

Glas The word for glass in Danish, Dutch, German, Letzeburgisch and Swedish.

Glasfabriek Leerdam Glassworks in Leerdam, Netherlands [–], see Leerdam.

Glasfabrik Oranienhütte See Losky, F.

Glasfabrik S Reich & Co Glassworks in Krasno nad Becvou, Czechoslovakia [–].

Glasfachschule School for glass making in Czechoslovakia located in Kamenický Šenov, [1856–1936] in Nový Bor, [1870–present] and in Železný Brod [c.1926–present]. There are similar schools in Germany located in Hadamar, Zwiesel, Lauscha and Rheinbach.

Glasgravören I Glasriket AB Glass refinery located in Nybro, Sweden [?–present], (engraving).

Glashütte Adlerhütten Glassworks in Penzig, Thuringen, Germany [–], active c.1930.

Glashütte Leichlingen GmbH See Gral-Glashütte)

Glashütte Rasch Glassworks in Nový Bor, Czechoslovakia [–], active c.1920.

Glashütte Schneegattern Ges. Glassworks in Schneegattern, near Kufstein, Austria [c.1961–c.1971], see Riedel.

Glashütte Zlatno Glassworks in Zlatno near Lucenec, Slovakia [1807–present], (pressed glass reported 1895, Stredoslovensko Sklárne, iridescent glass).

Glaskoch Glass dealer located in Bad Driburg, Germany [1972–present], (huge output of Leonardo tableware and giftware)

Glaskunst Lauscha GmbH Glassworks in Lauscha, Thüringen, Germany [1949–present], had various GDR name changes 1949–90, (lampwork, decorative items, giftware).

Glass ceramics Glass is amorphous (it does not contain crystals) but by allowing some controlled crystallisation the best of both worlds can be had. Some "glass ceramics" (lithium aluminosilicate glasses) are extremely resistant to thermal stock and are used in cookers, cookware, windows, gas or coal fires, astronomical telescopes and missile nose cones.

Glass Co Manufacturer of beads in Jabloneč nad Nisou, Czech Republic [?–present].

Glass Studio Glassworks in Thessaloniki, Greece [?–present], (recycled cast, slumped glass).

Glassboro Glassworks Glassworks in Glassboro, NJ, USA [1781–?], (bottles, flat glass, tableware).

Glassics Trade name used by Concorde Kristallglas.

Glassmaker's soap See Manganese.

Glastonbury Glass Factory Glassworks in Glastonbury, CT, USA [1816–27], (bottles).

Glažuta Glassworks See Osredek.

Gleason, EP Mfg Co Glassworks in USA [c.1871–c.1900], (lighting).

Gleason-Tiebout Glass Co Glassworks in USA [c.1904–c.1935], uses the trade name Celestialite, (burning fluid lamps).

Glimåkra Glassworks in Sweden [–], active c.1964.

Glimma Glasbruk Glassworks in Sweden [c.1954–c.1968], designers include Marcolin and Gunnar Nylund.

Globe Lighting Fixture Manufacturing Co

Glassworks in USA [c.1935–c.1940], (lighting).

Globe Lighting Products, Inc Glassworks in USA [–], active c.1949, (lighting).

Glöggler, Josef Glass designer from Germany [1907–], worked for WMF engraving, 1945–72.

Glory hole The working opening of a glass furnace.

Gluchowsky & Faber Glashütte Glassworks in Neu Petershain near Calau, NL, Germany [1898–c.1937], renamed Gluchowsky Glashütte in 1903. Sig: G+F on bottom.

Gob A drop of liquid glass for feeding into the forming machine when shaping bottles. The automatic Gob feeder was introduced in 1917.

Gobbe-Hocquemiller, Verreries E Glassworks in Lodelinsart, near Charleroi, Belgium [?–1960], merger with flat glass producer Sobelever/ Glaverbel 1960 ended the operations of their artistic department Art et Verre (worked 1946–60), handmade rustic tableware was designed by Frantz Bellaska and Thumson after 1951. This was aka Verre Antique in amethyst, ruby, blue, yellow and green, they exported to the US after 1956, other designers included Paule Ingrard, (publicity, neon, art glass).

Gobeleterie Inebrechable, Cie Intl De, SA Glassworks in Belgium [–], active c.1950, (tableware).

Gobeleterie Nationale, SA Glassworks in Belgium [1918–39]. Previously known as Notre Dame, it finally merged with Familleureux, Blanc-Nisseron in 1886 then with Verrerie de Crespin/F 1897 and continued as Gobeleterie Nationale between the two World Wars, (tableware, pressed glass, bottles, cut glass in clear glass and semi-crystal).

Goblet A large stemmed glass.

Goebel Porzellanfabrik, W Manufacturer of collectable porcelain figures from Rödental, Germany [19th–present]. Sig: Goebel W Germany before 1991 and Germany after 1991, (hummel figures after 1935 as well as crystal figures and collectables under the Goebel mark).

Gol, Jose Maria Glass designer from Barcelona, Spain [–], worked c.1920–c.1940, (floral, abstract, enamel).

Goldberg, Carl Glassworks in Nový Bor [1881–?], sigs: usually unmarked, (art glass, cut glass, enamel, gilding, engraving, silvering, iridescence).

Golding, Richard Glass designer from Great Britain [–], founder of Okra Glass in 1979.

Goldoni, Raoul Painter, sculptor and glass artist from Split, Croatia (1919–83), worked at Boris Kidrič in Rogaška Slatina after 1956, was their artistic director after 1967, then for the Kristal factory in Samobor, Zagreb and also worked at Barbini, Seguso, Nason and Signoreto in Murano after 1967, (art glass

esp. sculpture and tableware).

Golembovskaya, Svetlana V Glass designer from Odessa, Ukraine [1927–], worked at the Kiev Factory, Kiev after 1964.

Gomes, Catarina and Magda Glass designers from Portugal [–], worked for MGlass, Marinha Grande in c.1999.

Gondolieri Venini art glass designed by Tapio Wirkkala, 1966.

Gooderham, John Glass maker from Sault Ste Marie, Ontario, Canada [–], (paperweights in the 1970s).

Goofus Type of pressed glass made between 1900–20 by Indiana, Northwood, Dugan, Imperial, Crescent, LaBelle, Northwood and others under a variety of names. Goofus glass is painted in garish silvered colours that are not fired on – so they damage easily.

Gordiola, Vidrios de Glassworks in Spain [–], active c.1962, (tableware).

Gordon, Alastair D Studio artist from Sweden [–], worked for Kosta c.1973.

Gordon, Ernest Glass designer from Sweden [–], worked for Kosta 1952/3.

Görlitz Town in Oberlausitz, Germany, which is the location for various glassworks including Raffinerie Pietsch, Raffinerie Fiemsch & Heinsius and Raffinerie Felkenhauer.

Gosda Glashütte Glassworks in Gosda, Döbern near Sorau NL, Germany [1833–c.1937], founded by Greiner who was the owner of Friedrichshain until 1823. It moved to Haidemühl in 1835 and was later noted as Haidemühler Glashüttenwerke, D H Apelt & Sohn.

Goupy, Marcel Painter, potter and designer from France [–], was the artistic director for Géo Rouard 1909–54 (the outlet sold products for Lalique, Navarre, Décorchemont, Thuret and Goupy, esp. after 1918), worked with Auguste Heiligenstein 1919–23). Sig: sometimes M. Goupy, often unsigned, (enamelled tableware, art glass).

Gowans, Kent & Co Glassworks in Toronto, Canada [–], (tableware).

Gowans, Kent & Co, Ltd Glassworks in Great Britain [c.1900–c.1906], (tableware).

Gozo Glassworks in Gozo, Malta, [–], active c.1975.

Graal Technique developed by Orrefors in 1916 for cutting, etching or sand-blasting a design onto a cooled two-coloured core form. After reheating, the piece is covered in clear glass and finished in the usual way. Variations of this technique include Slipgraal (cut), Fishgraal (fish), Ariel (air pattern), Kraka (net) and Ravenna (mosaic).

Graal numbering 1=1936, 6=1937, 121=1938, 361=1939, 511=1940, 571=1941, 795=1942, 1213=1943, 1401=1944, 1,928=1945, 2,356=1946, 2,825=1947, 300B=1947, 651B=1948,

1,661B=1948, 200C=1949, 870C=1950,
1915C=1951, 200D=1951, 438D=1952,
1,836D=1953, 2,867D=1954, 200H=1954,
1,387K=1955, 101L=1956, 101M=1957,
100N=1958, 100Q=1959, 100P=1960,
100R=1961, 101S=1962, 101T=1963,
101V=1964, 101A=1965, 344A=1966,
101B=1967, 100D=1969, 100E=1970,
101F=1971, 100G=1972, 100E3=1973,
101E4=1974, 101E5=1975, 100E6=1976,
100E7=1977, 100E8=1978, 100E9=1979,
100F1=1980, 100F2=1981.
Graal numbering, early pieces 1=1916,
101=1917, 522=1918, 741=1919,
856=1920, 1,026=1921,
1,090–1,099=1922, 2,000=1922,
2,004=1923, 2,014=1924,
2,032–2,081=1925, 2,082–2,099=1926,
3,000=1926, 3,065=1927, 3,073=1928,
3,246=1929/30, 3,285–3,292=1931.

Grabar, Mirona V Glass designer from
Uzhgorod, Ukraine [1938–], worked at
Dyatkovsky Cut Glass after 1961.
Gracia, Margarida Glass designer from
Portugal [–], worked for Mglass in Marinha
Grande c.1999.
Graffart, Charles Glass designer from Belgium
[1893–1967], worked for Val St Lambert
1906–58 and from 1942 was their artistic
director, see Luxval.
Graffito Amaranto Barovier & Toso art glass
type by Ercole Barovier, 1969.
Gräfl von Arnimsche Glaserke Glassworks in
Jämlitz zu Muskau near Sorau, Germany
[1815–c.1937], operated by Count von Arnim.
Sig: company logo GA+crown+GJ c.1924.
Gräflich Harrachsche Glasfabrik, Neuwelthütte
See Harrach.
Gräflich Schafgötsch'sche See
Josephinenhütte.
Grahl, John Glass refiner located in Dublin,
Ireland [c.1800–c.1820], (cut glass).
Gral-glashütte GmbH Glassworks in Dürnau,
Göppingen and Leichlingen, Germany
[1930–85], designers include Karl Wiedmann,
Konrad Häbermeier and Hans R Janssen
c.1974/5. Sig: usually labels sometimes
engraved with name, date and Gralglas, (art
glass, florist glass).

Gramss, Horst Glass maker/designer from
Lauscha, Germany [1936–], worked at VLG
after 1957, (lampwork).
Granada Series glass by Orrefors, designed by

Edvard Hald in 1939.
Grand Crystal Co Glassworks in Peitou, Taipei,
Taiwan [1994–present], chief designer is
Heinrich Wang, there is a glass museum at
same location, (lost wax, pate-de-verre, limited
editions, traditional Chinese motifs).
Grand Depot, Le See Bourgeois, Emile.
Grande Verrerie de la Gare See Gare, Verreries
de la.
Granger, Geneviève Glass designer from
France [–], worked for Etling c.1920s.
Grandes Verreries de Croismare Aka Verreries
d'Art Muller Freres. See Croismare, Grandes
Verreries de; Muller Freres.
Granite glass 1. Type of glass made in
Murano, c.1845, with white flecks on colour
ground 2. Trade name used by Gill Brothers.
Granja, Real Fabrica de Cristales de
Glassworks in La Granja de San Ildefonso,
Segovia, Spain [1726–present], (luxury
tableware, cut glass, gilt engraving and
enamel).
Gränna Glasbruk AB Glass studio located in
Gränna, Sweden [c.1965–present], operated
by Germano Padoan. Sig: all items are needle-
signed, (art glass, gift items).
Granulare Type of art glass made by Venini
and designed by Carlo Scarpa, 1940.
Granville-Barker, J Glass engraver from Great
Britain [–], worked for Liberty & Co Ltd
c.1952/3.
Graphite A crystalline form of carbon used for
glassworking tools and moulds because it
does not burn or stick to hot glass.
Graville, Verreries De See Tourres & Cie.
Gravis, Verreries Glassworks in Anzin, France
[1968–], (bottles, cosmetic).
Gray Glassworks in Tyneside, Great Britain
[?–1885], their moulds were sold to Davidson
in 1885, (pressed glass).
Gray & Hemingray Based in Cincinnati, OH,
USA [1848–64], (bottles).
Gray, Milner Glass designer from Great Britain
[–], worked for George Davidson & Co
c.1962/3.
Gray-Stan Glass Glassworks in Battersea,
Great Britain [1926–36], designers include
Noel Billinghurst and Elisabeth Graydon-
Stannus. Sig: often unsigned; sometimes
engraved "Gray-Stan, British", (art glass
similar to Monart glass, reproduction Irish cut
glass and Venetian style).

Gray-Stan

Greasy lustre Having a greasy appearance;
see lustre.
Greathead, Davis See Davis, Greathead &
Green.
Green & Nephew, James Glass seller from
London, Great Britain [–], working c.1876, (cut
glass).
Greenalite See Emeralite.
Greener Glass Glassworks located on the River
Wear, Sunderland, Great Britain

[1858–present], was named Angus & Greener 1858–69, moved to Millfield, Sunderland in 1871, was renamed Greener & Co in 1885 and then James A Jobling & Co in 1921 and has produced Pyrex since 1921. It is currently operating as part of Corning and is producing technical glass/pyrex only, (tableware, novelties, pressed glass, opalique, jade; pyrex).

Greenfield Trade name of Greenfield Fruit Jar & Bottle Co, Greenfield, IN, [1888–1912], (bottles).

Greensburg Glass Co/National Glass 08 Glassworks in Greensburg, USA PA [1889–?] began as Greensburg Glass Co Ltd 1893–8, was sold to the Brilliant Glass Co in 1893, closed in 1898, became part of National Glass in 1900–1, was sold to LE Smith Glass Co in 1901, was operating as Greensburg Glass Co 1901–37, (pressed glass and depression glass).

Greentown Glass Glass made in Greentown, IN, USA [1894–1903], previously known as Indiana Tumbler and Goblet Co, became part of National Glass in 1899, burned down in 1903, (pressed glass, novelties, chocolate glass after 1900, "Golden agate" and "Rose agate" after 1902).

Gregory, Mary Type of enamel decoration on glass first made at Boston & Sandwich in the 1880s. Consists of white enamel pictures especially of children at play. Most examples were made in Czechoslovakia by companies such as Schmidt Glassworks in Kusov, and in Italy.

Greiner Glashütte, Gebr Glassworks in Penzig near Görlitz, Germany [1873–?], operated by Gebr Greiner, then located in Rauscha near Görlitz, Germany [after 1900] and located in Drebkau near Calau, Germany [1909–c.1937] and operated by Greiner & Co,.

Greiner, Glasraffinerie E Glass-decorating firm located in Rietschen, near Rothenburg, Germany [1885–present], owner is Dieter Sänger, (painting on glass).

Grenada glass Trade name for Amberina glass, by Josef Rindskopf c.1900.

Grenade An early fire extinguisher; a round bottle with a short neck. It was invented c.1850 and the first US patent was in 1863, the latest c.1910. It was introduced in the US in 1871 and used until it was until superceded by the fire extinguisher in 1905.

Gretsch, Hermann Architect/ceramicist from Augsburg, Germany [1895–1950], worked for VLG Weisswasser in the 1930s.

Grice, Edvin Glass engraver/cutter from Great Britain [1839–1913], was a decorator at J & J Northwood after 1861 and later worked at Guest Bros.

Griegst, Arje Goldsmith/glass designer from Denmark [1938–], worked for Holmegaard

after 1983.

Grierson & Co Glassworks, location unknown [–], active c.1875, (tableware).

Griesel Glassworks in Leitersdorf, Germany [–], operated by Steuer & Fink, (green glass, white tableware).

Griffe Montenapoleone See Empoli SpA, Vetererie de.

Grill plate A plate with sections (usually three).

Grinding Removing glass with abrasives (shaping, polishing, milling, sawing, edging, drilling).

Grizinkalns-2 Glassworks in Riga, Latvia [1992–present], (bottles, lighting shades).

Grog Pieces of broken crucible used to make new ones from.

Groot, Mieke Glass designer/artist from Alkmaar, Holland [1949–], worked for Leerdam c.1979.

Grosse, Farbenglaswerk Glassworks in Wiesau near Sprottau, NL, Germany [1873–c.1937].

Grossherzögliche Hessische Edelglasmanufaktur See Darmstadt.

Grossräschen Glassworks in Grossräschen, Pfännerhütte NL, Germany [–]. Sig: triangle shape.

Groszart Glass Co Glassworks, location unknown [–], active c.1947, (tableware).

Grotteschi Type of art glass made by Venini and designed by Fulvio Bianconi and Paolo Venini, 1957.

Groviglie Venini art glass designed by Toni Zuccheri, 1964.

Groviglio Barovier & Toso art glass type by Ercole Barovier, 1940.

Gruber, Jacques Glass artist from France [1870–1938], worked for Daum before 1897 and was later independent.

Gründemann, Elke Glass engraver from Germany [1960–], worked at Glaswerk Schönborn after 1983.

GSK & L Glassworks location, unknown [–], active c.1894, (lighting).

Guasco Trade name for an early perfume burner/Berger lamp c.1900.

Gudovskis, Dainis Contemporary designer from Latvia, designs for Livanu Stiklas.

Guêpière Bottle with inward-curving opening in the bottom, which is used for catching wasps (guêpes) in orchards and gardens [19thC–present], aka fly catcher.

Guericolas Signature found on glass believed to be designed by Michel Colle for Cristalleries de Nancy in c.1920s.

Guérin, David Glass artist possibly from Turkey who worked in France c.1925–c.1945 for Cristallerie de Compiègne and Degué.

Guéron Signature signed by Edouard Cazaux.

Guernsey Glass Co Glassworks in Cambridge, OH, USA [1970–?].

Guest & Co, Joseph Glassworks located in Dudley, Great Britain [c.1780s–1899], aka Castle Foot Glassworks, operated by Homer and Renaud 1842–99, (tableware and cut glass).

Guest Brothers Glass decoration firm located in Brethell Lane, Stourbridge, Great Britain [c.1864–1918], decorators include Edvin Grice, (etched glass).

Guillotière, La Glassworks in Lyon, France [–], active 19thC, (opalines).

Gulbrandsen, Nora Glass designer from Norway [1894–1978].

Gullaskruf Glassworks in Gullaskruf, Sweden [1895–1920] and [1926–77], was bought by Royal Krona 1975–7, by Orrefors 1977 and finally closed in 1983. Designers include Hugo Gehlin 1930–53, Arthur Percy 1951–70, Kjell Blomberg 1954–75. Sig: rarely marked, labels only, sometimes factory + designer + pattern no in full. Some examples: G=Gehlin, P=Percy, label "Gullaskruf + mirrored GG" used in the 1920s and "G Gehlin Gullaskruf Sweden" in the 1930s, (bottles, flat glass, pressed glass, tableware and art glass).

Gunderson Glass Works Glassworks in New Bedford, MA, USA [1938–c.1957], previously Pairpoint, therefore often referred to as Gunderson-Pairpoint.

Gunderson, Jon Glass designer from Norway [1942–], worked for Hadelands after 1967.

Gundrum, Ivan Glass artist from Croatia working in the early 20th century.

Gunnarson, Håkan Glass designer from Sweden [–], worked for Strombergshyttan.

Gunther, Alfred Glass designer from Bohemia/Germany [1906–], worked for Kamenický Šenov school then for Ichendorfer Glashütte c.1976.

Günther, Karl Glass engraver from Bohemia [1808–83].

Guretsky, A Artist from Russia [–], produced glass decoration in the 1920s

Gushin, Oleg I Glass designer from Kiev, Ukraine [1938–], worked at the Kiev Factory after 1969 and also for UkrGlass.

Gus-Krushtalny Glassworks in Gus-Krushtalny, Vladimir province, Russia [1756–present], belonged to the Maltsov family after c.1850s. Designers include Aksyonov after 1969, Bychkov who was both a designer and chief designer 1958–62, Chukanov after c.1967, Egorov 1931–41, Filatov after 1959 (was chief designer after 1963), Ibraghimov after 1966, Korneyev after 1962, Kurilov after 1968, Lipskaya; Matushevskaya after 1951, Maximova, Muratov after 1966, Nevskaya; Pivovarov after 1959, Rogov after 1936, Rostovtseva; Savalieva, Tarkovskaya and Verin 1964–9, (cut glass, tableware and art glass).

Gustafsson, Gunnel Glass designer from Finland [1909–48], worked for Nuutajärvi 1946–8, Riihimäki 1930–48, Karhula 1933–7 and Iittala 1946–8.

Gutgesell, Kunstglasbläserei André Glass studio located in Ernstthal, Germany [1991–present], (lampworked art glass).

G over W Westmoreland Glass mark.

Gylden, Eva Artst from Finland [–], worked for Riihimäki c.1920s.

H 1. Mark for Holt Glass Works, in combination with numbers only. 2. Engraved mark for Erik Höglund.

H co G (inside a circle) Hocking Glass Co mark

H in a square diamond Heisey or reproduction mark.

H in diamond Heisey mark.

H with an A in lower half Hazel Atlas mark.

H Heye Annahütte, Glasfabrik Glassworks in Grossräschen b. Döbern near Sorau, NL, Germany [1863–present], founded as Emilienhütte, merged into Annahütte 1872, operated by H Heye 1884–1945, known as VEB Glaswerk Annahütte 1945–72, VEB Grossräschen-Annahütte 1973 then became VEB Glaswerk Döbern, Section Annahütte from 1987, (pressed glass, cut glass, tableware, lighting, coloured glass, bottles).

Habel see Elisabeth Glassworks in Kostany near Teplice, Czechoslovakia [–].

Häbermeier, Konrad Glass designer from Germany [1907], worked for WMF and Gralglashütte, (engraving, and sand blasting).

Habert-Dys, Jules Graphic artist from Fresnes, France [1850–1922], illustrator/designer at Nancy school after 1907, worked in glass 1910–14, esp. colour with metal inclusions. Sig: engraved JHD over X on bottom.

Hackel, Hieronymus Glass engraver from Bohemia [19thC].

Hackmann Designor Oy AB Tableware conglomerate from Helsinki, Finland [?–present], includes the glassworks of Iittala, Nuutajärvi and Humppila.

Haddock, Robert English engraver [–], worked at Sunderland 1854–69.

Hadeland's Glassverk Glassworks in Jevnaker, Norway [c.1762–present], designers include AE Boman after c.1911, Sverre Petterson 1926–49, Willy Johansson after 1942, Herman Bongard 1947–55, Severin Brörby 1956–c.1967, Gerd Slang 1948–52 and 1963–72, Arne Jon Jutrem after 1950, Benny Motzfeld 1955–67, Tias Eckhoff c.1951, Arvid Bakkene 1964–76, Gro Bergslien after 1964, Jon Gunderson after 1967, Edler Freij after 1976 and Ulla-Marie Brantenberg after 1976. Sig: various stickers; some glass engraved "Hadeland + designer initials", some with a logo, (tableware, art glass, pressed glass after 1857).

Haden, Mullett & Haden Glassworks located at Stourbridge, Great Britain [c.1900–c.1925], operated the Coalbournebrook Glassworks, (decorative glass, tableware, ruby, turquoise, opal, Victorian style).

Haefeli, Carl, Kristallglasfabrik AG Glassworks in Sarnen, Switzerland [–], active c.1955, (tableware).

Haerdtl, Oswald Glass designer from Vienna, Austria [1899–1959], worked with Josef Hoffmann 1922–39 at Wiener Werkstaette, Bakalowitz and Lobmeyr.

Haidemühler Glashüttenwerke GmbH Glassworks in Haidemühl near Spremberg, NL, Germany [–], operated by F A Kaennichen, known as VEB Glaswerk Haidemühl after 1946. Sig: H over ~ over + over HAIDEMÜHL on bottom, (tableware, bottles).

Hainaut, Verreries du Glass group from Belgium [1975–86], aka Vereno, grouped Scailmont, Michotte, Wauty, Chanteclair in Manage, Dur-o-Bor Manuel, Braine-le-Comte, Doverbel, Boussu (from 1982) and Doyen. Designers include Jean-Claude Faidherbe 1975–84 and Francoise Bacquaert 1974–86.

Haine-Saint Paul, Verrerie Glassworks in Mons, Belgium [1786–?].

Haiplick, Franz Glass cutter/engraver from Germany [1911–82], worked at Weisswasser c.1945–80.

Halama, František Glassworks in Železný Brod, Czech Republic [?–present], designers include Jindřich Tockstein, Prof Medek, Prof Přenosil and Prof Metelák. Halama glass is related in style to Schlevogt, Desná and Lalika, (pressed glass flask, novelties, figures, frosted, clear and malachite glass).

Hald, Edward Glass designer from Sweden [1883–1980], worked for Orrefors 1907–47 and then was freelance until the late 1970s, see also Gate and Lindstrand.

Hald Expo numbering 1-47-53=1953, 1-46-54=1954, 47-66-55=1955, 67-69-57=1957, 70-58=1958, 71-72-61=1961, VX1, VX45=1963, 73-63=1963, 100-117-E3=1973, 118-73=1973 and 119-125-78=1978.

Hald numbering on engraved glass H35-51-90-116=1917/8, H91-130=1919, H131-193=1920, H194-248=1921, H249-293=1922, H294-350=1923, H351-472=1924, H473-509=1925, H510-589=1926, H590-673=1927, H674-840=1928, H841-860=1929, H861-890=1930 and H891-948=1931.

Halem, Harry Studio glass artist from USA [–].

Haley, KR Glassware Co Glassworks in USA [–], active c.1970.

Half-post technique Bottle-making technique in which additional glass covers an initial bottle up to the shoulder.

Hall, William & Co Glassworks, location unknown [c.1897–c.1906], (tableware).

Hallesche Pfännerschaft, Glashütte Glassworks in Senftenberg, Elster but location also reported as Grossräschen near Calau, Germany [1876–c.1937–?]

Hallet, L Glass designer from Belgium [–].

Halling-Koch, Anne-Grete Glass designer from Denmark [–], worked for Holmegaard.

Halophane Taiwan reproduction of Holophane shades.

Ham, Frank van der Glass artist from Holland [1952–], (fused & slumped objects).

Ham Mfg Co, CT Glassworks, location unknown [–], active c.1913, (lighting).

Hameln, Glashütte Glassworks in Hameln, Germany [?–present], part of Rolf Wiemers Glashütten.

Hamendes, Verreries des, L Lambert & Cie Glassworks in Hamendes, in Jumet near Charleroi, Belgium [1963–present] and in Merksem near Antwerp [1963–present], their production was mechanized in 1952. Sig: L on a bell (bottles, demijohns and tableware in Jumet; bottles only in Merksem).

Hamilton, Frank Glass maker from USA [–], worked for Gentile Glass Co in the 1960s, (paperweights).

Hamilton Glass Works Glassworks in Hamilton, Ontario, Canada [1865–72]. Sig: Hamilton, (bottles).

Hamm, Henri Glass artist from France [–], specialized in luxury perfume bottles c.1907–c.1914. His work is unsigned and is often mistaken for Lalique.

Hammar, Göran [–], designer for Stockholms Glasbruk.

Hammond, David Glass designer from Great Britain [1931–], worked for Thomas Webb c.1958/9 and Edinburgh Crystal.

Hammonton Glassworks Glassworks in Hammonton, NJ, USA [1817–?], (bottles, flat glass and tableware).

Hamon Glass Co Glassworks in WV, USA.

Hamon, Robert Glass maker from Scott Depot, WV, USA [–], (paperweights in the1970s).

Hamrad Selena Glass series by Orrefors, designed by Sven Palmqvist in 1947, has a "hammered" surface. Marks: PA3111/1, 2.

Hamza, Erzébeth N Glass artist from Parádsasvár, Hungary [1944–], has been exhibiting since 1979.

Hand blown Made by hand, as opposed to machine made.

Hand cooler A small egg-shaped paperweight.

Hand finished Bottle and lip mould blown and hand-finished (c.1890–1911).

Hand pressed Made on a hand-operated pressing machine.

Handel Co Glassworks in Meriden, CT USA [1885–1936], named Eyden and Glass Decorators 1885, Handel & Co 1892 and Handel Company Inc in 1904. Fittings were bought from Miller Co 1885–1902 their own production was started after this but decoration was always done on bought blanks. Handel fixtures are often complemented by Quezal and Steuben shades, (lighting, art glass and cameo glass).

Handkerchief vase A vase in the shape of a handkerchief with the corners pulled up. First designed by Fulvio Bianconi for Venini in 1950, often copied. Proper name is Fazzoletto.

Handl, Milan Glass artist from Příbram, Czech Republic [1952–], workied with Libenský 1972–8, was independent after 1978.

Handler The worker who specializes in making handles. In Fenton baskets, every handler had his own mark to allow identification.

Handles Handles applied top end first were customary until c.1860. Applying them to the lower end first was customary after c.1860.

Hanel, Anton Glass engraver from Kuřivody, Czechoslovakia [1870–1925], worked at Nový Bor school 1885–1923. Sig: engraved HA, (acid-etched vases after c.1906).

Hans, Eugene & Cie Glassworks in Jumet, Belgium [–].

Hansel, Franz Glass engraver from Bohemia [1802–83].

Hansen Glass Co Glassworks in Mackinaw City, MI, USA [c.1960s–c.1970s]. Sig: RGH 1960s, "Ronald Hansen" or "Robert Hansen" in italic script, (pressed glass, modern carnival).

Hansen, Johnny Glass designer from Denmark [–], worked for Holmegaard.

Hansen, Théophil von Architect/glass designer from Austria [1813–91], worked for Lobmeyr c.1867.

Hantich & Co Glassworks in Nový Bor, Czechoslovakia [–], active c.1930.

Hanus, Vaclav Glass designer from Czechoslovakia [–], worked for national companies after c.1950s.

Hanzel, Franz Glass engraver from Bohemia [1803–83], worked at Baccarat c.1830.

Harbridge Crystal Glass Co Glassworks in Stourbridge, Great Britain [1928–50], (cut glass).

Harcuba, Jiří Glass artist from Harrachóv, Czech Republic [1928–], worked as an engraver/medal maker at Umělecké Sklo, Nový Bor after 1948, in Prague after 1971 and in various locations after c.1990.

Hard glass Used to indicate borosilicate glass in order to distinguish it from soft or sodalime glass, (lampwork).

Hardenburg, Blair R Glass maker from Corning, NY, USA [–], (paperweights 1960s–1970s).

Hardening (aka tempering) Hot glass cooled slowly in animal fat or margarine. This technique was invented in France in 1874.

Harland Glass Glass studio located in Wick, Scotland [1970–5]. See Paul Ysart and William Manson, (paperweights).

Harmon, James R Studio glass artists from NY, USA [1952–].

Harmony Glassworks Glassworks in South Jersey, USA [1813–1918], renamed Whitney after merging with Olive Glassworks in 1824 and was then taken over by Owens Bottle Co in 1918, (bottles, flasks and tableware).

Harrachóv Glassworks in Harrachóv, Nový Svet, Czech Republic [1630–present], it was bought by the Counts of Harrach in 1798, the art director was Julius Jelinek after 1901. Designers include Bohdan Kadlec c.1880s–1901, Carl Lederle c.1900, Jan Kotera, Jaroslav Horejc, Vladislav Hofmann and Milos Metelák. Sig: Harrach glass is rarely marked, but you may find "Harrach" or "Graf Harrach" etched or enamelled on pieces from c.1900–c.1925, a crowned fleur-de-lys in a shield c.1930s, a crowned H over 1712 c.1980s and "Glassworks N&S Bohemia Harrachóv/Czech Republic" after 1991, (cut crystal, tableware c.1850–c.1900, enamelled glass, cased glass, sulfures 1820s–30s, cameo, luxury glassware).

Harris, WM Glass designer from Great Britain [–], worked for WE Chance & Co Ltd, c.1960/1.

Harrop, Hammond & Co, Ltd Located in Brierley Hill, Staffordshire, Great Britain, ran Harts Hill Glass Works [–], active c.1885, (tableware).

Harrtil glass Glassware made by Harrachóv, Nový Svet, Czechoslovakia from 1955, (with inlaid colour threads).

Hashimoto, Kazuyo Glass designer and flamework artist from Osaka, Japan [–], worked for Kamei Glass Co 1963–5 and Daiwa Glass Co 1973–89.

Hartelt, L Glassworks in Jabloneč nad Nisou, Czechoslovakia [–], active c.1931.

Harts Hill Glass Works Glassworks in Great Britain [–], active c.1885, see Harrop and Hammond.

Hartzviller, Cristallerie de Glassworks in Metz, France [?–1999], (tableware).

Harzing, W Glass designer from the Netherlands [1898–1978], worked for Leerdam 1927/28.

Harzkristall GmbH, Staatliche Glasmanufaktur Glassworks in Derenburg near Wernigerode, Germany [1946–present], (tableware, vases in full lead crystal).

Hasek, Alois Glass designer from Prague, Czechoslovakia [–], working in the 1920s.

Haselbauer, Joseph Glass engraver from Bohemia [–], worked for TG Hawkes & Co, Corning c.1866–c.1910.

Hateley, James Glass maker located in Birmingham, Great Britain, working c.1887.

Häubner & Dobschall, Glashütte Glassworks in Reichenbach near Görlitz, Germany [1892–c.1937].

Haute Bretagne, Cristalline de Glassworks in Fougères, France [1921–present], trade name is CHB. Sig: sand-blasted mark CHB, (bottles, perfume display bottles, tableware, art glass, giftware).

Havré-Ville, Verrerie et Gobeleterie d' Glassworks in Havré, near Mons [1910–18], renamed Doyen in 1918.

Hawkes, Thomas Glassworks located in Dudley, UK [c.1770–1842], aka Dudley Flint Glass Works, closed 1842 and materials sold to Richardson at Wordsley. Designers include William Haden Richardson 1810–28, (bottles, cut glass, tableware, lighting, enamel after 1794, etching after 1830, gold enamel after 1834, opaline after 1840 and chandeliers.

Hawkes, TG & Co Glassworks in Corning, NY, USA [c.1888–c.1962], co-founder of Steuben with Carder, 1903, (tableware, cut glass, Brilliant period, blanks).

Hazard, Charles-François Glassmaker from Paris, France [1758–1812], (glass figures of celebrities).

Hazel Trade name of Hazel Glass Co, Wellsburg, WV [1886–1902], (bottles).

Hazel Atlas Co Glassworks in Wheeling, WV, USA [1902–55], founded in Washington, PA, USA, operated several pressed glass factories in OH, PA, WV, USA (esp. depression glass). Was bought by Continental Can Co in 1956 and continued as Hazel Ware. The tableware division was finally sold to Brockway Glass Co. Some of the moulds went to Colony Glass Co. Sig: H with an A in bottom half.

Hazel Ware See Hazel Atlas Co.

Hazlegrove, Page Studio artist from Great Britain [–].

Heat resistant glass Glass with a low coefficient of expansion, which means it is less liable to thermal shock. Borosilicate glass is the most common type.

Heaton, Maurice Glass designer from Switzerland [1907–], moved to USA in 1914, had his own studio at Nyack, NY, (glazing, murals, lighting from 1931, enamel 1947 and laminated glass from 1961).

Hechter, Daniel Trade name for designer glass made at Boussu 1978–82.

Heckert, Fritz Glassworks in Piechowice (Petersdorf), Silesia, Poland (used to be in Germany) [1866–1945], aka Petersdorfer Glashütte, merged with Josephinenhütte in 1923. Sig: gold numbers only, sometimes full sig, many pieces usually attributed to Loetz are believed to have been made by Heckert, (bottles and mirrors 1866–89, historical glass after 1870, "Jodhpur" glasses etched, gilded and transparent enamel 1875–1900, "Cypriot" art glass vases after 1898 designed by Max Rade and Ludwig Sütterlin, floral cameo, iridescent glass "Changeant","Chämeleon" and "Marmopal", gold enamel).

Hédon, François Glass designer from France [–], see Papes, Cristallerie des.

Hedwigshütte Glassworks in Döbern near Sorau, NL, Germany [1900–?], located in Teplitz near Sorau 1888–1900, known as Fettke & Co after 1900, Glaswerke Döbern 1946–52, Glaswerke Döbern 1953–6, VEB Glaswerk Döbern 1956–87, aka Glaswerk

Döbern; Niederlausitzer Hohl- und Kristallglaswerke, (containers and barware, lead crystal, cased glass – from 1969 only lead crystal).

Heemskerck, Henri Glass designer from Belgium [1886–1932], worked for painting department at Scailmont after 1924. Sig: HH.

Heesen, Bernard Glass artist from Leerdam, Holland [1958–], worked at De Oude Horn glass studio, Acquoy.

Heesen, Willem Glass designer/artist from Utrecht, Holland [1925–], worked for Leerdam 1947–77 and produced unica after1991, becoming their chief designer after 1967, then worked at De Oude Horn glass studio in Acquoy after 1977.

Heesen, Unica Letters, year, quantity produced: HA=1957(12), HB=1958(23), HC=1959(24), HD=1960(31), E/HEB=1961(51), HF/HFB=1962(31), AH=1963(25), HK=1964(57), L=1965(48), HO=1966(135), HP=1967(43), HR=1968(132), HS=1969(28), HT=1970(74), HV=1971(71), HW=1972(68), HAA=1973(11), HAB=1974(104), HAC=1975(173), HAD=1976(90) and HAE=1977(unknown).

Hegenbarth Söhne, Franz, Kristallglasraffinerie Glassworks in Ceská Kamenice, Czechoslovakia [–], active c.1920.

Heiligenstein, Auguste Glass artist from St Denis, France [1891–1976], worked at Legras 1902–6, Baccarat 1907–10, for Goupy at Rouard 1919–23, was independent after 1923, then at Verrerie Souchon-Neuvese 1926–31, Pantin 1931–5, only worked on ceramics 1945–51, was at Verrerie de Clairay 1951 and 1960–65. Sigs include: Heiligenstein, M Goupy, Mont Joye, Daum Nancy and Clairistal, (enamelled glass and acid-etched glass c.1931–5).

Heilman, Christopher Studio artist from USA [–].

Heinz Trade name for HJ Heinz Company, Pittsburgh, PA, USA [1860–present]. Sig: HJ Heinz 1860–9, Heinz & Noble 1869–72, FJ Heinz 1876–88 and HJ Heinz Co 1888–present, (bottles).

Heinz Glass Glassworks operated by Heinz sauces in Sharpsburg, PA, USA [c.1885–c.1915], first Heinz sauce 1869 and first ketchup in 1889 (pickle bottles etc).

Heinz Gmbh & Co Kg Carl Aug Glassworks in Kleintettau, Germany [1661–present], (cosmetic bottles).

Heinzel, Fritz Engraver from Silesia [1910–], worked at Josephinenhütte 1924–8, Harrachóv 1928–32, Muskauer Hohlglas 1933–40, Georg Stange Weisswasser 1948–50 and Glasgestaltung Weisswasser 1951–79.

Heisey & Co, AH Glassworks in Newark, OH, USA [1893–1958]. Sig: H inside raised diamond and H inside a squared diamond, (cut glass, etched tableware, pressed glass and novelties).

Heisler, Herbert Glass decorator from Germany [1934–], worked at Rietschen c.1965–c.1985.

Heitzmann, Theodore SA Glassworks in France [–], aka Cristallerie Lorraine.

Held Art Glass, Robert Glassworks in Vancouver, BC, Canada [c.1980–present], (art glass, paperweights, perfume bottles and giftware).

Helenenhütte Glassworks in Hartmannsdorf near Sprottau, NL, Germany [1862–c.1937] .

Helios Electric Co Glassworks, location unknown [–], active c.1909, (lighting).

Heller, Karl Glass decorator/designer [1886–1932], worked for Verreries et Gobeleteries in Manage, Belgium. Sig: Novelty.

Novelty

Heller, Paul Glass designer from Belgium [–], son of Karl Heller; trained at Verreries et Gobeleteries Nouvelles, Manage then was head decorator at Boom after 1935. Sig: Paul Heller, ARTVER, (black glass sanded in Art Deco style).

Hellman, Tina Glass designer from Sweden [–], worked for Bergdala Glass.

Hellsten, Lars Glass designer from Sweden [1933–], worked for Skrufs 1964–72 and Orrefors after 1972

Helme Trade name George W Helme Co, Jersey City, NJ, USA [1870–95], (bottles).

Helmschmied Manufacturing Co, Carl V Lighting Manufacturer located in USA [c.1900–c.1920], (leaded glass shades).

Helzel, August Glass engraver from Bohemia [1851–1931], worked for Lobmeyr engraving studios in Kamenický Šenov c.1880s.

Helzen, Brüder Glassworks in Germany [–], active c.1928, (lighting).

Hemingray Glass Co. Glassworks in Covington, KY, USA [1864–c.1933], previously known as Hemingray Brothers & Co, (bottles and insulators).

Hennix, Erik and Margareta Glass designers from Sweden [both 1941–], worked for Johansfors and at Pukeberg.

Hens-on-the-nest Covered pressed glass animal dishes made their first appearance in Germany c.1895 and were an instant hit. The largest producer has been Valérysthal since 1907. Many Valérysthal originals were reproduced in the US after 1945.

Hentschel Glashütte Glassworks in Rauscha near Görlitz, Germany [1886–c.1937].

Hentschke, Glasschleiferei Lothar Glass-cutting works located in Weisswasser, Germany [?–present], (cut glass).

Heppell & Co, WH Glassworks in Newcastle, Great Britain [c.1874–85], their moulds were sold to Davidson in 1885 (pressed glass, clear, opaque white and marbled, lighting, lenses etc).

Heraut & Guignard Glass decorators from France and owners of Le Rosey shop for tableware/art glass, which bought Léveillé

in 1906.

Herbatte Glassworks in Herbatte, Belgium [1851–1934], in 1853 known as SA de Herbatte-lez-Namur, then merged with Namuroises in 1867. Exported to various countries worldwide, (tableware, pressed glass, cut glass, opaline, gilt and enamelled glass, pressed glass and from 1879–1934 produced blown semi-crystal, novelties and paperweights). The company actually briefly reopened 1946–9 after its closure in 1934 but just produced lighting.

Herbert, William Glass engraver from Stourbridge, Great Britain [1806–], worked for Thomas Hawkes at Dudley 1828–42 and was later based in Bristol.

Herman, Samuel Glass designer from USA [1936–], studied with Littleton, worked in Great Britain after 1966, founded The Glasshouse studio in 1969, worked for Val St Lambert c.1970 and his VSL items were produced until 1979, set up The Jam Factory in Australia 1974–8 and had his own glass studio in Chelsea Wharf, Great Britain after 1978.

Hermanova Hut Glassworks in Plzen, Czech Republic [1907–present], in 1909 the production of pressed glass was reported, part of Sklo Union, current name is Sklarna Hermanova Hut AS. Sig: HH, (pressed glass and still producing "beaded edge" or "Kugelrand" pattern).

Hermelin, Carl Glass designer from Sweden [1897–1979], worked for Orrefors after 1922, Sandvik 1926–30, Pukeberg 1930–40 and Alsterfors Glasbruk after 1941.

Hermès Dealer in luxury tableware from Pantin, France [?–present], marketed by Cie Des Arts de la Table.

Herminenhütte Glassworks in Rietschen near Rothenburg, Germany [1873–c.1937], operated by A F Vollprecht, and was previously known as Gebr Schober & Co, (lighting).

Hero Glass Works Located in Philadelphia, PA, USA [1884–1909], (bottles).

Heron Glass Glassworks in Ulverston, Cumbria, Great Britain [?–present], (paperweights, lamps and lighting, giftware, coloured and lustered glass).

Herrfeldt, JH & Co Glassworks in USA [–], (cut glass, Brilliant period).

Herrmann, Pepi, Crystal, Inc Glassworks in USA [–], active c.1976, (cut glass).

Herzog, Ernst Glass engraver from Frauendorf, Germany [1908–], worked at Hoffmann, Glashütte 1923–39 and VEB Ankerglas 1949–73.

Herzog, Glasbläserei Reinhard Glass blower located in Wertheim, Germany, working now.

Hessen-Glaswerke GmbH Glassworks in Stierstadt, Taunus, Germany [–], active c.1950, (tableware).

HF Signature used by Hubert Fouarge.

HFM Mark found on Fostoria giftware made for the Henry Ford Museum

HG Heraut & Guignard, see Léveillé.

HH Signature for Henri Heemskerck.

Hibbeln, Wilhelm German industrialist [1847–1903] set up a wholesale business in gas light in Amsterdam 1869–1914 supplying Holland, Germany, Belgium and northern France with gas light from his own factories in Wickede and Radeburg. Hibbeln supplied light fixtures for the Eiffel tower, 1896.

Hickisch Glassworks in Arnultovice near Bor, Czechoslovakia [–], active c.1905).

Hiesz, Géza Sculptor from Hungary [–], worked for Etling c.1920s, (animal figures).

Higbee Glass Co, John B Glassworks in Bridgeville, PA, USA [1897–1918], known as Bryce, Higbee 1879–1907, their trade mark is a raised bee, (pressed glass).

Higgins & Seiter Glassworks, location unknown [c.1898–c.1911], (cut glass).

Higgins, Frances Glass artist from the USA [–], had a glassworks with husband Michael 1948–58 then worked for Dearborn Glass Co after 1958.

Higgins, Michael Glass artist from Great Britain [1908–] had a glassworks with wife Frances 1948–58 then worked for Dearborn Glass Co after 1958, (enamel design on flat glass).

Hildebrand Glashütte Glassworks in Scheckthal near Hoyerswerda near Kamenz, Germany [1877–?], was reported to be located in Kunzendorf near Sorau, Germany [c.1937–?].

Hileley, PW Studio artist from USA [–].

Hill, James Glass engraver from Great Britain [–], worked for Stevens & Williams.

Hill Ouston Firm of retailers located in Birmingham and London [1920s–30s], (reproduction glassware, cut glass replicas, bubble glass, clear and coloured tableware).

Hiller, Rudolf Glass designer from Austria, worked for Ludwig Moser c.1880.

Hilton, Eric Glass designer from Great Britain [1936–].

Hindricks & Co Lighting manufacturer located in Germany [19thC], (student lamps).

Hingley L & S & Sons Glassworks in Stourbridge, Great Britain [–], active c.1928.

Hinks & Son Ltd, James Lighting manufacturer located in Birmingham, Great Britain with sales outlets in London, India, South Africa and Australia [1847–1970], taken over by Falk Stadelman 1925; trading ceased 1970, (lighting – oil, gas and electric, Duplex burner patented 1865, Art Nouveau lamps c.1907).

Hinz, Darryle Glass designer from Denmark [1949–], worked for Afors 1974/75, Boda 1975–8, Bornholm after 1978 and Holmegaard.

Hinzelin, Gobeletterie Glassworks in Croismare, Nancy, France [?–1919], bought by Muller Frères in 1919.

Hirota Glass Co Ltd Glass decorating company located in Tokyo, Japan [1899–present], (tableware, art glass, giftware, and barware in crystal, sodalime and opal).

Hirsch & Janke, Glashütte Glassworks in Weisswasser near Rothenburg, OL, Germany [1884–c.1937].

Hirsch AG, Glashütte Glassworks in Schmölln near Bautzen, OL, Germany [1896–c.1937].

Hirsch, Glashütte R Glassworks in Döbern near Sorau, Germany [1876–c.1937], known as Glashütte Adolf Hirsch & Co 1896, as

Glashütte Hirsch, Mielisch & Co 1902, also noted as Glashütte Gebr Hirsch and Adolf Hirsch & Co c.1907.

Hirschberg, Kristallglaswerk Glassworks in Allendorf, Marburg, Germany [–], active c.1954, formerly known as Kristallglaswerk Hirschberg der Steinkohlenbergwerke Mathias Stinnes AG Essen. Designers include Wilhelm Wagenfeld and Wilhelm Braun-Feldweg.

Hirtreiter Glaskunst Glassworks in Frauenau, Bavaria, Germany [?–present].

Historical glass Glass from the 19thC with heraldic enamelling, made by many glassworks in Germany and Bohemia c.1880–c.1920.

Hlava, Pavel Glass designer/artist from Prague, Czech Republic [1924–], worked for central institutions 1952–85, Borske sklo 1956–c.1964, ŽBS 1964/5, Včelnička works Ceský Křistal c.1974/5 and was then an independent artist after 1985.

Hlousek, R Glassworks in Czechoslovakia [–], active c.1920s.

Hoare, J & Co Glassworks in Corning, NY, USA [1854–1920], Hoare is the oldest cutting shop in the US and symbolizes more than 1,000 small cut glass workshops located in the eastern USA between 1880–1915 (known as the "Brilliant period"), all producing similar, mostly unsigned, cut glass patterns. Sig: block letters, acid-stamped HOARE 1900–20, (cut glass).

Hoare, John Glass maker located in Corning, NY, USA [1853–68], worked as Hoare & Burns, Hoare & Daily, Gould & Hoare, which became Hoare, J & Co, (cut glass).

Hobbs, Brockunier & Co/US Glass H Glassworks in Wheeling, WV, USA [1845–91], founded as Hobbs & Barnes, renamed Hobbs, Brockunier & Co in 1863, taken over by US glass and known as Factory H 1891, dismantled shortly after, (tableware, cut glass after 1845, pressed glass, paperweights 1880s, sodalime glass developed 1864, art glass after the 1880s including opalescent, spangled and amberina).

Hobnail cut See Diamond cut.

Hobnail, opalescent Developed by Hobbs Brockunier & Co, 1886.

Hoboken de Bie, A van Gin distiller from Rotterdam, Holland [1800–98], owned NV Bottleworks after 1855. Sig: AVH A (aka Van Hoboken & Co).

Hoboken, Gobeleterie d' Glassworks in Hoboken/ Antwerp, Belgium [1903–?], (tableware).

Hobson, Diana Studio artist from Great Britain [–].

Hocking & Co Glassworks in Lancaster, OH, USA [1905–69], merged with Anchor Cap & Closure into Anchor Hocking in 1937. Sig: H co G inside a circle, (pressed glass).

Hodgetts, Joshua Intaglio engraver from Great Britain [–], worked for Stevens & Williams; made cameo with the Northwood team c.1887–c.1897.

Hoff, Paul Glass designer from Sweden [1945–], worked for Kosta Boda 1972–82 and Studioglas AB/Strömbergshyttan c.1987.

Hoffmann, Arthur Glass designer from Germany [–], worked for Sachsenglas Ottendorf-Okrilla 1935–62.

Hoffmann, Emanuel Glass engraver from Bohemia [1819–78].

Hoffmann Glashütte Gebr Glassworks in Bernsdorf near Hoyerswerda, OL, Germany [1872–1945], known as Gebr Hoffmann, later as Ankerglas.

Hoffmann, Glashütte Max Glassworks in Neu Petershain near Calau, NL, Germany [1916–c.1937].

Hoffmann, Heinrich Glassworks in Jabloneč nad Nisou, Czechoslovakia [–], active c.1935.

Hoffman, Johan F Glass engraver from Karlovy Vary, Czechoslovakia [1840–1900].

Hoffmann, Johann Glass designer from Austria [?–1883], worked for Ludwig Moser c.1880.

Hoffmann, Josef Architect and glass designer from Moravia, worked in Vienna, Austria [1870–1956], founded Wiener Werkstätte in 1903, produced glass designs for Loetz c.1899–1913 and introduced new colours: cream white, dark blue, light green and red with black, dark blue and dark red. Worked for Lobmeyr 1910–25 – his 1925 tableware was also produced in 1955/6. His glass designs were produced by Oertel, Schappel, Meyr's Neffe, Moser and the Wiener Werkstätte, (geometrical shapes, cameo and innovative cut glass).

Hoffmann, Maximilian, Glaswerk Glassworks in Neu Petershain near Calau, NL, Germany [1916–c.1937].

Hofman, Robert Glass designer from Belgium [1910–81], worked for Scailmont and Familleureux after c.1938.

Hofmantorps Glasbruk Glassworks in Hovmantorp, Sweden [c.1873–c.1954].

Hofstätter, Franz Glass designer/decorator from Austria [1871–1958], worked for Loetz c.1900/11.

Hogan, James (aka Edmond) Glass designer from Great Britain [1883–1948], was the director at Whitefriars c.1920–c.1930.

Höglund, Erik Sylvester Glass designer from Sweden [1932–98], worked for Kosta Boda 1953–73, Pukeberg and Lindshammar 1978–81, was independent 1973–98, worked for Vrigstads in 1986 and Strömberg c.1987. Sig: H.

Höglund, Erika Glass designer and ceramicist from Sweden [–], has worked for Målerås Glasbruk since 1996.

Holl, Glas und Porzellanmalerei Marion Glass decorating firm located in Krauschwitz, Germany [?–present], (painting on glass).

Holly Amber Design by Indiana Tumbler, 1903, (art glass and pressed glass).

Holly Hall Glassworks See Joseph Stevens & Co.

Holmegaard's Glasvaerk Glassworks in Holmegaard, Denmark [1825–present], renamed Royal Copenhagen in 1985 and is currently part of Royal Scandinavia A/S. Designers include Michael Bang 1968–74, Per Lütken 1942–98, Ole Winther, c.1965/66, Sidse Werner, Darryle Hinz, Anja Kjaer, Torben Jørgensen, Lone Ostenfeld, Johnny Hansen,

Allan Scharff, Ole Kortzau after 1976, Arje Griegst after 1983, Anne-Grete Halling-Koch, Malene Lütken, Peter Svarrer after 1997, Tora Urup after 1995. Sig: usually marked HG or Holmegaard since c.1945, PL monogram for Per Lütken and/or pattern number since c.1945, crowned swan labels 1930s and Royal Copenhagen labels c.1990s, (tableware, bottles, art glass, cut glass, paperweights and flat glass), see also Kastrup.

Holmes, Peter Glass maker from Scotland [–], worked at Caithness Glass, Scotland 1960s–1977 and at Selkirk Glass, Scotland after 1977, (paperweights).

Holmgren, Christer Glass designer from Sweden [1933–], worked for Kastrup-Holmegaard after 1957.

Holmgren-Exner, Christel Glass designer from Austria [1940–], worked for Kastrup-Holmegaard after 1968.

Holophane Lighting Corp Manufacturer located in Paris, France [1879], in New York [1898–1900] and in Newark, USA, OH [1900–?], trade names include Flecfrac, Lunar, Polar, Prismolier, Satin Finish and Razl-Dazl, (lighting: shades, pressed, mostly signed; the glass was actually produced by neighbour Heisey).

Holophane, SA Francaise Glassworks in Andelys, France [–], (lighting), see also Holophane Lighting Corp and Verlys.

Holt Glass Works Located in West Berkley, CA, USA 1893–1906.

Holton, Paul Glass maker from Corning, NY, USA [–], (paperweights in the 1940s).

Holubetz, Robert Glass designer from Austria [–], worked for Loetz c.1901.

Holyrood Flint Glass Works Glassworks in Edinburgh, Scotland [1835–1904], designers include John Ford, (cut glass and paperweights).

Homer & Renaud See Guest & Co.

Homestead Glass Works Glassworks in Pittsburgh, PA, USA [1879–1911], aka Bryce, Higbee & Co, (pressed glass).

Honda, Norimichi Glass designer from Japan [–], worked for Sasaki Glass Co, Japan c.1967/8.

Honesdale Decorating Co Glassworks in Honesdale, PA, USA [1901–32], (cut glass, gold-decorated and Art Nouveau glass).

Honeycomb cane Paperweight cane with a honeycomb pattern. Baccarat and Islington both produced it.

Hongell, Göran Glass designer from Finland

[1902–73], worked for Karhula-Iittala 1933–54 but his "Aarne" glasses from 1948 are currently in production.

Honzik, Stanislav Glass designer from Czechoslovakia [–], worked for Borsic Skló c.1961/2.

Hoosier Glass Furniture works located in USA [–], gave away sets of depression glass with their cabinets.

Hope Glass Works Glassworks in Providence, RI, USA [1872–1951], (cut glass).

Hopea, Saara Glass designer from Finland [1925–84], worked for Nuutajärvi/Wärtsilä 1952–c.1960.

Hora, Ljubomir Glass artist from Brno, Czech Republic [1946–], had own lampwork studio in München, after Germany 1975 and own studio oven after 1983. Sig: all pieces are needle-signed "Hora + year" or "Studio Hora + year", (lampwork/oven and various techniques).

Hora, Peter Glass artist from the Czech Republic [–].

Horacek, Vaclav Glass designer from Czechoslovakia [1948–], (cut glass).

Horányi, Agnes Glass artist from Budapest, Hungary [1946], has been exhibiting since 1971.

Hordijk Signature found on commemorative slumped glass made by Maastricht c.1945–c.1953.

Horejc, Jaroslav Sculptor/glass designer from Prague, Czechoslovakia [1886–1963], worked for Artel after 1912, Lobmeyr c.1921/5 and also worked at Harrachóv. Worked until c.1960 but his designs were reissued at Borske Sklo in 1960.

Horn, de Oude Glass studio located in Acquoy, Holland [1977–present], operated by Bernard and Willem Heesen.

Horta, Victor Famous Belgian Art Nouveau architect [1861–1947] had some lighting realized by VSL 1894–7 but is not known to have contributed to factory production.

Hosch, Carl Glassworks in Nový Bor, Czechoslovakia [c.1864/68–c.1939], (tableware, art glass, and lighting).

Hosena Glaswerke Glassworks in Hosena-Hohenbocka near Hoyerswerda, OL, Germany [1896–?], known as Glaswerke Gebr von Streit GmbH in 1936 and VEB Glaswerk Hosena after 1945, (pressed glass).

Hospodka, Josef Glass designer from Czechoslovakia [–], worked for Borské Sklo c.1961/2.

Houdaille & Triquet Glassworks in Choisy-le-Roi, France [c.1912–28], merged with Choisy-le-Roi 1928 and was known under the new name Cristalleries et Verreries Réunies de Choisy-le-Roi, see Choisy-le-Roi.

Houillez, A Glass sculptor from Nancy who was a pupil of Colotte; made chiselled crystal on Daum blanks c.1930–c.1940.

House of Marbles See Teign Valley Glass.

Houserová, Ivana Industrial designer/Glass artist from Jablonec, Czech Republic [1957–] worked at Prague Academy 1976–82 and at Moser 1997.

Houston, James Glass designer from Canada [1921–], worked for Steuben after 1962.

Hovenden R & sons Glassworks in London, Great Britain [c.1875–?], (bottles).

Hoya Crystal Corporation Glassworks in Tokyo, Japan [1958–present], designers include Saburo Funakoshi after 1957, Fumio Sassa, Akira Shirahata and AK Kawakami, (crystal giftware, cut crystal, tableware, pressed glass, clocks, technical, optical glass, lenses and art glass after 1979).

Hoyerswerda Glassworks in Hoyerswerda, Germany [1877–1931], see Vereinigte Glasfabriken Strangfeld & Hannemann.

Hrastnik dd, Steklarna Glassworks in Hrastnik, Slovenia [1860–present], (barware).

Hrdina, W Glassworks, location unknown [–], active c.1931, (lighting).

Hrodek, Karl Glass artist from Bohemia [–], had an engraving studio at Umělecké Sklo, Nový Bor c.1948.

Hrtska, Miroslav Glass designer from Czechoslovakia [1933–83], worked for Venini.

HS Abbreviation for Hutchinson Stopper, (bottles).

HS (encircled) Trade name used by Twitchell & Schoolcraft.

Hudcov Glassworks in Hudcov, Czechoslovakia [?–1886].

Hudson, Thomas English engraver [–], worked at Newcastle c.1820s–c.1840s.

Huguet-Moreau Glassworks, location unknown [c.1890–c.1900], (lights).

Hultström, Gustaf Adolf ("Karl") Glass engraver from Sweden [1884–1973], worked for Kosta 1919–24. Sig: usually full name + year.

Humppila Glassworks in Humppila, Finland [?–present], operated as part of Hackman Designor/littala/Nuutajärvi group, designers include Pertti Santalahti 1971–81 and Kajja Aarikka 1972–87, (pressed glass and tableware).

Hungarian glass Glassworks include Ajkai Üveggyár in Ajka, Bereg Crystal in Vasarosnameny, Zlatno (Zahn) in Losoncz on the Slovakian border, Miskolci Üveggyár in Miskolci, Paradi Üveggyár in Parádsavár, Ujantalvölgy and Zayngróc in Northern Hungary and Zera-Crystal in Halimba.

Hunnebelle, André Glass manufacturer from France [1896–?], warehouse for luxury wares on the Champs Elysées in Paris 1927–38), sig A Hunnebelle, "Modèle de A Hunnebelle & R Cogneville-France", (art glass, tableware, lighting, geometric patterns and opalescent glass).

Hunt Glass Co Glassworks in Corning, NY, USA [1895–c.1912], (cut glass on blanks from Corning and Union, Brilliant period).

Huntington Glass Co Glassworks in New Brighton, PA, USA [1888–97] and in Huntington, WV 1891–7, then Royal Glass Co, Marietta OH 1897–99 and became part of National Glass in 1899.

Huntingdon Tumbler Co Glassworks in Huntingdon, WV, USA [–], active c.1925, (tableware).

Huntley, GW & Co Glassworks, location unknown [–], active c.1919, (tableware).

Hunyadi Janos Signature found on bottles produced by Andreas Saxlehner in Budapest,

Hungary 1863–1900.

Husted, Wayne Glass designer from the US [–], worked for Blenko 1953–64, (modernistic glass design).

Huta Skzla Gospodarczego 'Dabrowa' Glassworks in Huta Dabrowa, Poland [?–present], (vases, jugs etc).

Huta Skzla Gospodarczego Tadeusz Wrześniak Glassworks in Skrzyszów, Poland [?–present].

Huta Skzla Ozdobnego Makora sc Glassworks in Krosno, Poland [?–present]. See Makora

Hutchinson stopper Bottle-closing device that clamps a rubber ring to the inside of a bottle with a spring wire loop, in use 1879–1912.

Hütte German for glassworks.

Hutton, John Glass designer from New Zealand [1906–], moved to Great Britain in 1935, (engraving, panels and architectural glass c.1950s–c.1970s).

HWC See Egizia.

Hyalith Black opaque glass, developed in Czechoslovakia by Count Bucquoy c.1807, popular around 1840, especially with gold decoration. It was also made by Friedrich Egermann.

Hydmann-Vallien, Ulrica Glass designer from Sweden [1938–], worked for Afors after 1963, Kosta Boda after 1972 and Pilchuck 1981–8.

Hydrofluoric acid A highly corrosive acid that attacks glass. It is used for marking, matting, etching, polishing.

Hyllinga Glasbruk Glassworks in Malmö, Sweden [–], designers include Bengt Orup c.1963/66, (hand-blown crystal, tableware).

I inside O Owens Illinois mark (with or without a diamond through it).

Ibanez Glass refinery located in Marseille, France [1948–present], (decoration, bottles, cosmetic, tableware, lighting).

Ibraghimov, Fidail Glass designer from Azerbaijan [1938–], worked at Gus-Krushtalny after 1966 and at Workshops of Applied Art Moscow after 1969, (glass painting).

Ibraghimov, Jalil Baba Ogly Glass designer from Baku, Azerbaijan [1935–], worked at Baku Glassworks after 1967.

Ice glass 1. A Venetian technique from the 16thC whereby hot glass is dipped in cold water, reheated and finished. The result looks like cracked ice. Aka Cracquelé (Fr) or Crackle. 2. Technique whereby the glass is rolled in splinters, covering the surface with an ice-like appearance, usually referred to as overshot glass.

Ice lip US term referring to a guard at the spout of a pitcher to keep ice from falling out of it.

Ichendorf Dorotheenhütte Glassworks in Bergheim-Ichendorf, Germany [–], active c.1960, designers include Alfred Gunther c.1976, see also their operators, Dorotheenhütte.

Icknield Glass Works Glassworks in

Birmingham, Great Britain [c.1850–c.1900], see Osler, who produced at the glassworks.

Idahütte, Idathal Glassworks in Vimperk, Idino Údolí, Czechoslovakia [1852–1945], founded by Jan Meyr, part of Meyr's Neffe after c.1852 and W Kralik after 1898.

Ideal Cut Glass Co. Glassworks in Corning, NY, USA [1904–34], moved to Syracuse, NY in 1909, (cut glass, Brilliant period).

Ide, T & W Glassworks in Great Britain [–], active c.1975.

Ifavidro/Indústria de Fabricação de Vidros Glassworks in the Marinha Grande region of Portugal [?–present], (decorative glass, modern style), see Marinha Grande and Mglass.

Iglehart, Edward Glass maker from Scotland [–], (lampwork c.1975).

IGW See Islington Glass Works.

Ihmsen Glass Co Located in Pittsburg, PA [1870–95], bottle marks include I G Co, (bottles).

Iittala/Iittalan Lasitehdas Glassworks in Iittala, Finland [1881–present], designers include Alvar Aalto c.1936; Markku Salo 1985–present, Heikki Orvola 1972–present, Brita Flander 1998, Tapio Wirkkala 1946–85, Tina Nordström after 1988, Timo Sarpaneva after 1950, Nathalie Lahdenmäki after 1997, Irina Viippola 1997, Kerttu Nurminen 1972–present, Göran Hongell 1933–54, Aino Aalto 1932, Stefan Lindfors 1999, Kaj Franck 1946–73, Harri Koskinen after 1996, Elina Joensuu after 1995, Oiva Toikka 1981–present, Kati Tuominen-Niittylä 1993, Markus Eerola 1997. Sig: designer tableware sometimes marked with initials eg TW for Wirkkala, TS for Sarpaneva but usually unmarked, art glass marked with designer initials or name + factory name "Karhula" after 1946, iittala after 1946, sometimes with year or model number added, sand-blasted marks are recent, Karhula label printed with a bear and KARHULA label before 1946, circular IITTALA label over a decanter with two glasses until 1956, shield-shaped IITTALA label with a cut vase before 1956, oval IITTALA label until 1956, white I in a red dot 1956–present, see Hackman Designor, Nuutajärvi and Karhula, (tableware, art glass, pressed glass and cut glass).

iittala
FINLAND

Ikora 1. Trade name for glass internally decorated with metal oxides, air bubbles and white tin netting from WMF 1926–36 and c.1947–c.1955, main designer Karl

Wiedmann. 2. Ikora is also used as a trade name for silvered or enamelled hollow metalware.

Ilanit Glass refinery located in Israel [c.1980–?], acid stain décor on blanks from France and Italy.

Illenberger, Karl Glass designer/engraver from Germany [1907–], worked for WMF 1926–37 and 1946–72.

Illig, John N Glassworks in USA [–], active c.1900, (cut glass, Brilliant period).

Illinois Glass Co Glassworks in Alton, IL, USA [c.1890–c.1929], trade names include IG and IG Co. Sig: IG 1900–28, ILL Glass Co 1916–29, IG before 1890, IG Co in a diamond 1900–16 and IG Co monogram c.1914, (bottles).

Illinois Pacific Glass Co Based in San Francisco, CA [1902–32]. Sig: IPG in a diamond 1925–30, (bottles).

Illzach, Ringer Glass artist from France [–], made art glass in lost wax process at Burgun, Schwerer & Co 1904–15, see Ringer.

Ilmenau Town in Germany where glass was produced since 1675; glassworks include Alt AG, Fischer-Hütte, Ilmenauer Glashütte, Ilmkristall, Langs-Hütte, Rosalinglaswerk, Sophienhütte, Spessart-Hütte and Technisches Glas Ilmenau.

Ilmenauer Glashütte (II) Glassworks in Ilmenau, Germany [1836–60], production was transferred to Stützerbach in 1860 (hollow ware and tubes).

Ilmenauer Glaswerke GmbH/Sophienhütte Glassworks in Ilmenau, Germany [c.1980–c.1999], trade names include Ilmglas and Ilmkristall, (art glass).

Ilmkristall Art glass produced by Sophienhütte, Germany 1983–1990.

Imbert & Cie Glassworks in France [c.1870–c.1885], aka Verreries Réunies de Sars-Poteries (Nord).

Imex (Kyn) Glass dealer located in Bialystok, Poland [?–present], (tableware, decorative items, crystal and lead crystal).

Imperial Glass Co Glassworks in Bellaire, OH, USA [1904–84]. Imperial owned many Heisey and Cambridge moulds and even reproductions made by Imperial are collectable in the US. The company was owned by Lenox, Inc of New Jersey 1973–81, by A Lorch, in 1981, R Stahl 1981–4 and then went bankrupt and was sold to Lancaster Colony 1984. Sig: pressed items marked Nucut or Nuart or Iron Cross logo after 1914, IM*PE/RIAL over iron cross logo 1904–51, freehand ware unmarked, label only 1924–31, oval label used 1939, interlocked G and I on reissued carnival glass 1951–72, label in shape of USA 1970s (not shown), interlocked G and L for Imperial Glass Liquidation Corp 1973–81, ALIG 1981–2 and NI for New Imperial 1983–4, (pressed glass, carnival and tableware).

Imperial Glassworks Glassworks in St Petersburg, Russia [c.1800–?].

Imperial Lighting Products Glassworks in Bellaire, OH, USA [1901–72], part of Imperial Glass Co.

IMVAT Glassworks in Murano, Italy [–], active c.1967, (giftware, souvenirs).

Incalmo Two hot, open-sided pieces of blown glass are joined together along their two edges of equal circumference in order to obtain different colour zones in the same object.

Incalmo, A Venini art glass designed by Carlo Scarpa in 1942, by Gio Ponti in 1946 and by Fulvio Bianconi, 1948.

Incalmo Type of art glass made by Venini designed by Thomas Stearns, 1962, designed by Tapio Wirkkala in 1970/2 and designed by Ove Thorssen and Brigitte Karlsson in 1976.

Incamiciato (It) Having a double wall; colour-cased lattimo, aka opalina.

Incisi Venini art glass designed by Paolo Venini, 1956.

Inciso A surface that has been fine wheel engraved, creating a satinated appearance.

Indiana Signature found on poppy-decorated cameo art glass made by Legras c.1900/14

Indiana Glass Co Glassworks in OH Steubenville, USA [1907–present], originally known as Beatty-Brady Glass Co 1850–1907, also located Dunkirk, IN but currently based in Cincinnati, OH. There is also a works based in Sapulpa, OK known as Bartlett-Collins Glass Company 1907–present. The company was bought by Lancaster Colony but still operates under its own name, (pressed glass and depression glass).

Indiana Tumbler & Goblet Co Glassworks in Greentown, IN, USA [1853–1903], became part of National Glass in 1899 and burned down in 1903, (pressed glass).

Industria Vetraria Valdarnese See IVV

Industrie Vetri Artistici Murano Glassworks in Murano, Italy [1922–31], designers include

Industrial Glassmaking School

Libero Vitali and Flavio Poli after 1929.

Industrial Glassmaking School Glassworks in Kamenický Šenov, Czechoslovakia [–], active c.1890, see School of Glassmaking.

Informali Venini art glass designed by Fulvio Bianconi, 1967.

In-Fusão Glassworks in the Marinha Grande region of Portugal [?–present], (flat glass, fusing, slumping and architectural).

Inge-Glas GmbH&Co KG Glassworks in Neustadt, Germany [?–present], (glass Christmas ornaments).

Ingrand, Max Glass designer from France [–], worked for Fontana Arte, Italy c.1957–c.1964.

Ingridglas (IG) Glass dealer currently located in Germany, (florist supplier).

Ingrid Glashütte Glassworks in Braunau am Inn, Austria [1874–1924 and 1945–79], (lead crystal).

Inland Glass Co Glassworks in USA [–], active c.1924, known as Inland Glass Works Inc c.1936 and Inland Glass Works, a division of Chamberlain Inc c.1939, (lighting).

Inncrystal Glas GmbH Glassworks in Braunau am Inn, Austria [?–present], trade names include Lisa Mori since 2000. Sig: acid-etched mark on "Lisa Mori" tableware, (tableware, cut glass and crystal).

Institút Szkla I Kerámiki Glassworks in Kráków, Poland [?–present].

Insufflated glass Aka mould blown glass.

Intaglio Glass A decoration cut below the glass surface.

Intarsia Type of art glass produced by Steuben c.1920s.

Intarsio Barovier & Toso art glass type by Ercole Barovier, 1961/3.

Intercalaire Glass that has colour inclusions between clear layers of glass; first patented in 1899 by Daum.

Inverted baluster See Baluster.

Inwald, Josef Glassworks and refineries conglomerate with head office and subsidiaries located in Vienna, Budapest, Prague, London and Paris. It has factories in Vienna Floridsdorf, Deutsch-Schützendorf, Grosspriesen an der Elbe, Praha-Slichov, Bad Podebrad and Rudolfshütte, Teplice-Sanov [c.1914–c.1950]. Works include Koštánské, Kamenný Pahovek, Libochovice, Rudolfová Hut, Hermanová Hut and Elsahutte. Glass designers include Rudolf Schötter 1920s and 1930s. Trade names include Asteroid, Azunit, Imperator, Luxodin, Malvit, Pyroplex, Reflektin, Transmitin, Transopal, (tableware, carnival pressed glass and cut glass).

Iowa City Flint Glass Co Aka Flint Glass Manuf Co.

IPG Trade name used by Illinois Pacifc Glass Corp.

Ipsen, Kent F Glass artist from Milwaukee, WS, USA [1933–], works in Richmond, VA.

IRA-Glasveredelungs GmbH Glass refinery from Zwiesel, Germany [?–present], (tableware).

Irena S.A., Huta Szkla Gospodarczego Glassworks in Inowroclav, Poland [?–present], (cut glass giftware, crystal animal figures, enamel-painted barware, cut-to-clear, crystal and sodalime glass).

Iridato (It) Iridescent.

Iridescence A shiny metallic finish obtained by spraying metal oxides onto hot glass. Popular since the late 19thC, after the discovery of iridescent Roman glass in Pompeii. Iridized glass was first presented at the Vienna exhibition in 1873 by JG Zahn and by JG Zahn and this example was soon followed by Lobmeyr, Webb, Riedl Glass and Pantin in 1878 and Richardson after 1878. Iridescence is also the distinguishing characteristic of Carnival.

Iris 1. Production series of thickwalled glass by Orrefors, designed by Sven Palmqvist in 1939. 2. Trade name of Fostoria Glass Specialty Co.

Irish Glass Bottle Ltd Bottle plant located in Dublin, Ireland [–]. Sig: IYGE in a circle, (bottles).

Irving Cut Glass Co Glassworks in Honesdale, PA, USA [1900–30], its glass was exported to Spain, South Africa and Asia, (cut glass on Fry blanks, esp. flowers and figures, Brilliant period).

Irving, Joan Studio artist from USA [1954–].

IS Machine (independent or individual section) Forming machine for bottles.

Isaac Glass Glassworks in Colognola ai Colli, VR, Italy [1973–present], (vases, bowls, tubes and automotive).

ISK See Institút Szkla Kerámiki.

Island Studio Glass Glassworks in Guernsey, Great Britain [?–present], prunt signatures.

Isle of Wight Studio glass Glassworks in the Isle of Wight, Great Britain [1973–present], designers Michael Harris and Timothy Harris. Sig: impressed flame logo 1973–81, flame label in the 1970s, triangular Isle of Wight/Glass in the 1980s, square label in the 1990s and some items were needle-signed by Harris, (art glass and paperweights).

Islington Glass Works Glassworks in Islington, Great Britain [–], active 19thC. Sig: IGW, (paperweights 1840s).

Israel-Frister, AG Glassworks in Switzerland [–], active c.1931, (lighting).

Ital Export di Novello & Cie Glassworks in Murano, Italy [–], active c.1967, (giftware and souvenirs).

ITALIA2 srl Glass collection from San Dono di Massanzago, in Padova, Italy [1993–present], trade names include Allglass and the designers include Valerio Bottin, Roberto & Ludovica Palombo, Luca Rossire who was also art director, Kris Ruhs, David Sicari and Wolfgang Tolk. Sig: all items are needle-

marked "Allglass", (art glass and florist glass).
Italian glass Italy has been the world's dominant glass producer since Roman times, esp. Venice since the 13thC. Venetian Cristallo became the standard for luxury glass throughout the middle ages. Venetian glassmakers pioneered and rediscovered many techniques and glass types, including latticcio, schmelzglas, crackle, millefiori, lampwork etc. Venetian glass suffered serious competition from Bohemia, Great Britain and France in the 18thC and 19thC and it has had artistic revivals at the end of the 19thC, in the 1920s (Venini), 1940s and 1950s.

Italiane Foresta, Vetrerie Glassworks in Martino L/PD, Italy [1977–], (bottles, tableware & tubes).

Italiane Vetr I Spa, Vetrerie Glassworks in Dego/SV, Lonigo/VI, Villa Poma/MN, Gazzo Veronese/VR, Pescia/PT and Rimini/FO, Italy [1942–present], (bottles).

Ito, Setsu Glass designer from Japan [–], designed "Shinobu" glass for Colle.

Ito, Yukio Glass designer from Japan [–], worked for Sasaki Glass Co, Japan in c.1969/70.

Ivanischevsky Glassworks Glassworks in Ivanischi, Vladimir region, Russia [–], designers include Natalya Ganf; Yury Kolov from 1967 and chief designer from 1969 and Zhigalkina Ivanova, Evgheniya A Glass designer/chemist from St Petersburg, Russia [1906–], worked at Leningrad Factory 1950–9 and at Krasny May 1959–61. She was the inventor of Zinc-sulphide glass.

Ivanovo Polje Glassworks in Slavonia, Croatia [1804–1904], (bottles, tableware, flat glass and luxury items).

IVA See Industria Vidriera Argentina Sacifi.

IVA di Piero Gabbrielli Glassworks in Montelupo Fiorentino, FI, Italy [?–present], (tableware).

IVAM See Industrie Vetri Artistici Murano.

Ivima Glassworks in Marinha Grande, Portugal [1895–present], started as Companhia Nacional and went through many changes of name and ownership and has been part of the Atlantis group since 1998, see also Mglass and Marinha Grande, (tableware, pressed glass gift items, hens-on-nest etc).

IVR See Industrie Vetraria Reunite.

IVR Mazzega Glassworks in Murano, Italy [–], see Mazzega.

Ivrene Steuben art glass which is opaque white with pearly lustre.

IVV Industria Vetraria Valdarnese Glassworks in San Giovanni Valdarno, Italy [?–present] (tableware).

Iwata, Toshichi Studio artist from Japan [1893–1980].

J

J in a triangle or square Jeannette Glass Co mark.

J-Glass Glassworks in Crieff, Scotland

[1979–83], this is the name John Deacons works under, (paperweights).

Jablonec Full name Jabloneč nad Nisou, Czech Republic, this town is a centre for costume jewellery, artificial gemstones, beads etc. It has had a technical college since 1880.

Jablonex Exporter of glass beads from Jabloneč nad Nisou, Czech Republic [?–present].

Jablonski, Adam Glass maker from Poland [–], active 1952–present, own glassworks 1966–present. Sig: all Jablonski glass is signed "A Jablonski" in needle script, (art glass, paperweights, especially clear-cased, colour swirls, etc).

Jachmann, Erich Glass cutter/engraver from Geisslingen, Germany [1909–], worked for WMF 1923–7, at various works 1928–36, VLG 1936–42 and WMF again 1948–74.

Jack-in-the-pulpit A slender vase with exaggerated rim, curled up at the rear and curled down at the front. The term was coined by Tiffany around 1900 after an American wildflower of that name, but the model is much older. Popular around the turn of the century it is now referred to by collectors as "JIP".

Jackson Bros Ltd Glassworks in Knottingley, Yorkshire, Great Britain [–], active [c.1950], (bottles and jars).

Jackson, Thomas G Architect from Great Britain [–], produced Arts and Crafts glass designs from 1874 for William Morris, which were made by James Powell & Sons.

Jacob, Laurent Glass designer from Belgium [1955–], worked at VSL in 1984.

Jacobean 1. Aka Jacobite, see style periods. 2. Popular pressed glass pattern introduced in 1923 by London factor Clayton Mayer & Co. By 1930 the range included 250 items, which were produced at various locations in the UK and in Czechoslovakia. Some items are still in current production.

Jacoby, Heinrich, Lampenfabrik u. Glashüttenerzeugnisse Glassworks in Halle, Germany [–], active c.1925, (tableware).

Jacopo Poli Glassworks in Schiavon, Italy [?–present], (crystal tableware).

Jade Fountain Glassworks in Dalian, China [?–present], (giftware).

Jäderholm-Snellman, Greta-Lisa Glass designer from Finland [1894–1963], worked for Riihimäki 1937–49 and Iittala 1945–62.

JAF & Co, Pioneer & Folger Trade name used by JA Folger & Co.

Jäger, Hans JG Painter from Germany [1887–1950], produced designs for Glaswerk Bernsdorf after 1931.

Jahny, Margarete Glass designer from Mittenwald, Germany [1923–], worked at GDR design institutions after 1965.

Jai Mata Glass Ltd Glassworks in New Delhi, India [1981–present], (tableware, barware, giftware and lead crystal).

Jain Glass Factory Pty Ltd Glassworks in Firozabad, India [1928–86], (pressed glass and carnival glass).

Jakič-Divkovič, Ana Glass designer from Croatia [1963–], has been working since

1985.

Jambes Glassworks in Jambes near Namur, Belgium [1850–1931], was run by Namuroises after 1867 and was later closed by VSL in 1931, (lighting and fruit jars 1879–1931).

Jämlitz Glashütte Glassworks in Jämlitz/ Muskau near Sorau, Germany [1815–1930], it was founded by Ignatius Seedel, the owner of Friedrichshain, then moved to Weisskeissel in 1830. Was run by KA Warmbrunn in 1833 then Fürst Pückler in 1845 and was renovated in 1854. It was then run by Count Hermann von Arnim in 1883 and Count von Arnim 1889, see also Tschernitz, which had the same owner. Sig: Company mark is GA-GJ <crown>GJ-GJ for Gräflich Arnimsche Glaswerke zu Jämlitz bei Muskau c.1924, (art glass, cut glass, engraved glass, lead glass after 1927 and pressed glass has also been reported).

Janák, František Glass artist from Prague, Czech Republic [1951–]. He is a glass cutter who trained at Josefodol and ŽB school after 1966, then worked in Prague 1972–88, was an independent artist after 1989 and started working for Moser in c.1997.

Jancke-Björk, Eva Painter/Glass designer from Sweden [1882–], worked for Orrefors in 1917.

Janeš, Želimir Glass sculptor from Croatia [1916–].

Janke, Urban Artist from Bohemia [1887–1914], worked for Wiener Werkstätte and produced decorations for Lobmeyr

Janštejn, Sklárna Glassworks in Horní Dubenky, Moravia, Czech Republic [1809–present], (lighting including chandeliers and shades).

Janku, Miloslav Glass decorator from Bohemia who worked in the 1930s.

Janov Glassworks in Janov nad Nisou/Liberec, Czechoslovakia [1912–93], since 1993 known as Vitrum GmbH, (pressed crystal and jewellery).

Janovy Hute Glassworks in Nové Hrady v jižních Cechách, Czechoslovakia [1777–?], (pressed glass).

Jansen, Yje Theo Glass decorator/designer from Amsterdam, Holland [1926–], worked for Leerdam 1947–76 and produced Unica 1968–76 and 1980.

Jansen Unica letters, year, quantity produced: JR=1968(39), JS=1969(29), JT=1970(10), none=1971(unknown), none=1972(1), none=1973(unknown), none=1974(unknown), none=1975(1), AD=1976(1), none=1980(unknown).

Janssen, Hans R Glass designer from Germany [–], worked for Glashütte Leichlingen GmbH c.1974/5 and for Gral-Glashütte GmbH c.1974/5).

Jansson, Arthur A, Des Glassworks, location unknown [–], active c.1921, (tableware).

Japanese glass Glass making in Japan developed in the early 19thC. Centres include Edo, Osaka, Nagasaki, Tokyo and Satsuma.

Jardinière (Fr) Flower basket used as milieu-de-table.

Jaroslaw Huta Szkla Glassworks in Jaroslaw,

Poland [1974–present], (bottles).

Jarville Signature used by Delatte.

Jasper glass See Calcedonio.

JBS Trade name used by Schlitz Brewing, Milwaukee, WI [c.1900–?], (bottles).

JD26S Trade name used by Duncan, John & Sons.

Jean, Auguste Ceramist/glass maker from France [–], (similar glass produced by Pantin and Sèvres). Sig: A Jean in enamel, but this often has not survived, or sig prunt "AS", (coloured glass with rigarees and appliques, sometimes enamel and gold, first produced 1878).

Jeannette Glass Co Glassworks in Jeannette, PA, USA [1898–1983]. Sig: J in a triangle and J in a square, (pressed glass and depression glass).

Jeannette Shades and Novelty Co Glassworks in Jeannette, PA, USA [1890s–?], (gas shades).

Jedlice, Huta Szkla Glassworks in Jedlice, upper Silesia, Poland [1960–present], (packaging and bottles).

Jefferson Glass Co Ltd Glassworks in Toronto, Canada [c.1915–c.1923]. Sig: on shades, (lighting, reverse painted table lamps).

Jefferson Glass Co Glassworks in Steubenville, OH, USA [1900–33], moved to Follansbee, WV in 1907 and was then bought by Imperial in the 1920s, (pressed glass, lighting and reverse painted table lamps).

Jekel, Mijnssen & Co Glassworks in Leerdam, the Netherlands [1879–?], aka Leerdam.

Jelinek, Julius Glass designer from Czechoslovakia [–], worked for Harrach c.1910.

Jelinek, Vladimír Glass artist from Žižice, Czechoslovakia [1934–], studied with Kaplický 1952–8, was then a designer at Moravske Sklárny Karolinka 1961–8, worked at central institutions 1966–77 and after 1982. Also worked for Karlovarske Sklo/Moser c.1971/2 and made independent work 1978–82.

Jelly glasses Small dessert glasses for custard, jelly or syllabub. See also sweetmeat.

Jemeppe Glassworks in Jemeppe-sur-Meuse, Belgium [–], in 1951 they moved to Momignies and in 1961 merged into Verlica, (pressed glass and bottles).

Jemeppe-sur-Meuse Glassworks in Jemeppe near Liège [1881/3] also reported [1888–c.1928]. The company was taken over by VSL in 1883 and then managed by Gevaert 1897/1901–1928. Sig: VSL intertwined enamelled on most pieces), see Oignon de Jemeppe, (tableware, lighting, opal, soliflores, goblets and flasks).

Jenaer Glaswerk Schott & Gen See Schott & Gen.

Jenkins Glass Co, DC Glassworks in Kokomo, IN, USA [1894–1932], began as Jenkins Glass Co in Greentown, IN c.1894, was then known as The Kokomo Glass Co 1901–5 and then DC Jenkins Glass Co in Arcadia, IN 1906–32 Sig: J in a triangle c.1920s, (pressed glass).

Jersey Glass Co Glassworks in Jersey City, NJ, USA [1824–c.1870, (cut glass, tableware, bottles, pressed glass, engraved and moulded).

Jesser, Hilda Glass designer from Austria [–], worked for Ludwig Moser c.1920.

Jet black jewellery Black gemstone made popular by Queen Victoria when mourning the death of Albert in 1861. A glass version was made at Jablonec, Bohemia after 1865, a resin-bonded version after 1877, riveted after 1880 and wire fitted after 1880. This jewellery was at the height of its popularity 1880–90.

Jetique 1. Black glass by Bagley c.1930–c.1960. 2. White enamel dot decoration aka Jetique Polkadot post-WWII.

Jewel Cut Glass Co Glassworks in USA [–], (cut glass, Brilliant period).

Ježek, Pavel Glass artist from the Czech Republic [–], (studied with Libenský).

JHL Glassworks, location unknown [–], active c.1900, (lighting).

Jihlavské Sklárny Bohemia as Glassworks in Jihlava, Jablonec, Czech Republic [?–present], trade names include "Bohemia 1845", no sigs, (tableware, cut glass, pressed glass in lead crystal only).

JIP See Jack-in-the-Pulpit.

Jirikovo Údoli, Georgenthal Glassworks in Nové Hrady v jižich Cechách, Czechoslovakia [1774–?], (pressed glass).

Jizerska Glassworks in Jizerska, Vilémova výsina, Czechoslovakia [1827–1914], (coloured glass, flasks, tableware), Klein Iser, Wilhelmshöhe.

Jizerské Sklo Glassworks in Jabloneč nad Nisou, Czech Republic [1990–present], aka Jizera Glass, (technical glass, cruet sets, perfumes and giftware), see also Ludwig Breit.

Joachimstal Glassworks in Austria [–], active c.1835.

Jobling & Co Ltd, James A Glassworks located on the River Wear, Sunderland, Great Britain [1858–1940], began as Angus & Greener in 1858, moved to Millfield, Sunderland in 1871, named Greener & Co in 1885 then renamed James A Jobling in 1921, Greener was taken over by Corning in 1940, (pressed glass, pyrex after 1918, opalique after 1933 and Jade).

Jodhpur glass Type of art glass with etched decoration, gold and transparent enamel, produced by Fritz Heckert 1875–1900.

Joensuu, Elina Glass designer from Finland [1974–], worked for littala after 1995.

Joetsu Crystal Glass Co Ltd Glassworks in Japan [–], designers include Yoyi Fusamae c.1968/9 and Naoto Yokoyama c.1968–72 (tableware).

Jõgi, Eha-Pilvi Glass designer from Estonia [1938–], worked at Krasny Ghigant after 1967 and Krasny May after 1969.

Johann Lötz Witwe, Loetz Glassworks in Klásterský Mlyn, Czechoslovakia [1836–c.1947], aka Loetz.

Johannahütte Glassworks in Schönborn near Luckau, NL, Germany [1899–c. 1937].

Johannesthal Glassworks in Janova hut, Czechoslovakia [–].

Johannislund & Arima Glassworks in Finland [1813–1959], (tableware and bottles).

Johannisthal, Glashütte Glassworks in Johannisthal near Hoyerswerda, OL, Germany [c.1937–?].

Johansfors Glasbruk Glassworks in Broakulla, Småland, Sweden [1891–present], merged with Kosta Boda in 1972. Designers include Bengt Orup c.1955–70 and current designers include Ardy Strüwer, Catti Aselius-Lidbeck, Astrid Gate and Helén Tapper. Sig: Many items are unsigned or needle-marked "JG" or "J.G."or sometimes "Johansfors + pattern no + designer surname".

Johansson, Berit Silversmith/glass designer from Sweden [–], was independent from 1969, worked for Orrefors 1979–84 then for Venini, Salviati and Rosenthal. Then set up Art Design AB in Vadstena, Sweden with husband Jan in 1985.

Johansson, Jan Silversmith/glass designer from Sweden [1942–], worked for Orrefors after 1969 then set up Art Design AB in Vadstena, Sweden with wife Berit in 1985.

Johansson, Willy Glass designer from Norway [1921–], worked for Hadeland after 1942.

Jo-He-Ki Glassworks in Silesia, Poland [1923–5], after a merger of Heckert, Neumann & Stäbe and Josephinenhütte it was renamed Josephinenhütte in 1925.

Johnsen & Jorgensen Flint Glass Ltd Glassworks in Great Britain [–], active c.1950, trade names include Wembley.

Jonasson, Mats Glass engraver/designer from Sweden [–], worked for Målerås Glasbruk AB 1959–69 and 1975–present and for Kosta

1969–75. Has specialized in engraved animal figures in cast crystal since 1975.

Jones, Cavitt & Co Glassworks in Pittsburgh, PA, USA [1884–91], see Campbell, Jones & Co.

Jones, Tom Glass designer from Britain [1906–], worked for Stevens & Williams/Royal Brierly 1920–82.

Jordan Marsh Co Glassworks in USA [–], active c.1914, (cut glass).

Jørgensen, Torben Glass designer from Denmark [1945–], worked for Holmegaard after 1977.

Josef Inwald AG Glassworks in Male Brezno, Czechoslovakia and in Zlíchov u Praha, Czechoslovakia [?–1945], in 1945 became part of the Sklo Union, (cut glass), see Inwald.

Josef Inwald AG, Elsahütte Glassworks in Poděbrady, Czechoslovakia [1877–1945], in 1945 became part of Sklo Union, (cut glass, coloured glass and blanks for the Nový Bor refineries), see Inwald.

Josef Inwald AG, Rudolfshütte Glassworks in Rudolfova, Teplice Sanov, Czechoslovakia [1884–1945], after 1945 merged into Sklu Union, (pressed glass, carnival, cut glass), see Inwald.

Josefhütte, Koštany Glassworks in Koštany u Teplice v Cechách, Czechoslovakia [1878–1945], was taken over by Rindskopf in 1891 and in 1936 linked to Inwald, (pressed glass from the 1920s).

Josefihütte, Ostrovec Josefinské Hut, also Rohovka Glassworks in Ostrovec, Pocatek, Czechoslovakia [c.1860–c.1890], (pressed glass reported 1873).

Josefodol Glassworks in Kunemil, Svetlá nad Sazavou, Czechoslovakia [–], (pressed glass and flasks).

Josefův důl Glassworks in Tanvald u Jabloneč nad Jizerou, Czechoslovakia [1868–1910], Josefsthal, Kamnitzhütte, Kamenická/Josefů v Důl taken over by Jizerské Sklo, 1990, (pressed glass and flasks).

Josephinenhütte Glassworks in Schreiberhau and in Karlstal, Silesia, Poland [1842–present], its full name is Gräflich Schaffgottsch'sche Schreiberhau. Merged with Fritz Heckert, Petersdorf and Neumann & Staebe in 1923. Currently known as Graf Schaffgottsch'sche Josephinenhütte GmbH in Schwäbisch Gmünd, Germany. Designers include Prof Siegfried Härtl c.1900, (tableware, cut glass; art glass and iridescent "antique" glass for Ludwig Felmer, Mainz). See also JZSS and Julia.

Joska Crystal, Glasfabrik Glassworks in Bodenmais, Bavaria, Germany [?–present], (art glass, cut glass, giftware, Rauchtopaz).

Joska Waldglashütte Glassworks in Bodenmais, Bavaria, Germany [?–present], (blown tableware, old style).

Jover Glassworks in Cervelló, Spain [?–1908], merged into Union Vidriera de España in 1908.

Jozefina Huta Szkla Glassworks in Krosno, Poland [?–present], (art glass, chandeliers, lighting, tableware and novelties).

JR Trade name used by Stourbridge Flint Glass Works.

JSC Berezhany See Berezhanski Sklozavod.

JT Trade name used by Mantua Glass Works/Glass Co.

JT & Co Trade name used by Brownsville Glass Works.

Jugendstil The german term for Art Nouveau named after Die Jugend magazine, which first carried illustrations in that style.

Julia Glassworks in Silesia, Poland. This became the new name for Josephinenhütte in 1956.

Julien Trade name used for pressed glass made in France c.1930.

Julien, René Painter from Liège, Belgium [1937–], worked for VSL c.1978.

Jumet, Verrerie de Glassworks in Manage, Belgium [1772–1943], started in Jumet but moved to Manage in 1852, (tableware in sodalime and semi-crystal).

Juna, Zdenek Glass designer/decorator from Železný Brod, Czechoslovakia [1897–1975], (etched glass in the 1920s).

Jung, Walter/Vaiter Glass designer from Finland; [1879–1946], worked for Nuutajärvi from c.1905.

Jungnickel, Ludwig Heinrich Animal painter from Germany [1881–1965], was a member of Wiener Werkstaette and worked for Lobmeyr.

Jurgen, Leida Glass designer from Estonia [1925–], worked at the Leningrad Factory after 1955.

Justrite Trade name of Justrite Manufacturing Co [–].

Jutrem, Arne Jon Glass designer from Norway [1929–], worked for Hadeland after 1950, Holmegaard 1962–4 and Plus in 1967. Sig: A.JJ.

Juvé Glassworks in Barcelona, Spain [?–1908], merged into Union Vidriera de España in 1908.

JZSS Aka Josephinehütte. Glassworks in Szklarska Poreba (Schreiberhau), Silesia, Poland [1945–1956], the full name is Jelenogórskie Zjednoczone Zaklady Szklarskie Piechowice-Szklarska Poreba. After a merger with Josephinenhütte it was renamed Julia in 1956.

K

K K Fachschule One of the signatures used by the Nový Bor Glass-making school before 1918.

Kabey Ashi Glass artist from Japan [–], was active c.1975–6.

Kadlec, Bohdan Glass designer from Bohemia [1856–1901], director/designer at Harrachóv, Nový Svet, (Venetian-style work, chandeliers, tableware and art glass).

Kagami Crystal Glass Works Ltd Glassworks in Tokyo, Japan [–], founded by Kozo Kagami. Designers include Jyunshiro Satoh c.1954–6, Seitou Ochiai c.1969/70 and Takeo Yoshida c.1972/3.

Kajakki Boat-shaped object designed by Timo Sarpaneva in 1953.

Kaleidoscopio Glass-fusing studio located in

Marigliano/ Napoli, Italy [1987–present], (fused art glass, flat glass, windows and panels).

Kalinin Crystal Factory Glassworks in Moscow, Russia [–], aka Kalinin Cut Glass Factory. Designers include Berskinskaya 1955–7 and Makarenko 1955–7, (cut glass).

Kallenberg, Fritz Glass designer from Sweden [1902–], worked for Boda 1925–68.

Kallenberger, Kreg Studio artist from USA [–].

Kallio, Heikki Glass designer from Finland [1948–], has held various teaching posts and has own studio.

Kaltenbach, Wasserhütte, Nové Hute Glassworks in Nové Hute, Czechoslovakia [c.1829–1945].

Kamei Glass Co Glassworks in Osaka, Japan [?–present].

Kamenz GmbH Glashüttenwerk Glassworks in Kamenz, OL, Germany [1883–?], known as Glashüttenwerk Kamenz GmbH in 1889, AG in 1906, Max & Co Glashüttenwerke Kamenz AG in 1912, Max Kray & Co Glas-Industrie Schreiber AG in 1919. Merged into VLG Weisswasser in 1924 and was operated by VLG in 1930, was then dismantled in 1945, reconstructed as VEB in 1947, became part of VEB Ankerglas Bernsdorf 1953–69 and was finally linked to Glaswerk Schwepnitz in 1969, (lighting until 1930, pressed glass after designs by Wagenfeld 1934/35 and barware).

Kanawha Co Glassworks in Kanawha, WV, USA [1955–87], (pressed glass, novelties and covered animal dishes).

Kane, Michael Glass maker from Millville, NJ, USA [–], (paperweights 1880s–1900s).

Kannegieter, H L Glass designer from the Netherlands [1898–1991], worked for Maastricht after 1927.

Kantara Glass designed by Sven Palmqvist for Orrefors in 1944.

Kantarell Glass designed by Edvin Öhrström for Orrefors in 1939.

Kantarelli Glass designed by Tapio Wirkkala for Iittala in 1946.

Kaplan, Anatoly L Painter/glass designer from St Petersburg, Russia [1902–], art director at Leningrad Factory 1948–50.

Kappi, Th Glass engraver from Finland [–], worked for Riihimäki c.1956/7.

Karel, Marián Glass artist from the Czech Republic [1944–], studied with Libenský 1965–72 and has been independent since 1972.

Karhula-Iittala Glassworks in Iittala, Finland [1899–present], merged with Iittala in 1915. Sig: engraved marks are found until c.1946, Iittala used after 1946, "Bear" label in 1956 and Iittala label after 1956.

Karl Schappel Glassworks in Nový Bor, Czechoslovakia [1857–1914].

Karlovarske Sklo See Moser.

Karlsbader Kristallfabriken AG: New name after the merger in 1922 of Meyr's Neffe and Ludwig Moser. See Moser.

Karlshütte, Karlova Hut Glassworks in Smrcná, Czechoslovakia [1701–1916].

Karlslund Glassworks in Örebro, Sweden [?–present], see Glashyttan Ulven AB.

Karlsson, Brigitte Glass designer from Sweden

[1943–], worked for Venini 1971/74.

Karlström, Arnold Glass designer from Sweden [–], worked for Kosta 1923.

Karneol glass Type of art glass by Loetz, 1889.

Karolina See Osredek.

Karolinka Glassworks in Nového Hrozenkova, okr Vsetin, Czechoslovakia [1861–c.1972], currently operated by Morávske Sklárny, (pressed glass).

Karpanen, Mikko Glass designer from Finland [1955–], worked for Iittala 1983–88 and has been freelance since 1988.

Kashiwabara, Hiroyuki Glass designer from Japan [–], worked for Sasaki Glass Co, Japan c.1972/3.

Kaspar Cristal France Trade name used by Vosges du Nord, Cristallerie des.

Kaspar Kristallglaswerk KG, Franz Glassworks in Neckarzimmern, Germany [?–present], (coloured crystal).

Kastrup Glassworks in Kastrup, Denmark [1873–1965], merged with Holmegaard in 1965 and went by the new name of Kastrup og Holmegaards Glasvaerker A/S. Kastrup designers include OJ Nielsen c.1925, Jacob E Bang c.1956–63, Grethe Meyer c.1960/1 and Ibi Trier Mørch c.1960/1 while Kastrup & Holmegaards designers include E Kindt-Larsen c.1973/4, Per Lütken c.1967/8, Ibi Trier Mørch c.1968/9 and Sidse Werner c.1973/4. Sig: KG monogram on pressed items c.1940–65, KH for Kastrup Holmegaard after 1965, (tableware, bottles).

Katarinska Huta Glassworks in Zlatno, Czech Republic [?–present], operated by Slovglass Poltár, Slovakia, see Zlatno and Zahn.

Katona, Erzsébet Glass artist from Szeged, Hungary [1942–], produced designs for Ajka, Sagótarján and Parad glass factories 1962–91.

Kauklahti Glassworks in Finland [?–1941], merged with Riihimaki.

Kavalier Glassworks Ltd Glassworks in Sázava, Czech Republic [1837–present], has plants in Sazava, Hostomice, Votice and Otvovice. Currently has an export house in Libereč, Czech Republic. Trade names include Simax oven and labware, (bottles, cookware, tubes, bulbs & TV).

Kavalír, František Glass maker from Bohemia [1796–1853], founded glassworks in Ostyedek, and later in Sazava; invented and produced glass with silicon oxide for lab use after the 1830s.

Kawakami, AK Studio artist from Japan [–], worked for Hoya c.1980.

Kaziun, Charles Glass maker from Brockton, MA, USA [1919–]. Sig: K in cane or K in gold; early pieces have CK, (relaunch of paperweights 1942).

Kearns, Herdman & Gorsuch Located in Zanesville, OH, USA [1876–84], (bottles).

Kedelv, Paul Glass designer from Sweden [1917–], worked for Orrefors, Nuutajärvi, Flygsfors 1949–56, Reijmyre 1956/7 and Fåglavik 1957–76, (biomorphic glass c.1950–c.1970 and designed the Cocquille series for Flygsfors).

Kehlmann, Robert Studio glass artist from USA [1942–].

Kehr, Gunter Flamework artist from Wiesbaden, Germany [1934–], taught glass blowing at Glasfachschule in Hadamar 1967–1977, had own studio from 1977.

Kekäläinen, Päivi Glass designer/teacher from Finland [1961–].

Keller, Joseph Bohemian engraver who worked at Stevens & Williams c.1880s.

Keller, Vincent Bohemian engraver who worked at Couper in Glasgow c.1870s/80s.

Kelley & Steinman Glassworks in USA [–], (cut glass, Brilliant period).

Kelly, Thomas Studio glass artist from Corning, NY, USA [–], works at Vitrix Hot Glass Studio.

Kelva Opaque glassware hand-decorated with flowers in a metal frame and is made by C F Monroe Company.

Kemple Glass Works, John E Glassworks in East Palestine, OH, USA [1945–1970], known as Kemple Glass Works before 1956, later moved to Kenova, WV and renamed John E Kemple Glass Co, (pressed glass, reproduced McKee patterns from old moulds and covered animal dishes, novelties).

Kensington Glass Works Glassworks in Philadelphia, PA ,USA [1822–1932], (bottles).

Kent Glass Factory Glassworks in Kent, OH, USA [1824–?], (bottles and tableware).

Kentucky Glass Works Co Located in Louisville, KY [1849–55], (bottles).

Kerch Packaging Glassworks in Kerch, Ukraine [–], designers include Balabin 1964–8 and Filimonova.

Kerhartová-Peřinová, Marta Glass artist from Prague, Czech Republic [1935–], was an independent artist 1959–69 and produced incidental works only after 1970.

Kerosene lamps Kerosene was patented in 1854 and first distilled in 1846. Mass production of the lamps was possible after 1859 and they were widely used until c.1900.

Kerr Glass Manufacturing Co Located in Portland, OR, Sand Spring, OK, Chicago, IL and Los Angeles, CA [1912–present], aka Alexander H Kerr Glass Co. Sig: Kerr, (bottles).

Kerry Glass Glassworks located at Ring of Kerry, near Killarney, Irish Republic [?–present], (giftware, paperweights and lead crystal).

Keuchel, Fritz Glass cutter/designer from Germany [1933–], worked at Sachsenglas Schwepnitz after 1959.

Kew Blas Trade name of iridescent opaque art glass type produced 1890–1920 by Union Glass Co.

Keystone Glass Mfg Co Glassworks in Hawley, PA, USA [1902–18], aka Keystone Cut Glass Co, (cut glass).

Keystone Glass Works/National Glass 10 Glassworks in Rochester, PA [1897–99], aka Keystone Tumbler Works, became part of National Glass in 1899.

Khaikin, V Artist from Russia [–], (glass decoration in the 1920s).

KH&G Trade name used by Kearns, Herdman & Gorsuch.

Khrolov, Vladimir G Glass designer from Krasnomaysky, Kalinin region, Russia [1935–], worked at Krasny May 1960–1 and after 1964.

Kick The raised underside of a glass, which is sometimes called the "Soul" of a glass; aka kick-up.

Kidd, Thomas Glassworks in Manchester, Great Britain [–], active c.1860s, pressed glass after c.1860.

Kidrič, OZD Steklarna Boris Glassworks in Rogaška Slatina, Slovenia [?–present], designers include Ljubica Kočica 1958–69 and Raoul Goldoni after 1956 (also art director after 1967). See Rogaška.

Kiefer Brothers Cut Glass Co Glassworks, location unknown [–], (cut glass, Brilliant period).

Kiev Factory of Decorative Glassware Glassworks in Kiev, Ukraine [1950–?], designers include Apollonov 1960–6 and after 1970, Averkov was chief designer 1954–69, Balabin was a designer there after 1968, Ghenske after 1948, Golembovskaya after 1964, Gushin after 1969, Mityaeve 1950–6 and after 1964, Zaritsky after 1958, Zatynaiko after 1956 and Zeldich 1954-64.

Kiln A high-temperature oven used for burning, drying or heating. In glass working kilns are used to fuse enamel and used during kiln-forming processes.

Kiln forming: Any forming process involving a kiln, such as slumping, fusing, enamelling and casting.

Kilner & Sons, J Glassworks in Wakefield, Yorkshire, Great Britain [–], active c.1860s, 1870, (paperweights).

Kimax Trade name used by Kimball for borosilicate glass used for labware.

Kimball Glass Co Glassworks in Vineland, NJ, USA [1931–?], previously known as Durand (art glass and Cluthra glass). Part of Vineland Flint Glass.

Kimberley Co Glassworks, location unknown [–], active c.1912, (lighting)

Kimberley, CP Glass engraver from Great Britain [–], worked at Thomas Webb 1930–78.

Kimble Glass Inc Glassworks in Vineland, NJ, USA [1901–present], operates six plants, (bottles, household glass, lighting, labware, tubes and automotive), see Gerresheimer Glass.

Kindt-Larsen, E Glass designer from Denmark [–], worked for Kastrup & Holmegaards c.1973/4.

King, Son & Co Glassworks in Pittsburgh, PA, USA [1859–91], founded as Cascade Glass Works, became Johann, King & Co, King, Son & Co from 1864, then King Glass Co c.1879 and finally merged into US Glass in 1891, (tableware, pressed glass and lighting).

King's Lynn Glass Glassworks located at King's Lynn, Norfolk, Great Britain [late 1960s–?], designers include R Stennet-Wilson c.1967/8. Sig: etched LYNN mark after 1969. See Wedgwood.

Kirkpatrick, Joey Studio glass artist from USA [1952–], works in Seattle, WA, USA.

Kirschner, Marie Glass designer from Prague, Czechoslovakia [1852–1931], designed around 270 different vases for Loetz 1897–1914. Typical charateristics of her work are soft colours (violet, green) and transparent glasses with matt finish & iridescence. Was also known to use crackle and silver foil. Sig: MK monogram.

Kiss, Miklos Glass artist from Ajka, Hungary [1944–], exhibited after 1973 and worked for Ajka 1986–90.

Kisslinger Kristallglas GmbH &Co KG Glassworks in Rattenberg, Austria [?–present], (crystal tableware).

Kittel, Emanuel Glass cutter from Jablonec, Czechoslovakia [–], working early 19thC.

Kjaer, Anja Glass designer from Denmark [1956–], worked for Holmegaard after 1989.

Kjellander, Lars Glass designer/engraver from Sweden [–], worked for Kosta 1881–1925.

Klaar, Wilhelm Export house for beads/costume jewellery from Jablonec, Czechoslovakia [?–c.1939].

Klarahütte Glassworks in Polevsko, Czechoslovakia [1907–?], run by Carl Mühlbauer, (blanks for refineries in the Nový Bor area).

Kleiner & Baderschneider, Glashütte Glassworks in Döbern near Sorâu, NL, Germany [1866–c.1937].

Kleinert, Glashütte Glassworks in Halbau near Sprottau, NL, Germany [1876–c.1937].

Klepsch, Kristian Glassworks in Neuzeug-Sierning, Germany [–], active c.1980.

Klim, Karen Glass designer from Norway [1951–], worked for Frysja glass studio c.1978.

Klingenbrunn Kristallglas Glassworks in Klingenbrunn, Bavaria, Germany [?–present], trade names include Atelier K.

Klinger, Miroslav Glass designer from Czechoslovakia [1922–], worked for Železný Brod after c.1948.

Kloot en Mijnlieff, Glasfabriek van der Glassworks in Capelle an der IJssel, Netherlands [1861–1919], aka Zuid-Hollandse Glasblazerij, (bottles for Henkes Gin), see Anglo Dutch.

Klostermühle Glassworks in Klásterský Mlýn, Czechoslovakia [1836–1851], see Loetz which was based here.

Klumper, Vladena Studio artist from the Czech Republic [1956–].

Kluyskens, HF Glassworks, location unknown [–], active c.1929, (lighting).

Knab, Moritz Glass designer from Austria [–], worked for Lobmeyr c.1882–c.1886.

Knappe, Karl Glass maker from Bohemia, working 1840s.

Knickerbocker Glory Glass Ice cream glass, taller than a sundae.

Knight, Laura Artist from Great Britain [1877–1970], designed glass for Stuart & Sons c.1934.

Knittel, FA See Reinerzer.

Knizek, Josef Glass producer located in Czechoslovakia [–], was active c.1905.

Knöchel, Franz Glass engraver from Bohemia [1860–1943].

Knop A "knop" means a finial on a lid or a bulbous section on the stem of a goblet. Distinguished knop shapes are: acorn, angular, annulated, bobbin, cushion, cylinder, drop, egg, swelling and merese.

Knox Glass Associates Inc Glassworks in USA [–], active c.1970, (tableware).

Knoz & McKee Based in Wheeling, WV, USA [1824–9], (bottles).

Knurling A decorative band, aka Gadrooning.

Kny, Frederick Englebert Engraver from Great Britain [–], worked at Thomas Webb & Sons 1860–96 with sons Ludwig, Harry and William Sig: FEK.

Kobylinskaya, Olga M Glass artist from Moscow, Russia [1928–], worked at Workshops of Applied Art Moscow after 1956 and her works were produced at Dzerzhinsky, First of May and Vorovsky Glassworks.

Koch, Gérard Glass designer from France [1926–].

Kočica, Ljubica Ratkajec Glass designer/artist from Zagreb, Croatia [1935–], worked for Boris Kidrič Glassworks at Rogaška Slatina 1958–69, was an independent artist after 1969, taught at the Glassmaking school Rogaška Slatina, Steklo at Slovenska Bistrica, for Serbian Glass at Paraćin and for Ciril Zobec Glassworks, (art glass and tableware).

Köck, Kunsthandwerk Glasscherben Glass refinery located in Riedlhütte, Bavaria, Germany [?–present].

Kodrič, Franjo Glass sculptor from Zagreb, Croatia [1952–], been working since c.1979.

Koellmann, Gero Glass artist from Saarbrücken, Germany [1941–].

Koepping, Karl see Köpping

Kohinur Cut Glass Co Glassworks in Jermyn, PA, USA [1906–7], (cut glass), see Laurel Cut Glass Co.

Kohlfurth Glashütte Glassworks in Kohlfurt near Görlitz, OL, Germany [1874–?], operated by Schneider & Hirsch.

Kokko, Valto Glass designer from Finland [1933–], worked for Iittala after 1963.

Kokomo Glass Mfg Co Glassworks in Kokomo, IN, USA [1899–1932], (pressed glass). See DC Jenkins Glass Co.

Köln-Ehrenfeld Glassworks in Köln Ehrenfeld, Germany [c.1896–c.1904], aka Rheinische.

Kolodin, Ivan S Glass designer from Dyatkovo, Bryansk region, Russia [1940–], worked at Dyatkovsky Cut Glass after 1969.

Kolov, Yury G Glass designer from Ivanischi, Vladimir region, Russia [1939–], worked at Ivanischevski Glassworks from 1967 and became their chief designer after 1969.

Kölsch glass Thin-walled cylindrical glass for beer, used in Cologne, Germany.

Komorowska-Birger, Paulina Flamework artist

from Zielona Gora, Poland [1965–], has worked since 1992.

Kontes Glass Company Glassworks in USA [1943–1980s], run by James and Nontas Kontes, (paperweights).

Kopecký, Vladimir Glass artist from Czechoslovakia [1931–], has been independent since 1961.

Kopp Glass Glassworks in Swissvale, PA, USA [–], (lighting).

Koppel, Henning Glass designer from Denmark [1918–81], worked for Orrefors 1940–5 and after 1971.

Köpping, Karl Painter/glass designer from Dresden [1848–1914], worked in Berlin, (Art Nouveau style lampwork 1892–1900).

Kopřiva, Pavel Glass designer from Duchcov, Czech Republic [1968–], worked at Prague Academy until 1995, worked with his wife Karolina Kopřivová at Moser in 1997.

Koralli glass Bowls and vases made at Riihimäki, Finland, designer Tamara Aladin.

Kořenov Glassworks in Kořenov, Czechoslovakia [1700–1882].

Korge, Helga Glass designer from Tallinn, Estonia [1926–], worked at Tarbeklaas works, Estonia from 1953 and was their chief designer from 1960.

Korneyev, Vladimir V Glass designer from Ryazan province, Russia [1927–], worked at Gus-Krushtalny after 1962 and was their chief designer from 1968.

Kortan Sklo Bižuterie Glassworks in Jabloneč nad Nisou, Czech Republic [?–present], (beads, glass candy and lampwork).

Kortzau, Ole Architect/designer from Denmark [1939–], worked for Holmegaard after 1976.

Koskinen, Harri Glass designer from Finland [1970–], worked for Iittala after 1996.

Kosta Glasbruk Glassworks in Sweden [1742–present], founded by Koskall and Stael, merged with Boda in 1947. Currently operated by Orrefors. Artists include Bäckström, Bergh 1929–50, Branzell 1922–3, 1929–30 and 1950, Dahlskog 1926–9, Anna Ehrner, Kjell Engman, Erixson 1923 and 1929–32, Erik Höglund, Hultström 1919–24, Ulrica Hydmann-Vallien, Vicke Lindstrand 1950–1973, Lundgren 1934/6, Morales 1958–70, Ollers 1917–18 and 1931–2, Persson c.1974/5, Gunnel Sahlin, Rolf Sinnemark 1967–86, Skawonius 1933–5 and 1944–50, Snadeberg c.1966/7, Vallien after 1960, Ann Wärff 1964–74, Göran Wärff 1964–74, 1978–82 and since 1986, Ann Wåhlström, Wallander and Wennerberg. (Flat glass, tableware, art glass, cut glass, paperweights, pressed glass since 1840, floral cameo in 1897. innovative design since c.1920).

Kosta marks LX=special crystal, ELX=semi-crystal, HX=lead crystal, MX=machine made, SX=soda glass, PK=pressed glass; KK=art glass, U or UNIK=unique one-off pieces by Wärff; AEH=Ehrner; AWA=Wahlström, W or GWA=Wärff, BW=Bergh, GSA=Sahlin and P=Persson. Five-digit codes have been in use since the 1970s; the last 2 numbers are the year of design, not production.

Kosta signatures used today Art Glass pieces are marked with article number, Kosta Boda, artist's name and type of art glass: unique, edition or atelier. The article number has six pieces of information. The first is the brand number, the next is the designer's initials. Then comes the type of glass. After this is the year of introduction followed by the code for the product type. The last bit of information is the serial number. For instance, in the following example, "8 MBA AT 99 4 001/300", 8 refers to Kosta Boda, MBA is Monica Backstom's initials, AT stands for Atelier, 99 is the year of introduction, 4 is the code for the product type and 001/300 is the serial number.

The designer's marks are: AEH=Anna Ehrner AWA=Ann Wahlström BVA=Bertil Vallien GSA=Gunnel Sahlin GWA=Göran Wärff KEN=Kjell Engman MBA=Monica Backström UHV=Ulrica Hydman-Vallien. Other abbreviations: AT=Atelier: produced in series of at least 100 pieces; ED=Edition: produced in series of a maximum of 60 pieces individually numbered with an edition number and UN=Unique: one of a kind, signed by the artist.

Kosta unlimited collection Marked with the words Kosta Boda, the name of the artist and the article number (five positions). The exception is the Artist Collection, which is marked with the words Kosta Boda, Artist Coll or Art Coll, the name of the artist and the article number. Painted pieces are signed with a painted signature with the designer's and the painter's initials. Engraved pieces also carry the engraver's signature.

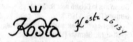

Kostanske Sklarny A Panvarny AS Glassworks in Kostany, Czech Republic [?–present], (lighting; shades, chandeliers and chimneys).

Kostka, Stanislav Glass designer from Kutná Hora, Czech Republic [1939–], was educated at Prague Academy 1961–7 and worked at Moser in 1997.

Kotěra, Jan Architect/glass designer from Prague, Czechoslovakia [1871–1923], taught in Prague 1899–1923, worked for Harrach 1904–10 and produced tableware designs for Artel c.1910.

Kothgasser, Anton Glass decorator from Austria [1769–1851], (Biedermeier style, transparent enamel), see Mohn and Mildner.

Kotik, Jan Glass artist from Turnov, Czechoslovakia [1916–], painter, engraver and designer who worked in glass at Škrdlovice 1950–65.

Kotov, Vladimir I Glass designer from Bryansk province, Russia [1944–], worked at Dyatkovsky Cut Glass after 1968.

Koula, Jan Glass designer from Bohemia [1855–1919].

Kovács & Szilágyi Designer team from Hungary [1947- and 1949–], active since

1974.

Kovačič, Kuzma Glass artist from Hvar, Croatia [1952–].

Kraft, Karl Glass maker from Toledo, OH, USA [–], (paperweights 1970s).

Kraka Type of art glass with internal fibre net, designed by Sven Palmqvist, in production at Orrefors from 1944–72. Sequential numbering starts 1=1944, 13=1945, 31=1946, 50=1947, 96=1949, 97=1950, 136=1951, 169=1952, 213=1953, 278=1954, 329=1955, 355=1956, 358=1957, 364=1958, 380=1959, 427=1960, 440=1961, 444=1963, 453=1965, 456=1967, 482=1969, 492=1971 and 521=1972. Serial production of Kraka from 1952 bears the number 3,364, 3,365, 3,366 or 3,367.

Kralik & Co Glashütte Glassworks in Finkenherd near Guben, Germany [1905–c.1937].

Kralik & Söhne, Wilhelm Glassworks in Lenora, Czechoslovakia [1881–?] was founded when Heinrich Kralik inherited the Eleonorenheim and Ernstbrunn Glassworks, which used to be part of Meyr's Neffe. No sig except on cameo, (art glass from 1899, iridescence, Peloton glass, Loetz type vessels and cameo glass).

Kralik, Wilhelm Glass maker from Adolfov, Bohemia [1806–77].

Kramsach Glashütte Glassworks in Tirol, Austria [1756–?], aka Tiroler.

Krantz, Helén Glass designer from Sweden [1953–], worked for Orrefors after 1988.

Krantz, Smith & Co Glassworks in the USA [–], (cut glass, Brilliant period).

Krásná Jizba Firm for interior decoration in Prague [–], active 1920s, commissioned glass by Smrčková, Sutnar and Meteläk.

Krasnik, Antoinette (Antonija) Glass designer from Croatia/Austria [–], worked for Loetz c.1903, Bakalowits, worked with Josef Hoffmann/ Wiener Werkstätte then emigrated to Italy in 1906.

Krásno nad Becvou Glassworks in Valašské Mezirici, Czechoslovakia [1855–present], aka Osvetlovaci Sklo before 1945 and after 1991, (pressed glass until end of the 19thC, lighting until 1945).

Krasny Ghigant Glassworks in Vladimir Province, Russia [–], active after the 18thC, previously known as Bakhmetyevsky Glassworks. Designers include Eryomin 1924–48, Jøgi after 1967, Mukhina 1938/9, Rostovtseva, Vertuzayev 1893–1938, Yakobson 1902–21 and Zhigalkina, (tableware, cut glass and art glass).

Krasny May Glassworks in Kalinin region, Russia [–], designers include Batanova, Berskinskaya after 1957, Dzivinskaya 1959–61, Fedorkov 1965–8, Fomina & Sazhin 1967–71, Ganf, Ivanova 1959–61, Jøgi after 1969, Khrolov 1960–1 and after 1964, Kobylinskaya, Marshumov & Marshumova after 1964, Matushevskaya, Ryazanova, Silko after 1952 (was their chief designer after 1956) and Zhigalkina. (Art glass, cut glass, tableware and Zinc sulphide glass.)

Krause, Karl Glass painter from Germany [1912–], worked at Arsall Weisswasser

1928–9 then had his own workshop 1945–50.

Krause Kunstglasbläserei Glassworks in Zwiesel, Bavaria, Germany [?–present].

Krebs-Glas-Lauscha GmbH Glassworks in Lauscha, Thüringen, Germany [?–present], (Christmas tree decorations).

Kreibitz Hütte Glassworks in Chribská, Czechoslovakia [–].

Krejcar, Jaromir Architect from Czechoslovakia [–], worked for Artel in the 1920s.

Kreutz, John Worked at Silverbrook Art Glass Co.

Krimmer, Eduard M Set designer from Odessa, Ukraine [1900–], worked at the Leningrad Factory 1948–50.

Kristal & Glasblazerij en Slijperij Fabrieken See Regout.

Kristal Glassworks Glassworks in Samobor, near Zagreb, Croatia [1957–present], designers include Raoul Goldoni 1963–5, (art glass and cut glass).

Krystallglasfabrik Steigerwald Regenhütte See Steigerwald, Kristallglasfabrik vorm

Kristalcolor Trade name of Cristalcolor.

Kristalia SRL Glassworks in Brugnera, Italy [?–present].

Kristallglasfabrik Carl Haefeli AG See Haefeli.

Kristallglas-Hüttenwerke Franz Wittwer See Wittwer.

Kristalunie NV Glassworks in Maastricht, Netherlands [1925–present], founded after merger of Regout and Stella 1925 and taken over by NV Verenigde Glasfabrieken in 1959, manual production ceased 1977 and from then on they produced bottles only, (tableware, pressed glass, art glass and bottles). See Maastricht.

Kristiánov Glassworks in Kristiánov, Czechoslovakia [1775–1887], (flat glass, tableware, pressed glass and beads).

Krizman, Tomislav Glass artist from Croatia [–], working in the early 20thC.

Kromer or Krommer, Emil Glass engraver working in Kamenický Šenov, Czechoslovakia [c.1930s–c.1948], used both variations on his name.

Kronex Trade name for pressed tableware (Duralex type) in Greece.

Krosno Town located in Poland, which has more than 10 operating glassworks, the largest being Krosno SA.

Krosno Krosnienskie Huty Szkla SA Glassworks in Krosno, Poland [1923–present], operates 5 plants. Sig: none. (Tableware, cut glass, barware, art glass, frosted, coloured and clear, paperweights, giftware, technical glass, fibres, tubes, lead crystal and sodalime glass).

Krüger, Otto Glass designer from Munich [1868–], worked for Valérysthal from c.1900.

Krugov Crystal Works Glassworks in Russia

[1835–?].

Krumholz, Eugen Glass artist from Germany [1944–].

Krys-Tol Trade name used by Jefferson Glass Co, USA for Chippendale pattern pressed glass 1908–19

Krystallglasfabrick Frauenau, J Gistl See Frauenau.

Krystallglas-Hüttenwerke Ruckers- F Rohrbach & Carl Bohme Glassworks in Silesia, Poland (was part of Germany) [c.1926–45], (cut glass).

Kuhn, John Studio artist from the USA [1949–].

Kuhnt, Georg Gottlieb Glass maker from Breslau, Poland [1805–85]. Sig: some items are signed, (mosaic panels).

Kuijers, Glasblazerij Harm Glassworks in Dedemsvaart, Netherlands [1863–85], (bottles for wine, beer and storage).

Kulasiewicz, Frank Studio glass artist from USA [–], had his own studio from 1964.

Kumbatović, Mila Glass artist from Krk, Croatia [1915–], worked until c.1987.

Kungsholm Glassworks in Stockholm, Sweden [1676–1815], (Venetian style, later Bohemian-style engraved glass)

Kuntz, Marcus Glass maker from Millville, NJ, USA [–], active in the 1900s, (paperweights).

Künzel Glashütte Glassworks in Uhsmannsdorf near Rothenburg, Germany [1890–c.1937].

Kurilov, Adolf S Glass designer from Vladimir Province, Russia [1937–], worked at Gus-Krushtalny after 1968/

Kurt Faustig See Faustig, Kurt

Kurz, Fritz Glass designer [–], worked for Orrefors c.1942. Sig: monogram KD.

Kutaisi Glassworks Glassworks in Kutaisi, Georgia [1950s–?].

Kvetna Hütte Glassworks in Kvetna, Moravia, Czech Republic [?–present], (tableware, gilded and engraved glass)

KYGW Co Trade name of Kentucky Glass Works Co.

Kyjov Glassworks in Morava, Rosice, Czechoslovakia [1858–present], moved to Rosice, operated by Sklárny Moravia, (flat glass, packaging, technical and pressed glass).

Kysela, Jan Architect/glass designer from Bohemia, working in the 1920s.

Kysela, František Glass designer from Bohemia [1881–1941], taught in Prague 1917–41.

L

L&W Trade name used by Lorenz & Wightman.

LIP Glassworks in Murano, Italy [–], active c.1981, (art glass).

La Chapelle SA, Verreries Glassworks in La Chapelle Saint Mesmin, France [?–present], Duralex/Bormioli Rocco plant.

La Murrina See Murrina, La

LaBelle Glass Works Glassworks in Bridgeport, OH, USA [1872–88], burned down in 1887, was sold to Muhleman Glass Works, in

LaBelle, OH in 1888, (pressed glass and engraved wares).

Labino, Dominick Glass artist from Grand Rapids, OH, USA [1910–87], a Studio movement pioneer 1962–87 and created paperweights 1963–65.

Lacato Venini art glass designed by Carlo Scarpa, 1940.

Lacework See Stitching.

Lace-de-Bohème A type of art glass that incorporates white enamelled decoration in order to resemble cameo glass. It was produced in Bohemia c.1880–90.

Lackawanna Cut Glass Co Glassworks, location unknown [–], active c.1903.

Lacy-pattern glass Pressed glass (1825–50) with all over pattern of stippling to produce a bright, lace-like effect to conceal wrinkles and glass imperfections. A similar style was used in England in the 1870s and 80s.

Laeken Crystal Glassworks in Brussels, Belgium [–], active c.1940s.

Laeken, Verreries de Glassworks in Laeken, Brussels, Belgium [1849–54], Bongard/Catou, Ledoux 1849–54 (tableware).

Lafiore, SA Glassworks in S'Esgleieta, Mallorca, Spain [1960–present]. Sig: Lafiore glass is never signed, (art glass, recycled glass, coloured glass, rough "antique" finishes, pontils ground, but not polished).

Lagerbielke, Erika Glass designer from Sweden [1960–], has worked for Orrefors since 1982.

Lagny Signature found on cameo-etched Art Nouveau glass, possibly manufactured by Baccarat.

Laguna Type of art glass made by Venini and designed by Tomaso Buzzi in 1932.

Lahdenmäki, Nathalie Glass designer from Finland [1974–], has worked for Iittala since 1997.

Laid-on-ring lip Bottle lip with applied ring in use c.1840–80.

Lake, John-Orwar Glass designer from Sweden [1921–], worked for Ekenäs Bruks 1953–c.1957.

Lalique, Cristal See Lalique René.

Lalique, Marc Glass artist from France [1900–70], worked at Lalique 1921–45 then took over management at the factory until 1970. It was then taken over by Marie-Claude Lalique.

Lalique, Marie-Claude Glass artist from France [1935–], manager at Lalique after 1970.

Lalique, René Jeweller and glass artist from Champagne, France [1860–1945]. Opened first glass studio in Clairefontaine, Rambouillet, near Paris in 1902, did lost wax casting, he pressed glass/art glass perfume bottles for perfumer Coty 1907 were made at Legras, he had own glassworks at Combs-la-Ville [1909–37]. He then opened a larger facility at Wingen-sur-Moder [1921–40], which was named "Verrerie d'Alsace, René Lalique". This was managed by his son Marc. It was destroyed in World War II, then rebuilt in 1945 as Cristalleine. There has been a comeback of colour there since the 1970s. Sig: none 1907–14, R Lalique 1914–25, R Lalique

France after 1925, VdA France 1925–30 and Lalique France after 1950.

R Lalique France

Lalique

Lallerstedt, Lars Glass designer from Sweden [1938–], worked for Johansfors after 1967.

Lamartine Glassworks in France [–], active c.1910.

Lamb Trade name of Lamb Glass Co, based in Mount Vernon, OH, USA [1855–64], (bottles).

Lambert GmbH, Günther Glass dealer from Mönchengladbach, Germany [?–present], (tableware).

Lambert & Cie, Sté V Glassworks in Namur, Belgium [1877–1931], (tableware, technical glass, refractories)

Lambert, L See Hamendes.

Lamberts, Glashütte Glassworks in Waldsassen, Germany [–], active c.1933–present, (flat glass for restoration, antique glass, window rondels, decorative flat glass and stained glass).

Lambou, Francois Glass engraver from Belgium [1858–1924], worked at VSL after c.1880.

Laminated glass Sandwich glass with two glass sheets and a sheet of polyvinyl butyral (PVB) in between. Used as safety glass for car windows etc. It is aka Feuilleté. Patented by Édouard Bénédictus in 1909 and marketed since 1920 under the name Triplex.

Lamp A burner or torch for lampworking.

Lampl, Fritz Glass designer from [–], worked for Orplid Glass Ltd, Great Britain c.1952–4.

Lampwork Small glass made out of pre-formed tubes and rods that are heated in the flame of a gas/air or gas/oxygen burner or lamp and used for making small decorative items, paperweights and labware.

Lancaster Colony Corp Glassworks in Lancaster, OH, USA [1908–present], (pressed glass), see Indiana Glass Co.

Lancaster Glass Co Glassworks in Lancaster, OH, USA [1908–37], was sold to Hocking in 1924 and closed in 1937, (pressed glass).

Lancaster Glass Corp Glassworks in Lancaster, OH, USA [1904–present], a subsidiary of Lancaster Colony, (lighting, tableware, barware, cookware, giftware and paperweights).

Lancaster Glass Works Glassworks in Lancaster, NY, USA [1849–?], (flasks, bottles, pharmaceutical glass and pitchers).

Land van Luik en de Kempen, Glasfabriek van het Glassworks in Mol, Antwerp, Belgium [?–present], (bottles).

Landberg, Nils Glass designer from Sweden [1907–], worked for Orrefors 1927–72.

Landberg Expo numbering 1-80-53=1953, 1-154-54=1954, 155-210-55=1955, 211-404-54=1956, 305-387-57=1957, 388-506-58=1958, 507-584-59=1959, 585-624-60=1960, 625-682-61=1961, 1-15-62=1962, 16-60-63=1963, 61-90-64=1964, 91-108-65=1965, 109-112-66=1966, 113-119-67=1967, 120-139-68=1968, 140-145-69=1969, 145-167-70=1970 and 168-170-72=1972.

Landier, A & Houdaille/Landier, A et Fils Glassworks in France [–]. See Sèvres.

Lane & Sons, Josiah Glassworks in Dudley, Great Britain [1888–1932], aka Eve Hill Glassworks, it is a subsidiary of Thomas Lane & Sons in Birmingham, (lighting, globes and chimneys).

Lang & Son, Jules Glass dealer located in Islington, London [c.1900–?], pressed glass from moulds acquired from Sowerby 1905, Edward Moore 1915 and Percival Vickers 1914 and had it produced at Valérysthal and Portieux, France.

Langham Glass Glassworks in Holt, Norfolk, Great Britain in the 1970s then relocated to Cambridge from the 1990s, founded by Ronald Stennett Wilson.

Langs-Hütte Glassworks in Ilmenau, Germany [1900–68], (technical glass and tubes).

Långviksgården Glashyttan Glassworks in Långvik, Rosvik, Piteå, Sweden [1798–1879], (bottles).

Laňka, Jaroslav Glassworks in Kamenice nad Lipou, Czech Republic [1894–1948] and then reopened after 1998 as Jihočeské Sklařské Závody, SRO, (tableware and art glass).

Lanooy Unica Letter, year and quantity produced: A=1926/27 (min of 223), B=1927 (min 442), C=1927/28 (unknown), D=1928 (min 383) and E=1929 (min 174).

Lanooy, Chris Ceramicist/decorator/designer from the Netherlands [1881–1948], worked for Leerdam 1919–29 and produced Unica after 1923. Sig: L/L back-to-back monogram on series glass and CJLanooy on Unica.

Lantern An enclosed lamp.

Lapp & Flershem Glassworks, location unknown [–], active c.1898, (cut glass).

Lapsinya, Malda Glass designer from Riga, Latvia [1940–], worked at Rigas Stikls Glassworks after 1964.

Larkin Co Glassworks, location unknown [–], active c.1917, (tableware).

Larson, Emil Glass maker from Sweden [–] who emigrated to the USA in 1889. Worked at Dorflinger, Pairpoint, Quezal 1919–20, at Sinclaire after 1920 and Durand after 1924. Had own works at Vineland, NJ after 1935, (tableware and paperweights).

Laser glass Chemically toughened glass for use in making dinnerware and springs since the 1960s.

Lasi The word for glass in Finnish.

Latalin, Yury P Glass designer from Zolotkovo, Vladimir region, Russia [1939–], worked at Sverdlov Glassworks after 1965.

Latticino Italian for lace. This is a Venetian technique from the 16thC onward for embedding a vessel of clear glass with threads of (opaque white) glass to form patterns of vertical stripes or spirals. See also Zanfirico.

Lattimo 1. White opaque glass. 2. Type of art glass made by Venini, designed by Carlo

Scarpa and Tyra Lundgren, 1936.

Latvian Glass Latvia has half a dozen Glassworks – the two major ones are Grizinkalns (produces bottles) and Livanu Stikls (tableware).

Lauke, Marita Glass designer from Germany [1958–], has worked at Sachsenglas Schwepnitz after 1981.

Lauke, Richard Glass cutter from Germany [1940–], worked at Weisswasser.

Launay, Hautin & Cie Glass wholesales company located in Paris, France [c.1830–57]. Their pattern books from 1834–50 are the main sources for identifying glass made by Saint Louis and Baccarat from that period, (tableware, pressed glass and cut glass).

Laurel Cut Glass Co Glassworks in Jermyn, PA, USA [1903–20], was founded as the German Cut Glass Co in 1903 then named Kohinur Cut Glass Co in 1906/7 and merged with Quaker City Cut Glass Co in 1918, (cut glass).

Laurent, Claude Glass designer from Belgium [–], worked for Boussu c.1965 and Atelier Gala c.1989.

Lausitz Important glass-producing region near the Czech border in Germany divided into Niederlausitz (NL) and Oberlausitz (OL).

Lausitzer Glashüttenwerke Glassworks in Kunzendorf near Sorau, NL, Germany [1889–c.1937].

Lausitzer Glasring eV Conglomerate of various manufacturers from the Lausitz glass-making region in Germany, located in Bad Muskau. Members include Werlich, Greiner, Holl, Renate Müller, Adam Kristall, Döbbrick, Hentschke, Micko, Noack, Petrucela, Stolzle-Oberglas Lausitz, Rainer Trumpf and Dieter Tusche.

Lava Glass Trade name used by Tiffany for a type of dark blue/grey art glass.

Lavaluna Black glass with reduction colours from WMF in the 1930s – it was never marketed.

Layton, Peter Studio artist from USA [–].

Lazy Susan US term for a revolving dish.

Le Progrès à Manage, Verreries Glassworks in Manage, Belgium [–]; (see Assn. Gobeletiers Belges)

Le Verre Francais Schneider's commercial art glass from the 1920s using an acid-engraved cameo technique, (flowers, leaves and geometric patterns).

Leach, Benjamin A Glass maker from Fowlerton, IN, USA [–], (paperweights in the 1890s).

Leaching Glass corrosion that can occur in glass that is stored in humid conditions. Sodium and potassium ions are dissolved from the structure, water molecules infiltrate the glass and the dissolved alkali ions eventually show up as sticky dullness.

Lead A soft metal (Pb) with a low melting point, used for cames in stained glass windows. Its oxides are used in crystal production.

Lead crystal Crystal that contains Lead oxide; crystal with 24% lead is called "half lead crystal" while crystal with more than 30% is full lead crystal.

Lead glass Glass that contains Lead oxide instead of Calcium oxide, and Potassium oxide instead of Sodium oxide. Any glass containing at least 24% PbO is lead crystal within the EC definition. Lead glass is easy to decorate by grinding, cutting and engraving as it has a high refractive index and a relatively soft surface. Glass with lead oxide contents of up to 65% is used as radiation shielding.

Leaded glass The technique of mounting coloured flat glass in lead channel profiles or "cames". Leaded glass shades were produced from c.1895 in the US by Tiffany, Handel, Dufner and Kimberly.

Lead oxides These are widely used for the production of crystal and optical glass, either as PbO (yellow lead) or as Pb304 (red lead) – the latter has a higher % of oxygen.

Lebeau, Chris Painter/Glass designer from the Netherlands [1878–1945], worked for Leerdam 1924–6 and Moser 1926–30. Sig: CLB monogram on series glass while his name and date produced is engraved in Unica, (tableware; Unica).

Lebeau, Geille & Cie, J Glassworks in Jumet near Charleroi, Belgium [1877–83], it closed 1883 after a takeover by SA des Gobeleteries de Jumet.

Lechevrel, Alphonse Engraver/gem cutter from Paris [–], designed cameo glass at Hodgetts, Richardson & Co in Stourbridge, Great Britain 1877–80, and also taught Joseph Locke.

Lecjaks, Maria Glass designer from Hungary [1943–], worked for Miskolci Üveggyár after 1969.

Lecoule, Thierry Glass designer from France [1954–].

Lederle, Carl glass designer from Friburg im Brisgau, Germany [–], worked at Harrach after c.1900 and at the Liberec museum 1890–1914.

Lednické Rovné Glassworks in Lednické Rovné, Trencina, Slovakia [1892–present]. Sig: labels incorporate a crowned LR, the trade name used in 1892 was Rona, (tableware, barware, pressed glass before 1945).

Ledoux Frères Glassworks in Jumet-Brûlotte, Belgium [1825–55], renamed Bauzot-Ledoux in 1855, (bottles, tableware, lamps and lighting, flat glass until 1849).

Ledru, Louis-Léon Painter from France [1855–1926], worked at VSL 1888–1926, (cut glass, Art Nouveau).

Leech jar Large covered counter jar used in pharmacies and barbers for keeping leeches. Popular in France and Great Britain 18thC–19thC.

Leerdam Glass Glassworks in Leerdam, Netherlands [1879–present], merged with Vereenigde Glasfabrieken in 1938, changed its name in 1953 to NV Koninklijke Nederlandse Glasfabriek Leerdam (Royal Leerdam), then a big merger in 1959 incorporated factories located in Schiedam, Delft, Leerdam, Nieuw-Buinen and Maastricht. It then became part of BSN Glasspack, France after 1998. Designers include Berlage, Copier, De Bazel, De Lorm, Heesen, Lanooy, Lebeau, Linssen, Meydam and Valkema. Limited edition pieces are called Serica; signed one-off pieces are called Unica. (Blown and pressed tableware, designer glass, art glass from c.1925–present; currently produces bottles and mechanical tableware in sodalime.)

Marks from top to bottom for: Copier, Lebeau, de Lorm/de Bazal, Berlage, Bloch/Lanooy, Serica mark, current factory mark

Leerdam year letters 1920/5, A=1926/7, B=1927, C=1927/8, D=1928, E=1928/9, F=1929/30, G and H=1930/1, K, L and M=1931/2, N=1932, O=1933–8, P=1939, R=1940, S=1941, T=1942, V=1943, W=1944, X=1946, Z=1947, AA=1949, AB=1950, AC=1951, AD=1952, AE=1953, AF=1954, AH=1955, AM=1956, CB=1958, CC=1959, CD=1960, CF=1962, CH=1963, CK=1964, CL=1965, CO=1966, CP=1967, MA=1957, MB=1958, MC=1959, MD=1960, ME=1961, MF=1962, MH=1963, MK=1964, ML=1965, MO=1966, MP=1967, MR=1968, MS=1969, MT=1970, MV=1971, MW=1972, MAA=1973, MAB=1974, MAC=1975, MAE=1976, MAE=1977, FM78–FM86=1978–86, A1–A910=1944–50, A911–A1307=1950–61, UB=1957–61, LL=1959–61 LLM=1962–76 and LEM=after 1973. See also listings for Copier, Heesen, Jansen, Lanooy, Meydam and Valkema.

Lega, Hubert Glass cutter from Amay, Belgium [1930–], worked at VSL 1970–86.

Legras & Cie Glassworks in St Denis, France [1864–1915], closed in 1915 and then reopened as Verreries de Saint-Denis in 1919, (tableware, art glass, enamelled glass, cameo glass and amberina).

Legras, Auguste Glass artist from France [–], bought Verreries et Cristalleries de St Denis in 1864 and Cristallerie Vidié and Verrerie Mellerio in 1897, merged with Pantin c.1906, but was then taken over by Souchon-Neuvesel in 1924. Sig: not always, but includes L, Legras, Mont Joye, Legras de St Denis Paris and Indiana. Legras cameo is always signed, (art glass, cameo, enamels, pastels, gold, production until 1914 then art glass Deco style 1918–24).

Lehr Annealing oven for gradually cooling glass over many hours. It usually has a moving belt to carry the glass through the controlled temperature zones at a controlled speed.

Leibovitz, Edward Glass artist from Romania [1946–], founded Anverre in 1972.

Leichlingen, Glashütte Glassworks in Germany [–]. See Gral-Glashütte.

Leinauer Glaswaren Glass refinery located in Leinau, near Kaufbeuren, Bavaria, Germany [c.1950–1986], trade names include LGW and Pfauenauge, (vacuum silvering on bought blanks, "carnival" finish).

Leippa, Glashütte Glassworks in Leippa near Rothenburg OL, Germany [1819–c.1937], operated by Carl Teubert, (cheap tableware).

Leivo, Inkeri Glass designer from Finland [1944–], worked for Nuutajärvi after 1971.

Leloup, Louis Glass sculptor from Seraing, Belgium [1929–], worked for VSL 1947–71, had his own independent studio after 1972.

Lemans, Maurisdes Glass designer from Belgium [–], worked at VSL c.1960–5.

Lemington Glass Works Glassworks in Newcastle-on-Tyne, Great Britain [1887–c.1950s], operated as Sowerby & Co, owned by George Sowerby, cousin to the more famous J G Sowerby of the Ellison Glassworks, (tableware).

Lemke, Theodore Studio artist from the USA [–].

Lengelé & Cie, Sté A Glassworks in Champ Baivy/ Namur, Belgium [1901–3], (vases, ornamental glass).

Leningrad Factory of Decorative Glassware Glassworks in St Petersburg, Russia [?–c.1940s], previously Leningrad Mirror Factory and became a workshop for decorative glassware after 1940/41. Designers include Antonova, Astvatsaturyan after 1965, Batanova 1952–4, Byakov & Byakova after 1965, Eismont 1950–2, Eryomin after 1948, Ivanova 1950–9, Jurgen after 1955, Krimmer 1948–50, Lipskaya, Mukhina 1940–53, Muntyan 1951–9 and occasionally after 1960, Ojamäa 1956–8, Pöld after 1956, Smirnov 1948–67, Smirnova after 1953 and Yanovskaya after 1949, (tableware, art glass, cut glass, colour).

Leningrad Mirror Factory Glassworks in St Petersburg, Russia [–], was renamed Leningrad Factory of Decorative Glassware after c.1940, designers include Mukhina, Vertuzayev 1939–41, Uspensky 1940–1 and Tyrsa 1940–1.

Lenox Producer of dinnerware from USA [?–2000], it was sold to Imperial in 1972 and its Mt Pleasant Glassworks, PA, which was sold to Nachtmann in 2000. Sig: LIG = Lenox Imperial Glass after 1972.

Lensfelt, Frits Glass designer from the Netherlands [1886–1945], worked for

Leerdam 1926–30, (lighting).
Lenti Barovier & Toso art glass type by Ercole Barovier, 1940.
Leon, Tina Glass designer from Tallinn, Estonia [1944–], worked at Tarbeklaas works, Tallinn after 1965.
Leonardo Trade name for Glaskoch.
Leonhardi Glashütte Glassworks in Schwepnitz near Kamenz, Germany [1867–c.1937].
Leperlier, Antoine et Etienne Studio for Pâte-de-verre located in Conches, France [1979–?], was run by grandsons Antoine [1953–] and Etienne [1952–] of François-Emile Décorchemont.
Lerche, Emanuel Bohemian engraver who worked in Edinburgh after c.1869.
Leucos SRL Glassworks in Scorzè, Venézia, Italy [?–present], (glass tiles).
Leune Glassworks in France [c.1904–c.1935]. Sig: most pieces were signed, but rubbed off easily so may not be evident, (art glass, enamel decoration on matt ground, landscapes, holly leaves, designs by Heiligenstein 1923–6 and cast glass in c.1930).
Léveillé, Ernest-Baptiste Glass artist from Paris [1841–1913], joined the works of Rousseau in 1885 and became manager in 1888. He took over Maison Toy in 1901 and produced tableware as Toy & Léveillé. The company was sold out to Heraut et Guignard in 1906. Sig: includes HG and Le Rosey c.1906–13, (art glass and tableware). See Rousseau.
Levine, Louis Glassworks, location unknown [–], (cut glass, Brilliant period).
Lewis, John Studio artist from the USA [1942–].
Lewis, Pete Glass maker from Millville, NJ, USA, (paperweights in the 1980s).
Lewis & Neblett Co Glassworks, location unknown [–], was active c.1915, (cut glass).
Lewis & Towers Glassworks in Edenbridge, Kent, Great Britain [1920–present], (pressed glass).
LG Co Trade name Louisville Glass Works, Louisville, KY, USA [–], active c.1880, (bottles).
Libbey Glass Inc Glassworks in Toledo, OH, USA [1818–present], (tableware, barware, household glass – all mechanical).
Libbey, Wh H & Sons, Co Glassworks in Toledo, OH, USA [1888–present], established by Edward Libbey after New England Glass Co closed in 1888. It become the largest cut glass factory in the world until 1918. Joseph Locke was part of the company from 1882–91 during which time he invented Agata, Amberina, Maize, Peachblow (Wild Rose) and Pomona. Other designers include A Douglas Nash c.1931. Libbey produced cut glass until c.1918 and is still in existence today as Libbey Glass Co making barware. Aka Libbey Glass Manufacturing Co, (pressed glass). See New England Glass Co and Libbey Glass Inc.

Libbey marks Etched mark "Libbey" over a curved sword 1896–1906, "Libbey" with L and Y linked 1906–13, logo on round paper label 1919–30, Libbey in script in a double circle 1924/29–45, Libbey Crystal in a circle 1933–5. Libbey-Nash glass is usually etched with "Libbey" in a circle, moulded tumblers from c.1950s are marked with L in a star with the year of manufacture on the left and quarters on the right. Logo "Libbey" with sabres top and bottom was used c.1959–70, Logo "Libbey" with sabres top and bottom c.1959–1968, "Libbey Glass" in a rectangle was used after 1970.
Libbey-Owens process Vertical drawing process for flat glass, which was first used in 1917. The drawing speed of the Libbey-Owens process is twice that of the Fourcault process.
Libellula Type of art glass made by Venini designed by Vittorio Zecchin, 1921.
Libenský, Stanislav Glass maker from artist from Bor, North Bohemia, Czech Republic [1921–], worked at Železný Brod school 1954–63, worked with Brychtová after 1954, then became independent (tableware, art glass, sculpture & architectural projects).
Libera Trade name of Bohemia Crystalex Trading.
Liberty & Co Sales outlet in London for art glass.
Liberty Works/Liberty Cut Glass Works Glassworks in Egg Harbor, NJ, USA [1903–32], (cut glass, pressed glass and tableware).
Liberty Glass Co Glassworks in Sapulpa, OK, USA [–]. Sig: L G 1924–46, L-G 1946–54 and LG after 1954, (bottles).
Libisch, Joseph Glass engraver from Hungary [–], worked in Vienna, Prague and at Steuben after 1921.
Libochovicke Sklárny as Glassworks in Litomerice, Czech Republic [1911–present], currently located in Libochovice, designers included Prof Drahonovsky in the1930s. Trade names include Barolac, part of Sklo Union, (pressed glass).
Licata, Riccardo Glass designer from Venice, Italy [1929–], worked for Archimede Seguso in 1952, Cenedese in 1952 and Venini in 1954.
Liégeoise See Stitching.
Lierke, Rosemarie Flamework artist from Schwalbach, Germany [1934–], had own studio after 1977. Sig: L° + number/year, (enamelling after 1964, slumping, fusing 1970–7 and crackle).
LIG Lenox Imperial Glass mark after 1972.
Lightning rod ball US term for a decorative glass ball used on lighting rods, esp. in rural areas [c.1875–c.1925].
Lighting stopper Bottle closing device with outside spring wire clasp introduced in 1875.

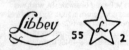

Lightolier Co Lighting manufacturer in New York [c.1920–c.1940].

Lily pad A decoration on art glass.

Limburg, Glashütte, Gantenbrink & Co Glassworks in Limburg, Germany [1947–present], (lighting, modern style).

Lime Calcined limestone stabilizes glass. (Insufficient lime can cause crizzling.)

Lime glass Light glass formula developed in 1864 by William Leighton. It replaced the heavier and more brilliant Flint glass.

Limmareds Glasbruk Glassworks in Limmared, Sweden [c.1872–c.1910], (tableware & bottles).

Lindberg, Bengt Glass designer from Sweden [–], worked at Bergdala Glass.

Lindberg, Stig Glass designer from Sweden [1916–82], also worked for porcelain maker Gustavsberg 1937–57 and 1970–80.

Lindblad, Gun Glass designer from Sweden [1954–], worked for Kosta Boda 1982–7, was independent in 1987 and worked for Strömbergshyttan after 1987.

Lindfors, Stefan Glass designer from Finland [1962–], worked for Iittala in 1999.

Lindner, Gerhard Glass painter from Weisswasser, Germany [1911–], worked for Arsall 1926–9, Bärenhütte 1947–68 and VEB KLG (Kombinat Lausitzer Glaswerke) until 1981.

Lindshammar Glasbruk Glassworks in Vetlanda, Sweden [1905–present], designers include Gunnar Ander c.1957/66, Christer Sjögren 1966/7, Catherina Åselius-Lidbeck and Birgitta Watz. Sig: unique pieces are usually engraved with the designer's name and pattern number from c.1945–80 and with "Unik" and the year after 1980. An engraved pattern number and edition is put on limited edition pieces while the L logo can be found on paper labels, (art glass and tableware).

Lindskog, Georg Glass designer from Sweden [–], worked for Kosta in 1923.

Lindstrand, Vicke Glass designer from Gothenburg, Sweden [1904–83], worked for Orrefors 1928–40, Sandvik and Kosta 1950–73.

Lindstrand numbers on Orrefors engraved glass (before 1954) L51–58=1929 and L59–118=1930.

Lindstrand signatures on Kosta glass (after 1955): LH=handmade, LU=unica, LC=Colora glass, LF=bird sculptures, LG=engraved, LS=cut glass.

LH numbers 1,001–1,259=before 1954, 1,265–1,627=before 1958 and 1,640–1,784=before 1962.

LG numbers 101–212=before 1954, 213–330=before 1958 and 335–407=before 1962.

LS numbers 501–590=before 1954,

599–682=before 1958 and 683-754=before 1962.

LU 2,004–2,036=before 1954
(Acid-etched or sand-blasted mark Lindstrand Kosta=1950–52.)

Linia Design Trade name of Glaswerk Olbernhau.

Linishing Refers to grinding or polishing glass on a continuous abrasive belt.

Linka, Vladimir Glass engraver from Bohemia [–], worked in Železný Brod c.1940s.

Linssen, Lodewijk JF (Lojo) Designer from the Netherlands [1936–], worked for Leerdam c.1962–67.

Lion Cachet, CA Glass designer from the Netherlands [1864–1945], worked for Leerdam 1928–30.

LIP Trade name of Lea and Perrins.

Lip-wrap See Wrap.

Lipa, Oldřich Glass designer from Rychvald, Czech Republic [1929–], was at the Prague Academy 1950–5 and worked for Moser after 1955, (engraved glass after 1962).

Lipofsky, Marvin Glass designer from Berkeley, CA, USA [1938–], worked for Leerdam and Venini.

Lipper Glass maker's tool for widening and forming jar and pitcher mouths.

Lippert, Oswald Designer from Stará Boleslav, Czech Republic [1908–], taught at Kamenický Šenov school 1933–45; and at Staatliche Glasfachschule Rheinbach, Germany 1949–73.

Lipskaya, Anna A Glass designer from Moscow, Russia [1902–], was art director at central offices 1938–57 and her main works were produced at Dyatkovsky Cut Glass, Gus-Krushtalny and the Leningrad Factory.

Lisková, Vera Glass artist from Prague, Czech Republic [1924–85], flamework, was an independent artist 1946–85, was based at the Lobmeyr workshop 1946–51, worked at Rath Studio, Karlovarske Sklo after 1950, Moser c.1956–67 and at central institutions in 1952.

Lithyalin(e) Slag glass imitating semi-precious stone, developed c.1840 by Friedrich Egermann in Czechoslovakia. Lithyalin is often facet cut to show off the colours. Its name is taken from the Greek Lithos, which means stone.

Littleton, Harvey Glass artist from Verona, WI, USA [1922–], was a co-founder of the Studio Glass movement after 1962 and worked at VSL in 1972. Now works at his studio, Spruce Pine, NC, USA, where he makes studio glass.

Livanu Stiklas Glassworks in Livani, Latvia [1887–present], the works were destroyed in WW1, were reconstructed in the 1920s, closed in 1935, reopened in 1944 and was privatized in 1994. Designers include Aida Ročenkova, Anda Munkevica, Raimonds Cirulis and Dainis Godovskis, (art glass after the 1970s, crystal after 1981 and decorative glass).

Livellara Srl, Cristallerie Glassworks in Milano, Italy [1920–present], (bottles, tableware, tumblers, vases, semi-crystal and lead crystal).

LKYGW Trade name used by Louisville Kentucky Glass Works.

Lobmeyr Atelier Glass studio located in

Kamenický Šenov, Czechoslovakia [–], active c.1957.

Lobmeyr, J & L Glass shop located in Vienna, Austria [1824–?] and run by the Lobmeyrs. They had their own glassworks from 1837. Many works were commissioned from artists including Girard & Rehlender, Knab Laufberger, Machytka & Schmoranz, Salb, Storck, Teirich and von Hansen. The place was managed by Stephan Rath after 1902. Designers after 1910 include Haerdtl, Hoffmann, Jungnickel, Prutscher and Powolny (1910–14 is known as "the Powolny era" when his designs dominated company production). J&L Lobmeyr's Neffe Stefan Rath production site founded in 1918. Artists after c.1920 include Fink, Horejc, Rath, Rottenberg, Strnad and Wieselthier. Sig: engraved or enamelled logo "LW" after 1864, circular labels "J&L Lobmeyr Wien" or "Lobmeyr Made in Austria" after 1925, (iridescence from 1878, tableware, cut glass and art glass).

Lobmeyr engravers' marks Monograms include RB=Robert Baluch, AB=August Bisschof, JH=Jaroslav Horejc, RK=Rupert Kolrus, AE=Alfred Opitz, EP=Erich Pohl and MR=Max Rössler.

Locke Art Glassware Co Glassworks in Mt Oliver, PA, USA [1891–1936].

Locke, Joseph Glass maker, engraver, painter and sculptor from Great Britain [1846–1936], worked at Guest Brothers, Stourbridge and Hodgett, Richardson & Co, emigrated to the USA in 1882 and worked at New England Glass Co, Libbey, US Glass after 1891 then founded Locke Art Glass Co, (invented Amberina in 1883 as well as Plated Amberina and Pomona).

Lodelinsart-lez-Charleroi See Saint-Roch.

Loetz Glass factory [1836–1947], founded by J B Eisner, taken over by Susanna, widow of Johann Loetz in 1852. The company name Glasfabrik Johann Loetz Witwe was retained until the end. It was taken over by Max Ritter von Spaun in 1879 until 1914. Etched pieces made on commission may be signed Richard, Lucidus, Veles, Velez or Lutetia (1926–9). Sig: Loetz glass is usually unsigned, but on export pieces for USA and Great Britain only you will find "Austria", "Austria" with crossed arrows and "Loetz Austria" on bottom; "Lötz" was put on special pieces made for the German market. Pontils are polished, sigs were applied with an oscillating point. Label with logo/Joh Lötz Wwe Klostermuehle was used after 1891, the oval label featuring a ram, a crown and "Klostermuehle" was used c.1913–38. See Asträa, Argentan, Chiné, Diaspora, Karneol, Malachit, Olympia, Onyx, Pampas, Papillon, Perglas, Phänomen, Rusticana, Schaumglas and Titania.

Loetz designers Leopold Bauer, Adolf Beckert (AB), Hans Bolek, Josef Hoffmann, Franz Hofstätter, Marie Kirschner (MK), Koloman Moser (KM), Arnold Nechansky, Dagobert Peche, Michael Powolny, Ed Prochazka, Otto Prutscher, Milla Weltmann, Marie Wilfert-Waltl and Carl Witzmann.

Löffelhardt, Heinrich Glass designer from Heilbronn, Germany [1901–73], worked with Wagenfeld for VLG 1937–41 and after 1949, and at Schott & Gen Farbenglaswerke Zwiesel 1950s–1970s.

Lomonosov Glassmaker from Russia [19thC], specialized in Smalti, mosaic, jet beads.

Lonaconing Glass Co See Dugan Glass Co.

London Tea Co Glassworks in London, Great Britain [–], active c.1897.

Lonja Manufacturas SA Glassworks in Paiporta, Valencia, Spain [1982–?], (lighting, chandelier drops and special cut glass).

Loo, Bert van Glass designer from the Netherlands [1946–], worked for VSL 1978.

Lorenz & Wightman Based in USA [1862–71], (bottles).

Lorenz, Gebrüder Glassworks in Kamenický Šenov, Czechoslovakia [–], active c.1926), (cut glass).

Lorestan Glass Co Glassworks in Tehran, Iran [1988–present], (household glass).

Lorio Glass studio located in Flemington, NJ, USA [c.1975–present], (cut glass, art glass and paperweights).

Lorm, Cornelis de Glass designer from the Netherlands [1875–1942], worked for Leerdam 1917–26. Sig: monogram LGcld.

Lorrain Trade name used by Daum for art glass produced at Verrerie de Croismare.

Lorrain, Verreries d'Art de Glassworks in France [1923–?], founded by Paul Daum to produce cheaply made cameo art glass. See Belle Etoile, Verreries de.

Lorraine 1. Glassworks in Montreal, Canada [1962–74]. Sig: paper label. 2. Trade name of C Dorflinger & Sons.

Lorraine, Cristallerie Glassworks in Lemberg, France [c.1961–c.1972], (tableware).

Lorraine Glass Company Glassworks in Gateshead, Great Britain [–], active 1860s, (pressed glass).

Lorraine, Verreries d'Art de Trade name of Meisenthal.

Losky F Glasfabrik Oranienhütte Glassworks in Seitenburg, Germany [–], active c.1911.

Lost wax This process involves a wax model being covered in clay, baked and then the resulting mould allows one single cast, aka cire perdu.

Lotton Glass Glass studio located in Crete, IL, USA [1973–], founded by former hairstylist Charles G Lotton. Sons David, Daniel and John Lotton all have their own art glass studios. (Art glass; his layered art glass is called "Multi Flora").

Lotus Crystal Co Ltd Glassworks in Pattaya, Thailand [?–present], (cut glass and crystal).

Lotus Cut Glass Co Glassworks, location unknown [–], active c.1920.

Lotus Glass Co Glassworks, location unknown [–], active c.1963.

Louisenthal Glassworks in Luisino Údolí, Dolní Dvur, Czechoslovakia [–], (pressed glass).

Louisville Glassworks Glassworks in Louisville, KY, USA [c.1855–73], (Christmas tree decorations).

Louisville Kentucky Glass Works Based in the USA [1873–90], (bottles).

Louit Frères & Co Glassworks in France [1870–90]. Sig: R, (bottles).

Loumani, Verrerie d'Art Glassworks in Valbonne, France [?–present], (art glass, lighting and stoppered bottles).

Louvre, Grands Magasins du Sales outlet in Paris [–], active c.1909, (cut glass and tableware).

Loving cup Describes a cup with three handles.

LR Sig found on smaller cameo pieces from Cristallerie La Rochère.

LR Crystal AS See Lednické Rovné.

LSA Trade name from Lubkowski Saunders & Associates Ltd, Sunbury-on-Thames, Great Britain [?–present].

Lucaný nad Nisou/Idahütte Glassworks in Lucaný nad Nisou, Czechoslovakia [1912–1945].

Lucaný nad Nisou/Jäckel Glassworks in Lucaný nad Nisou, Czechoslovakia [1840–1930], (beads).

Lucaný nad Nisou/Ludwig Breit See Breit.

Luce, Jean Glass artist from France [1895–1964]. Sig: monogram JL, (art glass, sand blasting, enamels 1913–c.1930).

Lucent Clear or transparent.

Luceo Trade name used by Jefferson Glass Co.

Lucidus Signature found on cameo pieces attributed to Loetz.

Lucinda Glassworks in Bellingen, NSW, Australia [1911–present], trade name is Planet, (household glass, art glass, lighting and bowls).

Lúcio, Isabel Glass designer from Portugal [–], worked for MGlass, Marinha Grande c.1999.

Lucky Cross Trade name used by Gill Brothers.

Ludlow Glass Factory Glassworks in Ludlow, MA, USA [18thC–19thC], (Chestnut bottles).

Ludwig, Frank Ceramicist from Berlin, Germany [1963–], produced tableware for Schott Gen. & Jenaer Glass c.1999.

Luh Glassworks in Luhu u Týniště u Preštic, okr. Plzen, Czechoslovakia [1838–40], (pressed glass).

Luigi, Mario de Glass artist from Italy, alias of Guido Bin; worked for Salviati (vetro Mosaico) c.1936.

Luisenhütte 1 Glassworks in Dobrilugk, OL, Germany [1817–?]. 2 Glassworks in Weisswasser near Rothenburg, OL, Germany [1897–c.1937]. 3 Glassworks in Vimperk, see Luisenhütte, Luisenthal.

Luisenhütte, Luisenthal Glassworks in Vimperk, Luisina Hut, Czechoslovakia [1850–1945], founded by Jan Meyr, operated by Meyr's Neffe and Wilhelm Kralik.

Luminarc Trade name from JG Durand for machine-made stemware, tableware and giftware, both clear and coloured. The name was introduced in 1960.

Luminescence The emission of visible rays under the influence of UV light; aka fluorescence (when the object emits light without being irradiated it is called phosphorescence).

Luminous Unit Co Manufacturer located in St Louis, MS, USA [–], active c.1900s, trade name is Brascolite, (lighting).

Lunar Trade name for Holophane.

Lundberg Studios Glassworks in Davenport, CA, USA [1970–present], designers include James and Steven Lundberg (art glass in Art Nouveau style and paperweights).

Lundgren, Tyra Glass designer from Sweden [1897–1979], worked for Riihimäki Glass in the 1930s, Kosta 1934–6, Venini c.1937–c.1966 and Reijmyre in 1960. Sig: on Kosta pieces: firm, year, model + number and "TL".

Lundin, Ingeborg Glass designer from Sweden [1921–], worked for Orrefors 1947–70.

Lundin numbering 1-70-53=1953, 1-71-54=1954, 72-95-55=1955, 1-19-56=1956, 20-43-57=1957, 1-8-58=1958, 9-24-59=1959, 25-51-60=1960, 52-86-61=1961, 87-119-62=1962, 120-183-63=1963, 184-219-64=1964, 220-261-66=1966, 262-336-67=1967, 337-414-68=1968, 415-440-69=1969 and 441-513-70=1970.

Lüner Glashüttenwerke GmbH Glassworks in Lünen, Germany [1907–present], (bottles).

Lunn & Sons, William H Glassworks in New York, USA [–]. Sig: five-pointed star.

Lusac Brand name for perfume burners from France produced until 1939.

Lusia-Ilona Ackermanova Glassworks in Lousnice, Czech Republic [1991–present], (household glass, giftware and cut glass).

Lustre 1 Sheen, brightness, gloss. Lustre is the light reflected at the surface; it depends on the refractive index of the surface and is independent of the basic colour. Types of lustre distinguished are Vitreous, Resinous, Silky, Pearly, Adamantine, Greasy, Waxy and Metallic. 2 Surface treatment; shiny metallic effect obtained by using metallic oxides, sprayed on and fired at 600° C, see iridescence. 3 Lighting device with hanging prismatic drops; or one such drop.

Lustre Art Glass Co, The Glassworks in Masbeth, Long Island, NY, USA [–], active c.1920, (lighting).

Lustry Glassworks Glassworks in Kamenický

89

Šenov, Czechoslovakia [–], designers include Milena Verlišková 1960–2.

Lutetia Signature found on cameo pieces attributed to Loetz.

Lutgen, Véronique Glass artist from Namur, Belgium [1962–], worked with Couffini in Gard and Umbdenstock, Haute Provence after the 1980s.

Lütken, Per Glass designer from Denmark [1916–], worked for Holmegaard 1942–98. Sig: Lütken glass is usually needle-etched with "Holmegaard"+ no + PL monogram.

Lutz, Nicolas Glass maker from Saint-Louis, France [–], worked for Dorflinger after 1860, New England 1867–9, Boston & Sandwich 1869–88, Mount Washington 1892–5 and Union Glass 1895–1904, (lampwork, millefiori, candy striped glass, filigrana and hollow-blown fruits).

Luxodine Trade name for Alexandrite glass by ŽBS/Železný Brod Glass.

Luxton, John Glass designer from Great Britain [1920–], worked for Stuart & Sons after 1949.

Luxval Trade name for Semi-crystal Art Deco pressed glass introduced in 1930 by VSL and produced until c.1940. Designers include Joseph Simon, Charles Graffart and René Delvenne.

Luzerne Cut Glass Co Glassworks in Pittson, PA, USA [c.1890–1920s], (cut glass).

Lvov Factory of Sculpture and Ceramics Glassworks in Lvov, Ukraine [c.1940s], aka Raduga Factory. Designers include Antonova, Berskinskaya, Dumich after 1963, Ginzburg after 1960, Mery after 1955 and chief designer in 1962; Pavlovsky 1947/63-, Ryazanova, Sergheyev, Shakh, Shushkanov, Stepanova and Zaritsky 1957–8, (art glass, tableware and colour).

Lyndeborough Glass Glassworks in Lyndeborough, NH, USA [–], (pressed glass).

Lyon & Co, JB Glassworks in Pittsburgh, PA, USA [c.1862–67], (pressed glass and tableware), see O'Hara.

Lyon Brothers Glassworks, location unknown [c.1905–c.1906], (tableware).

Lyon, Cristallerie de Glassworks in Lyon, France [c.1872–?], (tableware). See also Choisy-le-Roi, Cristalleries de & de Lyon.

M

M (underscored) Mark used by Mosser.

Maasikas, Miriam Glass designer from Tallinn, Estonia [1916–], worked at Tarbeklaas works, Tallinn after 1953.

Maastricht, Kristalunie NV Glassworks in Maastricht, the Netherlands [1830–1972], designers include Willem Jabob Rozendaal 1928–39, Piet Zwart 1927–8, Jan Eisenloeffel 1927, Ed Cuypers 1927, Jan de Meyer 1927, H L Kannegieter after 1927 and Max Verboeket was their chief designer 1953–70. Sig: designer monograms in five-pointed star after the 1920s: E=Eisenlöffel; JM=J de

Meyer; R=Roosendaal; PZ=Zwart and K inside C=Cuypers & Kannegieter. Verboeket pieces are usually needle-signed in full. The company used circular paper labels until 1972, (tableware, cut glass, art glass Manuvaria).

Mabut, Jules Owner of tableware and art glass outlet A la Paix at Avenue de l'Opéra, Paris [c.1890–c.1900], commissioned art glass and their designers included Desrousseaux. Sig: "Mabut" sometimes engraved; most often paper label only, (enamels, stone effects, satin pastel, engraving etc).

Macbeth Company, George A Glassworks in IN, USA [1899–?], (lighting).

Macbeth-Evans Glass Co Ltd Glassworks in Toronto, Canada [c.1900–c.1936], (lighting).

Macbeth-Evans Glassworks in Charleroi, PA, USA [1899–present], taken over by Corning Glass Co in 1936 but kept its own name.

Mace, Flora C Studio glass artist from Seattle, WA, USA [–].

Macedoine Mixed, scrambled colours.

Macek, Otto Sculptor from the Czech Republic [–], worked for BAG Vsetin after c.1994.

MacGrav Engraving studio located in St Petersburg, Russia [1990–present]. Sig: artist name engraved on major pieces only, (cameo cutting, cut-to-clear, both original work and museum replicas, unique pieces and limited editions).

Machař, Václav Glass artist from Nový Bor, Czech Republic [1945–], worked at Nový Bor school after 1978.

Machytka, Johann Architect and glass designer from Bohemia [1845–c.1886], worked for Lobmeyr c.1873–c.1886. Produced "Islamic" art glass together with Schmoranz.

Mackenna Y Mackenna SA Glassworks in Quilicura, Chile [1972–present], (bottles, barware and tableware).

Madesk Glass refinery located in Czechoslovakia [?–present], (raised enamel on gold, green/blue/black/red).

Mado, Nancy Signature found on enamelled floral art glass c.1910.

Maestri Muranesi Sas di Rossi Sergio & C Glassworks in Murano, Italy [c.1967–present], (scavo vases, antique finish art glass and tableware).

Maestri Vetrai Muranesi Cappelin & Co Glassworks in Murano, Italy [1925–31], artistic director Vittorio Zecchin. For their earlier work see Vetri Soffiati. See also Cappelin and Venini (founders).

Magdalenenhütte Glassworks in Grossräschen near Calau, Germany [1888–c.1937].

Magdalenenhütte Glassworks in Mstišov, Czechoslovakia [–].

Magistretti, Vico Architect and designer from Italy [c.1920–c.1980], worked for Vistosi c.1968.

Magnesium oxide (MgO, Magnesia) This chemical stops devitrification and improves working time.

Magnor Glasverk AS Glassworks in Magnor, Norway [1896–present], it was founded by Eda and has the same management as Johansfors. Designers include Per Spook, Gro Erikson and Stein Nilsen, (tableware).

Magnum A paperweight larger than 8cm (3¼ in) in diameter.

Mahmood Saeed Glass Industry Glassworks in Jeddah, Saudi Arabia [?–present], (bottles, tableware and household glass).

Mairesse, Léon Glass designer from Belgium [1903–85], founded decoration studio at Verreries du Centre, Manage, (enamel, acid cutback).

Maize Type of art glass from Libbey, designed by Joseph Locke c.1885.

Majella, Josephine Glass engraver from Great Britain [–], active c.1975.

Majo, de see De Majo.

Majorelle, Louis; Furniture maker from Nancy, France [1859–1926], collaborated with Daum c.1902–c.1925, (glass in metal frames).

Makarenko, Galina K Glass designer from Moscow, Russia [1930–], worked at Kalinin Cut Glass Factory, Moscow 1955–7, at Dyatkovsky Cut Glass 1957/8 and at Workshops of Applied Art Moscow after 1958. Main works were produced at Dyatkovsky Cut Glass, The Neman and Dzerzhinsky.

Makora Glassworks in Krosno, Poland [1991–present], no sigs, (ornamental glass; cased, coloured, spatter).

Malachite Dark green marbled glass imitating malachite. Made by Loetz from 1889, by Kurt Schlevogt of Jablonec since the thirties, by Halama at Železný Brod and at Desná until the present day. Malachite was first used as a trade name by St Louis in 1850.

Målerås Glasbruk AB Glassworks in Målerås, Sweden [1890–present], it was a part of Kosta Boda 1977–80 but has been independent since 1981. Designers include Rolf Sinnmerk, Eva Englund, Erika Höglund and Mats Jonasson. Sig: engraved Mats Jonasson Studio + date + edition number on limited editions, sometimes includes engraver's initials (engraved crystal with animal figures).

MÅLERÅS
SWEDEN

Málinec Glassworks in Lucence, Slovakia [1820–c.1972], aka Stredoslovenské Sklárne, (pressed glass reported from 1895).

Mallorca See Lafiore.

Mallorytown Glass Works Glassworks in Mallorytown, Ontario, Canada [1825–40], (tableware and bottles).

Maltsov Glass-making family from Russia [19thC], in the second half of the 19thC the Maltsov family had a virtual monopoly on glass making and sales in Russia and Persia, controlling all glass works including Gus-Krushtalny and Dyatkovsky.

Mambour, Louis Glass engraver from Belgium [–], worked at VSL 1885–1940.

Manage, Cristalleries de Glassworks in Manage [1881–1924], founded by Verreries de Manage and Verreries Bougard then taken over by Sté Des Pavillons in 1924, (tableware, lighting, cut glass, pressed glass, engraved glass and semi-crystal).

Manage, Verrerie et Gobeleterie de Glassworks in Manage [1853–?], (tableware glass and semi-crystal).

Manage-Scailmont See Scailmont.

Mandruzzato, Gianfranco Glass artist from Murano, Italy [–], active c.1980.

Manganese "Glass-maker's soap", this is used to discolour a glass batch. A high percentage of manganese will slowly turn the glass light purple when it is exposed to sunlight for an extended time.

Mangiarotti, Angelo Glass designer from Italy [1921–], worked for Vistosi c.1967.

Manhattan Oval Trade name used by Whitall, Tatum & Co.

Mano Volante Italian term for freehand.

Manship, Paul Glass designer from USA [–], worked for Steuben.

Manson, Joyce Glass maker from Scotland [–], worked for Caithness Glass 1980s–90s and for William Manson Paperweights, Perth after 1997.

Manson Sr, William Glass maker from Scotland [–], worked at Caithness Glass in the 1960s, 1980s and 1990s, at Harland Glass in the 1970s and at William Manson Paperweights, Perth after 1997.

Mantle Lamp Co of America Lighting manufacturer located in Chicago, IL, USA [1908–68], took over Lippincott Glass Co in 1926 and moved to Alexandria, IN in the same year, (lighting, including Aladdin kerosene lamps).

Mantua Glass Co Glassworks in OH Mantua [1822–9]; (bottles, flasks)

Manufacture de Glaces, Verres à Vitre, Cristaux et Gobeleteries Group from Seraing near Liège, [1836–?], included VSL, Mariemont, Drion in Jumet and Houtart in Lodelinsart. Aka Sté des Manufactures.

Manuvavia Handmade art glass produced by Maastricht in the 1930s.

Manuverbel Aka Manufacture Belge des Verres groups, tableware producers in Belgium [1968–73], Boussu and Doyen were later joined by De Rupel, Boom and Verreries Gobleteries Nouvelles (Manage).

Maple City Glass Co Glassworks in Honesdale, PA, USA [c.1904–.1923], (cut glass).

Mara Glashütte Glassworks in Lienz, Austria [1962–present], aka Rojko Glaskunsthandwerk, designers include Josef

Rojko, (giftware and sports trophies).

Marais, Verrerie du Glassworks in Boussu near Mons, Belgium [1849–?], (bottles and tableware).

Maraj, Jerzy Glass designer from Poland [–], worked at Tarnowiec Glass Works c.1999.

Marangoni, Federica Glass artist from Italy [1940–], produced designs for Salviati in the late 1970s.

Marbled glass Refers to glass that includes colour streaks in order to imitate marble. See slag, marmorite, schmelzglas, calcedonio and lithyalin.

Marcaurel Trade name used by Nachtmann Bleikristall for machine made tableware designed by Heinz Frisch.

Marcolin Art Crystal Glassworks in Ronneby, Sweden [1962–1994], the Marcolin trade name was taken over by Sardinia Crystal. Sig: FM Ronneby, FM Konstglas, Marcolini). (crystal figures).

Marcolin, Josef and Benito Glass artists from Venice, Italy [–], worked for Glimma Glasbruk, Sweden 1954–7 and Reijmyre 1957–61, started their own company Marcolini Art Crystal 1961–94 and worked for Sardinia Crystal Srl 1994–5. Their trade name Marcolin is currently in use at Sardinia.

Marcquebreucq, Michel Glass designer from Belgium [–], designed for Boussu c.1970.

Marel, Siem van der Glass designer from Holland [1944–], worked for Leerdam after 1966.

Mareš, Ivan Glass artist from Děčín, Czech Republic [1956–], worked with Libenský before 1983, was independent after 1983 and worked at Moser in 1997.

Mareschi Barovier & Toso art glass type by Ercole Barovier, 1957.

Margold, Emanuel Glass designer from Darmstadt, Germany [–], worked for Schappel, developed Borussia glass designs c.1913.

Marienhütten Glassworks in Penzig near Görlitz, Germany [–].

Marienthal Glassworks in Otvovice, Czechoslovakia [–].

Marinha Grande Glass-making region of Portugal. Factories based there include Atlantis Cristais de Alcobaça, Canvidrio, Centro Vidreiro do Norte de Portugal, Cristul, Dâmaso, Ifavidro Marividros, Neovidro, Nova Ivima, Tecnologia Tosel, Vetricor, Vicrimag, Vidrividro Produçao de Vidros. Currently produces a designer glass called MGlass.

Marinot, Maurice Glass artist from Troyes, France [1882–1960], first work c.1911, worked with enamels until c.1923, was production director at Viard c.1918–37. Last works made in 1937.

Marisa Dalla Pieta' Glass refinery located in Treviso, Italy [1980–present], (painting on glass).

Marividros Produçao de Vidros Glassworks in

the Marinha Grande region of Portugal [?–present], (clear glass tableware and lighting), see Marinha Grande and Mglass.

Markhbein SA Glass producer from France [–], designers include Dumond & Leloup c.1965/6, (tableware).

Marlboro Street Glassworks Glassworks in Keene, NH USA [1815–41], (flasks, tableware and moulded articles).

Marmopal Type of art glass produced by Fritz Heckert c.1900.

Marmorite Slag glass produced by Leerdam in the 1930s.

Marques, Paula and Virgilio Glass designers from Portugal [–], worked for MGlass, Marinha Grande c.1999.

Marquetry Trade name for mosaic art glass made by Gallé in 1898.

Marquis, Richard Glass designer from USA [1945–], worked for Venini after c.1969.

Marquot & Fils, Verreries Vve G Glassworks in Bayel, France [–], active c.1931 and 1933. See Bayel.

Marschner, Franz-Josef Bohemian engraver who worked in Edinburgh after c.1869.

Marsh, Honoria Diana Glass designer from Great Britain [1923], (engraving and stippling).

Marshumov, Mikhail M Glass designer from Kalinin, Russia [1938–], worked at Krasny May after 1964 and was then chief designer at Stekloremont, Kalinin.

Marshumova, Irina M Glass designer from Kalinin, Russia [1937–], worked at Krasny May after 1964 and at the Kalinin Glassworks after 1967.

Martel Opalescent glass produced in France c.1930s, source unknown.

Martelé 1 Cut surface resembling hammered finish, for example Battuto. 2 Type of art glass made by Daum after 1899. 3 Type of art glass made by Consolidated Lamp & Glass.

Martens, Dino Glass designer from Italy [1894–1970], worked for SALIR in 1925, Salviati 1925–35 and produced many designs for Aureliano Toso 1939-1970.

Martinez, Raymond Glass designer from France [1944–].

Martinske Udoli Glassworks in Martinske Udoli, Czechoslovakia [1793–1863].

Martinuzzi, Napoleone Glass designer from Italy [1892–1977], worked for Venini 1925–31, Vetreria Vetri Artistici e Mosaici Zecchin Martinuzzi 1931–6, Arte Vetro di Alberto Seguso 1950/2, Cenedese c.1950s and Barbini c.1960s.

Márton, Horváth Glass artist from Budapest, Hungary [1941–], has been an independent artist since c.1971. Sig: engraved HM, (iridized threaded art glass).

Martoret Sig found on paperweights from France c.1820s–c.1840s

Marver A flat marble or steel plate for shaping glass by rolling.

Marvering Pre-shaping hot glass by rolling it to and fro on a marvering table or marble plate. Colour decoration is picked up using this rolling action.

Maryland Glass Glassworks in Cumberland, MD, USA [–].

Maschio, Fabbrica Vetri Artistici C Glassworks in Murano, Italy [–], active c.1933, (art glass).

Maschio, Serena dal Glass designer from Italy [1920–74], worked for SALIR after 1951.

Masip SA, Vidrieras See Vidrieras Masip.

Maštová, Ivana Glass artist from the Czech Republic [1961–] has been an independent artist since 1988.

Mason Fruit Jar Co Glassworks in Philadelphia, PA, USA [–], the company invented the metal screw top for wide mouth jars in 1858. Trade names include Mascot, Mason, MFG Co 1885–90, see also Canning jars, (bottles).

Massanetz, Carl Glass decorator/designer from Kamenický Šenov, Czech Republic [1890–1918], had own studio in Kamenický Šenov after 1912, (feather pen decoration).

Massari, Noti Glass designer from Italy [1939–], worked for Leucos in 1971.

Massart Michel Glassworks in La Louvière, Belgium [c.1925–35].

Massiccio Italian term for a technique of manipulating glass on a solid pontil rod. This has been used since the 1930s.

Masson, Dieudonné Master glass blower/artist from Belgium [1850–1924], worked at VSL 1862–1924, (specialist in fine work, filigrane and Venetian-style glass).

Masson, Edouard Painter from Belgium [1881–1950], worked at VSL with father Dieudonné.

Matagne, F Glass engraver from Belgium, worked at VSL c.1920–1940.

Matarese Sas, Cristalleria Glassworks in Arzano, NA, Italy [?–present], (tableware).

Mataro SCOCL, Cristalerias de Glassworks in Mataro, Spain [1919–present], (lighting, shades and chimneys).

Match head cane (St.Louis) Solid opaque red paperweight cane used by Saint-Louis.

Matos, David Glass designer from Portugal [–], worked for MGlass, Marinha Grande c.1999.

Matous, Jaroslav Glass artist from the Czech Republic [–].

Matous, Josef Contemporary studio glass artist from the Czech Republic [–].

Mat-Su-No-Ke Art glass made by Stevens & Williams featuring applied flowers, after c.1885.

Matsushima, Iwao Flamework artist from Okayama City, Japan [–].

Matteis, De Glassworks in Florence, Italy [–], active c.1934.

Mattoni, Anton H Glass cutter from Karlovy Vary, Czechoslovakia [1840–1850s].

Mattsson, Johnny Glass designer from Sweden, worked for Reijmyre 1954–c.1958.

Matura, Adolf Glass artist from Bystřice, Czech Republic [1921–79], independent artist 1947–54, worked at central institutions 1954–79 and Rudolfova hut, Poděbrady, Exbor and Moser after c.1960, (cased glass after c.1955 and pressed glass after 1964).

Matushevskaya, Nadezhda P Glass artist from Podolsk, Moscow, Russia [1925–], worked at Gus-Krushtalny after 1951, Workshops of Applied Art after 1953. Main works produced at Gus-Krushtalny, Dyatkovsky Cut Glass, Krasny May)

Mauder, Bruno Glass designer from Munich, Germany [1877–1948], worked in Zweisel.

Maude-Roxby, David Howard Glass designer from Great Britain [1934], (engraving and stippling after 1961).

Mauser Manufacturing Co Glassworks, location unknown [–], active c.1890, (tableware).

Maveya, Alla I Glass designer from St Petersburg, Russia [1928–], worked at Leningrad Factory of Decorative Glassware 1957–64.

Maximov, Ernest S Glass designer from the St Petersburg region, Russia [1937–], worked at Vosstanie Glassworks 1967–70.

Maximova, Nadezhda N Glass decorator from St Petersburg, Russia [1911–], worked after 1956 and main works produced at Krasny May, Dyatkovsky Cut Glass and Gus-Krushtalny.

May, Kurt Glass engraver from Germany [–], worked at OLG, Weisswasser until 1965. OLG (VEB Oberlausitzer Glaswerke).

Maywood Glass Co. Glassworks in Compton, CA, USA [–]. Sig: M G c.1930, MG c.1940 and MG c.1950,(bottles).

Mazerski, Edward J Glass maker from USA [–], (paperweights at Union Glass Co, Sommerville, MA 1960s).

Mazoyer, Albert Glass decorator from Belgium [–], (enamelled glass).

Mazzega IVR Glassworks in Murano, Italy [1946–c.1981], has been dormant since 1983. Designers include Ermanno Nason 1954, Luigi Scarpa Croce 1954, Aldo Bergamini c.1954–c.1960, Carlo Scarpa 1957, Renzo Burchiellaro, Anzolo Fuga, Gianfranco Purisiol 1958–62 and Romano Mazzega c.1980. Sig: no signatures, (art glass).

Mazzega, AV Vetri d'Arte Glassworks in Murano, Italy [c.1967–c.1981], designers include Carlo Nason c.1980, (art glass, lamps and lighting).

Mazzega, Vetrerie d''Arte, Romano Several Mazzega firms operated in the 1930s. Romano Mazzega sold this workshop to Aureliano Toso in 1937 and it was renamed Vetri Decorativi Rag.Aureliano Toso. Fratelli Mazzega was founded in 1938, then renamed IVR in 1946.

Mazzuco, Successori Romano Glassworks in Murano, Italy [?–present], (conterie).

McConnico, Hilton Glass designer from USA [1943–], worked for Daum c.1987.

McCully, William & Co Located in Pittsburgh, PA [1869–85], (bottles).

McCutchen, Earl Glass designer from USA [1933–], worked after 1966.

McFaddin & Co, HG Glassworks, location unknown [–], active c.1885, (lighting).

McGlauchlin, Tom Studio artist from the USA [–].

McKanna Cut Glass Co Glassworks, location unknown [–], (cut glass, Brilliant period).

McKee & Brothers/National Glass 12 Glassworks in Pittsburgh, PA, USA [1843–1961], moved to Jeannette, PA in

93

1889, became part of National Glass in 1899, was known as McKee-Jeannette Glass Co 1904–10, McKee Glass Co 1910–52 then Jeannette Glass Co until 1961, (pressed glass, flat glass, barware, tableware and depression glass).

McKenny & Waterbury Co Glassworks, location unknown [c.1893–c.1920], (lighting).

Mdina glass Glassworks in Mdina, Malta [1968–present], founded by Michael Harris. Sig: Glass nearly always signed "Mdina" in large script. Further (spinoff) glass works on Malta are Mtarfa and Gozo. (Thick-walled glass and paperweights with abundant use of colour.)

Meadows, William Glass designer from Great Britain [1926–], (engraving, stippling after 1964).

Meaker, Charlie Glass designer [–], worked for Leerdam c.1979.

Medek, Božetech Glass engraver from Czechoslovakia [–], after the 1920s worked for Železný Brod and Halama.

Medici Trade name used by Cristalleria Corba.

Mediterranea Coop V, La Glassworks in L'Olleria, Valencia, Spain [1975–present], (recycled glass, household glass, tableware, decorative glass and art glass).

Mednis, Juris Glass designer from Ogre, Latvia [1937–], (worked for Rigas Stikls Glassworks after 1967).

Medusa Barovier & Toso art glass type by Ercole Barovier, 1938.

Medved, Ivan Glass artist from Zagreb, Croatia [1951–].

Meech, Annette Studio glass artist from Great Britain [–], working c.1975.

Meisenthal Glassworks in Meisenthal on the border of Alsace and Lorraine, France [1711–1969], after a merger in 1824 had the new name of Burgun, Schwerer & Co. The works closed in 1969 but currently it is a museum that is open in the summer only. Emile Gallé produced his works at Meisenthal after c.1867 and used blanks until 1895. BS & Co glass is much like Gallé's work, designed and/or executed by Désiré Christian until c.1903. Trade name used after 1901 is Verrerie d'Art de Lorraine. (Historical glass c.1875, pressed glass c.1900, lost wax art glass by Ringer d'Illzach 1904–15, tableware, blanks, cut glass, engraving and enamelling.)

Meissener Bleikristall GmbH Glassworks in

Meissen, Germany [1947–present], founded as Kristallschleiferei Horst Sändig, was nationalized 1972–1990 as VEB Meissener Bleikristall and has been named Meissener Bleikristall GmbH Marlies Sändig from 1994–present. Sig: needle-engraved M monogram on all pieces, (art glass, cut-to-clear, flashed, engraved crystal).

Meisser, Kleinert & Co Glashütte Glassworks in Penzig near Görlitz, OL, Germany [1884–c.1937].

Meitner, Richard Craig Glass designer/artist from Philadelphia, USA [–], worked in Holland since 1972, for Leerdam c.1979.

Mellerio Frères Glassworks in Aubervilliers, France [–], active c.1890.

Melloni & Moretti Glassworks in Murano, Italy [–], active c.1967, (smalti and enamel for mosaics);

Melon Orrefors glass designed by Nils Landberg in 1939, marks: NU2219/1-4.

Melort, Andries Engraver from Holland [1779–1849], (stippled copies of paintings on flat glass).

Mélotte-Nizet Glassworks in Quai d'Avroy, Liège [1816–1837], was previously known as Nizet-Melotte aka Avroy, (lighting, cut glass tableware)

Melt Molten glass obtained by melting a batch of raw materials.

Mendes, Carla Glass designer from Portugal [–], worked for MGlass, Marinha Grande c.1999.

Mendini, Allessandro Glass designer from Italy [1931–], worked for Venini.

Menghi, Roberto Glass designer from Italy [1920–], worked for Venini.

Mensa Glassworks in Barcelona, Spain [?–1908], merged into Union Vidriera de España in 1908].

Menzel, Johann Sigismund Glass maker from Warmbrunn, Silesia [1744–1810].

Menzelhütte Glassworks in Penzig near Görlitz, OL, Germany [1858–c.1937].

Mercury glass Patented (for door handles) in the US in the 1850s and produced in Great Britain, the US, France and Czechoslovakia until the beginning of the 20thC. Double-walled blown vessels were filled with a mixture of tin, lead, bismuth and mercury. The opening was sealed with a cut mirror disc or cardboard to prevent deterioration. Decoration of white or polychrome enamel was used. It was made in Great Britain by Varnish while in Czechoslovakia the decoration was done in cottage industries. One of the known producers is Hugo Wolff in Nový Bor. It is also known as Bauernsilber (Farmer's silver) or Silver glass.

Merese Ornamental knop or disc between stem and bowl.

Mériaux, Louis Artist from Sars Poteries, France [–], worked at Anverre Glasatelier in c.1988 and had own studio in Namur Bovesse.

Meriden Brittannia Co Glassworks in Meriden, CT, USA [19thC], (lighting).

Meriden Cut Glass Co Glassworks in Meriden, CT, USA [1895–1923], part of Meriden Silver Plate Co but was later known as International Silver Co, (cut glass, Brilliant period).

Meriden Flint Glass Co Glassworks in USA [–], active c.1877, (tableware).

Merikallio, Mikko Glass designer from Finland [1942–], had own studio after 1971.

Merker, Ursula Glass designer from Hohenstadt, Germany [1939–]

Merletto Italian term for glass with a "fishnet" pattern obtained by the inclusion of a fine glass-fibre netting.

Merritt, Douglas B Glass maker from Flemington, NJ, USA, [–], (paperweights after 1980s).

Mersey Flint Glass Works See Robinson, Skinner & Co Ltd.

Mery, Evghenia A Glass designer from Lvov, Ukraine [1918–?], worked at Lvov Glassworks after 1955, chief designer of Raduga 1962, designer for Steklopribor after 1968, for Striysky Glassworks after 1971.

Mesmer, P Glassworks in France [–] was active c.1890. See Gare, Gde Verrerie de la.

Metahütte Glassworks in Rauscha near Görlitz, Germany [1897–1937].

Metal Term used for molten glass.

Metal cased A glass object mounted in a metal covering.

Metallic lustre Shining like metal. See Lustre.

Metelák, Alois Glass designer from Czechoslovakia [1879–1980]. Director at school in Železný Brod 1924–48, designs for ŽBS, Halama.

Metelák, Lubos Glass designer from Czechoslovakia [1934], worked for Moser.

Metelák, Milan Glass designer from Bohemia [1928–93].

Meurice, Soupart & Cie Glassworks in Familleureux [1866–81], became Notre-Dame after 1867, aka Crystal, into Verreries Réunies c.1880.

Meursing, Jan Glassworks in Nieuw Buinen, Netherlands [1840–1938], merged NV Nederlandse Glasfabrieken Leerdam 1938, who closed it in 1967, (bottles).

Meydam, Floris Glass designer from the Netherlands [1919–]; worked for Leerdam 1945–80s, (tableware, Unica, Serica).

Meydam Unica letters, year and quantity produced: AC=1951(74app), AD=1953(526app), AE=1953(860app), AF=1954(621app), AH=1955(976app), AM=1956(1579app), AP=1957(3101), MB=1958(1679), MC=1959(1397), MD=1960(742), ME=1961(645), MF=1962(902), MH=1963(247), MK=1964(396), ML=1965(496), MO=1966(573), MP=1967(166), MR=1968(283), MS=1969(211), MT=1970(469), MV=1971(135), MW=1972(164), MAA=1973(28),

MAB=1974(149), MAC=1975(269), MAD=1976(241), MAE=1977(229), FM78=1978(143), FM79=1979(189), FM80=1980(348), FM81=1981(264), FM82=1982(47), FM83=1983(39), FM84=1984(125), FM85=1985(181), FM86=1986(147min), FM87=1987(107min).

Meyer, Grethe Glass designer from Denmark [1918–], worked for Kastrup c.1960–61.

Meyer, Jan de Glass designer from the Netherlands [1878–1950], worked for Maastricht Kristalunie NV 1927.

Meyr, Johann Glass maker from South Bohemia [1775–1841], founded several glassworks which passed on to Kralik, (crystal, coloured glass).

Meyr's Neffe, Adolfshütte Glassworks in Adolfov nad Vimperk, Czechoslovakia [1815–1922], also includes glassworks at Eleonorenheim; Ernstbrunn, Franzensthal, Idathal, Louisenhütte [c.1829–1922], owned by Wilhelm Kralik [1806–77], close association with Lobmeyr after 1851; split in 1883 when Adolf, Idathal and Louisenhütte continued under the name "Wilhelm Kralik Sohn" [1884–1944], merged with Ludwig Moser & Söhne in 1922 to form Karlsbader Kristallglasfabriken AG Ludwig Moser & Söhne und Meyr's Neffe; designers include E Eisenmenger, Theophil Hansen, Moritz Knab, Friedrich Schmidt, Josef Storck, al c.1880s, Koloman Moser, Prutscher, R Wille, c.1906; (tableware, cut glass, art glass; pressed glass after 1835).

Meysenthal, Verreries de Glassworks in Lemberg, France [–], was active c.1872. See Meisenthal, Burgun, Schwerer & Cie.

Mezza filigrana 1 Venini art glass designed by Carlo Scarpa and Paolo Venini, c.1935. 2 Composed of parallel threads of glass creating a diagonal pattern.

MFG Co See Mason

MG (italic) Trade name Maywood Glass, Maywood, CA, USA [1930–50], (bottles).

MG Co Trade name of Missouri Glass Co [–], was active c.1900, (bottles).

MG Co Modes Glass Co, Modes, ID, USA [1895–1904], (bottles).

MGW See Middletown Glass Co, New York, NY [c.1889].

MGlass Designer glass collection from Marinha Grande region, Portugal [present]. Consortium of glassworks lead by Vitrocristal. For participating manufacturers see Marinha Grande. Designers include Vítor Agostinho, Sandra Barateiro, Sylvia Bettencourt, Ricardo Cabral, Paulo Cardoso, Isabel Cunha, Ana Flôr, Paula Freitas, Catarina Gomes, Magda Gomes, Margarida Gracia, Isabel Lúcio, Paula Marques, Virgílio Marques, David Matos, Carla Mendes, Cláudia Pacheco, Rafael Pedro, Luis

Royal, Luis Silva, Cláudia Teixeira, Alda Tomás, Pedro Vieira.

Michel, Eugène Glass engraver from France [–], worked for Rousseau c.1867–77.

Michel & Co, E Glassworks location unknown [–], was active c.1931. See Hrdina, W, (lamps and lighting).

Michigan Cut Glass Co Glassworks in USA [–], (cut glass, Brilliant period).

Michlovkahütte Glassworks in Nový Bor, Czechoslovakia [1874–?], (crystal parts for chandeliers).

Michotte, Emile, Verreries Glassworks in Manage, Belgium [1939–1974], merged into Verreries du Hainaut 1974 (tableware).

Mickelsen, Robert A Flamework artist from Melbourne Beach, FL, USA [–], active since 1975.

Micko, Glasschleifmeister Harry Glass cutting works located in Neugersdorf, Germany [?-present], (cut glass).

Midland Industrial Glass Ltd Glassworks in Birmingham, Great Britain [1935–present], (cookware, giftware, paperweights, tableware and technical).

Mikasa Crystal/Kurasa Tableware dealer located in Secaucus, NJ, USA [?–present].

Mildner, Johann Josef Glass decorator from Gutenbrunn, Austria [1763–1808], (Zwischengoldglass, medallion cutting). See Mohn, Kothgasser.

Milieu de Table French term for centerpiece, a bowl for fruit or/and flowers set in the middle of the table, aka console bowl.

Milk bottle First USA patent 1880.

Milk glass White opaque glass, formulated with tin oxide, resembling milk, first made Venice where it was called Lattimo (milk glass), used for Zanfirico work, "Milchglas" in Germany, "Blanc-de-Lait" in France; much appreciated as an alternative to expensive porcelain in the 17thC and 18thC, and treated accordingly with enamel paint and gilding. Milk glass became popular for pressed wares at the end of the 19thC until the 1920s. The term applies to white glass only, not any coloured opaque glass.

Millar, J Glass seller from Edinburgh, Scotland [–], was active c.1876.

Milled edge Having a grooved edge like a coin.

Millefili Barovier & Toso art glass type by Ercole Barovier, 1956.

Millefiori Italian term for "Thousand Flowers", a technique used since roman times. Glass canes are fused bundles of colour threads, cut across to reveal the pattern inside. Widely used in Murano glass and paperweight manufacturing.

Miller & Co, Edward Lighting manufacturer located in Meriden, CT, USA, [1844–c.1920], (table lamps, sconces, hanging lamps, burners & leaded shades).

Miller Co, Ivanhoe Div Division of Miller & Co, based in Cleveland, OH, USA [c.1929–c.1932], (lighting).

Millersburg Glass Co Glassworks in Millersburg, OH, USA [1909–12], reopened [1920–24], (pressed glass, carnival glass, Rhodium ware, Radium ware), Radium Glass

Co. 1912; Jefferson Glass Co. 1913.

Millville Glassworks Glassworks in Millville, NJ, USA [1806–1844], sold to Whitall in 1844, became Whitall Tatum Co 1857, artists include Ralph Barber, Marcus Kuntz & Emil Stanger, (bottles, fruit jars & apothecary glass, paperweights 1860–1910s).

Millward, J Glass artist from Great Britain [–], worked for Stevens & Williams c.1940s, (cameo on old blanks).

Milovy Glassworks in Nové Mesto na Morave, Czechoslovakia [1835–1886] [1890–1893], (pressed glass, especially USA export).

MIM Trade name of Made in Museum SRL, Rome, Italy [?–present], (antique-inspired modern glass marked with MIM logo or "Canova").

MIMI Fenton customer mark 1973–74.

Ming Hou Chen Glass designer from Holland [–], works at Yumi Studio, Voorburg.

Miniature Small paperweight, maximum 5cm (2in) diameter.

Miniature bottles Have been around since the 19thC, surge in popularity after c.1930, especially 1950s & 60s.

Mirin Dol Glassworks in Slavonia, Croatia [19th C].

Mirosov Glassworks in Pelhrimova, Czechoslovakia [19thC–c.1900], (pressed glass c.1873).

Mirox, Miroiteries de Charleroi Mirror factory located in Charleroi, Belgium [1893–?], moved to Marchienne-au-Pont 1919, (mirrors & special flat glass)

Mirror glass Flat glass coated with silver (> 0,7 gm-2), copper and varnish. In 1996 Pilkington introduced mirrors made with CVD (Chemical Vapor Deposition) of 1 mm silicium. The companies Aurys and Charles André (part of Saint-Gobain) produce 4 million m2/year of mirror glass. Saint-Gobain makes ⅔ of European mirror glass, the rest is made by Glaverbel and Pilkington.

Miskolci Üveggyár Glassworks in Miskolci, Hungary [c.1969–c.1976].

Missouri Glass Co Glassworks in MS, USA [–] was active c.1902, (cut glass).

Mistretta, Giovanni Italian glass designer [–], worked for Josef Riedel Tiroler Glashütten c.1973.

Mitchell, Vance & Co Glassworks location unknown [–] was active c.1870, (lighting).

Mitoraj Glass artist [–], worked for Daum c.1989.

Mitre cut V-shaped groove.

Mityaeva, Lidia M Glass designer from Kiev, Ukraine [1923–], worked at Kiev Factory 1950–56 and after 1964).

MMA Mark found on replicas sold through the Metropolitan Museum of Art.

Mo, Jorun Kraft Glass designer from Norway [1949–], worked for Riis 1986.

Model Flint Glass Co Glassworks in Findlay, OH, USA [1888–1902], located in Albany, IN 1891–94, National Glass 1899, operated as Model Flint Glass Works 1900 until closure in 1902, (pressed glass).

Model, Hanns Glass designer from Germany [1907–], workshop in Stuttgart after 1933.

Modiano, D Glassworks location unknown [–], was active c.1890, (lighting).

Moe Bridges Corp Glassworks in Milwaukee, WI, USA [?c.1940]. Sig: Moe Bridges lamps are marked on the edge of the shade, not on the inside rim, which is the usual place, (lighting, reverse painted table lamps). See Inland Glass.

Mohn, Gottlob Samuel Glass decorator from Weissenfels, Austria [1789–1825], son of Samuel, (Transparent enamel).

Mohn, Samuel Glass decorator from Weissenfels, Austria [1761–1815], (Biedermeier style, discovered transparent enamel). See also Kothgasser, who improved the enamel technique further, and Mildner.

Moilanen, Harry Glass designer from Finland, [1931–1991], worked for Nuutajärvi 1960–63.

Moiseyenko, Stepan K Glass designer from Chudovo, Novgorod region, Russia [1922–], worked for Vosstanie Glassworks 1956–1970, chief designer 1960-70.

Moje, Klaus Glass artist from Hamburg, Germany [1936-].

Moje-Wohlgemut, Isgard Glass artist from Schwanewede, Germany [1941–]. Sig: full, or Moje, or IMW.

Molineux & Company Glassworks in Manchester, Great Britain [1827-?], renamed Molineux & Webb, renamed Molineaux, Webb & Co 1865. Sig: sometimes M,W&Co c.1850, (blown glass after 1827, pressed glass after 1846).

Möller, Tom Glass designer from Sweden [1914–], worked for Alsterbro 1959, Reijmyre 1963–67, Lindshammar after 1967.

Molnar, Pavel Glass designer from Czechoslovakia [b. 1940], works in Germany. Sig: MP & year.

Mombel-Bossart & Fils Glassworks in Belgium [–].

Momignies, Verreries de Glassworks in Momignies, Belgium [–], active c.1962, (art glass "Art Moderne" until 1962; since 1962 automatic production only).

Monarch Cut Glass Co Glassworks location unknown [–], (cut glass, Brilliant period).

Monart Art glass made in Perth, Scotland [c.1924–1939] by Salvador Ysart & family, and [1947–61] by Paul Ysart. See John Moncrieff Ltd.

Monax A thin white colour produced by MacBeth Evans.

Moncrieff, John Ltd Glassworks in Perth, Scotland [1865–1961], Monart art glass made c.1924–39 by Salvador Ysart and family, and by Paul Ysart only 1947–61); Sig: unsigned, raised and polished prunt over pontil mark, circular paper labels: at first only "Moncrieff's" and "Monart ware" in script, later "Moncrieff Scotland" around "Monart Ware" in script, and later "Moncrieff Scotland" and "Monart Glass" in script, the acid etched mark "Monart Glass/Made in Scotland" is found on US export pieces only. See Monart. After WWII the Ysart family split up. See Vasart 1946–65, Strathearn 1965–80, (bottles).

Monniot, Gervais, Lambalais Glassworks in France [–], (lighting).

Monod, Claude Glass artist from Biot, France [1944–90], worked Verrerie de Biot 1969–76, own art glass workshop after 1976.

Monod, Véronique Glass artist from Biot, France [1954–], (art glass).

Monod-Ferrière, Isabelle Glass artist [1945], has worked with Monod since 1976.

Monongah Glass Co Glassworks location unknown [c.1910–c.1920], (tableware).

Monot & Co, Monot & Fils See Pantin

Monot Père et Fils & Stumpf Glassworks in Pantin, France [–], See Pantin.

Monro, Helen Glass designer from Scotland [–], worked Edinburgh Crystal after 1941, Juniper workshop after 1956.

Monroe Co, C F Glassworks in Meriden, CT, USA [1898–1914], trade names include Kelva, Nakara & Wave Crest, (tableware & art glass).

Monschau, Glashütte in Glassworks in Monschau, Eifel, Germany [present], (figures).

Mont Joye Glass produced by Saint Hilaire, Touvier, De Vareaux & Cie in Pantin, France [1864–?]. See Pantin.

Montage "Assembly" lampwork technique developed in the 1960s in Lauscha, Germany by Albin Schaedel.

Montbronn, Cristallerie de Glassworks in Montbronn, France [1930–]. Sig: sand-blasted mark always present, (tableware, art glass, giftware, paperweights, cased crystal/cut-to-clear & sports prizes; full lead crystal only).

Montcenis Mont-Cenis see Creusot-Montcenis, Le.

Montelin, E Glass designer [–], worked at Reijmyre c.1979. Sig: EM.

Monterrey, Vidrios de Glassworks in Monterrey, Mexico [1906–c.1980], now a museum, (bottles).

Montferrand (Doubs) Verreries de Glassworks in Montferrand (Doubs), Paris, France [c.1879], (tableware).

Montgomery Ward & Co Glassworks location unknown [c.1910–c.1919], (lighting, flat glass).

Monthey, Verrerie de Glassworks in Monthey, Valais, Switzerland [1822–c.1910], operated by Contat & Cie.

Monti, Roberto Licenziato Glass designer from Italy [–], worked for Colle c.1999.

Moonlight Trade name of Moonlight Patent Lamp Co Ltd.

Moonshine Name given to clear Pearline made by Davidson's, (pressed glass).

Moonstone 1 Translucent stone with bluish-white schiller called adularescence. 2 Hobnail pressware by Anchor Hocking [1941–46].

Moore Bros Trade name of Moore Brothers, Clayton, NJ, USA [1864–1880], (bottles).

Moore, Edward Glassworks in South Shields, Great Britain [1860–1913], aka Tyne Flint

97

Glass Works, also recorded as Edgar Moore; failed 1913, moulds were sold to France, (pressed glass, tableware, vitroporcelain, marbled, caramel, Celadon green).

Moore, Simon Glass blower, designer from Great Britain [–], worked at Salviati, own studio in London, Dartington after 2000.

Morales-Schildt, Monica Glass designer from Sweden [b.1908], worked for Kosta 1958–70.

Morandiane Type of art glass made by Venini designed by Fulvio Bianconi, 1951 and by Paolo Venini, 1956.

Morassi Luigi Glassworks in Murano, Italy [–] was active c.1967, (beads and bangles).

Morava Glass Atelier Glassworks in Vizovice, Czech Republic [1991–present], (hand-made, mouth-blown stemware, art glass & Crystal).

Mørch, Ibi Trier Glass designer from Denmark [–], worked for Kastrup, Kastrup & Holmegaards c.1960–c.1969.

Morden, Samson Glass maker at Stevens and Williams [–], active c.1880s. Sig: initials "SM" (cameo, perfume bottles).

Moreau & Ducatel Glassworks in France [c.1890–c.1900].

Moretti Carlo SNC Glassworks in Murano, Italy [1958–present]. Sig: usually engraved "Carlo Moretti" after 1970, logo: MC in a square, (tableware, art glass).

Moretti & Fratelli, Ercole Glassworks in Murano, Italy [1911–present], artist: Ercole Moretti, (beads, lampwork, murrines; colour canes for lampworking.

Moretti Ulderico & Cie Glassworks in Murano, Italy [c.1934–c.1967], members of Quality Circle, (lighting).

Morey and Ober Lighting company in USA [19thC], (burning fluid lamps).

Morgantown Glass Works Glassworks in Morgantown, WV, USA [1898–1980], Martins Ferry, OH [1898–1902], Grafton, WV [1903–1906], Morgantown, WV [1913–1980], named Economy tumbler 1903, Economy Glass 1924, Morgantown 1939, trade name Old Morgantown 1924–39, (tumblers, pressed glass, cut glass & coloured glass after 1924).

Mori, Lisa Trade name for tableware from Inncrystal, Austria.

Morin, Claude Glass artist from Dieulefit, France [1932–], (art glass).

Moritzdorf Glassworks in Hermsdorf, Königsbrück OL, Germany [1869–?], operated by Sachsen Mitscherling & Baldermann and/or C A Walther & J Baldermann, (bottles & tableware).

Morley Brothers Glassworks location unknown [–] was active c.1919, (cut glass).

Morris, William Interior designer from Walthamsow, Great Britain [1834–1896], designed glassware for J Powell.

Mortevieille Glassworks in Mortevieille, près

Napoule, France [?–present], intertwined MV prunt.

Mortlock & Co, J Glass maker in London, Great Britain [–], active c.1880s.

Morton, M Glass wholeseller in London, Great Britain [c.1877–?], distributor for A J Beatty & Sons, (pressed glass).

Mosaico Tessuto Type of art glass made by Venini designed by Fulvio Bianconi and Paolo Venini, 1954.

Mosaico Veneziano, Il Glassworks in Marghera, Venezia, Italy [?–present], (Murrine & murrine giftware).

Moser Glasstudio, Tanja Glass studio in Bunsenberg, Austria [?–present], (fused glass).

Moser, Koloman Artist from Vienna, Austria [1868–1918], designed tableware, art glass and windows for Bakalowits after c.1900, Loetz c.1900/03, Wiener Werkstätte before 1908, Meyr's Neffe and Rheinische Glashütten.

Moser, Ludwig Glassworks in Karlovy Vary [1857–present], glass cutting workshop 1857–1893 named "Ludwig Moser Werkstatt für Glasveredlung", glassworks named "Ludwig Moser Glashütte" added 1893, named "Karlsbader Glasindustrie Gesellschaft Ludwig Moser & Söhne", 1900–1922, aka "Ludwig Moser Staatliche Glasmanufaktur AG", merged Meyr's Neffe, 1922 to form "Karlsbader Kristallglasfabriken AG Ludwig Moser & Söhne und Meyr's Neffe"; operated until 1938, designers include Rudolf Hiller, Johann Hoffmann, Joseph Urban, c.1880s, Hilda Jesser, D Peche, E J Wimmer, Julius Zimpel, c.1920, Oldrich Lipa, Lubos Meteläk c.1976, Vera Liskova c.1956–67; Milos Filip c.1963–4; Vladimir Jelinek c.1971–2, (tableware, art glass, cut glass, cameo, enamel & "rare earth glass" c.1930).

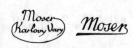

Moser marks "Moser" all caps in gilt or
enamel c.1880–93, "Moser" in linked script
engraved c.1880–90, acid-etched LMK
monogram in a square 1911–38, "Moser
Karlsbad" monogram script in an oval, R and K
linked, engraved, acid-etched, stamped,
coloured stamp or written in gold 1911–38,
acid-etched colour stamp 'WW' in use
1923–33, "Moser" in script over a curved line
engraved c.1926–present; acid-etched oval
mark "Moser M&M" incorporated in logo
c.1926–30, acid or colour stamp "Moser" in
script over a curved line 1926–50, acid-
etched stamp "Moser" in an oval 1926–36,
acid-etched "Moser Bohemia" in an oval
c.1928–30, acid-etched stamp "Moser MM
Czechoslovakia" in an oval 1936–1991, acid-
etched stamp "Moser" script 1936–38,
engraved mark + over 0 with two horizontal
stripes 1941–45, Acid etched stamp 'Moser
Karlovy Vary' in script 1946–present, acid-
etched stamp "Moser" with script underlined
c.1950–present, "Moser" underlined and
attached to the R 1992–present and used as
a sand-blasted mark 1995 onwards, sand-
blasted "Moser Studio" 1996–present.
Moser Stickers Circular label printed in thin
black lettering c.1880, circular label with
cluttered appearance printed in black
c.1880–90, circular label "Glassfabrik
Karlsbad" or "Moser/ Made in Austria" or
"Moser Austria" surrounding a glass black
print on coloured label 1898–1918 and in
smaller, modified version before 1938,
rectangular sticker printed in brown
c.1919–25, oval sticker with black print
1926–36, oval foil stickers "Moser" in script
underlined in yellow on silver c.1950–60s,
yellow on gold c.1960–70, violet on silver
1957 only, dark blue on silver 1962 only,
square sticker with flame logo
"Czechoslovakia" 1966–96 and "Czech
Republic" 1996–present, sticker black on gold
"Moser" with "Made in Czechoslovakia" in a
semi circle 1970s–80s, "Moser" over a semi
circle in black and red 1970s–80s, dark red
oval foil sticker with "Moser" in gold 1991–91.
Moser Trademarks "Orogravure" trade name
used 1919–29, "Oroplastique" used
1919–present, "Verroplastique" and
"Oropantogravur" used 1924–34, "Animor"
used 1925–35, "Acidoplastik",
"Argentoplastik" & "Patinor" in use 1928–38,
"Gipsy Gläser" used 1919–39, "Heliolit",
"Prasemit", "Alexandrit" trade names used
1929–present, "Royalit" used 1930–present,
"Eldor" used 1932–present.

Moskan and Hastings Manufacturing Co
Lighting manufacturer in Chicago, IL, USA [–],
(leaded glass shades c.1910–c.1920).
Moss agate Type of art glass named after the
semi-precious stone, first made by Rousseau
c.1880, Stevens & Williams after 1888, Trade
name by Steuben (red, brown marbled).
Moss cane Cane type in green and white,
typical for Clichy, (paperweights).
Mosser Glass Co Glassworks in East
Cambridge, OH, USA [c.1964–present]. Sig: M
underscored, N underscored inside C on repro
pressed glass 1980s, M 1980s–90s, M inside
Ohio state outline 1980–present, (pressed
glass, novelties & covered animal dishes).

Mother-of-pearl Layered type of art glass, the
inner layer blown into a pattern mould then
covered with clear or coloured glass to trap air
bubbles, often satinated. Patented 1886 by
Frederick S Shirley, made by Mt Washington &
Stevens & Williams, patterns include raindrop,
diamond quilted & herringbone. Collector's
term of endearment is MOP.
Motika, Antun Glass sculptor & artist from
Croatia [1902–], worked after 1952, at Nason
in Murano c.1961.
Motzfeld, Benny Glass designer from Norway
[1909–], worked for Hadeland 1955–67,
Randsfjords c.1950–c.1970, Plus after 1970.
Mould A form made of wood or metal, can be
open, enclosed, smooth or patterned. See also
dip mould.
Mould, block Cast iron single piece mould
used for pressed glass.
Mould blown Glass blown into a dip mould or
pattern mould, as opposed to freehand or
pressed.
Mould, dip Cylindrical one-piece open mould.
Moulineau, Verrerie du Glassworks in Ghlin-
lez-Mons, Belgium [18thC–1859], founded by
Delobel, switched to coal 1811, only blown
tableware and neogothic pressed glass after
1839, (flat glass, bottles, Demijohns, tableware
& pressed glass).
Mount Vernon Glass Co Glassworks in Mt
Vernon, NY, USA [1810–44], (bottles),
reopened late 19th C, (art glass; giftware &
novelties).
Mount Washington Glass Co Glassworks in
New Bedford, MA, USA [1837–94], located in
Boston until 1869, changed to Pairpoint Mfg
1894, (art glass, see Burmese, Crown Milano,
Peachblow, Peach Satin, Lava glass, Napoli
glass, Verona glass, cameo glass, cut glass,
paperweights 1870–76).

Mourgue, Pascal Glass designer from France [–].

Moyano, Lucrecia Glass designer from Argentina [–], worked for Rigolleau Crystal Works SA c.1950–57, (nail mould glass).

Mrzla Vodica Glassworks in Mrzla Vodica, Croatia [1812–27], (quality tableware).

MS/Moravske Sklarny Glassworks in Karolinka, in Kvetna and in Vrbno pod Pradedem, Czech Republic [?–present].

Mstišov See Tischau.

Mtarfa Glassblowers Ltd Glassworks in Ta'Qali, Malta [c.1975–present].

Muckley, William Jabez Glass engraver from Great Britain [1829–?], worked for Richardson before 1851.

Muffle Kiln A low-temperature kiln for refiring glass to fuse enamel, fix gilding and produce luster. See Kiln.

Mug A heavy handled cup.

Mugnoni Barovier & Toso type of art glass by Ercole Barovier, 1938.

Mühlbock, Glashütte Glassworks in Mühlbock near Bunzlau OL, Germany [c.1937–].

Muhleman Glass Works Glassworks in LaBelle, OH, USA [1872–?], took over LaBelle Glass Co in LaBelle, OH in 1888.

Mühlhaus & Co, Julius Glassworks or refinery in Nový Bor, Czechoslovakia [–] was active c.1985, (enamelled glass).

Mukhina, Vera I Glass artist from Russia [1889–1953], crystal works at Krasny Ghigant 1938/9, experimental workshop at Leningrad Factory 1940–53.

Mulcahy, Katherine Studio artist from USA [–].

Müller & Hoffmann, Glashütte Glassworks in Neu Petershain, near Calau NL, Germany [1896–c.1937].

Müller & Hruby Glass Studio Glassworks in Holice v Cechách, Czech Republic [?–present], (imitations of historical glass).

Müller & Poeschmann, Glashütte Glassworks in Döbern, near Sorau NL, Germany [1905–c.1937].

Müller, Erich Glass designer and decorator from Germany [1907], worked at Süssmuth 1924–39, Fürstenberg/Oder 1946–52, Eisenhütten 1952–57, institutions after 1957.

Müller, Eugène Glass designer from Belgium [–], worked for Val St Lambert 1906–08. See also Müller, Jean-Désiré.

Müller, Felix Glass decorator from Bohemia, worked 1830s–40s.

Muller Frères Glassworks in Lunéville, France [1895–]. There were nine brothers: Désiré & Eugène worked as decorators for Gallé c.1885, Henri, Victor & Pierre as apprentices. Decorator workshop founded by Henri 1895, used blanks from Gobeletterie Hinzelin in Croismare, which they bought up after WWI (art glass, cameo, acid-etching). Désiré and Henri worked on Fluorogravure for Val St Lambert 1906–07. During WWI Eugène died, Emile went to Choisy-le-Roi, Camille, Jean, Auguste to Sèvres. Ceased production 1933, closed 1936. Sig: various engraved, etched and cameo signatures exist; "Müller Croismare'" before 1914, "Müller Frères Lunéville" after 1919, "Butterfly mark", sometimes unsigned, "Grandes Verreries de Croismare" or GV de Croismare after 1918, (lighting, art glass, cast glass, etching & enamels).

Muller Frères, Val St Lambert Glassworks in Seraing, Belgium [–]. See Val St Lambert.

Muller, Gerard Glass designer, tableware outlet from Amsterdam, Netherlands [1877–1943], designed elegant tableware, commissioned from Josephinenhütte and VSL, and sold at Muller, Amsterdam 1905–43

Müller, Glas- und Porzellanmalerei Renate Glass decorating firm in Uhrmannsdorf, Germany [?–present], (painting on glass).

Müller, Jean-Désiré Glass designer from Belgium [–], worked for Val St Lambert 1906–08, brother of Eugène.

Müller, Josef Glass engraver from Bohemia [1839–1906].

Müller lamp See Berger lamp.

Mulvaney, Charles Glassworks in Dublin, Ireland [–]. Sig: CM&Co, (cut glass).

Münnerstadter Glaswarenfabrik Gmbh Glassworks in Münnerstadt, Germany [1920–present], (bottles & cosmetics).

Munkevica, Anda Contemporary designer from Latvia, designs for Livanu Stiklas.

Muntyan, Yury A Glass designer from St Petersburg, Russia [1921–], worked at Leningrad Factory 1951–59 and occasionally after 1960.

Muona, Toini Glass designer from Finland [1904–87], worked for Nuutajärvi 1963–4.

Murakami, Tatsuo Flamework artist from Chiba City, Japan [1950–], worked for Shibata Hario Co after 1970 designing heat-resistant glassware.

Murakhver, Vladimir S Glass designer from Tashkent, Uzbekistan [1931–], worked at The Neman, Belarus after 1959, chief designer from 1960.

Murano, Cristalleria Glassworks in Murano, Italy [c.1919–c.1920].

Murano, Cristalleria Glassworks in Murano, Italy [–], active c.1919/c.1930.

Murano, Eliodoro Glassworks in Murano, Italy [–].

Murano glass The island of Murano near Venice has been the domain of glassmakers since 1292. Its produce includes beads, mirrors, chandeliers, tableware, art glass, architectural glass, pressed glass – all types and all qualities are represented. In 1967 there were around 60 exporting glass factories on Murano.

Murano Glass Company di Fuga G & Barbini C Glassworks in Murano, Italy [–] was active c.1967, (cut glass & engraved glass).

Muratore, Rémi Glass designer from France [1954–].

Muratov, Vladimir S Glass designer from

Odessa, Ukraine [1924–], worked at Gus-Krushtalny after 1966.

Murphy, John Glass maker from Cameron, WV, USA [–] was active c.1970s, (paperweights).

Murray, Keith Architect and glass designer from New Zealand [1893–1981], worked for Whitefriars c.1932, for Stevens & Williams 1932–39.

Keith Murray
S ✶ W BRIERLEY

Murrina Slice of patterned glass cane used for decorating glass, also found as Murrhine, Murrini or Murrino. See Millefiori.

Murrina, La Glassworks in Murano, Italy [1968–present], designers include Peter Pelzel 1968–73 and Lino Tagliapietra, (art glass & lighting).

Murrine, A Venini art glass designed by Carlo Scarpa in 1940 by Fulvio Bianconi in 1948 and 1953 and by Tobia Scarpa in 1959.

Murrine Romane Type of art glass made by Venini designed by Paolo Venini in 1936.

Murrino Barovier & Toso type of art glass by Ercole Barovier in 1948.

Musashi Crystal Factory See Hoya Corp.

Musesti, Vetreria Glassworks in Cunettone, Italy [?–present], (tableware & giftware).

Muskauer Hohlglas Glassworks in Muskau, Germany [1889–], Arthur Sachmann vorm Raetsch & Co. Sig: MH-U-AS on bottom, (containers).

Musler Jay Flameworking artist from Sacramento, Berkeley, CA, USA [1949], glassblower at Maslach Art Glass 1971–81, autonomous works after 1981.

Mutual Lamp Manufacturing Co Glassworks location unknown [–] was active c.1922, (lighting).

Muurlanlasi Oy Glassworks in Muurla, Finland [1975–present], (giftware, tableware & pressed items).

MVM Cappellin Glassworks in Murano, Italy [1925–31], colour trailing edges, pasta 1929, Vetri Lattei 1929, white opaque silver crackle 1929, Neri e Argenti 1930. Designers include Vittorio Zecchin 1921–5, Carlo Scarpa after 1927–8. Sig: acid-etched script "MVM Cappellin Murano", sometimes "Italy", often unsigned. See Cappellin MVM.

Myagkova, Ludmila M Glass designer from Beryozovka, Grodno, Belarus [1929–], worked at The Neman after 1959.

Myers Co, SF Glassworks location unknown [–] was active c.1898, (tableware).

Myers, Joel Philip Glass designer from USA [b.1934], worked for Blenko 1964–72), also Studio glass.

Mykene technique Variation on Graal developed by Vicke Lindstrand for Orrefors, c.1936; involves carborundum powder bubble pattern.

Mylenberg og Aalborg Glasvaerker Glassworks in Aalborg, Denmark [–] was active c.1859, (tableware).

Myra Crystal Gold iridescent glass type based on silver oxide, made by WMF 1926–36; plates, bowls and vases were never signed. See Favrile and Aurene for similar items.

N

Northwood mark, N in circle, in double circle, N underscored in circle.

Nachtmann Bleikristallwerke GmbH, FX Glassworks in Neustadt an der Waldnaab and Riedlhütte, Germany [1834–present], includes tableware plant in Mt.Pleasant, PA, USA, ex Lenox after 2000. Trade name includes Marcaurel for tableware, designers include Heinz Frisch, (tableware, cut glass, pressed giftware & crystal).

Nacrocristal Trade name for Art Deco pressed glass made by VSL c.1920–30.

Nadir Figueiredo Glassworks in Sao Paolo, Brazil [?–present], (bottles, jars & domestic ware).

Nahariya Glass, Andreas Meyer Ltd Glassworks in Tefen, Israel [?–present], (souvenirs, bent, fused & gilded art glass.

Nail mould Glass-making mould has nails in a pattern for producing controlled air bubbles in thick-walled glass.

Nailsea glass Glass houses in Nailsea, near Bristol, Great Britain [1788–1873], clear or coloured glass with contrasting spatters, swirls, or loops, first produced in Nailsea, but also made elsewhere. At first Nailsea produced only decorative novelties, aka "friggers", but after c.1845 also produced tableware.

Nakara: Opaque glassware produced by C F Monroe Company after 1900.

Namuroises, Cie Anonyme des Cristalleries et Verreries Glassworks in Namur, Belgium [1867–79], over 600 different items produced c.1876, grouped together Zoude, Herbatte, Jambes and Ourthe works, merged into VSL 1879, (cut glass, tableware, flat glass, bottles, mirrors; pressed glass, lighting & coloured glass).

Nancy, Cristalleries de Glassworks in Nancy [c.1922–31], it has no relation to Daum. Main designer Michel Colle. Sig: round seal; Guericolas, (tableware, art glass cameo engraved, Art Deco style).

Nancy School Provincial grouping of arts industries founded 1900 folded 1914, members include Antonin Daum, Emile Gallé, Louis Majorelle.

Napco Mark found on pressed glass made by Jeannette for Napco stoneware manufacturer in Cleveland, OH, USA c.1945–c.1960.

Napoli glass Glass completely covered in gold, with or without enamel; made at Mt Washington after 1894 and continued after 1900.

Nappy Bowl.

Nash, A Douglas Associates Glassworks in Corona, Long Island, USA [1919–31], worked for the Tiffany factories until 1919 when he went independent, supported by Tiffany until 1928, failed 1931. Trade names Corona, ADNA & Nash, Nash joined Libbey Glass Co in Toledo, OH, USA 1931–35, various firms 1935–40, (art glass, lustred glass & cluthra style glass).

Nash, Arthur J Glass maker and technician from Great Britain [1849–1934]. Manager of White House Glass Works in Stourbridge before 1893; went to USA to work for Louis Comfort Tiffany 1895, developed Cypriot glass.

Nash, John Glass designer from USA [–], worked for Steuben c.1955/6.

Nash, Leslie Glassmaker from Great Britain [–], son of Arthur J Nash, brother of A Douglas Nash, worked for Tiffany, own glass factory at Woodside, Long Island, NY, not connected with his brother's factory A Douglas Nash Co.

Nason & Cie, Vincenzo Glassworks in Murano, Italy [c.1967–c.1989–present]. Sig: labels "VNC", "Opaline Véritable", current name V Nason & C in use since 1989, (tableware, & opalines).

Nason & Moretti Glassworks in Murano, Italy [c.1920s–present]. Sig: unmarked before 1990, labels are sandblasted NM logo from 1990, square logo featuring gold goblet on blue ground with "Nason & Moretti/ Glassfactory/Murano/Venice" in 1920s, circular logo "N M Murano" in 1940s, circular logo with goblet and "N M/Nason& Moretti" in 1950s, (tableware).

Nason, Aldo Glass designer from Italy [1920–], worked for AVEM 1934–67, independent 1968–80.

Nason, Emilio Glass designer from Italy [1891–1959], was one of founders of AVEM, 1932–58.

Nason, Ermanno Glass blower from Murano, Italy [b.1928], worked for IVR Mazzega, Gino Cenedese 1964–70.

Natale & Cie, Mancioli Glass producer from Italy [–], wicker covered tableware c.1958/9.

National Canton Glass Co/ National Glass 02 Glassworks in Marion, IN, USA [c.1883–present], was based in Canton, OH, USA c.1883–c.1903, National Canton Glass Co. 1898–present.

National Glass Co, The Glass syndicate in Pittsburgh, OH, USA [1898–1905]; syndicate of 19 factories including Canton, Central, Dalzell, Indiana Tumbler, McKee, Northwood and Riverside was announced 1899, but failed 1904. The glassworks were rented or sold out including the new Cambridge plant, final curtain 1908. Showroom in London, Great Britain 1900–02, (pressed glass).

National Glass Combine, The National Glass Glass conglomerate located in Harrisburg, PA, USA [1899–?], in Cambridge, OH, USA

[1901–59], (pressed glass).

National Glass Company Ltd Glass importing company in London, Great Britain [c.1908–28], imported large amounts of carnival pressed glass into the UK, exclusive Fenton and Chippendale distributor. Moved to York c.1932 and started manufacturing pressed glass, currently the makers of Redfearn glass.

National Glass Works Glassworks in Fishergate, York, Great Britain [c.1932–c.1950], (redfearn glass).

National Silver Deposit Ware Co Inc Glassworks in USA [–].

Nationales, Verreries Glassworks in Jumet-Brulotte, Belgium [1887–92], bought by SA des Verreries de Jumet in 1892, (bottles, flat glass; bottles before 1887, flat glass only after 1887).

Navarre, Henri Edouard Glass artist from Paris, France [1885–1971], worked c.1924–c.1960). Sig: usually signed, not always, (art glass, sculptures, thickwalled).

Nazeing Glass Works Ltd Glassworks in Broxbourne, Hertfordshire, Great Britain [1928–present], allegedly founded in Vauxhall, Surrey in 1612, named Albert Glassworks 1879–1920, moved to Broxbourne in 1928 and renamed Nazeing. Sig: Nazeing glass is unmarked, retail labels may include "Elwell's of Harlow", "Craftsman"; an oval logo featuring two fighting goats and "Nazeing/Made in England" was used in the 1930s, (tableware, art glass, barware, lighting; ornamental glass, paperweights, crystal, lead crystal, soda-lime, coloured glass; borosilicate, opal, manual & semi-aurtomatic).

Nazionali, Cristallerie Glassworks in Naples, Italy [c.1934–c.1950], aka Cavalieri Alice, (pressed glass).

NBBG Co Trade name for North Baltimore Bottle Glass Co, North Baltimore, OH, USA [1885–1930], (bottles).

NCE Glassworks location unknown [–], was active c.1910, (lighting).

Near Cut 1. Pressed glass imitating cut glass; 2. Trade name for Cambridge Glass.

Nebulite Trade name for Gillinder & Sons.

Nechaev-Maltsov, Turil Stepanovich Glassworks in Moscow, Russia [–] was active c.1898.

Nechansky, Arnold Glass designer from Czechoslovakia [–], worked for Loetz c.1914.

Necking Shrinking the end of a bubble to form a bottle neck.

Neck-ring Glassmaker's tool for making bottle necks.

Needle etching See Acid engraving.

Negreanu, Matei Glass designer from Romania [1941–], in France since 1981.

Nekovár, Jiri Glass artist from Pardubice,

Czech Republic [b.1956], with Libenský until 1983, independent after then.

Nelka, Margreitner Glass artist from Zagreb, Croatia [1964–], sculpture since 1987.

Nelson Bead Co Glassworks in USA [–].

Nelson, JA Glass refinery in USA [–], (cut glass, Brilliant period).

Neman Glassworks, The Glassworks in Berezovka, Grodno, Belarus [?–present], designers include Balabin 1962–64, Batanova, Dzivinskaya after 1967, Fedorkov after 1968, Ganf, Makarenko, Murakhver, Myagkova, Raudväa, Rostovtseva 1957–59, Wachs after 1967, Zhigalkina, (tableware, cut glass).

Németh, Magda Vadeszi Glass designer from Hungary [b.1941], worked for Ajka Üveggyayár 1960–present.

Nemsová Glassworks in Trencina, Slovakia [1901–present] , operated by Stredoslovenské Sklárne, (pressed glass).

Neolitica 1 Type of art glass made by Barovier & Toso 1935. 2 Name of glass designed by Ercole Barovier 1954.

Neomurrino Barovier & Toso art glass type by Ercole Barovier 1970.

Neovidro Glassworks in the Marinha Grande region of Portugal [?–present]. See Marinha Grande & M Glass, (tableware, decorative glass).

Netzglas Type of Latticino, aka Zanfirico.

Neu Bor Srl Glassworks in San Vito al Tagliamento/PN, Italy [1993–present], part of Bormioli Rocco, (tubes & vials).

Neubert, Tafelglashütte Glassworks in Triebel near Sorau NL, Germany [1903–c.1937], (tableware).

Neuglas, Glashütte Glassworks in Weisswasser near Rothenburg, OL, Germany [1904–c.1937].

Neuhütte Glassworks in Frauenau, Germany [–], was active after c.1820.

Neumann Glassworks in München, Germany [–], was active c.1920.

Neumann & Stäbe Glassworks in Germany [–], merged into Josephinenhütte 1923,

Neuwelthütte Glassworks in Nový Svet, Czechoslovakia [1712–1800].

Neuwiese Glassworks in Nová Louka, Czechoslovakia [–].

Neville Glassworks Glassworks in Gateshead, Great Britain [1871–80], (pressed glass, moulds sold to Davidson c.1880).

Nevskaya, Irina A Glass designer from Moscow, Russia [1926–], worked at Workshops of Applied Art after 1952, central offices 1966–69, main works produced at Gus-Krushtalny, Dyatkovsky Cut Glass, Sverdlov, Romanovsky, Stryisky Glassworks.

New Bremen Glass Manufactory Glassworks in New Bremen, MD, USA [1784–?], (tableware).

New Brighton Glass Co Glassworks in New Brighton, PA, USA [1888–91], became Huntington Glass in 1891.

New Carnival Reproduction carnival glass made since 1961.

New Cumberland Glass Co Glassworks in New Cumberland, WV, USA [c.1922–30].

New England Crystal Co Glassworks in Lincoln, RI, USA [1990–present], (cut glass &

pate-de-verre).

New England Glass Co Glassworks in East Cambridge, MA, USA [1818–90], founded as New England Glass Works, changed to W L Libbey & Son Co after 1880, later The Libbey Glass Co until present. Sig: cut or etched with a circle 1865. See Agata, Wild Rose Peachblow, Pomona, Amberina, (paperweights 1850–80; pressed glass, cut glass & art glass)

New Gold Glass Gold foil glass made by Joseph Webb c.1883.

New Granite Glassworks Glassworks in Zanesville, OH, USA [1816–49], (tableware & bottles). See Zanesville.

New Martinsville Glass Manufacturing Co Glassworks in New Martinsville, WV, USA [1901–44], sold and reorganized into Viking Glass Co 1944, (tableware, pressed glass, novelties & depression glass).

Newark Cut Glass Co Glassworks in USA [–], (cut glass, Brilliant period).

Newell, Steven Studio glass artist from Great Britain [–], was active c.1979/80.

Niagara Cut Glass Co Glassworks in USA [–] was active c.1906, (cut glass, Brilliant period).

Nickel Plate Glass Co Glassworks in Fostoria, OH, USA [1888–91], 1891 US Glass as Factory N, (pressed glass).

Nicolas, Paul Glass artist from Lorraine, France [1875–1952], worked for Gallé 1893–1918, first individual works after c.1908, worked for Saint-Louis after 1918. Sig: art glass Art Nouveau style signed St Louis or d'Argental, Paul Nicolas signatures sometimes survived but often rubbed off, (art glass, floral, geometric on blanks from Saint-Louis).

Nicolle, Dubois, Lissaute & Cie Glassworks in France [c.1865–c.1890]. See Aubervilliers, Verreries et Cristalleries d'.

Niederlausitzer Glas-Industrie GmbH Glassworks in Weisswasser near Rothenburg OL, Germany [–] was active c.1920.

Niederlausitzer Hohl- und Kristallglaswerke Glassworks in Döbern near Sorau NL, Germany [1902–90], Niederlausitzer Hohl- und Kristallglaswerke Brox & Mader, VEB Hohlglashütte Döbern 1946–52, Glaswerke Döbern 1953–56, VEB Glaswerk Döbern 1956–87, closed c.1990, (bottles & tableware). See also Döbern.

Niemen Glassworks Glassworks in Niemen (Memel), between Lida and Nowogródek, border of Lithuania/Belorussia [?–1945].

Niemi, Jaakko Glass designer from Finland [–], worked for Wärtsilä Notsjö c.1960/1.

Nienburger Glas Gmbh & Co Kg Glassworks in Nienburg, Germany [1889–present], took over Stralauer Glashütte, Berlin, (bottles).

Niké Exkluzivni Zdobene Sklo, Dworokova Magdalena Glass decorating plant in Jablunkov, Czech Republic [1986–present], with sister plant Niké – Artystyczne Recznie Malowane Sklo, Cieszyn, Poland, (decorative bottles, silvered, gilt & enamelled tableware).

Nikol'skoye Crystal Works Glassworks in Penza Province, Russia [c.1800–c.1930–], into Krasnyy Ghigant.

Nilsen, Stein Glass designer from Norway [–],

was active after 1934, worked for Magnor after 1972.

Nilsson, Anne Glass designer/ceramicist from Sweden [–] was active after 1953, worked for Orrefors after 1982.

Nippon Glass Co Bottle plant in Tokyo, Japan [–]. Sig: N inside a diamond.

Nirschl, Andreas Glass artist from Zwiesel, Germany [b. 1951].

Nizet, Verreries Glassworks in Quai d'Avroy, Liège, Belgium [1709–1802], aka Avroy, (tableware, lighting, crystal, pincered decorations, Venetian style tableware, black bottles & flat glass).

Nizet-Mélotte, Verreries Glassworks in Quai d'Avroy, Liège, Belgium [1802–52], aka Avroy, (cut glass & engraved tableware).

Noack, Heinz Glass cutting works in Bad Muskau, Germany [?–present], (cut glass). See Lausitzer Glasring EV.

Nocus, Jean & Joseph Glass makers from St.Mandé, France [–] were active 1841–57, (paperweights).

Nonesuch Flint Glass Factory Glassworks in Bristol, Great Britain [1805–20]. Sig: J Jacobs Bristol in gilt, (tableware, Bristol Blue).

Nordix Glass dealer/export house for Bohemian glass in Libereč, Czechoslovakia [?–present].

Nordström, Tina Glass designer from Finland [1957–], worked for Nuutajärvi 1985–88, littala after 1988, also freelance.

Norec Trade name Fostoria Glass Specialty Co.

Noritake Co Ltd Glassworks in Japan [–], designers include Naoto Yokoyama c.1966/7.

Norrala Glassworks Glassworks in Hälsingland, Sweden [c.1906–c.1910], designers include Axel Boman, (tableware).

Norris, Alister & Co Glassworks in USA [–], (cut glass, Brilliant period).

Norsk Glassverk A/S Glassworks in Norway [–], active c.1980, designers include Oysten Sandnes c.1957–80.

North American Glass Corp Bottle plant in Montreal, QUE, Canada 1883–90. Sig: NAGC.

Northrop, Agnes Designer from the USA [–], worked for Tiffany Studios c.1900.

Northstar Glassworks Glassworks in USA [–], specialized in (coloured) borosilicate glass for lampwork.

Northwood & Co, Harry/National Glass Glassworks in Wheeling, WV, USA [1888–1924], The Northwood Glass Works, Martins Ferry, OH, USA 1888–90, The Northwood Glass Co, Elwood City, PA, USA 1890–95, The Northwood Co, Indiana, PA, USA 1896–1904, National Glass 1899, H Northwood & Co, Wheeling, WV, USA 1902–24. Sig: Northwood script c.1890s, N, N in circle, N in double circle, and N underlined in circle 1908–25, (blown glass, spatter glass after 1888, pressed glass & carnival glass 1908–15).

Northwood, J & J Glass refinery in Wordsley, Great Britain [1860–1926], founded by John Northwood, decorators include Edwin Grice. Sig: special editions marked JNJ; Portland vase 1876, (acid engraved glass & pottery, cameo).

Northwood, John Glass maker from Great Britain [1836–1902], worked for W H B & J Richardson at Stourbridge after1848. Founded J & J Northwood at Wordsley 1860, worked for Stevens & Williams 1881/2, Portland vase copied 1876, Milton Vase 1878, Pegasus Vase 1882), (cameo glass).

Northwood, John II Glass maker from Great Britain [1870–1960], worked for Stevens and Williams, "Birth of Aphrodite" plaque 1906, (cameo glass).

Northwood, William Engraver worked for J & J Northwood on cameos c.1880s.

Notre-Dame, Verrerie Glassworks in Familleureux, Belgium [1866–81], aka Meurice, Soupart & Cie, joined Verreries Réunies c.1874, crystal manufacture after 1867.

Notsjö Glasbruk Glassworks in Finland [1852–?]. See Nuutajärvi, Wärtsilä-Yhtyma Oy.

Nourot Glass Studio Glassworks in USA [c.1973–present], (art glass)

Nouveau Art Glass Co Inc Glassworks in USA [–], (tableware).

Nouvelles d'Aigremont, SA des Verreries Glassworks in Awirs, near Engis, Liège, Belgium [1908–], only building elements and industrial glass after WWII, (household glass, tankards, ashtrays, lighting & pressed glass).

Nouvelles Verreries de Momignies Glassworks in Momignies [1898/1985–present], joined Gerresheimer Glas conglomerate in 1985, (bottles).

Nouvelles, Verreries et Gobeleteries Glassworks in Manage, Belgium [–], aka Wauty Frères, into Manuverbel 1968–73, Vereno 1975, designers include Karl Heller c.1930, Faidherbe after 1968. Sig: "Novelty" for Karl Heller 1930s, (tableware, decorated glass).

Nouvion Glassworks in France [–] was active c.1925.

Nová Hut, prev Kittelovská Hut Glassworks in Svor, okr. Nový Bor, Czechoslovakia [1750–1865], (pressed glass c.1851).

Nova Scotia Glass Glassworks in Nova Scotia, Canada [–].

Nová Ves nad Nisou Glassworks in Nová Ves nad Nisou, Czechoslovakia [1870–1914], Neudorf an der Neisse in German.

Novák, Bretislav Glass designer from Czechoslovakia [1913–], (cut glass at Železný Brod).

Novak Jr, Bretislav Studio artist from Czechoslovakia [1952–], worked at Železný Brod.

Novaro, Jean Claude Glass artist from France [1943–], worked at Biot 1957–77, own workshop after 1977.

Novelty See Verreries Nouvelles de Manage c.1930.

Novelty Glass Co Glassworks in LaGrange, OH, USA [1880–93], founded at LaGrange in

1880, moved to Brilliant, OH in 1882, entered USG as factory T in 1891, moved to Fostoria, OH in 1892, burned down in 1893, (pressed glass).

Novikov, Alexey I Glass designer from Odessa, Ukraine [1940–], worked at Krasny May after 1967.

Nový Svet Glassworks in Harrachóv v Podkrkonosi, Czechoslovakia [1712–after c.1972], pressed glass c.1833 until begin 20thC; Umitkove Sklo.

Nu Art Company Glassworks in USA; [–] was active c.1900s, (lighting & carnival glass).

Nucut, Nuart Trade name of Imperial Glass Co 1904–51.

Nuova CEV/Cristalleria Glassworks in Ponte a Elsa, SI (Empoli), Italy [1987–present], (cut glass, tableware, art glass, chandeliers & ornamental items in lead crystal).

Nurmesniemi-Eskolin, Vuokko Glass designer from Finland [1930–].

Nurminen, Kerttu Glass designer from Finland [1943–], worked for Nuutajärvi/Iittala 1972–present.

Nuutajärvi-Notsjö glass Glassworks in Urjala, Finland [1793–present]. (Notsjö is Swedish for Nuutajärvi.) Bought by Wärtsilä 1949, Arabia 1971–76, merged Iittala 1987. Part of Hackmann Design or OY Ab conglomerate. Designers include Hilkka Liisa Ahola c.1952–c.1960, Kaj Franck c.1956/7, Sara Hopea 1952–c.1960, Jaakko Niemi c.1960/1, Gunnel Nyman 1946/8, Oiva Toikka 1963–c.1975, (tableware, pressed glass & art glass).

Nuutajärvi marks Tableware is usually unmarked, art glass is pen engraved 1946–53; engraved 1954–65, unmarked 1965–67, engraved 1968–present. Marked designer name & Nuutajärvi, with or without Notsjö and year, year discontinued after 1965. Circular N sticker before 1953, fish logo and "Nuutajärvi/Notsjö 1793/Made in Finland" used 1953–71, 1977–83, 1987–92, "Arabia/Wärtsilä Finland" sticker 1971–76 and 1983–87, white I in red dot (Iittala logo) in use after c.1992.

Nyblom, Lennart Glass designer from Sweden [–], worked for Kosta 1919, Pukeberg 1926.

Nybro Glasbruk AB Glassworks in Nybro, Sweden [1935–present], designers include Göran Axelsson, Mia Branzell, Jon Eliasson, Paul Isling & Cilla Persson, (sports prizes, centrifugal casting; tableware, giftware, ornaments, paperweights, lighting, Christmas ornaments & handmade crystal).

Nylund, Gunnar Ceramicist and glass designer from Sweden [1904–], worked for Strömbergshyttan 1954–67, Glimma Glasbruk 1968.

Nyman, Gunnel Gustafsson Glass designer

from Finland [1909–48]; worked for Riihimäki 1932–47, Karhula 1935–37, Iittala 1946–47, Nuutajärvi Notsjö 1946–48.

Obas Glassworks Glassworks in Teplice, Czech Republic [–], part of Sklo Union, designers included Vratislav Sotola from 1979.

Oberstdorfer Glashütte GmbH Glassworks in Oberstdorf, Germany [1986–present], crystal, semicrystal, borosilicate. Mark: G inside crowned O, (art glass, paperweights; JIPs & vases in swirl colours).

Oberursel, Cristallerie Glassworks in Schmiedefeld, Thüringen, Germany [1912–present], privatized 1991, (technical glass & thermos bottles before 1945, cased, coloured & cut glass after 1945)

Obolensky Glassworks in Penza Province, Russia [–] was active c.1800s.

Obsidian glass Black glass, volcanic natural glass.

Ocean Glass Co PCL/Sasaki Glassworks in Samut Prakan, Thailand [1982–?], part of Sasaki Group, Japan after 1993, (tableware).

Ochiai, Seitou Glass designer from Japan [–], worked for Kagami Crystal Works c.1969/70.

Oedenkoven NV Glassworks in Brussels, Belgium [1921–present], (special flat glass).

Oertel & Co Glassworks in Welzheim, Germany [1945–present], (cut glass tableware, full range lead crystal & antique replicas).

Oertel & Co, Johann Glassworks in Nový Bor, Czechoslovakia [1869–1945], used independent workshops and technical schools for refining, designs from the Nový Bor Glassmaking school and from Wiener Werkstätte, relocated to Welzheim, Germany after 1945 until present. Sig: Ö, Ö in a square, Ö squared, (painted glass, cased, cut-to-clear, cut glass, enamel & engraving, especially after c.1913.

Ofallan, J M Glass engraver [–], (cameo).

Off-hand Free formed at the end of a blowpipe or pontil.

Ogee Semi-circular bowl shape.

Ogival Cutting pattern resembling large diamond, aka Venetian diamond, reticulated diamond or expanded diamond, (cut glass & pressed glass).

O'Hara Flint Glass Works Glassworks in USA [1852–91], aka Jas B Lyon & Co, O'Hara Glass Co, into US Glass 1891, (pressed glass & tableware).

Ohio Flint Glass Co/National Glass 14 Glassworks in Lancaster, OH, USA

[1893–1937], located Bowling Green, OH, USA before 1899, Lancaster, OH, USA 1899–1908, National Glass 1899, became independent after 1904 and closed in 1908, Lancaster Glass Co after 1908, Hocking Glass Co after 1937.

Öhrström, Edvin Glass designer from Sweden [1906–], worked for Orrefors 1936–57, also independent after 1936. See Edvin.

Öhrström Expo numbering 1-100-53 = 1953, 1-65-54 = 1954, 66-73-55 = 1955, 74-79-57 = 1957, 80-81-58 = 1958, 82-96-59 = 1959, 97-98-60 = 1960.

Oignon de Jemeppe Jemeppe Onion, vase shape with short bulbous body and long, drawn out neck produced from various opaque colours with colour inclusions in Jemeppe 1909–14 & 1918–21, aka Soliflore or Berluze, vase for a single flower, height up to 45cm (18")

Ojamäa, Pilvi Glass designer from Tallinn, Estonia [1930–], worked at Leningrad Factory 1956–58, at Tarbeklaas, Tallinn after 1965.

Okamoto Glassworks in Kashiwa Chiba, Japan [1928–present], (automotive lighting, lighting, bottles in Taiwan plant).

O'Keeffe, Michael Glass maker from Seattle, OR, USA [–], (paperweights after 1976).

Okkolin, Aimo Glass designer from Finland [1917–], worked for Riihimäki c.1959–67.

Okra Glass Glassworks in Great Britain [1979–present]. Sig: usually marked "okra", (iridescent art glass & Loetz type).

Olbernhau, Glaswerk Glassworks in Olbernhau OL, Germany [1946–present], operated as Olbernhauer Glas Pech & Kunte GmbH, VEB Glaswerk Olbernhau after 1956, trade name Linia Design, (cut glass, crystal, enamelled, cased, coloured glass; since 1961 technical glass; currently bent, fused glass & flat glass constructions).

Olbrich, Professor Josef Glass designer from Vienna, Austria [–]; worked for Bakalowits after c.1900.

Old Virginia Trade name used by Fenton 1950s–1970s.

Oliva, Ladislav Glass designer from Czechoslovakia [1933], designer at Borské Sklo 1957–64, at Bohemia Poděbrady 1964–69, at ZB school after 1969.

Olive Glassworks Glassworks in Glassboro, NY, USA [1780–1918], sold to Harmony Glassworks 1824 and renamed Whitney Glass Co, taken over by Owens Bottle Co 1918, (bottles).

Ollers, Edvin Glass designer from Sweden [1888–1959], worked for Kosta 1917–8 and 1931–2, Reijmyre 1918–9, Elme 1926–30, Limmared 1929–40, Alsterfors 1930–4, Åfors 1934–40, Ekenäs 1946–7 and Flygsfors 1945. Sig. on Kosta pieces c.1931/2 Ollers or O, plus model number.

Olsufyev, VA Glassworks in Smolensk, Russia [19thC].

Olympia Type of art glass made by Loetz, classically inspired, around 1894.

Ongaro & Fuga Glassworks in Murano, Italy [–] was active c.1967, (cut glass & engraved glass).

Ongaro, Romero Glass refinery in Venice, Italy [–] was active c.1948, (cut glass).

Onyx glass Type of art glass made by Loetz, dark with white streaks introduced in 1888.

Opal glass Semitransparent white glass, made by adding arsenic, tin or bone ash to the batch, aka milk-and-water glass, or opaline. See also: Milk glass, Opaline, Opalescent glass, Opalisation, Moonstone.

Opál sklarska dilna Glassworks in Železný Brod, Czech Republic [1992–present], (giftware, lampwork, fantasy glass & paperweights).

Opala, La Glassworks in Calcutta and Madhupur, India [1986–present], (tableware, lead crystal giftware, opal and dinnerware).

Opalescent glass Glass reflecting a milky blue or pearly light. First made in Great Britain in 1870, opalescent glass became popular in America around 1900 and throughout the 1920s and '30s. Manufacturers include Lalique, Sabino, Jobling, Etling, Verlys, Hunebelle, Dieupart at Simonet Brothers, Cesare, Daniolo, Ferjac, Paul d'Avesn, Martel, Barolac (Bohemia), Val St Lambert. Vernox and Verart were trade names from Sabino to compete with the cheaper opalescent glass from Verlys; Verlux is trade name from VSL. Opalescent hobnail was introduced by Hobbs, Brockunier & Co, 1886.

Opaline Semitransparent glass type originally made with bone ash (calcium phosphate), later with tin or arsenic (non-reflective surface). First occurrence France c.1780; pale green and rose pink after c.1835. Often enamelled and/or gilt mounted. Similar to Bristol glass. Variations include "Bulle-de-Savon", from 1822, with tiny bubbles, and a cheaper, greyish-white opaline with lower lead content (grainy, greasy texture) was produced 1825–50 called pâte-de-riz or Verre d'Albâtre (alabaster glass).

Opaline, French Popular from 1804–15 (boxes and large vases), becoming more feminine during the Restoration 1815–30 (flower vases, perfume sets and tableware), "Bulle-de-Savon" after 1822. Semi-crystal opaline 1833, the Golden Age of Opaline 1830–80, flowers, fruits (notably pineapples c.1870), flasks, candy dishes; also pressed glass & lighting. From 1880–1920, many glassworks produced opaline in large series – the cheaper variety (especially covered animal dishes) is referred to as "Opaline de Bazar" and was produced until the late 1950s. Manufacturers include Baccarat 1825–70, Saint-Louis, Cristalleries du Creusot 1783–1832, Bercy, Choisy-le-Roi, La Villette-Pantin, La Guillotière and Valérysthal.

Opalino a Fiamma Barovier & Toso art glass type by Ercole Barovier 1957.

Opalino Italian term for lattimo cased with a layer of clear coloured glass, aka incamiciato.

Opalique Trade name for opalescent pressed glass made by Jobling [1933–40], inspired by Lalique.

Opalisation Mottled play of colours as found in the opal.

Opaque glass Solid colour non-transparent glass.

Open work Perforated design/decor.

Oppitz, Moritz Glass engraver from Bohemia [–], worked 1840s.

Oppitz, Paul Glass engraver from Bohemia [–], worked in Great Britain at W T Copeland & Sons c.1873.

Optic mould; A patterned open mould.

Optical glass Glass types used in lenses and prisms requiring high refractive index and low dispersion. The refractive index represents the deviation of a ray of light striking the glass at an oblique angle; dispersion is the dependence of the refractive index on wavelength.

Oralit Marbled type of pressed glass made by A Walther, Germany 1932–c.1940; is sometimes mistaken for Davidson Cloud glass.

Oranienhütte, Glasfabrik Glassworks in Seitenburg, Germany [–], was active c.1911. Aka Losky, F.

Orchard, John Engraver at Stevens & Williams c.1880s–90s.

Orchid vase Vase for holding a single flower, especially made in Scandinavia, designers include Sarpaneva and Lütken.

Oreot Brand name for moulded and frosted glassware in the style of Lalique, made in France c.1930s, source unknown.

Organic fifties crystal Fifties glass in the Scandinavian style was produced by Baccarat, Bayel, AF Bischoff, Blenko, Daum, Dunbar, Fire Island, Flygsfors, Fostoria, Kanawha, Maastricht, Morgantown, Pilgrim, Rainbow, Scandia, Seneca, Sèvres, Steuben, Tiffin, Val St. Lambert, Vannes (Cofrac) and others.

Orient & Flume Glassworks in Chico, CA, USA [1972–present], (paperweights).

Orlov's Factory, Mikhail Glassworks in Milyutino, Kaluga, Russia [c.1825–62].

Orlovsky, P Artist from Russia [–], glass decoration 1920s.

Ormolu Gilt metal mounting or trimming.

Ornberg, Ann Glass designer from Sweden [–], worked for Strombergshyttan.

Ornela, Atelier Glassworks in Desná, Czech Republic [1847–present], trade names include Desná, pressed items made from original designs by, among others, Josef Drahonovsky (pressed glass, frosted statuettes & malachite/jade glass).

Oroide Art glass by Edward Webb c.1880s, includes foil.

Orplid Glass Ltd Glassworks in Great Britain [–], designers include Fritz Lampl c.1952–54.

Orr, Charles Glass designer from Scotland [–], worked for Caithness.

Orrefors Glasbruk AB (O~ Kosta Boda AB) Glassworks in Orrefors, Hovmantorp, Sweden [c.1726–present], operates 10 plants including Boda Glasbruk, Kosta Glasbruk, Sandviks Glasbruk, Sea Glasbruk, Afors Glasbruk, Älghults Glasbruk, The Glass Painting Studio in Lessebro, Glasma AB in Emmaboda, and the Orrefors Inn Restaurant. Founded in 1898, bought by Johan Ekman 1913 who contracted principal designers Simon Gate 1916–45 and Edward Hald 1907–47. Designers include Fagerlund, Landberg c.1950–63, Lindstrand c.1960/1,

Lundin c.1953–66, Öhrström 1936–57, Orup c.1958/9, Palmqvist 1930–72, Selbing 1927–70, and many others. Current designers include Lena Bergström, Gunnar Cyrén 1959–70 and 1976–present, Lars Hellsten 1972–, Jan Johansson 1969–, Helen Krantz 1988–, Erika Lagerbielke 1982–, Anne Nilsson 1982–, Martti Rytkönen 1994–,and Per Sundberg 1994–. Techniques developed include Graal 1916, Slottsglas 1923, Slipgraal 1940, Mykene 1936; Ravenna 1948, Kraka 1944, Ariel 1937, and Fuga, (tableware, art glass, pressed glass, cut glass & paperweights; subsidiary Sandvik produces tableware, flat glass & technical glass).

Orrefors artist monograms and codes
A=Alberius, AS=Strömberg, B=Cyren, C=Selbing, D=Lundin, F=Öhrström, G=Gate, H=Hald, J=Johansson, K=Koppel, KD=Kurz, L=Lindstrand, N=Landberg, P=Palmqvist, R=Fagerlund, S=Selbing, T=Hellsten, V=Englund; A=cut, AX=cut semicrystal, B=jewellery, D=lighting, E=frosted, F=cut-to-clear, P=pressed, S=graal, U=oven finished, UX= blown semicrystal, X=corona, Z=lustred. On early Cameo (1914–16): FB=Fritz Blomqvist, SG=Gate, HW=Heinrich Wollman, KB=Knut Bergkvist.

Orrefors engravers Name, monogram and the years in which they worked: Arthur Diessner AD 1920–63; Ake Karlsson AK 1924–45; Arne Lindahl AL 1938–?; Axel Nordgren AN 1927–30; Arthur Roos AR 1924–74; Ake Karlsson ARK 1927–46; Anders Svensson ASA-s 1923–?; Birger Gustafsson B 1923–27; Börje Eriksson BE 1946–?; Bertil Gustafsson BG 1926–75; Börje Hermansson BH 1923–41, 1948–65; Ernst Aberg EA 1947–58; Emil Goldman EG 1923–40; Edit Högsted EH 1925–31; Erich Pohl EP E–P 1950–75; Emil Weidlich EW 1922–29; Fritz Bohman FB 1923–31; Folke Karlsson FK 1923–27; Folke Walwing FW 1923–27; Fritz Hickisch FH 1920–c.30; Gustaf Abels GA 1915–59; Gösta Elgström GE 1926–46; Gustaf Ruud GR 1920–?; Gunnar Schultzberg GS 1926–36; Harals Axelksson HA 1946–64; Hans Carlsson HCn 1928–32; Hakon Gustavsson HG 1938–61; Harold Hansson HH 1922–28; Hjerton Rydh Hj 1924–39; Hilding Lindahl HL 1923–67; Henry Rydh HR 1925–43; Hugo Williamsson 1938–44 & 1973–76; Jan Andersson JA 1956–62; John Rosenstam JR 1923–62; Karl Müller KM 1923–27; Karl Rössler KR 1923–66; Liss Bergkvist LB 1924–59; Lars-erik Nilsson L-EN 1942–70; Ljupce Kocevski LjK 1971–79; Lennart Lindsten LL ?–?; Nils Landberg NL 1925–28; Ove Bjerding O 1928–70; Oskar Landas OL 1922–70; Olle Karlsson OK 1923–27; Olle Wigselius OW 1923–27; Olof

Petersson P 1925–30; Peder Lindahl PL 1943–65; Richard Bayer RB 1922–27; Ragnar Bergkvist RB 1921–30; Reine Hagsted RH 1925–28; Rickard Möller ?–?; Rune Pettersson RP 1940–?; Ragnar Rosenstam RR 1921–64; Sven Palmqvist SP 1928–33; Sten Pettersson SP 1922–69; Sigvard Wulff SW 1923–41; Thure Löfgren ThL 1922–58; Thutre Schultzberg TS 1926–56; Verner Abrahamsson VA 1926–46; Wilhelm Eisert WE 1920–34;

Orrefors marks on cut glass Cut décor matt with E-numbers beginning E1=before 1926, E54=1927, E78=1928, E99=1929, E103=1930, E140=1931, E182–E201=1931/32. Polished cut décor with A-numbers beginning A31–196=before 1926, A197=1927, A205=1928, A234=1929, A261=1930, A341=1931, A361=1932, A411=1933, A416=1934. All designs by Hald(H) or Gate(G).

Orrefors marks on engraved glass Model numbers 1000–1165=1931, 1166–1212=1932, 1213–1294=1933, 1295–1379=1934, 1380–1399=1935. See Hald, Gate & Lindstrand for earlier pieces.

Orrefors marks on production glass Sequential from 1935 beginning 1400=1935, 1521=1936, 1692=1937, 1910=1938, 2021=1939, 2261=1940, 2351=1941, 2651=1942, 2775=1943, 2885=1944, 2960=1945, 3081=1946/8, 3121=1949, 3171=1950, 3221=1951, 3351=1952, 3401=1953, 3501=1954, 3531=1955, 3571=1956, 3618=1957, 3696=1958, 3751=1959, 3801=1960.

Orrefors marks, other Enamelled glass marks I50–I68=1930, designers Gate or Lindstrand; pressed glass marked P=1920s/1930s, designed by Gate and Hald; limited edition green glass marked Z16–Z53=1929/30; oven ready glass marked U50–U115=1930–31, U116–140=1932, U141–155=1933, U156–168=1934/35.

Orrefors serial models Alaska, Colora, Fasett, Florida, Fuga, Iris, Granada, Kantara, Kantarell, Hamrad Selena, Melon, Platina, Rotary, Selena, Turkos, Stella Polaris, Tan-si.

Orrefors year letters A1–A9=1935–43; B1–9=1944–52; C1–9=1953–61; D1–9=1962–70; E1–9=1971–79 F1–9=1980–88, etc.

Orsoni Angelo Glassworks in Murano, Italy [c.1967], (Smalti, enamel for mosaics).

Ortlieb, Nora Glass designer from Germany [1904–84], worked independently 1933–77, own workshop in Stuttgart after 1943.

Ortner See Wolfram Ortner WOB.

Orup, Bengt Glass designer from Sweden [1916–], worked for Johansfors c.1955–70, Orrefors c.1958/9, Hyllinge Glasbruk 1963–66.

Orvola, Heikki Glass designer from Finland [1943–], worked for Nuutajärvi and Iittala 1968–present, (tableware, art glass & sculpture).

Osiris glass Stevens & Williams art glass with pulled up feathering after 1887.

Oskamp, Nolting & Co Glassworks location unknown [–] was active c.1902, (cut glass).

Oskar Karla See Karla

Osler, F & C Glassworks in Birmingham, Great Britain [c.1850–c.1900), Osler was one of the largest makers of cut glass in Victorian Britain, with extensive exports to Indian subcontinent, (cut glass & lighting).

Osram, Glashütte Glassworks in Weisswasser near Rothenburg OL, Germany [1899–c.1937–present], trade name "Osram" was deposited in 1906 by Auer-Gesellschaft; Osram Co was created 1919 in merger between AEG, Siemens & Halske and Auer, moved to Munich 1954, merged Sylvania 1993, currently Osram Sylvania, (lighting).

Osredek Glassworks in Osredek, near Samobor/Zagreb, Croatia [1839–1904], aka Glažuta Glassworks, owned by Baroness Kulmer 1839–47, frequent changes of ownership 1847–1904, new plant "Karolina" in Grdanjci 1872. Unrelated "Kristal" factory in Osredek opened 1957. (Biedermeier Bohemian style glass, cased, engraved, matt, cut-to-clear, enamelled glass, tableware, art glass, cut glass, goblets; tableware, paperweights, bottles, flat glass, lighting & pressed glass after 1870).

Osterfeld, Lone Glass designer from Denmark [–], worked for Holmegaard.

Ostglas, VVB Conglomerate of 12 glass making companies in Weisswasser, Germany [1950–90]. Sig: OG intertwined around "12" in a truncated diamond 1950–64.

Ostredek Glassworks in Benesova, Czechoslovakia [1715–1887], (pressed glass reported 1873).

Ostroumov, Adolf M Glass designer from St Petersburg, Russia [1934–], worked in Czechoslovakia and at Leningrad Factory after c.1960.

Osvětlovací Sklo -Lares, sro Glassworks in Valasské Mezirici (Krásno), Czech Republic [1855–1945 and 1991–present, previously under name of Reich, (lighting, leaded shades & coloured flat glass)

Ottlinger & Co Glashütte Glassworks in Döbern near Sorau NL, Germany [1903–after c.1937], Ottlinger & Co after 1903, Ottlinger Glashütte located in Teplitz near Sorau c.1937, Gebr Ottlinger located in Kunzendorf near Sorau, 1885–c.1937.

Ourthe, Cristallerie et Verrerie de l' Glassworks in Chênée, Liège, Belgium [1882–?], renamed Amiable, Baiwir et Cie 1883, (Filigrane, paperweights & art glass).

Overlay: A thin layer of clear or coloured glass on the outside of a piece; cased glass in which a layer is folded over another. See also flashing, casing, cut-to-clear.

Overshot glass Technique whereby hot glass is rolled in splinters covering surface with an ice-like appearance, which is then fused on by reheating, aka ice glass.

OVG overlapping Mark found on Fenton "Old Virginia Glass" mail order line c.1955–c.1972.

Ovington Mark found on Schneider pieces for New York retailer, Ovington.

Owens-Illinois Inc Glassworks in Toledo, OH, USA [1929–], formed by Michael J Owens, who invented mechanical bottles blowing in 1903, and Illinois Glass Co, trade name includes Duraglass. Sig: I inside O, I inside O with diamond, (pressed glass).

Owens machine Automatic bottles forming machine introduced in 1903; by 1917 nearly all bottles were machine produced.

Oxidizing Atmosphere rich in oxygen with little uncombusted gas. Coloured glass containing metal oxides reacts differently in oxidising or reducing atmospheres.

Ozdobnego Makora See Makora.

Özlem Kristal Sanayi ve Ticaret AS Glassworks in Istanbul, Turkey [?–present].

P

P&W Trade name of Perry & Wood/Perry & Wheeler, Perry Keene, NH, USA [1822–30], (bottles).

PCGW Mark for Pacific Coast Glass Works, (bottles).

PMG Fratelli Pitau Glassworks in Murano, Italy [–] was active c.1967, (giftware & souvenirs).

Pacheco, Cláudia Glass designer from Portugal [–], worked for MGlass, Marinha Grande c.1999.

Pachthütte Glassworks in Penzig near Görlitz OL, Germany [1861–c.1937].

Paddle Glass maker's tool.

Paden City Glass Manufacturing Co Glassworks in Paden City, WV, USA [1916–51], (pressed glass; depression glass & coloured tableware).

Padoan, Germano Glass maker from Italy [1934–], worked at Gränna Glasbruk, Sweden since c.1965.

Padula, Attilio da Glass designer from Italy [1917–81], worked for Venini.

Pagnin, Lucio Glass artist [–], worked at Gala, Liège, Belgium after c.1989.

Painted glass shades Lamp shades painted inside reverse, aka Pairpoint lamps c.1885–c.1920s, blown out, ribbed or scenic. Most made by Pairpoint; some by Consolidated.

Pairpoint Corp Glassworks in USA [c.1900–1920s], (cut glass).

Pairpoint Manufacturing Co Glassworks in New Bedford, MA, USA [1865–1958], merged with Mt Washington 1894 and became Pairpoint Corporation, sold to Gunderson in 1938 and operated as Gunderson Glass Works until Robert Gunderson died in 1952, then Gunderson-Pairpoint until 1956 when the works closed. Reopened as New Pairpoint in 1970, (paperweights 1910s–1920s, 1970s).

Paisley shawl Type of art glass made by Monart (colour enamel swirls, lustre).

Paix, A la Glass shop in Paris. See A la Paix.

Palatine Glass Co Ltd, The Glassworks in St Simon, Lancashire, Great Britain [–], was active c.1950.

Pallme-König und Habel Glassworks in Kostány, Czechoslovakia [1786–?], founded

1786 in Kamenický Šenov, inherited 1887 by Josef and Theodor Pallme-König, 1889 merged Elisabeth-hütte in Kostány owned by Wilhelm Habel, renamed "Vereinigte Glashüttenwerke Pallme-König & Habel, Jg Grossmann's Sohn GmbH" 1920. Sig: P, K & H glass is usually unmarked, (art glass from 1900, especially threaded Phänomenglas; many different art glass models and techniques, iridescence, no pontil marks).

Palme & Walter Glassworks in Kamenický Šenov, Czechoslovakia [c.1925–c.1970] , (lighting). Aka Swarovski.

Palme, Elias Glassworks in Kamenický Šenov, Czechoslovakia [–], was active c.1940.

Palme, Franz-Josef Glass engraver from Bohemia [–], worked at Dennis Glassworks/Thomas Webb & Sons 1882–1930). Sig: most works are signed, (animals)

Palmqvist, Sven Glass designer from Sweden [1906–84], worked for Orrefors 1930–72, then freelance until 1984. Kraka, Ravenna.

Palmqvist Expo numbering 1-79-53-1953, 1-56-54=1954, 1-41-55=1955, 1-16-56=1956, 17-87-57=1957, 88-115-58=1958, 116-165-59=1959, 166-199-60=1960, 200-228-61=1961, 229-248-62=1962, 249-329-63=1963, 330-352-64=1964, 353-376-65=1965, 377-427-66=1966, 428-447-67=1967, 448-519-68=1968, 520-539-69=1969, 540-585-70=1970, 586-747-71=1971, 748-802-72=1972, 803-74=1974, 804-809-77=1977, 810-817-78=1978, 818-823-79=1979.

Pamio, Roberto Architect/designer from Murano, Italy [–], was active c.1980, worked with Toso, Renato.

Pampas décor Type of art glass made by Loetz (threads rolled in with iridescence).

Panevezio Stiklas Glassworks in Panevezis, Lithuania [1965–present]. Sig: no signatures, polished ground on paperweights, (art glass, paperweights, bottles, flat glass & automotive).

Pannier, Frères Sales outlet in Paris for bronze mounted glass furniture named "A l'Escalier de Cristal" [c.1880s]. Sig: sometimes marked "Pannier", (art glass engraved, gilded, enamelled in Japanese style, bronze mounted).

Pantin, Cristallerie de Glassworks in Pantin, Paris [1851–1937], company names were Monot & Co 1851, Monot & Fils 1855, Monot Père et Fils & Stumpf 1868, Stumpf, Touvier, Viollet & Co 1888. Merged with Legras c.1906. Sig: "Cristallerie de Pantin", "STV & Co", "de Vez, CP", none on earlier works, (art glass, opaline painted c.1855, cut glass, ruby red, aventurine c.1878, paperweights c.1878, tableware designed by Berlage 1902, cut glass, art glass, iridescence after 1878, crackle after 1878, bronze mountings & cameo). See Mont Joye.

Pantograph Machine for copying needle etched decor onto glass, made possible and popular after the invention of mechanical blowing (1903) which ensured identical dimension of bowls.

Panvarny See Kostanske Sklarny A Panvarny.

Paperweights Classic period 1845–55 Bohemia, Silesia, Venice and France, Great Britain after 1848, US after 1851, continued in some places until 1880; revival 1878–1915, second revival c.1950–present. 19thC French makers include Baccarat, Clichy, St Louis, St. Mandé & Pantin, Belgian makers include Bougard, Verrerie Nationales & VSL, British makers include Bacchus, John Ford, Islington, Kilner, Apsley Pellatt & Whitefriar's, US makers include Gillinder, Mt Washington, New England, Sandwich & Whitall & Tatum, Italian makers include Franchini & P Bigaglia.

Paperweights, 20thC Makers include Ayotte, Baccarat, Banford, Buzzini, Caithness, Cape Cod, China, Choko & Lewis, Correia, d'Albret, John Deacons, Donofrio, Ebelhare, Fote, Grubb, Hacker, Hansen, Hartley Wood, Isle of Wight (Great Britain), Kaziun, Kontes bros, Kosta, Labino, Langham, Liskeard, Lotton, Lundberg, Malta Mayauel Ward, Monart, Murano, O'Keeffe, Okra, Orient & Flume, Orrefors (Sweden), Panavezio, Parabelle, Perthshire (Scotland), Michael Rayner, Rosenfeld, St Louis (France), Salazar, Sautner, Selkirk, Shaw, Smith, Stankard, Strathearn, Tarsitano, Thiewes, Trabucco, Vasart, Whitall Tatum, Whitefriar's, Whittemore (USA), William Manson, William Walker & Ysart.

Papes, Cristallerie des Glassworks in Avignon [1974–6] and Fontaine de Vaucluse, France [1976–present], the designer is François Hédon, (art glass, bubble, crackle and hand-blown glass).

Papillon Loetz type art glass with iridescent spots, made in colours Candia (gold), Ruby (red) and Cobalt (blue) from 1898.

Papini, Cristalerias SA Glassworks in Buenos Aires, Argentina [1896–present], now Crystalux SA, (tableware).

Parabelle Glass Glassworks in Portland, OR, USA [1983–], (paperweights). See Gary & Doris Scrutton.

Parabolica Barovier & Toso art glass type by Ercole Barovier, 1957.

Paracin Glassworks Glassworks in Paracin, Serbia [1907–present], (tableware, barware, bottles, decorative glassware, pressed items, thermos glass, technical & automotive, raised enamel and gold, cut-to-clear & colour cased glass).

Paradi Üveggyár Glassworks in Parádsavár, Hungary [1708–present], aka Parad Crystal Manufacture Ltd, designers include Judit Sipos after 1960.

Pargeter, Michael Glass engraver from Great Britain [–], worked at Royal Brierly c.1999.

Pargeter, Philip Glassworks in Stourbridge, Great Britain [–], was active c.1877, (tableware). See Red House Glass Works.

Parian Trade name of Gill Brothers.

Paris, E & Cie Glassworks in Le Bourget, Seine, France [c.1882–c.1900], Cristallerie et Emaillerie Saint Joseph du Bourget, Emile retired and company was continued by son, Charles, name changed to Charles Paris & Cie c.1900, (lighting & tableware)

Paris Musée Mark found on contemporary replica pressed glass tableware from Cristallerie La Rochère.

Parisienne, Verrerie See Aubervilliers.

Parison A small glass bubble at the end of a blowpipe. The French term is paraison.

Parlik, Michael Studio artist from Czechoslovakia [1941–].

Parramore, Roger Flameworking artist from Waynesville, NC, USA [–].

Pasabahce Cam Sanayi ve Ticaret AS Glassworks in Tuzla and Istanbul, Turkey [1935–present], subsidiary of Sisecam. Joint venture tableware production with Schott, (automatic tableware production; cookware, barware, pressed glass).

Passavant See Cristallerie Rochère.

Passglass Tall drinking vessel, 16th–19thC divided by horizontal bands.

Pasta Vitrea Opaca Venini art glass designed by Napoleone Martinuzzi, 1927.

Paste Artificial gem made from a vitreous paste developed by Josef Strassner, aka Strass.

Pâte-de-Riz See Opaline.

Pâte-de-verre Glassmaking technique using powdered glass in a plaster mould, which is then fused in a kiln. (Walter, Nancy; Bergé; Daum) The term is sometimes, erroneously in France, applied to opaline.

Patent numbers and dates, USA 1=1836, 110=1837, 546=1838, 1,061=1839, 1,465=1840, 1,923=1841, 2,413=1842, 2,901=1843, 3,395=1844, 3,873=1845, 4,348=1846, 4,914=1847, 5,409=1848, 5,993=1849, 6,981=1850, 7,865=1851, 8,622=1852, 9,512=1853, 10,358=1854, 12,117=1855, 14,009=1856, 16,324=1857, 19,010=1858, 22,477=1859, 26,642=1860, 31,005=1861, 34,045=1862, 37,266=1863, 41,047=1864, 45,685=1865, 51,784=1866, 60,658=1867, 72,959=1868, 85,503=1869, 98,460=1870, 110,617=1871, 122,304=1872, 134,504=1873, 146,120=1874, 158,350=1875, 171,641=1876, 185,813=1877, 198,733=1878, 211,078=1879, 223,211=1880, 236,137=1881, 251,685=1882, 269,820=1883, 291,016=1884, 310,163=1885, 333,494=1886, 355,291=1887, 375,720=1888, 395,305=1889, 418,665=1890, 443,987=1891, 466,315=1892, 488,976=1893, 511,744=1894, 531,619=1895, 552,502=1896, 574,369=1897, 596,467=1898, 616,871=1899, 640,167=1900, 664,827=1901, 690,385=1902, 717,521=1903, 748,567=1904, 778,834=1905, 808,618=1906, 839,799=1907, 875,679=1908, 908,436=1909, 945,010=1910, 980,178=1911,

1,013,095=1912, 1,049,326=1913, 1,083,267=1914, 1,123,212=1915, 1,166,419=1916, 1,210,389=1917, 1,251,458=1918, 1,290,027=1919, 1,326,899=1920, 1,364,063=1921, 1,401,948=1922, 1,440,362=1923, 1,478,996=1924, 1,521,590=1925, 1,568,040=1926, 1,612,790=1927, 1,654,521=1928, 1,696,897=1929, 1,742,181=1930, 1,787,424=1931, 1,839,390=1932, 1,892,663=1933, 1,941,449=1934, 1,985,878=1935, 2,026,516=1936, 2,066,309=1937, 2,104,004=1938, 2,142,080=1939, 2,185,170=1940, 2,366,154=1945, 2,492,944=1950, -2,698,434=1955, 2,919,434=1960, 3,163,865=1965, 3,487,470=1970, 3,858,241=1975. Patent data 1791–1835 were destroyed by fire in the patent office 1836. See also Design Registration and Trademark Registration.

Patent medicine bottles Specialist collectors' area in the USA, earliest c.1810, most c.1870, latest 1907.

Patskan, Yury P Glass designer from Lvov, Ukraine [1935–], worked at Workshops of Applied Art, Leningrad.

Pattern Glass Mass-produced pressed tableware made from Flint glass after 1840 to the Civil War; later made with soda lime glass ("non-flint"). Staggering volumes were produced 1880–1915 in thousands of patterns and colours; collectable since the 1930s.

Pattern mould Glass mould with a pre-shaped pattern. Pattern moulds are hinged; the glass bubble is enclosed before being inflated. See also Dip mould.

Paul, Bruno Glass designer from Munich, Germany [1874–1968], worked for Valérysthal after c.1900.

Paula, Frantisek de Glass engraver from Bohemia [19thC].

Paulin, Ida Glass decorator, worked in Augsburg, Germany c.1925.

Paulina Glassworks in Pavlína, Czechoslovakia [–].

Paulinenhütte Glassworks in Kohlfurt near Görlitz, Germany [1873–after c.1937], operated by Schneider & Hirsch.

Paulus, Claude Glass designer from Liège, Belgium [1932–], worked at VSL c.1977.

Pavanello Malvino & Figli Glassworks in Murano, Italy [–] was active c.1967, (lighting).

Pavanello, Eliodoro Glass refinery in Venice, Italy [–] was active c.1895.

Pavlovsky, Mechislav A Glass designer from Lvov, Ukraine [1922–], glass blower at Peskovsky Glassworks 1936–40, worked in Lvov after 1947 and at Lvov Factory of Sculpture & Ceramics from 1963.

Pays de Liège et de la Campine, Cie des Verreries de Glassworks in Liège, Belgium, active c.1920 and c.1930, (tableware). See La Sté Le Pyrex.

Peace, David Glass engraver from Great Britain [1915–].

Peachblow: Glass type patented in 1886 by Mt Washington, shades from pink to ivory, the opaque variety of Amberina. Found mainly with a satin finish, though gloss peachblow does exist. It was not a commercial success at the time. Other manufacturers were New England, Webb (Peach Bloom), Hobbs Brockunier (Coral, or Wheeling Peachblow), Libbey (Wild Rose), Mount Washington, New Martinsville, Gunderson-Pairpoint made replicas in the 1950s.

Pearce, Daniel Engraver from Great Britain [1817–1902], worked at Dobson & Pearce 1845–63, Phillips & Pearce 1863–84 and for Webb after 1878 and at Webb after 1884, when he gave up his own company. He specialized in tableware and ornamental & engraved glass.

Pearce, Lionel Engraver/designer from Great Britain [1854–1926], chief designer at Webb c.1900s.

Pearl Ornaments: Pressed glass with a décor of diagonal bandings, such as squares and diamonds.

Pearline Glass colour developed 1889 by Davidson's made in blue and lemon yellow with a white edge. Pearline glass remained popular until around 1914, with new designs released almost yearly between 1890–1903. The clear version is known as Moonshine. The glass is opalescent and contains uranium and arsenic, which turns opaque on re-heating hence the white edges. Greener's produced some patterns in a similar colour. Lemon Pearline (never the blue variety) falls within the American definition of Vaseline Glass. Sig: Pearline is mostly marked with a Rd No and/or the word Patent. Some designs are unmarked.

Pearly lustre Shining like a pearl. See Lustre

Pebaqué, Carlos R Glass artist from Montevideo, Uruguay [b.1950], worked at Orrefors school after 1981, founded Gullaskruv Glas Atelier 1984, Carlos R Pebaqué AB after 1991. Sig: needle-etched Gullaskruv/La Vida/numbers in full.

Peche, Dagobert Glass designer from Austria [1887–1923], worked for Loetz c.1914 and for Wiener Werkstätte 1915–23. Soft, enamelled decors are characteristic.

Pedestal Mushroom paperweight. See Piedouche.

Pedro, Rafael Glass designer from Portugal [–], worked for MGlass, Marinha Grande c.1999.

Pegging Inserting an airbubble or teardrop in hot glass.

Peill & Pützler Glashüttenwerke GmbH
Glassworks in Düren, Germany [1952–95],
designers include Wagenfeld and Wilhelm
Braun-Feldweg c.1959. Sig: etched P mark on
bottom after c.1960, circular stickers "Peill"
c.1920s–1970, circular sticker P-logo and
"Peill/WGermany" c.1970–95), (lighting,
crystal & art glass).

Peill & Sohn GmbH Glassworks in Düren,
Germany [1903–52], merged with Pützler in
1945, formalised in 1952. Sig: circular label
featuring two crossed arrows surrounded by
"Peill & Sohn/GmbH/ Glashüttenwerk Düren
(Rhld)" 1903–20, circular sticker "Peill"
c.1920–70.

Peiser, Mark Studio glass artist from Chicago,
IL, USA [1938–].
Peitz, Glashüttenwerke/Kristallglaswerke
Glassworks in Peitz near Cottbus NL, Germany
[1923–c.1937]. Sig: scalloped sticker with
knight and shield "Glashütte/Peitz/
Brandenburg/Qualitäts-Glas" c.1930s, (clear
glass after1923, clear crystal after 1927 & cut
crystal).
Peking Glass: First glass house in Peking
founded 1680, made imitation porcelain,
cameo cutting from 1725. Factory closed
1736–95; Po-Shan glass finished in Peking
is also called Peking Glass.
Pelgrimse Hut Glassworks in Leerdam, Holland
[1816–99], closed 1899, (bottles).
Pelikan, Eduard Glass engraver from Bohemia
[1822–1919].
Pelikan, Franz-Anton Glass engraver from
Meistersdorf, Bohemia [1786–1858],
Biedermeier engraving, several members of
the Pelikan family were also engravers.
Pellatt IV, Apsley Glass maker from Great
Britain [1791–1863], owner of the Falcon
Glassworks at Southwark, London; specialized
in sulfure/encrusted cameos introduced 1819,
aka cameo incrustations and crystallo-
ceramie. In business until at least 1878, had a
subsidiary at New Cross until 1895, ("Anglo-
Venetian" glass, revived "Ice" glass c.1851,
paperweights, tableware, scent bottles etc).
Peloton glass Kralik art glass type, 1880, with
colour threads rolled onto the vessel,
sometimes decorated with enamel. Found with
shiny or matt finish.
Pelzel, Franz Glass designer from
Czechoslovakia [1900–74], worked for
SALIR 1928–68.

Pelzel, Peter Glass designer from Murano, Italy
[b.1937], worked for SALIR after 1958, Vistosi
after 1962, La Murrina 1968–73 and Vetrelco
Treviso after 1969.
Penzig Town near Görlitz, Germany, location of
Penziger Glashütten AG 1872–1903,
previously Bänisch, Menzel & Co, (tableware,
lighting, chimneys, milk glass); Hoffmann &
Schopplick [–], active after 1872, (lighting);
Toepert, Breslau & Co [–], (lighting); J T
Büchner [–], previously Putzler & Büchner;
(tableware & lighting); Görlitzer Glasmacher
[–], active after 1858; Gebr Greiner; Krinke &
Jörn [–], Refinery; Meissner, Kleinert & Co [–];
Gebrüder Putzler [–], active after 1868,
(pressed glass & tableware); and Rodowe.
Pepita glass Iridised art glass type made by
Rindskopf at Barbarahütte.
Percival & Yates Glassworks in Manchester,
Great Britain [1846–?], later known as Percival
Vickers & Co, (cut glass, engraved glass,
pressed glass & tableware).
Percy, Arthur Glass designer from Sweden
[1886–1976], worked for Gullaskruf
1951–70.
Pereira Roidao e Filhos Lda., Manuel
Glassworks in Marinha Grande, Portugal [–] was
active c.1965, (tableware).
Perlasdorf Glass Glassworks in Delnice,
Croatia [1728–1834], founded by Spaniard
Perlas de Rialp, (bottles & tableware).
Periglas Type of art glass made by Loetz.
Perlmutt Glass type made by Eisch.
Perlmutter Type of iridescent art glass made
by WMF (1926–36) made with high amount of
lead oxide iridised at the surface resulting in
pink-green shimmer.
Persiano Fratelli Glassworks in Murano, Italy
[–] was active c.1967, (lighting).
Persson, Cilla Glass designer from Sweden
[–], worked for Nybro.
Persson, Leif Glass designer from Sweden [–],
worked for Strömbergshyttan.
Persson, Sigurd Glass designer from Sweden
[1914–], worked for Älghults glass after 1966
and for Kosta c.1974/5.
Persson, Sven Glass designer from Sweden
[–], worked for Kosta 1923.
Persson-Melin, Signe Glass designer from
Denmark [1925–], worked for Kosta Boda
1967–77 and BodaNova after 1970.
Perthshire Paperweights Glassworks in Crieff,
Scotland, Great Britain [1968–present]. Sig: P,
vague impressed P on repro items,
(paperweights, lampwork & reproductions of
Monart style glass).
Peruzzi & Bozzi Glassworks in Italy [–],
designers include Sergio Asti c.1970/1,
(tableware).
Pesci Type of art glass made by Venini
designed by Ken Scott, 1951.
Peskovsky Glassworks Glassworks in Lvov,
Ukraine [–], designers include Mechislav
Pavlovsky 1936–40 and Zeldich 1964–67.
Peters & Co, H J Glassworks in Chicago, IL,
USA [c.1914–15], (lighting, leaded glass
shades).
Peters, Eberhard Glass engraver from
Weisswasser, Germany [b.1936], at

Bärenhütte c.1960–c.86.

Petersdorf Glashutte See Fritz Heckert.

Petignot, J Glass maker from Belgium [–], head of Fluogravure at VSL after 1909.

Petroleum Lighting fluid, aka Coal oil.

Petrucela, Glasschleiferei P Glass cutting works in Turnow, Germany [?–present], (cut glass).

Pettersen, Sverre Glass designer from Norway [1884–1958], worked for Hadeland 1926–49.

Pezzato 1. Heavy object; 2. Type of art glass made by Venini designed by Fulvio Bianconi, 1950 and 1951; 3.. Barovier & Toso art glass type by Ercole Barovier, 1956.

PFW Trade name of Pacific Glass Works, San Francisco, CA, USA [1862–76], (bottles).

Pfeiffer, Anton H Glass engraver from Bohemia [1801–66].

Pfeiffer Glass studio in Netherlands [c.1970s–present], (giftware & paperweights).

Pfohl, Alexander Glass decorator from Bohemia [1868–1943].

Pfohl, Alexander Glass designer from Bohemia [1894–1953], worked for Heckert, Josphinenhütte.

Pfohl, Ervin Glass decorator from Bohemia [1906–75].

Pfohl, Karl Glass engraver from Bohemia [1826–94], worked at Egermann, in Wiesbaden, in Kamenický Šenov c.1850, in Paris 1858–64 and 66–72, his speciality was horses.

Phänomän Loetz art glass type introduced 1899, random pulled threads.

Pharmaceutical glass Aka apothecary glass it is used for potions, poisons, pills, pomades and perfumes. Abundant in Roman times, and from 15thC onward.

Philabaum, John Studio artist from USA [–].

Philadelphia Glassworks Glassworks in Philadelphia, PA, [1771–c.1926], (bottles, flat glass & tableware).

Philips process Process for tube and rod drawing.

Phillips, W P & G Glassworks in London, Great Britain [–] was active c.1862, (engraved, coloured glass & glass furniture).

Phoenician decoration Decoration consisting of contrasting threads on the surface of a vessel, combed to obtain loops.

Phoenix, Verrerie du Glassworks in Boussu near Mons, Belgium [1900–10].

Phoenix Glass Co Glassworks in Monaca, PA, USA and Beaver, PA, USA [1880–1970], bought by Anchor Hocking, 1970, (lighting; kerosene chimneys, lightbulbs, opalescent, frosted, etched, painted shades; patent for shades etched on the inside 1886; coloured glass, satin & mother-of-pearl).

Phoenix Glassworks Co Glassworks in Pittsburgh, PA, USA [–], was active c.1880, (art glass, cased milk glass & Mother-of-Pearl).

Phoenix Glassworks Glassworks in Dudley, Great Britain [1820–59], operated by Thomas Badger & Co, (cut glass).

Phoenix Oven Glass, British Heat-Resisting Glassworks in Bilston, Staffordshire, Great Britain [–] was active c.1950, (ovenware).

Phönixhütte Glassworks in Penzig near Görlitz OL, Germany [1887– after c.1937].

Photochromatic or Photochromic glass Self darkening glass. Invented by Corning.

Piacentini, Marcello Glass designer from Italy [–], worked for Venini.

Piana spa, Cristalleria Artistica La Glassworks in Siena, Italy [?–present], (tableware).

Planissimo Venini art glass designed by Tapio Wirkkala, 1966.

Pianon, Alessandro Glass designer from Italy [1931–84], worked for Vistosi after 1956, (lighting).

Piccardo, Cristalerias Glassworks in Buenos Aires, Argentina [–], was active c.1934.

Pichet French term for pitcher.

Pickle castors Silverplate set for holding pickle jars, often cut glass or pressed glass, popular around 1870–1900.

Pickle dish American term for a small serving dish for serving pickles.

Pick-up decoration A technique whereby hot glass is rolled in coloured glass chips, which are picked up, marvered in and blown out.

Piedouche French term for a stemmed paperweight, sometimes referred to as a "pedestal" or a "wig-stand". If the weight is flanged only, it is called a "footed weight".

Pieruzzi, Pierluigi Glass artist from Murano, Italy [–], worked for Barovier & Toso c.1970s, worked in Murano in the 1980s.

Pieschel & Hoffmann Glashütte Glassworks in Strassgräbchen near Kamenz, Germany [1888–after c.1937].

Pietsch, Friedrich Glass engraver from in Kamenický Šenov, Czechoslovakia [c.1900–c.1920s].

Pietsch, Karl Glass engraver from Bohemia [1828–83]

Pig bottle American term for a novelty whisky bottle shaped like a pig [after c.1850].

Pigeon Blood glass Orange-red glass with grey or brown hues, made from c.1835, especially in 1880s. Produced in France where it is called "gorge de pigeon" or pigeon's neck.

Pilchuck Glass school for studio artists in USA [1971–present], founded by Dale Chihuly and others.

Pilgrim Glass Co Glassworks in Ceredo, WV, USA [1949–?], previously Tri-states Glass Manufacturing Co. Designers include Robert Moretti. Sig: silver foil labels, (free-blown coloured, crackled and acid-finished glass, paperweights after 1960s, cameo & giftware).

Pilgrim Glass, The Glassworks in New York, NY, USA [?–present], (tableware, pressed glass & art glass; manual or semi-automatic; semi-crystal, soda-lime).

Pilkington Bros Ltd Glassworks in St Helens & Doncaster, Great Britain [–], (flat glass).

Pillar cutting Vertical parallel ribs on cut glass. See Fluted.

Pincers Glass maker's tool.

Pineapple 1. Hobnail pattern. 2. Strong yellow colour.

Pinnow, Glashütte Glassworks in Pinnow near Lübben NL, Germany [1713–after c.1937].

Pinzan Luigi Glassworks in Murano, Italy [–] was active c.1967, (giftware & souvenirs).

Pinzoni, Mario Glass designer from Italy [b.1927], worked for Seguso Vetri d'Arte 1954, art director 1963–71.

Pioneer Cut Glass Co Glassworks location unknown [–], (cut glass, Brilliant period).

Pisello Art Glass Glassworks in the USA [–].

Pitkin & Brooks Glassworks in Chicago, IL, USA [1872–1920], (cut glass & glassware distributor).

Pitkin flask American term for pocket bottle in ribbed, swirled etc design in half-post technique; made since 1788.

Pittori See Centro Studio Pittori.

Pittsburgh Flint Glass Works Glassworks in Pittsburgh, PA, USA [1808–], precursor to Bakewell, Pears & Co.

Pittsburgh Glass Flat glass and tableware were produced in the Pittsburgh area from before 1800. Around 150 glass companies sprung up, but many failed during the first half of the 19thC. By the mid-19thC, the survivors produced a wide range of glass items in pressed glass, cut glass, free-blown and mould-blown.

Pittsburgh Glass Works Glassworks in Pittsburgh, PA, USA [1798–1852], became known as James B Lyon Glass Co, associated with O'Hara Glass Co, Pittsburgh, 1891, US Glass, (pressed glass, lighting & flat glass)

Pittsburgh Lamp, Brass and Glass Co Manufacturer in Pittsburgh, PA, USA [c.1900]. Sig: on base P L B & G Co, but not always signed, (lighting; reverse painted table lamps).

Pittsburgh process Flat glass production process developed c.1920s. Glass is drawn up through a long annealing shaft prior to cutting.

Piumato Barovier & Toso art glass type by Ercole Barovier, 1942.

Pivovarov, Sergey K Glass designer from Almaty, Kazakstan [1935–], worked for Gus-Krushtalny after 1959.

Plaine-de-Walsch Area in northern Alsace, France, credited with invention of enamel decoration on semi-crystal, 1836. See Troisfontaines, Valérysthal.

Planet Trade name of Lucinda Glass, Australia.

Plate glass Flat glass made by casting or rolling and mechanically grinding and polishing.

Plate mould Full size bottle mould with interchangeable embossing plates introduced in the 1870s.

Plátek, Miroslav Glass engraver from Czechoslovakia [b.1922], worked for Železný Brod after 1950, (cut glass, engraving).

Plátek, Václav Glass engraver from Czechoslovakia [b.1917], worked for Železný Brod glassworks c.1940s and 50s.

Platina Series glass by Orrefors, designed by Vicke Lindstrand in 1939, cut surface décor. Marks: LA2253/1–10, LA2276/1–32.

Plating 1. Cover with gold or silver. 2. See flashing.

Platonite Type of heat resistant white glass made by Hazel Atlas.

Plesl, Rony Sculptor from Železný Brod, Czech Republic [–], worked for BAG Vsetin.

Pliva, Oldrich Glass artist from Czech Republic [b.1946], with Libenský until 1971, then independent after 1971.

Plum Glass Co Glassworks in Pittsburgh, PA, USA [present].

Plum, Susan Flamework artist from Berkeley, CA, USA [–], has been working since c.1986.

Plume and Atwood Manufacturer in USA [–], (lighting).

Plus Glasshytta Glassworks in Frederikstad, Norway [1958–present], designers include H Bongard 1960–64; A J Jutrem 1967; B Motzfeld from 1970 and Grete Ronning 1959–60. Sig: sanded PLUS/[ ]/NORWAY.

Plzen Glassworks in Plzen, Czechoslovakia [1879–1914], (pressed glass reported 1897).

Pocher, C A GmbH Glassworks in Nürnberg, Germany [–], was active c.1930s, (tableware).

Poděbrady Glassworks Glassworks in Poděbrady, Czechoslovakia [c.1850s–present], operated by Sklárny Bohemia (pressed glass).

Pohl Family of glass engravers and decorators included Alois, engraver, worked 1900s; Franz, engraver [1764–1834], Johann, worked at Harrach, Nový Svet specializing in marbling, millefiori and venetian inspired glass [1769–1850]; Josef M, decorator [1890–1962]; Karl, decorator, worked in the 1900s; Vincenz, decorator, worked in the 1830s and 40s; Wilhelm, worked at Edinburgh, Warrington, Manchester c.1860s and 70s.

Pohl, Vinzenz Glass refinery in Nový Svet, Czechoslovakia [c.1886–1914].

Poillerat, Gilbert Medal maker from France [1902–88], specialized in paperweights, especially sulfures, worked for Vianne.

Pokal German term for a stemmed goblet with a cover.

Polak, R F Glassworks in USA [–], (cut glass, Brilliant period).

Polar Trade name of Holophane.

Polczer, Glashütte M Glassworks in Laichingen, Germany [1990–present]. Sig: no signatures except on large, unique pieces, (decorative items – coloured, swirled & splattered).

Pöld, Helle Glass designer from Estonia [1928–], worked at Leningrad Factory after 1956.

Poli, Flavio Glass designer from Italy [1900–84], worked for IVAM after 1929, Seguso-Barovier-Ferro 1934–37, Seguso Vetri d'Arte 1937–63, Conterie e Cristallerie 1964–66 and Aureliano Toso 1963–8. His designs for Aureliano Toso include Vicenza 1963, Rudi 1966, Maja 1966, Macrostruttura, 1966, Sbocciati c.1967, Articolati c.1967 and Solchi colorato 1968.

Poli, Gino Glass designer from Murano [b.1919], worked for Venini after 1946, art director at Aureliano Toso from 1965–76.

Polishing Smoothing the surface of an object by holding it against a rotating wheel or using hand tools. Polishing agents are colcothar (Jewellers' Rouge) and cerium oxide.

Polishing wheels Traditionally made of wood or bristle, nowadays made of cork, polyurethane or bonded cloth; felt wheels are used for fine polishing.

Pollard, Donald Glass designer from USA [1924], worked for Steuben after 1950.

Polubny/Polaun 1. Czech/German name for the town of Desná, in the Jizerské mountains, Czech Republic; glassworks in operation 1847–present. 2. Glassworks in Polubny, Czechoslovakia [1846–c.1972–], (pressed glass c.1849 onwards).

Polyák, Janos Glass artist from Budapest, Hungary [1967–], has exhibited since 1988.

Polychromatic Having many colours.

Polychrome Having many colours.

Pomona Glass type patented 1885 by Joseph Locke of New England Glass Works, made until c.1900. Its appearance is frosted beige with amber edge, often decorated.

Pompeian Type of art glass made by John Walsh in the 1920s, surface imitating antique roman glass.

Poncet, Glashütte von Glassworks in Friedrichshain near Spremberg, Germany [1767–after c.1937]. See Friedrichshain.

Ponti, Gio Glass designer/architect from Milano, Italy [1891–1979], worked for Venini 1946, founded Domus in 1928.

Pontil rod Solid metal bar used to hold a piece in place while finishing the handles, rims, ruffles and applied trimming. The pontil rod is stuck on with hot glass, leaving a pontil mark, which can be left unfinished in a raised or footed piece or which can be ground and/or polished off. Pontil marks were generally polished on stemware after the 1780s allowing a flatter foot. In bottles the pontil disappeared c.1880.

Pope, G H Glass engraver from Great Britain [–],worked for Webb from 1929–70.

Porcelain imitations White milk glass decorated like porcelain was en vogue after the establishment of Meissen porcelain in 1710, most popular from 1775–1800. Mainly produced in Bohemia, Bristol, Sunderland and China.

Porpora Barovier & Toso art glass type by Ercole Barovier, 1959.

Porrón Spanish glass vessel with long spout for drinking wine.

Porter's Burning Fluid Lighting fluid patented 1834 in use until 1859, which contained turpentine and quicklime. It produced a clear flame, few fumes and was highly flammable.

Portieux, Cristalleries de Glassworks in Portieux, France [1705–present], merged with Valérysthal in 1872; re-established as "Art de Portieux" in 1982; was taken over by Groupe Faience Niderwiller from 1996 and is now currently Cristalleries de Portieux. Sig: impressed PORTIEUX on pressed items, PVP label, (tableware, pressed glass and covered animal dishes; typical colour includes a light blue/light amber combination; crystal only since 1996).

Portland Glass Co Glassworks in Portland, ME, USA [1863–73], later became the Portland Glass Works, (pressed glass).

Portland Vase A prime example of Roman cameo glass displayed in the British Museum in London, Great Britain.

Poschinger, Glashütte Freiherr von Glassworks in Frauenau b Zwiesel, Germany [1568–present]. Sig: crowned P in a shield, (tableware, art glass, cut glass, lighting & copies of historical glass).

Postal, Auguste Glass maker from Herbatte, Belgium [–], producing crystal with filigrane decoration after 1853; worked at Bauzot-Ledoux until 1858.

Postrednik, Ladislav Glass cutter from Bohemia [1897–1973], worked after c.1928.

Pot A pot containing molten glass; a modern pot contains approximately 500–800 kg (1100–1760 lb).

Pot arch A kiln used for preheating pots.

Potash Potassium carbonate, used as a flux in the manufacture of glass.

Potron, Eugene Glassworks location unknown [–], was active c.1901, (lighting).

Potstone A gritty glass contaminant, usually of refractory material.

Potz, Enrico Glass designer from Italy [b.1943], worked for Aureliano Toso 1962–65.

Powder Finely ground glass.

Powder box, jar, puff A covered dresser jar for holding facial powder; popular in Art Deco through 1950s, often part of a set.

Powell & Sons, James Glassworks in Whitefriars, Great Britain [1834–1980]. Aka Whitefriars.

Powell, Barnaby Glass maker from Great Britain [1871–1939], worked for Whitefriars 1919–39.

Powell, Harry Glass maker/designer from Great Britain [1835–1922], worked for Whitefriars 1873–1919, was succeeded by his son Barnaby.

Powell, William and Thomas Glass cutters from Temple Gate, Bristol, Great Britain, were active c.1820s, (cut glass).

Powolny, Michael Ceramicist/glass designer from Austria [1871–1954], worked for Lobmeyr 1910–14 and for Loetz c.1914, pioneered orange and black "Tango" glassware, which became a craze in the 1930s, a membert of Wiener Werkstatte.

Praha-Slíchov Glassworks in Zlíchov u Praha, Czechoslovakia [1862–1933], (pressed glass). See Josef Inwald.

Prasch, Sally Flamework artist from Montague, MA, USA [–], has worked since c.1980.

Prashant Glass Works Glassworks in Varanasi, India [1940–present], (household glass, beads, tubes & rods).

Pravec, Josef Glass designer from Czechoslovakia [b.1925], worked for Bohemia Poděbrady after 1951, (cut glass, engraving).

Preciosa Glassworks/refinery conglomerate located in Jabloneč Nad Nisou and Kamenický Šenov, Czech Republic [1946–present], (mechanically cut costume jewellery, chandelier drops, crystal giftware & rosaries).

Pre-heating Heating up a glass piece to prevent shock when it is exposed to a flame, either in a kiln or using a burner (flamework).

Preissler Manfred Glassworks in Schwäbisch Gmünd, Germany [1946–present], (cut glass, lighting, chandeliers & novelties).

Premium Trade name of the Premium Glass Co, Coffeyville, KS, USA [1908–14], (bottles).

Prenosil, Ladislav Glass engraver from Prisovice, Czechoslovakia [1893–1965], taught at Železný Brod from 1922–58, worked for Eiff, Stuttgart in 1927. Sig: LP.

Prescut Trade name of McKee-Jeannette Glass Works.

Preserve dish A tall, footed dish.

Press-and-blow Semi-automatic bottles making process for wide neck bottles, fruit jars and milk bottles introduced 1892.

Pressed glass Glassware pressed in a metal mould, positively shaping both inside and outside. In mould-blown glass the inside wall follows the outside mould shape. Pressing glass is one of the oldest glassworking techniques. It was applied to mass production after the 1820s, especially in the USA. Pressed glass has sharp edges and shows the closing lines of the mould, except when fire polished. See Fire Polishing.

Presser The worker who cuts off excess glass when the mould is filled.

Preston test Test for bursting strength during automatic inspection of bottles.

Pribic, Sanja Glass designer from Zagreb, Croatia [1960–].

Prim Rose Bordier Trade name for designer glass made at Boussu 1978–1982.

Prima, Crystallerie Glassworks in Murano, Italy [?–present].

Primavera di Cristallo Trade name of CALP.

Princess House Manufacturing Glassworks in Weston, WV, USA [?–present], (pressed glass, tableware & barware).

Prismolier Trade name of Holophane.

Prochaska, Eduard Glass designer from Austria [–], worked for Loetz c.1908.

Procter, Steven Studio artist from Great Britain

[1946–].

Progrès, Verreries du Glassworks in Manage, Belgium [1896–?], operated by Emile Michotte, (tableware).

Prokes, Petr Glass studio in Uhlioské Janovice, Czech Republic [1990–], (decorative labware)

Prokofiev, Vladimir F Glass designer from Minsk region, Belarus [1936–], worked at Dzerzhinsky Glassworks after 1964.

Prost E Glassworks in Paris, France [–], was active c.1925, (tableware).

Prostakov, Alexander A, Glass designer from St Petersburg, Russia [1941–], worked at First Communist VDG after 1969.

Prouve, Victor Painter/designer from Nancy, France [1858–1943], friend and associate of Emile Gallé, art director at Gallé factory 1904–13.

Prunt A blob of glass applied to a vessel. From the middle ages, the prunt was a decoration for German and Bohemian drinking glasses so they would not slip from greasy fingers. These prunts were smoothed, shaped like a raspberry (Raspberry prunt) or thorny. The Venetians also used prunts in the shape of a lion's head (Lion prunts) and several glass houses use a prunt to cover over the pontil mark; Vasart uses an angel logo, Mortevieille an intertwined MV.

Prutscher, Otto Glass designer from Austria [1880–1949], a member of Wiener Werkstätte, worked for Loetz c.1908, Lobmeyr, Bakalowits and Meyr's Neffe c.1907.

Pseudo-Cameo See Cameo-fleur.

Pucellas Glass maker's tool; tongs.

Pukeberg Glassworks in Pukeberg, Småland, Sweden [1871–present]. Designers include Erik Höglund and Göran Wärff c.1962/3. Contemporary designs are by Eva Engdahl, Margareta Hennix, Liselotte Henriksen, Börge Lindau, Rolf Sinnemark and Birgitta Watz. Marks: post war art glass is sometimes needle engraved with designer name and year; otherwise labels only.

Pulegoso Having fine bubbles, sometimes embellished with gold leaf, and may be slightly iridescent.

Putzler Glashütte, Martin Glassworks in Neu Petershain near Calau, Germany [1898/9–1945], see also Peill & Putzler.

Pumice Volcanic stone used in cut glass polishing.

Punch bowl A large bowl with a lid, ladle and

small punch cups (no saucers).

Puntini, A Venini art glass designed by Carlo Scarpa and Tyra Lundgren, 1938.

Punty 1 Pontil. 2 A cut facet on a paperweight.

Purisiol, Gianfranco Glass designer from Italy [b.1939], better known as Franco Purisiol, worked for IVR Mazzega 1958–62 and Archimede Seguso after 1963.

Purled Having applied ribbing around the base.

Push-up The base of a glass bottle, aka kick-up.

Puteaux, Cristallerie de Glassworks in Puteaux, France [–], was active c.1866, (tableware).

Putnam Flint Glass Works Glassworks in Putnam, OH, USA [1852–?]. Sig: Putnam Glass Works encircled, (bottles).

Putnam, Henry W Located in Bennington, VT, USA [1875–90], (bottles).

Putzer, Glashütte Gebr Glassworks in Penzig near Görlitz OL, Germany [1869–1945], merged with Peill after 1945. Sig: unmarked, stickers only "GEPU", "GEPE", "Putzler Gebr" or "Putzler/Glas".

Putzler, Martin Glassworks in Neupetershain NL, Germany [1899–]. Sig: P over N monogram.

P
N

Putzler, Thomas Class cutter from Germany [b.1947], worked at Döbern before 1987.

Puy de Dome S A, Verrerie de Glassworks in France [–]. Sig: pressed glass, (bottles).

PY Signature of Paul Ysart on paperweights and canes.

Pyle, Robert British engraver [–] worked at Sunderland 1827–53.

Pyrex, La Sté Le Glassworks in Liège, Belgium, active 1920s and 30s, (tableware). See also Pays de Liège.

Pyrex Trade name of Corning for heat resistant ovenware from borosilicate glass, invented in 1912 and launched 1915. Early clear glass ovenware items were wheel cut and engraved with ferns, flowers and wreaths from 1918–45. Hand-blown teapots were made 1922–34. Licence to Jobling, UK, 1921.

Q

Quaker City Cut Glass Co Glassworks in Philadelphia, USA [1902–27], (cut glass).

Quality Circle Members of the quality circle for traditional handmade venetian glass in 1967 included Barbini, Barovier, Arte Nuova, Cristalleria Santi, SALIR, Salviati, Archimede Seguso, Toso Rag Aureliano, Fratelli Toso, Moretti Ulderico, Venini, Seguso Vetri d'Arte, Vistosi.

Quast, Johan Z Glass decorator from Bohemia [1814–91].

Queen Trade name of Smalley, Kivian & Onthank, Boston, MA, USA [1906–19]. Sig: Queen scripted + Trade Mark in shield, (bottles).

Queensberry, Marquess of Glass designer from Great Britain [b.1929], worked for Webb & Corbett.

Quenvit, P Signature attributed to Legras c.1920–c.1925 on enamelled art glass; stylistic similarities with Goupy and Delvaux.

Quezal Art Glass Decorating Co Glassworks in Brooklyn, NY, USA [1901–25]. Established by Martin Bach and Thomas Johnson, former workers at Tiffany Studios. Sig: usually engraved "Quezal" on base or on lampshade edge after 1902, sometimes code number added, (art glass, lighting, similar to Favrile, Aurene and Myra).

quezal

Quilling Edge finishing using tongs to create a wavy pattern.

R

R Trade name, or bottle mark, of Louit Frères & Cie, France [1870–90], (bottles).

R & C Co Trade name of Roth & Co, San Francisco, CA, USA [1879–88], (bottles).

Rabane, Paco Trade name for designer glass made at Boussu in Belgium 1978–82.

Rachelkristall Weidensteiner Glass refinery in Frauenau, Bavaria, Germany [1959–present], (souvenir glasses after 1959, cut glass after 1966, chandeliers after 1973, cut-to-clear & lampwork, plus a retail operation).

Rade, Max Glass designer from Dresden, Germany [1840–1917], worked for Heckert, Petersdorf c.1898–c.1906.

Radeburger Glashüttenwerke Glassworks in Radeburg, near Dresden, Germany [c.1890–1914]; (lighting, domes & chimneys for gas lighting). See Hibbeln, Wilhelm.

Radi, Giulio Glass designer from Italy [1895–1952], worked for Rioda 1918–32 and AVEM 1935–52.

Radium ware See Millersburg.

Radke, Carl Glass maker from Harmony, CA, USA [–], founded Phoenix Studios, (art glass & lustre).

Raduga (Rainbow) Factory Glassworks in Lvov, Ukraine [c.1940s–]. See Lvov Factory of Sculpture and Ceramics.

Raetsch & Co Glashütte Glassworks in Muskau near Rothenburg OL, Germany [1899–after c.1937].

Raetsch, Schier & Co Glashütte Glassworks in Muskau near Rothenburg OL, Germany .[1884–after c.1937].

Rainbow Art Glass Co Glassworks in Huntingdon, WV, USA [1942–c.1972], bought by Viking in c.1972, (animal figures, decorative glass, crackle and cased glass & paperweights).

Raised enamel Type of decoration of thick enamel, often in combination with gold and/or a colour background. Made in Murano, especially souvenir pieces, from the 1920s. The largest producer is Crystalex, Nový Bor, Czech Republic and other Czech factories, plus various works in Italy, Hungary, Romania and Serbia.

Raman, Ingegerd Glass designer from Sweden [1943–], worked for Johansfors 1967–71, independent studio after 1972 and for Skruf after 1981.

Rance, Verrerie de Glassworks in Rance, Hainaut, Belgium [1806–50], jointly operated with Ghlin c.1820s, last of the wood fired glass huts in Belgium, (handmade tableware, pressed glass in neogothic style after c.1830s).

Randsfjords Glassworks Glassworks in Randsfjord, Norway [–], was active c.1950s–c.1960s.

Raos, Peter Studio glass artist from New Zealand [–], (art glass & paperweights).

Rapotin Glassworks in Sumperka, Czechoslovakia [1883–after c.1972], operated by Osvetlovaci Sklo, (pressed glass until start of 20thC).

Rare earth glasses 1 Glass coloured with rare earth elements developed in 1925 and introduced in1928 by Moser. 2 Laser glasses, mostly containing neodymium. When stimulated, Nd ions emit radiation at 1.06um, which is transformed into high-intensity coherent optical data for various measurement functions in industry.

Rasch, Clemens Glass maker from Bohemia [–], was active 1830s/40s.

Rasch, Glashütte Glassworks in Nový Bor, Czechoslovakia [–], was active c.1920.

Rasche, Adolf Glassworks in Nový Bor, Czechoslovakia [–], was active c.1925, (art glass).

Raspiller, G Glass artist from Alsace, France [–], operated c.1900–c.1914 and is believed to have worked for Gallé, (art glass & Cameo landscapes).

Raspiller & Cie Fenner Glashütte Glassworks in Fenne, Saarbrücken, Germany [1812–1939], founded as Karlsbrunner Hütte in 1812, became Dern Karcher & Cie after 1818, then Raspiller from the 1820s–1903, changed to Hirsh & Hammerl 1903–37, merged with Glasfabrik Dreibrunnen/Troisfontaines, Valérysthal in 1909, Saarglas AG Fenne-Saar after 1937 and closed in 1939. Sig: VTF impressed for

"Verrerie Troisfontaines" c.1903–35, "VTF Fenne", "Peinture VTF Fenne-Saar" c.1925–35, crown "SG" c.1910–39, "Saar" 1920s, yellow stickers "Fenne" in an oval 1920s–30s, circular yellow label "SAARGLAS" c.1937–39 and "Deutschland" c.1933–39, (tableware, pressed glass, guilloche/engraved glass, covered animal dishes & paperweights).

Rastal GmbH & Co KG Glass refinery in Höhr-Grenzhausen, Germany [1919–present], further plants are located in Gliwice, Poland and Chur, Switzerland, (enamel transfer printing, satination & cutting etc).

Rath, Hans Harald Glass designer from Austria [1904–68], worked for Lobmeyr c.1925–68, specialized in lustres.

Rath, Marianne Glass designer from Austria [–], worked for Lobmeyr c.1925.

Rath Studio, Stephan Glass engraving studio in Kamenický Šenov, Czechoslovakia [–], active c.1950s, works by Jaromina Lipska, and Vera Lisková, (engraved glass).

Rathmann & Kissmeyer Glassworks in Denmark [–]. See Mylenberg og Aalborg Glasvaerker.

Rau's Trade name of Fairmount Glass Works, Fairmount, IN, USA [1898–1908], (bottles).

Rauchtopaz German term for the smoky colour developed by WMF and used by Wilhelm Wagenfeld in the 1950s, but also used by other factories, such as Joska.

Raudväa, Silvia Glass designer from Estonia [1926–], worked at The Neman after 1961.

Rauscha Glashütte Glassworks near Görlitz OL, Germany, [1706–c.1937], aka O Schulze & Co, (tableware & lighting).

Ravanello Giuseppe & Cie Glassworks in Murano, Italy [–], was active c.1967, (giftware & souvenirs).

Ravenhead Glass Glassworks in St. Helen's, Merseyside, Great Britain [?–present], aka United Glass Bottle Manufacturers Ltd. Designers include Alexander Hardie Williamson 1930s–72. Sig: some beer glasses marked with raven's head logo, otherwise unmarked, oval logo with raven's head and "British/Ravenhead/Glassware" 1945–70, raven with spread wings logo after 1970. Currently owned by Durobor of Belgium, (tableware & barware).

Ravenna Type of art glass developed by Sven Palmqvist for Orrefors in 1948, in production until 1981; a mosaic variation on Graal.

Sequential numbering starts 1=1948, 173=1952, 609=1954, 914=1956, 1220=1958, 1568=1960, 1901=1962, 2305=1964, 2789=1966, 3039=1967, 4079=1968, 4497=1970, 5116=1972, 5889=1974, 6441=1976, 6952=1978, 7161=1980, 7232=1981.

Ravenna Glass Works Glassworks in Ravenna, OH, USA [–], (paperweights, late 19thC).

Ravenscroft Inventor of flint glass (crystal) in 1676.

Ravilious, Eric Glass designer from Great Britain [1903–42], worked for Stuart & Sons.

Rays Spoke-like designs on the bottom of a glass, (pressed glass).

Razl-Dazl Trade name used by Holophane Lighting Corp.

RCR Crystal Trade name of CALP (Royal Crystal Rock).

Reading Artistic Glass Works Glassworks in Reading, PA, USA [1884–86], (various styles of art glass).

Real Fabrica de Cristales See Granja.

Reamer 1 A flameworker's tool. 2 American term for a juice extractor for lemons, oranges and grapefruit, (pressed glass).

Rebard, Camille Glass maker in Liège, Belgium [–].

Recycling Glass SA Glassworks in Ayelo de Malferit, Spain [?–present].

Red Trade name of Safe Glass Co, Upland, IN, USA [1892–98], (bottles).

Red House Glass Works Glassworks in Great Britain [–], operated by Philip Pargeter. See Stuart and Sons.

Reducing Atmosphere containing uncombusted fuel that causes metallic oxides to react and colour the glass. A metallic deposit may appear on the surface.

Reed & Barton, Silversmiths Tableware producers in Great Britain [–], active c.1905.

Refining Any operation taking place after production of the blank: cutting, such as cold enamelling or painting, engraving, staining etc.

Reflexolier Trade name of Welsbach Company.

Refractories Heat-resistant materials used to build furnaces, kilns, ovens etc.

Regal Trade name of Lippincott Glass Co.

Regency cut glass Deep extravagant cut glass in the Empire style made possible after the arrival of steam power in 1790, made c.1810–1820s.

Regenhütte, Krystallglasfabrik Steigerwald See Steigerwald.

Registered See Design registration, British.

Regout, Petrus Glassworks/cutting shop in Maastricht, Netherlands [1835–1925], merged with Stella to form Kristalunie in 1925, (tableware & cut glass). See Kristal en Glasblazerij.

Reich & Co Glasfabrik, S Glassworks in Kràsno, Czechoslovakia [1855–1939], (lighting & shades).

Reichenbach Glassworks in Reichenbach near Görlitz, OL, Germany [1882–1983], operated by Cristallglaswerke Rohrbach und Böhme, by Reichenbacher Farbglashütte Häubner & Dobschall 1945–72, VEB Rubinglashütte 1972, VEB Reichenbacher Farbglaswerk 1977–83, merged with Reichenbacher Hütte and closed in 1983, (colour cased glass, bars and rods, beads & mosaic).

Reichenbacher Hütte Glassworks in Reichenbach near Görlitz, OL, Germany [1866–present], operated as Farbglas Schuster & Wilhelmy, as VEB Reichenbacher Farbglaswerk after 1946, as part of VEB Kombinat Lausitzer Glas Weisswasser after 1979 and Farbglashütte Reichenbach GmbH after 1990, (technical glass, coloured glass, lustered glass, pressed crystal, lighting & bottles; currently technical coloured glass only).

Reichenhall, Bad See Bad Reichenhall.

Reid, Colin Studio artist from Great Britain [1953–].

Reijmyre Glassworks in Reijmyra, Östergötland, Sweden [1810–1926 and 1937–present], designers include Betze Ählström 1901/2, Anna Boberg 1901/2, Sten Branzell, Monika Bratt 1937–58, Paul Kedelv 1956/7, Tyra Lundgren 1960, Johnny Mattsson 1954–c.1958, Tom Möller 1963–7, E Montelin c.1979, Edvin Ollers, Axel Törnemann and Alf Wallander 1908–14. Current designers include Margareta Hennix, Peter Gibson-Lundberg, John Larson, Filippa Reuterswärd and Klas-Göran Tinbäck. Trade names include Sial. Sig: Many pieces unmarked, cameo pieces usually engraved Reijmyre, with or without Suède, UNIK, designer name, pattern number and date; 1960s onward sometimes engraved Reijmyre with designer and/or engraver name (abbreviated); sometimes initials and year only; Bratt glass is usually unsigned; circular labels "R" with the 1810 date; various other labels include special Sial and Montelin labels, (tableware, art glass & pressed glass after 1836).

Reinerzer Kristallglaswerke FA Knittel Glassworks in Bad Reinerz, Germany [–], active c.1925, (tableware).

Renaissance, Verrerie de la Glassworks in Boussu near Mons, Belgium [1918–], named Verrerie Robette from 1897–1918.

Renard, Camille Glass decorator from Belgium [–], worked at VSL 1863–c.1910.

Renval, Essi Glass designer from Finland [1911–].

Replicas Historical glass, such as claw beakers, viking glass, stangenglas, berckemeyers, roemers and passglasses, are being manufactured in the Czech Republic, Italy and Sweden for museum shops. Replicas of pressed glass are common in the US.

Resinous lustre Shining like resin. See Lustre.

Resist Material applied to a specific portion of a glass surface to stop it from being etched or sandblasted.

Resonance The sound a glass makes when tapped. Tapping is used to distinguish glass (a dull sound) from crystal (a clear sound), although results can be misleading. The shape of the vessel accounts for some resonance and many glass and semi-crystal types ring clear.

Reticello Having a fine network of filigrana.

Reticello Zanfirico Venini art glass designed by Paolo Venini, 1954.

Retortoli Having twisted, spiral threads, aka Zanfirico.

Réunies, SA Verreries Glassworks in Blanc-Misseron, France and in Familleureux, Belgium [c.1880–?], active c.1880 and c.1900, member of Association Gobeletiers Belges, (tableware).

Reverse Amberina: See Amberina.

Reverse painting The technique of painting on the underside of glass, aka Verre Eglomisé. First noted in the early 18thC, popular in the 19thC in geman portraits, romanian icons and on advertising mirrors after 1900. Advertising mirrors are mostly 1980s.

Rexxford Signature found on bowls made in Bavaria, Germany c.1971.

Reyen, Alphonse-George Glass engraver from France, worked for Rousseau after c.1877.

RG Co Trade name of Renton Glass Co, Renton, WA, USA [–], active c.1911, (bottles).

Rheinbach Glass producing town in Germany, home to Glaskunst Fritz Berg, Glashaus am Wasserturm/Chris & Udo Edelmann, Glasmalerei Helga Feuser-Strasdas, Gescha Kristall, Lehmann-Glas, Kristall-Lüsterfabrik Christoph Palme GmbH, Posselt's Glasfabrikation, Cristallerie Baldur Schönberg, Glasmanufaktur Stanka, Stefanie Stanka, Franz Wendler refineries and Staatliche Glasfachschule.

Rheinische Glashütten AG Glassworks in Köln-Ehrenfeld, Germany [1864–1931], designers include Peter Behrens, Georges de Feure, Johann Vincent Gissarz, Erich Kleinhempel and Kolo Moser, (antique glass c.1880 and Art Nouveau tableware c.1900).

Rhetondes Manufacturer in France [–], (deco-style lighting).

Rhinestone Imitation stone made of cut mountain crystal, crystal or paste; aka Strass. Named after the Rhine where crystals were found.

Rhodium ware See Millersburg.

Ribbed mould Mould for making Rigadin glass (vertical ribbing).

Ribbon burner A neon worker's gas burner that has a series of flames to heat long sections of tubing.

Ribbon plate A pressed glass plate with an open edge for weaving a decorative ribbon through pressed glass.

Rice Harris & Co Glass firm located at the Islington Glass Works, Birmingham, Great Britain [19thC]. Sig: includes IGW, (pressed glass after 1830s, tumblers, goblets, sugars, stems and paperweights).

Rich Cut period: Cut glass period c.1850–c.1880.

Richard The signature found on cameo glass produced for Edmond Etling by Loetz; industrial cameo glass and landscapes c.1905–c.1920 were almost always signed.

Richards & Hartley Flint Glass Co/US Glass E Glassworks in Tarentum, PA, USA [1866–1918], in Pittsburgh, PA until 1884; USG 1891, taken over by Tarentum Glass Co in 1893, burnt down in 1918.

Richardson Glassworks in Stourbridge, Great Britain [1850–1930], companies included W H, B & J Richardson and Henry G Richardson & Sons, both involving Benjamin Richardson, taken over by Thomas Webb in 1930. Sig: "Richardson Stourbridge" in a circle surrounding P#; rarely P# without text; "Richardson Vitrified" with or without enamel colors before 1851, (opaque white glass gilded, painted or printed c.1851; etched and moulded glassware patented 1857; threading machine patented 1857; airlocks in hobnail pattern patented 1857; art glass & decorative ware c.1880s, many different techniques).

Richardson & Sons Ltd, Henry G Glassworks in Wordsley, Stourbridge, Great Britain [c.1800–?], trade names include "Wonder" and "Wordsley", (pressed glass 1840s, 1910s–1920s).

Richardson, William Haden Glass designer from Great Britain [1785–1876], worked for Hawkes 1810–28, one of the three founding brothers in W H B & J Richardson; the other two were Benjamin and Jonathan, (Regency cut glass).

Richter, Georg Glass cutter from Germany [b.1937], worked at Bärenhütte 1954–56 and KLG Weisswasser after 1959.

Richter & Phillips Glassworks location unknown [–] active c.1909, (tableware).

Richter, Vjenceslav Architect/Glass artist from Zagreb, Croatia [1919–], produced sculpture after 1949.

Rickard, Stephen Glass designer from Great Britain [b.1920], known for engraving after 1953.

Ricketts, Jacob Wilcox Industrialist from Bristol, Great Britain [–], invented single operation bottle making after 1811. Ricketts bottles were superseded by semi-automatic Ashley bottles in 1880 and by fully automatic Owens bottles in 1903.

Riedel Glassworks conglomerate in Polubný, Czechoslovakia [1849–], Klein-Iser after 1866, Wurzelsdorf after 1867, Maxdorf after 1878,

Polubný II after 1880, Glass refinery after 1883, Refinery Harrach'ov after 1885, Polubný III/Przichowitz after 1886, Polubný IV after 1889. Sig: mostly unsigned, cameo pieces are signed "Riedel", export pieces are marked "Elric", circular label features printed glassblower and "JRP" c.1925–39, (lighting, tableware, beads, art glass & technical glass).

Riedel Glassworks in Kufstein, Austria [1955–present], opened new facility in Tiroler Glashütte, Kufstein in 1957 and in Schneegattern, Austria in 1969. Designers included Giovanni Mistretta c.1973/4 and Claus-Josef Riedel c.1964/74. Sig: square sandblasted CJR monogram introduced in 1960, which is modified yearly; "Riedel" name in full on handmade tableware, (tableware).

Riedel

Riedel dynasty Glassmaking family includes Johann Cristoph [1673–1744], Johann Carl [1701–81], Johann Leopold [1726–1800] who founded the first family Glassworks, Anton Leopold [1761–1821], Franz Xaver Anton [1786–1844] the famous engraver, discovered uranium glass in 1830; Josef Riedel Sr [1816–94] nicknamed "The glass king of the giant mountains", Josef Riedel Jr [1862–1924] who created 600 colours and revolutionized jewellery production, Walter [1895–1974] who invented glass fibres, radar and TV screens, Claus-Josef [1925–] who re-established the family business in Kufstein after WWII, and Georg Josef [1949–] the current manager of Riedel Glassworks.
Riedinger, L A Glassworks location unknown [–], active c.1925, (lighting).
Riedl Glass Trade mark of Bad Reichenhall.
Riedlhütte Glassmaking town in Germany where the largest operation is Nachtmann Bleikristall.
Rietschen Glaswerk Glassworks in Rietschen near Rothenburg OL, Germany [1901–], Rietschener Hohlglashüttenwerk Berthold Greiner GmbH, Glaswerk Rietschen GmbH 1929, Glaswerk Rietschen H Eckert KG 1937, closed in 1943, re-opened in 1947, operated by VEB OLG Weisswasser after 1953, renamed 1954–58 Glaswerk Rietschen, state participation in 1958, VEB Glaswerk Rietschen 1972, merged into VEB KLG in 1976, (blown and pressed tableware, kitchenware, flat glass & barware).
Rigadin Thin ribbing obtained by blowing the object inside a mould. The glass may also be

twisted while hot to produce "rigadin ritorto", or twisted ribbing.
Rigaree Applied decoration of a crimped or pinched glass ribbon.
Rigas Stikls Glassworks Glassworks in Riga, Latvia [–], designers include Malda Lapsinya after 1964 and Juris Mednis after 1967.
Rigatti S N C Glassworks in Montelupo Fno, FI, Italy [1910–present], (bottles & tableware, mechanical or manual).
Rigolleau, Cristallerias Glassworks in Berazategui, Argentina [1882–present], designers include Lucrecia Moyano c.1950–57, trade names include Rigopal, (pressed glass, tableware, art glass & nail mould glass).
Rigopal Trade name for opal tableware produced by Rigolleau c.1960s–present, similar to Arcopal from J G Durand.
Rigot, Emile Glass designer from Germany/France [1885–?], worked for Villeroy & Boch 1929–31.
Riihimaki Glass/Riihimäen Lasi Oy Glassworks in Riihimaki, Finland [1910–present], designers include Tamara Aladin 1959–75, Arttu Brummer c.1913/52, Henri Ericsson c.1928, G L Jaderholm-Snellman 1937–49, Gunnel Nyman 1932–47, Aimo Okkolin.1959/67, Erkkitapio Siiroinen 1964–80, Nanny Still 1949–76 and Helena Tynell c.1952–57. Sig: tableware unmarked, art glass engraved "Riihimäen lasi oy" or "Oy Riihimäki" + designer name + year; or circular acid stamp featuring a lynx with engraved pattern number, logo of lynx with one paw raised over "Oy/Riihi/Mäki" encircled by "Riihimäen Lasitehdas ya Kriustallihiomo" in use 1912–1920s, free standing lynx with one paw raised over "Riihimäki" in use 1930s–1960s, transparent paw print label over "Riihimäen/lasi" 1970s, heart-shaped logo "Riihimäki"+ lynx + "Finland" 1980s, (pressed glass, art glass & tableware).

Riis Glasindustri AS Glassworks in Riis, Norway [–] active c.1986.
Rika, Eliahu Glass designer from Syria [b.1938], working in Israel since c.1955.
Rilievi, A Venini art glass designed by Carlo Scarpa, 1935.
Rimpler GmbH, Kristallglasmanufaktur Glassworks in Zwiesel, Bavaria, Germany [c.1920–1936, 1946–present], designers include Christine Schimkowski since c.1996. Sig: engraved R, (art glass & decorated glass,

flashed, cut-to-clear, gilded, engraved & enamelled in Biedermeyer style).

Rindskopf, Josef Glassworks in Kostaný u Teplice, Czechoslovakia [1891–1927], acquisition of Fannyhütte and Barbarahütte in 1900, (art glass, Baroque glass, iridized glass, Grenada (Amberina), Alhambra, Pepita, Diluvium & pressed glass 1920–27).

Ringel d'Illzach Alias of Jean Désiré Ringel [1847–1915], sculptor, potter and glass artist from Illzach, Alsace, France. He specialized in the lost wax process, art glass made in Meisenthal. Ringel worked c.1895–1915. Sig: "Ringel d'Illzach" in full or "R d'I"

Ringer The worker who applies threading etc to a glass.

Rioda, Andrea Glassmaker from Murano, Italy [1878–1921], manager at CVM until opened own works in 1910, co-founder of VSM Cappelin Venini in 1921. See Vetri Soffiati Muranese Cappelin, Venini & Co.

Rioda, Andrea Vetraria Artistica Glassworks in Murano, Italy [1910–?], Andrea Rioda died in 1921, but the company continued as Succesori Andrea Rioda c.1930, glass blowers A and E Ferro left in 1932 to found AVEM.

Ripley & Co Glassworks in Pittsburgh, PA, USA [1865–1918], co-founded by Duncan George & Sons, joined US Glass in 1891, moved to Connellsville, PA, USA 1910, became Capstan Glass Co after 1918, (lighting, tableware & pressed glass).

Rithner, Edward Glass maker from Wellsburg, WV, USA [–], was active c.1940s–1950s, (paperweights).

Ritzenhoff Glass printer from Germany [present], (designer beerglasses).

Ritzman, Jan-Erik Glass designer from Sweden [–], worked at Kosta; Transjö Hytta AB.

Riunite, Vetrerie Glassworks in Colognola ai Colli/VR, Italy [1980–present], (lighting, technical & automotive).

Riverbend Glass Works Glassworks in USA [–], (pressed glass, novelties & covered animal dishes).

Riverside Glass Co Glassworks in Wellsburgh, WV, USA [1879–1907], 1899 National Glass 15, closed 1907/1911, previously Crescent Glass Co, manufacturer of automobile lenses and blown tumblers, (tableware & pressed glass).

Riverton, Christopher Studio artist from USA [–].

Rizzetto, Ezio Glass designer from Venice, Italy [b.1917] who worked for various producers including Ferro-Lazzarini from 1954.

Robax Trade name for transparent glass-ceramic by Schott.

Robette, Verrerie Glassworks in Boussu near Mons [1897–1918], renamed Verrerie de la Renaissance in 1918, (cut glass engraved,

guilloche & lighting; stemware only after 1913).

Robinson Glass Co Glassworks in Zanesville, OH, USA [1893–1906], joined National Glass in 1899, burned down in 1906, (pressed glass).

Robinson, Skinner & Co Ltd Glassworks in Warrington, Great Britain [–], active c.1870, (tableware & pressed glass). See Mersey Flint Glass.

Rocailles See beads.

Rocenkova, Aida Glass designer from Latvia [–], current factory designer for Livanu Stikls.

Rochère La, Cristallerie Glassworks in Passavant-la-Rochère, France [1475–1636 and 1660–present], the oldest working maker of art glass in France. Sig: Rochère etched in cameo pieces and LR on small cameo items. "Paris Musée" on moulded tableware replica, (tableware, art glass, giftware, cameo glass, lighting, pressed glass, tiles, marbles, barware, gift items & paperweights).

Rochester Burner Co Manufacturer in Rochester, NY, USA [–], introduced the Rochester burner in 1888, a kerosene burner with a circular wick, (lighting).

Rochester Cut Glass Co Glassworks in Rochester, PA, USA [–], active c.1900–c.1910, (cut glass).

Rochester Tumbler Co/National 17 Glassworks in Rochester, PA, USA [1872–99]; joined National Glass in 1899, founded by H C Fry, aka Rochester Glass Works, (pressed glass).

Rock Crystal All over polished style of intaglio engraving, ornate copper wheel sculpted glass, speciality of Stourbridge c.1878, popular until 1900, out of fashion by 1906. Produced by Stevens & Williams after 1879 and Webb after 1878, among others. Three famous engravers were Kny, Fritsche and Kretschman.

Rock Trade name of Gill Brothers.

Rockware glass Trade name of Bailey & Co.

Rod A length of solid glass of a consistent diameter.

Roemer, Römer Traditional drinking glass with a bulbous cuppa on a conical foot, produced in Rhineland and Holland until c.1850.

Rogaška Slatina Town in Slovenia with two glassworks. See Steklarska Sola and Steklarna Rogaška.

Rogov, Evgeny I Artist from St Petersburg, Russia [1918–], worked at Gus-Krushtalny after 1936,

Rohrbach, F See Krystallglas-Hüttenwerke.

Rojko See Mara Glashütte.

Roka Glass Glassworks in Decin, Czech Republic [1993–], (raised enamel and gold).

Rolled edge Edge folded inwards or outwards from the centre.

Romanovsky Glassworks Glassworks, exact location unknown, Russia [–], designers include Irina Nevskaya.

Rona Trade name of L R Crystal.

Roná, Jaroslav Glass artist from Prague, Czech Republic [1957–], worked independently from 1984.

Rondelle A flat disk made by spinning a bubble.

Ronneaux Fils Glassworks location unknown, France [–], active c.1911, (lighting).

Ronning, Grete Glass designer from Norway [1937–], worked for Plus 1959–60.

Roosma, Max Glass decorator from Latvia [1909–71], worked at Nový Bor school 1937/8, as lecturer of glass decoration in Tallinn after 1938 and professor after 1960.

Root Trade name of Root Glass Co, Terre Haute, IN, USA [1901–32], (bottles).

Rope edge Glassware with an edge looking like a rope.

Ros, Antonio da Glass designer from Italy [1936–], worked for Cenedese after 1959.

Rosalinglaswerk See Sophienhütte.

Rosdala Glassworks in the Kingdom of Crystal, Sweden [?–present], (lighting).

Rose bowl 1 Squat, wide-necked vase with a metal grill for holding short-stemmed roses. 2 American term for a spherical bowl with a small centre hole and a scalloped or crimped rim, sometimes standing on three feet, for holding rose petals, produced by many factories in the US in the late 19thC.

Rosey, Le Sig found on art glass from Léveillé c.1906–13.

Roselli, Alberto Glass designer from Italy [1921–], worked for Salviati.

Rosenberg, M Glass artist from Croatia active during 20thC.

Rosenfeld, Ken Glass maker from North Hollywood, CA, USA [–], (paperweights after 1980).

Rosenthal A G Porcelain factory in Selb, Bavaria, Germany [1879–present], operates glass works in Bad Soden and Amberg, Germany. Designers include Michael Boehm, Ernest Fuchs, Hap Grieshaber, Berit Johansson, Marcello Morandini, Timo Sarpaneva, Nanny Still, Victor Vasárely, Björn Wiinblad, Tapio Wirkkala, and many others. Sig: etched with crowned R 1950s, sandblasted "Rosenthal" or "Rosenthal Studio-line" 1960s & 70s, printed in white 1980s, sandblasted mark 1990s, (tableware – studio line from 1950, artist designed glass from c.1960s, limited editions).

Rosice Glassworks in Brna, Czechoslovakia [1921–after c.1972], part of Sklo Union, (pressed glass & lighting).

Rosin, Loredano (Dino) Glass artist working in Murano, Italy [–], active c.1981, (sculptures).

Rosipal, Josef Czech designer [1885–1914], worked for Artel 1910–14.

Rosol, Martin Studio artist from USA [–].

Rosola, Yrjö Glass designer from Finland [1904–89], worked for Karhula c.1932 and Riihimäki c.1937.

Rossi Artistic Glass Glassworks in Cornwall, Ontario, Canada [1981–present], previously Chalet.

Rossi, M Glass artist from Murano, Italy [–], active c.1976.

Rossini Glass maker working in Empoli, Italy c.1950s. Sig: label "Rossini genuine Empoli glass Italy".

Rössler, Theodor Glass decorator from Bohemia [1893–1955].

Rosso Glass Co, Phil Glass dealer located in Port Vue, PA, USA [?–present], has replicas made. Sig: R in an outline, (reissued pressed glass & covered animal dishes)

Rostovtseva, Nina N Glass designer from Moscow, Russia [1903–], central offices after 1939, The Neman 1957–59, chief designer at Dzherzhinsky Glassworks 1959/60; her main works were produced at Gus-Krushtalny, Dyatkovsky Cut Glass and Krasny Ghigant.

Roszypal, Ivo Glass artist from Brno [1942–], worked for Borské Sklo 1963–66, Crystalex Nový Bor 1973–84 and became an independent glass sculptor after 1984.

Rotary Series glass by Orrefors designed by Edvin Öhrström 1940, marks: FA2402/1–4, FA2408.

Roth & Co Glassworks in San Francisco, CA, USA [1879–88], (bottles).

Rottenberg, Ena Glass designer from Austria [1893–1950], worked for Lobmeyr c.1925.

Rouard, Géo Sales outlet in Avenue de l'Opéra, Paris, aka Cristallerie de la Paix [1919–present]. Sold products for Lalique, Navarre, Décorchemont and Thuret and its own produced by artistic director Marcel Goupy (c.1909–54), assisted by Heiligenstein (1919–23).

Roubicek, René Glass designer from Prague, Czech Republic [b.1922], taught at Kamenický Šenov glass school 1945–52, was design director of Borské Sklo 1952–65 then worked independently after 1969.

Roubicková, Miluse Glass artist from Prague, Czech Republic [b.1922], designed tableware for Borske Sklo and Skrdlovice 1950s).

Round Oak Glass Works Glassworks in Brierly Hill, [–]. See Smart Brothers.

Round, John & Sons Glassworks in Sheffield, Great Britain [–], active c.1896, (tableware).

Rousseau, François-Eugène Glass artist from France [1827–91], artist and decorator with a decidedly japanese style, his first art glass items were presented in 1878. They had gem-like colour inclusions, enamels, foil and internal crackle. In 1885 Ernest-Baptiste Léveillé joined the company and became manager in 1888. Rousseau died in 1891, Maison Toy was taken over c.1901 and became Toy et Léveillé (tableware). The company was sold to Heraut et Guignard in 1906.

Roux, SA des Verreries Spéciaux Glassworks in Roux near Charleroi, Belgium [1919–?], (flat glass).

Rowatt & Sons, Thomas Glassworks location unknown [–], active c.1890, (lighting).

Royal, Luis Glass designer from Portugal [–], worked for MGlass, Marinha Grande c.1999.

Royal Brierly Crystal Glassworks in Brierly Hill, Great Britain [1776–1930–present], was Stevens & Williams before 1930. Current designers include David Redman; current engravers include Stewart Davies, Lenny Jones and Michael Pargeter. Sig: acid or sand mark, (crystal tableware & giftware).

Royal Copenhagen Conglomerate of Danish tableware manufacturers [?–present], Royal Copenhagen Crystal is a current label for Holmegaard & Kastrup. Designers include Michael Bang, Anne-Grete Halling-Koch, Johnny Hansen, Darryle Hinz, Torben Jorgensen, Anja Kjaer, Per Lütken, Lone Ostenfeld, Allan Scharff, Sidse Werner and Ole Winther c.1965/66) (tableware, art glass & pressed glass since 1875).

Royal Doulton British tableware group that includes Caithness (paperweights), Webb Corbett (cut glass, tableware, giftware & sports prizes), Royal Doulton Studio (art glass) and Royal Doulton Classics (tableware).

Royal Flemish Transparent glass type with raised gold enamel lines made to look like stained glass, made since 1890 and patented in 1894 by Mt Washington. Sig: red enamel mark RF back to back, linked in a diamond, is sometimes found, otherwise circular paper label only.

Royal Glass Co/National Glass 18 Glassworks in Marietta, OH, USA [1891–97], also found as Royal Glass Works, The Huntington Glass Co in Huntington, WV 1897–1900, National Glass 1899, burnt down in 1903.

Royal Krona Group Conglomerate of glass producers in Sweden [failed 1977], five glassworks including Målerås, Skruf, Gullaskruf and Björkshult.

Royal Leerdam See Leerdam.

Royal Scandinavia Conglomerate in Frederiksberg, Denmark [present], includes Royal Copenhagen/Holmegaard works, Orrefors, Kosta and Venini.

Royal, Richard Studio artist from USA [–].

Royale Germania Crystal Trade name for paperweights made in West Germany c.1970s.

Royales de Champagne, Cristalleries Glassworks in Bayel, France [1666–present], (tableware). See Bayel.

Royo Mark found on enamelled and gilded glass, allegedly a Moser name used in Spain c.1930s, but this can not be confirmed.

Rozátová, Eliska Glass artist from Prague, Czech Republic [b.1940], worked at ŽBS 1966–70, independent artist since 1970.

Rozendaal, Willem Jacob Glass designer from the Netherlands [1899–1971], worked for Kristalunie Maastricht 1928–39, taught in The Hague 1937–62. Sig: R in a five-pointed star on series work, Metz/&co/R on specials for retailer Metz, WJ R engraved on unica, with or without Maastricht, (tableware & art glass; Manuvaria & freehand crackle).

RTL Sarl See Roland Trinquart.

Rube, Cristallerie Glassworks in Paris, France [–], active c.1930, (tableware).

Rubena glass Glass with a colour shading from clear to ruby red, made by several firms in the late 19thC.

Rubena Verde Glass with a colour shading from red to green, introduced in the late 19thC by Hobbs, Brockunier & Company, Wheeling, WV, USA.

Rubino Art Glass Glass studio in Seattle, WA, USA [1988–present], operated by Bryan Rubino, (art glass).

Ruby flash Aka ruby stained glass, made by folding a thin layer of colour over clear glass. Produced especially in Bohemia, France and Belgium, particularly late 19thC.

Ruby red Expensive red glass made using gold. First produced in Venice in the 15thC, but the recipe was lost; rediscovered c.1680 in Potsdam, Germany by Johann Kunckel (1630–1703).

Ruckers See Krystallglas-Hüttenwerke Ruckers F Rohrbach.

Rückl's Glassworks, A Glassworks in Nizbor, Czech Republic [–], was active c.1929 and 1936–present], designers include J Drahonovsky 1931 and Ludvika Smržková 1936, produced "Tango" vases in orange and black enamel, 1930s, currently named Vcelnicka, (tableware).

Ruda Glassworks in Sweden [–], closed in the 1970s.

Rudolfova Hut/Rudolfshütte Glassworks in Rudolfova, Teplice Sanov, Czechoslovakia [1900–c.1930s], one of the Inwald works, designers include Adolf Matura, (cut glass).

Ruffner,Ginny Flamework artist from Seattle, WA, USA [–], active since c.1981.

Rugiadoso Barovier & Toso art glass type by Ercole Barovier, 1940.

Ruhr Kristall Glas Glassworks in Essen, Germany [1923–present], known as Stinnes AG in the1950s, currently part of Bormioli Rocco, (mechanical tableware & barware in semi-crystal and sodalime).

Ruhland GmbH Glashüttenwerke Glassworks in Ruhland near Hoyerswerda OL, Germany [1906–after c.1937].

Ruiz, Alejandro Glass designer from Argentina [1958–], worked for Venini 1980s.

Rupel, De See Boom.

Rupprecht, Louis Glassworks location uncertain [–], active c.1890, (tableware).

Rusi-Kristall Glassworks in Haidershofen, Austria [c.1969–present], (cut glass parts for chandeliers).

Russell, Henry and Nathan Manufacturer, location unknown [–], active c.1885, (lighting).

Russell-Poole, Kari Flamework artist from Centerbrook, CT, USA [1967–], produced work from 1990.

Rusticana Type of art glass made by Loetz.

Rutter, Winnfield Glass maker from Millville, NH, USA [–], active c.1940s, (paperweights).

Ryazanova, Svetlana G Glass designer from St Petersburg, Russia [1928–], worked at Workshops of Applied Art from 1960, main works produced at Dyatkovsky Cut Glass, The

First Of May, Krasny May and Lvov.

Rybák, Jaromir Glass artist from Plzen, Czech Republic [1952–], worked at Academy 1973–79, was independent from 1979 and worked for Moser in 1997.

Rydlo, Jiří Glass designer from Podbořany, Czech Republic [1949–], worked since 1970.

Rynkiewicz, Mariusz Studio artist from Bialystock, Poland [1962–], worked as a glass blower at Bialystock Glassworks 1978–85, has been working in Seattle since 1988 and operates his own studio since 1995.

Rýnovice Glassworks in Jablonec nad Nisou, Czechoslovakia [1881–1949], (pressed glass & crystal).

Rytkönen, Martti Glass designer from Sweden [1960–], worked for Orrefors since 1994.

Ryttylä Glassworks in Finland [?–1941], merged with Riihimaki in 1941.

S

S Trade name of the Southern Glass Co, Los Angeles, CA, USA [1920–29], (bottles).

S & C Trade name of Strebbins & Chamberlain, aka Coventry Glass Works, Coventry, CT, USA [1825–30], (bottles).

S & M Embossed mark of Stykes and MacVey, Castleford, Great Britain [1860–88], (bottles).

SAIAR Ferro Toso Glassworks in Murano, Italy [1901–35], (Societa Anonima Industrie Artistiche Riuniti) merged into Ferro Toso Barovier in 1935, designers include Luigi Toso 1918, Anna Åkerdahl 1921, Guido Balsamo Stella 1930 and Vittorio Donà 1932. Animal figures, glass types vetri chimici, vetri striati 1930 and vetri mugnoni 1934 were produced. Sig: no signatures, (art glass & tableware).

SALIR Glass refinery/works in Murano, Italy [1923–], full name is Studio Ars Labor Industrie Riuniti, used blanks from SAIAR 1923–34, member of the Quality Circle. Designers included Serena Dal Maschio 1951–58, Renzo Zaniol, Ettore Sottsass 1948, Giorgio Zecchin, Romeo Ongaro, Guglielmo Barbini, Riccardo Licata 1952, Gio Ponti, Pietro Fornasetti, Vinicio Vianello 1951–54, Franz Pelzel 1928–68, Guido Balsamo Stella 1926–c.1932 and Vittorio Zecchin c.1933. SALIR produced art glass types Soffiati after 1923, Milleocchi in 1954, Murano in 1954 and Vasi Astrali in 1954. Sig: often no signature, sometimes engraved on side near bottom, gold foil label c.1945–c.1950, (art glass, cut glass, engraved glass, mirrors, sanding, enamelling and gold engraving).

SAVAM See VAMSA.

SAVE SpA, Vetreria Glassworks in Empoli, (FI), Italy [?–present], full name is Societa Anonima Vetrerie Empoli.

SB & Co Glassworks location unclear [–], active c.1900, (lighting).

SGDG Mark found on silverplated mountings, lids, etc, on pre-WWII French items, meaning Sans Garantie Du Gouvernement – without government warranty.

SIP Trade name of Sklarny Industri Plovdiv.

STV & Co See Pantin.

SVA di Francesco & Roberto Scarpa Glassworks in Murano, Italy [–], active c.1967, (giftware & souvenirs).

Sabattini, Lino Designer from Correggio, (RE), Italy [b.1925], worked for Moser 1997.

Sabino, Marius-Ernst Sculptor/glass designer and maker from Paris, France [1878–1961], started producing lighting after 1900, business closed 1939, Sabino fils produced figures for US export c.1960s, moulds sold c.1975, reproductions found, especially in the US. Trade names include Verart and Vernox. Sig: almost always signed, either moulded or engraved "Sabino" or "Sabino France", (opalescent glass based on Arsenic colouring early 1920s, pressed glass, mould blown wares, novelties).

Šabóková, Gizela Glass artist from Nové Zámky, Czech Republic [b.1952], worked independently from 1979.

Sachse, Albert Export house from Jablonec, Czechoslovakia [1876–1931], (beads, jewellery & conterie).

Sachsenglas Ottendorf-Okrilla Glassworks in Ottendorf, Germany [1865–1932], merged August Walther & Söhne AG in 1932. Sig: "AWS" inside a heart before 1945, "SG" in a heart after 1945, "SG" in a crown, "Atlas Edelglas" around "SG" in a crown, (pressed glass & tableware)

Sachs-Glas Glassworks in Lauscha, Thüringen, Germany [?–present].

Saeed Glass Industry, Mahmood Glassworks in Jeddah, Saudi Arabia [1994–present], (pressed glass, tea sets, bottles & jars, often with gold trim).

Safe Glass Co Glassworks in Upland, IN, USA [1892–98], (bottles).

Saga Décor Glass decorating plant in Maxence, France [1992–], (bottles & perfumes).

Sahara Heisey, yellow colour

Sahlin, Gunnel Glass designer from Sweden [–], current designer at Kosta Boda.

Saint-Amans, Boudon de Glassmaker from France [–], active in the 19thC, sulfures patented 1810s–1830s, patent later ceded to Cristallerie du Creusot.

Saint Clair Glass Works Inc Glassworks in Elwood, IN, USA [1938–77], also reported as

St Clair Glass Co 1941–71, run by John St Clair 1930s, Ed St Clair, Joe St Clair 1960s and Bob St Clair 1970s. Sig: BOB/ST.CLAIR in a circle 1940–59, (pressed glass, paperweights).

Saint George Crystal Glassworks in Jeannette, PA, USA [1985–present], trade name Toscany, (pressed glass, crystal tableware & ornaments).

Saint Joseph du Bourget, Cristallerie et Emaillerie Glassworks in France [c.1882–c.1900], (lamps and lighting). See Paris, E & Cie.

Saint Laurent à Manage SA, Verreries des Glassworks in Manage, Belgium [1897–?], a member of the Association des Gobeletiers Belges.

Saint Louis Clock and Silverware Glassworks in USA [–], active c.1919, (cut glass).

Saint Louis Gemenos Glassworks in Marseille, France [–], active c.1830, (tableware).

Saint Mandé See Nocus, Jean & Joseph.

Sainte-Anne Glassworks in Vonêche near Beauraing in the Ardennes, Belgium [1779–1802], aka Verrerie Impériale et Royale, (a precursor to Cristallerie Vonêche, (table cast flat glass, mirrors, engraved & gilded tableware).

Saint-Anne/Baccarat Glassworks in Baccarat, France [1764–c.1820], merged with Baccarat.

Saint-Antoine, Verrerie Glassworks in Wasmuel-lez-Mons, Belgium [1900–10].

Saint-Denis, Verreries de Glassworks in St Denis, France [1919–]. See Legras.

Saint-Denis, Verreries et Cristalleries de Glassworks in St Denis, France [–], active c.1880, (bottles).

Saint-Ghislain, SA des Verreries de Glassworks in Saint Ghislain, near Mons, Belgium [1786–c.1870], (tableware).

Saint-Gobain, Chauny & Cirey Glassworks in France [c.1884–present], the largest producer of bottles and packaging glass in the world. Originally created in 1665 by Colbert to make mirrors for Louis XIV, the invention of casting 1688 quickly turned the company into world leader in mirror fabrication in the 18thC. Société Anonyme since 1830, operations in Germany since 1857, Italy since 1889, Spain since 1904 and a sales office in New York since 1831. 20thC diversification in glass wool, threads, hollow fibres. By 1920 Saint-Gobain had taken over various US businesses in flat glass, glass wool production with Certainteed 1967, merger with Pont-a-Mousson 1970, acquisition of Norton 1990 and Ball Foster Glass 1995. Saint-Gobain owns more than 1000 enterprises in 45 countries, the hollow glass division produces 30 billion bottles, jars and pots per annum. Operated glass works in Aniche (59),

Chantereine (60), Longjumeau (91), St Just sur Loire (42), Jouarre (77), Château Thierry (02), Salaise-sur-Sanne (38). Chantereine is the main works for flat glass production. It has factories in Chalon sur Saône (71), Cognac (16), Lagnieu (01), St Romain le Puy (42), Mers les Bains (80, the world's largest bottles plant), Oiry (51), Vauxrot (02), Sucy en Brie (94) and in Germany, Spain, Italy, Portugal and Brazil. Saint Gobain also operates 27 other sites with 67 glass ovens in Europe, (bottles & flat glass).

Saint-Hilaire, Touvier, de Varreaux et Cie Glassworks in Pantin, France [1864–]. See Pantin and Mont Joye.

Saint-Joseph Glassworks in Gers, France [–], active after c.1865, (tableware).

Saint-Louis, Cristalleries de Glassworks in Saint-Louis-les-Bitche, Münzthal (Moselle), France [1586–present], became known as Verreries Royales de Saint Louis in 1767, then Cie des Verreries et Cristalleries de St. Louis in1809, bought by Pochet et Hermès in 1989. Produced the first lead crystal in continental Europe in 1781. Designs by Goupy and Dufrène, and Jean Sala c.1933. Sig: "VS" before 1914 on art glass, "D'Argenthal" or "St Louis Münzthal" on cameo art glass, (paperweights 1845–48, reissued 1950s, annual editions since 1970s; malachite, agate and marble glass 1855; lead crystal cut glass & tableware, cut-to-clear, millefiori, pressed glass, art glass c.1900s enamel, gold, cameo & metal mounts; art glass 1920s Art Deco style enamel, engraved).

Saint-Louis à Neufville, Verreries Glassworks in Neufville, Manage, Belgium [1905–?], a member of the Association des Gobeletiers Belges.

Saint-Paul, Cristallerie de Glassworks in Condat-sur-Vienne, France [?–present], (colour glass and enamel powders).

Saint-Roch, Godefroid Glassworks in Château de Lodelinsart, Charleroi [1669–1834], (flat glass, tableware since 1824, apothecary glass, cut glass & engraved glass).

Sajószentpéteri Üveggyar RT Glassworks in Sajószentpéter, Hungary [1894-present], (bottles).

Sala, Bienvenue Glassmaker from Cataluña, Spain [–], worked with brother Jean c.1919.

Sala, Jean Glass designer from Cataluña, Spain [1895–1976], worked in France since 1905, worked with his father Dominique until c.1920, produced cut glass designs for St Louis c.1933, worked until 1953.

Salazar, David Glass maker from Santa Cruz, CA, USA [–], worked for the Lundberg studios, Davenport, CA in the 1970s, made paperweights after 1985.

Sallmann Glashütte Glassworks in Muskau

near Rothenburg OL, Germany [1889–after 1937].

Salmenhaara, Kyllikki Glass designer from Finland [1915–81], worked for Kauklahti-Riihimäen 1943–46.

Salmenlinna, Antti Glass designer from Finland [1897–1968].

Salo, Markku Glass designer from Finland [1954–], worked for Nuutajärvi/Iittala 1985–present.

Saltpeter Potassium nitrate, used as flux to lower the melting point of a batch.

Salvadori, Fratelli Glassworks in Murano, Italy [–], active c.1967, (giftware & souvenirs).

Salviati & Co Glassworks in Murano [1859–present], mosaic workshop 1859–66, renaissance revivalist glass since 1866, renamed "The Venice and Murano Glass and Mosaic Compagny, Salviati & Co" in 1872. Salviati left the company in 1877, which was renamed "Compagnia Venezia Murano". He founded another works "Salviati & Co", but withdrew in 1883. The company split in 1896 and its new name was "Artisti Barovier". Member of the Quality Circle. Designers include Dino Martens 1932, Luciano Gaspari c.1950–68, Sergio Asti c.1961–c.1983, Marcello Seganti, Giorgio Taverniti, Federica Marangoni, Beth & Steff Sarasin, Dino Martens c.1925–35, Mario de Luigi c.1936, Romano Chirivi 1960–c.1981, Renzo Camerino since 1960, Claire Falkenstein c.1971–80. Current designs are by Sergio Asti, Marc Coulon, Piero Gaeta, Luciano Gaspari, Anna Gili, Johanna Grawunder, Maria-Christina Hamel, Berit Johansson, Giovanni Levanti, Simon Moore, Heinz Oestergaard, Guido Rosati, Laura de Santillana, J B Sibertin-Blanc & Marcel Wanders, (art glass, tableware & lighting).

Salviati signatures No signatures from 1877–1910, retail labels refer to Barovier before 1919, acid stamped "Salviati" in script 1921–37, no sigs after 1945, silver foil circular label with scalloped edge c.1958–65, circular foil label with a smooth edge in the 1970s and an engraved "Salviati" since c.1970s.

Salviati, Antonio Glass maker from Murano, Italy [?–1909].

Salzburger Kristallglas GmbH Glassworks in Salzburg, Austria [–], active c.1954.

Samaritaine, Grands Magasins de la Sales outlet in Paris for all types of glass [c.1909–present].

Samoshkina, Valeria P Glass designer from St Petersburg, Russia [1936–], trained in Czechoslovakia, worked at Vosstanie after 1967.

Sampson Trade name of Gill Bros.

Samuels Glass Co, AR Glassworks in Philadelphia, PA, USA [1855–72], marks include ARS, (bottles).

San Miguel See Vidrios San Miguel.

Sand (Silica) Basic ingredient for making glass. Sand with iron impurities will turn green (see Waldglas). Before being used, sand is washed, heat cleaned and sifted. Silica alone melts at approx. 1980°C and is then called fused quartz or silica, but it is usually mixed with a flux to melt at a lower temperature. Many recipes exist.

Sand blasting (Flat glass, art glass) 1 Surface matting technique using a stream of sand or grit propelled by compressed air, invented by Benjamin C Tilghman in 1870. 2 To blast away the top layer; matted window panes are covered in glue before sandblasting to obtain a clear/matt decorated surface, technique pioneered by Val St Lambert in c.1907.

Sandcast Made in a sand mould.

Sändig, Horst See Meissener Bleikristall.

Sandnäs Glassworks in Munsala, Finland [1847–90], (flat glass, bottles & tableware in green and clear).

Sandnes, Eystein Glass designer from Norway [1924–], worked as art director at Magnor 1951–55, worked for Norsk Glasverk c.1957–80.

Sandra Crystal Glassworks in Slovakia [?–present], (cut glass).

Sandviks Glasbruk Glassworks in Hovmantorp, Sweden [c.1905–present], a subsidiary of Orrefors. Designers include Gate, Hald, Landberg, Lindstrand, Lundin and Palmqvist. Current designs are by Erika Lagerbielke. Colours include light green, light blue, clear, topaz, emerald green and steel blue, (tableware).

Sandwich See Boston and Sandwich Glass Company.

Sandwich Alabaster Type of white cloudy art glass imitating alabaster, made at Cape Cod Glass Works.

Sanford & Klinne Glassworks in USA [–], active in the 19thC, (lighting).

Santa Lucia Glassworks in Cartagena, Spain [?–1908], merged into Union Vidriera de Espana in 1908.

Santa Marina Glassworks in Sao Paolo, Brazil [?–present], aka Companhia Vidraria Santa Marina.

Santalahti, Pertti Glass designer from Finland [1941–], worked for Nuutajärvi in 1963 and 1969–70 and Humppila 1971–81.

Santi, Cristalleria Glassworks in Murano, Italy [c.1967–c.1980], (tableware).

Santos Barosa Vidros SA Glassworks in Lisbon, Portugal [1889–present], (bottles).

Sao Paulo e Rio, Cia Industrial Glassworks in Rio de Janeiro, Brazil and Sao Paolo, Brazil [1917–present], (machine-made bottles, tableware & barware).

Saphira Glass Trade name for dealer's collection by Stil-Glas, Bocholt, Germany [?–present], (tableware & giftware).

Sarasin, Betha & Teff Glass artists from Switzerland [b.1930 & 1931], worked for Salviati since 1963 and Carlo Moretti in 1960.

Sardinia Crystal Srl Glassworks in Alghero, Sardinia [?–present], trade names include Marcolini since 1995, (Murano-style art glass

& giftware).

Sarner Cristal Glassworks in Uetendorf, near Thun, Switzerland [1957–present]. Sig: modern items are sand blasted with logo and "Sarner Cristal"; older items have a sanded "zs" logo only, (tableware, giftware & vases in clear and coloured crystal).

Sarpaneva, Timo Designer from Finland [1926–], worked for Iittala from 1950, ran his own design studio from 1962 and worked for Rosenthal after 1970 and Venini from 1988.

Sars-Poteries (Nord), Verreries de Glassworks in Sars-Poteries (Nord), France [c.1871–c.1977], now a museum (tableware).

Sasaki Glass Co Glassworks in Japan [–], designers include Norimichi Honda c.1967/8, Yukio Ito c.1969/70, Hiroyuki Kashiwabara c.1972/3, Nobuyasu Sato c.1966–68, Yuji Takahashi c.1967–71 and Denji Takeuchi c.1967/8. Sig: Starfish and SSS reversed, (tableware).

Sassa, Fumio Studio artist from Japan [1924–], worked for Hoya.

Satin finish 1 See acid finish. **2** Trade name used by Holophane.

Satin glass Glass with an acid-matt finish, often with a white lining, sometimes called "frosting", associated with art glass produced in the US in the last quarter of the 19thC. Hobbs, Brockunier was the principal manufacturer, but it was also produced by Webb in Great Britain and elsewhere in Europe during the same period. Beware of reproductions in the US.

Satinato Glass is given a glazed "satinato" effect by a mechanical process in which sand is projected at high speed onto the surface. To obtain a "misted velato" effect, the glass is lightly ground at the wheel.

Sato, Nobuyasu Glass designer from Japan [–], worked for Sasaki Glass Co, c.1966–68.

Satoh, Jyunshiro Glass designer from Japan [–], worked for Kagami Crystal Glassworks c.1954–56.

Saturneo Barovier & Toso art glass type by Ercole Barovier, 1951.

Sauerbier & Mijnlieff, Glasfabriek Fa Glassworks in Nieuwerkerk ann de IJssel [1861–1923], renamed De Struisvogel v/h Sauerbier en Mijnlieff after 1892, (bottles).

Saulterre, Georges Sculptor from France [1943–], produced clear vases for VSL c.1977.

Sautner, Barry Glass maker from Flemington, NJ, USA [–], active after 1984, specializing in diatreta.

Sauwery, Léon Glass designer from Belgium [1910–], worked for Verreries du Centre.

SAVA See Societa Artistico Vetraria di Altare.

Savelieva, Lyubov Glass designer from Moscow, Russia [1940–], worked at Workshop of Applied Art after c.1969, works produced at Gus-Krushtalny, Dyatkovsky Cut Glass & Trud Glassworks.

Savonese A Voglienzone SA, Vetrerie Glassworks in Milan, Italy [–]. Sig: S inside a circle, (bottles).

Savoy vase Art glass vase designed by Alvar Aalto for Iittala, 1937.

Sawing Glass cutting using a motorized diamond blade.

Saxlehner Andreas Bottle plant in Budapest, Hungary [1863–1900]. See Hunyadi.

Sazhin, Timur P Glass artist from Moscow, Russia [1943–], worked at Krasny May 1967–71 with L Fomina.

Scailmont, Verreries de Glassworks in Scailmont, Manage, Belgium [1901–70], designers included Charles Catteau and Henri Heemskerck, (pressed glass vases in frosted geometric decor c.1925–c.1935, bottles, tableware, cut glass, lighting & pressed glass).

Scalloping Undulating (ruffled) shape used on the rims of vases, plates, bowls and other objects.

Scancrystal Glassworks in Tallinn, Estonia [1934–present], (manually produced tableware, giftware & paperweights).

Scanglas AB Glassworks in Täby, Sweden [?–present], specializes in historical replicas of Waldglas, Viking glass, etc.

Scarpa Croce, Luigi Glass designer from Italy [1901–67], worked after 1925, worked for VAMSA 1940–42, AVEM 1950–56, IVR Mazzega and Scarpa-Schiavon.

Scarpa Fulvio & Cie Glassworks in Murano, Italy [–], active c.1967, (giftware & souvenirs).

Scarpa, Carlo Glass designer from Italy [1906–78], worked for Cappellin 1927–28, Venini 1932–46 then 1961 and 1968, and for IVR Mazzega c.1956.

Scarpa, Romualdo Painter from Italy [b.1919], worked for SALIR before 1980.

Scarpa, Tobia Glass designer from Italy [1935–], worked for Venini after 1958.

Scavo The process where corrosive chemical material is added to the surface of hot glass to give a matt finish. The final piece has a rough texture or "excavated" look. Scavo vases are made by Maestri Muranesi and by Lafiore, Mallorca.

Schachtenbachhütte Glassworks in Rabenstein, Germany [1820–].

Schäfer, Manfred Glass engineer/designer from Germany [b.1937], worked at KLG Weisswasser 1968–83.

Schagemann, Bernhard Glass designer from Lindberg Germany [b.1933].

Schappel, Karl Glass refinery located in Nový Bor, Czechoslovakia [1857–1945], had various owners 1868–98, bought by Stier und Wanderle 1898–1910, conducted by Stier und Wanderle after 1910 and closed in 1945. Designers included Prutscher, Hoffmann and Margold c.1913. Used blanks from Borské Sklo, (enamelled work c.1900, Jugendstil, floral, cameo, gilding; cut glass from 1913, 'Borussia' cut-to-clear glass).

Scharff, Allan Silversmith/glass designer from Denmark [b.1945], worked for Holmegaard since 1987.

Schaschl-Schuster, Reni Designer from Istria [1895–1979], a member of the Wiener Werkstätte.

Schaumglas Type of art glass with fine foamy air bubbles made by Loetz in the 1930s. Similar to some WMF Ikora and Pulegoso.

Schechinger, Gerhard Glass designer from

Germany [b.1939], ran his own workshop in Schwäbisch Gmünd 1961.

Scheckthal Glassworks in Kamenz OL, Germany [–], operated by H Hildebrand, (lighting, bottles & tableware).

Schiavon Alfio & Figli Glassworks in Murano, Italy [–], active c.1967, (giftware & souvenirs).

Schie, Glasfabriek de Glassworks in Schiedam, Holland [1897–1923], merged with Vereinigde Glasfabrieken in 1923, (bottles; Owens machine installed 1912).

Schiedt, Wilhelm Glassworks in Leipzig, Germany [–], active c.1878–c.1890, (tableware).

Schiller Bohemian engraver who worked at Stevens & Williams c.1860–76.

Schiller, Peter Studio artist from USA.[–].

Schimkowski, Christine Glass artist from Zwiesel, Germany [–], worked at Rimpler Kristall, Zwiesel after c.1996. Sig: needle "Christine" and year; needle "R" monogram for Rimpler, (art glass goblets).

Schlevogt, Curt Glassworks in Jabloneč nad Nisou, Czechoslovakia [1934–39], designers included Eleon von Rommel c.1935, style is close to Lalique and Halama, (malachite and clear frosted pressed glass figures, vases).

Schlitz Brewing Based in Milwaukee, WI, USA [c.1900–?], (bottles).

Schlyter-Stiernstedt, Margaretha Glass designer from Sweden [b.1927], worked for Björkhults Glass after 1953.

Schmelzglas German term for marbled glass or calcedonio.

Schmid & du Houx Glassworks in Fains, France [–], active c.1879, (tableware).

Schmid, Karl, Die Glasbläserei Glassworks in Lindberg and Zwiesel, Germany [1976–?], (art glass, giftware, tableware & decorative objects in crystal and borosilicate).

Schmidt Glassworks Glassworks in Kusov, Czechoslovakia [c.1850–?], (enamelled decorative wares & Mary Gregory-type glass).

Schmidt, Ludwig Glass designer from Bohemia [1882–], associated with the Wiener Werkstätte after 1912.

Schmitt à Clichy Glassworks in Clichy-la-Garenne, France [–], active c.1890, (lighting).

Schmoranz, Franz Architect and glass designer from Bohemia [1845–92], worked for Lobmeyr after c.1873, produced "Islamic" art glass together with Machytka.

Schmoranz, Gustav Glass artist from Bohemia [1858–c.1936], worked for Lobmeyr c.1886–c.1900.

Schneckendorf, Joseph Emile Glass designer from Germany [1865–1949], worked for Darmstadt c.1907–c.1911.

Schneegattern Glashütte Glassworks in Schneegattern, Kufstein, Austria [1949–present]. See Riedel.

Schneider Glassworks in Epinay-sur-Seine, France [1911–40] and [1949–57] and in Lorris, Loiret, France [1962–81], founded by Ernest Schneider and Charles Schneider, was the largest modern glassworks in France c.1926. Was called Verrerie Schneider before 1949, Cristallerie Schneider after. Charles Jr led the company from rebuilding in 1949 to

closure in 1981, brother Robert-Henri was art director 1952–77. Sig: usual gold or red enamel on pieces 1920–24, if preceded by amphora, produced for Au Vase Etrusque, a Paris sales outlet; also found are customer sigs "De Baker", "Finnigans" and "Ovington"; sandblasted sinature in caps after 1925, "Le Verre Français" on cameo pieces after c.1920, sometimes also "Charder" for Charles Schneider, (art glass "coupe a bijoux" cased enamels, black feet after 1918).

Le Verre Français **Charder**

Schneider, Charles Glass designer from France [1881–1953], his first works were exhibited in 1906, he worked for Daum before 1910, ran Verrerie Schneider in 1911–14 and 1919–40 and Nouvelle Verrerie Schneider 1946–53.

Schneider, Ernest Glass entrepreneur from France [1877–1937], worked for Daum 1903–09, founded Verrerie d'Epinay-Schneider in 1911.

Schoder, Marianne Glass decorator from Germany [b.1918], had her own workshop in Stuttgart after 1938.

Schöffel, Peter Glass studio located in Höchstädt, Germany [1997–present]. Sig: all items needle signed in full, (coloured fused panels & slumped dishes).

Schollain & Brauer, Glashütte Glassworks in Welzow near Spremberg NL, Germany [–], active 1904 until after c.1937.

Schönwälder Kristall Glassworks in Schwäbisch Gmünd, Germany [?–present].

School of Glassmaking Three schools: the first established in Kamenický Šenov in 1856, the second established in Nový Bor after 1870 (a secondary school specializing in glass making education, Střední Průmyslová Škola Sklářská, an older school existed 1763–1870; engraving from 1881, glass cutting from 1909, manufacture for various glassworks from 1912, sales department 1927, technical glass from 1947) and the third established in Železný Brod in 1920.

Schöppenthau & Wolf, Glashütte Glassworks in Senftenberg an der Elster near Calau NL, Germany [1875–after c.1937.

Schott & Genossen, Jenaer Glaswerk Glassworks in Mainz, Germany [1884–present], located in Jena, 1884–1945 and Mainz after 1951, current name is Schott Jena-er Glas GmbH. Trade names include Amiran (antireflective), Antique75 (drawn), Duran (lab glass), Okalux, Oklasolar, Borofloat (Borosilicate flat glass), Foturan (photoetchable), Ceran (ceramic flat glass) and Robax (transparent glass-ceramic). Sig: circle in a square with "Schott & Gen Jena" and "Schott & Gen Mainz" before 1980, flame inside a square under "JENAerGLAS" 1981–94, "SCHOTT" in a circle inside a square 1981–94, (cookware, technical glass & borosilicate household glass).

129

Schott-Zwiesel-Glaswerke AG Glassworks in Zwiesel, Landshut and Mittereich, Germany [1927–present], designers include Rolf Krüger, Heinrich Löffelhardt and Wilhelm Wagenfeld. Produces around 60 million wine glasses per year in an automated process; a second plant in Husinec, Czech Republic, produces mouth-blown tableware and cut glass. Operates Wiesenthalhütte, Schwäbisch Gmünd. Sig: tableware unmarked, handmade tableware sometimes markes "S", Zwiesel art glass marked "SA" for Serica Arte or "Unica" for one-offs, (tableware).

Schötter, Rudolf Glass designer who worked for Josef Inwald in the 1920s & 30s.

Schowanek, Johann Export house for beads and costume jewellery from Jablonec, Czechoslovakia [–], active until the 1940s.

Schrader Studio Glass engraving studio in Scandinavia [–], engravers include Åse Voss Schrader c.1951/2.

Schreiber & Neffen, J Glassworks in Zay-Ugróc, Hungary [c.1890s–c.1910s], (enamelled glass).

Schreibner, Frank Glass engraver [–], worked for Stevens & Williams.

Schuch & Co, J Glassworks location unknown [–], active c.1928, (lighting).

Schulte, E Glassworks location unknown [–], active c.1910, (lighting).

Schulz, Richard Salesman/designer from Berlin, Germany [–], designed tableware for VLG in the 1930s.

Schulze, Paul Glass designer from USA [1934–], worked for Steuben after 1961 and was design director from 1970.

Schwab, A G & Sons Glassworks location unknown [–], active c.1921, (tableware).

Schwarz, David J Studio artist from USA.[1952–].

Schwarzlot painting Black or sepia decorating technique where the ink is fired on; developed in Nürnberg after c.1650.

Schwarzthal Glassworks in Cernodol, Cerný Dul, Czechoslovakia [–].

Schwepnitz, Glaswerk Glassworks in Schwepnitz near Kamenz OL, Germany [c.1936–?], originally known as Glasfabrik Horst Walter GmbH, became VEB Glaswerk Schwepnitz in 1951, Glaswerk Kamenz in 1969, a section of VEB Ankerglas Bernsdorf in 1969, Glaswerk August Leonardi in 1972, VEB Rabima Radeberg in 1976, more recently merged with VEB Sachsenglas Ottendorf-Okrilla into VEB Sachsenglas Schwepnitz in 1979. Sig: "Sglas" in a scalloped circle, (white tableware & bottles).

Scolpiti Type of art glass made by Venini designed by Toni Zuccheri, 1966.

Scott, Ken (George Kenneth) Glass designer from USA [1918–], worked for Venini in 1951.

Scozzese Venini art glass designed by Fulvio Bianconi and Paolo Venini in 1957.

Screen printing Glass decoration process in which ink is forced through a fine-mesh screen (mask) onto the glass surface. The automated process allows high printing speeds.

Screw top In use after c.1900, threads for bottle tops were standardized in 1924.

Scrutton, Gary & Doris Glass makers from Portland, OR, USA [–], worked for Parabelle Glass from 1983, (paperweights).

Sculpting Free-forming solid glass while hot.

Sea Glasbruk AB Glassworks in Kosta, Sweden [1956–present], part of the Orrefors Kosta Boda group, designers include Björn Ramél from 1969, Rune Strand from 1978, Renate Stock from 1989, Lena Engman and Göran Anneborg from 1990, (tableware, art glass, crystal giftware & recycled glass).

Seager, Harry Glass designer from Great Britain [b.1931].

Seam mark A protruding line of excess glass left on a moulded object where the sections of a mould meet.

Sebino Porcellane srl Mosaic-making company in Villongo/BG, Italy [?–present]. (mosaic panels & trays in glass).

Sechrist Manufacturing Co, Albert Lighting manufacturer in Denver, CO, USA [–], (lighting; leaded glass shades c.1920).

Securit Trade name of Saint-Gobain for safety glass, introduced in 1929.

Seeds Small bubbles less than 0.4 mm diameter; points at insufficient fining.

Seemann Kunstglasbläserei Glassworks in Zwiesel, Bavaria, Germany [?–present].

Segmentati Barovier & Toso art glass type by Ercole Barovier, 1942.

Seguso, Angelo Glass designer/blower from Murano [b.1921], worked for Seguso Vetri d'Arte 1933–72 and Archimede Seguso after 1988.

Seguso, Antonio Glass blower/designer from Murano, Italy [1884–1965], worked for Soffiera Cerruti, Fratelli Toso until 1933 and for Barovier Seguso Ferro 1933–64.

Seguso, Archimede Glass artist from Murano, Italy [1909–], a member of the Quality circle, worked for Seguso Vetri d'Arte 1933–45, ran his independent workshop Vetreria Archimede Seguso from 1947. He produced art glass – filigrana, zanfirico, merletto and incalmo after 1947, Vetri a nastro lilla in 1952, spiraline in 1954, composizione lattimo in 1954, a piume in 1955, filigrana stellata in 1968 and spina di pesce in 1972. Sig: usually unmarked, sometimes engraved "Seguso Archimede", with or without year and "Murano", red and silver foil on paper oval relief label "Archimede Seguso/Murano/Made in Italy", (art glass).

Seguso Dalla Venezia & Cie Glassworks in Murano, Italy [c.1952–69], operated by Guido Seguso, (art glass, tableware & decorative items).

Seguso Dynasty Famous family name in Murano glass since c.1400. It includes Antonio [1829–1903], master at Salviati/ Venice & Murano Co; Isidoro [1858–96], master at Salviati/ Venice & Murano Co; Giovanni [1853–1931], son of Antonio, master at Venice & Murano until 1895, Seguso Zanetti after 1895, Cappelin Venini after 1921 and MVM Cappelin until 1931; Antonio [–], son of Giovanni, worked at Vetreria Artistica Barovier c.1919; Archimede [1909–], son of Antonio; Gino and Giampaolo [–], sons of Archimede, working with Seguso Viro since 1993.

Seguso, Ernesto Glass blower from Murano, Italy [1908–86], worked for Barovier Seguso Ferro 1933–66.

Seguso, Livio Glass sculptor from Murano, Italy [1930–], worked from c.1975.

Seguso, Mario Glass worker located in Murano, Italy [–] active c.1967, (cut glass & engraved glass).

Seguso, Mario Glass maker working in Sao Paolo, Brazil [–] active c.1960–present, (art glass).

Seguso Viro srl Glassworks in Murano/Venezia, Italy [1993–present], operated by Giampaolo Seguso with sons Pierpaolo and Gianluca, (art glass, tableware; filigrana, incalmo, pulegoso, sommerso, gold foil, zanfirico, murrhine).

Seguso Vetri d'Arte Glassworks in Murano, Italy [1933–present], founded 1933 as Artistica Vetreria e Soffiera Barovier Seguso e Ferro, changed to its present name in 1937, is a member of the Quality circle. Designers include Vittorio Zecchin 1933–35, Flavio Poli 1934–63 art director 1937–63, Mario Pinzoni, art director 1963–71, Vittorio Rigattieri after 1971 and Angelo Seguso 1933–72. Archimede Seguso left to found his own company in 1945. Sig: rarely engraved, mostly labels with model numbers, numbers run 3500–1937 to 14200–1969; b/w labels before 1948; paper label "Seguso Murano" <blank> Made in Italy 1948–after c.1960; transparent labels 1951–after c.1960; paper label shield c.1962–1970s, (art glass, decorative objects, figures & lighting).

seguso

Seidensticker Glashütte Glassworks in Senftenberg/Elster near Calau NL, Germany [1883–c.1937–].

Seidl, Alfred Glass designer from Austria [–], worked for Stölzle Glasindustrie AG c.1966/7.

Selbing, John Glass designer and photographer from Sweden [b.1908], worked for Orrefors 1927–70.

Selbing Expo numbering 1-17-53=1953, 1-27-54=1954, 1-12-55=1955, 1-56=1956, 1-21-57=1957, 22-25-58=1958, 26-27-59=1959, 28-35-60=1960, 36-67-61=1961, 68-74-62=1962, 75-85-63=1963, 86-110-64=1964, 111-112-65=1965, 1-3-66=1966, 113-135-67=1967.

Seldon line Type of lighting glass made by the Phoenix Glass Co, Monaca, PA, USA.

Selena Series glass by Orrefors, 1940s/1950s, designed by Sven Palmqvist; opalescent "moonstone" colouring. Marks: PU3090/1-13,15,17,21.

Selenium Used with sulphur to produce yellow glass; used with cadmium disulphide it produces red and orange colours.

Selfsealing Trade name of the Kerr Glass Manufacturing Corp.

Selkirk Glass Ltd Glassworks in Selkirk, Scotland [1977–present], operated by main artist Peter Holmes, (paperweights).

Sellner Glashütte Glassworks in Lohberg, Germany [1998–present], designers include Theodor Sellner, (art glass).

Sellner, Theodor Glass artist from Bayerisch Eisenstein, Germany [1947–], founded Sellner Glashutte.

Seneca Glass Co Glassworks in Morgantown, WV, USA [1891–present], (tableware, cut glass; rock crystal 1930s; coloured tableware, ornaments & gift items).

Sent, Guglielmo Glassworks in Murano, Italy [c.1946–c.1967], (cut glass & engraved glass).

Serenella Industria Vetraria Glassworks in Murano, Italy [–], active c.1967, (lighting).

Serghevev, Yuri P Glass artist from Russia [1934–], made free form sculptures made at MCIA studio, Moscow and Lvov factory.

Serica Limited edition piece produced by Leerdam.

Serpentina Art glass vase series designed by Nils Landberg for Orrefors, produced only in 1945, numbered 4–33.

Serrurier-Bovy, Gustave Architect from Belgium [1858–1910], worked for VSL after c.1902, produced bronze mounted vases 1905–10, and worked for Loetz.

Serruys, Yvonne Glass designer from Belgium [1874–?], worked in Paris for Despret and others.

Sestante, Il Glass producer located in Italy [–], designers include Sergio Dello Strologo c.1964/5.

Sestervik, Lars Glass designer from Sweden [–], worked for Lindshammar.

Settat Trade name of Classic Light.

Severin, Bent Glass designer from Denmark [1925–], worked for Kastrup c.1957 and Holmegaard.

Severosklo AS Glassworks in Nový Bor, in Kamenický Šenov and in Svor, Czech Republic [1951–present], (pressed glass, paperweights & tableware; semi-crystal, sodalime).

Sèvres et Clichy Reunies, Cristalleries de Glassworks in Sèvres, France [–], active c.1890 and c.1905.

Sèvres, Cristallerie de Glassworks in Sèvres [–], active after 18thC, taken over by Landier in 1870 and master technician Houdaille, acquired Cristallerie de Clichy in 1885; new name is Cristalleries de Sèvres et de Clichy Réunies, (cut glass, coloured tableware, invented enamel decoration on lead crystal 1837, enamel, crackle glass, aventurine, tortoise shell glass, marbled glass, cased, acid etched cameo).

Sèvres, Cristal de Trade name of CFC, owners of Daum and Vannes, where Sèvres crystal is manufactured.

Shades, Art Glass (US) Lamp shades in art glass first made by Tiffany (favrile shades in green, brown, red, blue, yellow, gold lustre and platinum iridescent Cypriot glass), followed by Fostoria Glass Specialty Co in c.1899 (Iris trade name after 1912), Quezal in 1901–24 (opal, red, green, blue, platinum, gold, yellow, brown), Steuben in 1907–33 (plain gold and blue Aurene; Verre-de-Soie, Alabaster, Calcite, Ivrene), Lustre Art Glass Co. after 1920, Victor Durand at Vineland Flint 1924–31 (cracked). Mountings and bases were supplied by Tiffany, Edward Miller Co, Bradley & Hubbard and Handel.

Shakh, Roman Y Glass designer from Lvov, Ukraine [1932–], worked at Raduga Glassworks Lvov after 1957 where he was chief designer from 1968.

Shard A glass fragment; coloured shards can be rolled or melted into a piece for decoration.

Sheared lip Cut-off bottle top in use before 1840.

Shears Glassmaker's scissors used for cutting and trimming hot glass.

Sherbet A small footed ice cream or dessert dish.

Sherdley Glass Glass producer from Great Britain [–], introduced the swastika as a trade name in 1933, (pressed glass).

Shevchenko, Viktor Y Glass designer from St Petersburg, Russia [1935–], worked at Dyatkovsky Cut Glass from 1966.

Shimada Glass factory Glassworks in Osaka, Japan [–], active c.1890, (tableware).

Shirahata, Akira Studio artist from Japan [–], worked for Hoya c.1980.

Shirley, Frederick S Glass technician at Mount Washington Glass Co [–], patents and trade name include Crown Milano, Burmese, Peach Blow, and Peach Satin c.1880–c.1886.

Shushkanov, Dmitry N Glass artist from Moscow, Russia [1923–], produced decorative glass from 1965, works produced at Lvov and Dyatkovsky Cut Glass.

Shushkanova, Ludmila N Glass artist from St Petersburg, Russia [1926–], worked with D Shushkanov.

Shuvalov, Evgraf S Glass designer from Perm, Russia [1912–], chief designer at Dyatkovsky

Cut Glass from 1950.

Sial Trade name of Reijmyre.

SI-AN Cristallerie SrL Glass refinery in Empoli, Italy [1960–present], trade name SI-AN, (decorated tableware & giftware).

Sick, J F & Co Glassworks in Hamburg, Germany [–], active c.1920, (tableware)

Sickness Chemical deterioration. See Cloudiness, Disintegration and Crizzling.

Side seams If there is no side seam then a bottle was free blown before 1860 or turned in a mould c.1900–20. If a bottle was blown in a mould (BIM), the side seams end below the top of lip, if a 3-piece mould (3PM) was used, no seams appear on the bottom half, but there will be a circular one ¾ of the way up and shoulder seams end just below the lip. If produced by an automatic bottle machine (ABM), the side seams extend over the top of the lip after c.1913.

Sidereo Barovier & Toso art glass type by Ercole Barovier, 1966.

Sidone Barovier & Toso art glass type by Ercole Barovier, 1957.

Siege A stone pedestal on which a crucible rests in the oven

Siesbey, Alev Glass designer from Turkey [1938–], worked for Royal Copenhagen 1963–68 and Rosenthal after 1975.

Signoreto Glass studio located in Murano, Italy [–], designers include Raoul Goldoni c.1970.

Sigvard, Gosta Glass designer from Sweden [b.1939], worked for Lindshammar after 1965.

Siiroinen, Erkkitapio: Glass designer from Finland [1944–], worked for Riihimäki 1964–80.

Silber and Fleming Glassworks in London, Great Britain [–], active c.1885, (tableware).

Silberberg Glashütte Glassworks in Stříbrný vrch, Czechoslovakia [–], active c.1834.

Silesia Glass making region in Poland after c.1370 bordering on northern Bohemia; it was part of Germany until 1945. Glassworks include Josephinenhütte (Julia, JZSS) and Fritz Heckert, (tableware, art glass, lighting & historical glass).

Silesian stem Faceted baluster stem, aka moulded pedestal (1715–65).

Silica Is the main ingredient of glass ($SiO2$).

Silko, Anatoly M Glass designer from Moscow, Russia [1927–], worked for Krasny May after 1952 and as chief designer after 1956.

Silky lustre Having a silk-like sheen. See Lustre.

Silva, Luis Glass designer from Portugal [–], worked for MGlass, Marinha Grande c.1999.

Silver & Co Lighting Manufacturer located in Brooklyn, NY, USA [–], active c.1880s.

Silver City Cut Glass Co Glassworks in Meriden, CT, USA [–]. Sig: 5-point star, filled.

Silver deposit Technique for electroplating on glass first developed in Great Britain by Stevens & Williams in 1889, at VSL after c.1890s, in the USA until c.1915, aka "American Overlay". Used on art glass.

Silverbrook Art Glass Co Glassworks in Flanders, NY, USA [–], active 1960s, (paperweights). See John Kreutz.

Silver overlay Glass decorated with a cut-out

pattern of sterling silver fixed to the surface.

Silvered glass See Mercury glass.

Silveria Type of art glass with all over encased silver foil developed by John Northwood II for Stevens and Williams, 1900.

Simax Trade name for borosilicate 3.3 glass; heat resistant ovenware from Kavalier, Czech Republic.

Simm, Anton Glass engraver from Gablonz/Jablonec nad Nisou, Bohemia [1799–1873], specialized in town panoramas.

Simon, Jacqueline Glass designer from Liège, Belgium [1944–], worked at VSL c.1978 producing Art Nouveau remakes.

Simon, Joseph Glass designer from Belgium [1874–1960], worked for Val St Lambert 1888–1940, designed Luxval pressed glass c.1930.

Simonet Frères Company specialized in lighting located in Paris [–], active 19thC, designer was Henri-Germain-Etienne Dieupart after 1924. Sig: "Dieupart", "Simonet Frères Editeur", (luxury pressed glass lighting since 1919; art glass vases & novelties in pressed or cast glass).

Simonis Glassworks in Bruxelles, Belgium [–], active c.1971, (tableware).

Simpson, Hall, Miller & Co Glassworks location unknown [–], active c.1895, (tableware).

Sinclaire, H P & Co Glass refinery in Corning, NY, USA [1904–28], produced translucent coloured, hand-blown glass often confused with Steuben. Sig: often unmarked, sometimes acid etched "S", acid stamp "SINCLAIR" in block letters on tableware, (cut glass, Brilliant period).

Singleton Bailey Glass Co Glassworks in USA [–]. Sig DBS, (pressed glass).

Sinnemark, Rolf Glass designer from Sweden [1941–], worked for Kosta Boda 1967–86 and at Pukeberg.

Sinumbral See Astral lamps.

Sipek, Boris Glass designer from Czechoslovakia [b.1949], worked in Holland since 1983.

Sipos, Judit Kekesi Glass designer from Hungary [b.1937], worked for Paradi Üveggyár after 1960.

Sirene Type of art glass made by Venini designed by Fulvio Bianconi, 1950.

Sirtaine, Emile Glassworks location unknown [–], active c.1919 and c.1921, (lighting).

Sisecam Glass Packaging Glassworks in Ayazaga, Turkey [1969–present], largest glass producer in Turkey, works includes Pasabahce, (bottles).

Sjögren, Christer Glass designer from Sweden [b.1926], worked for Lindshammar Glasbruk c.1966/7.

Skawonius, Sven Erik Glass designer from Sweden [1908–81], worked for Kosta 1933–35, Karlskrona 1933–39 & 1960–68, Uppsala-Ekeby 1935–39 & 1953–57 and Kosta 1944–50. Sig: most works for Kosta were signed with name, model number, company name, year.

Skibska, Anna Flamework artist from Wroclaw, Poland [1959–], taught at Academy of Art in Wroclaw, Poland since 1985, followers include Paulina Komorowska-Birger and Barbara Idzikowska.

Skinner-Hill Co, Inc Glassworks location unknown [–], active c.1930, (tableware).

Sklarny Bohemia Glassworks in Podebrady, Czech Republic [?–present].

Sklarny Cesky Kristal Glassworks in Chlum u Trebone, Czech Republic [?–present].

Sklo Bohemia Glass conglomerate located in Svetla nad Sazavou, Czech Republic [?–present], (cut glass & tableware).

Sklo Fiser Liberec See Fiser.

Skrdlovice Sklarska Hut Glassworks in Skrdlovice, Czech Republic [c.1942–present], (tableware & art glass). See Beranek.

Skrufs Glassworks in Sweden [1897–present], closed in 1980 and reopened in 1981. Designers include Bengt Edenfalk 1953–78 and Ingegerd Råman 1959. Techniques include Thalatta glass 1959. Sig: usually unmarked, Edenfalk pieces bear designer name + Skruf + pattern number + Thalatta; label "Skruf" inside a crowned oval or "Skrufs Kristall" with a goblet in an oval c.1920s, (tableware).

Slade, Tenney & Weadley Glassworks location unknown [–], active c.1912, (tableware).

Slag glass Opaque glass with marble like trails of colour, base colour most often purple or brown (purple slag, caramel slag). First made in Venice and in Germany as "Schmelzglas", became popular for pressed glass c.1870–1930s. The effect is obtained by adding blast furnace slag to the melt.

Slang, Gerd Glass designer from Norway [1925–], worked for Hadeland 1948–52 and 1963–72, was freelance 1952–63.

Slavetin Glassworks in Pacova, Czechoslovakia [18thC–end 19thC], pressed glass reported 1873.

Slavia Glassworks Glassworks in Nový Bor, Czech Republic [?–present], known as Sklárna Slavia in Czech, (decorated giftware, high enamel on gold, coin spot glass, stained and spatter ware).

Slipgraal Variation on the Graal technique in which the submerged pattern is achieved by cutting (Swedish: slip), produced by Orrefors since 1940. Signature S.Graal + sequential number 1940–50, after 1950 encoded. Sequential numbers (year): S21=1940, S91=1941, S151=1942, S251=1943, S291=1944, S421=1945, S601=1946, S931=1947, S1291–S1689=1949. Encoded S51L=1950, S400L=1951, S848L=1952, S1176L=1953, S1601L=1954, S2309L=1955, S50M=1955, S100N=1956, S510=1957, S2260=1958, S345P=1959, S441P=1960, S559R=1961, S574S=1962, S586T=1963, S620V=1964, S639A=1965, S651C=1968, S665D=1969, S723E=1970, S738F=1971, S814G=1972, S855E3=1973,

S1321E4=1974, S1797E5=1975, S1961E6=1976, S2112E7=1977, S2282E8=1978, 2449E9=1979, 2559-80=1980, 2567F1=1980, 2640F2=1981.

Slottsglas (Castle Glass) Orrefors art glass type designed by Simon Gate executed by Knut Bergqvist 1926/1928. Olive green and brown semi-crystal in 20 different models, marked A thru V. Sig: eg GXT 16/100 Gate=G Semi-crystal=X model 19=T 16/100=number 16 out of 100.

Slovenske Zavody Medical-Glass Glassworks in Bratislava, Slovakia [1962–], (technical).

Slovglass Glassworks in Poltár, Slovakia [?–present], operates Katarinska Huta glassworks in Zlatno, (tableware & cut glass in lead crystal and sodalime).

Slug bottom A sloping or uneven base in a defective glass container.

Slug plate Embossing plate in bottles mould.

Slump Flat glass heated over a mould will slump and assume its shape.

Smalti Soft, colourful Venetian glass mosaic squares.

Smart Brothers Glassworks at Round Oak Glassworks, Brierly Hill [–], active c.1880s, (tableware, cranberry glass, baskets, clear handles and rigarees, lampshades, late 19thC).

Smetana, Agnes Glass artist from Hungary [1961–], has been exhibiting since c.1985.

Smirnov, Boris A Architect from St Petersburg, Russia [1903–], worked at Leningrad Factory 1948–67 and trained many USSR glassmakers.

Smirnova, Lidia D Glass designer from St Petersburg, Russia [1927–], worked at Leningrad Factory after 1953.

Smith Brothers Decorating Co Glassworks located at Mount Washington, PA, USA [1871–75], originally a decorating studio for Mt Washington, opened own business in 1875, (tableware). See Smith Bros.

Smith Bros Glass Co Glassworks in New Bedford, MA, USA [1875–]. Sig: either marked on base with rampant lion in a shield and "Trademark"; beware of reproductions, (bottles & opalescent decorated ware).

Smith Co, John D Glassworks location unknown [–], active c.1910, (lighting).

Smith, David Glass designer/engraver from Great Britain [–], worked at Webb Corbett c.1975.

Smith, Earle Glass maker, location unknown [–], active c.1946, (tableware).

Smith Glass Co, L E Glassworks in Mt Pleasant, PA USA [1907–present], known as as Libbey-Owens Ford 1979–present. Sig: S in shield or SGC moulded, current glass with paper label, (pressed glass, novelties, covered animal dishes, baskets, tabletop, giftware, punch bowls, platters & lighting).

Smith, Gordon Glass maker from Mays Landing, NJ, USA [–], (paperweights after 1981).

Smith, Michael Glass designer [–], designed for Boussu c.1981.

Smith & Co, Wilfrid Glass studio located in New York, NY, USA [–], active c.1900s, (paperweights).

Smoke bell Lighting shade for use with kerosene or gas is freely suspended.

Smržková, Ludvika Glass designer from Czech Republic [1903–91], produced functional pieces, worked for various Czech glass producers 1930–70, for Riedel c.1930s, worked with Matura after 1941, worked for Inwald 1948–52, central institutions 1950–58, for Krásná Jizba, worked independently after 1958, for Škrdlovice 1950s, Umělecké Sklo at Nový Bor 1952, Borske Sklo c.1962/3, Karlovarske Sklo Moser 1950s and Crystalex 1970s.

Smržova Town near Jabloneč nad Nisou, Czech Republic, involved in glass manufacture since c.1800, especially jet black jewellery after 1861.

Smyser-Royer Co Glassworks location unknown [–], active c.1925, (lighting).

Snadeberg, Ove Glass designer from Sweden [–], worked for Kosta c.1966/7.

Snap tool, Snap case A gripper, which clamps around the hot bottle replacing the pontil rod, sometimes leaving lateral grip marks. Introduced c.1850 and widely used 1870–1903, (bottles).

Sneath Glass Co Glassworks location unknown [–], active c.1894, (lighting).

Snellman-Jaderholm, G L Glass designer from Finland [–], worked for Riihimäki c.1950/1.

Snowball Round candle holder looking like a snowball; modern icon designed by Ann Wärff, made by Kosta Boda.

Soak To keep glass in the annealing oven at a specific temperature for proper annealing.

Sobelever – Sté Belge d'Exploitations Verrieres Glassworks group located in Lodelinsart, Charleroi, Belgium [1939–1960], became part of the Glaverbel conglomerate after 1960, (flat glass & various special items). See Verreries Gobbe-Hocquemiller, E.

Sobodec Glass decorating company in Artigues, Bordeaux, France [1960–], (bottles).

Societa Artistico Vetraria di Altare Glassworks in Altare, Italy [c.1913–c.1925], (bottles).

Società Italiana Vetri Speciali Glassworks in Murano, Italy [–], the official name of Cristalleria Murano.

Societa Veneziana Conterie e Cristallerie See Conterie.

Société Industrielle de Verrerie Glassworks in Pantin, France [–]. See Pantin.

Soda glass Light, clear type of glass developed by Venetian glassmakers. Shows yellowish under UV-light.

Soda, Soda ash, Sodium carbonate (Or potash) Commonly used as the alkali ingredient of glass. As a flux it lowers the fusion point of the silica in the melt. Soda ash (Na_2CO_3) or sodium carbonate is the main source of sodium oxide (Na_2O) in the batch.

Sodalime glass Normal industrial standard glass, typically composed of silica (71–75%), soda (12–16%) and lime (10–15%), with small amounts of other materials added. It transmits a high percentage of visible light; a disadvantage is its relatively high thermal expansion. Silica does not expand much when heated but the addition of soda increases the expansion enormously. The higher the soda content, the poorer its resistance to thermal shock. An improved formula was developed in 1864 by William Leighton of Hobbs, Brockunier.

Sodis-Uhart Glassworks in Biarritz, France [?–present], (bottles).

Sodium chloride (Salt, NaCl) Is used in the melting of high-silica borosilicate glass; at high temperatures it becomes volatile and poisonous.

Sodium flare The bright, harmful light given off by the reaction of an oxygen-rich flame and the surface of sodium containing glass in a kiln; protective eyewear requires didymium glass.

Sodium silicate Aka water glass (Na2O.SiO2), has almost equal portions of silica and soda. It dissolves in water and is used in ceramics and in hardening concrete.

Soer, Glasblazerij M Glassworks in Schiedam, Holland [1920–21], (bottles).

Soffiato Type of art glass made by Venini designed by Napoleone Martinuzzi, 1925.

Soffieria Bertolini Glassworks in Candiolo/TO, Italy [1935–present], (tubes & vials).

Soffieria Luigi Dal Moro Glassworks in Murano, Italy [–], active c.1980.

Soft glass Any glass other than borosilicate, which is hard glass.

Soga Glass Co Ltd Glassworks in Komaki-City, Japan [?–present].

Soho and Vesta Glassworks See Walsh Walsh, John Ltd.

Soignies, Verreries de Trade name Durobor, Belgium

Soliflore French term for a vase with a bulbous body and a long, drawn out neck for a single flower.

Solvay process Process for making soda ash from salt, ammonia and carbon dioxide. Discovered in Belgium in 1865 by Ernest Solvay.

Solven, Pauline Glass designer from Great Britain [b.1943], worked for Glasshouse London after 1969, ran her own studio after 1974.

Sölvesborg Glassworks in Sweden [–], active c.1963.

Sommerso Submerged glass; coloured glass cased with a clear outer layer.

Sophienhütte Glassworks in Rauscha near Görlitz OL, Germany [1883–c.1937–].

Sophienhütte Glassworks in Ilmenau, Germany [1852–1991], factory known as Rosalinglaswerk after 1972, produced Ilmkristall art glass after 1983, (fire extinguishers, bottles, perfume flasks & thermic hollowglass).

Soria SA Glassworks in Bordeaux, France [?–present], (tubes & vials)

Sotancro - Embalagem De Vidro SA Glassworks in Portugal [?–present], (bottles).

Šotola, Vratislav Glass artist from Helmanův Mestec, Czech Republic [b.1931], studied at the Prague Academy 1949–54, worked at Borske Sklo 1958–69, worked at central institutions 1962–78, Sklo Union/Obas after

1979 and Moser 1997, (specialized in cut glass, cut-to-clear glass and tableware early on, utilitarian later).

Sottsass, Ettore Glass designer from Austria/Italy [1917–], ran his own design studio, worked for SALIR in 1948, Vistosi c.1969 and Venini 1980s.

Sotuver - Societe Tunisienne De Verrerie Glassworks in Megrine, Tunisia [1963–present], (bottles & pressed glass tableware).

Souchon-Neuvese, Verrerie de Glassworks in France [–], new name for Legras. Designs by Heiligenstein 1926–1931.

Soufflée Mécanique, Verrerie Glassworks in Andeville, France [?–present], aka VSM, (packaging glass).

Sousa, Catherine de Glass designer from the USA [–], designed animal figures for VSL since 1980s.

South Boston Flint Glass Works Glassworks in Boston, MA, USA [–], active c.1816, (bottles).

South East Glass Co Ltd Glassworks in Bangkok, Thailand [?–present], (machine made tableware, cookware & technical glass).

South Jersey Glass Referring to various glassworks in the USA active c.18thC.

Sovánka, István Glass designer from Hungary [1858–1945], worked for Zayngróc and Ujantalvölgy, (art glass, acid etching, cameo in Gallé style).

Sowerby Glassworks in Gateshead, Great Britain [1807–1972], located at New Stourbridge Glassworks 1807–52, moved to Ellison Glassworks 1852–1972, became Sowerby & Co in 1870, became Sowerby's Ellison Glass Works Ltd in 1870. It was the largest pressed glass works in the world in 1882. It operated an art glass workshop 1870–c.1888 where Venetian-style glass was made by Italian workers, but it was best known for pressglass, which was made c.1870–c.1970. It was renowned for the quality of its moulds and pressglass versions of designs by Dresser, Crane, and copies from Wedgwood's Egyptian and Japanese items were made 1876–88. Many products were made in vitroporcelain (imitation China); colours included white, turquoise, ivory, slag in purple, blue and brown, and clear flint. The company declined from the turn of the century with a slight upturn upon the introduction of its "Tyneside" range in the 1920s. Further decline after WWII resulted in final closure in 1972. Sig: the company mark – a peacock's head – was used on most pieces 1876–1930.

Spa glass A tumbler used at fashionable spas, such as Aix-les-Bains, Karlsbad and Baden-Baden, in the 19thC. A spa glass often has a measure and a flat oval cross section so it will fit in the pocket of a gown. Originally issued as

part of the spa treatment, later as a souvenir.

Spahr, Carl Glass designer from Germany [1899–1979], worked for WMF on Ikora and tableware after 1927.

Spangled glass Type of art glass that has an interior layer of shimmering mica flakes. Made in Europe and the US in the last quarter of the 19thC; reproductions made by Fenton in the 1960s. One manufacturer was Dr Flower of Sandwich, MA at Cape Cod after c.1880s whose products were sold through distributor Vasa Murrhina.

Spatter glass Glass with flecks of contrasting colour rolled in, first made in the 1840s in Murano as "Granite glass" and since made by many companies, especially in Bohemia. Beware of reproductions in the US.

Spaun, Max Glass maker from Bohemia [1837–1909]. See Loetz.

Specialty Glass Co, The Glassworks in East Liverpool, OH, USA [1889–1985], known as the East Liverpool Glass Co 1882–1889, the Specialty Glass Co in Grapeville, PA 1892–1923 and Westmoreland Glass Co in Grapeville, PA 1923–85. It closed in 1985.

Spencer, Jeff Flamework artist from Grant's Pass, OR, USA [–], worked since 1968.

Spessart-Hütte Glassworks in Ilmenau, Germany [1904–50], taken over by Spessarter Hohlglaswerke c.1936, (coffee and tea pots from "Vitrex" borosilicate; various glass).

Spicchi, A Venini art glass designed by Fulvio Bianconi, 1951.

Spiegelau GmbH, Kristallglasfabrik Glassworks in Spiegelau, Bavaria, Germany [1521–present], taken over by Rosenthal in 1997. Sig: sandblasted crowned S mark, (crystal tableware).

Spiegelhütte Glassworks in Buchenau, Germany [–], active c.1926.

Spina A Barovier & Toso art glass designed by Ercole Barovier, 1958.

Spindler, Charles Artist from Strassbourg, France [1865–1938], worked for Valérysthal after c.1898.

Spinning, Hollow Ware Manufacturing method for the production of technical items, such as glass columns, funnels and television tubes. Molten glass is fed into a rotating steel mould.

Spira Aurata Barovier & Toso art glass type by Ercole Barovier, 1966.

Spirali Type of art glass made by Venini designed by Thomas Stearns, 1961.

Spittoon See Cuspidor.

Splintex Mirror works in Gilly near Charleroi, Belgium [1929–], (mirrors, safety glass & car windows).

Spook, Per Glass designer from Norway [1939–], worked for Magnor since 1995.

Spun glass Lampwork technique involving fine glass threads for making baskets, birds, ship models etc. From early 19thC, especially used in the British Midlands and Liège.

Sputtering Metal coating process for glass.

Squibb Trade name of E R Squibb MD, Brooklyn, NY, USA [1858–95], (bottles).

Šrámková, Ivana Glass artist from Liberec, Czech Republic [b.1960], painter, engraver and sculptor, worked at ŽBS 1980–81, then independent from 1987.

ST-Glass Glassworks in Salgótarján, Hungary [1893–present], (tableware, barware, pressed glass, bottles, lighting, chandeliers & hand painted items).

Stadelmann, Guido Flamework artist from Switzerland [1952–],his own studio opened in Zürich in 1976.

Stained glass Method of making windows, lamp-shades, boxes etc, using pieces of flat glass (flashed or enamelled) mounted in lead strip.

Standard Trade name of the Standard Cooperative Glass Co/ Standard Glass Co, Marion, IN, USA [1894–1932], (bottles).

Standard Glass Manufacturing Co Glassworks in Lancaster, OH, USA [1908–24], later merged with Hocking Glass Co.

Stangenglas Tall German drinking glass from the Middle Ages. See Replicas.

Stanger, Emil Glass maker from Millville, NJ, USA [–], active 1900s, (paperweights).

Stankard, Paul Flameworking artist from Mantua, NJ, USA [1943–]. Sig: S or PS, (paperweights after 1969; naturalistic floral paperweights after 1972).

Star cutting On the underside of feet, if star cutting crosses at the centre and rays do not extend to the edge, a piece was probably made after c.1830. Fine radial grooves extending to the edge of the foot with a clear ground out pontil mark indicate earlier production.

Star Glass Co Trade name of the Star Glass Co, New Albany, IN, USA [1867–1900], (bottles).

Starck, Philippe Designer from France [1949–], worked for Daum c.1988/90.

Stardust cane A cane with opaque white stars, (paperweights).

Staszic Glassworks in Poland [–], active c.1980, artistic director was Ludwik Fiedorowich.

Staszów, Huta Szkla Gospodarczego Glassworks in Staszów, Poland [?–present].

Sté de Charleroi pour la Fabrication de Verre et de Gobeleterie Manufacturing group in Charleroi, Belgium [1836–], it groups 7 factories making flat glass and bottles in Charleroi and Jumet.

Sté des Manufactures Manufacturing group in Seraing near Liège/Val St Lambert [1836–]. See Manufacture de Glaces.

Stearns, Thomas Glass designer from Philadelphia, PA, USA [b.1936], worked for Venini 1960–62.

Stebih, Mihael Glass artist from Čakov, Croatia [1948–], produced sculpture from 1983.

Steigerwald, F Glass dealer from Munich, Germany [–], active c.1855, (cut glass, coloured glass & engraved glass).

Steigerwald, Kristallglasfabrik vorm Glassworks in Regenhütte, Germany [1831–?], active c.1920 and c.1935, location also reported as Lindberg, Zwiesel.

Steimer Glass Co Glassworks in Buckhannon, WV, USA [c.1870–1906], (pressed glass, known as Valley glass).

Steinbatchek, Larry Glass artist [–], worked at

Anverre from 1988.

Stein Beer tankard made in Germany, normally from stoneware with a pewter lid, but also found in glass.

Steinwald & Co, Ernst Glassworks, location unknown [–], active c.1920, (lighting).

Steklarna Rogaška Slatina – Boris Kidric Glassworks in Rogaška Slatina, Slovenia [1927–present], trade name Rogaška Crystal. Sig: acid mark "Rogaška", (tableware, cut glass & semi and full lead crystal).

Steklarska Šola Rogaška Slatina Glassworks in Rogaška Slatina, Slovenia [1947–present], (tableware, cut glass, engraved, enamelled, art glass & semi and full lead crystal).

Steklopribor Glassworks location unknown, Russia [–], designers include Evghenia Mery from 1968.

Stekloremont Glassworks in Kalinin, Russia [–], designers include Marshumov from 1966 and Marshumova from 1967.

Stella Glassworks in Meersen, the Netherlands [1902–25], merged with Kristalunie in 1925.

Stella Polaris Series glass produced by Orrefors, designed by Vicke Lindstrand in 1939 (clear blue). Mark: LU2251/10-10.

Stelle, A Barovier & Toso art glass designed by Ercole Barovier, 1942.

Stelvia Coop r l Glassworks in Empoli (FI), Italy [?–present], (tableware).

Stem bead A tiny piece of glass between a stem and bowl, aka merese, (tableware).

Stem types Baluster 1685–1735, inverted baluster 1685–1735, plain 1730–1775, air twist 1745–1770, opaque twist 1755–1780, faceted 1760–1810, silesian 1715–1765, balustroid 1725–1760, composite 1745–1770, incised twist 1745–1770, mixed and colour twist 1755–1775.

Stenberg, William Glass designer from Sweden [–], worked for Gullaskruf 1927–61.

Stenberg-Andersson, Marianne Glass designer from Sweden [–], worked for Gullaskruf after 1927.

Stenhytta Glassworks in Kosta, Sweden [–]. See Transjö Hytta.

Stennett-Willson, Ronald S Glass designer from Great Britain [–], worked for D Wuidart & Co Ltd c.1955–57, founded King's Lynn Glass c.1967/8 and Wedgwood Glass c.1970s.

Stepanova, Antonina Y Glass designer from Russia [1927–], worked at central design institutions from 1952, was chief artist after 1962 and director of Workshops of Applied Art after 1965. Her main works were produced at Dyatkovsky Cut Glass and Lvov.

Steuben Glass Works Glassworks in Corning, NY, USA [1903/1933–present]. Designers include Sidney Waugh after 1933 and Walter Dorwin Teague c.1930s. Sig: some pieces marked with a facsimile signature F Carder or FC 1903–32; iridescent glass is usually marked "Aurene" or "STEUBEN Aurene", sometimes with pattern #; some pieces are acid stamped with fleur-de-lis with "STEUBEN" banner 1903–32; diamond engraved "Steuben" after 1932. Heritage re-issues have a special mark after 1978, (tableware, art

glass, limited editions, unica, crystal and paperweights 1940s–1970s). See Carder.

Stevens & Co, Joseph Glassworks in Dudley, Great Britain [c.1783–1854], aka Holly Hall Glassworks, Parkes, Grainger & Green 1800–17, Major Parkes & Co 1817–21, Edward Page 1821–28 and Joseph Stevens 1828–54, (tableware, cut glass & bottles).

Stevens & Williams Glassworks in Brierly Hill, Great Britain [1776–1847] at Stourbridge, Great Britain [1870–1930], became Brierly Crystal in the 1930s. Designers included John Northwood from 1882, John Northwood II from 1902, Frédérick Carder until 1903 and Keith Murray after 1932. Sig: "Brierly/Royal/Crystal" with a fleur-de-lis etched mark 1924–27, circular stamp S*W after 1927, Keith Murray signature over S*W from 1934–39, sandblasted marks after 1945, "Royal/Brierly/England" 1945–50, "Royal/Brierly/Crystal" 1950s, "Brierly", "RBC" or "Royal Brierly" from the 1960s, (art glass, satination over mother-of-pearl, amberina, iridescence, cut glass, engraving, enamelling, rigarees etc; cameo glass neoclassical style; Silveria; Tapestry ware, Jewell ware, Threaded ware, Intaglio ware, Mat-su-no-ke; Moss agate c.1880s).

Stevens, Irene Glass designer from Great Britain [–], worked for Webb & Corbett Ltd 1946–60 and Stourbridge 1961–77.

Sticerom Glassworks in Bucharest, Romania [1990–], (hand made glassware and ceramics, giftware, ornamental items, vases & lighting).

Stiegel Glass Glassware produced in Pennsylvania, USA after 1760 by Baron Henry Stiegel.

Stilart Glassworks in Buzău, Romania [1992–present], (cameo glass replicas marked "Tip Gallé", "Tip Daum", "Müler" or other fantasy names).

Still, Nanny Glass and porcelain designer from Finland [1926–], worked for Riihimäki

1949–76, Val St Lambert c.1966/68, Hackmann, WMF & Rosenthal.

Stippling: 1 Decorating technique developed in Holland in the 17thC and 18thC. Tiny dots tapped onto the glass with a diamond point resulting in a detailed picture, often portraits. Most surviving stippled glasses are in museum collections. 2 In lacy-patterned pressed glass, stippling is part of the decoration of the mould to cover up striae.

Stirom Glassworks in Bucharest, Romania [1966–present], (bottles, vials & technical).

Stitching Making glass shapes out of fine loops drawn from the tip of a rod. Used for small ornaments, baskets, ship's models, etc. Also known as Liégeoise, crocheting, weaving or lacework.

Stiver-Soc Coop rl Glassworks in Colle Val d'Elsa, Italy [1952–present], located in Poggibonsi 1952–81. Sig: no sigs or marks, (pressed glass, tableware, moulded replicas of lacy glassware & goblets; all colours, also frosted).

Stoccolma Venini art glass designed by Fulvio Bianconi and Massimo Vignelli, 1953.

Stock, Renate Glass designer from Sweden [–], worked for Sea Glasbruk.

Stockholms Glasbruk Glassworks in Skansen, Sweden [1936–present], full name is Stockholms Glasbruk Karin Hammar Skansen. Designers include Ture Berglund 1936–80, Goran Hammar, (pressed glass, art glass, flasks, giftware, novelties & animals).

Stoltenberg-Lerche, Hans-Stephan Glass designer from Germany [1867–1920], worked for Fratelli Toso 1912–14.

Stölze Flaconnage Glassworks in Knottingley, Great Britain [1994–], (bottles).

Stölzle Kristall GmbH, Neue Glassworks in Alt-Nagelberg, Austria [?–present], (tableware).

Stölzle-Oberglas AG Glass conglomerate in Vienna, Köflach and in Bärnbach, Austria [?–present], includes Stölzle Glasindustrie AG, Stölzle Kristall and Stölze-Oberglas Lausitz. Designers include Alfred Seidl c.1966/7, (pressed glass, tableware & giftware).

Stölze-Oberglas Lausitz GmbH Glassworks in Weisswasser, Germany [?–present], part of the Stölze-Oberglas glass conglomerate from Austria, (machine produced tableware).

Stones Small particles of grit in the glass from disintegrating refractory material or unmelted batch causing a defect.

Stoppers Internal screw thread after 1861; Matthews gravitating stopper after 1864; glass marble stopper 1873–1930s; Codd stopper after 1873; Hutchinson blob top 1879–1912; Lightning stopper after 1875; Crown Top after 1900, patented 1875; screw top in use after 1900, standardized in 1924; applied lip before c.1880–1900; tooled lip after c.1890, (bottles).

Storck, Joseph Glass designer from Vienna, Austria [1830–1902], worked for Lobmeyr c.1870s.

Stourbridge D G Ware Ltd Glassworks in Amblecote, Stourbridge, Great Britain [–], active c.1950.

Stourbridge Flint Glass Works Located in

Pittsburgh, PA, USA [1823–8], (bottles).

Stourbridge Glass Co Ltd Glassworks in Audnam, Stourbridge, Great Britain [c.1928–c.1950], produced Tudor range after 1929.

Stráhlíková, Maria Glass designer from Czechoslovakia [–], worked for Borske Skló c.1960/1.

Strain Mechanical stress in glass remedied by annealing.

Stralau Glaswerk Bottle plant in Stralau, Berlin, Germany [1945–92]. Sig: Fish.

Stralauer Glashütte GmbH [1992–present], (bottles). See Nienburger Glashütte.

Strand, Rune Glass engraver from Sweden [–], worked for Strömbergshyttan c.1975 and Sea Glasbruk.

Strangfeld & Hannemann Hoyerswerda, Glasfabriken Glassworks in Scheckthal/Hoyerswerda near Kamenz OL, Germany [1877–1931], founded as Legel & Co in Schlegel, moved to Scheckthal in 1888, new factory in Hoyerswerda in 1890, Strangfeld & Hannemann, Ver Hoyerswerdaer Glaswerke, renamed Vereinigte Glasfabriken Strangfeld & Hannemann in 1891, became AG in 1922, but failed in 1931. Sig: "Hoyerswerda HVG Glasgut" in a roofed circular monogram, (lighting & pressed glass).

Strass 1 Artificial gemstone made from vitreous paste, first developed by Josef Strassner. 2 Glass with high lead content used for fake jewellery, invented by 18thC Paris jeweller G F Strass. See Paste, Rhinestone.

Strathearn Glass Co Glassworks in Crieff, Scotland [1965–80], previously Vasart, taken over by Stuart Crystal and renamed Stuart Strathearn in 1980. Sig: raised prunt over pontil mark with leaping salmon impressed, (art glass in the Monart style & paperweights).

Strauss & Sons, L Glassworks in USA [1888–1915]. Sig: 5-point star in circle, (cut glass, Brilliant period).

Strauss Frères & Cie Glassworks in France [–], active c.1912, (lighting).

Strauss-Likarz, Maria Designer from Austria [1893–1971], worked for Wiener Werkstätte 1912–14 and 1920–31.

Straw drop A tubular drop, (lighting).

Straw opal Glass type developed by Whitefriar's c.1878, pale yellow, opalescent.

Strawberry cut See Diamond cut.

Strawbridge & Clothier Glassworks in USA [–], (cut glass, Brilliant period).

Strebelle, Rodolphe Painter/graphic designer from Belgium [1880–1959], designed at least 87 Unica for Leerdam c.1926/7, year letter A.

Streit Nachfolger, Gebrüder von Glass decorating works in Berlin, Germany [1872–1935], (pressed glass, novelties & painting on pressed glass).

Streit, Glashütte von Glassworks in Hosena-Hohenbocka near Hoyerswerda OL, Germany [1906–], Glaswerke Gebrüder von Streit GmbH, Hohenbocka-Hosena in 1936, VEB Glaswerk Hosena after 1945, (pressed glass & covered animal dishes).

Stretch glass American term for glass with a cracked iridescence made 1900–30 by Northwood, Imperial, Fenton and the US Glass Co and others. Similar wares were made by Leerdam and Maastricht. See Tin Craquelé.

Striae, striations Clear swirls inside thick glass in, for example, paperweights.

Striato Barovier & Toso art glass type by Ercole Barovier, 1954.

Strike Glass "strikes" if it changes colour when re-heated, for example, Amberina, opalescent glass. Borosilicate colours are based on germanium strike from clear to deep red.

Strlulli Vetri d'Arte Glassworks in Murano, Italy [1991–present], (Venetian style tableware & lighting).

Strnad, Oskar Architect/glass designer from Austria [1879–1935], worked for Lobmeyr c.1925, member of Wiener Werkstatte.

Strologo, Sergio dello Glass designer from Italy [–], worked for Il Sestante, Italy c.1964/5.

Strömberg, Asta Glass designer from Sweden [–], worked for Strömbergshyttan 1946–76, incidentally for Orrefors.

Strömberg, Edvard Glass technician from Sweden [1872–1946], worked for Kosta 1891/7, bought Sandvik 1905–17, Kosta 1917–18, Orrefors 1918–28, Eda 1927–33 and Strömbergshyttan 1933–46.

Strömberg, Gerda Glass designer from Sweden [1879–1960], worked for Eda 1927–33 and Strömbergshyttan 1933–55.

Strömbergshyttan Glassworks in Hovmantorp, Småland, Sweden [1933–81–present], bought by Orrefors in 1979. Designers include Asta Strömberg and Gunnar Nylund; current designers include Anna Örnberg, Mikael Axenbrandt, Leif Persson and Håkan Gunnarson, (modern scandinavian style art glass, tableware, lighting & giftware in thickwalled blue crystal).

Strömbergshyttan numbers Signatures are mostly needle etched in full or S-hyttan; letters encode type of vessel: A=plate B=vase, C=bonbon, E=decanter, F=jamjar, H=ashtray, K=drinking glass, N=jug, O=liqueur set, S=service, T=dish; highest number B111(1936), B318(1941), B388(1944), B401(1947), B642(1954), B974(1962), E54(1936), E125(1941), E152(1947), E171(1954), E200(1962), T73(1936), T164(1941), T180(1944), T197(1947), T264(1954), T377(1962).

Struisvogel See Sauerbier & Mijnlieff.

Stryisky Glassworks Glassworks location unknown, Ukraine [–], designers include Irina Nevskaya and Evghenia Mery after 1971.

Stuart & Sons Ltd Glassworks in Stourbridge, Great Britain [1881–present], Red House Glassworks taken over from Pargeter in 1881. Chief designer Ludwig Kny after c.1930s, designers c.1936 include Gordon & Moira Forsyth, Eric Ravilious, Graham Sutherland,

Dod & Ernst Procter, Laura Knight and Paul Nash. Sig: unmarked before 1927, etched "Stuart" or "Stuart England" after 1927, some pieces marked L. Kny 1930s, "Designed by" + artist name after 1934, etched "Stuart" or "REGISTERED/Stuart/TRADEMARK" after 1945, (cut glass, tableware, medallion cameo & perfume bottles c.1880s; lead crystal, cut glass & air twist stems c.1955/6).

Stubelius, Thorsten Glass designer from Sweden [–], worked for Färe Glassworks in 1914.

Student lamps Light fixture with directional reflector; first produced in Germany in the 1860s.

Studio Bormioli Rocco See Bormioli.

Studio Glashyttan I Åhus AD Glassworks in Åhus, Sweden [1977–present], designers include Hanne Dreutler-Zirnsack, Arthur Zirnsack, Martin Zirnsack and Lennart Nissmark. Sig: all pieces are needle signed in full, additional monogram on Graal, (art glass, decorative glass & crystal).

Studio Skla Galerie Hlučín Glass studio in Hlucin near Opava, Czech Republic [?–present], (stained glass & leaded lamps).

Stump, Loren Flamework artist from Elk Grove, CA, USA [–], (stained glass after c.1980, lampwork, beads & paperweights after 1993).

Stumpf, Touvier, Viollet & Co See Pantin.

Štursa, Jaroslav Glass designer from Olomouc, Czech Republic [b.1943], worked with Libenský 1962–68.

STV Glass Glassworks in Valasské Mezirící, Czech Republic [1995–present], owned by Schott, (TV tubes).

Stykes & Macvay Co, Albian Glassworks Glassworks in Yorkshire, Great Britain [–], active c.1863.

Style periods Tudor 1485–1533 (1603), Elizabethan 1533–1603, Jacobean 1603–88, Jacobite c.1688–c.1750, Georgian 1714–1830, Regency 1810–20, Victorian 1837–1901, Edwardian 1901–10, Louis XIV 1643–1715, Louis XV (Rococo) 1715–74, Louis XVI 1774–92, Napoleon 1799–1815, Empire 1804–15, Restoration/Charles X 1815–30, Louis-Philippe 1830–48, Napoleon 3 1848–71, Franco-Prussian War 1870, Biedermeyer 1815–50, Arts & Crafts c.1860–c.1900, Secession 1897–1903, Wiener Werkstätte 1903–39, US Civil War 1861–65, Art Nouveau c.1890–1915, Art Deco 1925–36.

Succesori Andrea Rioda

Succesori Andrea Rioda See Rioda.

Suck-blow process Bottle-making process.

Sucker Glashütte Glassworks in Bischofswerda, near Bautzen OL, Germany [1895–c.1937–].

Šuhájek, Jiri Glass designer/artist from Pardubice, Czech Republic [b.1943], studied with Libenský, worked at Moser 1962–64, 1972–78 and present, worked at central institutions after 1979, and for Crystalex and BAG Vsetín.

Sulfure Portrait or cameo paperweights first made Bohemia c.1750, perfected and patented by Apsley Pellatt, Great Britain in 1819. Most popular in France c.1800–c.1850. Makers include Apsley Pellatt, Boudon de Saint-Amans, Le Creusot, Harrach, New England Glass Co and Bakewell.

Sulphate glass Soda glass in which the soda has been replaced by natrium sulphate; it has a greenish tint.

Sumava Glassworks in Sumava, Czechoslovakia [1820?], (enamelled glass c.1880s).

Summit Art Glass Co Glassworks in Ravenna, OH, USA [1972–present], previously in Akron, OH and Rootstown, OH. Sig: S or V in a circle, (pressed glass, novelties & covered animal dishes).

Sun coloured glass See desert glass.

Sun Glo Studios Glassworks in USA [–], part of Phoenix Glass Co.

Sundberg, Per B Glass designer from Sweden [1964–], worked for Orrefors since 1994.

Sunset Lighting Fixture Co Glassworks in USA [–], part of Mutual Lamp.

Superbolle Barovier & Toso art glass by Ercole Barovier, 1942.

Surabhi Ceramics Ceramics decorator plant in Bombay, India [1994–present], (bottles printing).

Surface mix burner A burner in which gases are mixed at the tip when ignited. It is said to be safer, quieter and more efficient than pre-mix burners.

Surjan, Valerie Studio artist from USA [–], worked for Nourot.

Sušica Glassworks in Sušica, Croatia [1766–?], founded by Czech Franjo Holub, (bottles & tableware).

Süssmuth Glashütte, Richard Glassworks in Immenhausen, Germany [1945–present], current name Süssmuth Glashütte GmbH. Designers include Richard Süssmuth and Egon Eiermann. Sig: engraved RS monogram 1920s-30s, angular S inside triangle mark after 1945, angular S over Süssmuth in a triangular label after 1945, (tableware & art glass).

Süssmuth, Richard Glass engraver from Silesia [1900–74], worked at Adlerhütte after 1915,

designed for Ankerglas in the 1930s, ran his own works in Penzig, Silesia before 1945, moved to Immenhausen 1945–70.

Sutherland, Graham Glass designer from Great Britain [1903–80], worked for Stuart c.1934.

Sutnar, Ladislav Functionalist glass designer from Plžen, Czech Republic [1897–1976], worked for Krásná Jizba and taught at Prague before 1939 and in the USA after 1939.

Sütterlin, Ludwig: Glass designer from Berlin, Germany [1865–1917], worked for Heckert Petersdorf.

Sv Sidonie Glassworks in Vlárského prusmyku, Slovakia [1788–1932], (pressed glass reported 1895).

Svanland, Kylle (Elisabeth) Glass designer from Denmark [1921–], worked independently from 1955 and for Holmegaard 1961–70 and 1970–77.

Svanström, Per Hilmer Glass designer from Sweden [–], worked for Kosta 1923.

Svarc, Josef Glass designer from Czechoslovakia [–], worked for Bohemia Poděbrady c.1975.

Svarrer, Peter Glass artist from Denmark [b.1957], worked for Holmegaard after 1997.

SVE – Società Vetreria Empolese srl Glassworks in Empoli, Italy [1953–present], (recycled household glass, bottles).

SVE – Sté des Verreries pour l'Eclairage Glassworks in France [–], active c.1915.

Svenska Kristallglasbruken Glassworks conglomerate in Stockholm, Sweden [c.1904–c.1930], (tableware). See Kosta, Eda.

Sverdlov Glassworks Glassworks in Sverdlov, Ukraine or Russia [–], designers include Yuri Latalin after 1965 and Irina Nevskaya.

Švertašek, Bojana Glass artist from Zagreb, Croatia [1952–].

Svoboda, Jaroslav Glass sculptor/artist from Poděbrady, Czechoslovakia [b.1938], worked in cutting workshop in Prague 1959–68 and as director at Škrdlovice 1969–87, as a designer from 1987.

Svoboda, Mislava Glass artist from Czechoslovakia [–], lives in Belgium, worked at Škrdlovice and Anverre in the 1980s.

Svor, Hut Tereza Glassworks in Nový Bor, Czech Republic [1872–c.1972–], (pressed glass reported 1928 & optical glass).

SVUS AS Glassworks in Hradec Králové, Czech Republic [1923–present], (technical & scientific).

Swahn, Bo Glass engraver from Sweden [–], worked for Måleras, for Kosta and independently since c.1985. Mark: BS.

Swan & Whitehead Manufacturer in USA [–], (lighting).

Swarovski & Co, D Glassworks in Wattens, near Salzburg, Austria [c.1960s–c.present], started as Palme & Walter. (cut crystal ornaments, jewellery, giftware & collectables).

Swayzee Trade name of Swayzee Glass Co, Swayzee, IN, USA [1894–1906], (bottles).

Sweetmeat A small glass or comport, usually with a handle, for serving sweets, custard, jelly, syllabub etc. Used in the 18th and 19thC. Can be distinguished from champagne coupes because they are not suitable for drinking.

Stykes & MacVey Glassworks in Castleford, Great Britain [1860–88]. Sig: S&M, (bottles).

Szabó, Erzsébet Glass designer from Budapest, Hungary [1935–], studied with Julia Báthory 1954–7, with Libenský 1963–4 and worked for Ajka in 1961–2 and Peill & Pützler after 1965.

T

Tableware set A classical set of tableware consists of 50 pieces: 12 water, 12 red wine, 12 white wine, 12 champagne flutes, 1 decanter and one jug, sometimes completed by glasses for port, whisky, other alcohols and fruit juice.

Taddei & Co, Soc Vetrerie T Glassworks in Empoli, Italy [–], active c.1934.

Tadeusz Wrześniak, Huta Szkła Gospodarczego Glassworks in Ladna near Tarnów, Poland [?–present], (hand-made table glass and vases in clear sodalime and blue glass; silver nitrate reduction glass).

Tafelglashütte See Neubert.

Tag, Konrad Sculptor/cutter/engraver from Geischen, Germany [1903–54], worked in Breslau before 1929, Kaiserswalde before 1932, Glatz, Silesia after 1932, Wroclaw 1945–48, Menzel&Co, and Lautawerk from 1948. Sig: K over T monogram.

Tagliapietra, Lino Glass maker from Italy [b.1934], master at Effetre, worked with many artists after c.1980, independent artworks since the 1990s.

Takahashi, Yuji Glass designer from Japan [–], worked for Sasaki Glass Co, Japan c.1967–71.

Takeuchi, Denji Glass designer from Japan [–], worked for Sasaki Glass Co, Japan c.1967/8.

Tank The removable crucible in a furnace, used in larger glass factories since the 19thC.

Tan-Si Series Glass by Orrefors, 1951 designed by Nils Landberg. Marks: NU3300/1-20.

Tantalus Lockable decanter box, 19thC.

Tarbeklaas Glassworks in Tallinn, Estonia [–], designers include Helga Kõrge after 1953, who was chief designer from 1960, Tina Leon after 1965, Miriam Maasikas after 1953 and Pilvi Ojamäa after 1965.

Tarentum Glass Co Glassworks in Tarentum, PA., USA [1866–1894–1918], previously Richards & Hartley 1866–93, USG as Factory E 1891, known as the Tarentum Glass Co after 1894, burnt down in 1918, (pressed glass).

Target ball Hollow glass ball, free- or mould-blown, used for target practice filled with confetti, feathers or ribbon. First used in Great Britain in the 1830s, in the US after c.1855; popular until c.1880 (when the clay pigeon was invented); latest c.1893.

Tarkovskaya, Nina A Glass designer from Moscow, Russia [1907–], main works produced at Gus-Krushtalny Dyatkovsky Cut Glass and First Communist VDG after 1949.

Tarnow Crystal Crystal made in Tárnow, Poland [?–present].

Tarnowiec Glass Works Glassworks in Tarnowiec, Poland [?–present], designers include Jerzy Maraj. Sig: no sigs, (art glass & decorative glass; cased, crackled and frosted).

Tarrida Glassworks in Barcelona, Spain [?–1908], merged into Union Vidriera de Espana in 1908.

Tarsitano, Debbie Paperweights artist from MS, USA [–], made paperweights with her father Delmo after 1970s. Sig: DT.

Tarsitano, Delmo Paperweights artist from Long Island, NY, USA [1921–], made paperweights also with his daughter Debbie. Sig: AT.

Taylor Bros & Co, Inc Glassworks location unknown [–], active c.1904, (cut glass).

Taylor, Dorothy Dealer in pressed glass collectables, based in Kansas City, MO, USA [?–present].

Taylor, Michael Studio artist from USA [1944–].

TBMBR This bottle must be returned.

TBNTBS This bottle not to be sold.

TBINS This bottle is not sold. Markings on US bottles c.1880–1910. Federal law forbids sale or re-use of this bottle on bottles produced in the US 1933–64.

TCW Trade name T C Wheaton Co, Millville, NJ, USA [1888–present], (bottles).

Teal A deep blue-green colour, popular in English wine glasses since the end of the 18thC. The colour was again popular in the 1930s, the 1950s and on and off in recent times.

Teams Glass Works Glassworks in Great Britain [1867–], (pressed glass). Set up by George Davidson.

Teardrop A tear shaped airbubble.

Technical Glass Co, Inc Glassworks location unknown [–], active c.1930, (tableware).

Technisches Glas Ilmenau/VEB Werk für Technisches Glas Glassworks in Ilmenau, Germany [1976–present], (technical glass, hollow wares, bottles & tubes).

Teign Valley Glass Glassworks in Newton Abbot, Devon, Great Britain [1981–present], aka House of Marbles, (toys, marbles & tableware).

Teirich, Valentin Glass designer from Austria [1845–1904], worked for Lobmeyr c.1870.

Teixeira, Cláudia Glass designer from Portugal [–], worked for MGlass, Marinha Grande c.1999.

Tejml, František Glass artist from Prague, Czech Republic [b.1933], worked for various glassworks 1957–70.

Temný Důl, Dorotina Hut Glassworks in Marsova, okr Zaclér, Czechoslovakia [1854–end 19thC], (pressed glass & crystal).

Tempering See toughening.

Terris, Colin Glass engraver from Scotland [–], worked for Caithness Glass since 1968, (paperweights).

Teschner, Richard Glass designer from Austria [–], worked for Loetz c.1906/08.

Tessere 1 The tessere technique is a mosaic of coloured strips or rectangles. 2 Barovier &

Tessere Ambra Toso art glass designed by Ercole Barovier, 1956.

Tessere Ambra Barovier & Toso art glass by Ercole Barovier, 1957.

Tessere Policrome Barovier & Toso art glass by Ercole Barovier, 1962/4.

Tessere Tessuto Venini art glass designed by Paolo Venini, 1957.

Tessuto Type of art glass made by Venini designed by Carlo Scarpa, 1939/40.

Tetterode Glasindustrie, van Glassworks in Amsterdam, Netherlands [1925–present], (technical glass, architectural glass & monuments).

Tetterode Glas Atelier, F van Glass studio in Voorthuizen, Netherlands [1968–present], (bent/slumped art glass & objects).

Thalatta technique Developed at Skruf by Bengt Edenfalk 1959 involving an enclosed air pattern made while the glass is hot.

Theresienthal Fachschule Glass school in Zwiesel, Germany [–], active c.1920.

Theresienthaler Krystallglasmanufaktur GmbH Glassworks in Zwiesel, Germany [1863–present], various glassworks located here from 1421 with first factory recorded in 1836. Glassworks operated by Poschinger 1863–1963. Sig: etched TH monogram in oval c.1920s–30s, oval label with goblet encircled by "Theresienthaler Krystallglas-Fabrik-Bayern" 1920s–30s, crowned "TH" encircled by "Kristall Theresienthal Germany" after 1940s, a crown, "Theresienthal", (luxury tableware, Venetian style glass, giftware & Art Nouveau replicas).

Thermal conductivity Heat transfer property of materials; isolators have low thermal conductivity, metals have high thermal conductivity.

Thermal linear coefficient of expansion The relative amount that a material will expand when heated; soft glass COE is usually between 90 and 105.

Thermal shock The strain caused by suddenly heating or cooling of a piece of glass.

Thermocouple Bimetal probe that measures kiln temperature.

Thermos Ltd Glassworks in Brentwood, Essex and Thetford, Great Britain [1907–present], (vacuum bottles).

Thermex Glassworks in Semily, Czech Republic [1990–present], (decorative).

Thesmar, André Fernand Glass designer from France [1843–1912], (enamelled glass, cloisonné & flowers and plants, japanese style after c.1875).

Thiel, Ana Glass artist from Mexico [b.1958], has worked since c.1980.

Thomas & Co Glashütte Glassworks in Welzow near Spremberg, Germany [1914–c.1937–?].

Thomassen, Gerard Glass designer from

Holland [b.1926], worked for Leerdam before c.1951–1967.

Thomczyk, Manfred Glass designer/cutter from Germany [b.1936].

Thompson Glass Co Ltd/National Glass Glassworks in Uniontown, PA, USA [1889–98], became National Glass in 1901, later Patterson-Fry Specialty Co run by George Fry, brother of H C Fry, (glass decorating & pressed glass).

Thompson, George Glass designer from USA [b.1913], worked for Steuben after 1967.

Thomson, Alan Glass designer from Great Britain [b.1935], (lampwork, borosilcate glass).

Thône, J H & Co Glassworks in Nieuw-Buinen, Netherlands [1838–1921], taken over by Bakker in 1921, (bottles).

Thorell, G Glass designer from Sweden [–], worked for Kosta in 1923.

Thorpe, Dorothy, Inc Glass decorating firm located in Los Angeles, CA, USA [1930s–c.1970], (sanding, etching & silver overlay on blanks from Heisey, Cambridge and others).

Thorssen, Ove Glass designer from Sweden [1945–], worked for Venini 1971–74.

Threaded glass Threads of glass, usually in contrasting colours, which can be wound around the glass. The technique was first used by the Egyptians. An automatic glass thread application machine was developed c.1875.

Three piece mould/3PM See Side seams.

Thrower, Frank Glass designer from Great Britain [b.1932], worked for Dartington Glass 1967–c.1973.

Thun, Matteo Glass designer from Italy [b.1952], worked for Memphis in 1979, Sottsass in 1979 and Barovier e Toso in 1989.

Thuret, André Glass artist from France [1898–1965], worked as an engineer for Verrerie de Bagneux in 1922, Verrerie de Bezons 1924–58. First works produced in 1924, together with Henri Navarre at Verrerie d'Alfortville. He worked until 1958. Sig: most Thuret pieces are signed, (art glass with colour and metallic inclusions, air bubbles).

Thüringen Traditional glassmaking region of Germany known for lampwork and figures, art glass in ultralight lampwork with enamels c.1900 and c.1920. Sig: none.

Thüringer Pharmaglas Gmbh Glassworks in Neuhaus, Germany [1990–], (tubes & vials).

Tiara glass Various types of glass marketed in the USA consisting of both original and replica pressed glass patterns [1970–98].

Tichý, Dalibor Glass artist from Kolín, Czech Republic [1950–85], worked for Crystalex Nový Bor 1976–80 and independently 1980–85.

Tid Bit American term for a cake stand on a metal centre pole.

Tiefenfurth Glashütte Glassworks in Tiefenfurth near Bunzlau OL, Germany [1744–c.1937–].

Tiepolo Venini art glass designed by Fulvio Bianconi, 1951.

Tietzehütte Glassworks in Penzig near Görlitz OL, Germany [1864–c.1937–].

Tiffany Glassworks & Decorating Co

Glassworks in Corona, NY, USA [1893–1920], previously Louis C Tiffany & Co, Associated Artists 1878–93, split into Tc Studio and Tc Furnaces in 1920. Sig: engraved LCT with 4 digit number and letter code, signatures were sometimes just LCT or "Louis C Tiffany Favrile Inc"; prefix A starts in 1894, suffix W ends in 1928; no prefix/suffix letters 1892/3, just numbers 1–9999; a printed TGDCO label surrounded by "Tiffany Favrile Glass Trademark Registered" was used 1892–1901, items made 1892–95 were often marked with a paper label only, (art glass, tableware & lamps).

Tiffany Furnaces Glassworks in Corona, NY, USA [1920–33], was the continuation of Tiffany Glassworks after studio split in 1920, run by Nash until 1932. Sig: Nash pieces are normally marked ADNA 1924–28, "Nash" with colour code letter and size code number 1929–31; not all Nash pieces are signed, some do not have the ADNA, but just "Nash" and a number; labels with colour LCT monogram + "Favrile" were used 1904–24; X=experimental piece; prefix S=blown glass shades and globes; EX=exhibition piece; o=special order; A-COLL=Louis Tiffany's private collection, (art glass & tableware).

Tiffany, Louis Comfort (1848–1933) Son of the famous New York jeweller. Started designing luxury glass and lamps around 1885, in production from 1893–1933 in Long Island. The height of his popularity was around 1900–15. Tiffany glass, which he named "Favrile" and signed "LCT", was and still is expensive. It is iridescent and freely formed glass in vivid colors ranging from deep blue to purple and from yellow-gold to green. The surfaces have a silky lustre.

Tiffany Studios Glassworks in Corona, NY, USA [1920–38], Tiffany lamps were first made in 1899, after 1920 the light division continued separately. Sig: Tiffany Studios New York plus a number that represented the pattern on the base, (leaded lamps).

Tiffin Art Glass Corp, Tiffin Glass, Tiffin Glass Co Inc Glassworks in Tiffin, OH, USA [–].
Tiffin, A J Beatty & Sons Glassworks in Tiffin, OH, USA [1888–1980], joined US Glass as Factory R in 1892, previously known as Beatty & Stillman, later Tiffin Glass, Tiffin Glass Co Inc. Sig: paper label after 1916, (quality pressed glass, depression glass; "Black Satin"

black glassware 1923–36).
Tildon and Sleeper Lighting works in Freemont, NH, USA [–], active 19thC, (lard oil lamps).
Tin cracquelé Decorative network of matt coating stretched out, pioneered by Copier, used extensively in Leerdam in the 1930s and 1940s. The technique is related to stretch glass.
Tinbäck, Klas-Göran Glass designer from Sweden [1951–], worked for Kosta Boda 1976–81 and Orrefors from 1982, also at his own studio in Skruf.
Tinker, Frank B Glassworks in USA [–], (cut glass, Brilliant period).
Tiozzo, Claudio Glass artist from Murano, Italy [–].
Tiozzo, Sergio Glassworks in Murano, Italy [1952–present], designers include Sergio Tiozzo and his son Claudio, (murrines, murrine vases, panels, plates, etc).
Tip 1 The hot end of a burner used in flamework. 2 Signature found on contemporary cameo glass replicas produced by Stilart in Romania [1992–].
Tiroler Glashütten Glassworks in Kramsach, Tirol, Austria [1756–?]. See Riedel, Claus Josef and Kramsach.
Tischau, Barbarahutte German name for Barborina Hut in Mstišov, Czech Republic. Other works known as "Tischau" are Eintrachthutte and Magdalenenhutte.
Tišljar, Jeronim Glass artist from Zagreb, Croatia [b.1963].
Titania 1 Type of Loetz glass. 2 Art glass by Edward Webb c.1880s, includes foil.
Titanised glass Developed in the early 1970s to lengthen the life of returnable glass bottles, titanized glass involves spraying bottles with a titanium compound to form a durable coating to reduce friction and lessen hairline cracks.
Tixhon, Jeanne Glass decorator from Belgium [1875–1955], wife of Romain Gevaert, worked at VSL).
Toastmaster's glass Thick-walled glass with small content used for formal toasting so the toastmaster would not get drunk. (UK, 18th–19thC) aka firing glass or bumper.
Tockstein, Jindřich Glass engraver from Bohemia [1914–75], worked for Halama and Železný Brod c.1940s–1959.
Toffolo, Cesare Flamework artist from Venice, Italy [1961–], started lampwork in his father's studio at age 15, worked with Venini, Fratelli Toso, Barovier & Toso and La Murrina.
Toffolo, Florino Master blower at Venini [–], father of Cesare, later specialized in avantgarde lampwork.
Toffolo, Giaccomo Master blower at Venini at age 17 [–], father of Florino.
Toikka, Inkeri Glass designer from Finland [1931–], worked for Nuutajärvi after 1970.
Toikka, Oiva Glass designer from Finland [1931–], worked for Nuutajärvi Notsjö 1963–c.1975 and Iittala 1981–present.
Tokyo Seibin Ltd Glassworks in Tokyo, Japan [–]. Sig: T inside a circle, (bottles).
Tomás, Alda Glass designer from Portugal [–], worked for MGlass, Marinha Grande c.1999.

Tomaszewski, Henryk Albin Sculptor and glass cutter from Poland [–], worked for Josephinenhütte c.1945–50.

Tomeo, Bonboniere srl Glass maker in Napoli, Italy [?–present], (decorated glass, colour, applications & metal mounts).

Tomeš Glassworks in Jabloneč nad Nisou, Czech Republic [?–present], (giftware, lighting, tableware, cut glass, engraved, flashed, enamelled & raised enamel).

Tommasi Glassworks in Murano, Italy [?–present], (decorated glass, stoppers, ornaments, gilding, rigadin & venetian style, lampwork).

Tongs Glassmaker's tool for picking up and transferring hot glass objects.

Tongue & Bros Inc, R E Glassworks location unknown [–], active c.1930, (tableware).

Toprak Enerji AS Glassworks in Bilecik, Turkey [1985–], (tableware, pressed glass & light bulbs).

Törneman, Axel Glass designer from Sweden [–], worked for Reijmyre 1923.

Torpedo Egg shaped bottles patented in 1809 by William Hamilton of Dublin. These bottles would lie on their sides so the cork would stay moist. They were less likely to break, easier to fit in crates and encouraged customers to drink faster.

Tort Glassworks in Cornellà, Spain [?–1908], merged into Union Vidriera de Espana in 1908].

Tortoise shell glass Glass type imitating tortoise shell, using brown and yellow flecks on a clear base. Made in the US (Boston & Sandwich), Czechoslovakia, Murano, patented in England in 1880 and made in Germany since the end of the 19thC. Popular in the 1950s, it has various contemporary manufacturers.

Torun Bülow-Hübe, Vivianna Silver smith/glass designer from Sweden [b.1927], worked for Holmegaard.

Toscane, Vetreria in Glassworks in Empoli, Italy [2000–], formed from the merger of CIVE and Fornace da Vinci.

Toscany Trade name of St George Crystal.

Tosel Tecnologia Produçao de Vidro de Cristalaria Glassworks in the Marinha Grande region of Portugal [?–present], (lighting). See Marinha Grande and MGlass.

Toso & Cie, Alberto Glassworks in Murano, Italy [–], active c.1954, designers include Vinicio Vianello.

Toso, Arnoldo Glassworks in Murano, Italy [–], active c.1980, (art glass).

Toso, Aureliano Accountant from Italy [1884–1979], worked for Fratelli Toso until 1932, Andrea Rioda 1932–38 and ran his own company after 1938.

Toso, Aureliano Glassworks in Murano, Italy [1938–], founded in 1938, full name Vetri Decorativi Rag Aureliano Toso, a member of the Quality circle. Designers include Dino Martens 1939–70, Enrico Potz 1962–65, Flavio Poli 1963–8, Gino Poli 1965–76, Aldo Bon 1939–55 and Mario Zanetti after 1960. Made zanfirico 1944, eldorado 1950, oriente 1950, battuti 1954, mezzafiligrana 1954,

vicenza 1965 and rudi 1965. Sig: circular silver foil label "Vetreria Aureliano Toso Murano" c.1940–60, rectangular label with blank for number c.1956–c.1968, engraved sigs only on Dino Martens exhibition pieces, (art glass & lighting, lustres). See Martens, Poli.

Toso Bagnoli Glassworks in Empoli, FI, Italy [c.1940–], produced "The green glass of Empoli". See Vetreria Etrusca.

Toso, Cesare Glassworks in Murano, Italy [–], active c.1967, (giftware & souvenirs).

Toso, Ermanno Glass designer from Italy [1903–73], worked for Fratelli Toso 1924–73 where he was art director 1939–73.

Toso, Fratelli Glassworks in Murano, Italy [1854–1982], was a member of the Quality circle. Designers include Ermanno Toso 1924–39–73, M Yoham, Vittorio Zecchin 1938, Vinicio Vianello 1952, Giusto Toso 1960, Renato Toso 1960 and Rosanna Toso c.1970–82, art director from 1974–80. Aureliano Toso left in 1932 to join Andrea Rioda, and founded his own company in 1938. Sig: no signatures except on incidental exhibition pieces; plastic label after c.1967, (art glass, lighting, lustres & paperweights).

Toso, Giusto Glass artist from Murano, Italy [1939–], worked for Fratelli Toso after c.1960, Leucos in 1969 and Barovier e Toso in 1985.

Toso, Rag Aureliano See Toso, Aureliano.

Toso, Renato Glass artist in Murano, Italy [1940–], worked with Roberto Pamio.

Toso Vetri d'Arte Glassworks in Murano, Italy [–], active c.1980, Fulvio Bianconi c.1980, (art glass).

Toughening (also tempering or hardening) The thermal or chemical process to make flat glass resistant to breakage. In thermal hardening the glass is heated to just below its softening point and then cooled by jets of air; the outside layer will harden before the inside solidifies under compression. The result is 2 to 3 times stronger than untreated glass. In chemical hardening, sodium glass is cooled slowly in a potassium salt bath; sodium ions in the glass surface migrate into the salt to be replaced by potassium ions. Chemically tempered flat glass is 5 to 8 times stronger than untreated flat glass.

Tourneau Frères Glassworks location unknown [–], active c.1933, (tableware).

Tourres & Cie, Verreries De Graville Glassworks in Le Havre, France [?–present], (bottles).

Tovil (Tosel Vidro E Iluminacão Lda) Glassworks in Leiria, Portugal [1982–], (lighting, chandeliers, shades & chimneys).

Tower Manufacturing and Novelty Co Glassworks location unknown [–], active c.1903, (tableware).

Townsend, Milon Flamework artist from Hilton, NY, USA [–].

Toy, Maison Glass retailer in Rue de la Paix, Paris, France [?–1901], bought by Léveillé in 1901, (tableware & cut glass, engraved).

Trabucco, Jon and David Glass makers from Clarence, NY, USA [–], (paperweights since 1986).

Trabucco, Victor Flamework artist from Clarence, NY/Buffalo USA [–], (sculpture, lampwork after 1974 & paperweights after 1978).

Trademark registration numbers, USA 1=1870, 122=1871, 608=1872, 1,099=1873, 1,591=1874, 2,150=1875, 3,288=1876, 4,277=1877, 5,463=1878, 6,918=1879, 7,790=1880, 8,139=1881, 8,973=1882, 9,920=1883, 10,822=1884, 11,843=1885, 12,910=1886, 13,939=1887, 15,072=1888, 16,131=1889, 17,360=1890, 18,775=1891, 20,537=1892, 22,272=1893, 23,956=1894, 25,757=1895, 27,586=1896, 29,429=1897, 31,070=1898, 32,308=1899, 33,957=1900, 35,678=1901, 37,606=1902, 39,612=1903, 41,815=1904, 43,932=1905, 48,446=1906, 59,014=1907, 66,892=1908, 72,083=1909, 76,267=1910, 80,506=1911, 84,711=1912, 89,931=1913, 94,796=1914, 101,613=1915, 107,875=1916, 114,666=1917, 120,005=1918, 24,066=1919, 128,274=1920, 138,556=1921, 150,210=1922, 163,215=1923, 177,785=1924, 193,597=1925, 207,437=1926, 222,401=1927, 236,987=1928, 251,129=1929, 265,655=1930, 278,906=1931, 290,313=1932, 299,926=1933, 309,066=1934, 320,441=1935, 1,338=1936, 342,070=1937, 353,324=1938, 363,536=1939, 374,062=1940. See Design Registration and Patent dates.

Trädgårdh, Björn Glass designer from Sweden [–], worked for Reijmyre 1937.

Trail A strand of glass either drawn out from a gather or applied to a vessel.

Transjö Hytta AB Glassworks in Transjö near Kosta, Sweden [1978–], designers include Jan-Erik Ritzman and Sven-Åke Carlsson, runs Stenhytta glassworks.

Traspària snc of Venturi V & C Glassworks in Sasso Marconi, Bologna, Italy [?–present], (art glass, fused).

Tre Bockar, Glashyttan Glassworks in Hudiksvall, Sweden [1983–present], (lighting, tableware, flasks & vases; flecked and mottled glass).

Trevaise Type of art glass produced by Alton Manufacturing Co 1907–08; made by ex-Tiffany workers, closely resembles Favrile, Aurene and Kew Blas.

Triebel, Hohlglashütte Glassworks in Triebel near Sorau, Germany [1891–c.1937–].

Trinquart Laboratoire, Roland Glassworks in Venerque, France [1987–present], aka RTL SARL, (labware).

Triplex Layered flat glass first made after 1910. See laminated glass.

Triventa, Vetrerie SpA Glassworks in Vicenza, Italy [–], trade name Ve-Tri. Sig. VT, (bottles).

Trivet A three-footed, small cake plate.

Trnka, Pavel Glass artist from Poděbrady, Czech Republic [b.1948], worked independently since 1973.

Troisfontaines See Valérysthal, Raspiller/Fenne.

Tronchi Venini art glass designed by Toni Zuccheri, 1966.

TRS Glasraffinerie Glass refinery in Riedlhütte, Bavaria, Germany [?–present], (cut glass).

Trud Glassworks Glassworks location unknown, Russia [–], designers include Savelieva.

Trumpf, Glasgestaltung Rainer Glass studio in Görlitz, Germany [?–present], (art glass).

TS Trade name of the Coventry Glass Works/Glass Factory Co, Coventry, CT, USA, mark used on bottles 1820–24.

Tschernitz, Glaswerk Glassworks in Tschernitz near Sorau NL and/or Muskau near Rothenburg, Germany [1884–], founded by August Klein and Karl August Warmbrunn from Friedrichshain, Warmbrunn, Quilitz & Co, VLG AG 1909, VEB Glaswerk Tschernitz 1946. Sig: T in a downward, pointed triangle, impressed, (electric bulbs, tableware, pressed glass, cut glass & bottles). See Jämlitz.

Tschirnhaus Glashütte Glassworks in Kieslingswalde near Görlitz OL, Germany [17thC–c.1937–?].

Tube drawing See Danner process.

Tubing Prefabricated hollow tubes used by flameworkers to make labware and fluorescent lighting.

Tullival Glass decorating plant in Moncada, Valencia, Spain [1996–], (lighting, chandeliers, shades & chimneys).

Tumble American term for a bottle with a wide neck and a tumbler serving as the bottle top. Aka water decanter.

Tumbler Drinking glass without stem, foot or handle.

Tuominen-Niittylä, Kati Designer from Finland [b.1947], worked for Iittala 1993.

Turchese Neri Venini art glass designed by Tomaso Buzzi, 1932.

Turkos Series glass designed by Sven Palmqvist for Orrefors, c.1947, turquoise variant of Selena. Marks: PU3090/1-21.

Turkovic, G Glass artist from Croatia [–], active 20thC.

Turnbull, Matthew Glassworks in Sunderland, Great Britain [–], active 19thC, (pressed glass).

Turquoise opaque Colour introduced by Friedrich Egermann c.1835.

Tusche, Glaskunst Lausitz Dieter Glass studio in Rietschen, Germany [?–present], (art glass).

Tutbury Glassworks Glassworks in Great Britain [–]. See Webb Corbett Ltd.

Tweedsmuir Paperweights Glassworks in Tweedsmuir, Scotland [?–present].

Twist Decoration in stems of drinking glasses made in 18thC and later; twisted threads of white or coloured glass, air bubbles (air twists), or a combination of all three. Twists allow precise dating of the glass.

Twitchell & Schoolcraft Located in Keene, NH, USA [–], active 1815/6, (bottles).

Tygart Valley Glass Co Glassworks in Grafton, WV, USA [1906–26], previously Beaumont Glass Co, burnt down in 1926 and relocated to Washington, PA, (tableware, small items, bottles & tumblers after 1918).

Tyne Flint Glass Works See Edward Moore.

Tynell, Helena Glass designer from Finland [b.1918], worked for Riihimäen Lasi c.1952–c.1957.

Tyrian glass Type of art glass produced by Frederick Carder at Steuben.

Tyrsa, Nikolay A Glass maker from St Petersburg, Russia [1887–1942], worked at Leningrad Mirror Factory 1940–41.

U

Uberti, Giacomo Leone Glass designer from Italy [b.1928], worked for Venini 1954–85.

Ufford, S N & H C Lighting works in Boston, USA [–], (lighting; lard oil lamps c.1840).

Uhrmann, G J Glassworks in USA [–], active c.1969, (tableware).

Uhsmannsdorf Glassworks in Uhsmannsdorf near Rothenburg OL, Germany [–], Künzel Glashutte.

Uiterwaal, Stef Sculptor/artist from the Netherlands [1889–1960], worked for Leerdam 1925–33 (religious themes).

Ujantalvölgy Glassworks Glassworks in Ujantoavölgy, Northern Hungary [–], in Slovakia after the border change. Designers include István Sovánka, (art glass & cameo glass c.1890s).

Uście Glassworks Glassworks in Uście, Poland [1812–present], renamed Neufriedrichstaler Glashütten in 1822, A G Für Glasfabrikation – a Siemens company – after 1900 and Polish after 1920. It was destroyed in c.1939–45, but reconstructed after 1946, (flat glass after 1812 & bottles after 1860.

UkrGlass Trust Glassworks in Kiev, Ukraine [–], designers include Apollonov 1966–69 and Gushin.

Ullmann, Franz Glass engraver from Bohemia [1846–1921].

Ultraviolet Absorbing Glass Ultraviolet radiation is absorbed by normal glass; transmitted by quartz glass.

Ultraviolet lamp Light for distinguishing different crystal refraction; soda shows yellow, leadglass and crystal show blue, uranium, vaseline and peachblow glass show bright green. Baccarat glass shows up blue, Saint-Louis is pinkish, Clichy greenish, replica cut glass fluoresces purple-pink. Also used for checking vessels for hairline cracks and stress faults.

Ulva Kvarn See Ulven.

Ulven AB, Glashyttan Glassworks in Sweden [1983–present], operates Ulva Kvarn in Uppsala and Karlslund in Örebro, designers include Håkan Blom, (tableware, giftware & art glass.

Umbdenstock, Jean-Pierre Glass artist from France [1951–], worked on glazing at Le Chevalier studio 1973–78, Sars-Poteries in 1978, Claude Morin in 1979 and ran his own workshop in St Etienne-les-Orgues from 1980.

Umelecké Sklo Glassworks Conglomerate of nationalized Czech art glass producers founded in 1948, became Crystalex in 1974. Conglomerate included various works including Lobmeyr in Kamenický Šenov, Harrachóv and Mstišov.

Underlay A thin layer of clear or coloured glass on the inside of a piece. See Overlay.

Unger Bros Glassworks in USA [–], active c.1885, (cut glass, Brilliant period).

Unica Term used by Leerdam for a one-off piece.

Union Flint Glass Works Glassworks in Pittsburgh, PA, USA [1854–82], sold to Dithridge Flint Glass Works in 1882, (pressed glass).

Union Glashütte Glassworks in Weisswasser near Rothenburg OL, Germany [1897–c.1945].

Union Glass Co Glassworks in Somerville, MA, USA [1851–1924], became bankrupt and reorganized in 1860, designers included Bunamo and Mazerski in the 1860s, (pressed glass and blanks for cutting; art glass from 1893, Venetian style glass and iridescent "Kew Blas" glass).

Union Professionnelle des Gobeleteries Belges Manufacturing group located in Manage, Belgium [1929–40], groups producers of tableware and bottles in Hainaut.

Union Supply Co Glassworks location unknown [–], active c.1870, (tableware).

Union Vidriera de Espana SA Glass conglomerate from Barcelona, Spain [1908–45], groups together Santa Lucia, Cadalso, Tarrida, Juvé, Farrés I Cia, Tort, Mensa, Jover and 2 works in Mataró.

Unik, Uniq Terms used by Kosta for one-off pieces.

United Cut Glass Co Glassworks in USA [–], (cut glass, Brilliant period).

United Glass Bottle Manufacturers Ltd Glassworks in London, Great Britain [–], active c.1950. "Sherdley" used as a brand name until the late 1930s. Designers include A H Williamson c.1958/9 for Johnsen & Jorgensen Flint Glass Ltd, Ravenhead Barware.

United States Glass Co Glass conglomerate located in Pittsburgh, PA and Glassport, PA, USA [1891–1963]. Bought up many companies and reorganized the industry, calling the companies Factory A, O, R etc. The 18 factories they bought include: Beatty, Bellaire, Block Light, Bryce, Central, Challinor Taylor, Duncan, Gillinder, Hobbs, King and O'Hara. Showroom opened in London, Great Britain after 1902, (pressed glass & tableware).

Universal Lamp Manufacturing Co Glassworks location unknown [–], active c.1940, (lighting).

Uranium Glass Glass (never crystal) coloured with uranium oxide resulting in a brilliant greenish-yellow colour that lights up under UV light and is, in fact, slightly radioactive. First made in 1830 by Franz-Anton Riedel in Czechoslovakia who named it Annagrün, Annagelb, Eleonorengrün after his daughters Anna Maria (b.1819) and Eleonora (b.1820). Made by Riedel 1830–48, Choisy-le-Roi after 1838, VSL, Webb after 1837, Baccarat after 1843, Saint-Louis, Richardson, Leerdam, Fenne/Saar, US Glass, Cambridge, Fostoria, Imperial, Northwood, Westmoreland, and many other works. Widely used during the 19thC, its popularity turned into a fashion after the discovery of radioactivity, but fell sharply when Marie Curie died of radiation exposure (1934). Aka Canary, Canaria, Citrine, Chartreuse, Florentine, Golden green, Topaz and Vaseline (in the US only). See Vaseline, Pearline, Custard, Chrysoprase, Dichroide.

Urbainz Glashütte Glassworks in Muskau near Rothenburg OL, Germany [1898–c.1937–].

Urban, Anton Glass engraver from Bohemia [1845–1909].

Urban, Joseph Glass designer from Austria [?–1895], worked for Ludwig Moser c.1880.

US Art Bent Glass Co Glassworks in CT, USA [–], (bent flat glass for lighting and tableware c.1920–c.1960).

US Glass See United States Glass.

Uspensky, Alexey A Glass designer from St Petersburg, Russia [1892–1941], worked at Leningrad Mirror Factory 1940–41.

UTO Glasfabriek Glassworks in Schiedam, Holland [1909–22], aka Herman Jansen, (bottles for Dutch gin, fish floats & jars).

Uzilkovlesklo N C Glassworks in Cezechoslovakia [–], active c.1975.

Uzur, Branka Glass artist from Croatia [1954–].

V

VAE See Vetri Artistici Esclusivi

VAMSA See Vetreria Artistica Muranese SA.

Vachtová, Dana Glass artist from Prague, Czech Republic [b.1937], worked independently after 1963 and produced tableware for Kvetná in 1967.

Val Signature found on art glass from c.1901–14 said to be from Daum but unsubstantiated; also found with "Lorrain", a Daum mark; may be short for "Verrerie d'Art de Lorrain". Trade name Meisenthal. In many cases Val is misread for Vsl.

Val St Lambert Glassworks in Seraing, near Liège, Belgium [1826–present], cut glass, luxury glass, crystal, semi-cristal, lighting, ecclesiastical glass, barometers and fish tanks produced from 1826; coal fuelled ovens used after 1828; goblets, flasks, inkwells, toys and mould blown ware produced from 1830; pressed glass, cut glass, tableware, pressed glass, toys, lighting lenses, filigrane and cut-to-clear produced from 1839; bought by Sté Génerale in 1836 and renamed SA des Manufactures de Glaces, Verre, Vitres; Cristaux et Gobeleteries; produced blue, green, violet & opal, filigrane, gilt, engraved, vines and flowers, pressed glass, lighting, opal crystal, semi-crystal and wooden trays from c.1855; produced candle sticks with prismatic drops1862/72; VSL Basse-Neuville closed in 1879 and Namuroises merged into VSL; semi crystal, coloured, decorated glass at Herbatte c.1880; tableware and mining lamps in Jambes c.1880; acid satination, pantograph, guilloche, enamel after c.1883; took over Jemeppe-sur-Meuse in 1883; acid engraved cameo 1888–1920s; printing; sanded lighting after 1888; export to Russia, Turkey, India, China, Australia and USA c.1890; c.1900 VSL produced 160,000 articles per day with 5,000 workers, 90% for export; c.1900 lighting: 930 different shade models, olive cut, stars, acid etched, sanded, engraved, portraits, flowers, animals, guilloche and pantographed; electric shades after 1905; acid engraving, enamelling; sand blasting developed after 1908; pressed glass colours included uranium green, opaque blue, pearl grey, iridised, cobalt blue, opal, ivory, opalescent blue, yellow and bright green in 1913; closed 1914–18; galvanic silvering on blue glass in 1918; inhouse iridescence after 1923; dormant 1939–45; Jambes closed in 1931; sand blasted glass in production after 1933; Herbatte closed in 1935; Jemeppe-sur-Meuse only tumblers & bottles after 1931; automatic stemware production after 1963; Herbatte reopened & reclosed 1946-49; some press moulds sold 1952/54. Today, VSL is much smaller company, (stem- and tableware, cut crystal, cut-to-clear crystal, figures and giftware). Cut-to-clear glass designed by Henri Fourage after 1883, art glass by Art Nouveau designer Philippe Wolffers 1895–1903, art glass Art Deco designers were Joseph Simon 1888–1940, Louis-Léon Ledru 1888–1926, Marcel Traipont c.1925, Charles Graffart 1906–58, Désiré and Henri Müller 1906–7, Modeste Denoël, Gevaert, Masson and Vanneste. Current production was designed by Romano Carrera, Leo Copers, Eric Delvaux, Katherine De Sousa, Pierre Dias, Hubert Lega, Louis Leloup, Jacques Royen, Boris Sipek, Philippe Starck, Martin Szekely, Robin Winters and Jan Zoricak. (tableware, sodalime, semicrystal, lead crystal, all colours; pressed glass, cut glass, art glass, refining, etc).

Val St Lambert marks Many pieces are needle etched with full factory name or "VSL"; Graffart engraved pieces signed "Graffart/VSL/Pièce unique" + date; Graffart pieces engraved by others CG+pattern number+V; art glass carries designer signature or monogram after c.1965; abbreviations include ADP= shown in the 1925 Paris exhibition, B= shown in the 1935 Brussels exhibition, EL= shown in the 1930 Liège exhibition, EV= engraved at VSL engraving school, S=designed by Simon; pressed star mark surrounded by "Val St Lambert Déposé" or "Val St Lambert Belgium" in the 1930s; label with cut star logo surrounded by "Val St Lambert/Cristal Belgium/Déposé" or "Val St Lambert/ Belgique/Déposé" in the 1930s; trade marks include Verlux and Lega.

Valentin, F Glass decorator from Bohemia [–], active 1880s.

Valérysthal Glassworks in Valérysthal/Troisfontaines, Nancy region, France [1838–present], Valérysthal came under the same management as Portieux in 1854, found itself in Germany after border shift 1870–1918, and merged with Portieux to keep market access in 1872. Taken over by Groupe Faïence Niderwiller from 1996, together with Portieux, operated as Cristallerie. Art glass production 1880–95, Gallé type cameo pieces designed and/or executed by Désiré Christian who worked for Meisenthal, Valérysthal, and Gallé. Designers include Charles Spindler c.1898, Otto Krüger 1900 and Bruno Paul 1900, their works discontinued after c.1910. Covered animal dishes were produced after 1880; those are from 1914–33. Sig: not always, "Valérysthal", "Portieux", "SV" or "PV" on pressed items, (tableware, clear, matt, purple slag, milk and blue opaque pressed glass, opalines & art glass; currently produces hand-blown tableware & pressed items from old moulds).

Valérysthal & Portieux See Valérysthal.
Valkema, Durk Glass blower/designer from Holland [b.1951].

Valkema, Sybren Glass designer from the Netherlands [b.1916], worked for Leerdam 1948–67 and independently, studio glass. Sig: V#.
Valkema Unica Letters, year and quantity produced: VA=1957(53), VB=1959(146), none=1960(1min), D=1960(97), VE=1961(73), VP=1962(248), VH=1963(53), VK=1964(47), L=1965(142), VO=1966(143), VP=1967(39), none=1968(unk), none=1969(unk), none=1970(unk), VV=1971(14), W=1972 (4), VAA=1973(11), VAB=1974(3), VAC=1975(7), none=1976(unk), VAE=1977(10), none=1978(10), none=1979(13), none=1980(46), none=1981(17), none=1982(13), none=1983(unk), none=1984(unk), none=1985(11)
Valle, Valerio Glass artist based in Murano, Italy [–], active c.1980.
Valley Glass Co 1 Glassworks in Buckhannon, WV, USA [1900–06]. See Steimer. 2 Glassworks in Beaver Falls, PA, USA [1887–90], aka Whitla Glass Co, taken over by Valley Glass Co in 1890.
Vallien, Bertil Glass designer from Sweden [1938–], worked for Kosta Boda Afors after 1963 and Pilchuck after 1980.
Vallon, G Signature found on opalescent glass from France, possibly a trade name .
Valva Mussel shaped vases in sommerso glass designed by Flavio Poli, 1954 for Seguso Vetri d'Arte.
Van de Velde, Henri Belgian architect [1863–1957], often thought to have worked for VSL 1898–1920, but this has not been substantiated.
Vannes-le-Chatel, Verreries de Glassworks in Meurthe-et-Moselle, France [1765–present], founded in 1765, was Verreries de until 1960, Cristallerie after 1960, became part of CFC after 1970, glass school CERFAV. Sigs: Art Vannes, Cristal de Sèvres, Daum, (tableware & art glass).
Vanneste, Jean Painter from Belgium [–], head of painting studio at VSL after 1897.
Vantine & Co, A A Glassworks location unknown [–], active c.1910, (lighting).
Vañura, Karel Glass artist from Prague, Czech Republic [b.1937], various postings after 1957, worked with Libenský 1965–88.
Vargas, Mauricio Studio glass artist from Mexico [1960–], worked at Devidrio Glaswerk, Germany since 1994.
Variegato Type of art glass made by Venini designed by Carlo Scarpa, 1942.
Varnish & Co, Edward Glassworks in London, Great Britain [c.1850–], designers include Edward Varnish and Frederick Hale Thompson, (silvered glass).
Vasa Murrhina 1 Dark glass with metallic hues developed by Dr Flower at Flower Medicine Co, Boston early 1870s, produced at Cape Cod Glass Works, which he operated until 1882, (barber bottles). 2 Vasa Murrhina Glass Co located in London c.1881. See D'Humy.
Vasart Glass Ltd Glassworks in Perth, Scotland [1946–65], Vasart was used as a trade name by precursor Ysart Brothers Glass from 1946,

Vasart Glass Ltd was taken over by Teacher's Whisky, renamed Strathearn and relocated to Crieff in 1965. Sig: "Vasart" in script acid etched mark c.1947–56, round black labels "Vasart" c.1947–56, label "Vasart Glass/Hand Made in Scotland" c.1956–64, (art glass). See Ysart, Monart.

Vaseline glass 1 Yellow-greenish glass with an oily opalescence resembling petroleum jelly; used mainly for small table ornaments, coloured with uranium and hence lights up under UV-light. Made in Czechoslovakia and Great Britain (Webb, Richardson) in the late 19thC and by US Glass, Cambridge, Fostoria, Imperial, Northwood and Westmoreland as late as the 1930s. 2 Known in the US only as any kind of glass that lights up under UV light. See Uranium glass.

Vashlsing, Conrad Glassworks in Brooklyn, NY, USA [–], son of Martin Bach who co-founded Quezal, (lighting).

Vasi Rigati Venini art glass designed by Napoleone Martinuzzi, 1926.

Vaupel, Louis Glass engraver from Germany [1824–1903], worked at Breitenstein after 1836, emigrated to the USA in 1850, worked at New England Glass Co 1853–85.

Vaux-sous-Chèvremont, SA de Verreries de Glassworks in Vaux-sous-Chèvremont, Liège, Belgium [1872–], active c.1880, Verrerie de Chênée taken over 1888, Amiable, Louvet operated 1888-95, (tableware for export). Vauxrot, Usine de Glassworks in France [–]. Sig: VX, (bottles).

VB Pressmark for Villeroy & Boch.

VCA See d'Arques, Verrerie Cristallerie.

Včelnička Works, Český Kristal Glassworks in Nizbor, Czech Republic [1991–present], previously A Rückl & Sons until WWII, was then part of Ceskycristal until c.1990 when it was returned to its previous owners. Designers include Pavel Hlava c.1974/5, (tableware & decorative glass).

VDA Signature found on glass from Verrerie D'Alsace/René Lalique

VDG SA Glassworks in Rive de Gier, France [?–present], made Duralex, was sold to Bormioli Rocco in 1997.

VEB Name for collective state operated works in GDR times c.1950–c.1990 (Volks Eigener Betrieb or People's own Company).

VE-TRI See Trivemta.

Vedart Signature found on enamelled glassware made in Venice c.1920s/1930s, short for Vetri d'Arte.

Velab Glass maker in Talsano, TA, Italy [?–present], (lampworked giftware).

Velato alla Mola e Inciso Venini art glass designed by Carlo Scarpa, 1940.

Velato Glass is given a misted or "velato" effect by sand blasting it lightly at the wheel.

Vele, Bohumil Glass designer from Prague, Czechoslovakia [–], active 1920s.

Vele, J Glassworks in Czechoslovakia [–], active c.1920s.

Veles, Velez Signature found on cameo pieces attributed to Loetz

Velišek, Marin Glass artist from Teplice, Czech Republic [b.1963], worked with Libenský 1983–89 then independently from 1989.

Velké Karlovice, Mariánská Hut Glassworks in Vsetína, Czechoslovakia [1862–1932], (pressed glass c.1880).

Velké Losiny Glassworks in Šumperka, Czechoslovakia [1857–early 20thC], owned by the Brno Museum from 1878, (pressed glass).

Vello process Drawing process for glass tubing.

Veluria Trade name of the Fostoria Glass Specialty Co.

Venetian glass A style of glass-making that uses soda glass. It produces light, thin, fragile glasses, often including colours, threads, elaborate stems, aventurine or gold leaf. Produced in Venice/Murano from the 13thC. Also produced as "Façon de Venise" ("in the Venetian style") in France, Great Britain, Germany and the Netherlands in the 17thC. There was a revival in the 1890s by various producers including Whitefriar's, Sowerby, Venice & Murano, Lutz, Union Glass, Steuben 1903–23 and Dorflinger.

Venezia e Murano, Compagnia di Glass company from Murano, Italy [1877–1910], produced until 1910 then continued as a dealer, but resumed production 1925/36. Sig: acid-etched CVM, crown.

Veneziana gia Franchetti, Cristalleria e Veteria Glassworks in Murano, Italy [–], active c.1907.

Venice and Murano Glass and Mosaic Company, Salviati & Co, The Glassworks in Murano and London [1872–], (copies of antique glass). See Salviati.

Venini e Co Glassworks in Murano, Italy [1925–present], members of the Quality Circle, founded by Paolo Venini, formerly Vetri Soffiati Muranesi Venini e Co. Designers include Martinuzzi 1925–32, Tommaso Buzzi 1932–4, Tyra Lundgren 1934–49, Carlo Scarpa 1932–46 (was art director from 1934) and in 1961 and 1968, Fulvio Bianconi 1946–55, J Carpenter, Eugene Berman, Massimo Vingelli, Riccardo Licata, Charles Linn Tissot, Ove Thorssen 1971–74, Birgitta Carlsson c.1974/5, Toni Zuccheri, Thomas Stearns, Tobia Scarpa, Tapio Wirkkala, Timo Sarpaneva, Marco Zanini, Toots Zynsky, Laura de Santillana and Ludovico de Santillana c.1980. Current designers include Gae Aulenti, Emmanuel Babled, Mario Bellini, Rodolfo

149

Dordoni, Guggisberg & Baldwin, Alessandro Mendini, Alejandro Ruiz, Ettore Sottsass, Gianni Versace, Giorgio Vigna and Marco Zanini. Art glass produced: soffiati 1925, rigati 1926, pasta vitrea 1927, incamiciato 1927, pulegoso 1928, calcedonio 1930, corrosi 1933, alga, laguna & tramonta 1933, sommersi 1934, pesanti 1934, lattimo sommerso 1936, tessuti 1939, murrine 1940, a fasce 1942, incalmo 1942, a canne 1946, fazzoletti 1946, Commedia dell'Arte 1948, a fasce verticali 1951, vetro pezzato 1951, forati 1951, morandiane 1951, mosaico tessuto 1954, scozzese 1957, grotteschi 1957, clessidre 1957, battuti 1960, occhi 1960, spirali 1961, colletti 1962, crepuscoli, groviglie 1964, pioggia 1965, tronchi 1966, ninfee 1966, scolpiti 1966 and Cardin 1969; many designs are in current production, (art glass).

Venini signatures A 2-line acid stencil script "venini italia" 1925–40, a 2-line acid stencil "venini murano" after 1930, a 2-line acid stencil "MADE IN ITALY" as a second stamp from c.1935 and incidentally until 1966, a 3-line acid stencil script "venini murano ars" c.1939–45, various paper labels "venini & C" c.1925–32, "Venini" after 1932, a 3-line acid stencil "venini murano italia" 1946–66, an acid stencil circular "Venini Murano" with or without "italy" in the middle c.1955–c.1959, a 2-line diamond engraved "venini italia" 1966–70, a 1-line engraved sig after 1970, a 1-line engraved sig with year added after 1975, "Venini"+year since 1985.

Venini, Paolo Lawyer from Italy [1895–1959], founded Cappelin-Venini 1921, Venini 1925–59.

Vennola, Jorma Glass designer from Finland [1943–], worked for Corning ovenproof 1973–75 and Iittala after 1975.

Venon, J H Glassworks in USA [–], (cut glass, Brilliant period).

Ver-Sace Vetrerie Cristallerie srl Glassworks in Barberino Val d'Elsa/Fi, Italy [?–present], (tableware).

Vera Walther See Walther.

Verart Signature found on art glass made by Sabino, France, (pressed glass/art glass, opalescence).

Verboeket, Max Glass designer from Holland [1922–], worked for Maastricht as chief designer 1953–70.

Vercentre Glassworks in Manage, Belgium [–], full name is Verreries du Centre, designers include L Mairesse, (heavy, deep etched vases with art deco floral motives made c.1927–c.1930.

A Verchi Venini art glass designed by Carlo Scarpa and Tyra Lundgren, 1938.

Vercribel Manufacturing group located in Val St Lambert, Seraing, Belgium [1949–59], full

name is Depot des Verreries et Cristalleries de Belgique, grouped various manufacturers in central sales office.

Verdalite See Emeralite.

Vereinigte Driburger Glashüttenwerke GmbH Glassworks in Bad Driburg, Germany [–], active c.1950, (tableware).

Vereinigte Farbenglaswerke AG Glassworks in Zwiesel, Germany [1870–], currently Schott-Zwiesel Glaswerke AG. Designers include Heinz Löffelhardt 1945–53, (art glass dishes in Murano style, tableware, decorative glass).

Vereinigte Glashüttenwerke Pallme-König & Habel, Ig Grossmann Sohn GmbH Glassworks in Koštany u Teplice, Czechoslovakia [1920–?].

Vereinigte Lausitzer Glaswerke, VLG Glassworks in Weisswasser, nr Rothenburg, OL, Germany [1905–45], designers include Wilhelm Wagenfeld. See Weisswasser VLG.

Vereno See Hainaut.

Verin, Stanislav P Glass designer from Moscow, Russia [1942–], designer at Gus-Krushtalny 1964–69.

Verko Trade name of Florence Talbot Westbrook.

Verlica Glassworks in Momignies and in Ghlin near Mons, Belgium [?–present], (specials & flasks).

Verlišková, Milena Glass artist from Czech Republic [b.1917], worked for Českomoravske Sklárny in Krásno nad Bečvou, 1942–45, Škrdlovice 1950–60 and Lustry Glassworks 1960–62.

Verlux Mark found on opalescent or satinated pressed glass, probably used by VSL c.1925–c.1930.

Verlys Glassworks in Andelys/Eure, France [–], aka Verreries d'Andelys, part of Holophane Co, produced art glass from c.1924, air trap vases, large floral satinated pressed glass vases and dishes 1933–55. Sig. point or pressed, (lighting, art glass, pressed glass & opalescent glass).

Verlys art glass Opalescent glass produced since 1931 by Verlys, operated by Holophane Co, in France and since 1935 in a second plant at Newark, OH, USA. Both factories signed "Verlys" – the French signature is moulded; the American one is etched.

Verlys of America Glassworks in Newark, OH, USA [1935–?], (opalescent pressed glass).

Vernox Trade name used by Sabino.

Veronese 1 Venini art glass designed by Vittorio Zecchin and Paolo Veronese, 1921. 2 Retail outlet in Paris, France [–], active after c.1945. Sig. acid stamp "Veronese Seguso Italia".

Verre Antique Bubbly glass produced at Gobbe-Hocquemiller c.1970s.

Verre de Fougère See Waldglas.

Verre de Nevers Aka Verre filé de Nevers. Lampwork figures, statuettes and groups made in the French city of Nevers, late 17thC–19thC. Also covers items made in Paris and Marseilles; similar products were made in Thüringen.

Verre de Soie Pale iridescent art glass produced by Steuben c.1910.

Verre Eglomisé See Reverse painting.

Verre Moiré Glass with evenly dispersed white spots on a coloured background, from c.1880, France, Nailsea.

Verre parlante ("Talking glass") Works by Emile Gallé decorated with poetic quotations.

Verre trembleur A tall stemmed glass on a twist/filigrane stem designed by Dieudonné Masson and produced at VSL after 1885.

Verrerie Cristallerie d'Arques See Arques and Durand & Cie, J G.

Verrerie d'Art de Lorrain Trade name of Meisenthal after 1901.

Verrerie d'en Bas See Bas, Verrerie d'en.

Verrerie de Belle-Etoile See Belle-Etoile, Verrerie de.

Verrerie des Hamendes L Lambert SA See Hamendes.

Verrerie Doyen See Doyen, Verrerie et Gobeletiere.

Verrerie Soufflée Mécanique See Soufflée Mécanique, Verrerie.

Verreries & Cristalleries de Saint-Denis See Legras and Saint-Denis.

Verreries & Gobeleteries Nouvelles See Nouvelles.

Verreries Anversoises SA See Anversoises.

Verreries Brosse See Brosse, Verreries.

Verreries d'Art de Costebelle See Costebelle.

Verreries d'Art 'Lorrain' See Belle-Etoile, Verreries de.

Verreries d'Art Muller Frères See Muller Freres.

Verreries de & á Saint-Ghislain SA Glassworks in Saint-Ghislain, Belgium [–].

Verreries de Braine-le-Comte See Association.

Verreries de Chênée See Chênée.

Verreries de Fauquez See Fauquez, Verreries de.

Verreries de la Gare SA See Gare.

Verreries de l'Est, Les See l'Est, Les Verreries de.

Verreries de Meisenthal See Meisenthal.

Verreries de Scailmont See Scailmont and Association.

Verreries de Vaux-sous-Chèvremont, SA des See Vaux-sous-Chevremont, SA des Verreries de.

Verreries de Vannes-le-Chatel See Vannes.

Verreries du Centre Trade name VSL for traditional collections in the 1920s and 30s.

Verreries du Pays de Liège et de la Campine, Cie. Des See Pays de Liège.

Verreries Gravis See Gravis, Verreries.

Verreries La Chapelle SA See La Chapelle SA, Verreries.

Verreries Nationales See Nationales, Verreries.

Verreries Nouvelles d'Aigremont, SA des See Nouvelles d'Aigremont, SA des Verreries.

Verreries Réunies, SA See Réunies, SA Verreries.

Verreries Saint-Louis See Saint-Louis.

Ver-Sace Vetrerie Cristallerie Srl Glassworks in Barberino Val d'Elsa/FI, Italy [1985–present], (tableware, art glass, barware & giftware; silverplate, lead crystal).

Vertuzayev, Mikhail S Glass maker from Russia [1882–1951], glass blower at Krasny Ghigant Glassworks 1893–1938, worked at Leningrad Mirror Factory 1939–41.

Vesanto, Erkki Glass designer from Finland

[1915–].

Vèssière Frères Engravers and glass decorators in Nancy, France [–], active c.1902–c.1905. Sig: "Justin Véssière", C Véssière, sometimes includes Croismare, Baccarat or Nancy to identify the blank supplier.

Vesta glass Lighting designed by Walter Gilbert for John Walsh Walsh, 1929.

Vesta Glassworks See Walsh Walsh, John Ltd.

Vetreria Artistica Muranese SA Glassworks in Murano, Italy [1936–45], co-founder was Alfredo Barbini, founded in 1926 as SAVAM. Designers include Ermenegildo Ripa 1938, Luigi Scarpa Croce 1940–42 and Alfredo Barbini 1936–44. Sig: shield shaped paper label "Mvrano Vamsa", (figures and sommerso vases).

Vetreria Cattelan Glassworks in Murano, Italy [c.1967]; (lighting);

Vetreria di Borgonovo Glassworks in 29011 Borgonovo/PC, Italy [1950–present], (mechanical tableware & lighting).

Vetreria Etrusca See Etrusca.

Vetreria Fratelli Toso See Toso Fratelli.

Vetreria Galliano Ferro See Ferro.

Vetreria in Toscane See Toscane.

Vetreria Musesti See Musesti.

Vetreria SAVE SpA See SAVE.

Vetreria VAE srl See VAE.

Vetrerie Betti Torino See Betti Torino.

Vetrerie d'Arte Romano Mazzega See Mazzega.

Vetrerie di Empoli SpA See Empoli.

Vetrerie Italiane Foresta See Italiane Foresta, Vetrerie.

Vetrerie Italiane Vetr I Spa See Italiane Vetr I Spa, Vetrerie.

Vetrerie Riunite See Riunite, Vetrerie.

Vetri Artistici Esclusivi Glassworks in Montelupo Fiorentino, Florence, Italy [1949–present], (blown coloured tableware).

Vetri d'Arte Briati srl See Briati, Vetri d'Arte.

Vetri delle Venezie Glassworks in Colognola ai Colli, Italy [1960–present], trade name Caldier, (automotive glass after 1960; Caldier glass line after 1999).

Vetri Murano Trade name for glass made in Murano used by various manufacturers. Sig: vetri murano vm sticker in grey-on-black.

Vetri Soffiati Muranesi Cappellin, Venini & Co Glassworks in Murano [1921–25], split into Vetri Soffiati Muranesi Venini & Co and Maestri Vetrai Muranesi Cappelin & Co in 1925, artistic director was Vittorio Zecchin.

Vetricor/Fábrica de Vidros Glassworks in the Marinha Grande region of Portugal [1995–present], (decorated tableware & coloured glass). See Marinha Grande and MGlass.

Vetro Appanato Venini art glass designed by Carlo Scarpa, 1940.

Vetro Paini Srl Glass decorating plant in San Polo di Torrile /PR, Italy [1974–], (pressed glass & tumblers).

Vetropack Holding Glassworks in Ruelach, Switzerland [1969–present], operates 9 bottle plants in Switzerland, Austria, Czech Republic and Croatia.

Vez, de See De Vez, Pantin.

VFA, Verreries Flaconnages Agussol Glassworks in Nanterre, France [?–present], (bottles, flasks & jars).

VHG See Strangfeld & Hannemann, Vereinigte Hoyerswerdaer Glaswerke.

Vials Small closed vessel for holding liquids.

Vianello, Vinicio Glass designer from Italy [–], worked for Barbini in 1950, Fratelli Toso in 1952 and SALIR in 1954. He produced Vaso a reazione nucleare 1952, milleocchi 1954 and atomici 1954 for SALIR. Worked with Alberto Toso 1952–54 and ran his own design studio after 1957.

Vianne, Cristallerie et Verrerie de Glassworks in Vianne, near Guyenne, Gascogne, France [1918–present], trade names include Cristal d'Albret for paperweights 1967–82, produced oil lamps after the 1930s and sulfures by Poillerat. Sig: paperweights signed "Cristal d'Albret", which is a trade name, (lighting deco style, art glass, tableware & incrusted paperweights).

Viard Frères Glassworks in Bar-sur-Seine, near Troyes, France [?–1937], production director was Maurice Martinot c.1918–37, (pressed glass flasks & boxes 1922–37).

Vibesal See Vidrios Beniganim.

Vickers, Percival Glassworks in Manchester, Great Britain [19thC–1914], (pressed glass c.1860–1914).

Vicrimag/Vidrios Artisanais da Marinha Grande Glassworks in the Marinha Grande region of Portugal [?–present], (quality glass, one-offs). See Marinha Grande and MGlass.

Victoriahütte Glassworks in Welzow near Spremberg NL, Germany [1903–c.1937–].

Victory Flasks Co Pvt Ltd/Sun Flask Glassworks in Bombay, India [1942–], (bottles & vacuum flasks).

Victory Glass & Industries Glassworks in Bangalore, India [1984–present], (bottles).

Vida, La Glass collection from Glasverlag Edita Geissler, Immenhausen, Germany [?–present].

Vida, Zsuzsa Glass designer from Budapest, Hungary [–], at work since 1970.

Vide-poche French term for a small ornamental dish for depositing keys, coins, etc, at night.

Vidrala SA Glassworks in Llodio, Alava and Caudete, Albacete, Spain [1965–present], (bottles).

Vidriera Centroamericana Sa (Vicesa) Glassworks in Cartago, Costa Rica [1978–], (bottles, tableware & tumblers; all mechanical).

Vidriera Leonesa SA – Vilesa Glassworks in Leon, Spain [1965–?], (bottles & jars).

Vidrieria Rovira SA Glassworks in Barcelona and Castellbisbal, Spain [1903–present], (bottles).

Vidrieras Canarias Glassworks in Las Palmas, Spain [1978–present], (bottles).

Vidrieras Masip Glassworks in Cornellà Llobregat, Barcelona, Spain [1945–present], (bottles).

Vidrieros de Levante sal Glassworks in l'Olleria, Valencia, Spain [?–present], (coloured giftware).

Vidrios Beniganim sal, Vibesal Glassworks in Beniganim (Valencia), Spain, [?–present].

Vidrios de Gordiola See Gordiola.

Vidrios San Miguel scv Glassworks in Ayelo de Malferit, Valencia, Spain [1986–present], (factory designs, art glass, tableware & giftware; recycled and new sodalime).

Vidrividro/ Produçao de Vidros Glassworks in the Marinha Grande region of Portugal [?–present], (lighting, domestic glass & welded glass). See Marinha Grande and MGlass.

Vidroporto SA Glassworks in Sao Paolo, Brazil [–], (bottles).

Vieira, Pedro Glass designer from Portugal [–], worked for MGlass, Marinha Grande c.1999.

Vignelli, Massimo Glass designer from Italy [b.1931], worked for Venini after 1953.

Viippola, Irina Glass designer from Finland [b.1973], worked for littala 1997.

Viking Glass 1 Glassworks in New Martinsville, WV, USA [1944–98], formed from New Martinsville Glass Co, Rainbow Art Glass Co joined in c.1972. (Viking was purchased by Kenneth Dalzell of the Fostoria glass family 1987 to become Dalzell-Viking), patterns include Epic and Georgian. 2 Early drinking vessels used in Scandinavian countries. See Replicas.

Vilbiss Atomiser, de See De Vilbiss.

Vilca Glassworks in Colle Val d'Elsa, Italy [1958–present], designers include Ambrogio Pozzi, Giorgio Pinchiorri, Sandro Bessi, Shiro Kuramata, Gio Ponti, David Palterer; Charles Rennie Mackintosh and Le Corbusier. Sigs: all items signed in diamond point "Vilca+artist name", sandblasted "Vilca" mark on small pieces, (pressed glass, cut glass, giftware & figures in clear and coloured crystal).

Villeroy & Boch Glassworks in Wadgassen, Saar, Germany [1842–1934] and [?–present], designers include Emile Rigot 1929–31. Sig: cameo pieces usually signed, "VB" pressed glass, (blown and pressed tableware & art glass from 1902, floral cameo).

Villette-Pantin, La Glassworks in Pantin, France [–], active c.1855, managed by Monot, (enamel painting). See Monot.

Vilniaus Stiklo Studija Glassworks in Vilnius, Lithuania [1920–present], produced bottles from 1950–75 and art glass after 1975, (art glass, coloured, decorated, swirled, crackled; handmade; figures & gifts).

Vilvoorde, Verrerie de Glassworks in Vilvoorde, Belgium [?–present], (bottles).

Vilyss Signature found on Art Deco glass, provenance unknown.

Vincent, Christian Glass designer from Belgium [–], creative director at Boussu 1974–86.

Vineland Flint Glass Works Glassworks in Vineland, NJ, USA [1897–?], named Kimble-Durand Glass Co 1912–18, Durand Art Glass Co 1920–31 and Kimble Glass Co after 1931, (tableware, art glass & lighting after 1920).

Viokef Glassworks N Kakkos SA Glassworks in Koropi, Greece [1955–present], (lampshades).

Violetta SA Glassworks in Stronie ¢laskie, Poland [?–present], (cut glass, tableware & crystal).

Viscosity The relative stiffness of hot glass;

measured in "poises".

Vistosi, Gino Glass designer from Murano, Italy [1925–80], worked for Vetreria Vistosi since 1952.

Vistosi, Guglielmo Glass artist from Murano, Italy [1901–52], founded his own workshop in 1945.

Vistosi, Luciano Glass artist in Murano, Italy [1931–], worked for Vetreria Vistosi since 1952.

Vistosi, Oreste Glass artist located in Murano, Italy [1917–82], worked for Vetreria Vistosi after 1952.

Vistosi, Vetreria Glassworks in Murano, Italy [1945–92], member of the Quality Circle, designers include Paolo Audifreddi, Gae Aulenti, Fulvio Bianconi, Enrico Capuzzo, Vico Magistretti c.1980, Angelo Mangiarotti, Eleonore Peduzzi-Riva c.1980, Peter Pelzel, Alessandro Pianon 1956, Ettore Sottsass, Gino Vistosi and Luciano Vistosi since 1952. Sig: circular foil label "Made in Italy Murano" and rectangular paper label "vistosi" 1957–c.1969, rarely engraved sigs in the 70s, (lighting, art glass & decorator objects).

Vitreous lustre A glassy shine. See Lustre.

Vitrex Trade name for Borosilicate. See Spessart-Hütte.

Vitrocrisa SA de CV Glassworks in Monterry NL, Mexico [1940–present], aka Vitro. Trade names include Pyr-o-rey for ovenware and Crisa for tableware. Sig: "Mexico" on pressed glass only, (tableware, marigold; barware, giftware, ovenware, pressed glass, flat glass & bottles).

Vitrocristal Designer collection from MGlass. See Marinha Grande.

Vitroporcelain China-like pressed opaque glass patented by Sowerby in 1877. Similar wares were made by Davidson and Moore. Colours include yellow, cream, white, turquoise and green.

Vitrosilicon SA Glassworks in Jtowa, Poland [?–present], (bottles & jars).

Vitrum Glassworks in Janov nad Nisou, Czech Republic [1993–present]. See Janov.

Vizner, František Glass artist from Žďár nad Sázavou, Czech Republic [b.1936], worked at Academy Prague 1956–62, at Sklo Union Teplice 1961–67, at Škrdlovice 1967–75 then as an independent artist after 1975.

VLG Vereinigte Lausitzer Glaswerke See Vereinigte Lausitzer Glaswerke, VLG and Weisswasser, VLG.

V-Linea SpA Glassworks in Murano, Italy [–], active c.1967, (lighting).

Vlkovec Glassworks in Benešova, Czechoslovakia [1855–?], (pressed glass reported 1873).

VMC Verrerie Mécanique Champenoise Glassworks in Reims, France [1985–present], part of Bormioli Rocco, (bottles, mechanical tableware & pressed glass).

VMG Vetropack Moravia Glass [?–present], (bottles).

V Nason & C See Nason, Vincenzo.

VNC Trade name found on Glassworks from Vincenzo Nason & Cie, especially on coloured glass, opalines.

Vonêche à Baccarat Glassworks located at Baccarat, France [1816–43]. See Baccarat.

Vonêche, Cristallerie de/ Verrerie Impériale Glassworks in Vonêche near Beauraing, Ardennes, Belgium [1802–30], founded by d'Artigues, owner of Saint-Louis and founder of Baccarat, known as Fabrique Royale des Glaces since 1822, sales outlet was l'Escalier de Cristal, Paris, (flat glass, cast glass, cut glass & tableware all of very high quality)

Vorovsky Glassworks Glassworks location unknown, Russia [–], designers include Batanova and Kobylinskaya.

Vos, Hanrath en Wiegel Glasfabriek Glassworks in Nieuwer Amstel, Netherlands [1836–88], (bottles in red, green and blue & various items).

Vosges du Nord, Cristallerie des Glassworks in Montbronn, Vosges, France [1965–present], operated by Leon Brunner, includes Kaspar Cristal France since 1991, (cut glass, tableware & mirrors).

Voss Schrader, Åse Glass engraver from Norway [–], worked for Schrader Studio c.1951/2.

Vosstanie Glassworks Glassworks location unknown, near St Petersburg, Russia [–], designers include Astvatsaturyan 1961/2, Maximov 1967–70, Moiseyenko 1956–70 who was chief designer 1960–70, Samoshkina after 1967 and Zhulyev after 1966, (flat glass, art glass & tableware).

Vrbno Glassworks in Bruntálu, Czechoslovakia [1863–1932] and [1945–after c.1972], (pressed glass reported 1895).

Vrigstads Kristallhytta Glassworks in Sweden [–], active c.1986.

VSL See Val St Lambert.

VSM See Soufflée Mécanique, Verrerie.

VTAF – Regard Glassworks in Montpothier, France [1989–], (small bottles).

VTF Verrerie Trois Fontaines. See Raspiller.

VVB (Z) Mittelglas Conglomerate of VEBs (people's own companies) during GDR years, located in Cottbus NL, Germany [1950–90], Vereinigung Volkseigener Betriebe.

VVB (Z) Ostglas Conglomerate of VEBs (people's own companies) during GDR years, located in Weisswasser, near Rothenburg OL, Germany [1950–90].

Vycor Trade name of Corning. See Fused silica.

W

W (underscored or encircled) Mark of L G Wright.

W & Co Trade name of Thomas Wightman & Co, Pittsburg, PA, USA [1880–89], (bottles).

W T Co Mark for Whitehall TatumGlass Co,

(bottles) .

Wachs, Kersti Glass designer from Estonia [1940–], worked at The Neman from 1967.

Wadgassen, Kristallfabrik Glassworks in Germany [–]. See Villeroy & Boch.

Wagenfeld, Wilhelm Glass designer from Germany [1900–90], worked for VLG 1935–47, Schott 1931–35 and WMF in 1947 until after c.1960, freelance after 1950; he ran his own design studio 1954–78 and worked for Peill & Pützler, Rosenthal and Hirschberg.

Wåhlström, Ann Glass designer from Sweden [–], current designer at Kosta Boda.

Wainwright, Kenneth Glass designer from Great Britain [b.1923], worked for Walsh Walsh 1937–51 and Stourbridge 1951–55.

Wakefield Glass Glass produced at Wakefield, Yorkshire, Great Britain c.1850s–c.1890s, various producers specializing in dumps, door Stops and paperweights.

Waldglas Green coloured glass made in Germany/Bohemia since the Middle Ages until c.1850. Aka Verre-de-Fougère (fern glass; made with fern ashes) in France and forest glass. See replicas.

Walker, Bruce Engraver from Scotland [–], active c.1975.

Wallace and McAfee Glassworks in Pittsburgh, PA, USA [–], active c.1893, merged into Consolidated.

Wallander, Alf Glass designer from Sweden [1862–1914], worked for Kosta 1908–09 and Reijmyre 1908–14.

Wallenstein, Mayer & Co Glassworks location unknown [–], active c.1910 and c.1913, (tableware & cut glass).

Wallstab, Kurt Flamework artist from Griesheim in Thüringia, Germany [1920–], trained instrument maker, worked at the Technical School of Glass in Thüringen after 1946, as a laboratory glassblower before 1975 and produced flamework after 1975. His company name is Kurt Wallstab Glasgestaltung.

Wallstab-Breitwieser Modernglas Glass studio in Griesheim, Germany [1993–present], (flameworked art glass).

Walsh Walsh Ltd, John (Soho & Vesta Glassworks) Glassworks in Birmingham, Great Britain [1851–1951], run by W G Riley after 1928. Produced New Opaline Brocade after 1897, "Vesta Ray", "Walsh", "Pompeiian", lustre glass, glass panel designs by Walter Gilbert after 1929, cut glass designs by W Clyne Farquharson 1936–42, paperweights 1920s–50s often featuring fake 1848 canes. Sig: no marks before 1926, etched WALSH 1926–30, "GScRFec" moulded on lighting panels by Walter Gilbert, etched "WALSH/ENGLAND" 1930–50, Clyne Farquharson designs engraved with name, production year after 1936 and "NRD" added 1939–42, (art glass, cut glass, lighting & tableware).

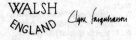

Walter, Almaric Glass artist from France [1869–1959], produced pâte-de-verre from 1903, production at Daum 1906–15, then worked independently in Nancy 1918–35 and 1945–early 1950s, designs by Henri Bergé, early works transparent; colour from 1906.

Waltersperger, Verrerie Glassworks in Blangy-sur-Bresle, France [1916–present]; (bottles, pressed glass; sodalime, lead crystal, opal)

Walther, August & Söhne Glassworks in Ottendorf, Germany [1936–51], merged with Sächsische Ottendorf-Okrilla AG in 1932, VEB Sachsenglas after 1951. Sig: AWS or SG inside heart, (pressed glass tableware & barware; gold frieze pressed glass in Moser style).

Walther Glasmanufaktur, Vera Glassworks in Willebadessen, Germany [?–present]. Sig: engraved "Vera Walther" or "Walther", (art glass & artglass).

Walther-Glas GmbH Glassworks in Bad Driburg, Germany [1951–present]. Sig: none, (pressed glass only; tableware, giftware & automotive).

Walton, George Architect and glass designer from Great Britain [1867–1933], worked for Couper on Clutha designs c.1890.

Walwing, Folke Glass designer from Sweden [b.1907], worked for Målerås.

Wand, F Glassworks in Herstal, Belgium [–], active c.1910, (tableware).

Wander Glassworks Glassworks in Bedřichov, Czechoslovakia [18thC–1820s].

Wang, Heinrich Author, actor and glass designer from Taiwan [–], founded New Workshop glass studio in Taiwan in 1988, founded Grand Crystal Co in 1994, (lost wax, pate-de-verre).

Wangum Cut Glass Co Glassworks location unknown [–], active c.1914, (cut glass).

Warburg-Ossendorf, Glashütte Glassworks in Warburg-Ossendorf, Germany [?–present]. See Rolf Wiemers Glashütten.

Ward, Mayauel Glass artist from USA [–], worked at Abelmann Art Glass, (paperworks).

Wärff, Ann See Wolff.

Wärff, Göran Glass designer from Sweden [1933–], worked for Pukeberg 1959–64 and Kosta Boda 1964–74, 1978–82 and since 1986.

Warmbrunn & Quilitz, Glashütte Glassworks in Tschernitz near Sorau NL, Germany [1830–c.1945].

Warmensteinach See Frankonia.

Warren-Wilson, H Glass engraver from Great Britain [–], active c.1959/60.

Wärtislä-Yhtyma Oy Glassworks in Notsjö, Finland [–]. See Nuutajärvi Notsjö.

Water set Pitcher plus six tumblers popular in the 19thC and 20thC, especially in the US.

Waterford Glassworks in Waterford, Ireland [1729–1851]. Sig: include "Waterford Penrose", (high quality Irish cut glass & tableware).

Waterford Crystal/Waterford Glass Ltd Glassworks in Waterford, Ireland [1951–present]. Sig: usually etched "Waterford", shamrock label "Waterford Glass Limited/Made in the Republic of Ireland" after 1950s, seahorse logo 1990s, (cut crystal tableware & giftware).

Waterloo Company Crystal manufacturer in Cork, Ireland [–], active after c.1830s, (old Irish cut glass).

Waterstone Glassware Ltd Glassworks in Wath-upon-Dearne, South Yorkshire, Great Britain [1945–present], (bottles, tableware, pressed glass, giftware & paperweights; semi-crystal, full lead crystal, sodalime, borosilicate, opal.

Watkins, James Studio artist from USA [1955–].

Watson, John British engraver [–], worked at Sunderland 1823–34.

Watz, Birgitta Glass designer from Sweden [–], worked at Lindshammar and Pukeberg.

Waugh, Sidney Sculptor from USA [1904–63], designed for Steuben after 1933. His designs include Gazelle Bowl 1935, Zodiac Bowl 1935 and Merry-Go-Round 1947, (moulded, cut glass, engraving).

Wauty Frères, Manage See Verreries et Gobeleteries Nouvelles in Manage.

Wave Crest Ware Trade name of C F Monroe Company, (art glass).

Waxweiler, Philippe Painter from Liège [1943–], worked at VSL 1972 and 1979.

WCut Glass Co Trade name of the West Coast Glass Co, Los Angeles, CA, USA [1908–30], (bottles).

Wear Flint Glass Company Glassworks in Deptford, Sunderland, Great Britain [–], active c.1824, (cut glass & tableware, Regency style).

Wear Glass Works Glassworks in Sunderland, Great Britain [1858–], founded by James Angus and Henry Greener, became Greener & Co after 1886, then became Jobling, then Corning, (pressed glass, currently technical glass/Pyrex only).

Weathering Surface degradation caused by chemical reaction with the environment. Alkali leaches out by exposure to water and leaves a weathered, siliceous surface, which is sometimes iridescent. Roman vessels with their weathered surface inspired the development of applied iridescence. See iridescence.

Weaving See Stitching.

Webb, Thomas/Thos & Sons Glassworks in Dennis Park, Stourbridge, Great Britain [1837–?], bought by Webb's Crystal Glass Co in 1920. Run by Thomas Webb until his death in 1869 when the company was run by his sons Wilkes and Charles. Cameo engravers include G & T Woodall, William Hill, Tom Farmer, Harry Davies and J T Fereday. Designers include Sven Fogelberg 1932–58, Anna Fogelberg 1930s, Homery Folkes c.1930s and David Hammond c.1958/9. Sig: some items etched "Thomas/Thos Webb & Sons" after 1880s, Woodall cameo pieces usually signed by name or initials, sometimes with date, etched Webb 1906–35, etched "Made in/Webb/England" 1936–49, etched Webb/ENGLAND 1950–66, sandblasted THOS/WEBB/ENGLAND 1966–80, THOMAS/WEBB/ENGLAND 1980–90, (tableware, colour glass, art glass; cameo, bronze, peach bloom, Queen's Burmese, Old Roman, Satin, Tricolour c.1889).

Webb & Corbett Ltd, T Glassworks located at Coalburnhill, Stourbridge, Great Britain [1897–present], incorporates Tutbury Glassworks from 1906, part of the Doulton group from 1969. Designers include Irene Stevens 1946–60. Sig: engraved "W&C England" on some agate flambé pieces 1920s, etched "Webb Corbett" curved over "Made in/England" 1930–47, etched "WEBB CORBETT ENGLAND" in a circle 1947–65, S for Stourbridge, T for Tudbury, * for both 1947–52, production year marked 1952–9, etched Webb/Corbett/Crystal 1965–72.

Webb, Edward Glass maker from Great Britain [–], operated White House Glass Works c.1880s, (cut glass, ornaments & art glass; "Argentine", "Oroide", "Titania" glass featuring metallic foil, last quarter 19thC).

Webb, Joseph Glassworks located at Coalburn Hill Glassworks [1883–], ("New Gold Glass" 1883, cut glass).

Webb, Philip Architect and designer from Great Britain [1831–1915], Arts and Crafts glass design after 1859 for William Morris, made by James Powell & Sons.

Webb, Thomas Glass maker from Great Britain [1802–69], worked at White House Glass Works 1835–37, Richardson & Webb at Wordsley Flint Glassworks before 1836, founded Thomas Webb & Sons at Platts Glasshouse 1837–56 and a new glasshouse at Dennis Hall, Amblecote 1856 aka Dennis Glassworks. Retired in 1863.

Webbs' Crystal Glass Company Ltd Glassworks in Stourbridge, Great Britain [–], active c.1921, now Dema Glass. See Edinburgh & Leith, Webb Thos.

Webster Co Glassworks location unknown [–], active c.1921, (tableware & cut glass).

Webster, Jane Glass designer from Great Britain [c.1934–], (copper wheel engraving).

Weck Glaswerk GmbH Glassworks in Bonn, Germany [c.1900–]. (bottles, packaging glass & fruit jars).

Wedgwood Glass Glassworks in King's Lynn, Norfolk, Great Britain [1970s–1986], founded as King's Lynn Glass by Ronald Stennett Wilson and sold to Wedgwood, factory sold to Caithness Glass in 1986. Sig: Lemington glass unmarked, King's Lynn glass unmarked before 1969, etched LYNN mark with crown after 1969, Wedgwood Glass etched "Wedgwood" 1969–87.

Weeping glass See leaching.

Weidensteiner See Rachelkristall.

Weidlich, Sebastian Glass decorator from Bohemia [–], active 1880s.

Weinfurtner Bergglashütte Freyung Glassworks in Freyung, Bavaria, Germany [?–present], (cut glass).

Weinfurtner Glassworks in Arnbruck, Bavaria [1969–present], open to the public and very popular, (cut glass & chandeliers).

Weinich, Valentin Glass engraver from Bohemia [1844–1927], worked in Manchester, Blackpool, Stourbridge 1870s–1910s.

Weinman, Frank X Glass maker from Boston, MA, USA [–], (paperweights 1940s).

Weisswasser Glassmaking town near Rothenberg/Oberlausitz, Germany. Glassworks include: Hirsch, Janke & Co 1906; Raffinerie Mostetzky, Raffinerie Grabner & Berger; Ladiges, Greiner & Co; Malky, Müller & Co; Gelsdorf; Menke; Gelsdorf, Grimm & Co; Mudra; Raffinerie Rex & Co; Schweig & Co; Schweig, Müller & Co; Thormann; Zwahr, Neubauer & Co 1873; Raffinerie May; Weisswasser AG 1897–1945. See VLG.

Weisswasser Bärenhütte Glassworks in Weisswasser, Germany [1897–1945–]. Sig: 2 champagne flutes over a wave in a rectangle 1954–69. See VLG.

Weisswasser, Farbenglaswerk Glassworks in Weisswasser near Rothenburg OL, Germany [1899–c.1937–].

Weisswasser, Glashüttenwerke Weisswasser AG/ Aktienhütte Bought by VLG in 1913 (pressed glass); VLG also buys Germania-Glaswerk in 1920, Max Kray & Co AG, Kamenz in 1924, Max Kray & Co and Fürstenberg/O in 1930. By 1928 VLG was one of the largest producers of tableware in Germany. New artistic director Wilhelm Wagenfeld re-

designed the assortment 1935–47. Sig: "Arsall" or "Lusa" in cameo script on Arsall cameoware 1918–29, impressed mark of circles with "GLV" after 1910, 3 consecutive overlapping diamonds with "VLG" before 1936, designed by Wagenfeld to <VXLXG> 1936 and used until 1947, <OXLXG> mark used 1945–68, logo L in circle used after 1968.

Weisswasser, VEB Lausitzer Glas Weisswasser Continuation of VLG Weisswasser; VEB Oberlausitzer Glaswerke Weisswasser after 1946, takes over Germaniahütte in 1951, Glashütte Weisswasser W Gelsdorf in 1952, VEB Kombinat Lausitzer Glas Weisswasser in 1969, part of OLG of the VEB Kombinat Lausitzer Glas Weisswasser, (medicine bottles, kitchenware, cut glass, tableware, automatic goblet production & screen printing)

Weisswasser, Vereinigte Lausitzer Glaswerke AG Neue Oberlausitzer Glashüttenwerke Schweig & Co AG 1905, buys Warmbrunn, Quilitz & Co, Tschernitz 1909, merged into VLG AG in 1909, (tableware, pressed glass). New VLG after 1920 includes VLG and the Tschernitz works, VLG AG 1909, takes over Tschöpelner Werke and Lignite works 1911, buys Glasswerks Weisswasser AG/Aktienhütte and Schweiger'sche Glas- und Porzellan AG in 1913, affiliation of labware maker Lausitzer Glaswerke AG 1921, (tableware, pressed glass & Osram/AEG light bulbs).

Vereinigte Glaswerke AG/Stölzle-Oberglas Lausitz took over parts of VLG Weisswasser in 1999.

Welch, Robert Glass designer from Great Britain [b.1929], worked for Bridge Crystal Glass Co c.1965.

Welsbach Co Glassworks location unknown [–], active c.1904 and c.1906, trade names include Reflexolier, (lighting).

Welsh Royal Crystal Glassworks in Rhayader, Powys, Wales [?–present], (cut glass).

Wennerberg, Gunnar Gunnarson Glass designer from Sweden [1863–1914], worked for Kosta 1898–1901, (art glass, cameo).

Wenzel Glasgravur, Annegret Glass engraver from Flensburg, Germany [–], currently active.

Werlich, Hans-Georg Glass engraver working in Weisswasser, Germany [–], currently active.

Werner, Sidse Glass designer from Denmark [b.1931], worked for Kastrup & Holmegaard after 1971.

Wersin, Wolfgang von Architect and designer from Munich, Germany [1882–1976], designed for Artisti Barovier, 1913/14, Peill & Sohn, Düren c.1917, Theodor Greiner from Rausacha c.1920, Rasch Haida c.1920, Neumann München c.1924, Kramsach c.1924, V A Barovier c.1926, Spiegelhütte c.1926, Regenhütte c.1935, Moser c.1940, Salzburger Kristallglas c.1957 and Lobmeyr c.1960.

West Virginia Glass Co/National Glass 19 Glassworks in Martins Ferry, OH, USA [1861–], became known as The Elson Glass Co 1882–94, then West Virginia Glass Mfg Co 1894–1900, joined National Glass conglomerate as Factory 19 in 1899, aka The West Virginia Glass Manuf Co and The West Virginia Glass Works, (tableware & pressed glass).

West Virginia Glass Specialty Co Glassworks in Weston, WV, USA [–], active c.1920, c.1958, c.present, (tableware).

Western Glas Fixture Co Glassworks location unknown [–], active c.1910, (lighting).

Westford Glass Co Glassworks in Westford, CT, USA [–], active before 1865, (bottles, carboys).

Westite Glassworks in USA [?–1931], moulds sold to Akro in 1931, (pressed glass).

Westman, Marianne Glass designer from Sweden [1925–], worked for Skruf after 1972.

Westmoreland Glass Co Glassworks in Grapeville, PA, USA [1924–85], previously Westmoreland Specialty Co. Sig: marks include V, B, R, G over W, (pressed glass).

Westmoreland Specialty Co Glassworks in Grapeville, PA, USA [1892–1924], previously The Specialty Glass Co in East Liverpool, OH 1889–92, became Westmoreland Glass Co in Grapeville, PA 1924–85, (tableware & pressed glass).

Wetting off Marking the separation line with a ring of water for easy removal of the blow pipe.

Wetzel Glass Co, R Glassworks in USA [?–present]. Sig: R/WETZEL or RW, (pressed glass).

Weule Gmbh & Co, Wilhelm Glassworks in Goslar, Germany [1896–present], (lighting, lenses & reflectors).

WF & S MILW Trade name of William Franzen & Son.

WGW Woodbury Glass Works, Woodbury, NJ, USA [1882–1900], (bottles).

Whale oil Lighting fluid in use c.1800–65; gives a bright light and hardly any odour. The best quality was oil from the sperm whale in use on ships and in public buildings. Whale oil burners have a single or double wick of simple construction. Whale oil lamps produced at New England from 1818, at Sandwich from 1825, at Blakewell and at Meriden Brittannia; 500 patents were issued between 1800–45.

Wheaton Do Brasil SA Glassworks in Sao Paolo, Brazil [1952–present], (tableware, barware & bottles).

Wheaton Glass Co Glassworks in Millville, NJ, USA [1888–present], specialized in commemmorative and novelty items and bitters bottles, (bottles & novelty items).

Wheel engraving Surface decoration using a fixed grinding wheel to which a vessel is pressed. Different diameters of wheel achieve different depth and width of cut.

Wheeler Reflector Co Glassworks location unknown [–], active c.1887, (lighting).

Whistler, Laurence Glass designer from Great Britain [b.1912], engraving after 1935 on blanks from Whitefriar's, Leerdam and Steuben. Sig: usually LW, date.

Whistler, Simon Glass designer from Great Britain [b.1940], (engraving).

Whitall Tatum Co Glassworks in Millville, NJ, USA [1844–1935], (bottles & paperweights). See Millville Glassworks

White Glassworks Glassworks in Zanesville, OH, USA [1815–51], (tableware). See Zanesville.

White House Glass Works Glassworks in Great Britain [–]. See Webb, Edward.

White Star Trade name of Gill Brothers Co.

Whitefriar's Glass Glassworks in Whitefriars, Great Britain [1834–1980], Whitefriars Glassworks was bought by James Powell in 1834. Moved to Wealdstone in 1923, switched to simpler designs. Failed and closed down 1980/1; name sold to Caithness. Important art glass production c.1880–c.1920, historical glass, Arts & Crafts glass, Art Nouveau glass and Venetian style glass; industrial art glass after 1920. Designers include Alfred R Fisher c.1967/8, W J Wilson c.1952–62 and Geoffrey Baxter c.1954–61. Sig: unsigned except for S numbers on studio line 1969–70, silver mounts are hallmarked J P & S 1906–30, otherwise labels only. Circular label POWELL WHITEFRIARS ENGLISH GLASS c.1870–1923, circular label featuring a friar holding "Whitefriars" encircled by "POWELL'S ENGLISH GLASS" 1923–50, arched rectangular friar label has "WHITEFRIARS" above and "CRYSTAL" below 1940–63, rounded rectangle with friar encircled by "WHITEFRIARS CRYSTAL MADE IN ENGLAND" 1950–63, rectangular "Whitefriars/hand made crystal" 1963–80, (art glass & industrial).

Whitefriar's Paperweights Many paperweights previously thought to have been made at Whitefriar's, some with 1848 date cane, are now traced to Arculus or Walsh Walsh.

Whitla Glass Co See Valley Glass Co..

Whitney Glass Co Glassworks in Glassboro, NY, USA [1824–1918], merger of Harmony and Olive 1824, taken over by Owens Bottle Co in 1918, (bottles).

157

Whittemore, Francis Lampwork artist from Lansdale, PA, USA [1921–], lives and works in New Jersey. Sig: black W in yellow cane, (paperweights after 1940s).

Whittle marks Rough dimpled or wavy marks caused by insufficient heating of a mould.

Whittled Curved line/vertical stretch marks along the neck of a bottle due to hand finishing when the lip is turned onto the neck.

Whorl A concentric cane in a paperweight.

Wickeder Glashüttenwerke W Hibbeln Glassworks in Wickede/Ruhr, Germany [1889–1913], (lighting, domes, chimneys, etc, for gas light). See: Hibbeln, Wilhelm.

Wiedmann, Karl Glass designer from Germany [1905–], worked for WMF 1924–36, Daum 1945–48, WMF 1949–51 and Gral-Glashütte 1954–after c.1970. Developed Ikora, Myra and Lavaluna.

Wiegel, Albert Glass engraver from Kassel, Germany [1869–1943], (sculpting, carving & engraving).

Wiemers Glashütten GmbH, Rolf Glassworks in Hameln, in Warburg-Ossendorf, in Bad Karlshafen and in Clausthal-Zellerfield, Germany [?–present].

Wiener Werkstätte Workshop for design, architecture, decoration and art founded by Josef Hofmann in 1903, failed 1932/39. Glass designs were normally commissioned from Lobmeyr or Bakalowits. Designers included Hoffmann, Haerdtl, Jungnickel, Janke, Krasnik, Koloman Moser, Peche, Powolny, Prutscher, Schaschl-Schuster, Schmidt, Strauss-Likarz, Strnad, Wieselthier and Zimpel. Decorators included Brunner-Frieberger, Flögl, Jesser-Schmidt and Rottenberg.

Wier, Don Glass designer from USA [b.1903], worked for Steuben before 1950–69.

Wieselthier, Vally Ceramicist and glass designer from Austria [1895–1945], member of the Wiener Werkstätte after 1920, worked for Lobmeyr c.1925.

Wiesenthalhütte Glassworks in Schwäbisch Gmünd, Germany [?–present], operated by Schott Zwiesel.

Wig-stand Tall, footed paperweight, aka Piedouche.

Winblad, Björn Glass designer from Denmark [1918–], worked for Rosenthal after 1957.

Wild & Wessel Glashütte Glassworks in Wiesau near Sprottau NL, Germany [1854–c.1945];

Wilfert-Walti, Marie Glass designer from Austria [–], worked for Loetz c.1906.

Wilhelmy Glashütte Glassworks in Reichenbach near Görlitz Rb Liegnitz, OL, Germany [1866–c.1945].

Wilkes, Richard Glass cutter from Dudley, Great Britain [–], ran Campbell Street Glass Works c.1870–1900.

Wilkerson, Fred Paperweights artist from Moundsville, WV, USA [–], active 1970s.

Wille, R Painter and glass decorator from Berlin [–], worked for Meyr's Neffe c.1906.

Williams, Christopher Studio artist from Great Britain [b.1949].

Williams, John British engraver [–], worked at Newcastle 1820s–30s.

Williamson, Alexander Hardie Glass designer from Great Britain [1907–94], worked for Bagley after 1933 and for Ravenhead Glass 1930s–72.

Williamson and Company, The Lighting manufacturer located in Chicago, IL, USA [–], leaded glass shades c.1919–20.

Willington Glass Co Glassworks in West Willington, CT, USA [1814–72], (black and green bottles).

Wilson, Robert Glass designer from USA [–], worked for Fratelli Toso.

Wilson, William J Glass designer from Great Britain [b.1914], worked for Whitefriars 1928–73, managing director 1950–73.

Wimmer, E J Glass designer from Austria [–], worked for Ludwig Moser c.1920.

Windsor Jr, Charles B Glass maker from USA [–], worked for Blenko Glass Co 1960s, (paperweights).

Windsor Glass Co Glassworks in Pittsburgh, PA, USA [1886–90].

Winner, V de Manufacturer located in Liège [1930–53], aka Ateliers Artistique, (lighting, satinated, blown, pressed).

Winther, Ole Glass designer from Denmark [–], worked for Holmegaard c.1965/66.

Wiped top Mould line ends before top since neck was wiped smooth after the top was tooled on. Dated pre-1915.

Wirkkala, Tapio Glass designer from Finland [1915–85], worked for Iittala 1946–85, Rosenthal 1956–85 and Venini 1959–85.

Wirths Mark found on blown opal glass painted souvenir items made in Dolhain, Belgium [c.1900–c.1920], blanks possibly supplied by VSL.

Wisteria Trade name for Alexandrite glass made by Steuben and Fostoria.

Witch Ball Large silvered ball used for home and garden decoration in the belief that when a witch flies into the room and sees herself, she will fly straight out again... Popular from the 1860s, especially in the German regions of Thüringia and Bavaria.

Witt, Anton Peter Glass engraver from Prague, Czechoslovakia [1900–1950s], engraving after 1922, worked in Karpitz until 1945 and at Weisswasser 1945–50s.

Wittwer, Franz Glassworks in Altheide-Bad, Silesia [–], active c.1930–1945, (cut crystal & tableware).

Witzmann, Carl Glass designer from Austria [–], worked for Loetz c.1913.

WJ Latchford Glass Co Glassworks based Los Angeles, CA, USA [1932–8], (bottles).

WMF, Württembergische MetallwarenFabrik: Kitchen and tableware producer located in Geisslingen, Germany [19thC–present], own glass production 1884–1984; now buy it in. Designers include Karl Wiedmann 1924–36 and 49–51, Karl Illenberger 1926–37 and 1946–72 and Wilhelm Wagenfeld 1947–60s. Sig: WMF glass is unmarked, except for some Ikora pieces retrosigned by Wiedmann, sometimes a serial number, a circular paper label was used depicting a tower in a circle and "IKORA HANDARBEIT" above WMF and GES GESCH. in a banner before 1950s, square label "WMF/ GLAS" c.1970–84. See Ikora, Myra Crystall and Lavaluna.

Wohlgemuth, Roderich Glass designer from Germany [b.1939], Sig: W.

Wolfers, Marcel Glass designer from Belgium [1886–1976], worked for Val St Lambert c.1935/36

Wolff, Ann (Wärff pre-1986) Glass designer from Denmark/Sweden [1937–], worked for Pukeberg 1959–64, Kosta Boda 1964–74 and Stenhytta 1978.

Wolff, Hugo Glassworks in Nový Bor, Czechoslovakia [c.1870–], worked for Mercury Glass, (silvered glass).

Wolf-Ferrari, Teodoro Glass artist from Italy [1878–1945], worked for Artisti Barovier c.1913, (Murrine).

Wolffers, Philippe Artist from Belgium [1858–1929], worked at VSL 1895–1903 where he created 20 different cameo vases; pumpkins, lilies, orchids, cyclamens before 1898; bats, newts and other animals 1898–1903. Gave up working in glass after 1903.

Wolfram Ortner, WOB Glassworks in Kleinkirchheim, Austria [?–present], (tableware).

Wolomin Huta Szkla Glassworks in Wolomin, Poland [?–present], (labware).

Wonder Trade name of Henry G Richardson & Sons Ltd.

Wondrejs, Fritz Glass designer and decorator from Bohemia [1911–70], worked in North Bohemia after 1936, Krasna 1938, Moser 39/40 and Weisswasser 1949–60.

Wood Brothers Glass Co Ltd Glassworks in Barnsley, Yorkshire, Great Britain [–], active c.1950], "Schola".

Woodall, George Glass engraver from Great Britain [1850–1925], brother of Thomas, apprentice of John Northwood until 1874, retired in 1911. Sig: T & G Woodall 1889–99, (cameo).

Woodall, Thomas Glass engraver from Great Britain [1849–1926], brother of George, apprentice of John Northwood until 1874, worked for Thomas Webb & Sons, retired in 1911. Sig: T & G Woodall 1889–99, (cameo).

Woods, O J Glass maker from Millville, NJ, USA [–], (paperweights 1900s–1910s).

Wordsley Trade name of Henry G Richardson & Sons Ltd.

Workshops of Applied Arts Glassmaking centre in Moscow, Russia [c.1947–], artists include Antonova after 1947, Filimonova after 1954, Ganf after 1950, Ibraghimov after 1969, Kobylinskaya after 1956, Makarenko after 1958, Matushevskaya after 1953, Nevskaya after 1952, Patskan; Ryazanova after 1960, Savelieva after 1969 and Stepanova after 1962.

WR Sig found on early cup plates from the Birmingham area, believed to be a die cutter's mark.

Wrap: A hot ribbon of glass applied to a vessel; applied strand of contrasting glass on the edge of a bow.

Wright Glass Co, L G Glassworks in New Martinsville, WV, USA [1936–99], manufacturing was subcontracted to L E Smith and Fenton, at liquidation the moulds were sold to Weishar (for the Moon & Stars pattern), to Fenton and to A & A Importing. Sig: W underlined in a circle c.1960s, leaning W underlined in a circle on Dugan moulds 1970s, W in a circle recent, (pressed glass, novelties and covered animal dishes).

Wrythen moulding Twisted ribbing, rigadin ritorto.

Września See Huta Skla.

W T & Co Trade name of Whitall, Tatum & Co, Millville, NJ, USA [1857–1935], (bottles).

Wuidart & Co Ltd, D Glass producer from Great Britain [–], designers include R Stennett-Wilson c.1955–57, (tableware).

Wünsch, Karel Glass artist from Bor, Czech Republic [b.1932], at Borske Sklo 1959–69 then independent after 1969.

Wyszkow Huta Szkla Glassworks in Wyszkow, Poland [?–present], (bottles).

Wytwarzanie Szkla Gospodarczego Glassworks in Florynka, Poland [?–present], (tableware, bottles, pressed glass & lighting; crystal, sodalime, borosilicate, opal).

Y

Yakobson, Adel Y Glass designer from Russia [1876–1942], worked at Krasny Ghigant 1902–21 and central design institutions before 1941, (tableware).

Yall Signature found on contemporary imitation Gallé cameo pieces made in China.

Yamo Glass designer from France [1959–].

Yanovskaya, Ekaterina V Glass designer from St Petersburg, Russia [1913–], worked at Leningrad Factory after 1949, chief designer there after 1953.

Yernel'yanovka Glassworks in Russia [19thC].

Yoke A support for a blowpipe during reheating in a glory hole.

Yokoyama, Naoto Glass designer from Japan [–], worked for Joetsu Crystal Glass Co Ltd c.1968–72 and for Noritake Co Ltd c.1966/7.

Yoshida, Takeo Glass designer from Japan [–], worked for Kagami Crystal Glass Works Ltd c.1972/3.

Yoshimoto, Yumiko Flamework artist from Tokyo, Japan [–], worked since c.1974.

Young, Brent Kee Studio artist from USA [–].

Ysart, Antoine Spanish glass maker born in France [1911–42], worked at Moncrieff 1935–42.

Ysart, Augustine Glass maker from Spain [1907–56], worked at Moncrieff 1930s–1946 and for Ysart Brothers Glass 1946–56.

Ysart Brothers Glass Glassworks in Perth, Scotland [1946–56], trade name: Vasart.

Ysart, Paul Glass blower and artist from Spain [1904–91], apprenticed at Edinburgh & Leith Flint Glass Works after 1917, worked at Moncrieff 1930s–1961, made his first paperweights 1932, worked at Caithness Glass 1963–70, ran his own studio at Harland, Wick 1971–75. Founded Paul Ysart Glass Co, Wick 1975–82 with Jokelson and Highland Paperweights 1977–79. Retired in 1979.

Ysart, Salvador Glass artist from Barcelona, Spain [1877–1955], worked at various glassworks in France 1909–14, Schneider frères et Wolf 1914, Edinburgh & Leith Flint Glassworks after 1915, A & R Cochran after 1916, Moncrieff 1922–46, made paperweights after 1923, worked for Monart art glass 1924–39 and set up Ysart Brothers Glass in 1946.

Ysart, Vincent Glass maker from Perth, Scotland [1909–71], worked at Moncrieff 1930s–1946, at Ysart Brothers 1946–56, at Vasart 1956–65 and Monart glass 1937–39. Vincent stopped glass making when Vasart was taken over by Teacher's Whisky in 1965, renamed Strathearn and moved to Crieff.

Yukhvets, Boris M Glass designer from Russia [1943–], worked at First Communist VDG after 1968.

Yumi Sales outlet for art glass/tableware in The Hague, Netherlands [?–present], own glass studio located in Voorburg, designer Ming Hou Chen.

Z

Zabkowice Huta Szkla Gospodarczego Glassworks in Dabrowna Gornicza, Poland [?–present], designers include Ludwik Fiedorowich c.1973 (tableware & pressed glass, sodalime, decorating).

Zach, Franz Paul Glass engraver from Bohemia [1821–81], worked in München, Germany c.1855.

Zach, Jan Vincenc Glass engraver from Bohemia [–], active 19thC, worked in Bavaria.

Žážko, Askold Glass artist from Bratislava, Slovakia [b.1946], independent 1971–78, lecturer after 1978, tableware designs for Lednické Rovne c.1986.

Zaffiro Barovier & Toso art glass type by Ercole Barovier, 1938 and 1940.

Zahn, J G Glassworks in Zlátno, Slovakia [–]. Zahn was the first glasshouse to present iridised glass at the Vienna exhibition in 1873. See Iridescence.

Zahour, Vladimír Glass designer from Czechoslovakia [b.1925], worked for Bohemia Poděbrady after 1954.

Žák, Juna and Oldřich Glass engravers from Železný Brod, Czechoslovakia [–], worked 1920–30s.

Zalivskaya Glassworks in Russia [–], active 19thC.

Záménčniková, Dana Architect, set designer and contemporary studio glass artist from the Czech Republic [b.1945], worked independently after 1985.

Zancanaro, Tono Glass producer in Padua, Italy [–], active c.1954.

Zanesville Glassware produced in Zanesville, OH, USA [–], active c.1815 and c.1851, made by manufacturers White Glassworks, New Granite. Characteristic patterns include diamond faceted, broken swirl, vertical swirl, perpendicular fluting and plain, with strap handles and scalloped or fluted rims. Colours include amber, light green and light aquamarine, also paperweights 1850s.

Zanetti, Fratelli/Zanetti Vetreria Artistica Glassworks in Murano, Italy [c.1980–present], (figures & art glass).

Zanetti, Vincenzo Glass historian from Murano, Italy [1824–83], founder of the Murano Glass School and glass museum.

Zanfirico 1 The process of reheating canes of glass with a spiral pattern of white or coloured threads and gathering them to blow into a shape. Aka Filigrana, Latticino or Latticinio. 2 Venini art glass designed by Napoleone Martinuzzi, 1929.

Zanini, Marco Glass designer from Italy [b.1954], member of the Memphis group of designers since 1981, worked for Toso Vetri d'Arte 1980s and for Venini 1989.

Zaniol, Arturo Glassworks in Murano, Italy [–], active c.1954, designers include Renzo Zaniol c.1954.

Zanon, Laura Glass dealer/refinery in Venice, Italy [–], active c.1960.

Zaritsky, Ivan V Glass designer from Kiev, Ukraine [1929–], worked at Raduga, Lvov 1957–8 and at Kiev Factory after 1958, where he was chief designer from 1970.

Zasche, Adolf Glass maker from Jablonec [–], produced metallised art glass c.1900.

Zatynaiko, Vladimir T Glass designer from Kiev, Ukraine [1937–], worked at Kiev Factory after 1956.

Zay-Ugróc Glassworks in Northern Hungary [c.1890s–c.1910s], operated by Schreiber & Neffen, designers include Istvan Sovánka.

ŽBS Short for Železný Brod Sklo.

Zebrati Barovier & Toso art glass type by Ercole Barovier, 1949.

Zecchin, Francesco Glass maker and engineer from Italy [1894–1986], worked for VSM Venini 1925–32 and Zecchin Martinuzzi

1932–39.

Zecchin, Giorgio Glass designer from Murano, Italy [1923–48], worked for SALIR 1938–43.

Zecchin Martinuzzi Vetri Artistici e Mosaici Glassworks in Murano, Italy [1932–39], named Ing F Zecchin 1936–39, designers include Alfredo Barbini, Giovanni Guerrini, Francesco Martinuzzi, Napoleone Martinuzzi, Otello Nason and Francesco Zecchin. Sig: no signatures; square paper label "Vetri Artistici e Mosaici – Zecchin Martinuzzi", (art glass; pasta, incamiciato, pulegoso).

Zecchin, Vittorio Glass designer from Italy [1878–1947], worked for Artisti Barovier 1913, VSM Cappelin-Venini 1921–25, AVEM 1932, Barovier Seguso Ferro 1933–35 and Fratelli Toso 1938.

Zehmenhütte Glassworks in Hohenbocka near Hoyerswerda OL, Germany [1874–c.1937–].

Zeiss, Carl Optical industry located in Jena, Thüringen, Germany [1846–present] and in Oberkochen, Ulm [1946–91]. Optical workshop established in 1846, first microscope 1847, first compound microscope 1857, optical theories developed by Ernst Abbe 1866, founded Schott & Gen in 1884, ultramicroscope 1903, UV-microscope 1904, fluorescence microscope 1904, planetarium 1923, factory bombed 1945, brain drain US and Russia 1945, refounded as Opton Optische Werke in Oberkochen 1946–51, renamed Zeiss 1951, VEB Carl Zeiss Jena state enterprise 1946–91, Carl Zeiss Jenoptik and Carl Zeiss Jena GmbH 1991–present. See Abbe, Ernst.

Zeldich, Asya D Glass designer from Lvov, Ukraine [1928–], worked at Kiev Factory 1954–64 and as chief designer at Peskovsky Glassworks 1964–67.

Železný Brod Glass/ ŽBS Glassworks located in Železný Brod, Czech Republic [1860–present], School of Glassmaking founded in 1920, merger of many small studios and glassmaking school in 1948, operates 7 Glassworks. Designers include Pavel Hlava c.1964/5, Stanislav Libenský c.1957/8 and Jindrich Tockstein c.1940s–1959. Sig: usually unsigned, labels only, (all glass types including costume jewellery).

Zeman, Otto Glass designer/decorator from Bohemia [–], active since the 1920s.

Zemek, František Glass designer from Czechoslovakia [–], furnace work glass at Pallme-König factory.

Zera-Crystal rt Glassworks in Halimba, Hungary [?–present].

Žertová, Jiřina Glass artist from Prague, Czech Republic [b.1932], worked independently from 1956, worked for Škrdlovice, Crystalex, Karlovarske Sklo and Bohemia Poděbrady, sculpture after 1970.

Zetland Glass Works Glassworks in Waterloo, Sydney, Australia [?–1927], merged with Crown Crystal in 1927.

Zeuner Artist from Amsterdam, Netherlands [c.18thC–1810], (gilt glasses; verre églomisé c.1810).

Zhigalkina, Elisaveta S Glass designer from Moscow, Russia [1923–], works produced at Dyatkovsky Cut Glass, Ivanischevsky, The Neman, Krasny Ghigant and Krasny May.

Zhulyev, Yuri V Glass designer from Rostov, Russia [1939–], worked at Vosstanie Glassworks after 1966 where he was chief designer from 1971.

Zibo Zhaohai Light Industrial Products Co Glassworks in Zibo, Shandong Province, China [?–present], (paperweights, mass produced).

Zich, Johann Glass maker located in Joachimstal, Austria [–], active c.1830.

Zich, Josef Glass maker located in Schwarzau, Austria [–], active c.1825.

Zignago Vetro Glassworks in Fossalta di Portogruaro/VE, Italy and in Empoli/FI, Italy [?–present], (tableware & pressed glass).

Zimmerman Art Glass Co Glass company located in Corydon, IN, USA [–], active 1960s–1980s, founded by Joseph Zimmerman, designers include Joseph Zimmerman and Gene Baxley, (paperweights 1960s–80s).

Zimmermann, Jörg F Glass designer from Uhingen, Germany [b.1940]. Sig: number only.

Zimpel, Julius Glass designer from Austria [1896–1925], member of the Wiener Werkstätte, worked for Ludwig Moser c.1920.

Zinc sulphide glass Glass formula developed by A Kirienen and E Ivanova, Russia 1950s; has a large range of thermal colour and opacity changes.

Zinovyev Glassworks in Russia [–], active 19thC.

Zircon Heisey blue-green colour later renamed Limelight.

Zirnsack, Arthur Glass designer from Russia [1944–], worked at Studio Glashyttan i Åhus, Sweden after 1977.

Zitzmann, Friedrich Glass designer and lamp worker from Wiesbaden, Germany [1840–1906], worked for Karl Köpping and designed for Rheinische Glashütte Köln-Ehrenfeld.

Zlatno, Verrerie Glassworks in Zlatno, Slovakia [?–present], aka Katarinska Huta, (operated by Slovglass).

Zmitko Decorative Glass Glassworks in Bilina, Czech Republic [1990–present], (hand-made bottles, tableware, giftware, ornamental glass, Borosilicate glass & Christmas ornaments).

Zoričák, Jan Glass artist from Ždiar, Slovakia [1944–], studied with Libenský, worked at Baccarat, Daum 1970–76 and at VSL after 1976.

Zoude & Cie, Louis Glassworks in Namur [1819–67], new factory in Jambes near Namur in 1849, Louis died in 1854 and the company merged with Herbatte 1865/7, was closed by VSL in 1879, (pressed glass after 1839; semi-crystal and crystal; made blanks for Regout; coloured crystal; lighting; matt and engraved items; lenses & flasks).

Zoude, Sébastien Glass maker from Namur [1709–79], founded the Zoude works, produced full lead crystal 1762/69.

Zoude, Verreries Sébastien Glassworks in Namur, Belgium [1753–1818], (tableware, crystal & milk glass).

Zoude-Drion, Veuve Glassworks in Jumet-Brûlotte, Charleroi, Belgium [1825–78], merged with SA des Manufactures in 1878, (bottles).

Zuber, Czeslaw Glass designer from Poland [1948–].

Zuccheri, Toni Glass designer from Venice, Italy [b.1937], worked for Venini c.1965 and Barovier e Toso c.1974–c.1990s.

Zvečevo Glassworks in Slavonia, Croatia [1842–1904], operated by Josef Lobmeyr until 1857, (bottles, cut glass, pressed glass, tableware; enamelled glass, flashed glass &

Annagrün).

Zwar, Neubauer & Co, Glashütte Glassworks in Weisswasser near Rothenburg, Germany [1873–1945], (tableware).

Zwart, Piet Glass designer from Holland [1885–1977], worked for Maastricht 1927–60s.

Zwiesel Town in Germany, location of Schott industries. The Zwiesel plant produces around 60 million wine glasses per year in an automated process.

Zwijndrechtse Glasfabriek See Bottleworks NV.

Zwischengoldglass Double walled glass decorated with gold leaf between the layers, produced in Bohemia, developed c.1725, popular c.1730–50, revival at the end of the 18thC and again at the end of the 19thC.

Zynsky, Toots Glass designer from USA [1951–], worked for Venini 1981–83.

BOTTLE MARKS

Anchor Glass Container
Corp., USA

Holzminden GmbH & Co.,
Glashüttenwerke,
Germany

Redfearn Glass, England

A.V.I.R., Aziende Vetrarie
Italiane Ricciardi SpA, Italy

Irish Glass plc, Ireland

Rockware Glass, England

Beatson Clark PLC, England

NV Verenigde
Glasfabrieken, Holland

Saint-Gobain Emballage,
France

Vetreria Parmense
Bormioli Rocco SpA, Italy

Nouvelles Verreries de
Momignies SA, Belgium

Verlipack, Belgium

BSN Emballage, France

Nienburger Glas, Himly,
Holscher GmbH & Co.,
Germany

Vetrerie Italiane VETR.I., Italy

Gerresheimer Glas AG,
Germany

Oberland Glas AG,
Germany

Vetropack, Switzerland

Giralt Laporta SA, Spain

Owens-Illinois, Owens-
Brockway, USA

Vicasa SA, Spain

H. Heye Glasfabrik, Germany

PLM Euroglas, Holland

Vidrala SA, Spain

Holmegaards Glasvaerker,
Denmark

European conformity mark;
(75 cl 83mm means
guaranteed to contain 75
ml if filled to 83 mm from
the top)

MUSEUMS WITH GLASS COLLECTIONS

AUSTRIA

Austrian Museum of Applied Art, Stubenring 5, A-1010 Vienna Tel. (+43) 1 71136 0
www.mak.at/indexe.html
*Website is in German. Contains a rich collection of glass and ceramics from Middle Ages to
present with emphasis on Venetian glass, cut and engraved glass, cased and cut-to-clear,
enamelled, iridescent, lustre and painted glasses. Recent acquisitions focus on 20th century
glass from Art Deco to the 1950s.*
Erstes Wiener Glasmuseum der Fa. Lobmeyr, 1 Kärntner Straße 26/2, Vienna
Tel. (+43) 512 05 08
www.magwien.gv.at/ma53/museen/glas.htm www.info.wien.at/e/mus/glasmus.htm
Both websites are in German.
Glas und Steinmuseum, Stadtplatz 34, Gmünd Tel. (+43) 02852 52506 18 or 38
www.gmuend.at/pages/sehenswuerdig/steinglas.htm
Collection of fine Biedermeier glass.
Sammlung der Neuen Stölzle Kristall GmbH Nagelberg-Glashütte Altnagelberg,
Hauptstraße 45, Alt-Nagelberg A3871 Tel. (+43) 02859 7531
www.volkskulturnoe.at/museen/0415.htm
Website is in German.
Steirisches Glaskunstzentrum und Glasmuseum Bärnbach Hochtregisterstraße 1,
A-8572 Bärnbach Tel. (+43) 03144 706800/03142 62950
Collection of Stölzle glass.

AUSTRALIA

National Gallery of Victoria, 285–321 Russell St, Melbourne VIC 8004 Tel. (+61) 3 9208 0222
www.ngv.vic.gov.au
Nicholson Museum, The University of Sydney 2006, Sydney Tel. (+61) 2 9351 3142
www.archaeology.usyd.edu.au/profile/nicholson_museum
*Museum of antiquities includes Anglo-Saxon jewellery, glass and pottery of the 6th
and 7th century.*

BELGIUM

Musée du Verre/ M.A.A.D.Musée des Antiquités et Arts Décoratifs, Quai de Maastricht 13/16,
B-4000 Liége, Tel. (+32) 4 221 94 04
www.ping.be/isllg/Doc/musees.htm
Website is in French. Large collection of Venetian glassware, façon de Venise, Val St.Lambert.
Royal Museums of Art and History, Parc du Cinquantenaire 10, 1000 Bruxelles
Tel. (+32) 02 741 7211
www.kmkg-mrah.be
Website is in French and Dutch.

CANADA

Glanmore National Historic Site, 257 Bridge St East, Belleville, Ontario Tel. (+1) 613 962 2329
www.suckercreek.on.ca/glanmore
Guelph Civic Museum, 6 Dublin St, Guelph, Ontario Tel. (+1) 519 836 5280
www.museum.guelph.on.ca/guelph.htm
Lambton Heritage Museum, Highway 21, Grand Bend, Ontario Tel. (+1) 519 243 2600
www.grandbend.com/lambton/museum.htm
Montreal Museum of Decorative Arts/Musée des Beaux Arts de Montreal, 1379 Sherbrooke,
Montreal, Quebec Tel. (+1) 514 285 1600
www.mbam.qc.ca
www.madm.org
A comprehensive collection of modern Italian and Scandinavian Art glass.
Royal Ontario Museum, Toronto, Ontario Tel. (+1) 416 586 5551
www.rom.on.ca

SWITZERLAND

Museum Ariana, Avenue de la Paix 10, 1202 Geneva Tel. (+41) 22 418 54 50
www.geneva.guide.ch/culture/museums/ariana_museum.html
*Website is in French. The Geneva municipal collection of 18,000 items mainly in porcelain
and pottery but also some glass.*
Musée d'Art et d'Histoire de Neuchâtel, Esplanade Léopold-Robert 1, CH2001 Neuchâtel
Tel. (+41) 32 717 79 20/5
www.nenet.ch/musees/musee_art_hist.htm

CUBA

Museum of Decorative Arts, Calle 17 No.502 e/ D y E, Vedado Havana
Glass collection includes Baccarat, Venetian and Catalonian crystal.

CZECHOSLOVAKIA

Museum of Decorative Arts, Umelecko-Prúmyslove Museum. Ul. 17 Listopadu, Prague
Important collections of Czech glass.
Muzeum skla a bižuterie (MSB) Jiráskova 4 CZ466 01 Jabloneč nad Nisou
Tel. (+420) 0428 311681
Fine collection of Bohemian glass.

GERMANY

Dorotheenhütte Wolfach Geschwister Hillebrand GmbH, Glashüttenweg 4, D77709 Wolfach
Tel. (+49) 7834 83980
www.dorotheenhuette.de
Website is in German.
Germanisches Nationalmuseum, Kartäusergasse 1, D-90402 Nürnberg Tel. (+49) 911 13310
www.gnm.de
Website is in German. 14,000 objects including glass, ceramic, metal, textiles, wood.
Glasmuseum Alter, Hof Letter Berg 38, 48653-Coesfeld-Lette, Hessisches Landesmuseum
Darmstadt, Friedensplatz 1, D-64283 Darmstadt Tel. (+49) 6151 165703
*Collections include Art Nouveau glass by Olbrich, Behrens, Lalique, Gallé, Ashbee,
Van de Velde, Hoffmann, Eisenloeffel and Tiffany.*
Glasmuseum Boffzen, Bahnhofstr 9, D-37691 Boffzen Tel. (+49) 5271 49909
Glasmuseum Burg Dringenberg, Burgstraße 33 D-33014 Driburg Tel. (+49) 052 59/15 51
Glasmuseums Frauenau, Am Museumspark 1, D94258, Frauenau Tel. (+49) 099 26 / 94 99 35
www.eisch.de/glasmuse.htm
www.glasmuseum-frauenau.de
Both websites are in German. Contemporary glass.
Glasmuseum Hentrich im Kunstmuseum, Ehrenhof 5, D-40479 Düsseldorf
Tel. (+49) 211 8992460
www.kunstmuseum-duesseldorf.de
*Website is in German. One of the largest glass museums in Europe with a vast collection of glass
from Roman times to contemporary Studio glass. All variations of Art Nouveau are represented,
and the collection of Gallé, Tiffany, Koepping, Lötz and Schneider glass is world famous. Other
collections in the museum include medieval glass, Persian, Indian and Chinese glass, and modern
Italian, Scandinavian and German glass.*
Glasmuseum Immenhausen/Süssmuth; Am Bahnhof 3, D34376 Immenhausen
Tel. (+49) 567 32060
http://immenhausen.de/pages/museen.htm www.polytechnik.uni-kassel.de/museen/ks-
l/glas.htm
Website is in German.
Glasmuseum, Oberwarmensteinacher Str.420, D95485 Warmensteinach Tel. (+49) 927 71401
GlasMuseum Rheinbach, Himmeroder Weg 6, D53359 Rheinbach Tel. (+49) 2226 14224/14231
Glasmuseum Weisswasser, Forster Strasse 12, D-02943 Weisswasser Tel. (+49) 3576 204000
www.glaskompetenzzentrum.de/glasmuseum/museum01.htm
Website is in German.
Glasmuseum Wertheim, Mühlenstr 24, D-97877 Wertheim Tel. (+49) 934 26866
www.glasmuseum.wertheim.de
Kunstgewerbemseum, Matthäikirchplatz, D10785 Berlin Tiergarten Tel. (+49) 402 662902
www.smb.spk-berlin.de/kgm
Museum für Angewandte Kunst, An der Rechtschule, 50667 Köln Tel. (+49) 221 2212/6714
www.museenkoeln.de/museenkoeln/mak/index.html
*Website is in German. Italian glass 16th century, German glass from 17th–18th century and Art
Nouveau.*
Passauer Glasmuseum, Am Rathausplatz, 94032 Passau Tel. (+49) 851 35071
www.passau.de/passau/Kultur/glasmuse.htm
*Website is in German. One of the largest collections of Bavarian and Bohemian Art Nouveau glass
in the world.*
Rheinisches Landesmuseum, Weimarer Allee 1, D54290 Trier Tel. (+49) 651 97740
www.uni-trier.de/trier/lm/rlmt.htm
Website is in German.

DENMARK

Danish Museum of Decorative Arts, Bredgade 68, DK1260 Copenhagen Tel. (+45) 3314 9452
www.mus-kim.dk/kim.htm
*European glass: drinking glasses etc, from Venice, Bohemia, Silesia and Norway. Special collection
of Zwischengoldglas.*
International Glass Museum of Denmark, Strandvejen 8, DK8400 Ebeltoft Tel. (+45) 8634 1799
www.glass.dk
Contemporary Studio glass.
Rosenborg Castle, Øster Voldgade 4 A, 1350 Copenhagen Tel. (+45) 3315 3286
www.aok.dk/E/V/CPHDK/0006/13/86/cs2.html

ESTONIA

Tarbekunstimuseum/Applied Art Museum, Lai Street 17 EE-10133, Tallinn, Estonia

EIRE

The Civic Museum, City Assembly House, 58 South William St, Dublin 2 Tel. (+353) 1 6794260
www.visit.ie/countries/ie/dublin/top_at/23_nationalmuseum.htm
Historic museum.

The National Museum of Ireland, Collins Barracks, Dublin 7 Tel. (+353) 1 6777444
Irish cut glass and tableware from the 17th–19th century.

FRANCE

Atelier-Musée Du Verre De Trelon, rue Clavon, F59132 Trélon Tel. (+33) 3 27606611
www.univ-lille1.fr/ush/accueil/index.htm
Website is in French. Museum dedicated to bottles and bottle production.

Musée des Arts Décoratifs, rue Bouffard F-33000 Bordeaux Tel. (+33) 5 5600 7250/5 5600 7251
www.ucad.fr/ucadgb/artydeco_eng.html
French decorative art of the 18th and 19th century; Bordeaux historical items. Paintings, furniture, sculpture, ceramics, glass and silver.

Musée des Arts Décoratifs, Palais du Louvre, 107/111 rue de Rivoli, F75001 Paris 1
Tel. (+33) 1 44555750/42604948
www.paris.org/Musees/Decoratifs www.ucad.fr/ucadgb/index.html
Collections contain glass from early times to the present day: cut and engraved crystal tableware, Art Nouveau glass, French glass, Bohemian glass, contemporary glass. There is a study collection at the Centre du Verre which has limited opening hours, so check first.

Musée d'Art et d'Histoire de Provence/Musée International de la Parfumerie, 2 rue Mirabeau,
F-06130 Grasse Tel. (+33) 4 9336 0161
www.museesdegrasse.com
Perfume bottles.

Musée Atelier du Verre de Sars-Poteries, 1 rue du Général de Gaulle, F-59216 Sars-Poteries
Tel. (+33) 3 2761 6144
http://www.cr-npdc.fr/tourisme/toursimindust/sars.htm
Website is in French. Said to be the most important collection of contemporary Studio glass in France.

Musée Baccarat, 30 bis, rue de Paradis 75010 Paris X Tel. (+33) 1 4022 1167/4770 6430
www.paris.org/Musees/Baccarat/info.html
Includes showpieces created for world exhibitions.

Musée des Beaux Arts, 3 pl. Stanislas, F-54000 Nancy Tel. (+33) 3 8385 3072/6
www.mobydoc.fr/utilis/lorraine/nancyba.html
Website is in French.

Musée Cluny, 6 Place Paul Painlevé, 75005 Paris Tel. (+33) 1 5373 7800.
Medieval museum.

Musée du Cristal Baccarat, R.N.
A nice selection of Baccarat showpieces in a village with several dozen glass shops.

Musée du Cristal, 20 rue des cristalleries, 54000 Nancy Tel. (+33) 3 8376 6006
Factory museum for Daum/Sèvres glass.

Musée de l'Ecole de Nancy, 36–38 rue du Sergent Blandan, F-54000 Nancy
Tel. (+33) 3 8340 1486

Musée de La Verrerie, Manoir de Fontaine, F-76340 Blangy-sur-Brestle Tel. (+33) 2359 44479

Verrerie-Crystallerie de la Rochère, Galerie d'Art Contemporain, F-70210 Passavant-La-Rochere
Tel. (+33) 3 8478 6100

FINLAND

Design Forum Finland, Fabianinkat 10, Fin 00130, Helsinki Tel. (+358) 9 6220 810
www.designforum.fi/eng
Contemporary design.

Finnish Glass Museum, Tehlaankatu 23, Riihimäki, Finland Fin 11910, Riihimäki
Tel. (+358) 1 9741 494/1 9741 7494
www.riihimaki.fi/lasimus

Museum of Art and Design, Korkeavuorenkatu 23, Fin 00130, Helsinki Tel. (+358) 9 6220 540
www.designmuseum.fi

National Museum of Finland, P.O. Box 913, Fin 00101, Helsinki Tel. (+358) 9 40501
www.nba.fi/NATMUS/kmeg.html

Nuutajärven Lasimuseo, SF31160 358, Nuutajärvi Tel. (+358) 2 0439 6504

GREAT BRITAIN

Ashmolean Museum of Art And Archaeology, Beaumont St, Oxford, OX1 2PH
Tel. (+44) 0186 527 8000
www.ashmol.ox.ac.uk

Brighton Art Gallery and Museum, Church St, Barnsley, BN1 1EE Tel. (+44) 0127 329 0290

British Museum, Great Russell St, London, WC1B 3DG Tel. (+44) 020 7636 1555
www.thebritishmuseum.ac.uk
Antiquities.
Broadfield House Glass Museum, Compton Drive, Kingswinford, W. Midlands, DY6 9NS
Tel. (+44) 0138 481 2745
www.aboutbritain.com/BroadfieldHouseGlassMuseum.htm
The collections cover a broad range from 18th century to contemporary work, from Regency cut decanters to Victorian cameo, Art Deco clocks and pressed glass.
Caithness Visitor's Centre, Inveralmond, Perth, PH1 3TZ Tel. (+44) 0173 863 7373
Caithnessglass.co.uk/caithness.htm
Paperweights and paperweight manufacture.
The Fitzwilliam Museum, University of Cambridge, Turpington St, Cambridge, CB2 1RB
Tel. (+44) 0122 333 2904
www.fitzmuseum.cam.ac.uk
Extensive collection of pottery, furniture, silver and glass especially. Arts and Crafts but also some Peking glass.
Harvey Wine Museum, 12 Denmark St, Bristol, BS1 5DQ Tel. (+44) 0117 927 5036
www.soc.surrey.ac.uk/~scs1sp/hwm/main.htm
National Glass Centre, Liberty Way, Sunderland, SR6 OGL Tel. (+44) 0191 5155555
Pilkington Museum of Glass, Presot Road, St Helen's, Merseyside, WA10 3TT
Tel. (+44) 0174 428 882
Royal Scottish Museum, Kelvingrove, Glasgow, GS 8AG Tel. (+44) 0141 287 2699
www.g3web.co.uk/glasgow_museum
Large and well balanced 20th century Art glass collection includes Scottish, Italian and Scandinavian glass.
Turner Museum of Glass, Dept. of Engineering Materials, Sir Robert Hatfield Building, Mappin St, Sheffield, S. Yorkshire, S1 4DU Tel. (+44) 0114 275 4325
The Victoria and Albert Museum, Cromwell Road, South Kensington, London SW7 2RL
Tel. (+44) 020 7938 8500
www.vam.ac.uk
One of the top three glass museums in Europe with a wide collection throughout the ages, shown in the purpose built glass gallery. Well presented study collection.
World of Glass, St Helen's Lyd, Shalon Way East, St Helen's, Merseyside, W8N 1BX
Tel. (+44) 0174 422 766
www.worldofglass.com

HUNGARY

Hungarian National Museum, 14–16 Múzeum krt, Budapest Tel. (+36) 1 1382 122
http://www.fsz.bme.hu/hungary/budapest/bpmuz/bpmuz14.htm
Museum of Applied Arts, 33-37 Üllöi út, Budapest Tel. (+36) 1 2175 222

CROATIA

Muzej za Umjetnost I Obrt MUO, Trg Maršala Tita 10, Zagreb
www.tel.hr/muo/ www.artplus.hr
www.accson.se/almi/glasmuseum/hinfo.html/muo

ITALY

Museo Barovier e Toso, Isola di Murano, Palazzo Contarini, F.ta Vetrai 28, Venezia
Tel. (+39) 041 739049
Museo del Vetro di Altare, Via Restagno 2, I-17041 Altare/SV Tel. (+39) 19 584734
www.imm.it/isvav/italiana.htm
Museo Vetrario di Murano, Murano Tel. (+39) 516 6269200
www.castellobanfi.com/tour/glass.html
Museo del Vetro di Murano, Fta. Giustian 8, I-30141 Venezia Tel. (+39) 417 39586
www.castellobanfi.com/tour/glass.html
Website is in Italian.

JAPAN

Hokkaido Museum of Modern Art, Kita1, Nishi17, Chuo-ku, Sapporo, Hokkaido 060-0001, Japan
Tel. (+81) 011 644 6881
www.dnp.co.jp/museum/doritsu/hokkaido-e.html
Contemporary art, especially glass.
Niijima Contemporary Glass Art Center
www.guild.ne.jp/niijima/museum/index.html

MEXICO

Vitro's Museum of Glass, Zaragoza S17, Col. Treviño, Monterey, CP 64570
Tel. (+52) 8 3291070 (ext.1105)
www.vto.com/vto/frame2.htm

Website is in Spanish.

NORWAY

Hadelands Glassmuseum
Kunstindustrimuseet, St.Olavsgate 1, N-0165 Jevnaker Tel. (+47) 2 2036540
http://jevnaker.guiden.no
Website is in Norwegian. Glass, ceramics, textile, furniture and industrial design.

NETHERLANDS

Nationaal Glasmuseum, Lingedijk 28, 4142LD Leerdam Tel. (+31) 34 5612714
http://www.royalleerdamcristal.nl/ned/museumfra.htm
Website is in Dutch. Specializes mainly in Leerdam glass. Changing exhibitions.
Rijksmuseum, Stadhouderskade 42 , Amsterdam Tel. (+31) 20 6732121
The collection of the Rijksmuseum includes glass from the Middle Ages through to Art Nouveau.

POLAND

Museum of Applied Art/Muzeum Sztuk Uzytkowych, ul. Góra Przemyslawa 1, PL61768 Poznan
Tel. (+61) 8522035
www.info.poznan.pl/Culture/Museums/AppliedArt.html

RUSSIA

Dyatkovo Glasshouse, 184 Lenin str, Dyatkovo, 242630 Bryansk reg
Tel. (+7) 08333 22897/21799
www.admin.debryansk.ru/~press/Dyatkovo.html
Website is in Russian. Showing the 200-year factory history plus antiquities, 19th–20th century decorative crystal and contemporary pieces.

SWEDEN

Eda Glass Museum, Folkparken Eda, S67392 Chalottenberg Tel. (+46) 05 71231 01
www.edaglas.com
Website is in Swedish.
Flygsfors Glasbruk, SE 380 40 Orrefors Tel.(+46) 04 81301 11
Small museum, tours of old factory
Glasbruksmuseet i Surte, Kvarnvägen 6, S44555 Surte Tel. (+46) 03 0333 0939/0106
Dedicated to bottles and bottle production.
Johansfors Glasbruk, Kvarnvagen 2, SE 361 53 Broakulla Tel. (+46) 04 71402 70
Small but interesting; historic glass.
Kosta Glasbruk, SE 360 52 Kosta Tel. (+46) 04 78345 00
Excellent presentation, large number of exhibits.
Kulturhistoriska Museet, Box 1095, SE 221 64 Lund
Lindshammar Glasbruk, Box 1005, SE 574 24 Vetlanda Tel. (+46) 383 21050
Small but interesting exhibition features pieces by Ohrstrom.
National Museum, Södra Blaiseholmshamnen, S10324 Stockholm
Tel. (+46) 08 5195 4300/08 6113803
www.nationalmuseum.se
Website is in Swedish.
Orrefors Glasbruk - Orrefore Museum, SE 380 40 Orrefors Tel. (+46) 481 34195
Excellent presentation, large number of exhibits.
Pukebergarnas Vag., SE 38234 Nybro, Tel. (+46) 481 80029
Excellent presentation. New exhibition hall.
The Röhss Museum, Vasagatan 37–39, S-40015 Göteborg Tel. (+46) 31 613850
Museum of applied art and design has exhibitions of European arts and crafts from the 17th century to the present, and an important section on 20th century Scandinavian design.
Rohsska Konstslojdmuseet, Box 53178, SE 400 15 Göteborg
Smålands Museum, Box 102, SE 351 04 Växjö Tel. (+46) 470 451 45
www.smalandsmuseum.g.se/engelsk.htm
Fantastic exhibition, the best museum in Sweden for both historic and contemporary glass
Skruf Glasbruk, SE 360 53 Skruv, Tel. (+46) 478 20133
Sundsvall Hantverks Museum, SE 85250 Sundsvall
lhttp://www.xs4all.nl/~abel/
Swedish Glass Museum, Södra Järnvagsgatan 2, Box 102, SE-351 04 Växjö
Tel. (+46) 047 07042 00
www.smalandsmuseum.g.se/engelsk.html
Sveriges Glasmuseum/Smålands Museum, Växjö Tel. (+46) 470 45145
www.telemuseum.se/museer

SLOVENIA

National Museum of Slovenia, Muzejska ul. 1, SI-1000 Ljubljana, Slovenija
Tel. (+38) 61 241 4400

http://www.narmuz-lj.si
Slovenian glass from the Middle Ages to, the present, including archeological finds.

TURKEY

Pasabahce Glass Museum, Istanbul Tel. (+90) 2163 955473
488 pieces dating from 600 BC to the present. Roman and Byzantine glass, Beykoz and European glass. Important Beykoz glass collection includes clear and coloured glasses, opal glassware and 'cesm-i bulbuller' glass; bottles, ewers, decanters, sugar bowls, rose water flasks, bowls, vases, plates and ornaments.

UNITED STATES

Arkansas State University Museum, Jonesboro, Continuing Ed. Bldg, P. O. Box 60 State University Tel. (+1) 870 972 2074
http://ohwy.com/ar/a/arstunmv.htm
Museum of Science & History, MacArthur Park, Little Rock AR72202 Tel. (+1) 501 324 9231
American pattern glass.
Old State House Museum, 300 W. Markham, Little Rock AR72201 Tel. (+1) 501 324 9685
The Bead Museum, 5754 W. Glenn Drive, Glendale, Arizona Tel. (+1) 623 931 2737
www.thebeadmuseum.com
Los Angeles County Museum of Art 5905 Wilshire Bd, Los Angeles CA90036 Tel. (+1) 213 857 6000
www.lacma.org/lacma.htm
1,000 pieces from China, Asia, Mediterranean, Western Europe and USA. Also contains American pressed and blown pieces. W. Randolph Hearst and the W. Dan Quattlebaum Collections of Lacy and non-Lacy glass from Sandwich, New England and Bakewell.
San Diego Museum of Art, 1450 El Prado, Balboa Park, San Diego Tel. (+1) 619 232 7931
www.sddt.com/sdma.html
Fine Arts Museum of San Francisco, Golden Gate Park Tel. (+1) 415 750 3636
www.famsf.org
Bowers Museum, 2002 N. Main St, Santa Ana, California Tel. (+1) 870 972 2074
www.bowers.org
Redlands Historical Glass Museum, 1157 Orange St, Redlands CA92373 Tel. (+1) 909 798 0868
www.rth.org/lookingglass
Wadsworth Athenaeum, 600 Main St, Hartford CT06103 Tel. (+1) 203 278 2670
www.wadsworthatheneum.org
www.hartnet.org/~wadsworth
2,000 pieces of glass from around the world. Fine enamelled, engraved, Venetian glass. Collection of Lacy glass and pattern glass.
Yale University Art Gallery, 111 Chapel St, New Haven CT06520 Tel. (+1) 203 436 0574
www.yale.edu/artgallery
2,600 Ancient, Islamic pieces, plus 18th and 19th century American free blown, pattern moulded, cut and pressed glass. Also examples of Tiffany, Dorflinger, Steuben, Amelung tumblers, Boston & Sandwich.
Lyman Allyn Museum, 625 Williams St, New London CT06320 Tel. (+1) 203 443 2545
800 pieces of mostly New England glass.
Winterthur Museum, Route 52, Winterthur DE19735 Tel. (+1) 800 448 3883
www.winterthur.org
1,200 American, English, Irish and European pieces. Colonial American tableware, drinking vessels and lighting devices. Also an extensive collection of Amelung, South Jersey, blown-three-mould, figured flasks, Steigel and European glass.
The Lannan Foundation, 601 Lake Ave, Lake Worth FL23460
600 American & European pieces – ancient and 20th century.
Laymon Memorial Collection-American Glass, Anne Pfeiffer Chapel, Florida Southern College, Lakeland FL33802 Tel. (+1) 863 855 1302
500 American and European pieces – mostly American.
Pensacola Historical Museum, 405 South Adams St, Pensacola FL32501 Tel. (+1) 805 443 5455
400 American and English pieces including Tiffany, Carder, Mt. Washington, Webb, Quezal, Lutz, Gallé and Lalique.
Lightner Museum, St. Augustine FL32084 Tel. (+1) 904 824 2874
www.lightnermuseum.org
500 pieces; Mostly American, some French. Art Glass and large collection of brilliant cut glass, compotes, salts. Much is not on display but can be made available with prior arrangement.
The Morse Gallery of Art, 133 E. Welbourn Ave, Winter Park FL32789 Tel. (+1) 305 644 3686
450 American and European pieces from mid 19th to 20th century. Tiffany, Gallé, Steuben, Loetz, Quezal.
Brunnier Gallery Iowa State University, 290 Scheman Blvd, Ames IA50011 Tel. (+1) 515 294 3342
www.museums.iastate.edu/Bam/brunnierartmuseum.html
400 engraved English and German glass including Art Nouveau, Biedermeier tumblers, etc.
Chicago Historical Society, Clark St at North Ave, Chicago IL60614 Tel. (+1) 312 642 4600

www.chicagohistory.org
1,000 American and European pieces from 18th–20th century. Emphasis on glass used in the settlement of Chicago and the Midwest.
The Art Institute of Chicago, Michigan Ave at Adams St, Chicago IL60603 Tel. (+1) 312 443 3600
www.artic.edu/aic/index.html
4,000 comprehensive pieces of ancient to modern glass including a collection of cup plates and pressed milk glass.
Illinois State Museum, Spring & Edwards Streets, Springfield IL62706 Tel. (+1) 217 782 7386
www.museum.state.il.us
1,100 pieces of mostly American glass, paperweights, Depression and pressed glass in period room settings.
Greentown Glass Museum Greentown, 112 N. Meridian, Greentown IN46936
Tel. (+1) 317 628 7386
www.eastern.k12.in.us/gpl/museum.htm
http://birch.palni.edu/~lhurst/gplhome/museum.htm
5,000 pieces of glass made by the Indiana Tumbler & Goblet Co. that produced unique forms and colours, including Chocolate Glass, Golden Agate (Holly Amber), Nile Green, etc.
Indianapolis Museum of Art, 1200 W.38th St, Indianapolis IN46208 Tel. (+1) 317 923 1331
www.ima-art.org
Contains several collections, including the Lion Pattern and Lacy glass. The collection is not regularly on display.
Thomas County Museum, 1525 W. 4th St, Colby KS67701 Tel. (+1) 913 462 6972
3,000 American and European pieces of Art glass, Sandwich, Mt. Vernon, Stiegel-type, Gallé, etc.
Spencer Museum of Art, The University of Kansas, Lawrence KS66045 Tel. (+1) 913 842 1646
1,000 American, European and Far Eastern pieces. Including 19th century American wineglasses and snuff bottles.
New Orleans Museum of Art, City Park Le Long Ave, New Orleans LA70179
Tel. (+1) 504 488 2631
www.noma.org/noma2.html
3,000 pieces of ancient to modern American, English, European and Asian glass including Amelung, Stiegel, South Jersey and Midwestern blown, three-mould and pattern-mould glass. Also Art Nouveau to contemporary.
R.W. Norton Art Gallery, 4747 Creswell Ave, Shreveport LA71106 Tel. (+1) 318 865 4201
www.softdisk.com/comp/norton
1,250 American and European pieces, Steuben and paperweights. Much of the pressed glass collection represents three patterns: Lion, Westward Ho! and U.S. Coin that are permanently displayed. Also has a collection of Steuben glass.
New Bedford Glass Museum, New Bedford MA02742 Tel. (+1) 617 994 0115
http://www.infonavigate.com/boston/60.htm
Sandwich Glass Museum, 129 Main St, PO Box 103, Sandwich MA02563
Tel. (+1) 617 888 0251
Baltimore Museum of Art, Art Museum Drive, Baltimore MD21218 Tel. (+1) 410 396 7100
www.artbma.org
650 European, English, Irish and American pieces from ancient to modern.
The Jones Gallery of Glass & Ceramics, East Baldwin ME04024 Tel. (+1) 207 787 3370
1,500 Glass and Ceramics from ancient to modern American, European and Asian including N.E. Glass, Steuben, Carder, Tiffany, Webb, etc.
Portland Museum of Art, 111 High St, Portland ME04101 Tel. (+1) 207 775 6148
www.portlandmuseum.org
1,000 American and European pieces from 18th century to present, particularly Portland glass.
Greensboro Historical Museum 130 Summit Ave, Greensboro NC27401 Tel. (+1) 919 373 2043
www.library.greensboro.lib.nc.us/museum
800 American and European pieces. Blown bottles, lab and medical equipment, goblets, pressed pattern glass, tableware, oil lamps and some Tiffany. Robert and Capelia McKinney Collection of American Commemorative Glass. representing the history of the United States in glass. It includes pattern glass, novelties, flasks, bottles, etc.
New Hampshire Historical Society, 30 Park St, Concord NH03301 Tel. (+1) 603 225 3381
1,300 18th to 20th century pieces of American and European glass with emphasis on New Hampshire. Tableware, lighting devices, decorative items and containers.
Currier Gallery of Art, 201 Myrtle Way, Manchester NH03104 Tel. (+1) 603 669 6144
www.currier.org
3,000 late 18th to 20th century pieces of American and European glass with the emphasis on New Hampshire and New England. Free blown, mould-blown and pattern-moulded. Art glass from all well known houses.
Museum of American Glass, Millville NJ08332 Tel. (+1) 800 998 4552
www.wheatonvillage.org
Over 7,000 pieces on display. American, particularly 18th to 20th century Colonial. Outstanding Art glass, Art Nouveau and Studio glass. Early Art glass, housewares, etc. One of the largest museums in the U.S. devoted to American glass.

Newark Museum, 49 Washington St, Newark NJ07101 Tel. (+1) 201 733 6600/596 6550
2,500 pieces of ancient glass to present, from Middle East, Europe, America and Asia. New Jersey glass, Art Nouveau, Art Deco, paperweights, pressed and cut glass.

Salem County Historical Society, 79–83 Market St, Salem NJ08079 Tel. (+1) 609 935 5004
500 pieces of 18th to 20th century glass from South Jersey. Housewares, bottles, pharmaceutical jars, etc.

New Jersey State Museum, 205 West State St, Trenton NJ08625 Tel. (+1) 609 292 6300
www.state.nj.us/state/museum/musidx.html
500 pieces of New Jersey glass. 1750–1980. Wistarburgh to Paul Stankard. Pressed and blown, (by appointment only: Tel. (+1) 609 292 5421).

Brooklyn Museum, Eastern Parkway, Brooklyn NY11238 Tel. (+1) 212 638 5000
www.brooklynart.org
3,000 ancient to contemporary pieces including Tiffany, Dorflinger, New England glass and Libbey. Several major collections.

Corning Museum of Glass, Corning Glass Center, Corning NY14831 Tel. (+1) 607 937 5371
www.cmog.org
The ultimate glass museum. Many collections, mostly American, European and ancient glass items. It is the largest in the United States devoted exclusively to glass. Exhibits include art, science and history of glassmaking from ancient times to present day. There is a 900 piece collection of Lacy glass.

Tuthill Cut Glass Co. Museum, Middletown NY10940 Tel. (+1) 914 361 3211
500 pieces from 1900–1923 including Tuthill cut glass, wineglasses and punch bowls.

Cooper-Hewitt Museum, 2 East 91st St, New York City NY10028 Tel. (+1) 212 860 6868
1,000 American, European, Middle Eastern, Asian and Scandinavian pieces. Emphasis on design elements.

Metropolitan Museum of Art, 82nd St & Fifth Ave, New York City NY10028–0198
Tel. (+1) 212 879 5500
www.metmuseum.org
20,000 pieces from 2000 BC to present from Western Europe, Near East and North America. Collections of American glass from all Eastern US glass houses.

Museum of Modern Art, 11 West 53rd St, New York City NY10019
Tel. (+1) 212 956 6100/212 708 9400
www.moma.org
600 pieces – Art Nouveau to present. Tiffany to Studio. Joseph Heil Collection of Gallé, etc.

Museum of the City of New York, Fifth Ave at 103rd St, New York NY10029
Tel. (+1) 212 534 1672
www.mcny.org
1,000 American, English and Continental pieces. The glass is not exhibited except in the 1906 room.

New York Historical Society, 170 Central Park West, New York City NY10024
Tel. (+1) 212 873 3400
www.nyhistory.org
2,000 pieces from Eastern and Midwestern United States and Western Europe. Includes Sandwich, Stiegel-type, Favrile, 400+ paperweights from the Jennie H. Sinclair collection. The pressed glass collection is mainly Lacy and coloured Sandwich glass, including cup plates, vases and candlesticks.

Margaret Woodbury Strong Museum, One Manhattan Square, Rochester NY14607
Tel. (+1) 716 263 2700
www.strongmuseum.org
7,500 pieces from mid 1800s to present. American and European Art glass and Asian. Extensive pressed/pattern glass representing the social and cultural northeastern America from 1820 to the present.

Degenhart Paperweight & Glass Museum, 177 & Rt. 22, Cambridge OH43725
Tel. (+1) 614 432 2626
www.carnivalglass.net
5,000 pieces. Almost every category of American Glass especially Midwestern pattern glass, Cambridge glass and Degenhart paperweights.

Cincinnati Museum of Art, Eden Park, Cincinnati OH45202 Tel. (+1) 513 7215204
www.cincinnatiartmuseum.org
500 pieces from ancient times to present. 19th century American glass; jugs, flasks, English cameo, Roman and Persian glass. William T. Howe Collection, N. Jersey, Pittsburgh and Ohio glass.

COLLECTORS' CLUBS & ASSOCIATIONS

The Akro Agate Collectors' Club
10 Bailey Street, Clarksburg, WV 26301, USA

American Carnival Glass Association
PO Box 235, Littletown, PA 17340, USA

American Cut Glass Association
PO Box 482, Ramona, CA 92065, USA

Association of Bottled Beer Collectors
http://ourworld.compuserve.com/homepages
/john_mann/abbchome.htm

Avon Collectors Club with links and message
board
www.icollectavon.com

Bytown Bottle Seekers Club, Canada
www.cyberus.ca/~pmarchan/bbsc

Cambridge Collectors
PO Box 416, Cambridge, OH 42735, USA
www.cambridgeglass.org

Cambridge Paperweight Circle
www.adc-ltd.demon.co.uk/paperweights

Canadian Depression Glass Association
www.members.home.net/cdga

Candlewick Club
275 Milledge Terrace, Athens, GA 30606, USA

Collectible Carnival Glass Association
2360 N. Old S R 9, Columbus, IN 47203, USA

Collectors of Findlay Glass
PO Box 256, Findlay, OH 45839, USA

Custard Glass Collectors' Society
591 SW Duxbury Ave, Port St Lucie, FL
34983, USA

Czechoslovakian Collectors Guild
PO Box 901395, Kansas City, MO 64190, USA

Early American Pattern Glass Society
PO Box 266, Colesburg, IA 52035, USA
www.eapgs.org

Federation of Historical Bottle Collectors
www.fohbc.com

Fenton Art Glass Collectors
PO Box 384, Williamstown, WV 26187, USA
www.collectoronline.com/club-FACCA.html

Fostoria Glass Collectors
PO Box 1625, Orange, CA 92668, USA
www.fostoriacollectors.org

Fostoria Glass Society
PO Box 826, Moundsville, WV 26041, USA
www.fostoriaglass.org

Fostoria Glass Assoc.
109 N Main St, Fostoria, OH 44830, USA

Glass Collectors Club of Toledo
6122 Cross Trails Rd, Sylvania, OH 43560, USA

Heisey Collectors' of America
www.ahheisey.com

International Paperweight Society
www.paperweight.com

Marble Collectors' Society of America
www.blocksite.com

Miniature Bottle Collector Online
www.bottlecollecting.com

National American Glass Club
www.glassclub.org

National Association of Milk Bottle Collectors
www.collectoronline.com/club-NAMBC-
wp.html

National Fenton Glass Society
www.axces.com/NFGS

National Imperial Glass Collectors' Society
PO Box 534, Bellaire, OH 43906, USA

www.imperialglass.org

National Milk Glass Collectors' Society
500 Union Cemetery Road, Greensburg, PA
15601, USA

National Milk Glass Collectors' Association
www.nmgcs.org

National Reamer Collectors' Association
www.reamers.org

National Westmoreland Glass Collectors' Club,
PO Box 625, Irwin, PA 15692, USA

New England Carnival Glass Club
10 Seminole Road, Canton, MA 02021, USA

Old Morgantown Glass Collectors' Club
PO Box 894, Morgantown, WV 26507, USA

Pacific Northwest Fenton Association
PO Box 881, Tillamook, OR 97141, USA
www.glasscastle.com/pnwfa.htm

Pairpoint Cup Plate Collectors
Box 52D, E Wetmouth, MA 02189, USA

Painted Soda Bottle Collectors' Association
www.collectoronline.com/PSBCA/PSBCA.html

Paperweight Collectors Association
PO Box 1263, Beltsville MD 20704, USA

Paperweight Collectors Society
www.paperweight.org

Phoenix/Consolidated Collectors
41 River View Drive, Essex Junction, VT
05452, USA

Port Nicholson Miniature Bottle Collectors'
Club
www.voyager.co.nz/~dsmith/index

Rose Bowl Collectors
1111 Delps Road, Danielsville, PA 18038, USA

Salt Shaker Collectors' Society
www.cbantiques.com/SSC

Stretch Glass Society
508 Turnberry Lane, St Augustine, FL 32084,
USA
http://members.aol.com/stretchgl

Southeastern Antique Bottle Club
http://home.attn.net/~Fred-Taylor

Surrey Bottle Collectors' Club
www.surreyad.co.uk/bottle/sbccl.html

Tiffin Glass Collectors Club
PO Box 554, Tiffin, OH 44883, USA
http://zeus.kspress.com/woodsland/duncan/i
ndex3.htmTiffin Glass Collectors Club

Toothpick Holder Collectors
PO Box 417, Safety Harbor, FL 34695, USA

Vaseline Glass Collectors
PO Box 125, Russellville, MO 65074, USA
www.icnet/users/davepeterson

Wavecrest Collectors' Club
PO Box 2013, Santa Barbara, CA 93120, USA

Westmoreland Glass Society
513 Fifth Avenue, Coralville, IA 51141, USA

Whimsey Glass Club
20 William Street, Danville, NY 14437, USA

World Wide Web Carnival Glass Club
www.woodsland.com/carnivalglass/pages/w
wwcga.html

INTERNET RESOURCES

The following list is a guide to what sites might be of interest to the glass collector on the Internet. Most sites offer additional links to other areas of interest. All the sites listed below were correct at the time of going to press but please remember the Internet is a rapidly changing world with sites constantly on the move. Be sensible if you wish to purchase anything online and make sure you take all precautions to protect yourself and your purchase.

MAGAZINES & NEWSLETTERS

Antique Bottle Collector Magazine includes online auctions www.glswrk-auction.com
Antiques Trade Gazette has information about all UK fairs & auctions plus news
www.atg-online.com
AntiqueWeek Online is packed with information for collectors & dealers www.antiqueweek.com
Bottles & Bygones Magazine for UK bottle collectors
www.members.tripod.com/MikeSheridan/page2.htm
Depression Era Glassware Magazine is a subscriber magazine www.dgshopper.com
Glass and Art is a quarterly magazine from Japan, printed in English
www.eikoh.com/galleryNiki/glassasrt_E.htm
Glass Collectors' Digest has articles and pictures on all types of glass
www.glasscollectormagazine.com
Guide to Czech and Slovak Glass http://homepages.together.net/~czechrep
Just Glass Online Magazine www.mindspring.com/~reyne/index.html
Miniature Bottle Collector Online www.bottlecollecting.com
Network is Carnival Glass quarterly magazine www.woodsland.com/thistle/pages/network.htm
Newsletters for Antique Bottle Collectors www.antiquebottles.com/newsletters

REFERENCE & INFORMATION SITES

Antique Glass Bottles www.antiquesbottles-glass.com antique glass bottle information site
Australian Carnival Glass Club www1.loom.net.au/home/rborrow/acg
Carnival Glass www.woodsland.com/carnivalglass
Contemporary Carnival glass from 1950s – 1990s (pay to access site) www.carnivalglass.net
Elegant Glassware site http://eapglass.hypermart.net
Flameworked Glass Art www.global-flamework.com A history of lampworking and artists work
Goofus Glass Information Centre http://sundial.net/~gballens
History of Glass www.interalpha.net/customer/cbrain
Internet Art Resources www.artresources.com Search the Internet for a gallery, museum, school of glassmaking, etc
Loetz Glass http://gallery.uunet.be/Loetzweb
Thistlewood Carnival Glass www.geocities.com/Yosemite/Geyser/1799/home.html with network, articles, sales and links
Through the Looking Glass www.fly-by-net.com/lookingglass4.html offers a reflection of art glass on the web with additional links
Tiffany Studios Resource Centre www.geocities.com/Vienna/Choir/7564
Virtual Glass Museum www.glass.co.nz/encyclopedia
Walden's Index of Glass and China Related Terms www.spiritone.com/~walden/dictionary.html
World Wide Arts Resource http://wwar.com/Index4.html a searchable 'gateway to arts on the net'
Worldwide Museums www.musee-online.org Reviews museums and art galleries from around the world
Collector Online has extensive information on clubs, shops books, news and resources
www.collectoronline.com

MUSEUMS

See also websites in individual museums entry on pages 164–171
Corning Museum of Glass www.cmog.org
Dorflinger Glass Museum www.dorflinger.org
Duncan & Millar Glass Museum www.duncan-glass.com/Lobby.htm
Fostoria Glass Heritage Gallery
www.wcnet.org/businesses/f/Fostoria_Glass_Heritage_Gallery.html
Heisey Collectors of America Museum www.ahheisey.com
International Glass Museum of Denmark www.glass.dk
Museum of American Glass www.wheatonvillage.org/museum/mus-a-g.html
Museum of Glass, Tacoma (Opens 2002) www.museumofglass.org/Index.html
National Cambridge Collectors' Museum www.cambridgeglass.org
Swedish Glass Museum www.smalandsmuseum.g.se/engelsk.htm
World of Glass www.worldofglass.com

BIBLIOGRAPHY

"Biedermeier in Wien 1815–1848, Sein und Schein einer Bürgeridylle", Verlag Philipp von Zabern, Mainz, 1990

"Ceramics and Glass"– Arabia Centenary Issue, Arabia, Helsinki, 1973

"Charles Schneider, Maitre-Verrier – Verreries Schneider France de 1913 à 1940", Le Louvre des Antiquaires, Paris, 1984

"Fins Glas – van Modern tot Heden", Museum voor Sierkunst, Gent, 1992

"Fins Glas", Stedelijk Museum, Amsterdam, 1972

"Gli Artisti di Venini", Fondazione Giorgio Cini, Electa Editori, Milano, 1996

"Kaj Franck, Teema ja muunnelmia", Heinola Town Museum publications, Lahden Tuotepaino Oy, Lahti, 1997

"La Verrerie Européenne des Années 50", Michel Aveline Éditeur/ Musées de Marseillè, 1988

"Le Val St. Lambert, Âme de la Création et de la Tradition Verrières en Wallonie et à Bruxelles", Ed. Lean-Noël Bloom, Bruxelles, 1994

"Ljubica Ratkajec Kočica, Staklo 1963–1988", Muzej za umjetnost I obrt, Zagreb, 1988

"Mistrovská Díla Sklárství ve Francii od 19. Století po Dnešek", Umēleckoprūmyslové Muzeum, Praha, 1991

"Orrefors Gallery 100 – 1898–1998", Orrefors, Sweden, 1998

"Raoul Goldoni", Muzej za umjetnost I obrt, Zagreb 1967; "Raoul Goldoni Skulptura 1972–1980", Muzej za umjetnost I obrt, Zagreb 1980; "Raoul Goldoni, Staklo Bronca Crtež", Muzej za umjetnost I obrt, Zagreb, 1984;

"Sybren Valkema", Uitgeverij De Prom, Baarn, 1994

"Venini and the Murano Renaissance; Italian Art Glass of the 1940s & 50s", Fifty-50, New York, 1984

Adlerova, Alena: "Czech Studio Glass", in Glass Style 2/2000

Aloi, Roberto: "Essempi di Decorazione Moderna di Tutto in Mondo – Vetri d'Oggi", Ulrico Hoepli Editore, Milano, 1955

Arwas, Victor: "The Art of Glass, Art Nouveau to Art Deco", Andreas Papadakis Publisher, Windsor, 1996

Asharina, Nina and Malinina, Tamara and Kazakova, Liudmila: "Russian Glass of the 17th–20th Centuries", Corning Museum of Glass and USSR Ministry of Culture, Moscow, 1990

Bacri, Clotilde, Daum, Noel et Petry, Claude: "DAUM Masters of French Decorative Glass", Rizzoli, New York, 1992

Baer, Ilse and Bloch, Peter and Riederer, Joseph and Ricke, Helmut and Klinge, Ekkart and Zacher, Inge: "Glas und Steinzeug, Original, Kopie oder Fälschung", Verlag Kunst & Antiquitäten GmbH, Hannover, 1979

Bana, Pawe": "Wspanialy Krajobraz, Artyści I Kolonie Artystyczne w Karkonoszach w XX wieku", Muzeum Okregowe, Jeleniej Górze

Bangert, Albrecht: "Glaswerk", Moussault, Bussum, 1981

Bangert, Albrecht: "Le Verre Art 1900 et Art Déco", Editions Duculot, Paris, 1980

Barovier, Marina and Dorigato, Attilia: "Animaux en Verre, le Bestiaire de Murano", Canal Éditions, Venice/Paris, 1996

Bauer, Ingolf: "Glas zum Gebrauch", Verlag Gerd Hatje und Bayerisches Nationalmuseum, München, 1996

Beard, Geoffrey: "International Modern Glass", Barrie & Jenkins Ltd, London, 1976

Brand, Jan; De Muijnck, Catelijne and Van der Sande, Brigitte: "Het Drinkglas", Stichting Leerdam Glasmanifestatie, Waanders Uitgeverij Zwolle, 1997

Breitkopf, Ursula: "Farbglas von L.Moser & Söhne", in Trödler 197/1996

Bröhan, Torsten and Berg, Thomas: "Avant Garde Design 1880–1930", Benedikt Taschen Verlag GmbH, Köln, 1994

Brozková, Helena and Drahotová, Olga and Mergl, Jan: "Bohemian Glass", Museum of Decorative Arts, Prague, 1992

Bruyn, Esther A.H. and de Bruyn, W.F.: "Argos Global Price Guide of Art and Antiques", Argos Publishing (HK) Ltd, Hong Kong, 1995

Burschel, Carlo: "Wilhelm Wagenfeld – Entwürfe für die WMF", in Trödler 225/1998

Cappa, Giuseppe: "100 jaar Europese Glaskunst"; Generale Bankmaatschappij, Brussel, 1983

Causa, Marina: "L'Art du Verre de la Renaissance à nos Jours", Payot, Paris, 1966/1987

Chambrillon, Paul: "Le Verre et les Arts du Feu", Editions France-Empire, Paris, 1963

Comisso, Durdica: "Osredek Staklo 1839–1904", Muzej za umjetnost I obrt, Zagreb, 1989

Daum, Noël: "Daum Maîtres Verriers", Trois-Continents/Edita S.A., Lausanne, 1999

Dolez, Albane: "Glass Animals, 3,500 years of Artistry and Design", Harry N.Abrams Inc., publishers, New York, 1988

Dorfles, Gillo: "Der Kitsch", Verlag Ernst Wasmuth Tübingen ©1969 and Prisma Verlag GmbH, Gütersloh, 1977

Dorigato, Attilia: "Murano Glass Museum"; Edizioni Electa SpA Milano, 1986

Drahotová, Olga, "European Glass", Excalibur Books, New York, 1983

Duits, T.G. te: "Antiek Herkennen – Glas", Kosmos Uitgeverij, Utrecht/Antwerpen, 1995

Duits, T.G.te: "Geperst Glas uit Leerdam", Assen, Drents Museum and Leerdam, Nationaal Glasmuseum, 1991

Duits, T.G.te: "Glas van buiten de Grenzen", Nijgh en Van Ditmar, Haags Gemeentemuseum, 1986

Dušánek, Jiri and Franz, Josef and Zatloukal, Pavel: "Střední Průyslová Škola Sklářská 1870–1995", School of Glassmaking, Nový Bor, 1995

Edwards, Bill and Carwile, Mike: "Standard Encyclopedia of Pressed Glass", Second Edition 1860–1930. Identification & Values, Collector Books, Schroeder Publishing Inc., Paducah Ky, 2000

Electa Editrice: "Vetri Murano Oggi"; Gruppo Editoriale Electa, Milano, 1981

Eliëns, T.M. and Singelenberg-van der Meer, M.: "Lexicon Moderne Nederlandse Glaskunst 1900–1992", Uitgeversmaatschappij Antiek, Lochem, 1993

Engen, Luc: "Het Glas in België", Mercatorfonds Paribas, Belgium, 1989

Erlhoff, Michael: "Designed in Germany since 1949", Prestel Verlag, München, 1990

Evers, Jo: "Cut Glass, Ever's Standard Value Guide", Collector Books, Paducah KY, 1975

Fahr-Becker, Gabriele: "Wiener Werkstaette 1903–1932", Benedikt Taschen Verlag, Köln, 1995

Feild, Rachael: "Collector's Style Guide Victoriana", Ballantine Books, New York, 1988

Fiell, Charlotte and Peter: "Decorative Art 50s", Benedikit Taschen Verlag, Köln, 2000

Fiell, Charlotte and Peter: "Decorative Art 60s", Benedikt Taschen Verlag, Köln, 2000

Fiell, Charlotte and Peter: "Decorative Art 70s", Benedikt Taschen Verlag, Köln, 2000

Florence, Gene, "Collectible Glassware from the 40s, 50s, 60s..", Collector Books, Paducah KY, 1992

Fouchet, Nelly: "Opaline, La Verrerie aux Couleurs de l'Arc-en-ciel", in Antiquités Brocante 11/1998

Fütterer, Ansgar: "Bauernsilber, Luxusobjekte des 19. Jahrhunderts", in Trödler 185/1995

Geiselberger, Siegmar: "Pressglas-Korrespondenz Ausgaben 1998/1999/2000", Geiselberger, München, 1999

Haase, Gisela: "Lausitzer Glas Geschichte und Gegenwart", Museum für Kunsthandwerk, Dresden, 1987

Hajdamach, Charles R.: "British Glass 1800–1914", Antique Collectors' Club Ltd., Woodbridge, Suffolk, 1991.

Hanebutt-Benz, Eva-Maria and Neerincx, Riet: "Zeitgenössisches deutsches und niederländisches Kunsthandwerk", Museum für Kunsthandwerk Frankfurt am Main, 1981

Hedges, A.A.C.: "Bottles and Bottle Collecting", Shire Books, Princes Risborough, 1975

Heiremans, Marc: "Andries Dirk Copier, Leerdams Glas 1923–1971, Unica, Serica, Gebruiksglas", Marc Heiremans, Galerij Novecento, Gent, 1986

Heiremans, Marc: "Art Glass from Murano 1910–1970"; Arnoldsche, Stuttgart, 1993

Heiremans, Marc: "Leerdam Unica 1923–1987", Marc Heiremans, Gent, 1987

Heiremans, Marc: "Murano Glas 1945–1970", Marc Heiremans, Antwerpen, 1989

Herlitz-Gezelius, Anne-Marie: "Orrefors, a Swedish Glassplant", Atlantis Publishers, Stockholm, 1984

Hibbeln, Mr. J.G.: "De Glasmof – Wilhelm Hibbeln", Uitgeverij Jan van Arkel, Utrecht, 1995

Hlaveš, Milan: "The Glass of Stanislav Libenský and Jirina Brychtová", Glass Style 2/2000

Hughes, Therle: "Sweetmeat and Jelly Glasses", Lutterworth Press, Guildford Surrey, 1982

Hurst Vose, Ruth: "Glass", Collins Archaeology, London, 1980

Jenks, Bill and Luna, Jerry and Reilly, Darryl: "Identifying Pattern Glass Reproductions", Wallace-Homestead Books, Radnor PA, 1993

Jokelson, Paul and Ingold, Gerard: "Les Presse-Papiers XIX et XX Siècles", Hermé Editions, Paris, 1988

Juras, Maja: "Bidermajer u Hrvatskoj 1815–1848", Muzej za umjetnost I obrt, Zagreb, 1997

Ketchum Jr., William C.: "A Treasury of American Bottles", Rutledge/ Bobbs-Merrill, Indianapolis, 1975

Kley-Blekxtoon, A. van der: "Floris Meydam Leerdam Glas 1944–1986", De Tijdstroom, Lochem, 1986

Kley-Blekxtoon, A. van der: "Leerdam Glas 1878–1930", De Tijdstroom, Lochem, 1984

Kley-Blekxtoon, A. van der: "Leerdam Glas 1878–1998", Uitgeversmaatschappij Antiek Lochem BV, 1999

Langhamer, Antonin: "Czech Traditions in Glass Manufacturing and Designing"; in Glass Style 2/2000

Lechaczynski, Danièle: "La Verrerie de Biot, le souffle de la Creation", Biot, 1999

Leibe, Frankie and Hayhurst, Jeannette: "Glass of the '20s and '30s", Miller's, London, 1999

Leonhardt, Jochen: "Farbiges Glas, eingefärbte und bemalte Gläser", in Trödler 180/1994

Lindkvist, Lennart: "Crystal Clear – New Glass from Sweden", Föreningen Svensk Form, Stockholm, 1982

Lloyd, Ward: "Investing in Georgian Glass", Barrie & Rockliff, The Cresset Press, London, 1969

Lutzeier, Sabine: "Modenes Glas von 1920–1990", Battenberg, Augsburg, 1993

Lynggaard, Finn: "La Verrerie Artisanale", Dessain et Tolra, Paris, 1975/1981

Mariacher, Giovanni: "Glassware Murano/ I Vetri di Murano", Carlo Bestetti Edizioni d'Arte, Milano/Roma, 1967

Maril, Nadja: "American Lighting 1840–1940", Schiffer Publishing Ltd, West Chester PA, 1989

Marsden, Josie A.: "Lamps and Lighting", Guinness Publishing Ltd, London, 1990

Mergl, Jan: "Bohemian Art Nouveau Glass 1890–1915", Museum of Decorative Arts, Prague and

The Mainichi Newspapers, 1992

Mergl, Jan: "Ceské Secesní Sklo a jeho Technologie", Umĕleckoprůmyslové Muzeum v Praze Sklárské Muzeum Nový Bor, 1991

Miller, Muriel M.: "Glass", Guinness Publishing Ltd, London, 1990

Namiat, Robert: "Barber Bottles", Wallace-Homestead Book Co., Des Moines, Iowa, 1977

Neuwirth, Waltraud: "Glas/Glass/ Verre/ Vetri 1950–1960 I", Dr. Waltraud Neuwirth, Wien, 1987

Notley, Raymond: "Carnival Glass", Shire Books, Princes Risborough, 1983

Notley, Raymond: "Pressed Flint Glass", Shire Publications Ltd., Princes Risborough, 1986

Opie, Jennifer Hawkins: "Scandinavia Ceramics & Glass in the Twentieth Century – the Collections of the Victoria and Albert Museum", Rizzoli International Publications Inc, New York, 1990

Ortmann, Andreas: "Wilhelm Wagenfeld, Designer", in Trödler 209/1997

Over, Claudia: "Murano Glaskunst 1910–1970", in Trödler 175/1994

Palmer, Geoffrey and Lloyd, Noel: "The Observer's Book of Victoriana", Bloomsbury Books, London, 1976

Payton, Mary and Payton, Geoffrey: "The Observer's Book of Glass", Bloomsbury Books, London, 1976

Petrová, Sylva and Olivié, Jean-Luc: "Verres de Bohème 1400–1989, Chefs-d'oeuvre des Musées de Tchechoslovaquie", Flammarion, Paris, 1989

Phillips, Phoebe: "The Collectors' Encyclopedia of Antiques", Bloomsbury Books, London, 1989

Phillips, Phoebe: "The Encyclopedia of Glass", Spring Books, London, 1981

Pickvet, Mark: "Official Price Guide to Glassware", House of Collectibles, New York, 1995

Polak, Michael: "Bottles Identification and Price Guide", Avon Books, New York, 1997

Reilly, Pat: "Paperweights", Courage Books, Quintet Publishing Ltd., London, 1994

Richter, Gerd: "Kitsch-Lexicon von A bis Z", Prisma Verlag, Gütersloh, 1985

Ricke, Helmut and Gronert, Ulrich: "Glas in Schweden", Prestel Verlag, München, 1986

Ricke, Helmut and Kuyken-Schneider, D and Geraeds, H: "A.D. Copier, Trilogie in Glas", A.D.Copier/Uitgeverij De Hes, Rotterdam, 1991

Ricke, Helmut and Thor, Lars: "Schwedische Glasmanufakturen Produktionskataloge 1915–1960", Prestel Verlag, München, 1987

Ricke, Helmut: "Art Nouveau & Art Deco Glas", Gemeentemuseum Arnhem, 1992

Sarpaneva, Timo: "Lasiaika GlasZeit", Cramers Kunstanstalt Verlag, Dortmund, 1985

Schreiner, Nina: "Glas – Auktionspreise", Battenberg Verlag, Augsburg, 1997

Schrijver, Elka: "Glas en Kristal I en II", C.A.J. van Dishoeck, Bussum, 1962

Schrijver, Elka: "Glas en Kristal", Unieboek BV, Bussum, 1980

Schwandt, Jörg: "WMF Glas- Keramik- Metall 1925–1950", Kunstgewerbemuseum, Staatliche Museen Preußischer Kulturbesitz, Berlin, 1980

Seger, Juliane: "Schneekugeln, Bunte Welt im Glas", Fackelträger-Verlag GmbH, Hannover, 1985

Soetens, Johan: "In Glas Verpakt: kunst, kitsch en koopmanschap", Uitg. De Bataafse Leeuw, Amsterdam, 1999

Spillman, Jane Shadel: "Glass from World's Fairs 1851–1904", The Corning Museum of Glass, Corning, New York, 1986

Stennett-Willson, Ronald: "Neues Glas", Verlag Ernst Wasmuth, Tübingen, 1975

Subotič, Vesna Mažuran: "Staklo u suvremenom hrvatskom kiparstvu", Galerija 'Karas', Zagreb, 1988

Thunissen, Claudia: "Echt/Vals, Schemergebieden van de Authenticiteit", Kunsthistorisch Centrum Amsterdam, 1990

Tischbein Schroy, Ellen: "Warman's Glass", Wallace-Homestead Book Company, Radnor PA, 1992

Truman, Charles: "English Glassware to 1900", Victoria and Albert Museum, HMSO, London, 1984

Vallières, Jean: "Le Soufflage du Verre, Art Perdu et Retrouvé", Les Éditions Leméac Inc, Ottawa, 1979

Vondruška, Vlastimil and Langhamer, Antonín: "Bohemian Glass, Tradition and Present", Crystalex Nový Bor, 1991

Voronov, N. and Rachuk, E: "Soviet Glass Verre Sovietique Sowjetisches Glas", Aurora Art Publishers, Leningrad, 1973

Walker, Alexandra: "Scent Bottles", Shire Publications Ltd, Princes Risborough, 1987

West, Mark: "Miller's Antiques Checklist - Glass", Reed International Books Ltd, London, 1994

Zerwick, Chloe: "A Short History of Glass", The Corning Museum of Glass, Corning, New York, 1980

Ziffer, Alfred: "Wolfgang von Wersin 1882–1976; vom Kunstgewerbe zur Industrieform", Klinkhardt & Biermann, München, 1991

ACKNOWLEDGMENTS

Thanks to: Frank Andrews - Andy Bell - John Bell - Lisa Beatty - Renée Dekker - Reyne Haines - Kevin Holt - Messe Frankfurt GmbH - Siegmar Geiselberger - David Issitt - Jean-Claude Klissak - Emile de Leeuw - Peter Pommerencke - Jeff Rose - Sandra Kandukar - Sylvia Schleif - Pierpaolo Seguso - Bob Smith. The Publisher would like to thank Joy McCall for her assistance.